AMERICAN HISTORY:

Recent Interpretations

BOOK I: TO 1877

BOOK I: TO 1877

Second Edition

Edited by ABRAHAM S. EISENSTADT   Brooklyn College

AMERICAN HISTORY:
Recent Interpretations

New York, Established 1834   THOMAS Y. CROWELL COMPANY

For Elizabeth, Laura, Jonathan

Preface
to the
Second
Edition

In preparing a second edition of this anthology, I have tried to achieve the purposes that guided me in preparing the first edition: above all, to afford the novice the opportunity of meeting first hand many of today's principal writers of American history, and of becoming familiar with many of the newer viewpoints on the American past. The criteria I observed in drawing up my original list I have observed again in revising it; I refer the reader to the preface to the first edition for a statement of these criteria. The newer selections, which constitute about two-fifths of the revised edition and which represent the historical literature of the 1960's, have been culled almost entirely from periodicals; in a few instances, however, selections have been taken from recent books of notable importance, because they better served the purposes of the anthology than what the periodicals offered.

It is a commonplace that every age is one of transition, and it is fair enough to expect that what historians are writing about our past is similarly undergoing change. While the change is far from being radical, it has however been characterized by an increasing concern with two new themes of major significance: 1) Out of the whole conflict over the Negro's place in today's America, a new view has emerged of his role in the American past. If some younger historians are urging the thesis that the Negro is central to American history, many more are exploring anew those elements in our society's development in which the Negro's centrality is universally recognized: the colonial economy, the ante-bellum plantation system, the Civil War and Reconstruction, the New South, and the shaping of Negro life in the Southern and

Northern communities during the first half of the twentieth century. 2) America's role vis-à-vis the new world of nations has served today's historians as a point of departure in reconsidering some basic aspects of the American past, viz.: the diplomacy of the American Revolution, the formation of parties in the new republic, the beginnings of the whole process of industrialization, the conduct of our foreign affairs, the premises and policies of American imperialism, and the impact of our revolutionary origins on the evolution of our institutions and values.

I should like to express my gratitude to the individuals whose help made it possible for me to prepare this new edition. I am, as ever, indebted to the authors whose writings are represented in the anthology and to the journals and publishing houses which permitted me to reprint these writings. I am indebted, too, to the staffs of the Brooklyn College Library, the New York Public Library, and the Baker Library of Dartmouth College, for serving me generously in my work, at their respective libraries, in the recent literature of American history. Three individuals at the Thomas Y. Crowell Company were particularly helpful to me: Mr. Stanley Duane, who patiently and perseveringly urged me on, Miss Penelope Post, whose editorial suggestions were most helpful in improving the manuscript, and Mrs. Phyllis Greenbaum, who lent me her invaluable assistance with unfailing good humor. I am grateful, too, to Mrs. Barbara Berg, for checking a variety of details, and to Mrs. Freda Limberg, for her usual job of superb typing. I wish, finally, to thank my younger colleagues at Brooklyn College, Thomas B. Furcron, Donald F. Gerardi, and Robert Muccigrosso, who were kind enough to read the introductory notes to the newer selections and to let me have the benefit of their criticism.

May, 1968   A.S.E.

Preface
to the
First
Edition

This collection is designed to meet the need for supplementary readings in basic courses in American history. The need for such readings is clear enough. A textbook has, after all, the limitations of its author's knowledge and approach. A class in history requires the stimulus of different views and expert knowledge, both of which may be found in a book of collateral readings. Such a book affords, moreover, a satisfactory answer to the question of how to bring large groups of students in touch with a wide range of literature and opinion under conditions of limited library facilities.

The basic problem in editing a book of supplementary readings is to define what one seeks to achieve and how one seeks to do it. The editing of this book has been guided by the following purposes:

The collection as a whole undertakes to present the newer viewpoints in American history. All too frequently the textbook is based on approaches that have to be substantially modified if not altogether discarded. The selections in this book, on the other hand, date almost entirely from 1945—for the greater part, indeed, from 1950. They constitute in this way an anthology of American historical writing since World War II. They indicate the newer directions of American historical thought.

The selections have been drawn, wherever possible, from a broad field of periodicals which include the following:

Agricultural History   *Journal of Religion*
American Archivist   *Journal of Southern History*

American Heritage
American Historical Review
American Scholar
Atlantic Monthly
British Journal of Sociology
Business History Review
Centennial Review
Columbia University Forum
Commentary
Current History
Daedalus
History and Theory
Indiana Magazine of History
Journal of American History
Journal of Economic History
Journal of the Illinois State Historical
    Society
Journal of Negro Education

Labor History
Marine Corps Gazette
Mississippi Valley Historical Review
Pacific Affairs
Pacific Historical Review
Pacific Northwest Quarterly
Political Science Quarterly
Proceedings of the American
    Antiquarian Society
Proceedings of the American
    Philosophical Society
Proceedings of the South Carolina
    Historical Association
Progressive
U.S. Naval Institute Proceedings
William and Mary Quarterly
Wisconsin Magazine of History

It is in the rich essay literature of such periodicals that the new American history is being defined. It is in this essay literature, too, that the contributions of the foremost historians will often be found at their condensed and argumentative best. Though clearly of great importance, these writings are usually inaccessible to the class. Many college libraries do not have the wide collection of periodicals from which the readings in this volume have been taken; and even if they did, it would be very difficult, if not impossible, for large classes to use them at any given time. In the relatively few instances where selections were taken from recent books, the reason has generally been that these selections recommended themselves as clearly preferable to what was afforded by the periodicals.

The anthology consists entirely of complete essays. Each selection is a self-contained unit. The excerpts and fragments that usually make up a book of readings have been avoided. In composing an anthology of essays the purpose has been to do justice to their writers by letting them speak their minds fully on subjects on which they are authorities, without the arbitrary interruption of an editor. The desire has also been to do justice to the instructor and his students by letting them read and analyze in its entirety a noteworthy essay by a major historian on an important issue in the American past.

The choice of a particular essay has been made for one or more definite reasons. The essay is concerned with a major problem, development, or individual in American history. It summarizes the findings of an expert in the specific area of his research. It is often revisionist in approach. It is well written. It presents a provocative thesis, designed to stimulate the mind of the student and the discussion of the class. It has, as Carl Becker put it, something to say and says it in its own way.

The essays as a whole seek to present history as wider in scope than merely past politics. In order to underscore the historian's interest in all aspects of human activity, the editor has included a relatively larger number of selections dealing with economic, social, religious, and intellectual developments in the American past.

Introductory notes have been written for all of the essays. The notes discuss the contribution and approach of the historian who wrote each essay. They define the nature and importance of the subject with which the essay is concerned. They suggest lines of inquiry about the subject, both in its particular context in the American past and in the broader frame of American historical development. The effort has been to see the significance of a historical issue for our own times, not only for the purpose of using the student's interest in the present as a point of departure for his study of the past but also to encourage him to see the present in its deeper perspective as a phase of the past in evolution. The effort has also been made to throw open to the student the challenging questions posed by the study of history—such questions, for example, as whether the past is to be explained by determinism or by accident, what the nature and meaning of causation are, how much the great man influences the course of historical development, and whether or not an objective truth about the past can be attained. In terms of its introductory notes, therefore, the collection may be used as a "problems" approach to the study of the American past and may serve also as a primer for the study of the historical discipline.

The attempt has been made throughout to include articles of a high level of competence and interest and to represent as many approaches, to canvass as many problems, and to seek as catholic an orientation toward the whole American past as is possible. The footnotes that originally appeared with the essays have, as a rule, been omitted for reasons of length; in a few instances, however, where the theme of the essays is historiographical, the footnotes have by necessity been retained. Full information is given with each essay concerning the journal from which it has been taken, and the footnotes accompanying the essay may, of course, be readily consulted there. Obvious typographical errors have been corrected and abbreviations have been spelled out, but all stylistic preferences have been retained.

It is my hope that this volume will afford the student a broad and deep outlook on the American past as well as a real sense of the vitality of its study today. I also hope that he will thereby be encouraged to seek out its wider reaches and dimensions on his own.

November, 1961   A.S.E.

Contents

Civil War and Reconstruction

Part 1

THE STUDY AND WRITING
OF HISTORY

New Lamps for Old in History
ALLAN NEVINS

The study of American history extends an invitation and a challenge. Even at first glance one can see that here is an epic drama, extending over some three and a half centuries, in which the frontiers of life are pushed from the Atlantic seaboard across a continent, from primitive and far-flung settlements to the advanced and teeming society of our own times. It is exciting to contemplate the larger themes of the drama as they unfold, the transplanting of a European civilization to an American wilderness, the rebellion against the British dominion, the growth of a democratic and materialistic society, the gigantic war between the North and the South, the industrialization of American life, the advent of the United States to world power. It is no less exciting to contemplate the titanic figures who move through the scenes of the drama, investing it with all the vibrancy and tension of man's character: his magnanimity, striving, friendship, success, despair, frustration, and hope.

The study of the American epic also presents a challenge. Several questions require careful consideration, if the study is to have any value. What, to begin with, do we mean by history? What is to be gained from studying the American past? What qualifications do we need in order to undertake such a study? To what extent will it yield us a true picture of what actually occurred? To what extent is history an art, to what extent a science? What utility will our knowledge of the past have in today's world?

Some of these questions are answered in the following essay by Allan Nevins, who, after his retirement as De Witt Clinton Professor of American History at Columbia University, became senior research associate at the Henry E. Huntington Library in San Marino, California. Professor Nevins is particularly well qualified to answer the larger questions about the nature and study of American history. He has written and edited more than fifty volumes covering virtually every major era of our past, and is presently engaged in work on a multi-volume study of the nation from the Mexican War through the age of Reconstruction. Professor Nevins's achievement has

SOURCE: *American Archivist*, XVII (January, 1954), 3–12. Reprinted by permission of the author and The Society of American Archivists.

been recognized in many ways: he has been president of the American Historical Association; he has served as Harmsworth Professor of American History at Oxford; he has twice won the Pulitzer Prize in biography. His particular interest and ability in opening up to the novice all the tasks and rewards of studying the past are especially evident in his volume entitled The Gateway to History *(1938). The same interest and ability are apparent too in the essay below, in which Professor Nevins analyzes the problem of how and why the American past is being freshly explored and newly interpreted by succeeding generations.*

There are many reasons for the study of American history. If, as Professor Nevins suggests, the present touches on our view of the past, it is also true that the past touches on our view of the present. Our study will afford us a better ability to meet the problems which now confront us. Seeing them in deeper perspective, we will understand them in fuller measure. We will get a truer sense of the substance and proportion of the present act of the American drama if we examine more extensively and more analytically the acts which have already taken place.

One curious thing about history, as Guedalla said, is that it really happened. Another curious fact about history is that while it was happening, nobody really understood its meaning.

John Fiske, pausing one day in his young manhood before the window of Little, Brown in Boston, saw a volume within entitled "Pioneers of France in the New World" and noted that its author was identified as the man who had written "The Conspiracy of Pontiac." He remembered that when that earlier volume appeared, he had wondered whether Pontiac was a barbarous chieftain of medieval Europe. He recalled also that some teacher at Harvard had once expressed the view that the French and Indian War was a dull squabble of no real significance to students of history. Passing on, Fiske wondered why anyone should write about French pioneers in America. He lived to pen an essay on Francis Parkman which not only placed that author at the head of American historians (where he yet stands) but recognized that the epic significance of the struggle of Britain and France for the mastery of North America—a significance which Parkman had first expounded—could hardly be overstated. An interpretation of our continental history which nowadays we assume no child could miss had been beyond the grasp of the brilliant young John Fiske in the 1860's.

This idea that history can ever be so well written that it does not need rewriting can be held only by those foolish people who think that history can ever ascertain exact truth. It cannot. We can go further than the assertion of that truism: we can say, "Fortunate for history that it cannot ascertain exact truth!" If history were a photograph of the past it would be flat and uninspiring. Happily, it is a painting; and like all works of art, it fails of the highest truth unless imagination and ideas are mixed with the paints. A hundred photographs of London Bridge look just alike and convey altogether a very slight percentage of the truth, but Turner's Thames and Whistler's Thames, though utterly different, both convey the river with a deeper truth.

All parts of our history are always being rewritten; no segment of it is not now in need of vigorous rewriting. Whenever an expert applies himself to the scrutiny of a special area, he at once sounds a lusty call for more searching exploration of the terrain. Douglas Freeman, carrying Washington through the Revolution, agreed with Bernard Knollenberg, writing a history of that war, that every part of the Revolutionary struggle needs the most searching re-examination and the boldest reinterpretation. Merrill Jensen states in the preface to his study of the Confederation that the entire period 1783–89 demands a study that will embrace every State and every act of Congress. There are men who believe that the historical study of the Civil War period has but just begun—and they are right. Margaret Leech, just completing a study of the McKinley administration, is convinced that a hundred research workers should be set to exploration of the dark nooks and secret crannies of the time.

"In vain the sage, with retrospective eye," writes Pope, "would from the apparent what conclude the why." The three main reasons why history constantly needs reinterpretation include something more than the impossibility of ever learning all the truth about all the motives and actions of the past.

The chief of the three reasons is the need of every generation for a reinterpretation to suit its own preconceptions, ideas, and outlook. Every era has its own climate of opinion. It thinks it knows more than the preceding era; it thinks it takes a wider view of the universe. Every era, too, is affected by cataclysmic events which shift its point of view: the French Revolution, the Metternichian reaction, the movement for national unification in Italy, the United States, and Germany, the apogee of Manchester liberalism, and so on down to the multiple crisis of our atomic age. We see the past through a prism which glows and sparkles as new lights catch its facets. Much of the rewriting of history is a readjustment to this prism. George Bancroft's spectrum was outmoded a few years after his laborious "last revision"; Charles A. Beard's begins to be outworn today, for we possess what Beard would have called a new frame of reference.

As a second reason, new tools of superior penetrative power are from time to time installed in the toolshed of even our rather unprogressive race of historians. Our council for research in the social sciences (it should be studies) justly emphasizes the value of overlapping disciplines. Much could be said for the contention that the best historians nowadays are prepared in some other field than that of history. Thus Wesley Clair Mitchell, the historian of the greenbacks, of business cycles, and of the ebb and flow of economic activity, whose National Bureau of Economic Research inspired so much fruitful historical writing, was trained as an economist. (He also was trained by John Dewey, who gave courses under all sorts of titles, but "every one of them dealt with the same subject—how we think.") Beard was trained as a political scientist. Parrington was trained as a student of literature. Carl Becker was trained in European history but wrote in the American field. James Henry Breasted was first trained in theology, a fact which stood him in good stead when this pioneer of Egyptology in America began to trace the development of conscience and religion in the ancient East. Not one historian in fifty knows as much as he should of the tool called statistics, or of psychology, or of economic geography, or of ecology. The kinship between Halford J. Mackinder, the geographer, and Frederick J. Turner, the historian, in loosing seminal ideas showed what the geographer could learn from history and the historian from geography.

But the third great reason why history is rewritten is simply because the constant discovery of new materials necessitates a recasting of our view of the past. We might think that this would one day cease, but it never does. Everyone who has laboriously mapped any historical subject knows how steadily the dust of new facts falls upon that map, blurring some lines and defining new ones. Happy are those who live to rewrite their books, as even Parkman rewrote one of his—"LaSalle and the Great West." One would have said that all the materials for a history of the Revolution had been assembled in print by the innumerable agencies, local, State and national, devoted to that effort, but Freeman assures us that the great depositories like the Massachusetts Historical Society, the American Philosophical Society, and the main State libraries, bulge with unstudied documents. One would have said that all the material for the history of the Confederate War Office had been studied and restudied; but, behold: the diary of the third officer of that department, Kean, is suddenly deposited in the University of Virginia, and we find a complete reassessment of the Southern military administration possible.

Thus the idea that history is photography is set at naught. It is art; it constantly requires a new mixture of pigments, new points of view, new manipulation of light and shade; and as an art it presents an endless challenge to the writer who perceives that the highest truth of history will always transcend a statement of fact; that indeed, historical fact is but a foundation for the truth won by imagination and intellectual power.

The best history is always interpretive, but this does not mean that the best history is consciously or ostentatiously interpretive. The work of the historical masters, from Thucydides to Trevelyan, illustrates the fact that interpretation is most effective when implicit rather than explicit. The true historical attitude is a search for truth about a situation, force, or event—the War of 1812, the abolitionist impulse, Pearl Harbor—which slowly, painfully, accurately, dredges up an unforeseen interpretation. That is, history properly operates by the inductive, not the deductive, method. The merit of an Olympian historian like Parkman is that he says, in effect: "Let us collect and collate all the relevant facts, and find what conclusions emerge from their impartial analysis." The cardinal weakness of a controversial historian like Beard is that he repeatedly gave the impression—perhaps falsely—of having said to himself: "Let us take this provocative theory of the fact, and see how impressive an array of facts we can collect in its support." Ideas in history, that is, should be applied in subordination to the ascertainment of all the facts, and not in control of the ascertainment of one picked body of facts. Hence it is that nothing could be more absurd than to try to predict in advance the interpretations to be applied to our history by future writers—who will certainly go their own way. But we may legitimately make some guesses as to the general drift of some of the new interpretations lying ahead of us.

As American history lengthens and the past falls into longer perspective, we tend not so much to discard major interpretations entirely as to place new ones beside them; not so much to substitute one simple synthesis for another as to embrace old monistic views in a new and complex synthesis. Let us take a sweeping view of the first century of our national history, 1775–1875. In that tremendously variegated and baffling sea of events, forces, personalities, tendencies, and fortuities, let us assume that three great dominant developments lift themselves above all others.

These three—let us assume—are the establishment of American independence, political, economic, and finally cultural, from Europe; the westward movement for the conquest and development of the continent; and the abolition of slavery and a Southern way of life in a civil war which vindicated national unity. Some students, to be sure, would select other elements in our historical fabric, but three special students out of five and nine lay readers out of ten would, I believe, choose these. Now it is evident to a cursory view that each of the three lent itself at first to a simple monistic interpretation, expounded in the work even of subtle historians, and that within one or two generations this simple view of the past was replaced by a dual or multiple interpretation. What had been a flat telescopic image was given depth and reality by a stereopticon lens.

The Revolution seemed to our primitive historians, down to and including George Bancroft, simply a political upheaval; richly interesting as it was, it was the epic story of the establishment of political liberty in a new nation in a new world, as a guiding torch to all mankind. Before long, however, historians doubled the lens. They showed that the Revolution was a social no less than a political convulsion; that the internal transformation of America was quite as significant as the external; that a broad sequence of changes was set in motion, or rather accelerated, which rolled inexorably on through the Jeffersonian and Jacksonian eras. Some of this truth was visible to that early historian Richard Hildreth, who was as realistic as he was conservative; more of it to Moses Coit Tyler and John Bach McMaster; and all of it to a later school headed by J. Franklin Jameson, Parrington, and others.

The westward movement and the taming of the continent were first treated in terms of the transforming impact of man on nature; the expulsion of the Indian and wild beast, the hewing out of pioneer farms, the building of roads, and the ultimate planting of school and factory where the fur trader had trod. Then arose the eminent historian who perceived an equally rich meaning in the impact of nature, the wilderness, upon man; who explained how the frontier converted the European into an American, how it transformed men of caste-ridden minds into belligerently democratic individualists, how it manufactured nationalists out of separatists, and how, in short, it altered the whole pattern of thought, emotion, and conduct. This binocular view of the westward march was infinitely more interesting and arresting than the old monocular view. Parkman, Justin Winsor, Reuben Gold Thwaites, Edward Eggleston, Theodore Roosevelt, H. H. Bancroft, had been roughly accurate in their delineation of the westward thrust, but their interpretation had lacked depth and distinctness. When Turner substituted his perceptive and penetrating image of the frontier for this flat photograph, it flashed into life, color, and meaning; and behind Turner came a new body of writers who saw with his eyes.

To Hermann Von Holst the abolition of slavery seemed to mark the climax of 70 years of national life. America, to this German of Lithuanian birth, this hater of Russian and Prussian tyrannies, was the home of freedom and democracy; and the development and exemplification of these two inestimable gifts had been its principal mission in the world. But Liberty in America had suffered from a cancerous social institution—slavery—which sadly impaired her usefulness in the sisterhood of nations and threatened her very life. This interpretation possessed more validity than some recent writers have been willing to allow; indeed, within limits it was entirely valid. But it was too obvious, and it left too many historical phenomena of the period unexplained. The antagonism of North and South by 1860 transcended slavery, even though the conflict over slavery was certainly its central element. The simple monistic view of our great upheaval in the middle of the nineteenth century had to be amplified.

Hence arose the interpretation of that upheaval as one which included conflicts of economic interest, of philosophies of life, and of ingrained prejudice; a conflict between the eighteenth-century and the nineteenth-century mind; a conflict between the nascent industrialism of the North and the entrenched agrarianism of the South. Such an interpretation had been adumbrated by Southern politicians and publicists like Yancey during the war; it was stated with emphasis by a Southern historian, Percy A. Greg, soon after Appomattox. It had the merit of both widening and deepening the canvas. It demonstrated the links which joined Thaddeus Stevens, the antislavery covenanter, with Thad Stevens, the ironmaster, and Thad Stevens, the high-tariff legislator. Used as a constructive interpretation and not as a cloak for our political shortcomings and errors or as a means of glozing over the hideous blot of slavery, it had immeasurable value.

So much for three great developments in American history: the severance from Europe, the conquest and settling of the continent, and the elimination of slavery and the State rights doctrine as retarding agencies in our national growth. The character of a fourth great development, accomplished and sealed in the last 50 years of our national life, can hardly be missed. On that new phase of our history, too, general agreement will perhaps be found. We have become first a great world power, and then the great world power. We have moved first into the open arena of world affairs, and then into the very center of that arena. We now view our national past from the vantage point of this new turn and with the changed perspective which it gives us.

Just as John Fiske saw our history from 1607 to 1789 as an evolutionary preparation for the gift to the world of practical democracy and the Anglo-American principle of self-government in the shape of our Constitution and Federal system, just as Von Holst saw the whole period from 1776 to 1861 as a preparation for the vindication of human liberty and national unity, so now we have historians who view our whole national life as an unconscious preparation for the time when we should become Protector of the Faith for all democratic peoples; when, having turned away from Western European affairs until we gained first place among the nations, we returned to them as the pivot and support of Western European civilization. These writers regard American history not in terms of the Western continent but in terms of an Atlantic community. We find, indeed, that we never left that community; that the Seven Years War was our first world war, the Revolution our second; that we have but awakened to our consciousness of a global role. And when these historians write of our national future, they speak not of short-term objects, but of what Lincoln called "man's vast future."

This tremendous change of the past 40 or 50 years—this emergence of America to the leadership of the Western World—will undoubtedly affect our children's children, and the long generations to come, in the most sweeping way. It will loom up, in time to come, as tremendously as the great changes which preceded it—as the Revolution, internal and external, the American conquest of the frontier and the frontier's conquest of the American, the death of slavery, and the birth of machine industry. But the full significance of this development will not become evident until it, too, is given the dual or multiple interpretation that historians gave these older developments. We shall not understand its essential character until all the accompanying phenomena, social, economic, and intellectual, have been analyzed, and some mind as electric as Parrington's and as penetrating as Turner's has pierced nearer its heart. When then will be its significance? That is a question we cannot answer; it is for the oncoming generation of historians.

My own guess is that this great development by which America has been projected into world leadership, with all the exhilarations and perils, the opportunities and costs of that position, will in some fashion be connected, by future interpreters, with the advent of an age of mass action, mass production, and mass psychology in American life. From being one of the most unorganized, the most invertebrate of nations, in 1860, we have grown into the most powerfully and efficiently organized people on the globe. Our population disposes of its resources through such mass combinations, political, social, and economic, as mankind never saw before. Our thinking in 1865 was still individual thinking; today it is largely mass thinking, shaped and colored by mass media of unparalleled and sometimes dismaying potency—press, radio, television, cinema. No one can go to what were recently primitive frontier communities in America—say Texas and California—without being struck, and a little appalled, by the complexity and efficiency with which they have organized their life. It was our mass production which won the two last world wars; it is our genius for making big organizations work which has built the means for saving Western democracy since the latest world war. Our national outlook, once that of the individualistic pioneer, has become a social outlook. Without this pervasive internal change, our new position in the world would have been impossible.

The striking shift in our character and our world position in the last half century of course has some direct results, already visible, in our interpretation of history. We are evincing a greater militancy in asserting the virtues of our political and social system. The apologetic attitude of the years of the Great Depression is gone. We can henceforth be more confident and more energetic in asserting that our way of life, called decadent by our enemies, has proved itself historically to be freer, more flexible, and more humane than any other in history. We can be as emphatic and frank as ever in describing our past weaknesses, from slavery to slums, but we shall insist more rigorously on the fundamental healthiness of our system and on its proved ability to mend its defects and give us a constantly self-regenerating society.

We shall also evince, I think, a tendency to insist more emphatically on the fundamental unity of the United States with Western Europe and the various other nations sprung from Western Europe. All kinds of Western institutions and virtues now find their principal stronghold in the United States. The literature written in the English tongue increasingly has its main center of vitality in America, a fact well recognized by the London *Times* Literary Supplement. The Roman Catholic Church, like the Protestant churches, finds its chief springs of wealth and power in the United States. The Atlantic Community, as many publicists term it, has taken the place of the former division between Europe and the Americas. Oldtime quarrels between America and Western Europe have lost a great part of the significance which was once attached to them. What does the War of 1812 count for, compared with the maintenance and growth of the political, social, and cultural ties that have made the English-speaking nations so nearly a unity? The nationalistic view of our history will increasingly be replaced by the international view, treating America as part of a great historic civilization with the Atlantic its center, as the Mediterranean was the center of the ancient world; with the tides of population, power, and influence first moving from Europe to America, and then beginning to flow in the opposite direction.

We may look forward also to a more appreciative attitude toward our material strength and to a more scientific treatment of the factors which have created this material power. In the past our historians were apologetic about our love of the dollar, our race to wealth, our interest in material objects; they deprecated our worship of size and deplored our boastfulness about steel tonnage, grain production, and output of machinery. Clio, with her tradition of devotion to moral values, was scornful of any others. Our writers in general—for the historians but followed the poets, the novelists, and the dramatists—intimated that America has grown too fast, too coarsely, too muscularly; they exalted the rural virtues as against industrial might, the rarefied air of the study as against the smoky atmosphere of the mill.

Without denying that many accompaniments of our swift industrialization were unhappy, we can now assert that this historical attitude was erroneous. The nation grew none too fast. We can see today that all its wealth, all its strength, were needed to meet a succession of world crises—and we still dwell in a crisis era. Had we applied restrictions to keep our economy small, tame, and timid, we would have lost the First World War. Had the United States not possessed the mightiest oil industry, the greatest steel industry, the largest automotive factories, the most efficient machine-tool industry, the best technological schools, and the most ingenious working force in the world, we would indubitably have lost the Second World War. Were we significantly weaker today in technical skills, in great mills and factories, and in the scientific knowledge which gave us priority with the atomic bomb and hydrogen bomb, all Western Europe would be cowering—we ourselves would perhaps be cowering—before the knout held by the Kremlin. The architects of our material growth—the men like Whitney, McCormick, Westinghouse, Rockefeller, Carnegie, Hill, and Ford—will yet stand forth in their true stature as builders of a strength which civilization found indispensable. As that realization spreads, industrial archives like that created in Dearborn by the vision of the Ford Motor Company will take their place as equal in importance to the political and cultural archives so long indispensable to students of our past.

It will yet be realized that the industrial revolution in the United States came none too soon and none too fast; and that the ensuing mass-production revolution, as yet so little understood by Americans, was not born a day too early. That is a fact which may well be stated in this birthplace of mass production—Detroit. It is a fact well appreciated in Manchester and London, in Paris and Berlin, and in Moscow. We shall also come to realize that the turmoil and human suffering which inescapably accompanied the industrial revolution and the mass-production revolution were not after all a tremendous price to pay for their benefits. The price was smaller in the United States than in foreign lands. The industrial revolution cost less in human travail here than it did in England, where it first came to birth; less than in Germany or Japan; far less than it is costing in Russia. Here is a wide field for the rewriting of American history and for the re-education of the American people, a field in which all archivists may contribute their due share.

Our material might, to be sure, is valuable only as it supports and carries to victory great moral ideas, only as it buttresses a civilization in which spiritual forces are predominant. But the fundamental difference between the democratic world and the totalitarian world lies precisely in the superior position which we give to moral and spiritual values. It is we, not our enemies, who have the right to talk about what Lincoln called man's vast future, for we really value men as individual souls. Behind our dreams of man's vast future, we mobilize an unconquerable strength. In time, when future historians look back on this period, which to us is so full of struggle, sacrifice, and anxious uncertainty, they will perhaps give it an interpretation of exalted character. They may say: "The era in which the United States, summoning all its strength, led democracy in winning the First World War, the Second World War, and the ensuing struggle against the Communist tyranny, was one of the great eras of history. It stands invested with all the radiance of the Periclean era, the Elizabethan era, and the era of Pitt and the long struggle against Napoleon."

Part 2

COLONIZATION AND REVOLUTION, TO 1783

COLONIAL BEGINNINGS

2

Myths That Hide the American Indian
OLIVER LA FARGE

It is fair enough that a study of the American past should begin with a study of the first Americans—the Indians. Even a minimal consideration of their society and achievements is all too frequently omitted from courses in American history. This omission is regrettable, because it deprives the student of an opportunity to see history in its full breadth as the study of contrasting cultures in evolution. It is regrettable too because the student's knowledge of the North American Indian tends to remain at the level of myths that have been questionably collected and inadequately explored.

The following essay by the late Oliver La Farge will serve admirably as an introduction both to the distinctive features of Indian culture and to the myths about it that we have fashioned for our own convenience. La Farge, a highly qualified guide on this subject, devoted his creative life to a concern with the present and past of the American Indian. It was a deep and warm concern, variously reflected in his novels, his career as a professional anthropologist, and his activities in organizations interested in the problems and welfare of American Indians today.

The root question about any myth in history is why it grew. The question becomes all the more challenging if the myth has undergone substantial change. Why, for example, did the first European settlers regard the red man as noble, and their descendants regard him as ruthless? The image of

SOURCE: *American Heritage, The Magazine of History*, VII (October, 1956), 5–9, 103–7. Copyright © 1956 by Oliver La Farge. Reprinted by permission of the author.

the noble Indian must, as La Farge explains, have served the need of the explorers and colonizers. Similarly, the image of the ruthless Indian must have served the needs of an independent, foreign nation seizing control of a continent and having to justify its doing so. To wage war one must have an enemy, and the enemy must, whatever else, arouse enmity. In the war for the land, the Indian was made over into an unqualified agent of barbarism and treachery. Only when the war had finally been won, in the later decades of the nineteenth century, could the myth be allowed to rest. Only then could the understanding begin to spread that the Indian had been presented too plainly and too starkly, that he had actually belonged to a variety of cultures, that the cultures had been in a constant process of evolution and interaction, and that they had been far removed from complete barbarism.

La Farge clears away the myths by portraying the three Indian areas— Southeast, Southwest, and Northwest Coast—which had achieved the highest cultural level at the time the white man came to settle in North America. He does more than explain the various patterns into which Indian societies formed themselves; he provides a broad view of cultures in interplay. La Farge surveys the effects of Meso-America upon North America as well as the reciprocal impact of Indian and European ways. In proceeding to the study of American history and of a culture which is so markedly European in its origins and evolution, one cannot but profit by keeping this larger cultural picture in mind.

Ever since the white men first fell upon them, the Indians of what is now the United States have been hidden from white men's view by a number of conflicting myths. The oldest of these is the myth of the Noble Red Man or the Child of Nature, who is credited either with a habit of flowery oratory of implacable dullness or else with an imbecilic inability to converse in anything more than grunts and monosyllables.

That first myth was inconvenient. White men soon found their purposes better served by the myth of ruthless, faithless savages, and later, when the "savages" had been broken, of drunken, lazy good-for-nothings. All three myths coexist today, sometimes curiously blended in a schizophrenic confusion such as one often sees in the moving pictures. Through the centuries the mythical figure has been variously equipped; today he wears a feather headdress, is clothed in beaded buckskin, dwells in a tepee, and all but lives on horseback.

It was in the earliest period of the Noble Red Man concept that the Indians probably exerted their most important influence upon Western civilization. The theory has been best formulated by the late Felix S. Cohen, who, as a profound student of law concerning Indians, delved into early white-Indian relations, Indian political economy, and the white men's view of it. According to this theory, with which the present writer agrees, the French and English of the early seventeenth century encountered, along the East Coast of North America from Virginia southward, fairly advanced tribes whose semi-hereditary rulers depended upon the acquiescence of their people for the continuance of their rule. The explorers and first settlers interpreted these rulers as kings, their people as subjects. They found that even the commonest subjects were endowed with many rights and freedoms, that the nobility was fluid, and that commoners existed in a state of remarkable equality.

Constitutional monarchy was coming into being in England, but the divine right of kings remained firm doctrine. All European society was stratified in many classes. A somewhat romanticized observation of Indian society and government, coupled with the idea of the Child of Nature, led to the formulation, especially by French philosophers, of the theories of inherent rights in all men, and of the people as the source of the sovereign's authority. The latter was stated in the phrase, "consent of the governed." Both were carried over by Jefferson into our Declaration of Independence in the statement that "all men are created equal, that they are endowed by their Creator with certain unalienable Rights" and that governments derive "their just powers from the consent of the governed. . . ."

Thus, early observations of the rather simple, democratic organization of the more advanced coastal tribes, filtered through and enlarged by the minds of European philosophers whose thinking was ripe for just such material, at least influenced the formulation of a doctrine, or pair of doctrines, that furnished the intellectual base for two great revolutions and profoundly affected the history of mankind.

In the last paragraph I speak of "the more advanced" tribes. Part of the myth about the first Americans is that all of them, or most of them, had one culture and were at the same stage of advancement. The tribes and nations that occupied North America varied enormously, and their condition was anything but static. The advent of the white men put a sudden end to a phase of increasingly rapid cultural evolution, much as if a race of people, vastly superior in numbers, in civilization, and above all in weapons, had overrun and conquered all of Europe in Minoan times. Had that happened, also, the conquerors would undoubtedly have concluded, as so many white men like to conclude about Indians, that that peculiar race of light-skinned people was obviously inferior to their own.

Human beings had been in the New World for at least 15,000 years. During much of that time, as was the case in the beginning everywhere, they advanced but little from a Palaeolithic hunting culture. Somewhere around 2,500 B.C. farming began with the domestication of corn either in Peru or in Meso-America[1] in the vicinity of western

---

[1] Meso-America denotes the area in which the highest civilizations north of Peru developed, extending from a little north of Mexico City into Honduras.

Guatemala. Farming brought about the sedentary life and the increased food supply necessary for cultural progress. By the time of the birth of Christ, the influence of the high cultures, soon to become true civilizations, in Meso-America was beginning to reach into the present United States. Within the next 1,500 years the Indians of parts of North America progressed dramatically. When the white men first landed, there were three major centers of high culture: the Southeast-Mississippi Valley, the Southwest, and the Northwest Coast. None of the peoples of these regions, incidentally, knew about war bonnets or lived in tepees.

The Southeast-Mississippi Valley peoples (for brevity, I shall refer to the area hereafter simply as "Southeast") seem to have had the strongest influences from Meso-America, probably in part by land along the coast of Texas, in part by sea across the Gulf of Mexico, whether direct from Mexico or secondhand through the peoples of the West Indies. There is a striking resemblance between some of their great earthen mounds, shaped like flat-topped pyramids, with their wood-and-thatch temples on top, and the stone-and-mortar, temple-topped pyramids of Meso-America. Some of their carvings and engravings strongly suggest that the artists had actually seen Meso-American sculptures. The full list of similarities is convincingly long.

There grew up along the Mississippi Valley, reaching far to the north, and reaching also eastwards in the far south, the high culture generally called "Mound Builder." It produced a really impressive art, especially in carving and modeling, by far the finest that ever existed in North America. The history of advancing civilization in the New World is like that of the Old—a people develops a high culture, then barbarians come smashing in, set the clock part way back, absorb much of the older culture, and carry it on to new heights. A series of invasions of this sort seems to have struck the Mound Builders in late prehistoric times, when they were overrun by tribes mainly of Muskhogean and Iroquoian linguistic stock. Chief among these were the ancestors of the well-known Five Civilized Tribes—the Seminoles, Creeks, Choctaws, Chickasaws, and Cherokees. When white men first met them, their culture was somewhat lower than that of the earlier period in the land they occupied. None the less, they maintained, in Florida, Alabama, Mississippi, Louisiana, and Georgia, the highest level east of the Rockies. A late movement of Iroquoian tribes, close relatives of the Cherokees, among them the Iroquois themselves, carried a simpler form of the same culture into Pennsylvania, New York, Ohio, and into the edge of Canada.

All of these people farmed heavily, their fields stretching for miles. They were few in a vast land—the whole population of the present

United States was probably not over a million. Hunting and fishing, therefore, were excellent, and no reasonable people would drop an easy source of abundant meat. The development of their farming was held in check quantitatively by the supply of fish and game. They farmed the choice land, and if the fields began to be exhausted, they could move. They moved their habitations somewhat more freely than do we, but they were anything but nomadic. The southern tribesmen lived neither in wigwams nor tepees, but in houses with thatched roofs, which in the extreme south often had no walls. They had an elaborate social structure with class distinctions. Because of their size, the white men called their settlements "towns." The state of their high chiefs was kingly. They were a people well on the road towards civilization.

The Natchez of Mississippi had a true king, and a curious, elaborate social system. The king had absolute power and was known as the Sun. No ordinary man could speak to him except from a distance, shouting and making obeisances. When he went out, he was carried on a litter, as the royal and sacred foot could not be allowed to touch the ground. The Natchez nation was divided into two groups, or moieties: the aristocracy and the common people. The higher group was subdivided into Suns (the royal family), Nobles, and Honored Ones. The common people were known simply as Stinkers. A Stinker could marry anyone he pleased, but all the aristocrats had to marry out of their moiety, that is, marry Stinkers. When a female aristocrat married a Stinker man, her children belonged to her class; thus, when a Sun woman married a Stinker, her children were Suns. The children of the men, however, were lowered one class, so that the children of a Sun man, even of the Sun himself, became Nobles, while the children of an Honored One became lowly Stinkers.

This system in time, if nothing intervened, would lead to an overwhelming preponderance of aristocrats. The Natchez, however, for all their near-civilization, their temples, their fine crafts and arts, were chronically warlike. Those captives they did not torture to death they adopted, thus constantly replenishing the supply of Stinkers (a foreigner could become nothing else, but his grandchildren, if his son struck a royal fancy, might be Suns).

The Indians of the Southeast knew the Mexican-West Indian art of feather weaving, by means of which they made brilliant, soft cloaks. The Sun also wore a crown of an elaborate arrangement of feathers, quite unlike a war bonnet. In cloak and crown, carried shoulder-high on a litter, surrounded by his retainers, his majesty looked far more like something out of the Orient than anything we think of ordinarily when we hear the word "Indian."

The Natchez were warlike. All of the southeasterners were warlike. War was a man's proper occupation. Their fighting was deadly, ferocious, stealthy if possible, for the purpose of killing—men, women, or children, so long as one killed—and taking captives, especially strong males whom one could enjoy torturing to death. It is among these tribes and their simpler relatives, the Iroquois, that we find the bloodthirsty savage of fiction, but the trouble is that he is not a savage. He is a man well on the road towards civilization.

With the Iroquois, they shared a curious pattern of cruelty. A warrior expected to be tortured if captured, although he could, instead, be adopted, before torture or at any time before he had been crippled. He entered into it as if it were a contest, which he would win if his captors failed to wring a sign of pain from him and if he kept taunting them so long as he was conscious. Some of the accounts of such torture among the Iroquois, when the victim was a member of a tribe speaking the same language and holding to the same customs, are filled with a quality of mutual affection. In at least one case, when a noted enemy proved to have been too badly wounded before his capture to be eligible for adoption, the chief, who had hoped that the man would replace his own son, killed in battle, wept as he assigned him to his fate. At intervals between torments so sickening that one can hardly make one's self read through the tale of them, prisoner and captors exchanged news of friends and expressions of mutual esteem. Naturally, when tribes who did not hold to these customs, including white men, were subjected to this treatment it was not well received.

This pattern may have come into North America from a yet more advanced, truly civilized source. The Mexicans—the Aztecs and their neighbors—expected to be sacrificed if they were captured, and on occasion might insist upon it if their captors were inclined to spare them. They were not tortured, properly speaking, as a general rule, but some of the methods of putting them to death were not quick. What we find in North America may have been a debasement of the Mexican practices developed into an almost psychopathic pleasure among people otherwise just as capable of love, of kindness, of nobility, and of lofty thoughts as any anywhere—or what the conquistadores found in Mexico may have been a civilized softening of earlier, yet more fearful ways. The Aztecs tore fantastic numbers of hearts from living victims, and like the people of the Southeast, when not at war said "We are idle." They were artists, singers, dancers, poets, and great lovers of flowers and birds.

The Iroquois and Muskhogeans had a real mental sophistication. We observe it chiefly in their social order and what we know of their religions. The Iroquois did not have the royalty and marked divisions of classes that we find farther south, but their well-organized, firmly knit tribes were what enabled them, although few in numbers, to dominate the Algonkians who surrounded them. The Iroquois came nearer to having the matriarchy that popular fable looks for among primitive people than any other American tribe. Actual office was held by the men, but the women's power was great, and strongly influenced the selection of the officers.

Five of the Iroquois tribes achieved something unique in North America, rare anywhere, when in the sixteenth century they formed the League of the Five Nations—Senecas, Onondagas, Mohawks, Cayugas, and Oneidas—to which, later, the Tuscaroras were added. The league remained united and powerful until after the American Revolution, and exists in shadowy form to this day. It struck a neat balance between sovereignty retained by each tribe and sovereignty sacrificed to the league, and as so durable and effective a union was studied by the authors of our Constitution.

The league was founded by the great leader Hiawatha. Any resemblance between the fictional hero of Longfellow's poem and this real, dead person is purely coincidental. Longfellow got hold of the name and applied it to some Chippewa legends, which he rewrote thoroughly to produce some of the purest rot and the most heavy-footed verse ever to be inflicted upon a school child.

The Iroquois lived in "long houses," which looked like extended Quonset huts sheathed in bark. Smaller versions of these, and similarly covered, domed or conical structures, are "wigwams," the typical housing of the Northeast. Many people use the word "wigwam" as synonymous with "tepee," which is incorrect. A tepee, the typical dwelling of the Plains Indians of a later period, is a functional tent, usually covered with hides or, in recent years, canvas, and one of its essential features is that it is the shelter of constantly mobile people. A tepee, incidentally, is about the most comfortable tent ever invented, winter or summer—provided you have two or three strong, competent women to attend to setting it up and striking it.

The great tribes we have been discussing showed their sophistication in a new way in their response to contact with Europeans. Their tribal organizations became tighter and firmer. From south to north they held the balance of power. The British success in establishing good relations with many of them was the key to driving the French out of the Mississippi area; to win the Revolution, the Americans had to defeat the Iroquois, whose favor up to then had determined who should dominate the Northeast. The southern tribes radically changed their costume, and quickly took over cattle, slaves, and many arts. By the time Andrew Jackson was ready to force their removal, the Cherokees had a stable government under a written constitution, with a bicameral parliament, an alphabet for writing their language, printing presses, a newspaper, schools and churches.

Had it not been for the white men's insatiable greed and utter lawlessness, this remarkable nation would have ended with a unique demonstration of how, without being conquered, a "primitive" people could adapt itself to a new civilization on its own initiative. They would have become a very rare example of how aborigines could receive solid profit from the coming of the white men.

After the five Civilized Tribes were driven to Oklahoma, they formed a union and once again set up their governments and their public schools. Of course we could not let them have what we had promised them; it turned out that we ourselves wanted that part of Oklahoma after all, so once again we tore up the treaties and destroyed their system. None the less, to this day they are a political power in the state, and when one of their principal chiefs speaks up, the congressmen do well to listen.

The tribes discussed until now and their predecessors in the same general area formed a means of transmission of higher culture to others, east and west. Their influence reached hardly at all to the northwards, as north of the Iroquois farming with native plants was difficult or impossible. On the Atlantic Coast of the United States the tribes were all more or less affected. Farming was of great importance. Even in New England, the status of chiefs was definite and fairly high. Confederacies and hegemonies, such as that of the Narragansetts over many of the Massachusetts tribes, occurred, of which more primitive people are incapable. Farther south, the state of such a chief as Powhatan was royal enough for Europeans to regard him as a king and his daughter as a true princess.

To the westward, the pattern of farming and sedentary villages extended roughly to the line that runs irregularly through Nebraska and Kansas, west of which the mean annual rainfall is below twenty inches. In wet cycles, there were prehistoric attempts to farm farther west, and in historic times the Apaches raised fair crops in the eastern foothills of the southern tip of the Rockies, but only the white men combined the mechanical equipment and the stupidity to break the turf and exhaust the soil of the dry, high plains.

An essay as short as this on so large a subject is inevitably filled with almost indefensible generalizations. I am stressing similarities, as in the case of the Iroquois-Southeast tribes, ignoring great unlikenesses. Generalizing again, we may say that the western farmers, whose cultures in fact differed enormously, also lived in fairly fixed villages. In the southern part, they built large houses covered with grass thatch. At the northwestern tip of the farming zone we find the Mandans, Hidatsa, and Crows, who lived in semi-subterranean lodges of heavy poles covered with earth, so big that later, when horses came to them, they kept their choice mounts inside. These three related, Siouan-speaking tribes living on the edge of the Plains are the first we have come to whose native costume, when white men first observed them, included the war bonnet. That was in the early nineteenth century; what they wore in 1600, no one knows.

The western farmers had their permanent lodges; they also had tepees. Immediately at hand was the country of the bison, awkward game for men on foot to hunt with lance and bow, but too fine a source of meat to ignore. On their hunting expeditions they took the conical tents. The size of the tepees was limited, for the heavy covers and the long poles had to be dragged either by the women or by dogs. Tepee life at that time was desirable only for a short time, when one roughed it.

The second area of Meso-American influence was the Southwest, as anthropologists define it—the present states of New Mexico and Arizona, a little of the adjacent part of Mexico, and various extensions at different times to the north, west, and east. We do not find here the striking resemblances to Meso-America in numbers of culture traits we find in the Southeast; the influence must have been much more indirect, ideas and objects passing in the course of trade from tribe to tribe over the thousand miles or so of desert northern Mexico.

In the last few thousand years the Southwest has been pretty dry, although not as dry as it is today. A dry climate and a sandy soil make an archaeologist's paradise. We can trace to some extent the actual transition from hunting and gathering to hunting plus farming, the appearance of the first permanent dwellings, the beginning of pottery-making, at least the latter part of the transition from twining and basketry to true weaving. Anthropologists argue over the very use of the term "Southwest" to denote a single area, because of the enormous variety of the cultures found within it. There is a certain unity, none the less, centering around beans, corn, squashes, tobacco, cotton, democracy, and a preference for peace. Admitting the diversity, the vast differences between, say, the Hopi and Pima farmers, we can still think of it as a single area, and for purposes of this essay concentrate on the best-studied of its cultures, the Pueblos.

The name "Pueblo" is the Spanish for "village," and was given to that people because they lived—and live—in compact, defensible settlements of houses with walls of stone laid up with adobe mortar or entirely of adobe. Since the Spanish taught them how to make rectangular bricks, pure adobe construction has become the commoner type. They already had worked out the same roofing as was usual in Asia Minor and around the Mediterranean in ancient times. A modern Pueblo house corresponds almost exactly to the construction of buildings dating back at least as far as 600 B.C. in Asia Minor.

The Pueblos, and their neighbors, the Navahos, have become well enough known in recent years to create some exception to the popular stereotype of Indians. It is generally recognized that they do not wear feathers and that they possess many arts, and that the Pueblos are sedentary farmers.

Farming has long been large in their pattern of living, and hunting perhaps less important than with any people outside the Southwest. Their society is genuinely classless, in contrast to that of the Southeast. Before the Spanish conquest, they were governed by a theocracy. Each tribe was tightly organized, every individual placed in his niche. The power of the theocracy was, and in some Pueblos still is, tyrannical in appearance. Physical punishment was used to suppress the rebellious; now more often a dissident member is subjected to a form of being sent to Coventry. If he be a member of the tribal council, anything he says at meetings is pointedly ignored. If he has some ceremonial function, he performs it, but otherwise he is left in isolation. I have seen a once self-assertive man, who for a time had been a strong leader in his tribe, subjected to this treatment for several years. By my estimation he lost some thirty pounds, and he became a quiet conformist.

The power of the theocracy was great, but it rested on the consent of the governed. No man could overstep his authority, no one man had final authority. It went hard with the individual dissident, but the will of the people controlled all.

The Pueblos had many arts, most of which still continue. They wove cotton, made handsome pottery, did fine work in shell. Their ceremonies were spectacular and beautiful. They had no system of torture and no cult of warfare. A good warrior was respected, but what they wanted was peace.

The tight organization of the Pueblo tribes and the absolute authority over individuals continues now among only a few of them. The loosening is in part the result of contact with whites, in part for the reason that more and more they are building their houses outside of the old, solid blocks of the villages, simply because they are no longer under constant, urgent need for defense.

It is irony that the peace-loving southwestern farmers were surrounded by the worst raiders of all the wild tribes of North America. Around A.D. 1100 or 1200 there began filtering in among them bands of primitives, possessors of a very simple culture, who spoke languages of the Athabascan stock. These people had drifted down from western Canada. In the course of time they became the Navahos and the Apaches. For all their poverty, they possessed a sinew-backed bow of Asiatic type that was superior to any missile weapon known to the Southwest. They traded with the Pueblos, learned from them, stole from them, raided them. As they grew stronger, they became pests. The Navahos and the northeastern branch of the Apaches, called

Jicarilla Apaches, learned farming. The Navahos in time became artists, above all the finest of weavers, but they did not give up their raiding habits.

These Athabascans did not glorify war. They made a business of it. Killing enemies was incidental; in fact, a man who killed an enemy had to be purified afterwards. They fought for profit, and they were about the only North Americans whose attitude towards war resembled that of the professional soldier. This did not make them any the less troublesome.

The last high culture area occupied a narrow strip along the Pacific Coast, from northern California across British Columbia to southern Alaska, the Northwest Coast culture. There was no Meso-American influence here, nor was there any farming. The hunting and fishing were so rich, the supply of edible wild plants so adequate, that there was no need for farming—for which in any case the climate was unfavorable. The prerequisite for cultural progress is a food supply so lavish that either all men have spare time, or some men can specialize in non-food-producing activities while others feed them. This condition obtained on the Northwest Coast, where men caught the water creatures from whales to salmon, and hunted deer, mountain sheep, and other game animals.

The area was heavily forested with the most desirable kinds of lumber. Hence wood and bark entered largely into the culture. Bark was shredded and woven into clothing, twined into nets, used for padding. Houses, chests, dishes, spoons, canoes, and boats were made of wood. The people became carvers and woodworkers, then carried their carving over onto bone and horn. They painted their houses, boats, chests, and their elaborate wooden masks. They made wooden armor, including visored helmets, and deadly wooden clubs. In a wet climate, they made raincloaks of bark and wore basketry hats, on the top of which could be placed one or more cylinders, according to the wearer's rank. The chiefs placed carvings in front of their houses that related their lineage, tracing back ultimately to some sacred being such as Raven or Bear—the famous, so-called totem poles.

I have said that the finest prehistoric art of North America was that of the Mound Builders; in fact, no Indian work since has quite equaled it—but that is, of course, a matter of taste. The greatest historic Indian art was that of the Northwest Coast. Their carvings, like the Mound Builder sculptures, demand comparison with our own work. Their art was highly stylized, but vigorous and fresh. As for all Indians, the coming of the white men meant ruin in the end, but at first it meant metal tools, the possession of which resulted in a great artistic outburst.

Socially they were divided into chiefs, commoners, and slaves. Slaves were obtained by capture, and slave-raiding was one of the principal causes of war. Generosity was the pattern with most Indians, although in the dry Southwest we find some who made a virtue of thrift. In the main, a man was respected because he gave, not because he possessed. The Northwest Coast chiefs patterned generosity into an ugliness. A chief would invite a rival to a great feast, the famous potlatch. At the feast he would shower his rival and other guests with gifts, especially copper disks and blankets woven of mountain sheep wool, which were the highest units of value. He might further show his lavishness by burning some possessions, even partially destroy a copper disk, and, as like as not, kill a few slaves.

If within a reasonable time the other chief did not reply with an even larger feast, at which he gave away or destroyed double what his rival had got rid of, he was finished as a chief—but if he did respond in proper form, he might be beggared, and also finished. That was the purpose of the show. Potlatches were given for other purposes, such as to authenticate the accession of the heir to a former chief, or to buy a higher status, but ruinous rivalry was constant. They seem to have been a rather disagreeable, invidious, touchy people. The cruelty of the southeasterners is revolting, but there is something especially unpleasant about proving one's generosity and carelessness of possessions by killing a slave—with a club made for that special purpose and known as a "slave-killer."

The Meso-American culture could spread, changing beyond recognition as it did so, because it carried its food supply with it. The Northwest Coast culture could not, because its food supply was restricted to its place of origin.

North and east of the Northwest Coast area stretched the sub-Arctic and the plains of Canada, areas incapable of primitive farming. To the south and east were mountains and the region between the Rockies and the Coastal ranges called the Great Basin. Within it are large stretches of true desert; most of it is arid. Early on, Pueblo influences reached into the southern part, in Utah and Nevada, but as the climate grew drier, they died away. It was a land to be occupied by little bands of simple hunters and gatherers of seeds and roots, not strong enough to force their way into anywhere richer.

In only one other area was there a natural food supply to compare with the Northwest Coast's, and that was in the bison range of the Great Plains. But, as already noted, for men without horses or rifles, hunting bison was a tricky and hazardous business. Take the year 1600, when the Spanish were already established in New Mexico and the English and French almost ready to make settlements on the East Coast, and look for the famous Plains tribes. They are not there. Some are in the mountains, some in the woodlands to the northeast, some farming to the eastward, within the zone of ample rainfall. Instead we find scattered bands of Athabascans occupying an area no one else wanted.

Then the white men turned everything upside down. Three elements were most important in the early influence: the dislodgment of eastern tribes, the introduction of the horse, and metal tools and firearms. Let us look first at the impact on the centers of high culture.

White men came late to the Northwest Coast, and at first only as traders. As already noted, early contact with them enriched the life of the Indians and brought about a cultural spurt. Then came settlers. The most advanced, best organized tribes stood up fairly well against them for a time, and they are by no means extinct, but of their old culture there are now only remnants, with the strongest survivals being in the arts. Today, those Indians who are in the "Indian business," making money from tourists, dress in fringed buckskin and war bonnets, because otherwise the tourists will not accept them as genuine.

The tribes of the Atlantic Coast were quickly dislodged or wiped out. The more advanced groups farther inland held out all through colonial times and on into the 1830's, making fairly successful adjustments to the changed situation, retaining their sovereignty, and enriching their culture with wholesale taking over of European elements, including, in the South, the ownership of Negro slaves. Finally, as already noted, they were forcibly removed to Oklahoma, and in the end their sovereignty was destroyed. They remain numerous, and although some are extremely poor and backward, others, still holding to their tribal affiliations, have merged successfully into the general life of the state, holding positions as high as chief justice of the state supreme court. The Iroquois still hold out in New York and in Canada on remnants of their original reservations. Many of them have had remarkable success in adapting themselves to white American life while retaining considerable elements of their old culture. Adherents to the old religion are many, and the rituals continue vigorously.

The British invaders to the New World, and to a lesser degree the French, came to colonize. They came in thousands, to occupy the land. They were, therefore, in direct competition with the Indians and acted accordingly, despite their verbal adherence to fine principles of justice and fair dealing. The Spanish came quite frankly to conquer, to Christianize, and to exploit, all by force of arms. They did not shilly-shally about Indian title to the land or Indian sovereignty, they simply took over, then granted the Indians titles deriving from the Spanish crown. They came in small numbers—only around 3,000 settled in the Southwest—and the Indian labor force was essential to their aims. Therefore they did not dislodge or exterminate the Indians, and they had notable success in modifying Indian culture for survival within their regime and contribution to it.

In the Southwest the few Spaniards, cut off from the main body in Mexico by many miles of difficult, wild country, could not have survived alone against the wild tribes that shortly began to harry them. They needed the Pueblo Indians and the Pueblos needed them. The Christian Pueblos were made secure in their lands and in their local self-government. They approached social and political equality. During the period when New Mexico was under the Mexican Republic, for two years a Taos Indian, braids, blanket, and all, was governor of the territory. Eighteen pueblos survive to this day, with a population now approaching 19,000, in addition to nearly 4,000 Hopis, whose culture is Pueblo, in Arizona. They are conservative progressives, prosperous on the whole, with an excellent chance of surviving as a distinctive group for many generations to come. It was in the house of a Pueblo priest, a man deeply versed in the old religion as well as a devout Catholic, that I first saw color television.

The Spanish, then, did not set populations in motion. That was done chiefly from the east. The great Spanish contribution was loosing the horses. They did not intend to; in fact they made every possible effort to prevent Indians from acquiring horses or learning to ride. But the animals multiplied and ran wild; they spread north from California into Oregon; they spread into the wonderful grazing land of the high Plains, a country beautifully suited to horses.

From the east, the tribes were pressing against the tribes farther west. Everything was in unhappy motion, and the tribes nearest to the white men had firearms. So the Chippewas, carrying muskets, pushed westward into Minnesota, driving the reluctant Dakotas, the Sioux tribes, out of the wooded country into the Plains as the horses spread north. At first the Dakotas hunted and ate the strange animals, then they learned to ride them, and they were off.

The Sioux were mounted. So were the Blackfeet. The semi-civilized Cheyennes swung into the saddle and moved out of the farming country onto the bison range. The Kiowas moved from near the Yellowstone to the Panhandle; the Comanches came down out of the Rocky Mountains; the Arapahos, the Crows, abandoning their cornfields, and the Piegans, the great fighting names, all followed the bison. They built their life around the great animals. They ate meat lavishly all year round; their tepees, carried or dragged now by horses, became commodious. A new culture, a horse-and-bison culture, sprang up overnight. The participants in it had a wonderful time. They feasted, they roved, they hunted, they played. Over a serious issue, such as the invasion of one tribe's territory by another, they could fight deadly battles, but otherwise even war was a game in which shooting an enemy was an act earning but little esteem, but touching one with one's bare hand or with a stick was the height of military achievement.

This influx of powerful tribes drove the last of the Athabascans into the Southwest. There the Apaches and the Navahos were also mounted and on the go, developing their special, deadly pattern of war as a business. In the Panhandle country, the Kiowas and Comanches looked westward to the Spanish and Pueblo settlements, where totally alien peoples offered rich plunder. The Pueblos, as we have seen, desired to live at peace. The original Spanish came to conquer; their descendants, becoming Spanish-Americans, were content to hold what they had, farm their fields, and graze their flocks. To the north of the two groups were Apaches and Utes; to the east, Kiowas and Comanches; to the south, what seemed like unlimited Apaches; and to the west the Navahos, of whom there were several thousands by the middle of the seventeenth century.

The tribes named above, other than the Kiowas and Comanches, did not share in the Plains efflorescence. The Navahos staged a different cultural spurt of their own, combining extensive farming with constant horseback plundering, which in turn enabled them to become herdsmen, and from the captured wool develop their remarkable weaving industry. The sheep, of course, which became important in their economy, also derived from the white men. Their prosperity and their arts were superimposed on a simple camp life. With this prosperity, they also developed elaborate rituals and an astoundingly rich, poetic mythology.

The Dakotas first saw horses in 1722, which makes a convenient peg date for the beginning of the great Plains culture. A little over a hundred years later, when Catlin visited the Mandans, it was going full blast. The memory of a time before horses had grown dim. By 1860 the Plains tribes were hard-pressed to stand the white men off; by 1880 the whole pattern was broken and the bison were gone. At its height, Plains Indian culture was brittle. Materially, it depended absolutely on a single source of food and skins; in other aspects, it required the absolute independence of the various tribes. When these two factors were eliminated, the content was destroyed. Some Indians may still live in tepees, wear at times their traditional clothing, maintain here and there their arts and some of their rituals, but these are little more than fringe survivals.

While the Plains culture died, the myth of it spread and grew to become embedded in our folklore. Not only the Northwest Coast Indians but many others as unlikely wear imitations of Plains Indian costume and put on "war dances," to satisfy the believers in the myth. As it

exists today in the public mind, it still contains the mutually in-
congruous elements of the Noble Red Man and the Bloodthirsty Savage
that first came into being three centuries and a half ago, before any
white man had ever seen a war bonnet or a tepee, or any Indian had
ridden a horse.

3

Imperial Prosperity from Southern Plantations
LOUIS B. WRIGHT

*A man's reach, wrote Browning, should exceed his grasp, or what's a
heaven for? History ought to be as much concerned with man's reach as
with his grasp. It ought to consider the heaven in men's lives no less than
their earth. If history is the record of what men have thought and done,
then their hopes are as properly a part of the record as their achievements.
Unfortunately, only their successes tend to live after them; the visions they
could not fulfill are "oft interred with their bones." History tends to concentrate on plans that were realized. It does not linger over actions which,
however significant in their day, have not for various reasons become part
of the more permanent ways of society.*

*Here is the particular appeal and importance of the following essay by
Dr. Louis B. Wright, Director of the Folger Shakespeare Library of Washington, D.C. Dr. Wright has earned a wide reputation as a historian of American colonial society, his interest centering largely on its English sources
and connections. His contribution to our knowledge and understanding of
the period consists not only in his own appraisals of colonial culture but also
in his excellent editions of important primary materials.*

*In the spring of 1951, Dr. Wright delivered a series of lectures at Alabama
College on the theme of "The Colonial Search for a Southern Eden." He*

SOURCE: Louis B. Wright, *The Colonial Search for a Southern Eden* (University:
University of Alabama Press, 1953), pp. 21–39. Reprinted by permission of the
author and publisher.

wished to relive with Englishmen of the sixteenth and seventeenth centuries the persistent dream they had of establishing profitable colonies in the Southern part of the Atlantic seaboard. In the second of his lectures, which is reprinted here, Dr. Wright directs his attention to the enthusiastic plans of Elizabethans and Jacobeans for the colony of Virginia. What they hoped and what actually occurred were very different things.

But it is the special theme of Dr. Wright's essay that both are essential components of the past. What man proposed and nature disposed has to be understood no less than what nature and other historical factors helped realize. Only through such understanding can one appreciate the fullness of the American adventure.

If the delusion of quick riches from the discovery of gold died hard as Englishmen contemplated the resources of America, another dream almost as intoxicating took its place. Indescribable good things might be found in the vegetable and animal kingdoms, and prosperity and plenty would flow from the fields and streams of the New World. Even more exciting to many an Englishman nursing his gout or other ailment was the belief that curative herbs of wondrous potency were to be had overseas for the picking. Since 1577, English readers had been wistfully contemplating a book called *Joyfull Newes Out Of The Newe Founde Worlde,* translated by a merchant named John Frampton from the Spanish of Nicholas Monardes. This volume assured the public that cures for most of the ills of mankind would be forthcoming from America. And that portion of America most productive of desirable products was the southern region. In popular belief the sun-drenched climates were most like paradise and would produce all of the good things which man had possessed before the fall of Adam. Both California and Florida still employ press agents to keep that doctrine alive.

In the 1560's someone in contact with Spanish America, probably John Hawkins, introduced tobacco, believed to be a strong and beneficent medicine, and its use set in motion a chain reaction which had far-reaching effects on the development of the British Empire. Also introduced soon thereafter were other vegetable products, notably potatoes, both white and sweet, which proved to be valuable supplements to the diet. In addition to their food value, physicians assured potato-eaters that this food had other virtues including the power to stimulate the affections of tender love. The price of potatoes responded accordingly.

Men had once thought of America as a series of gold mines; now they began to talk of the country as one vast herb garden or plantation of good things, especially those vegetables and fruits which grew in tropical climates. Ponce de Leon had believed that Florida would reveal a fountain of youth. More prosaic Anglo-Saxons contented themselves with an array of new herbs, fruits, gums, and drugs which might confer some of the same benefits. The early promotional literature is filled with extravagant descriptions of Nature's abundance in the land to the south.

The bounty of Nature would provide the commodities, said propagandists and pamphleteers, to make England prosperous. The unpeopled land across the seas would also make a place for the surplus population and create a market for more English goods. The English have been called a "nation of shopkeepers"—a nation whose primary interest is business and commerce. We Americans have attained our own commercial civilization by a natural inheritance. This instinct for commerce—as contrasted with the mere search for treasure—is evident from the earliest proposals for English expansion in the New World.

The first book describing Virginia, for example, gives an excellent statement of the mercantilist point of view and follows it with an enumeration of the multitude of merchantable commodities by which Virginia would enrich itself and the mother country. This work, *A briefe and true report of the new found land of Virginia* (1588), by Thomas Hariot, a scientific observer, is worth our attention for the way it emphasized a point of view which dominated English policy for the next two centuries. The first chapter of the book, Hariot promises, "will make declaration of such commodities there alreadie found or to be raised, which will not onely serue the ordinary turnes of you which are and shall bee the planters and inhabitants, but such an ouerplus sufficiently to bee yelded, or by men of skill to bee prouided, as by way of trafficke and exchaunge with our owne nation of England, will enrich your selues the prouiders, those that shal deal with you, the enterprisers in general, and greatly profit our owne countrey men, to supply them with most things which heretofore they haue bene faine to prouide, either of strangers or of our enemies: which commodities for distinction sake, I call Merchantable."

The notion of a self-sufficient closed commercial empire, which would not need to buy from strangers and enemies, was to grow stronger with the passing years. Already Hariot in 1588 thought he had discovered in Virginia (really the coast of what is now North Carolina) a source for some of the exotic commodities which England was to seek, usually in vain, during the next century.

Significantly Hariot begins his chapter of "merchantable" commodities with a discussion of silk, for silk had to be imported from Asia, or bought from Italians, Frenchmen, Portuguese, or Spaniards. In contemporary thinking, its purchase represented a great drain on the economy.

Silk was to be a greater will-o'-the-wisp than gold mines had ever been. From Raleigh's colony to the settlement of Georgia, the imperial economy would demand the production of silk, and always success evaded the planners. Englishmen unhappily had to pay dearly for an extravagant fashion which made courtiers and gentlemen rustle in silk doublets and hose. Even after the eighteenth century had introduced a more subdued fashion in dress for men, satin and taffeta gowns for women consumed an enormous yardage of silk. One has only to look at a few portraits of ladies by Gainsborough, Reynolds, and Romney to realize that even if the world of fashion was small, it took thousands of yards of silk to clothe it. At the time of Oglethorpe's project for settling Georgia, England's annual silk bill averaged approximately £500,000 sterling, and for the preceding century and a half England had been paying huge sums for this fabric.

Hariot thought that Virginia would soon supply silk for home consumption and for commerce. He had observed a silk-fibred grass similar to a type common in Persia "which is in the selfe same climate as Virginia, of which very many of the silke workes that come from thence into Europe are made." He also was hopeful of worm silk, for "in manie of our iourneyes we founde silke wormes fayre and great" and "there is no doubt but if art be added in planting of mulberry trees and others fitte for them in commodious places . . . there will rise as great a profite in time to the Virginians, as thereof doth now to the Persians, Turkes, Italians, and Spaniards." A warm climate like that of Persia was what Hariot thought he had found in Virginia, and undoubtedly the products which the Levant Company and the East India Company had brought from the East would soon be flowing from the New World.

Among the merchantable commodities which Hariot believed Virginia could produce were many others which England had imported: drugs and rare gums, oils, wine, cedar wood, furs, iron, copper, alum, pitch, tar, rosin and turpentine. Among the drugs was sassafras, a fragrant shrub used to this day as a folk remedy. Sassafras tea, drunk in April and May, is supposed to cure spring fever. So highly was it prized by the early seventeenth century that many cargoes of sassafras were shipped back to English markets.

Second only to silk in the volume of money required for its purchase was wine. Foreigners from the warmer countries, notably Portugal and Spain, had long profited from English thirst, and English merchants looked forward hopefully to colonies in a climate where grape vines would flourish. Consequently Hariot's observations on the grapes of Virginia stirred new hope: "There are two kinds of grapes that the soile doth yeeld naturally: the one is small and sowre of the ordinarie bignesse as ours in England: the other farre greater & of himselfe lushious sweet. When they are planted and husbanded as they ought, a principall commoditie of wines by them may be raised." The big luscious grapes were muscadines or scuppernongs, and Hariot's words were at least partially prophetic, for though wine-making never succeeded in bolstering the economy of Virginia, homemade scuppernong wine has comforted many a Southerner from that day to this.

The promise of wine production in Virginia impressed other early travellers, some of whom were even more enthusiastic than Hariot. William Strachey, for example, writing about 1610, comments that "we have eaten there as full and lushious a grape as in the villages between Paris and Amiens, and I have drunck often of the rathe [early] wine, which Doctor Bohune and other of our people have made full as good, as your French British wyne. Twenty gallons at a time have bene sometimes made without any other helpe then by crushing the grape with the hand, which letting to settle five or six daies, hath in the drawing forth proved strong and headdy. Unto what perfection might not these be brought by the art and industry of manie skillful vineroones [vignerons], being thus naturally good."

Like the desire for silk production, the hope of growing grapes and making wine for commerce persisted for many generations. At the beginning of the eighteenth century Robert Beverley made elaborate attempts to produce wine commercially at his plantation in King and Queen County, Virginia. He was scarcely more successful than others had been. John Fontaine, a French Huguenot, with characteristic French logic, accounted for Beverley's failure by pointing out that he followed Spanish instead of French methods in wine production.

Most of the early writers on English expansion had the mercantilist point of view and realized that the greatest profits eventually would come from the colonial production of raw materials which England had to buy outside of what today we would call the "sterling area." Captain John Smith in 1606 emphasized the commercial possibilities of Virginia: "Muscovia and Polonia [Russia and Poland] doe yearely receive many thousands for pitch, tarre, sope-ashes, Rosen, Flax, Cordage, Sturgeon, Masts, Yards, Wainscot, Firres Glasses and such like; also Swethland [Sweden] for Iron and Copper. France in like manner for wine, Canvas, and Salt. Spaine as much for Iron, Steele, Figges, Reasons [raisins], and Sackes [wine]. Italy with Silkes and Velvets consumes our chiefe Commodities. Holland maintaines it selfe by fishing and trading at our owne doores." Virginia, Smith assured the reader, could provide all of these commodities within the scope of a hundred miles, "either ready provided by nature, or else to be prepared were but industrious men to labour."

The Muscovy Company which imported from the Baltic forests most of the naval stores required by English vessels was at the mercy of the whims of Russia, which was as difficult to deal with in the seventeenth century as it is in the twentieth. One thing our own diplomats ought to know is that Russian behavior is historically consistent, whether the ruler be Ivan the Terrible or Joseph Stalin. If the magnificent forests of Virginia could supply all of the needs of the royal navy and English shipping, that service alone would justify the expense of colonization. For various reasons Virginia's forests did not meet expectations for forest products, but eventually the long leaf pines of South Carolina and Georgia supplied a profitable trade in rosin and turpentine— valuable commodities in international trade to this day.

So important was the colonization of the earthly paradise in Virginia by Englishmen that the endeavor became a patriotic crusade. The Virginia Company enlisted the services of the clergy, a very good substitute in the seventeenth century for the British Broadcasting Company. Preachers extolled the virtues of Virginia in the pulpit and pictured the new country as little short of celestial in its promise. For example, the Reverend Daniel Price, a fashionable London preacher and chaplain to Prince Henry, delivered a sermon on May 28, 1609 which is typical of the clergy's extravagant praise of Virginia. Published by authority of the Virginia Company under the title of *Saul's Prohibition Staide . . . with a reproofe of those that traduce the Honourable Plantation of Virginia. Preached in a Sermon Commaunded at Pauls Crosse* (1609), this sermon condemned to hell all those who libelled Virginia and pictured the new country as "the Barne of Britaine, as Sicily was to Rome, or the Garden of the world as was Thessaly, or the Argosie of the world as is Germany." Virginia, said Price, would soon surpass Persia, Tyre, Babylon, Arabia, Spain, and other countries, ancient and modern, in the supply of spices, silks, dyes, oils, rare woods and other precious commodities. Moreover, investors in this godly enterprise would have an insurance not vouchsafed other speculators, for God himself would grant them an "vnspeakable blessing" for bringing the message of salvation to the Indians. "You will make . . . A Sauadge country to become a sanctifyed Country; you will obtaine their best commodities; they will obtaine the sauing of their Soules; you will enlarge the boundes of this Kingdome, nay the bounds of heauen."

Here openly asserted with ecclesiastical authority is the statement of profit in the saving of heathen souls for Protestant Christianity with the distinct implication that Virginia is presently to be a corner of heaven itself. English travellers in the nineteenth century were to ridicule Americans for their bumptiousness in declaring that the United States was "God's country," as if it had the special favor of the Deity. That assertion was made in the early seventeenth century by Daniel Price and scores of other pious promoters of English colonization.

The Virginia Company and later the royal authorities under James I and Charles I took steps to see that Virginia became a source of the commodities which were causing the greatest drain of cash into foreign pockets, namely silk and wine. The newly-established House of Burgesses in 1619, on instructions from London, passed a law that every man in Virginia owning land should plant six mulberry trees annually for seven years to nourish silk worms. The mulberry trees flourished all right but the worms suffered from sundry mishaps. Just when it looked as if the infant industry would get a start, rats destroyed the cocoons.

King James himself busied his royal brain with schemes to encourage silk production. Already religious refugees from France and other Continental countries had set up silk-spinning and weaving shops in England and the King hoped to produce the raw silk for this hopeful industry in his new colony of Virginia. To promote this enterprise—and some others almost as important—he instructed one John Bonoeil, a Frenchman in charge of the Royal silk works, to compile a treatise.   When the book was done, James himself wrote a preface and the whole thing was published under the title of *His Maiesties Gracious Letter To The Earle of South-Hampton, Treasurer, and to the Councell and Company of Virginia heere: commanding the present setting vp of Silkworkes, and planting of Vines in Virginia. . . . Also a Treatise of the Art of making Silke: Or, Directions for the making of lodgings, and the breeding, nourishing, and ordering of Silkewormes, and for the planting of Mulbery trees, and all other things belonging to the Silke Art. Together with instructions how to plant and dresse Vines, and to make Wine, and how to dry Raisins, Figs, and other fruits, and to set Oliues, Oranges, Lemons, Pomegranates, Almonds, and many other fruits, &c.   And in the end, a Conclusion, with sundry profitable remonstrances to the Colonies.   Set foorth for the benefit of the two renowned and most hopefull Sisters, Virginia and the Summer-Ilands. By Iohn Boneil Frenchman, seruant in these imployments to his most Excellent Maiesty of Great Brittaine, France, Ireland, Virginia, and the Summer-Ilands. Published by Authority* (1622). With all the weight of the Crown behind it, this treatise ought to have been effective, but like government efforts in the promotion of analogous enterprises in later times, it failed.   Recently we have read in the newspapers about British efforts to relieve the shortage of fats at home by raising groundnuts [peanuts] in Africa and the enormous losses incurred, and of the plan to produce poultry and eggs for home consumption on African farms.   From King James' time to Mr. Attlee's, the government has had ill-luck in promoting these enterprises of imperial benefit. Ignorance, weather, and pests often confound the dreams of statesmen.

King James' letter prefatory to Bonoeil's treatise is indicative of the seriousness with which the government viewed the necessity of producing silk and wine within the empire.   "Whereas We vnderstand that the Soyle in Virginia naturally yeeldeth store of excellent Mulberry trees," wrote the English Solomon, "We haue taken into Our Princely consideration the great benefit that may grow to the Aduenturers and Planters, by the breed of Silkewormes, and setting vp of Silkeworkes in those parts. And therefore of Our gracious Inclination to a designe of so much honour and aduantage to the publike, Wee haue thought good, as at sundry other times, so now more particularly to recommend it to your speciall care, hereby charging and requiring you to take speedy order, that our people there vse all possible diligence in breed-ing Silkewormes, and erecting Silkeworkes, and that they rather bestow their trauell in compassing this rich and solid Commodity then in Tobacco, which besides much vnnecessary expence, brings with it many disorders and inconueniences. And for as much as Our Seruant, Iohn Bonoeil hath taken paines in setting downe the true vse of the Silkeworme, together with the Art of Silkemaking, and of planting Vines, and that his experience and abilities may much conduce to the aduancement of this business; We doe hereby likewise require you to cause his directions, both for the said Silkeworkes and Vineyards, to bee carefully put in practice thorowout our Plantations there, that so the worke may goe on cheerfully, and receiue no more interruptions nor delayes."

To his royal majesty, it must have seemed simple to decree the pro-duction of these commodities which would redress the balance of trade with the rest of the world, but unhappily, about the time Bonoeil's book reached Virginia, the Indians fell on the settlements in the terrible massacre of 1622, a calamity which nearly wiped out the colony. For several years, the Virginians were more concerned about survival than with King James' plans for the empire.

It is worth noting that the King here makes an attack in passing on the production of tobacco, a commodity which he had condemned the year after he ascended the throne in *A Counter Blaste To Tobacco* (1604). Having gone on record as opposed to the use of tobacco, the King felt obliged to continue his hostility. Already, however, signs indicated that tobacco might prove the most profitable crop produced in Virginia.

About 1612, John Rolfe began to experiment with the growing of tobacco. Within four years it had become a staple crop and was planted even in the streets and marketplace of Jamestown. The use of tobacco had already taken such a firm hold on Englishmen that in 1614 it was estimated that England's annual tobacco bill amounted to £200,000 sterling and someone complained in Parliament that even preachers smelled of smoke and poor men each night spent a large portion of their daily wages on pipe tobacco. Even though King James might not ap-prove, it was clear that here was a product which would have to be produced within the empire or else the drain on the economy would be almost as great as that for silk and wine.

Some tobacco was produced in England, but before Rolfe's experiments most of it had come from Spain, to the distress of English imperialists. In 1620 one Edward Bennett published *A Treatise deuided into three parts touching the inconueniences that the Importation of Tobacco out of Spaine hath brought into this Land.* Using some of the same arguments made by the advocates of silk culture, Bennett urged the production of tobacco within the empire. "The maine decay of Trade," he pointed out, "and the chiefe cause that hindreth the importation of Bullion out of Spaine is Tobacco, for there is consumed by all computation, yearely in this Land, three hundred thousand weight." The Spanish tobacco trade, Bennett argues, has hindered the development of Virginia and the Bermudas. The encouragement of tobacco production in these colonies, he asserts, would create prosperity and establish a strong bulwark against Spain. Incidentally, Bennett insisted that the Spaniards were very uncleanly in the way they handled their tobacco. He is probably the first to use a theme which tobacco advertisers in a later time appear to have found effective.

The popularity of tobacco and its potentialities for the trade of England had not been anticipated by the economic planners who were slow to realize that at last a luxury product had been discovered which could be produced within the frame of empire. Once that fact was demonstrated, the government took steps to see that England reaped the maximum benefits from the tobacco trade. Government regulations from the time of James I onward forbade the growing of tobacco in England itself and decreed that tobacco grown in the colonies should be shipped directly to English ports for processing. Thus the government reaped a substantial revenue from duties and brought in a product in great demand in the foreign trade. The sale of tobacco abroad, even in competition with Spanish and Dutch tobacco, helped to offset the unfavorable cash position created by purchases of non-empire products like silk and wine.

The production of tobacco, which had come into English trade almost by the backdoor, occupied a place of first importance in the imperial economy in the later seventeenth and eighteenth centuries. So profitable was the trade that many merchants of London and Bristol devoted themselves exclusively to it, and the production of tobacco was the main concern of planters in Virginia, Maryland, and in a portion of the Carolinas. Such a concentration was not without its penalties because a crop failure, or a glut of the market by overproduction, might cause a widespread financial disaster. Wise leaders in the colonies argued earnestly against the hazards of the one crop system, a system which has often been the ruin of the South, but profits were large in good years, and the pressures were great, both at home and abroad, to raise more and more tobacco. When the Reverend James Blair at the end of the seventeenth century was arguing with the Board of Trade that they should help establish a college to save the souls of Virginians, Sir Edward Seymour, a Lord of the Treasury, exclaimed, "Souls? Damn your souls! Make tobacco!" To the empire builders, tobacco was more important even than salvation, and they prized the tobacco colonies on the Chesapeake above those sometimes recalcitrant and always competitive offspring to the north.

Tobacco was an ideal commodity from the point of view of the seventeenth- and eighteenth-century mercantilists. It was produced in the raw state in the colonies; it was shipped from the colonies to the mother country, paying an export tax in the colony and an import tax at home; and it could be processed in England to become a lucrative article of export. Furthermore it could be raised with unskilled labor, such labor as could be supplied by African slaves, themselves an article of profitable commerce to the Royal African Company. The usefulness of the rawest slaves from the west coast of Africa in the tobacco fields of Virginia, Maryland, and Bermuda helped to fasten a system of labor and a racial problem upon the Southern colonies which had evil consequences persisting to our own day.

Although the very success of tobacco as a money crop was a hindrance to the production of other desired commodities, the planners did not abandon hope that Virginia would eventually compete with France, Spain, Italy, Persia, and the East Indies in exotic products. The distribution of John Bonoeil's treatise in 1622 was accompanied by orders from the Virginia Company commanding efforts to produce silk and wine. Skilled artisans from Southern Europe came to Virginia to instruct the settlers in these crafts, and experimentation led some Virginians to believe as late as 1649 that silk and wine would supersede in time tobacco in popular favor, but their optimism was ill-founded. The profits from sugar in Barbados induced a few planters to try to plant sugar cane, but nothing came of this. The grapes, lemons, oranges, ginger, and figs, recommended to the planters, likewise failed, and tobacco ruled supreme. In 1705 Robert Beverley the historian complained that Virginians were so entrapped in the one crop system and so lacking in enterprise that they would not even use their abundant timber for making their own wooden ware but instead imported it from England. By this time, however, the Board of Trade in London had come to approve of Virginia and Maryland's complete concentration upon tobacco, which fitted well with mercantile theory. They would try elsewhere to produce the other desired materials.

One of the commodities which international trade in the Elizabethan period had popularized, and which England now wanted to produce, was sugar. Sugar like silk was a product which cost England cash, cash which went to Italian, Spanish, and Portuguese producers.

In early times, Englishmen had depended on the bees to provide their sweets, and many ancient recipes specified honey for sweetening. But in the sixteenth century, trade with the Canary and Madeira Islands brought sugar into fairly common use. By the early seventeenth century it was an essential.

Sugar was believed to have great curative values and to be a preservative of health. John Gerard, the herbalist, asserted that "It drieth and cleanseth the stomacke, maketh smooth the roughness of the breast and lungs, cleareth the voice, and putteth away hoarseness, the cough, and all sournesse and bitternesse." And a seventeenth century physician had a saying that

> If Sugar can preserve both Pears and Plumbs,
> Why can it not preserve as well our Lungs?

Even if sugar had not possessed these healing virtues, it was pleasant to the taste and Englishmen even used it to qualify their drinks. But England was not a sugar-producing nation, and the government was troubled.

Sugar canes had been taken from the Canaries to Brazil and had flourished. From Brazil, sugar cane had spread to the Spanish islands of the West Indies. Perhaps Englishmen might find a place where they too could produce sugar. About 1640 conditions on Barbados forced the planters there to think of a crop to take the place of tobacco. Stimulated by the demand for tobacco on the European market, the Barbadians had raised more of the weed than they could sell. Faced with bankruptcy because of the glut of the tobacco market, they were ready to try anything and sugar cane looked promising. The cane grew so luxuriantly on Barbados that within a short time sugar had superseded tobacco as the principal industry on that island, and it quickly spread to other British territory in the Caribbean.

On the mainland of North America English planters had no success with sugar cane in the colonial period. But Barbados became a sugar paradise. Since sugar making required expensive equipment, only those planters with large capital could operate the plantations and refineries. Consequently many of the smaller planters, who had done well with tobacco, had to leave Barbados in search of greener pastures. Many of them came to South Carolina and helped to establish the economy of that colony on a sound basis, as we shall see later.

The sugar making of Barbados was so profitable in imperial trade that by 1675 over four hundred vessels were engaged in the transport of sugar and molasses. A by-product of molasses, rum, became a national drink and another commodity enormously important in international commerce. The sugar islands were so prized by the mother country that when the Peace of Paris in 1763 ended the Seven Years War, some English politicians wanted to allow France to retain Canada on condition that she cede the French islands in the West Indies to Great Britain.

These French West Indian possessions had proved so enormously valuable as sources of sugar and molasses that English merchants were anxious to obtain them. The demand for rum had long outstripped the capacity of Barbados and the other British islands to supply the necessary raw material, namely molasses, but nevertheless England tried to prevent the colonies from developing an independent trade with the French West Indies. As early as 1733, England passed the first Molasses Act to restrict the trade to the British possessions and succeeded only in stimulating wholesale smuggling between the French islands and New England, where the manufacture of rum had become an important factor in the Northern colonies' prosperity. This disrespect for imperial regulations by the Northern colonies was one more reason why the home government found the Southern colonies more to their liking.

By the middle of the seventeenth century, England had succeeded in developing two profitable tropical products within the empire, namely tobacco and sugar. The cash which these commodities brought into England confirmed still further the belief held by many of the mercantile imperialists that the most desirable colonies would be those established in the South. Pleased with the profits from tobacco and sugar, Englishmen for the next century continued their endeavor to find a modern counterpart of the Garden of Eden in the warmer parts of America where they might yet produce all of those exotic commodities which had previously defied the best efforts of their statesmen.

God's Bridge Falling Down:
"Another Approach" to New England Puritanism Assayed
DARRETT B. RUTMAN

It is widely agreed that the beginnings of American life and thought were, in many basic respects, Puritan. But just what these Puritan beginnings were, no less than what they signified, has long been a matter of disagreement. A notable contribution to the study of this subject is a recent book by Darrett B. Rutman, of the University of New Hampshire, entitled Winthrop's Boston: Portrait of a Puritan Town, 1630–1649 *(1965). In his book Professor Rutman arrives at the following conclusions: John Winthrop, the leader of the Puritan migration to Massachusetts Bay, had wished to pattern the American colony after the ideal of a medieval community. But actual conditions made it impossible for him to realize the ideal. The materialism and individualism of others thwarted his hope for action that would be based on a sense of community. Far from being united in purpose and deed, society was early divided into classes. Seeking salvation became less a matter of Christian "love" and a self-effacing celebration of God, and more a pursuit of the moral and good life. Diversity in religion supplanted an earlier belief in a unified society. In sum, the actual course taken by the development of institutions in Boston during the Puritans' first two decades marked a real decline from the ideal "city upon a hill" that Winthrop had conjured up, in the spring of 1630, in his address to his transatlantic fellow travelers on the flagship Arbella.*

It is precisely the theme of decline that Professor Rutman explores in the article reprinted below. He is, in doing so, sustaining his larger thesis about the beginnings of American Puritan experience and, in particular, responding to the suggestion of Edmund S. Morgan, one of our outstanding authori-

SOURCE: *The William and Mary Quarterly,* Third Series, XIX, 3 (July, 1962), 408–421. Copyright © 1962 by Darrett B. Rutman. Reprinted by permission of Curtis Brown, Ltd. The original footnotes have been omitted.

ties on early American history, that what we have hitherto accepted as evidence of religious decline may in fact have been evidence of increasing religious sophistication and scrupulosity. The exchange between the two scholars poses some significant questions. Are they perhaps talking about developments that were not mutually exclusive, but possibly even complementary, so that decline in one aspect of early Puritan life may have been accompanied by growing sophistication and scrupulosity in another? To what extent is Professor Rutman correct in arguing that Winthrop and his cohorts had projected a bridge between this world and the next? Indeed, was Winthrop's ideal of a "city upon a hill" ever meant to be a practicable program? As Morgan has elsewhere suggested, is it possible that Rutman has made too much of Winthrop's speech? Has he converted into a civic plan what the Puritan leader meant to use only as a literary device?

But however separate their paths in other respects, Morgan and Rutman converge on at least two important points. The first is that generalizations about American Puritan beginnings must be tested by a close examination of particulars. To this goal, Rutman has made a very valuable contribution in Winthrop's Boston, a book that takes its place alongside of Sumner C. Powell's Puritan Village (1963), a study of the formation of Sudbury, Massachusetts. Their second point of agreement is what is universally apparent: that in the soil of early Puritan experience was rooted much of what American life later became, and that a careful probing of the one is essential to meaningful understanding of the other.

In a recent article, Edmund S. Morgan has suggested "another approach" to New England Puritanism, calling for a "town by town and church by church" study of the section, for an examination of "every known individual in a town, to discover how much land he owned, where he lived, how much he paid in taxes, whether he belonged to the church, how many children he had."

There should be no argument with Morgan's method. Advocates of one school of thought or another regarding New England Puritanism and the section as a whole have long drawn generalities from generalities; Morgan would have generalities built upon specifics. But he goes beyond method. He tucks into his methodological argument figures reflecting the proportion of church communicants to the whole congregation in the mid-1770's and writes that these "suggest a strange paradox: that the non-members may have had more religious scruples than the members." Persons accepting halfway membership in one New England church, as against full communion, he muses, "evidently had scruples against accepting the privileges which the more easygoing full members held out to them."

If such was the case in the eighteenth century, what are we to think of the non-members of the seventeenth century? Were they perhaps more

Puritan and more scrupulous than some of those who sought and obtained membership? . . . The very fact that the half-way covenant was
needed may be testimony, not to the decline of religion, but to the rise of an
extraordinary religious scrupulosity, which still existed in the eighteenth
century. The second generation of Puritans may have become so sophisticated in the morphology of conversion that they rejected, as inconclusive,
religious experiences that would have driven their parents unhesitatingly
into church membership.

These last surmises are startling, certainly, but they are open to
serious question. Historians have long been aware of the inadequacy
of monistic interpretations and have come increasingly to distrust the
variety of either/or equation which Morgan employs. There may well
have been a tendency toward "extraordinary religious scrupulosity,"
as he implies, but this fact does not necessarily rule out the element of
decline. Indeed, "scrupulosity" might well have been one symptom of
decline. Moreover, to ignore the element of decline is to shrug off in a
moment mountains of evidence to the contrary, much of it readily
obtainable by the very method Morgan advocates. The clear indication
is a steady disintegration of the ideal of the founders, a slow collapse
of that bridge which the Winthrops and Cottons were attempting to
build between this world and the next—a bridge consisting of a worldly
society in which men would be united in willingly performing their
duty to God, to the community, and to their fellow-men.

A survey of the rolls of the First Church of Boston and a comparison
with the known inhabitants of the town indicate the nature of the
original ideal. In the first years of settlement, the great majority of
the town's population was oriented in its religious feelings toward the
church. Out of 145 adult men and women known to have come to the
town from the Winthrop fleet of 1630, seventy-one were to join the First
Church prior to 1633 and eighty-nine, prior to 1636, while of forty-eight
families arriving in 1630, forty-two were to be represented in the church
by at least one adult member. This arrangement reflected the intention
of these first Puritans to have an absolute homogeneity—the congregation (in the sense of members) to be synonymous with the town's
population, and the population, excluding servants, to be synonymous
with the propertied elements of the town.

The early Puritan leaders constantly implied this intention. "Wee
must be knitt together in this worke as one man," John Winthrop told
his fellow passengers aboard the *Arbella* in the lay sermon "A
Modell of Christian Charity," "allwayes haveing before our eyes our
Commission and Community in the worke, our Community as members of the same body, soe shall wee keepe the unitie of the spirit in
the bond of peace, [and] the Lord will be our God and delight to dwell
among us, as his owne people." John Cotton, in his farewell to the

Winthrop fleet, referred to the settling of "a City or Commonwealth" such as God in the past had "blessed and prospered exceedingly, and made . . . a glorious Church," and commanded the settlers to "Goe forth, everyman that goeth, with a publicke spirit, looking not on your owne things onely, but also on the things of others." Our practice, wrote the men of Plymouth to Massachusetts in 1632, "was and hath been" to accept "only of shuch as come to dwell and inhabite, whether as servants or free men; and not sojourners," but the Bay commonwealth went further in this direction: when sixty passengers aboard the *Handmaid* desired "to plant here" in 1630, the authorities "would not receive them," they "having no testimony."

The interrelationship of land and church membership in the early years is clear, too. In 1633 the congregation of the First Church in Boston was setting out "men's lands, etc." Subsequently, the town meeting established a commission "to devide and dispose of all such lands belonging to the towne . . . to the inhabitants of the towne"; it was agreed that "all the inhabitants" should plant in a given area, "every able man fitt to plant" to have two acres, "and for every able youth one acre to be allotted out." Moreover, "noe further allotments shalbe graunted unto any new comers, but such as may be likely to be received members of the Congregation." But any people admitted to the colony or town during these early years—even servants—were to be those "of inoffensive Carryage" and "likely to be received members of the Congregation." The idea of potential conversion was strong, for while the theologians could and did rationalize the process into an awakening of God-implanted "grace" and hence adhere to a form of Calvinism, the laity all too often implied a literal conversion from sin to grace. Edward Howes, for example, sent John Winthrop, Jr., four wolf dogs "with an Irish boy to tend them" and assured Winthrop that, though a Roman Catholic, "with gods grace he will become a good convert."

In this monolithic society, the government of the colony and the towns was the prerogative of the freemen who were to be, in early theory, church members, landowners, and the great bulk of the adult male population. The election law itself (that of May 1631 providing that "noe man shalbe admitted to the freedome of this body polliticke, but such as are members of some of the churches within the lymitts of the same") together with the clear implication that church membership was superior to freemanship in the case of Nicholas Willis of Boston—who became a member of the First Church in May 1634, took part in a General Court on May 14, and was admitted a freeman in September—points up as much. For if the law established church membership as a prerequisite of freemanship, and if the towns held as a matter of practice that only those "likely to be received members of the Congregation" should receive allotments in the town, and that all male inhabitants should receive allotments, then eventually freemen, property holders, and male church members (excluding servants) would be the same. In the light of this ideal, the entrusting of government to the assistants in October 1630 "by the generall vote of the people, and erection of hands" should not be surprising. The people—all the people—were in theory God's people joined together by covenants with God and among themselves, and God, through them, would select their rulers.

From the beginning, however, the decline of the Puritan ideal was apparent. That all were not of like minds in regard to "Christian charity" led John Winthrop, Sr., shortly after arrival, to complain that "Sathan bends his forces against us, . . . so that I thinke heere are some persons who never shewed so much wickednesse in England as they have doone heer." In 1635 the people of Ipswich were concerned: "Our Towne of late but somewhat too late," wrote Nathaniel Ward, "have bene carefull on whome they bestowe lotts, being awakned therto by the confluence of many ill and doubtfull persons, and by their behaviour since they came in drinking and pilferinge." The Godly, he went on, "have made an ill change, even from the snare to the pitt," and "must mediate some safer refuge if God will afford it." Two years later a writer in Old England commented "that many in your plantacions discover much pride, as appeareth by the lettres we receave from them, wherein some of them write over to us for lace. . . . cuttworke coifes; and others, for deep stammell dyes; and some of your owne men tell us that many with you goe finely cladd." Sumptuary and prudential laws were passed, in part for economic reasons, in part to command men to follow God's dictates toward their fellow-men when they would not do so voluntarily. The problem concerned not only the unregenerates in the colony. "Divers of the elders' wives, etc., were in some measure partners in this general disorder"; cases of church discipline increased rapidly in the years after 1635; and in December 1638 a general fast was proclaimed in part in atonement for "the apparent decay of power of religion, and the general declining of professors to the world." The very next year a fight broke out among the members of the First Church as to the placement of a new meeting-house: "Some were for the green . . . ; others, viz., the tradesmen, especially, who dwelt about the market place, desired it might stand still near the market, lest in time it should divert the chief trade from thence."

All the while, the idea of homogeneity was being submerged by the influx of servants, tradesmen, and merchants. More and more, the congregation was becoming something apart from the greater number of inhabitants. In Boston, the congregation numbered about 110 in mid-1632, the town approximately 325; by 1650, the congregation numbered 625 while the town had grown to about 3,000. The appearance of people with no interest in the church accounts in part for this proportionate decrease. Equally important was the greater selectivity exercised by the church in admitting members. For a time, the commonwealth tried to maintain the line against the nonmembers participating in town affairs, enacting in September of 1635 that "none but freemen shall have any vote in any towne." By 1637, however, the nonmembers were voting for militia officers, and by 1647 all the inhabitants of the towns were free to take part in town government. Earlier, the idea of conversion had lost strength, and the church had begun the tendency toward that inward looking "tribalism" which Morgan has so well described in *The Puritan Family.* John Cotton, in 1641, taught out of Revelation, "None could enter into the temple until, etc.," and delivered the doctrine "that neither Jews nor any more of the Gentiles should be called until Antichrist were destroyed, viz. to a church estate, though here and there a proselyte."

The purity of independent congregationalism, too, was disappearing. The collapsing homogeneity was introducing diversity where the ideal of the founders had embraced a perfect joining together of all "in one mind, and one judgement, and one speech, in one truth" —not by coercion, but by the very strength of the truth itself. The ideal failing, the power of an organized ministry, supported by the power of the state, was brought to bear to enforce "truth." The maintenance of the church by both members and nonmembers was made mandatory by statute, though notably the church of John Cotton refused to make use of the legal provisions and clung to the idea of voluntary offerings. Subtle changes in the conduct of church business shifted power from the members to the ministers and elders, and from the individual churches to the assembled presbyteries of all the churches, culminating in the latter part of the second decade when the Cambridge Synod of 1646–48 and the *Platform of Church Discipline* which emerged from it were foisted upon the protesting members of the First Church. Inexorably, the church administration was hardening, institutionalizing.

Disaster lay in this direction, for the resultant protective shell of New England Puritanism, having sacrificed the substance of the ideals of the first years by attempting to impose conformity, could neither maintain the ideals nor withstand the pressures of coming generations. But the ministers could see no other way. Decline and formalism were going hand in hand, the decline of the ideals of the first years being sensed by the ministers and elders who attempted to counteract it by formalism, itself a further decline. Indeed, the ministers themselves were changing, becoming more and more adamant in their defense of what was emerging as a unique "New England Way." The gentle John Wilson, during the trial of the Quakers in 1651, struck one of the defendants, cursing him, "saying, the Curse of God or Jeusus goe with thee," and on his deathbed cited as "those sins amongst us, which provoked the displeasure of God" the rising up of the people *"against their Ministers . . . when indeed they do but Rule for Christ,"* and *"the making light of, and not subjecting to the Authority of* Synods, *without which the Churches cannot long subsist";* becoming, too, more and more mere purveyors of religion, anxious for preferments, squabbling over fees.

Most serious, however, was the failure of the children of the church members to complete—by undergoing the process of obtaining full membership—that covenant first offered when a parent presented them for baptism. The Christian education of children was basically the responsibility of the parents, though from the early 1640's, when criticism of the low spiritual state of the children began, the churches more and more imposed compulsory catechism. But the agonizing public soul-searching attendant upon full membership dissuaded many, while more worldly pursuits offering tremendous opportunities for material gain in this New World took the mind off the pursuit of heaven. As early as 1646, in calling the Cambridge Synod, the General Court noted the problem and the fact that "the aprehentions of many persons in the country are knoune not a litle to differ" in regard to the baptism of children of those who failed to "profess" the "father's covenant" by obtaining membership in the church. Most churches in the commonwealth, the court stated, "doe [baptize] only such children whose neerest parents are one or both of them setled members in full comunion with one or other of these churches," but others "doe baptize the children if the grandfather or grandmother be such members *though* the imediate parents be not," while still other churches, and "many persons living in the country, who have binn members of the congregations in England, but are not found fitt to be receaved at the Lords table here," "doe much encline . . . as thinking more liberty and latitude in this point ought to be yeelded then hath hetherto binn donne."

It is in this climate of a declining ideal, the emergence of the church as a hardening institution, and the failure of the church to accommodate to both its and their satisfaction baptized newcomers to the area and the baptized children and unbaptized grandchildren of the first generation that the halfway covenant of the 1650's and 1660's must be viewed. That this decline was accompanied by a heightened interest in religion as Morgan implies would seem highly improbable. Moreover, there is little in the extant material of the mid-seventeenth century to support the musings about "scrupulosity" and religious sophistication from which Morgan derives his idea of a heightened interest.

Some such evidence exists, certainly. But in view of the overwhelming evidence as to decline it would appear that what little there is reflects not a heightened interest in religion, but a falling away from the religion of the founders. For example, a Mrs. Bartrow, although baptized herself in infancy, offered her child for baptism "albeit she judged not herself as yet so meet for the Lord's supper." The scrupulosity displayed would not seem symptomatic of a quickened spirituality or a greater refinement of religious feeling, but of a morbid, crabbed, fearful introspection; an evaluation of her individual experience according to the forms of a hardened church rather than the regular and personal discovery of the "comfort in God, and delight in heavenly things" of John Winthrop. Indeed, the scrupulosity of Mrs. Bartrow might well have been but a step away from that of Dorothy Talbye of Salem, who broke the neck of her three-year-old daughter "that she might free it from future misery." The contrast between the spirituality of Winthrop and the scrupulosity of those of Mrs. Talbye's persuasion would seem to be adequate testimony of decline.

The halfway covenant was, in actuality, a compromise covenant, expanding the basis of the church within the population as demanded by the realities of the New England situation and yet preserving the church "in its purity" as desired by the ministry. To say otherwise is to ignore the nature of the halfway covenant itself. The new covenant admitted the halfway member to the least of the sacraments—baptism of his children—but not to the highest—communion, and it was not accepted in all the churches, or by all the ministers, many of whom clung adamantly to the absolute purity of the old way despite the pressures of reality.

It is to ignore, too, the statements of such men as John Cotton in advocating that system by which "all the Infants of the Church-members bee baptized; yet none of them are received . . . unto Communion at the Lords Table, nor unto liberty of power in the Government of the Church, untill they doe approve themselves both by publick Profession before the Church, and also by their Christian conversation, to take hold of the Covenant of their Fathers." By "this primitive practise," Cotton maintained, "there will bee no more feare of pestering Churches with a carnall Generation of members baptized in their Infancy. . . . Either the Lord in the faithfulnesse of his Covenant, will sanctifie the hearts of the baptized Infants to prepare them for his Table: or else hee will discover their hypocrisie and profanenesse in the presence of his Church, before Men and Angels, and so prevent the pollution of the Lords Table, and corruption of the Discipline of the Church, by their partaking in them."

It is to ignore the actions of the congregation at Chelmsford, for example, which, in 1656, voted to put into practice virtually those same ideas, including the requirement that baptized persons satisfy the church "touching there further fitnes ere they yeeld them the liberty of partakeing in the Lords Supp and of voteing in church affaires" by "A Confession of the faith, and a Relation of the manner of Gods working with there soules."

It is to ignore, finally, a public and private literature of tremendous extent, all bemoaning the state of the commonwealth and its churches. Thomas Shepard: "I saw that hypocrites are fat for humbling"; "men wonder why, in this country, men are more vile than ever they were, men that gave great hopes; the reason is this, they have seemed to be under Christ's government, but secretly cast it off." Theophilus Eaton: "our holy and Righteous father, hath Just cause of controversy with all the Colonyes, and churches, in these parts, for . . . declining, from their first love, zeale, workes etc." Edward Johnson: "An over-eager desire after the world hath so seized on the spirits of many, that the chief end of our coming hither is forgotten; and notwithstanding all the powerful means used, we stand at a stay, as if the Lord had no farther work for his people to do, but every bird to feather his own nest." John Hull: "Self-interest is too predominant in many. Want of subjection of inferiors to superiors, and too much want of religious care to contain in subjection these under them, is a visible evil among us. Disacknowledgement of the ordinances of councils, and that great breath of a ministerial judge, is very visible in many churches. Non-acknowledgement of the children of the church to be members thereof, nor taking care that their knowledge and life might answer their relation, is also manifest. And many other evils." The General Court in appointing January 2, 1662, a day of humiliation: "It being obvious to all pious and serious persons amongst us that wee are called of God deeply to humble ourselves for the many and great sins and evills of the Country, as our unproffitablenes under the glorious meanes of grace soe long continued to us, the decay of our first love, neglect and indisposednes to a full enquiry and practice of the order of the Gospell, the great ignorance and inclination of the riseing generation to vanity, prophanes, and disobedience, the sinfull indulgence." Boston, more influenced by the outer world as it turned increasingly to trade and commerce, lost far more of the ideals of the past than the inland towns. One diarist recorded the story of the exciseman meeting a countryman on the road: "The Devil is Dead," the exciseman called out. "How?" said the countryman, "I believe not that; Yes, said the other, he is dead for certaine: Well then, said the Countryman, if he be dead, he hath left many fatherless Children in Boston." But the whole commonwealth, the whole of New England, had lost, and it was in an attempt to call the ideals back that Hubbard wrote his *History,* that Mather wrote his *Magnalia,* that Boston's own Joshua Scottow wrote his *Old Men's Tears for their own Declensions, mixed with Fears of their and Posterities further falling off from New-England's Primitive Constitution,* and that, years before, William Bradford, resorting to poetry, had warned his children:

> When I think on what I have often read,
> How, when the Elders and Joshua were dead;
> Who had seen those great works, and them could tell,
> What God had done and wrought for Israel;
> Yet they did soon forget and turn aside,
> And in his truth and ways did not abide;
> But in the next age did degenerate;
> I wish this may not be New England's fate.

Much has been written in the past decades to counter that opinion of Puritan New England which Charles Francis Adams and Brooks Adams set forth in the late nineteenth century, and which James Truslow Adams, Thomas J. Wertenbaker, and others have kept alive in the twentieth. The view of a "glacial age" has been relegated to the historical ashcan; the view of an absolute oligarchy is heading in the same direction. More will be written in the future. In this regard, Morgan is to be commended for again pleading the case for a close examination of sources, particularly on a local level, before arriving at generalizations. But any re-examination of the complex subject of Puritanism should encompass the fact of its decline in New England from the ideals and spirituality of the first years, and the institutional hardening of its Church of Christ; any commentary on the halfway covenant should place it in the context of this decline and institutionalization.

5

Errand into the Wilderness
PERRY MILLER

History is a narrative of social self-consciousness. It is the cumulative story of how and why each generation's sense of purpose has been altered by that of the next generation. It deals with the fundamental questions facing men in society: what they construe to be their identity, the goals they set for their existence, the ways in which they hope to achieve them, the awareness they have of failing to do so.

No group offers the student a more challenging and fascinating means of exploring these questions and gaining the larger perspective of history which they open than the Puritans who came to settle English America during the 1630's and who were so important in molding its values and institutions during the course of the seventeenth century. Conscious of their purpose, the Puritans regarded themselves as having been sent on an "errand into the wilderness." But what exactly was this errand? How was it interpreted by the first generation of Puritans? How did they translate it into the terms of civil and religious polity? How did the sense of their errand change among the second and third Puritan generations? What accounts for it? How was it reflected in the jeremiads of their ministers?

These are the questions answered in the following essay by the late Perry Miller, who was for many years Professor of American Literature at Harvard. Professor Miller's principal interest was in the intellectual history of New England during the seventeenth and early eighteenth centuries and during the decades before the Civil War. His works on the earlier period include a superb trilogy on the intellectual anatomy of New England during its first century: Orthodoxy in Massachusetts, 1630–1650 *(1933),* The New England Mind: The Seventeenth Century *(1939), and* The New England Mind: From Colony to Province *(1953). The essay below*

SOURCE: Perry Miller, *Errand into the Wilderness* (Cambridge, Mass.: The Belknap Press of Harvard University Press), pp. 2–15. Copyright © 1956 by the President and Fellows of Harvard College and reprinted with permission. This essay appeared originally in *The William and Mary Quarterly,* Third Series, X (January, 1953), 3–19.

first appeared in The William and Mary Quarterly *(January, 1953) and subsequently in a collection of essays which carried its title:* Errand into the Wilderness *(1956). In it Professor Miller explored the changing attitude of the Puritans toward their purpose and their movement from a vision which had been universal to one which was becoming merely American.*

The essay has a double importance. It extends our knowledge about the Puritans and therefore our understanding of them. It restores the Puritans to the premises and realities of the seventeenth century and thus gives renewed validity to their purpose and their actions. In this respect, the essay, and for that matter the rest of Professor Miller's brilliant contribution, may be seen as part of the larger effort of our generation to come to terms with, indeed to rehabilitate, the Puritans. The historians of the late nineteenth and early twentieth centuries saw the Puritans as intolerant, unlearned, inflexible, severe, strait-laced, sexually constricted, unchanging— Calvinist in the worst sense of the word. In recent decades, however, historians have adopted a less monolithic and more favorable outlook. Samuel Eliot Morison, for example, has stressed the intellectual and educational attainments of the Puritans, Clifford K. Shipton their contributions to American democracy, Alan Simpson their real sense of inspiration and enthusiasm, Perry Miller their larger philosophy and its validity and vitality in the world of the seventeenth century.

Professor Miller's essay is important, moreover, for its bearing on the question of a philosophy for our own times. What, indeed, is our sense of purpose? What do we understand to be the ends of existence and by what means do we seek to attain them? What are the circumstances around us shaping our view of ends and means? What are our jeremiads and how valid are the charges our consciences level against us? Do we still, in any wise, have a covenant with God? If, as Professor Miller suggests, we found ourselves alone with America in the seventeenth century, have we restored ourselves to Europe in the twentieth? Or is the essence of our problem that, having made America a mission for ourselves, we are now seeking to make it one for the world? And if, throughout its history, America has been on an errand, what was it in the generations following the Puritans, and what is it today?

It was a happy inspiration that led the staff of the John Carter Brown Library to choose as the title of its New England exhibition of 1952 a phrase from Samuel Danforth's election sermon, delivered on May 11, 1670: *A Brief Recognition of New England's Errand into the Wilderness.* It was of course an inspiration, if not of genius at least of talent, for Danforth to invent his title in the first place. But all the election sermons of this period—that is to say, the major expressions of the second generation, which, delivered on these forensic occasions, were in the fullest sense community expression—have interesting titles; a mere listing tells the story of what was happening to the minds and emotions of the New England people: John Higginson's *The Cause of God and His People In New-England* in 1663, William Stoughton's *New England's True Interest, Not to Lie* in 1668, Thomas Shepard's *Eye-Salve* in 1672, Urian Oakes's *New England Pleaded With* in 1673, and, climactically and most explicitly, Increase Mather's *A Discourse Concerning the Danger of Apostasy* in 1677.

All of these show by their title pages alone—and, as those who have looked into them know, infinitely more by their contents—a deep disquietude. They are troubled utterances, worried, fearful. Something has gone wrong. As in 1662 Wigglesworth already was saying in verse, God has a controversy with New England; He has cause to be angry and to punish it because of its innumerable defections. They say, unanimously, that New England was sent on an errand, and that it has failed.

To our ears these lamentations of the second generation sound strange indeed. We think of the founders as heroic men—of the towering stature of Bradford, Winthrop, and Thomas Hooker—who braved the ocean and the wilderness, who conquered both, and left to their children a goodly heritage. Why then this whimpering?

Some historians suggest that the second and third generations suffered a failure of nerve; they weren't the men their fathers had been, and they knew it. Where the founders could range over the vast body of theology and ecclesiastical polity and produce profound works like the treatises of John Cotton or the subtle psychological analyses of Hooker, or even such a gusty though wrongheaded book as Nathaniel Ward's *Simple Cobler*, let alone such lofty and rightheaded pleas as Roger Williams' *Bloudy Tenet*, all these children could do was tell each other that they were on probation and that their chances of making good did not seem very promising.

Since Puritan intellectuals were thoroughly grounded in grammar and rhetoric, we may be certain that Danforth was fully aware of the ambiguity concealed in his word "errand." It already had taken on the double meaning which it still carries with us. Originally, as the word first took form in English, it meant exclusively a short journey on which an inferior is sent to convey a message or to perform a service for his superior. In that sense we today speak of an "errand boy"; or the husband says that while in town on his lunch hour, he must run an errand for his wife. But by the end of the Middle Ages, errand developed another connotation: it came to mean the actual business on which the actor goes, the purpose itself, the conscious intention in his mind. In this signification, the runner of the errand is working for himself, is his own boss; the wife, while the husband is away at the office, runs her own errands. Now in the 1660's the problem was this: which had

New England originally been—an errand boy or a doer of errands? In which sense had it failed? Had it been despatched for a further purpose, or was it an end in itself? Or had it fallen short not only in one or the other, but in both of the meanings? If so, it was indeed a tragedy, in the primitive sense of a fall from a mighty designation.

If the children were in grave doubt about which had been the original errand—if, in fact, those of the founders who lived into the later period and who might have set their progeny to rights found themselves wondering and confused—there is little chance of our answering clearly. Of course, there is no problem about Plymouth Colony. That is the charm about Plymouth: its clarity. The Pilgrims, as we have learned to call them, were reluctant voyagers; they had never wanted to leave England, but had been obliged to depart because the authorities made life impossible for Separatists. They could, naturally, have stayed at home had they given up being Separatists, but that idea simply did not occur to them. Yet they did not go to Holland as though on an errand; neither can we extract the notion of a mission out of the reasons which, as Bradford tells us, persuaded them to leave Leyden for "Virginia." The war with Spain was about to be resumed, and the economic threat was ominous; their migration was not so much an errand as a shrewd forecast, a plan to get out while the getting was good, lest, should they stay, they would be "intrapped or surrounded by their enemies, so as they should neither be able to fight nor flie." True, once the decision was taken, they congratulated themselves that they might become a means for propagating the gospel in remote parts of the world, and thus of serving as steppingstones to others in the performance of this great work; nevertheless, the substance of their decision was that they "thought it better to dislodge betimes to some place of better advantage and less danger, if any such could be found." The great hymn that Bradford, looking back in his old age, chanted about the landfall is one of the greatest passages, if not the very greatest, in all New England's literature; yet it does not resound with the sense of a mission accomplished—instead, it vibrates with the sorrow and exultation of suffering, the sheer endurance, the pain and the anguish, with the somberness of death faced unflinchingly:

> May not and ought not the children of these fathers rightly say: Our fathers were Englishmen which came over this great ocean, and were ready to perish in this wilderness; but they cried unto the Lord, and he heard their voyce, and looked on their adversitie. . . .

We are bound, I think, to see in Bradford's account the prototype of the vast majority of subsequent immigrants—of those Oscar Handlin calls "The Uprooted": they came for better advantage and for less danger, and to give their posterity the opportunity of success.

The Great Migration of 1630 is an entirely other story. True, among the reasons John Winthrop drew up in 1629 to persuade himself and his colleagues that they should commit themselves to the enterprise, the economic motive frankly figures. Wise men thought that England was overpopulated and that the poor would have a better chance in the new land. But Massachusetts Bay was not just an organization of immigrants seeking advantage and opportunity. It had a positive sense of mission—either it was sent on an errand or it had its own intention, but in either case the deed was deliberate. It was an act of will, perhaps of willfulness. These Puritans were not driven out of England (thousands of their fellows stayed and fought the Cavaliers)—they went of their own accord.

So, concerning them, we ask the question, why? If we are not altogether clear about precisely how we should phrase the answer, this is not because they themselves were reticent. They spoke as fully as they knew how, and none more magnificently or cogently than John Winthrop in the midst of the passage itself, when he delivered a lay sermon aboard the flagship *Arbella* and called it "A Modell of Christian Charity." It distinguishes the motives of this great enterprise from those of Bradford's forlorn retreat, and especially from those of the masses who later have come in quest of advancement. Hence, for the student of New England and of America, it is a fact demanding incessant brooding that John Winthrop selected as the "doctrine" of his discourse, and so as the basic proposition to which, it then seemed to him, the errand was committed, the thesis that God had disposed mankind in a hierarchy of social classes, so that "in all times some must be rich, some poor, some highe and eminent in power and dignitie; others mean and in subjeccion." It is as though, preternaturally sensing what the promise of America might come to signify for the rank and file, Winthrop took the precaution to drive out of their heads any notion that in the wilderness the poor and the mean were ever so to improve themselves as to mount above the rich or the eminent in dignity. Were there any who had signed up under the mistaken impression that such was the purpose of their errand, Winthrop told them that, although other peoples, lesser breeds, might come for wealth or pelf, this migration was specifically dedicated to an avowed end that had nothing to do with incomes. We have entered into an explicit covenant with God, "we haue professed to enterprise these ACCIONS vpon these and these ends"; we have drawn up indentures with the Almighty, wherefore if we succeed and do not let ourselves get diverted into making money, He will reward us. Whereas if we fail, if we "fall to embrace this present world and prosecute our carnall intencions, seekeing great things for our selves and our posterity, the Lord will surely breake out in wrathe against us be revenged of such a periured people and make us knowe the price of the breache of such a Covenant."

Well, what terms were agreed upon in this covenant? Winthrop could say precisely—"It is by a mutuall consent through a specially overruleing providence, and a more than ordinary approbation of the Churches of Christ to seeke out a place of Cohabitation and Consorteshipp under a due forme of Government both civill and ecclesiasticall." If it could be said thus concretely, why should there be any ambiguity? There was no doubt whatsoever about what Winthrop meant by a due form of ecclesiastical government: he meant the pure Biblical polity set forth in full detail by the New Testament, that method which later generations, in the days of increasing confusion, would settle down to calling Congregational, but which for Winthrop was no denominational peculiarity but the very essence of organized Christianity. What a due form of civil government meant, therefore, became crystal clear: a political regime, possessing power, which would consider its main function to be the erecting, protecting, and preserving of this form of polity. This due form would have, at the very beginning of its list of responsibilities, the duty of suppressing heresy, of subduing or somehow getting rid of dissenters—of being, in short, deliberately, vigorously, and consistently intolerant.

Regarded in this light, the Massachusetts Bay Company came on an errand in the second and later sense of the word: it was, so to speak, on its own business. What it set out to do was the sufficient reason for its setting out. About this Winthrop seems to be perfectly certain, as he declares specifically what the due forms will be attempting: the end is to improve our lives to do more service to the Lord, to increase the body of Christ, and to preserve our posterity from the corruptions of this evil world, so that they in turn shall work out their salvation under the purity and power of Biblical ordinances. Because the errand was so definable in advance, certain conclusions about the method of conducting it were equally evident: one, obviously, was that those sworn to the covenant should not be allowed to turn aside in a lust for mere physical rewards; but another was, in Winthrop's simple but splendid words, "we must be knit together in this worke as one man, wee must entertaine each other in brotherly affection." We must actually delight in each other, "always having before our eyes our Commission and community in the worke, our community as members of the same body." This was to say, were the great purpose kept steadily in mind, if all gazed only at it and strove only for it, then social solidarity (within a scheme of fixed and unalterable class distinctions) would be an automatic consequence. A society despatched upon an errand that is its own reward would want no other rewards: it could go forth to possess a land without ever becoming possessed by it; social gradations would remain eternally what God had originally appointed; there would be no internal contention among groups or interests, and though there would be hard work for everybody, prosperity would be bestowed not as a consequence of labor but as a sign of approval upon the mission itself. For once in the history of humanity (with all its sins), there would be a society so dedicated to a holy cause that success would prove innocent and triumph not raise up sinful pride or arrogant dissension.

Or, at least, this would come about if the people did not deal falsely with God, if they would live up to the articles of their bond. If we do not perform these terms, Winthrop warned, we may expect immediate manifestations of divine wrath; we shall perish out of the land we are crossing the sea to possess. And here in the 1660's and 1670's, all the jeremiads (of which Danforth's is one of the most poignant) are castigations of the people for having defaulted on precisely these articles. They recite the long list of afflictions an angry God had rained upon them, surely enough to prove how abysmally they had deserted the covenant: crop failures, epidemics, grasshoppers, caterpillars, torrid summers, arctic winters, Indian wars, hurricanes, shipwrecks, accidents, and (most grievous of all) unsatisfactory children. The solemn work of the election day, said Stoughton in 1668, is "Foundation-work" —not, that is, to lay a new one, "but to continue, and strengthen, and beautifie, and build upon that which has been laid." It had been laid in the covenant before even a foot was set ashore, and thereon New England should rest. Hence the terms of survival, let alone of prosperity, remained what had first been propounded:

> If we should so frustrate and deceive the Lords Expectations, that his Covenant-interest in us, and the Workings of his Salvation be made to cease, then All were lost indeed; Ruine upon Ruine, Destruction upon Destruction would come, until one stone were not left upon another.

Since so much of the literature after 1660—in fact, just about all of it— dwells on this theme of declension and apostasy, would not the story of New England seem to be simply that of the failure of a mission? Winthrop's dread was realized: posterity had not found their salvation amid pure ordinances but had, despite the ordinances, yielded to the seductions of the good land. Hence distresses were being piled upon them, the slaughter of King Philip's War and now the attack of a profligate king upon the sacred charter. By about 1680, it did in truth seem that shortly no stone would be left upon another, that history would record of New England that the founders had been great men, but that their children and grandchildren progressively deteriorated.

This would certainly seem to be the impression conveyed by the assembled clergy and lay elders who, in 1679, met at Boston in a formal synod, under the leadership of Increase Mather, and there prepared a report on why the land suffered. The result of their deliberation, published under the title *The Necessity of Reformation*, was the first in what has proved to be a distressingly long succession of investigations into the civic health of Americans, and it is probably the most pessimistic. The land was afflicted, it said, because corruption had proceeded apace; assuredly, if the people did not quickly reform, the last blow would fall and nothing but desolation be left. Into what a moral quagmire this dedicated community had sunk, the synod did not leave to imagination; it published a long and detailed inventory of sins, crimes, misdemeanors, and nasty habits, which makes, to say the least, interesting reading.

We hear much talk nowadays about corruption, most of it couched in generalized terms. If we ask our current Jeremiahs to descend to particulars, they tell us that the republic is going on the rocks, or to the dogs, because the wives of politicians aspire to wear mink coats and their husbands take a moderate five per cent cut on certain deals to pay for the garments. The Puritans were devotees of logic, and the verb "methodize" ruled their thinking. When the synod went to work, it had before it a succession of sermons, such as that of Danforth and the other election-day or fast-day orators, as well as such works as Increase Mather's *A Brief History of the Warr With the Indians*, wherein the decimating conflict with Philip was presented as a revenge upon the people for their transgressions. When the synod felt obliged to enumerate their enormities of the land so that the people could recognize just how far short of their errand they had fallen, it did not, in the modern manner, assume that regeneration would be accomplished at the next election by turning the rascals out, but it digested this body of literature; it reduced the contents to method. The result is a staggering compendium of iniquity, organized into twelve headings.

First, there was a great and visible decay of godliness. Second, there were several manifestations of pride—contention in the churches, insubordination of inferiors toward superiors, particularly of those inferiors who had, unaccountably, acquired more wealth than their betters, and, astonishingly, a shocking extravagance in attire, especially on the part of these of the meaner sort, who persisted in dressing beyond their means. Third, there were heretics, especially Quakers and Anabaptists. Fourth, a notable increase in swearing and a spreading disposition to sleep at sermons (these two phenomena seemed basically connected). Fifth, the Sabbath was wantonly violated. Sixth, family government had decayed, and fathers no longer kept their sons and daughters from prowling at night. Seventh, instead of people being knit together as one man in mutual love, they were full of contention, so that lawsuits were on the increase and lawyers were thriving. Under the eighth head, the synod described the sins of sex and alcohol, thus producing some of the juiciest prose of the period: militia days had become orgies, taverns were crowded; women threw temptation in the way of befuddled men by wearing false locks and displaying naked necks and arms "or, which is more abominable, naked Breasts"; there were "mixed Dancings," along with light behavior and "Company-keeping" with vain persons, wherefore the bastardy rate was rising. In 1672, there was actually an attempt to supply Boston with a brothel (it was suppressed, but the synod was bearish about the future). Ninth, New Englanders were betraying a marked disposition to tell lies, especially when selling anything. In the tenth place, the business morality of even the most righteous left everything to be desired: the wealthy speculated in land and raised prices excessively; "Day-Labourers and Mechanicks are unreasonable in their demands." In the eleventh place, the people showed no disposition to reform, and in the twelfth, they seemed utterly destitute of civic spirit.

"The things here insisted on," said the synod, "have been often-times mentioned and inculcated by those whom the Lord hath set as Watchmen to the house of Israel." Indeed they had been, and there-after they continued to be even more inculcated. At the end of the century, the synod's report was serving as a kind of handbook for preachers: they would take some verse of Isaiah or Jeremiah, set up the doctrine that God avenges the iniquities of a chosen people, and then run down the twelve heads, merely bringing the list up to date by in-serting the new and still more depraved practices an ingenious people kept on devising. I suppose that in the whole literature of the world, including the satirists of imperial Rome, there is hardly such another uninhibited and unrelenting documentation of a people's descent into corruption.

I have elsewhere endeavored to argue that, while the social or economic historian may read this literature for its contents—and so construct from the expanding catalogue of denunciations a record of social progress—the cultural anthropologist will look slightly askance at these jeremiads; he will exercise a methodological caution about taking them at face value. If you read them all through, the total effect, curiously enough, is not at all depressing: you come to the paradoxical realization that they do not bespeak a despairing frame of mind. There is something of a ritualistic incantation about them; whatever they may signify in the realm of theology, in that of psychology they are purgations of soul; they do not discourage but actually encourage the community to persist in its heinous conduct. The exhortation to a reformation which never materializes serves as a token payment upon the obligation, and so liberates the debtors. Changes there had to be: adaptations to environment, expansion of the frontier, mansions constructed, commercial adventures undertaken. These activities were not specifically nominated in the bond Winthrop had framed. They were thrust upon the society by American experience; because they were not only works of necessity but of excitement, they proved irresistible—whether making money, haunting taverns, or committing fornication. Land speculation meant not only wealth but dispersion of the people, and what was to stop the march of settlement? The covenant doctrine preached on the *Arbella* had been formulated in England, where land was not to be had for the taking; its adherents had been utterly oblivious of what the fact of a frontier would do for an imported order, let alone for a European mentality. Hence I suggest that under the guise of this mounting wail of sinfulness, this incessant and never successful cry for repentance, the Puritans launched themselves upon the process of Americanization.

However, there are still more pertinent or more analytical things to be said of this body of expression. If you compare it with the great productions of the founders, you will be struck by the fact that the second and third generations had become oriented toward the social, and only the social, problem; herein they were deeply and profoundly different from their fathers. The finest creations of the founders—the disquisitions of Hooker, Shepard, and Cotton—were written in Europe, or else, if actually penned in the colonies, proceeded from a thoroughly European mentality, upon which the American scene made no impression whatsoever. The most striking example of this imperviousness is the poetry of Anne Bradstreet: she came to Massachusetts at the age of eighteen, already two years married to Simon Bradstreet; there, she says, "I found a new world and new manners, at which my heart rose" in rebellion, but soon convincing herself that it was the way of God, she submitted and joined the church. She bore Simon eight children, and loved him sincerely, as her most charming poem, addressed to him, reveals:

> If ever two were one, then surely we;
> If ever man were loved by wife, then thee.

After the house burned, she wrote a lament about how her pleasant things in ashes lay and how no more the merriment of guests would sound in the hall; but there is nothing in the poem to suggest that the house stood in North Andover or that the things so tragically consumed were doubly precious because they had been transported across the ocean and were utterly irreplaceable in the wilderness. In between rearing children and keeping house she wrote her poetry; her brother-in-law carried the manuscript to London, and there published it in 1650 under the ambitious title, *The Tenth Muse Lately Sprung Up in America*. But the title is the only thing about the volume which shows any sense of America, and that little merely in order to prove that the plantations had something in the way of European wit and learning, that they had not receded into barbarism. Anne's flowers are English flowers, the birds, English birds, and the landscape is Lincolnshire.

So also with the productions of immigrant scholarship: such a learned and acute work as Hooker's *Survey of the Summe of Church Discipline,* which is specifically about the regime set up in America, is written entirely within the logical patterns, and out of the religious experience, of Europe; it makes no concession to new and peculiar circumstances.

The titles alone of productions in the next generation show how concentrated have become emotion and attention upon the interest of New England, and none is more revealing than Samuel Danforth's conception of an errand into the wilderness. Instead of being able to compose abstract treatises like those of Hooker upon the soul's prepara- tion, humiliation, or exultation, or such a collection of wisdom and theology as John Cotton's *The Way of Life* or Shepard's *The Sound Believer,* these later saints must, over and over again, dwell upon the specific sins of New England, and the more they denounce, the more they must narrow their focus to the provincial problem. If they write upon anything else, it must be about the halfway covenant and its manifold consequences—a development enacted wholly in this country —or else upon their wars with the Indians. Their range is sadly con- stricted, but every effort, no matter how brief, is addressed to the per- sistent question: what is the meaning of this society in the wilderness? If it does not mean what Winthrop said it must mean, what under Heaven is it? Who, they are forever asking themselves, who are we? —and sometimes they are on the verge of saying, who the Devil are we, anyway?

This brings us back to the fundamental ambiguity concealed in the word "errand," that *double entente* of which I am certain Danforth was aware when he published the words that give point to the exhibition. While it was true that in 1630, the covenant philosophy of a special and peculiar bond lifted the migration out of the ordinary realm of nature, provided it with a definite mission which might in the secondary sense be called its errand, there was always present in Puritan thinking the suspicion that God's saints are at best inferiors, despatched by their Superior upon particular assignments. Anyone who has run errands for other people, particularly for people of great importance with many things on their minds, such as army commanders, knows how real is the peril that, by the time he returns with the report of a message delivered or a bridge blown up, the Superior may be interested in something else; the situation at headquarters may be entirely changed, and the gallant errand boy, or the husband who desperately remem- bered to buy the ribbon, may be told that he is too late. This tragic pattern appears again and again in modern warfare: an agent is dropped by parachute and, after immense hardships, comes back to find that, in the shifting tactical or strategic situations, his contribution is no longer of value. If he gets home in time and his service proves useful, he receives a medal; otherwise, no matter what prodigies he has performed, he may not even be thanked. He has been sent, as the devastating phrase has it, upon a fool's errand, than which there can be a no more shattering blow to self-esteem.

The Great Migration of 1630 felt insured against such treatment from on high by the covenant; nevertheless, the God of the covenant always remained an unpredictable Jehovah, a *Deus Absconditus*. When God promises to abide by stated terms, His word, of course, is to be trusted; but then, what is man that he dare accuse Omnipotence of tergiversation? But if any such apprehension was in Winthrop's mind as he spoke on the *Arbella*, or in the minds of other apologists for the enterprise, they kept it far back and allowed it no utterance. They could stifle the thought, not only because Winthrop and his colleagues believed fully in the covenant, but because they could see in the pattern of history that their errand was not a mere scouting expedition: it was an essential maneuver in the drama of Christendom. The Bay Company was not a battered remnant of suffering Separatists thrown up on a rocky shore; it was an organized task force of Christians, executing a flank attack on the corruptions of Christendom. These Puritans did not flee to America; they went in order to work out that complete reformation which was not yet accomplished in England and Europe, but which would quickly be accomplished if only the saints back there had a working model to guide them. It is impossible to say that any who sailed from Southampton really expected to lay his bones in the new world; were it to come about—as all in their heart of hearts anticipated—that the forces of righteousness should prevail against Laud and Wentworth, that England after all should turn toward reformation, where else would the distracted country look for leadership except to those who in New England had perfected the ideal polity and who would know how to administer it? This was the large unspoken assumption in the errand of 1630: if the conscious intention were realized, not only would a federated Jehovah bless the new land, but He would bring back these temporary colonials to govern England.

In this respect, therefore, we may say that the migration was running an errand in the earlier and more primitive sense of the word—performing a job not so much for Jehovah as for history, which was the wisdom of Jehovah expressed through time. Winthrop was aware of this aspect of the mission—fully conscious of it. "For wee must Consider that wee shall be as a Citty upon a Hill, the eies of all people are uppon us." More was at stake than just one little colony. If we deal falsely with God, not only will He descend upon us in wrath, but even more terribly, He will make us "a story and a by-word through the world, wee shall open the mouthes of enemies to speake evill of the wayes of god and all professours for Gods sake." No less than John

Milton was New England to justify God's ways to man, though not, like him, in the agony and confusion of defeat but in the confidence of approaching triumph. This errand was being run for the sake of Reformed Christianity; and while the first aim was indeed to realize in America the due form of government, both civil and ecclesiastical, the aim behind that aim was to vindicate the most rigorous ideal of the Reformation, so that ultimately all Europe would imitate New England. If we succeed, Winthrop told his audience, men will say of later plantations, "the lord make it like that of New England." There was an elementary prudence to be observed: Winthrop said that the prayer would arise from subsequent plantations, yet what was England itself but one of God's plantations? In America, he promised, we shall see, or may see, more of God's wisdom, power, and truth "then formerly wee have beene acquainted with." The situation was such that, for the moment, the model had no chance to be exhibited in England; Puritans could talk about it, theorize upon it, but they could not display it, could not prove that it would actually work. But if they had it set up in America—in a bare land, devoid of already established (and corrupt) institutions, empty of bishops and courtiers, where they could start *de novo,* and the eyes of the world were upon it—and if then it performed just as the saints had predicted of it, the Calvinist internationale would know exactly how to go about completing the already begun but temporarily stalled revolution in Europe.

When we look upon the enterprise from this point of view, the psychology of the second and third generations becomes more comprehensible. We realize that the migration was not sent upon its errand in order to found the United States of America, nor even the New England conscience. Actually, it would not perform its errand even when the colonists did erect a due form of government in church and state: what was further required in order for this mission to be a success was that the eyes of the world be kept fixed upon it in rapt attention. If the rest of the world, or at least of Protestantism, looked elsewhere, or turned to another model, or simply got distracted and forgot about New England, if the new land was left with a polity nobody in the great world of Europe wanted—then every success in fulfilling the terms of the covenant would become a diabolical measure of failure. If the due form of government were not everywhere to be saluted, what would New England have upon its hands? How give it a name, this victory nobody could utilize? How provide an identity for something conceived under misapprehensions? How could a universal which turned out to be nothing but a provincial particular be called anything but a blunder or an abortion?

If an actor, playing the leading role in the greatest dramatic spectacle of the century, were to attire himself and put on his make-up, rehearse his lines, take a deep breath, and stride onto the stage, only to find the theater dark and empty, no spotlight working, and himself entirely alone, he would feel as did New England around 1650 or 1660. For in the 1640's, during the Civil Wars, the colonies, so to speak, lost their audience. First of all, there proved to be, deep in the Puritan movement, an irreconcilable split between the Presbyterian and Independent wings, wherefore no one system could be imposed upon England, and so the New England model was unserviceable. Secondly—most horrible to relate—the Independents, who in polity were carrying New England's banner and were supposed, in the schedule of history, to lead England into imitation of the colonial order, betrayed the sacred cause by yielding to the heresy of toleration. They actually welcomed Roger Williams, whom the leaders of the model had kicked out of Massachusetts so that his nonsense about liberty of conscience would not spoil the administrations of charity.

In other words, New England did not lie, did not falter; it made good everything Winthrop demanded—wonderfully good—and then found that its lesson was rejected by those choice spirits for whom the exertion had been made. By casting out Williams, Anne Hutchinson, and the Antinomians, along with an assortment of Gortonists and Anabaptists, into that cesspool then becoming known as Rhode Island, Winthrop, Dudley, and the clerical leaders showed Oliver Cromwell how he should go about governing England. Instead, he developed the utterly absurd theory that so long as a man made a good soldier in the New Model Army, it did not matter whether he was a Calvinist, an Antinomian, an Arminian, an Anabaptist or even—horror of horrors— a Socinian! Year after year, as the circus tours this country, crowds howl with laughter, no matter how many times they have seen the stunt, at the bustle that walks by itself: the clown comes out dressed in a large skirt with a bustle behind; he turns sharply to the left, and the bustle continues blindly and obstinately straight ahead, on the original course. It is funny in a circus, but not in history. There is nothing but tragedy in the realization that one was in the main path of events, and now is sidetracked and disregarded. One is always able, of course, to stand firm on his first resolution, and to condemn the clown of history for taking the wrong turning: yet this is a desolating sort of stoicism, because it always carries with it the recognition that history will never come back to the predicted path, and that with one's own demise, righteousness must die out of the world.

The most humiliating element in the experience was the way the English brethren turned upon the colonials for precisely their greatest achievement. It must have seemed, for those who came with Winthrop in 1630 and who remembered the clarity and brilliance with which he set forth the conditions of their errand, that the world was turned upside down and inside out when, in June 1645, thirteen leading Independent divines—such men as Goodwin, Owen, Nye, Burroughs, formerly friends and allies of Hooker and Davenport, men who might easily have come to New England and helped extirpate heretics—wrote the General Court that the colony's law banishing Anabaptists was an embarrassment to the Independent cause in England. Opponents were declaring, said these worthies, "that persons of our way, principall and spirit cannot beare with Dissenters from them, but Doe correct, fine, imprison and banish them wherever they have power soe to Doe." There were indeed people in England who admired the severities of Massachusetts, but we assure you, said the Independents, these "are utterly your enemyes and Doe seeke your extirpation from the face of the earth: those who now in power are your friends are quite otherwise minded, and doe professe they are much offended with your proceedings." Thus early commenced that chronic weakness in the foreign policy of Americans, an inability to recognize who in truth constitute their best friends abroad.

We have lately accustomed ourselves to the fact that there does exist a mentality which will take advantage of the liberties allowed by society in order to conspire for the ultimate suppression of those same privileges. The government of Charles I and Archbishop Laud had not, where that danger was concerned, been liberal, but it had been conspicuously inefficient; hence, it did not liquidate the Puritans (although it made halfhearted efforts), nor did it herd them into prison camps. Instead, it generously, even lavishly, gave a group of them a charter to Massachusetts Bay, and obligingly left out the standard clause requiring that the document remain in London, that the grantees keep their office within reach of Whitehall. Winthrop's revolutionaries availed themselves of this liberty to get the charter overseas, and thus to set up a regime dedicated to the worship of God in the manner they desired—which meant allowing nobody else to worship any other way, especially adherents of Laud and King Charles. All this was perfectly logical and consistent. But what happened to the thought processes of their fellows in England made no sense whatsoever. Out of the New Model Army came the fantastic notion that a party struggling for power should proclaim that, once it captured the state, it would recognize the right of dissenters to disagree and to have their own worship, to hold their own opinions. Oliver Cromwell was so far gone in this idiocy as to become a dictator, in order to impose toleration by force! Amid this shambles, the errand of New England collapsed. There was nobody left at headquarters to whom reports could be sent.

Many a man has done a brave deed, been hailed as a public hero, had honors and ticker tape heaped upon him—and then had to live, day after day, in the ordinary routine, eating breakfast and brushing his teeth, in what seems protracted anticlimax. A couple may win their way to each other across insuperable obstacles, elope in a blaze of passion and glory—and then have to learn that life is a matter of buying the groceries and getting the laundry done. This sense of the meaning having gone out of life, that all adventures are over, that no great days and no heroism lie ahead, is particularly galling when it falls upon a son whose father once was the public hero or the great lover. He has to put up with the daily routine without ever having known at first hand the thrill of danger or the ecstasy of passion. True, he has his own hardships—clearing rocky pastures, hauling in the cod during a storm, fighting Indians in a swamp—but what are these compared with the magnificence of leading an exodus of saints to found a city on a hill, for the eyes of all the world to behold? He might wage a stout fight against the Indians, and one out of ten of his fellows might perish in the struggle, but the world was no longer interested. He would be reduced to writing accounts of himself and scheming to get a publisher in London, in a desperate effort to tell a heedless world, "Look, I exist!"

His greatest difficulty would be not the stones, storms, and Indians, but the problem of his identity. In something of this sort, I should like to suggest, consists the anxiety and torment that inform productions of the late seventeenth and early eighteenth centuries—and should I say, some thereafter? It appears most clearly in *Magnalia Christi Americana,* the work of that soul most tortured by the problem, Cotton Mather: "I write the Wonders of the Christian Religion, flying from the Depravations of Europe, to the American Strand." Thus he proudly begins, and at once trips over the acknowledgment that the founders had not simply fled from depraved Europe but had intended to redeem it. And so the book is full of lamentations over the declension of the children, who appear, page after page, in contrast to their mighty progenitors, about as profligate a lot as ever squandered a great inheritance.

And yet, the *Magnalia* is not an abject book; neither are the election sermons abject, nor is the inventory of sins offered by the synod of 1679. There is bewilderment, confusion, chagrin, but there is no surrender. A task has been assigned upon which the populace are in fact intensely engaged. But they are not sure any more for just whom they are working; they know they are moving, but they do not know where they are going. They seem still to be on an errand, but if they are no longer inferiors sent by the superior forces of the Reformation, to whom they should report, then their errand must be wholly of the second sort, something with a purpose and an intention sufficient unto itself. If so, what is it? If it be not the due form of government, civil and ecclesiastical, that they brought into being, how otherwise can it be described?

The literature of self-condemnation must be read for meanings far below the surface, for meanings of which, we may be so rash as to surmise, the authors were not fully conscious, but by which they were troubled and goaded. They looked in vain to history for an explanation of themselves; more and more it appeared that the meaning was not to be found in theology, even with the help of the covenantal dialectic. Thereupon, these citizens found that they had no other place to search but within themselves—even though, at first sight, that repository appeared to be nothing but a sink of iniquity. Their errand having failed in the first sense of the term, they were left with the second, and required to fill it with meaning by themselves and out of themselves. Having failed to rivet the eyes of the world upon their city on the hill, they were left alone with America.

6

Communications and Trade: The Atlantic in the Seventeenth Century
BERNARD BAILYN

Americans in the seventeenth century were located on the frame of an Atlantic world. The ocean no less than the land defined their existence. Land has so much fashioned our history since 1776 that we tend to forget how much the ocean fashioned it before 1776. The frontier of the colonists was not only terrestrial but oceanic. It was indeed only by means of their commercial lifelines across the ocean that they were able to master the land. No less significant, the oceanic trade posited the central characteristics of their society.

It is this impact of trade on colonial life which Bernard Bailyn considers in the following article. Winthrop Professor of American History at Harvard University, Bailyn is one of our leading authorities on the colonial period, particularly on the nature and origins of the American Revolution. An

SOURCE: *The Journal of Economic History,* XIII (Fall, 1953), 378–387. Reprinted by permission of the author and publishers.

earlier work of his, The New England Merchants of the Seventeenth Century *(1955), is an excellent study of social history, construed in the broadest sense, exploring as it does the interplay between family ties, status mobility, religious connections, and the course of politics, on the one hand and the mercantile group's economic 'nterests on the other. In the article below, Professor Bailyn seeks to answer several important questions about the role of transoceanic trade in the colonial world. What was the larger structure of England's commercial system? What part did kinship play in Atlantic trade? How did trade help shape the character of colonial urban development? How did the advent of an English official class in the colonies affect the merchant community?*

In his answers, Professor Bailyn adds a dimension to the story of American origins in the seventeenth century. He provides a view of the larger Atlantic world without which our colonial past is only partly seen. He construes history as a complex of forces at once economic, social, and political. And he reminds us that this complex, and indeed all history, may ultimately be understood only in terms of people and their interrelations.

In the first half of the seventeenth century the northern mercantile nations of Europe followed Spain and Portugal in flinging their commercial frontiers westward to the New World. By the end of the century they had surpassed the Iberian nations in western trade and made of the Atlantic basin a single great trading area. Their economic enterprises created not only a crisscrossing web of transoceanic traffic but also a cultural community that came to form the western periphery of European civilization. The members of this community were widely separated, scattered across three thousand miles of ocean and up and down the coasts of two continents. But the structure of commerce furnished a communication system that brought these far-flung settlements together. The same structure proved to be a framework upon which certain important elements in colonial society took form. My purpose is to sketch certain characteristics of the Atlantic colonies in the seventeenth century which relate to these social consequences of commercial growth.

The formative period of northern Atlantic trade was the second third of the seventeenth century. In those years there were important commercial developments on the American continent by the English, the Dutch, and the French; but the swiftest advance took place in the Caribbean. "After 1625," A. P. Newton writes, "swarms of English and French colonists poured like flies upon the rotting carcase of Spain's empire in the Caribbean, and within ten years the West Indian scene was changed forever." The Lesser Antilles became a battleground of the expanding European empires. The island of St. Christopher in the Leewards was jointly possessed by the French and English; Barbados, Nevis, Antigua, and Montserrat were indisputably English; Guadeloupe and Martinique were French; and Curaçao, St. Eustatius, and Tobago were in the hands of the Dutch.

The feverish activity that lay behind these developments resulted from the belief of numerous Europeans that wealth could be readily extracted from the places in the New World with which they were acquainted. But for every success there were a dozen failures. Hopes were held for commercial designs that strike us now as ill-conceived, even stupid. Yet to contemporary merchants, cautious men who built fortunes on their ability to judge investments shrewdly, they were at least as promising as the schemes that succeeded.

Remarkable only for its subsequent fame but typical in its results was the Plymouth Company's colony at the mouth of the Sagadahoc River in New Hampshire. Behind the failure of this venture lay the belief that exploiters of North America, like those of Asia, had only to build coastal trading factories, to which throngs of natives would haul precious piles of goods to exchange for tinkling bells and snippets of bright cloth. English merchants invested approximately £15,000 in the Lynn Ironworks, which collapsed within two decades of its promising start in the early 1640's. At least three major fur companies foundered on the belief that the heartland of American pelts lay in the swampy margins of a mythical "Great Lake of the Iroquois," from which were supposed to flow all the main rivers emptying into the Atlantic. The Virginia settlements after the mid-twenties gradually gained a solid economic base, but only after a decade and a half of continuous failure. In the Caribbean islands, experimentation in all sorts of commodities preceded and accompanied the development of sugar as a staple crop.

Patterns of trade were established, of course, around the poles of successful economic ventures, and it was, therefore, only after the broad wave of failures had receded, leaving behind clear indications of natural possibilities, that the commercial system in its familiar form became evident.

The result was a network of trading routes woven by the enterprises of merchants, shipmasters, and colonists representing all the leading mercantile nations of western Europe. The character of each nation's involvement in the web of traffic was determined largely by the resources it controlled and its place in European affairs. Holland's concentration on the carriage of other nations' goods shaped its position; the commerce of France came to rest upon Canadian furs and West Indian sugar; England's position was determined by the very variety of her colonial products and of the interests of her merchants.

The form of England's commercial system was an interlocked group of irregular circles linking the fixed points of port towns in the British Isles, Newfoundland, the American mainland, the West Indies, the

Wine Islands, and the continent of Europe. Outward from the larger ports in the British Isles flowed shipping, manufactures, and investments in colonial property, the enhanced value of which returned as colonial products to be sold at home or abroad. No important part of this flow was self-sufficient. Merchants in the colonies, who profited by injecting into the flow goods of their ownership which would be carried one or more stages closer to the ultimate resolution, became important agents in maintaining the efficiency of this mechanism. Their commerce was not independent, and if it appeared to be so to some of them that was because the efficiency of the system permitted them to operate successfully within a limited area. A breakdown in any major part of the mechanism affected all other parts. When, at the outbreak of the American Revolution, the link between England and her colonies was broken, the whole system, in so far as it affected the colonial merchants, was destroyed.

To contemporaries, the commercial system, which we may describe in abstract, geometrical terms, was not something impersonal existing above men's heads, outside their lives, to which they attached themselves for purpose of trade. Unconcerned with abstract economic forces, they knew that their trade was the creation of men and that the bonds that kept its parts together were the personal relationships existing among them.

Overseas commerce in the seventeenth century was capricious. Arrangements were interminably delayed by the accidents of sailing. Demand fluctuated almost incalculably, as one unforeseen crop failure could create a market which the arrival of a few ships could eliminate overnight. Reliable factors and correspondents were, therefore, of paramount importance, for the success of large enterprises rested on their judgment. In such a situation the initiation and continuance of commerce demanded deep personal commitments between people separated by hundreds of miles of ocean. How could such commitments be made? Not, in these early years, by impersonal correspondences between men brought into temporary contact by complementary business needs. The logic of the situation demanded that they follow pre-existent ties of blood or long acquaintance.

To a striking degree first commercial contacts were secured by the cement of kinship. Very frequently brothers, sons, and "in-laws" became the colonial agents of their European relatives. In the middle years of the seventeenth century a number of European—especially English and French—trading families spread out over the Atlantic world. Sons of Londoners seeking their fortunes entered trade in the West Indies and drew on their London connections who were themselves anxious to profit from the importation of colonial goods. Thus Richard Povey, brother of the famous London merchant-politician

Thomas Povey, looked after the family interests in Jamaica, while another brother, William, attended to affairs in Barbados. Not infrequently the same family had other relatives on the American mainland who joined in the growing enterprise. The Winthrop family, starting with representatives in England and Massachusetts, ended with ties to Rhode Island, New London and Hartford, Connecticut, Teneriffe in the Canaries, and Antigua in the West Indies. Typical of the reports by young Samuel Winthrop of his progress in securing the last-named contacts are these sentences from a letter of 1648 to his father:

> Captain Clement everet a Justice of peace [in St. Christopher], who being our country man and hearing our name vsed me verry Courtiously, and assisted me much in my law suites which were there verry many. Justice Froth, who was of your acquantance in England (as he informes me), was his Granfather. I haue left in his handes my busines in St. Christpors.

Jean Bailly of La Rochelle conducted his West Indian trade through two relatives in the Caribbean islands, especially Clerbaut Bergier in Martinique. But the most complete family commercial system of which we have any knowledge is that of the Hutchinsons; it is an almost ideal type of this sort of arrangement.

The Hutchinson family trading unit was based upon the continuous flow of manufactures exported from London by the affluent Richard Hutchinson to his brothers Samuel and Edward and his nephews Elisha and Eliakim in Boston, Massachusetts. They, together with Thomas Savage, who had married Richard's sister, retailed the goods in the Bay area and, through middlemen, sold also to the inland settlers. They conducted a large trade with the West Indies, sending provisions and cattle in exchange for cotton and sugar which they sold for credit in London.   This West Indian trade of the Hutchinsons was largely handled for them by Peleg Sanford of Portsmouth, Rhode Island, whose mother was another sister of Richard and who was, hence, cousin and nephew of the Boston merchants of the family. Peleg, who had started his career as a commercial agent in the West Indies, exported their horses and provisions to Barbados where they were sold by his brothers, the Barbadian merchants William and Elisha Sanford.

The Hutchinsons with their Rhode Island and West Indian relations formed a self-conscious family group which considered it unfortunate but not unnatural that Edward Hutchinson should go to jail, as he did in 1667, as a consequence of his support of his nephew Peleg in a law suit.

Since commerce was so dependent upon personal relationships, the weaving of a network of correspondences was greatly facilitated by the migrations within the colonial area. Many mainland settlers transplanted themselves to the Caribbean islands and became factors in the West Indies for the merchant friends they had left behind. On the other hand, several merchants were involved in the movement of people among and out of the West Indies, and some of them became residents of the continental colonies. Thus, John Parris, a relative of the New Englander John Hull, moved from the West Indies to Boston where he engaged in large operations in an attempt to stock his Barbados plantation with slaves. Men who moved south to the Indies or north to the continent carried with them friendships and a knowledge of affairs in their old home towns which were used in broadening the foreign contacts of the colonial merchants.

A further consequence of the personal nature of commercial ties in this early period was the consistency, long before mercantilist legislation became effective, with which Frenchmen and Britishers dealt with their fellow nationals in trade. Correspondences with foreigners were difficult to establish and maintain. To British colonials in this period, it seemed that little reliance could be placed on the bonds of Frenchmen who desired nothing more than the collapse of the British settlements in the New World. In long-distance transactions Englishmen preferred to deal with their relatives and friends who, if necessary, could be brought to law in the British courts far more easily than could Frenchmen. Richard Wharton, one of the most enterprising colonial merchants of the seventeenth century, failed to extend his contacts into the French West Indies because of his inability to secure reliable French correspondents. The later enforcement of mercantilist legislation was greatly facilitated by this early tendency of overseas merchants to favor connections with, if not relatives or old friends, at least fellow countrymen.

Through channels of trade created by personal ties among Europeans scattered about the Atlantic world flowed not only physical commodities but the human communications that related the settlers to European life. The orbits of commerce formed by lines drawn between the fixed points of correspondents helped shape the character of urban development and the structure of society in the colonial settlements.

On the American continent, as certain trading centers became poles in the primary cycles of trade, others slipped back toward ruralism. In the passage of generations the communities involved in the major orbits came into closer cultural relations with Europe than they did with some of the neighboring backwoods villages. The Boston merchants' meeting place in their Townhouse Exchange was in every way, except geographically, closer to the "New-England walke" on the London Exchange than to the market places of most inland towns. Study of any of the continental trading regions reveals the varying degrees of provincialism that followed the solidification of the routes of commerce.

In New England, the most important commercial center in North America during the seventeenth century, Boston, with its excellent harbor and access to the provincial government and to flourishing agricultural markets, became the major terminus of traffic originating in Europe. With the exception of Salem and Charlestown, the other promising mercantile centers of the 1630's and 1640's fell back into secondary economic roles and relative seclusion from the cultural life of the Atlantic community. Plymouth, which had been the first trading center east of Manhattan, was described in 1660 as "a poor small Towne now, The People being removed into Farmes in the Country," and New Haven, whose optimistic merchant leaders had laid out "stately and costly houses," was "not so glorious as once it was," with its "Merchants either dead or come away, the rest gotten to their Farmes." This is not to say that these essentially rural districts had no trade. On the contrary, there were men in the Connecticut River towns and along Long Island Sound who managed a considerable exchange of goods; but their dealings were different from those of the Bostonians. Engaged in secondary orbits of trade, they sent small but steady flows of local produce only to other American colonies or occasionally to the West Indies. The Connecticut River grandees were, like the younger Pynchon, primarily landed squires and only secondarily merchants. The few men in the small coastal villages who did devote themselves primarily to trade operated within a commercial sphere subordinate to that of the Bostonians and the Dutchmen.

Life in the inland areas and in the minor ports came to differ significantly from that in the commercial centers in direct contact with Europe. While Boston and New York assumed characteristics of British provincial outports and while their leading residents groped for an understanding of their place as colonials in British society, towns like Scarborough, Maine, and Wethersfield, Connecticut, became models of new types of communities; and their inhabitants, restricted in experience to the colonial world, came to lack the standards by which to measure or even to perceive their provincialism. Fashion, patterns for styles of living, and the emulative spirit of provincialism followed the routes of trade, which, throughout the colonial world, became important social boundaries.

This fact became particularly evident in the last third of the century when national rivalries, both military and economic, required the presence of official representatives in the colonies from the home countries. These officers, civil and military, settled for the most part in the large trading centers, close to the main objects of their supervision. Their presence in what might be called the focuses of the primary trading orbits had a most important social consequence. These home country representatives were quickly surrounded by a number of Europeans new to the colonies: men seeking careers in the quickly expanding colonial administrations. Customs functionaries, lesser bureaucrats, fortune hunters in official positions—these newcomers, grouped around the chief European representatives, came to constitute colonial officialdom, which in all the main colonial ports became a major social magnet for the residents. For not only did it represent cosmopolitan fashion and political influence, but, in its access to those who controlled government contracts and who wielded the weapon of customs regulations, it offered great economic opportunities.

Toward these groups, therefore, moved every colonial with ambition and the slightest hope of success. The threshold of officialdom became a great divide in the society of the commercial towns. Next to this principle of association, "class," in the traditional European sense, was meaningless. In Europe the word "merchant" meant not only an occupation but a status and a way of life. In America, where, as Madam Knight discovered in her famous journey of 1704, they gave the title of merchant to every backwoods huckster, trade was not so much a way of life as a way of making money, not a social condition but an economic activity. Similarly, how could the well-known American mariner, Captain Cyprian Southack, be prevented from describing himself, as he did on occasion, as "gent."?

The limits of officialdom, however, were palpable. No merchant would confuse failure with success in obtaining favors from customs officials or in gaining contracts for provisions and naval stores. It was well worth a merchant's noting, as Samuel Sewall did in his *Diary*, that he was not invited to the governor's dinner parties or to the extravagant funerals staged by the members of his group.

It was as true in the seventeenth century as it is now that the introduction of an important new social barrier necessarily intrudes upon a variety of interests. The advent of officialdom was attended by upheavals throughout the Atlantic world. Wherever we turn in this period we find evidence of social dislocation as successful resident entrepreneurs came to terms with this important new force in the colonial world.

One of the first successful agricultural districts in Carolina was Albemarle County. Behind the barrier of shifting sand bars that blocked Albemarle Sound to all but the most shallow-draft ocean-going vessels. lived, in the 1670's, approximately 3,000 settlers—farmers, coastal backwoodsmen, many of them tough, stubborn refugees from better-organized communities. Their one cash crop was tobacco, of which they prepared nearly one million pounds a year. This they disposed of to northerners on peddling voyages in exchange for the commodities they needed. The Navigation Law of 1673 levied duties on tobacco at the port of lading, and Albemarle, like all other commercial centers, was soon visited by a customs collector. The settlers resisted, fearing an increase in the price of goods if their tobacco was taxed, and they forced the governor to remit to the traders three farthings in every penny taken. In 1677 the appointment of an imperious collector of customs determined to enforce the law led to a rebellion of the settlers headed by one John Culpeper. Until the legal authorities could regain control, Culpeper acted as collector, formed a temporary government, and barred the royal comptroller and surveyor of the customs at Albemarle from the exercise of his office.

Culpeper's rebellion, though it was soon quelled and finds little mention in American history, was a significant event. It is a simplified example of what was taking place throughout the colonies. We do not yet have a full account of Leisler's rebellion which kept New York in turmoil for two years. But when we do, it will be found that it was in great part the culmination of resentments that accompanied the introduction of English officialdom into that province. Leisler's career, in fact, can only be understood against the background of family rivalries that grew up around this pre-eminent principle of association. Edmund Andros, famous for his difficulties as the governor of the Dominion of New England, had a less notorious but equally important reign as the Duke of York's governor in New York. In this position he precipitated social differences among the merchants who resisted when they could not take advantage of his influence. He was finally recalled on charges of excessive fee-taking and profiteering.

The rebellion of 1689, which overthrew his administration of the Dominion of New England, divided the northern merchants on lines not of ideology but of interests defined by the degree of proximity to officialdom. No ideology, no religious belief, no abstract political principle or party loyalty separated the Boston merchants Richard Wharton and Charles Lidget, but in 1689 they were on opposite sides of the political fence. Lidget ended up in the Boston jail with Andros because his connections, inherited from his father who had built the family fortune on the timber he sold to the Navy mast contractors, linked him to the leaders of the official group. Wharton died in the midst of his fight for the removal of Andros whose favor he had been denied. The fact that Lidget was one of the founders of the first Anglican Church in New England does not indicate a religious or ideological orientation different from Wharton's. The latter, if he was not an active Anglican, certainly was not a dissenter. Both men married heiress daughters of nonconformist New Englanders.

In the West Indies the same principle was at work during most of the seventeenth century. But toward the end of the century controversies touched off by the intrusion of officialdom diminished in the islands as a consequence of the consolidation of large plantations and the growth of absenteeism. The resident nonofficial population became less active politically as the large planters returned to the home country, leaving their estates in the hands of managers and agents. But battles over the economic benefits of political and social advantage were not ended; they were merely transferred to London where they punctuated the history of the West India interest.

By the end of the century this principle of association in the commercial centers was deeply woven into the fabric of American society. Its importance did not diminish thereafter. Recently, Oliver Dickerson in his book *The Navigation Acts and the American Revolution* destroyed a number of myths by pointing out the importance of what he called "customs racketeering." From his researches it appears that the merchant group was as deeply divided on the eve of the Revolution as it was in 1689. Both John Hancock and Thomas Hutchinson were leading Boston merchants, but the former was clearly victimized by the strategy of the Hutchinson-Bernard clique which controlled the channels of prerogative. And in South Carolina, Henry Laurens, probably the richest merchant in the southern colonies, whose mercantile connections were with the opponents of the King's Friends, suffered equally from the rapacity of the official group.

Further study of the merchants as a social group may reveal that this principle of association, which emerged as an important social force when the nations of Europe undertook to draw together the threads of trade spun by seventeenth-century entrepreneurs, was a major determinant of the movement that led to Revolution.

7

The Role of the Lower Houses of Assembly in Eighteenth-Century Politics

JACK P. GREENE

*In 1898 Charles M. Andrews, speaking before the American Historical
Association, invited the attention of his peers to the decades between 1690
and 1750. To him, these decades of transition "between colonization and
revolution" were the great "neglected period" of American colonial history.
That important developments had characterized the period was clear enough.
It was the training time of the men who led the Revolution. The mainland
colonies shed an essentially English identity and assumed one that was
essentially American. The conflict between Britain and France for hegemony
over the continent of Europe also settled the kind of European civilization
that would prevail on the continent of North America.*

*The period between 1690 and 1750 has, since Andrews's address of 1898,
been the subject of many significant studies on particular subjects, and it is
surely no longer the dark age, neglected and misunderstood, that he then
considered it to be. But no historian has as yet fully answered Andrews's
call, none has attempted to explore, in a comprehensive way, the process
by which an American polity emerged. In this sense, the period between the
accessions of William of Orange and George III has remained pretty much
what Andrews considered it to be: neglected.*

*It is in his attempt to offer a larger survey of this period that one will find
the special importance of Jack P. Greene's recent monograph,* **The Quest**

SOURCE: *The Journal of Southern History,* XXVII (November, 1961), 451–474.
Copyright © 1961 by the Southern Historical Association. Reprinted with
the author's additions and by permission of the Managing Editor. The original
footnotes have been omitted.

for Power: The Lower Houses of Assembly in the Southern Royal Colonies, 1689–1776 (1963). And here too is the importance of the follow- ing article by Professor Greene, in which he extends his survey to all the mainland colonies. His concern is to define the regularities and common features which were basic to the political development of the lower houses and to present a "comprehensive synthesis" of the process whereby they advanced from a position of subordination to one of ascendancy.

In anatomizing the development and process, he offers his reader answers to the following questions: In what respects did the lower houses move con- tinuously, during the course of the eighteenth century, to increase their power and authority? What were the two divergent concepts of their constitutional positions held by the colonial lower houses and the imperial authorities respectively? How did British policy after 1763 challenge the newly won position of the lower houses and, consequently, precipitate a constitutional crisis within the empire?

It is fair to say that Professor Greene's contribution was anticipated, in some respects, by the work of other historians, notably that of Charles M. Andrews and Leonard W. Labaree. What is fresh about his contribution is his massive presentation of the details by which the colonial legislators gained their ascendancy. It becomes clear from Greene's account that the colonists, over a period of decades, were growing both in sophistication and in control, and that, after 1763, they countered British attempts at imperial "reform" with an already clearly defined constitutional theory of their own. The significance of what Greene is saying lies in this, then: that in the process of offering a large-scale analysis of the "neglected period" of American colonial history, he is also helping to explain the coming of the American Revolution.

The rise of the representative assemblies was perhaps the most signi- ficant political and constitutional development in the history of Britain's overseas empire before the American Revolution. Crown and pro- prietary authorities had obviously intended the governor to be the focal point of colonial government with the lower houses merely subordinate bodies called together when necessary to levy taxes and ratify local ordinances proposed by the executive. Consequently, except in the New England charter colonies, where the representative bodies early assumed a leading role, they were dominated by the governors and councils for most of the period down to 1689. But beginning with the Restoration and intensifying their efforts during the years following the Glorious Revolution, the lower houses engaged in a successful quest for power as they set about to restrict the authority of the executive, undermine the system of colonial administration laid down by imperial and proprietary authorities, and make themselves paramount in the affairs of their respective colonies.

Historians have been fascinated by this phenomenon. For nearly a century after 1776 they interpreted it as a prelude to the American Revolution. In the 1780's the pro-British historian George Chalmers saw it as the early manifestation of a latent desire for independence, an undutiful reaction to the mild policies of the Mother Country. In the middle of the nineteenth century the American nationalist George Bancroft, although more interested in other aspects of colonial history, looked upon it as the natural expression of American democratic principles, simply another chapter in the progress of mankind. The reaction to these sweeping interpretations set in during the last decades of the nineteenth century, when Charles M. Andrews, Edward Channing, Herbert L. Osgood, and others began to investigate in detail and to study in context developments from the Restoration to the end of the Seven Years' War. Osgood put a whole squadron of Columbia students to work examining colonial political institutions, and they produced a series of institutional studies in which the evolution of the lower houses was a central feature. These studies clarified the story of legislative development in each colony, but this necessarily piecemeal approach, as well as the excessive fragmentation that characterized the more general narratives of Osgood and Channing, tended to emphasize the differences rather than the similarities in the rise of the lower houses and failed to produce a general analysis of the common features of their quest for power. Among later scholars, Leonard W. Labaree in his excellent monograph *Royal Government in America* presented a comprehensive survey of the institutional development of the lower houses in the royal colonies and of the specific issues involved in their struggles with the royal governors, but he did not offer any systematic interpretation of the general process and pattern of legislative development. Charles Andrews promised to tackle this problem and provide a synthesis in the later volumes of his magnum opus, *The Colonial Period of American History,* but he died before completing that part of the project.

As a result, some fundamental questions have never been fully answered, and no one has produced a comprehensive synthesis. No one has satisfactorily worked out the basic pattern of the quest; analyzed the reasons for and the significance of its development; explored its underlying assumptions and theoretical foundations; or assessed the consequences of the success of the lower houses, particularly the relationship between their rise to power and the coming of the American Revolution. This essay is intended to suggest some tentative conclusions about these problems, not to present ultimate solutions. My basic research on the lower houses has been in the Southern royal colonies and in Nova Scotia. One of the present purposes is to test the generalizations I have arrived at about the Southern colonies by applying them to what scholars have learned of the legislatures in the other colonies. This procedure has the advantage of providing perspective on the story of Southern developments. At the same time, it may serve as one guidepost for a general synthesis in the future.

Any student of the eighteenth-century political process will sooner or later be struck by the fact that, although each of the lower houses developed independently and differently, their stories were similar. The elimination of individual variants, which tend to cancel out each other, discloses certain basic regularities, a clearly discernible pattern— or what the late Sir Lewis Namier called a morphology—common to all of them. They all moved along like paths in their drives for increased authority, and although their success on specific issues differed from colony to colony and the rate of their rise varied from time to time, they all ended up at approximately the same destination. They passed successively through certain vaguely defined phases of political development. Through most of the seventeenth century the lower houses were still in a position of subordination, slowly groping for the power to tax and the right to sit separately from the council and to initiate laws. Sometime during the early eighteenth century most of them advanced to a second stage at which they could battle on equal terms with the governors and councils and challenge even the powers in London if necessary. At that point the lower houses began their bid for political supremacy. The violent eruptions that followed usually ended in an accommodation with the governors and councils which paved the way for the ascendancy of the lower houses and saw the virtual eclipse of the colonial executive. By the end of the Seven Years' War, and in some instances considerably earlier, the lower houses had reached the third and final phase of political dominance and were in a position to speak for the colonies in the conflict with the imperial government which ensued after 1763.

By 1763, with the exception of the lower houses in the corporate colonies of Rhode Island and Connecticut, which had virtually complete authority, the Pennsylvania and Massachusetts houses of representatives were probably most powerful. Having succeeded in placing its election on a statutory basis and depriving the Council of direct legislative authority in the Charter of Privileges in 1701, the Pennsylvania House under the astute guidance of David Lloyd secured broad financial and appointive powers during the administrations of Daniel Gookin and Sir William Keith. Building on these foundations, it gained almost complete dominance in the 1730's and 1740's despite the opposition of the governors, whose power and prestige along with that of the Council declined rapidly. The Massachusetts House, having been accorded the unique privilege of sharing in the selection of the Council by the royal charter in 1691, already had a strong tradition of legislative supremacy inherited from a half century of corporate experience. During the first thirty years under the new charter first the benevolent policies of Sir William Phips and William Stoughton and then wartime conditions during the tenures of Joseph Dudley and Samuel Shute enabled the House, led by Elisha Cooke, Jr., to extend its authority greatly. It emerged from the conflicts over the salary question during the 1720's with firm control over finance, and the Crown's abandonment of its demand for a permanent revenue in the early 1730's paved the way for an accommodation with subsequent governors and the eventual dominance of the House under Governor William Shirley after 1740.

The South Carolina Commons and New York House of Assembly were only slightly less powerful. Beginning in the first decade of the eighteenth century, the South Carolina lower house gradually assumed an ironclad control over all aspects of South Carolina government, extending its supervision to the minutest details of local administration after 1730 as a succession of governors including Francis Nicholson, Robert Johnson, Thomas Broughton, the elder William Bull, and James Glen offered little determined opposition. The Commons continued to grow in stature after 1750 while the Council's standing declined because of the Crown policy of filling it with placemen from England and the Commons' successful attacks upon its authority. The New York House of Assembly began to demand greater authority in reaction to the mismanagement of Edward Hyde, Viscount Cornbury, during the first decade of the eighteenth century. Governor Robert Hunter met the challenge squarely during his ten-year administration beginning in 1710, but he and his successors could not check the rising power of the House. During the seven-year tenure of George Clarke beginning in 1736, the House advanced into the final stage of development. Following Clarke, George Clinton made a vigorous effort to reassert the authority of the executive, but neither he nor any of his successors was able to challenge the power of the House.

The lower houses of North Carolina, New Jersey, and Virginia developed more slowly. The North Carolina lower house was fully capable of protecting its powers and privileges and competing on equal terms with the executive during the last years of proprietary rule and under the early royal governors, George Burrington and Gabriel Johnston. But it was not until Arthur Dobbs' tenure in the 1750's and 1760's that, meeting more regularly, it assumed the upper hand in North Carolina politics under the astute guidance of Speaker Samuel Swann and Treasurers John Starket and Thomas Barker. In New Jersey the lower house was partially thwarted in its spirited bid for power during the 1740's under the leadership of John Kinsey and Samuel Nevill by the determined opposition of Governor Lewis Morris, and it did not gain superiority until the administrations of Jonathan Belcher, Thomas Pownall, Francis Bernard, and Thomas Boone during the Seven Years' War. Similarly, the Virginia Burgesses vigorously sought to establish its control in the second decade of the century under Alexander Spotswood, but not until the administrations of Sir William Gooch and Robert Dinwiddie, when first the expansion of the colony and then the Seven Years' War required more regular sessions, did the Burgesses finally gain the upper hand under the effective leadership of Speaker John Robinson.

Among the lower houses in the older colonies, only the Maryland House of Delegates and the New Hampshire House of Assembly failed to reach the final level of development in the period before 1763. The Maryland body made important advances early in the eighteenth century while under the control of the Crown and aggressively sought to extend its authority in the 1720's under the leadership of the older Daniel Dulany and again in the late 1730's and early 1740's under Dr. Charles Carroll. But the proprietors were usually able to thwart these attempts, and the Delegates failed to pull ahead of the executive despite a concerted effort during the last intercolonial war under the administration of Horatio Sharpe. In New Hampshire, the House had exercised considerable power through the early decades of the eighteenth century, but Governor Benning Wentworth effectively challenged its authority after 1740 and prevented it from attaining the extensive power exercised by its counterparts in other colonies. It should be emphasized, however, that neither the Maryland nor the New Hampshire lower house was in any sense impotent, and along with their more youthful equivalent in Georgia gained dominance during the decade of debate with Britain after 1763. Of the lower houses in the continental colonies with pre-1763 political experience, only the Nova Scotia Assembly had not reached the final phase of political dominance by 1776.

The similarities in the process and pattern of legislative development from colony to colony were not entirely accidental. The lower houses faced like problems and drew upon common tradition and imperial precedents for solutions. They all operated in the same broad imperial context and were affected by common historical forces. Moreover, family, cultural, and commercial ties often extended across colony lines, and newspapers and other printed materials, as well as individuals, often found their way from one colony to another. The result was at least a general awareness of issues and practices in neighboring colonies, and occasionally there was even a conscious borrowing of precedents and traditions. Younger bodies such as the Georgia Commons and Nova Scotia Assembly were particularly indebted to their more mature counterparts in South Carolina and Massachusetts

Bay. On the executive side, the similarity in attitudes, assumptions, and policies among the governors can be traced in large measure to the fact that they were all subordinate to the same central authority in London, which pursued a common policy in all the colonies.

Before the Seven Years' War the quest was characterized by a considerable degree of spontaneity, by a lack of awareness that activities of the moment were part of any broad struggle for power. Rather than consciously working out the details of some master plan designed to bring them liberty or self-government, the lower houses moved along from issue to issue and from situation to situation, primarily concerning themselves with the problems at hand and displaying a remarkable capacity for spontaneous action, for seizing any and every opportunity to enlarge their own influence at the executive's expense and for holding tenaciously to powers they had already secured. Conscious of the issues involved in each specific conflict, they were for the most part unaware of and uninterested in the long-range implications of their actions. Virginia Governor Francis Fauquier correctly judged the matter in 1760. "Whoever charges them with acting upon a premeditated concerted plan, don't know them," he wrote of the Virginia burgesses, "for they mean honestly, but are Expedient Mongers in the highest Degree." Still, in retrospect it is obvious that throughout the eighteenth century the lower houses were engaged in a continuous movement to enlarge their sphere of influence. To ignore that continuity would be to miss the meaning of eighteenth-century colonial political development.

One is impressed with the rather prosaic manner in which the lower houses went about the task of extending their authority, with the infrequency of dramatic conflict. They gained much of their power in the course of routine business, quietly and simply extending and consolidating their authority of passing laws and establishing practices, the implications of which escaped both colonial executives and imperial authorities and were not always fully recognized even by the lower houses themselves. In this way they gradually extended their financial authority to include the powers to audit accounts of all public officers, to share in disbursing public funds, and eventually even to appoint officials concerned in collecting and handling local revenues. Precedents thus established soon hardened into fixed principles, "undoubted rights" or "inherent powers," changing the very fabric of their respective constitutions. The notable absence of conflict is perhaps best illustrated by the none too surprising fact that the lower houses made some of their greatest gains under those governors with whom they enjoyed the most harmony, in particular Keith in Pennsylvania, Shirley in Massachusetts, Hunter in New York, and the elder and younger Bull in South Carolina. In Virginia the House of Burgesses made rapid strides during the 1730's and 1740's under the benevolent government of Gooch, who discovered early in his administration that the secret of political success for a Virginia governor was to reach an accord with the plantation gentry.

One should not conclude that the colonies had no exciting legislative-executive conflicts, however. Attempts through the middle decades of the eighteenth century by Clinton to weaken the financial powers of the New York House, Massachusetts Governors Samuel Shute and William Burnet to gain a permanent civil list, Benning Wentworth to extend unilaterally the privilege of representation to new districts in New Hampshire, Johnston to break the extensive power of the Albemarle Counties in the North Carolina lower house, Dinwiddie to establish a fee for issuing land patents without the consent of the Virginia Burgesses, and Boone to reform South Carolina's election laws each provided a storm of controversy that brought local politics to a fever pitch. But such conflicts were the exception and usually arose not out of the lower houses' seeking more authority but from the executives' attempts to restrict powers already won. Impatient of restraint and jealous of their rights and privileges, the lower houses responded forcefully and sometimes violently when executive action threatened to deprive them of those rights. Only a few governors, men of the caliber of Henry Ellis in Georgia and to a lesser extent William Henry Lyttelton in South Carolina and Bernard in New Jersey, had the skill to challenge established rights successfully without raising the wrath of the lower houses. Clumsier tacticians—Pennsylvania's William Denny, New York's Clinton, Virginia's Dinwiddie, North Carolina's Dobbs, South Carolina's Boone, Georgia's John Reynolds—failed when pursuing similar goals.

Fundamentally, the quest for power in both the royal and the proprietary colonies was a struggle for political identity, the manifestation of the political ambitions of the leaders of emerging societies within each colony. There is a marked correlation between the appearance of economic and social elites produced by the growth in colonial wealth and population on the one hand and the lower houses' demand for increased authority, dignity, and prestige on the other. In the eighteenth century a group of planters, merchants, and professional men had attained or were rapidly acquiring within the colonies wealth and social position. The lower houses' aggressive drive for power reflects the determination of this new elite to attain through the representative assemblies political influence as well. In another but related sense, the lower houses' efforts represented a movement for autonomy in local affairs, although it is doubtful that many of the members recognized them as such. The lower houses wished to strengthen their authority within the colonies and to reduce to a minimum the amount of supervision, with the uncertainties it involved, that royal or proprietary authorities could exercise. Continuously nourished by the growing desire of American legislators to be masters of their own political fortunes and by the development of a vigorous tradition of legislative superiority in imitation of the imperial House of Commons, this basic principle of local control over local affairs in some cases got part of its impetus from an unsatisfactory experience early in the lower houses' development with a despotic, inefficient, or corrupt governor such as Thomas, Lord Culpeper, or Francis, Lord Howard or Effingham, in Virginia, Lionel Copley in Maryland, Sir Edmund Andros in Massachusetts, Seth Sothell in North Carolina, or the infamous Cornbury in New York and New Jersey.

With most of their contemporaries in Great Britain, colonial Americans were convinced that men were imperfect creatures, perpetually self-deluded, enslaved by their passions, vanities, and interests, confined in their vision and understanding, and incapable of exercising power over each other without abusing it. This cluster of assumptions with the associated ideals of a government of laws rather than of men and of a political structure that restrained the vicious tendencies of man by checking them against each other was at the heart of English constitutionalism. In Britain and in the colonies, wherever Englishmen encountered a seeming abuse of power, they could be expected to insist that it be placed under legal and constitutional restraints. Because the monarchy had been the chief offender in seventeenth-century England, it became conventional for the representative branch to keep an especially wary eye on the executive, and the Glorious Revolution tended to institutionalize this pattern of behavior. The necessity to justify the Revolution ensured both that the specter of Stuart despotism would continue to haunt English political arenas throughout the eighteenth century and that representative bodies and representatives would be expected—indeed obliged—to be constantly on the lookout for any signs of that excess of gubernatorial power that would perforce result in executive tyranny. When colonial lower houses demanded checks on the prerogative and sought to undermine executive authority, they were, then, to some extent, playing out roles created for them by their predecessors in the seventeenth-century English House of Commons and using a rhetoric and a set of ground rules that grew out of the revolutionary conditions of Stuart England. In every debate, and in every political contest, each American legislator was a potential Coke, Pym, or Hampden and each governor, at least in legislators' minds, a potential Charles I or James II.

But the lower houses' quest for power involved more than the extension of legislative authority within the colonies at the expense of the colonial executives. After their initial stage of evolution, the lower houses learned that their real antagonists were not the governors but the proprietors or Crown officials in London. Few governors proved to be a match for the representatives. A governor was almost helpless to prevent a lower house from exercising powers secured under his predecessors, and even the most discerning governor could fall into the trap of assenting to an apparently innocent law that would later prove damaging to the royal or proprietary prerogative. Some governors, for the sake of preserving amicable relations with the representatives or because they thought certain legislation to be in the best interest of a colony, actually conspired with legislative leaders to present the actions of the lower houses in a favorable light in London. Thus, Jonathan Belcher worked with Massachusetts leaders to parry the Crown's demand for a permanent revenue in the 1730's, and Fauquier joined with Speaker John Robinson in Virginia to prevent the separation of the offices of speaker and treasurer during the closing years of the Seven Years' War.

Nor could imperial authorities depend upon the colonial councils to furnish an effective check upon the representatives' advancing influence. Most councilors were drawn from the rising social and economic elites in the colonies. The duality of their role is obvious. Bound by oath to uphold the interests of the Crown or the proprietors, they were also driven by ambition and a variety of local pressures to maintain the status and power of the councils as well as to protect and advance their own individual interests and those of their group within the colonies. These two objectives were not always in harmony, and the councils frequently sided with the lower houses rather than with the governors. With a weakened governor and an unreliable council, the task of restraining the representative assemblies ultimately devolved upon the home government. Probably as much of the struggle for power was played out in Whitehall as in Williamsburg, Charleston, New York, Boston, or Philadelphia.

Behind the struggle between colonial lower houses and the imperial authorities were two divergent, though on the colonial side not wholly articulated, concepts of the constitutions of the colonies and in particular of the status of the lower houses. To the very end of the colonial period, imperial authorities persisted in the views that colonial constitutions were static and that the lower houses were subordinate governmental agencies with only temporary and limited lawmaking powers—in the words of one imperial official, merely "so many Corporations at a distance, invested with an Ability to make Temporary By Laws for themselves, agreeable to their respective Situations and Climates." In working out a political system for the colonies in the later seventeenth century, imperial officials had institutionalized these views in the royal commissions and instructions. Despite the fact that the lower

houses were yearly making important changes in their respective constitutions, the Crown never altered either the commissions or instructions to conform with realities of the colonial political situation and
continued to maintain throughout the eighteenth century that they
were the most vital part of the constitutional structure of the royal
colonies. The Pennsylvania and to a lesser extent the Maryland proprietors were less rigid, although they also insisted upon their theoretical constitutional and political supremacy over the lower houses.

Colonial lower houses had little respect for and even less patience
with such a doctrinaire position, and whether or not royal and proprietary instructions were absolutely binding upon the colonies was
the leading constitutional issue in the period before 1763. As the political
instruments of what was probably the most pragmatic society in the
eighteenth-century Western world, colonial legislators would not likely
be restrained by dogma divorced from reality. They had no fear of
innovations and welcomed the chance to experiment with new forms
and ideas. All they asked was that a thing work. When the lower
houses found that instructions from imperial authorities did not work
in the best interests of the colonies, that they were, in fact, antithetic to
the very measures they as legislatures were trying to effect, they openly
refused to submit to them. Instructions, they argued, applied only to
officials appointed by the Crown.

> Instructions from his majesty, to his governor, or the council, are binding
> to them, and esteemed as laws or rules; because if either should disregard
> them, they might immediately be displaced,

declared a South Carolina writer in 1756 while denying the validity of
an instruction that stipulated colonial councils should have equal
rights with the lower houses in framing money bills. "But, if instructions should be laws and rules to the people of this province, then there
would be no need of assemblies, and all our laws and taxes might be
made and levied by an instruction. Clearly, then, instructions might
bind governors, but never the elected branch of the legislature.

Even though the lower houses, filled with intensely practical politicians, were concerned largely with practical political considerations,
they found it necessary to develop a body of theory with which to
oppose unpopular instructions from Britain and to support their claims
to greater political power. In those few colonies that had charters, the
lower houses relied upon the guarantees in them as their first line of
defense, taking the position that the stipulations of the charters were
inviolate, despite the fact that some had been invalidated by English
courts, and could not be altered by executive order. A more basic
premise which was equally applicable to all colonies was that the constituents of the lower houses, as inhabitants of British colonies, were

entitled to all the traditional rights of Englishmen. On this foundation the colonial legislatures built their ideological structure. In the early charters the Crown had guaranteed the colonists "all privileges, franchises and liberties of this our kingdom of England . . . any Statute, act, ordinance, or provision to the contrary thereof, notwithstanding." Such guarantees, colonials assumed, merely constituted recognition that their privileges as Englishmen were inherent and unalterable and that it mattered not whether they stayed on the home islands or migrated to the colonies. "His Majesty's Subjects coming over to America," the South Carolina Commons argued in 1739 while asserting its exclusive right to formulate tax laws, "have no more forfeited this their most valuable Inheritance than they have withdrawn their Allegiance." No "Royal Order," the Commons declared, could "qualify or any wise alter a fundamental Right from the Shape in which it was handed down to us from our Ancestors."

One of the most important of these rights was the privilege of representation, on which, of course, depended the very existence of the lower houses. Imperial authorities always maintained that the lower houses existed only through the consent of the Crown, but the houses insisted that an elected assembly was a fundamental right of a colony arising out of an Englishman's privilege to be represented and that they did not owe their existence merely to the King's pleasure.

> Our representatives, agreeably to the general sense of their constituents [wrote New York lawyer William Smith in the 1750's] are tenacious in their opinion, that the inhabitants of this colony are entitled to all the privileges of Englishmen; that they have a right to participate in the legislative power, and that the session of assemblies here, is wisely substituted instead of a representation in parliament, which, all things considered, would, at this remote distance, be extremely inconvenient and dangerous.

The logical corollary to this argument was that the lower houses were equivalents of the House of Commons and must perforce in their limited spheres be entitled to all the privileges possessed by that body in Great Britain. Hence, in cases where an invocation of fundamental rights was not appropriate, the lower houses frequently defended their actions on the grounds that they were agreeable to the practice of the House of Commons. Thus in 1755 the North Carolina Lower House denied the right of the Council to amend tax bills on the grounds that it was "contrary to Custom and Usage of Parliament." Unintentionally, Crown officials encouraged the lower houses to make this analogy by forbidding them in the instructions to exercise "any power or privilege whatsoever which is not allowed by us to the House of Commons . . . in Great Britain."

Because neither fundamental rights nor imperial precedents could be used to defend practices that were contrary to customs of the mother country or to the British Constitution, the lower houses found it necessary to develop still another argument: that local precedents, habits, traditions, and statutes were important parts of their particular constitutions and could not be abridged by a royal or proprietary order. The assumptions were that the legislatures could alter colonial constitutions by their own actions without the active consent of imperial officials and that once the alterations were confirmed by usage they could not be countermanded by the British government. They did not deny the power of the governor to veto or of the Privy Council to disallow their laws but argued that imperial acquiescence over a long period of time was tantamount to consent and that precedents thus established could not be undone without their approval. The implication was that the American colonists saw their constitutions as living, growing, and constantly changing organisms, a theory which was directly opposite to the imperial view. To be sure, precedent had always been an important element in shaping the British constitution, but Crown officials were unwilling to concede that it was equally so in determining the fundamental law of the colonies. They willingly granted that colonial statutes, once formally approved by the Privy Council, automatically became part of the constitutions of the colonies, but they officially took the position that both royal instructions and commissions, as well as constitutional traditions of the mother country, took precedence over local practice or unconfirmed statutes. This conflict of views persisted throughout the period after 1689, becoming more and more of an issue in the decades immediately preceding the American Revolution.

In the last analysis it was the imperial denial of the validity of the constitutional defenses of the lower houses that drove colonial lawmakers to seek to extend the power of the lower houses at the very time they were insisting—and, in fact, deeply believed—that no one individual or institution should have a superiority of power in any government. No matter what kind of workable balance of power might be attained within the colonies, there was always the possibility that the home government might unleash the unlimited might of the parent state against the colonies. The chief fear of colonial legislators, then, was not the power of the governors, which they could control, but that of the imperial government, which in the circumstances they could never hope to control, and the whole movement for legislative authority in the colonies can be interpreted as a search for a viable constitutional arrangement in which the rights of the colonists would be secured against the preponderant power of the Mother Country. The failure of imperial authorities to provide such an arrangement or even to formalize what small concessions they did make, meant, of course, that the search could never be fulfilled, and the resulting anxiety, only partly conscious and finding expression through the classic arguments and ringing phrases of English political struggles of the seventeenth century, impelled the lower houses and the men who composed them relentlessly through the colonial period and was perhaps the most important single factor in the demand of patriot leaders for explicit, written constitutions after the Declaration of Independence.

It is nonetheless true that, if imperial authorities did not grant the validity of the theoretical arguments of the lower houses, neither did they make any systematic or concerted effort to force a rigid compliance with official policies for most of the period after 1689. Repressive measures, at least before 1763, rarely went beyond the occasional disallowance of an offending statute or the official reprimand of a rambunctious lower house. General lack of interest in the routine business of colonial affairs and failure to recognize the potential seriousness of the situation may in part account for this leniency, but it is also true that official policy under both Walpole and the Pelhams called for a light rein on the colonies on the assumption that contented colonies created fewer problems for the administration. "One would not Strain any point," Charles Delafaye, secretary to the lords justices, cautioned South Carolina's Governor Francis Nicholson in 1722, "where it can be of no Service to our King or Country." "In the Plantations," he added, "the Government should be as Easy and Mild as possible to invite people to Settle under it." Three times between 1734 and 1749 the ministry failed to give enthusiastic support to measures introduced into Parliament to insure the supremacy of instructions over colonial laws. Though the Calverts were somewhat more insistent upon preserving their proprietary prerogatives, in general the proprietors were equally lax as long as there was no encroachment upon their land rights or proprietary dues.

Imperial organs of administration were in fact inadequate to deal effectively with all the problems of the empire. Since no special governmental bodies were created in England to deal exclusively with colonial affairs, they were handled through the regular machinery of government—a maze of boards and officials whose main interests and responsibilities were not the supervision of overseas colonies. The only body sufficiently informed and interested to deal competently with colonial matters was the Board of Trade, and it had little authority, except for the brief period from 1748 to 1761 under the presidency of George Dunk, Earl of Halifax. The most useful device for restraining the lower houses was the Privy Council's right to review colonial laws, but even that was only partly effective, because the mass of colonial statutes annually coming before the Board of Trade made a thorough scrutiny impossible. Under such arrangements no vigorous colonial policy was likely. The combination of imperial lethargy and colonial aggression virtually guaranteed the success of the lower houses' quest for power. An indication of a growing awareness in imperial circles of the serious-ness of the situation was Halifax's spirited, if piecemeal, effort to restrain the growth of the lower houses in the early 1750's. Sympto-matic of these efforts was the attempt to make Georgia and Nova Scotia model royal colonies at the institution of royal government by writing into the instructions to their governors provisions designed to insure the continued supremacy of the executive and to prevent the lower houses from going the way of their counterparts in the older colonies. However, the outbreak of the Seven Years' War forced Halifax to suspend his activities and prevented any further reformation until the cessation of hostilities.

Indeed, the war saw a drastic acceleration in the lower houses' bid for authority, and its conclusion found them in possession of many of the powers held less than a century before by the executive. In the realm of finance they had imposed their authority over every phase of raising and distributing public revenue. They had acquired a large measure of independence by winning control over their compositions and proceedings and obtaining guarantees of basic English Parlia-mentary privileges. Finally, they had pushed their power even beyond that of the English House of Commons by gaining extensive authority in handling executive affairs, including the right to appoint executive officers and to share in formulating executive policy. These specific gains were symptoms of developments of much greater significance. To begin with, they were symbolic of a fundamental shift of the constitu-tional center of power in the colonies from the executive to the elected branch of the legislature. With the exception of the Georgia and Nova Scotia bodies, both of which had less than a decade of political ex-perience behind them, the houses had by 1763 succeeded in attaining a new status, raising themselves from dependent lawmaking bodies to the center of political authority in their respective colonies.

But the lower houses had done more than simply acquire a new status in colonial politics. They had in a sense altered the structure of the constitution of the British Empire itself by asserting colonial authority against imperial authority and extending the constitutions of the colonies far beyond the limitations of the charters, instructions, or fixed notions of imperial authorities. The time was ripe for a re-examination and redefinition of the constitutional position of the lower houses. With the rapid economic and territorial expansion of the colonies in the years before 1763 had come a corresponding rise in the responsibilities and prestige of the lower houses and a growing aware-ness among colonial representatives of their own importance, which had served to strengthen their long-standing, if still imperfectly defined, impression that colonial lower houses were the American counterparts of the British House of Commons. Under the proper stimuli, they would carry this impression to its logical conclusion: that the lower houses enjoyed an equal status under the Crown with Parliament. Here, then, well beyond the embryonic stage, was the theory of colonial equality with the mother country, one of the basic constitutional principles of the American Revolution, waiting to be nourished by the series of crises that beset imperial-colonial relations between 1763 and 1776.

The psychological implications of this new political order were profound. By the 1750's the phenomenal success of the lower houses had generated a soaring self-confidence, a willingness to take on all comers. Called upon to operate on a larger stage during the Seven Years' War, they emerged from that conflict with an increased awareness of their own importance and a growing consciousness of the implications of their activities. Symptomatic of these developments was the spate of bitter controversies that characterized colonial politics during and immediately after the war. The Gadsden election controversy in South Carolina, the dispute over judicial tenure in New York, and the contests over the pistole fee and the two-penny act in Virginia gave abundant evidence of both the lower houses' stubborn determination to preserve their authority and the failure of Crown officials in London and the colonies to gauge accurately their temper or to accept the fact that they had made important changes in the constitutions of the colonies.

With the shift of power to the lower houses also came the development in each colony of an extraordinarily able group of politicians. The lower houses provided excellent training for the leaders of the rapidly maturing colonial societies, and the recurring controversies prepared them for the problems they would be called upon to meet in the dramatic conflicts after 1763. In the decades before Independence there appeared in the colonial statehouses John and Samuel Adams and James Otis in Massachusetts Bay; William Livingston in New York; Benjamin Franklin and John Dickinson in Pennsylvania; Daniel Dulany the younger in Maryland; Richard Bland, Richard Henry Lee, Thomas Jefferson, and Patrick Henry in Virginia; and Christopher Gadsden and John Rutledge in South Carolina. Along with dozens of others, these men guided their colonies through the debate with Britain, assumed direction of the new state governments after 1776, and played conspicuous roles on the national stage as members of the Continental Congress, the Confederation, and, after 1787, the new federal government. By the 1760's, then, almost every colony had an imposing group of native politicians thoroughly schooled in the political arts and primed to meet any challenge to the power and prestige of the lower houses.

Britain's "new colonial policy" after 1763 provided just such a challenge. It precipitated a constitutional crisis in the empire, creating new tensions and setting in motion forces different from those that had shaped earlier developments. The new policy was based upon concepts both unfamiliar and unwelcome to the colonists such as centralization, uniformity, and orderly development. Yet it was a logical culmination of earlier trends and, for the most part, an effort to realize old aspirations. From Edward Randolph in the last decades of the seventeenth century to the Earl of Halifax in the 1750's colonial officials had envisioned a highly centralized empire with a uniform political system in each of the colonies and with the imperial government closely supervising the subordinate governments. But, because they had never made any sustained or systematic attempt to achieve these goals, there had developed during the first half of the eighteenth century a working arrangement permitting the lower houses considerable latitude in shaping colonial constitutions without requiring crown and proprietary officials to give up any of their ideals. That there had been a growing divergence between imperial theory and colonial practice mattered little so long as each refrained from challenging the other. But the new policy threatened to upset this arrangement by implementing the old ideals long after the conditions that produced them had ceased to exist. Aimed at bringing the colonies more closely under imperial control, this policy inevitably sought to curtail the influence of the lower houses, directly challenging many of the powers they had acquired over the previous century. To American legislators accustomed to the lenient policies of Walpole and the Pelhams and impressed with the rising power of their own lower houses, the new program seemed a radical departure from precedent, a frontal assault upon the several constitutions they had been forging over the previous century. To protect gains they had already made and to make good their pretensions to greater political significance, the lower houses thereafter no longer had merely to deal with weak governors or causal imperial administrators; they now faced an aggressive group of officials bent upon using every means at their disposal, including the legislative authority of Parliament, to gain their ends.

Beginning in 1763 one imperial action after another seemed to threaten the position of the lower houses. Between 1764 and 1766 Parliament's attempt to tax the colonists for revenue directly challenged the colonial legislatures' exclusive power to tax, the cornerstone of their authority in America. A variety of other measures, some aimed at particular colonial legislatures and others at general legislative powers and practices, posed serious threats to powers that the lower houses had either long enjoyed or were trying to attain. To meet these challenges, the lower houses had to spell out the implications of the changes they had been making, consciously or not, in the structures of their respective governments. That is, for the first time they had to make clear in their own minds and then to verbalize what they conceived their respective constitutions in fact were or should be. In the process, the spokesmen of the lower houses laid bare the wide gulf between imperial theory and colonial practice. During the Stamp Act crisis in 1764–1766 the lower houses claimed the same authority over taxation in the colonies as Parliament had over that matter in England, and a few of them even asserted an equal right in matters of internal policy. Although justified by the realities of the colonial situation, such a definition of the lower houses' constitutional position within the empire was at marked variance with imperial ideals and only served to increase the determination of the home government to take a stricter tone. This determination was manifested after the repeal of the Stamp Act by Parliament's claim in the Declaratory Act of 1766 to "full power and authority" over the colonies "in all cases whatsoever."

The pattern over the next decade was on the part of the home government one of increasing resolution to deal firmly with the colonies and on the part of American lawmakers a heightened consciousness of the implications of the constitutional issue and a continuously rising level of expectation. In addition to their insistence upon the right of Parliament to raise revenue in the colonies, imperial officials also applied, in a way that was increasingly irksome to American legislators, traditional instruments of royal control like restrictive instructions, legislative review, the governors' power to dissolve the lower houses and the suspending clause requiring prior approval of the Crown before laws of an "extraordinary nature" could go into effect. Finally Parliament threatened the very existence of the lower houses by a measure suspending the New York Assembly for refusing to comply with the Quartering Act in 1767 and by another altering the substance of the Massachusetts constitution in the Massachusetts Government Act in 1774. In the process of articulating and defending their constitutional position, the lower houses acquired aspirations well beyond any they had had in the years before 1763. American representatives became convinced in the decade after 1766 not only that they knew best what to do for their constituents and the colonies and that anything interfering with their freedom to adopt whatever course seemed necessary was an intolerable and unconstitutional restraint but also that the only security for their political fortunes was in the abandonment of their attempts to restrict and define Parliamentary authority in America and instead to deny Parliament's jurisdiction over them entirely by asserting their equality with Parliament under the Crown. Suggested by

Richard Bland as early as 1766, such a position was openly advocated by James Wilson and Thomas Jefferson in 1774 and was officially adopted by the First Continental Congress when it claimed for Americans in its declarations and resolves "a free and exclusive power of legislation in their several provincial legislatures, where their right of representation can alone be preserved, in all cases of taxation and internal polity."

Parliament could not accept this claim without giving up the principles it had asserted in the Declaratory Act and, in effect, abandoning the traditional British theory of empire and accepting the colonial constitutional position instead. The First Continental Congress professed that a return to the *status quo* of 1763 would satisfy the colonies, but Parliament in 1774–1776 was unwilling even to go that far, much less to promise them exemption from Parliamentary taxation. Besides, American legislators now aspired to much more. James Chalmers, Maryland Tory, in 1776 correctly charged that American leaders had "been constantly enlarging their views, and stretching them beyond their first bounds, till at length they have wholly changed their ground." Edward Rutledge, young delegate from South Carolina to the First Continental Congress, was one who recognized that the colonies would not "be satisfied with a restoration of such rights only, as have been violated since the year '63, when we have as many others, as clear and indisputable, that will even then be infringed." The simple fact was that American political leaders, no matter what their professions, would not have been content to return to the old inarticulated and ambiguous pattern of accommodation between imperial theory and colonial practice that had existed through most of the period between 1689 and 1763. They now sought to become masters of their own political fortunes. Rigid guarantees of colonial rights and precise definitions of the constitutional relationship between the mother country and the colonies and between Parliament and the lower houses on American terms—that is, imperial recognition of the autonomy of the lower houses in local affairs and of the equality of the colonies with the mother country—would have been required to satisfy them.

No analysis of the charges in the Declaration of Independence can fail to suggest that the preservation and consolidation of the rights and powers of the lower houses were central in the struggle with Britain from 1763 to 1776, just as they had been the most important issue in the political relationship between Britain and the colonies over the previous century and a half. Between 1689 and 1763 the lower houses' contests with royal governors and imperial officials had brought them political maturity, a considerable measure of control over local affairs, capable leaders, and a rationale to support their pretensions to political power within the colonies and in the Empire. The British challenge after 1763 threatened to render their accomplishments meaningless and drove them to demand equal rights with Parliament and autonomy in local affairs and eventually to declare their independence. At issue was the whole political structure forged by the lower houses over the previous century. In this context the American Revolution becomes in form, if not in essence, a war for political survival, a conflict involving not only individual rights as traditionally emphasized by historians of the event but assembly rights as well.

8

The Farmer in the
Eighteenth Century Almanac
CHESTER E. EISINGER

The image we Americans have of ourselves reflects the meaning and direction of American life. The image is a compound of what is real and of the hopes with which we invest what is real. Thus, what we see in the national mirror is part fact, part fancy. The myths we live by, no less than the realities, are important factors in the things we do and in the way we go. The study of American history must therefore be concerned with the changing image we have had of ourselves and with the reasons it has changed.

What view of itself did the agrarian society of the eighteenth century take? This is the question posed by Chester E. Eisinger, Professor of English at Purdue University. For the answer, Professor Eisinger has widely canvassed the almanacs which enjoyed great vogue and popularity among Americans at that time. The almanac is a particularly felicitous source of information about agrarian values and the American image. Dangling near the fireplace, it was endlessly consulted for its information about sunrises and sunsets, for its homely advice, for its simple poetry. It served as an eighteenth-century combination of Reader's Digest *and* Edgar Guest, *of*

SOURCE: *Agricultural History,* XXVIII (July, 1954), 107–112. Reprinted by permission of the author and the Agricultural History Society.

Ladies' Home Journal *and Dr. Spock. It was full of preachment and morality; it prescribed details for the good life; it commended farmers for the simplicity of their ways and the ruggedness of their individualism; it encouraged a do-it-yourself society to continue doing it. If to work is to pray, then farm work afforded its own morality. The almanac, as Professor Eisinger stresses, spoke for more than agrarian virtues. In an age when America was an open and mobile frontier of Europe, it was inevitable that Americans should define the differences between themselves and Europeans. In their image of themselves, Americans stressed their freehold tenures, their equality, their abundance, their freedom, their independence. The parts of the image made a whole which Professor Eisinger aptly calls agrarian nationalism.*

The image is a challenging one. It elicits both interest and inquiry. What part of the image of the farmer in the eighteenth-century almanac was fact, what part fancy? How did this image contrast with that given us by such notable visitors as Crèvecoeur and Kalm? In what ways did this image reflect larger political, social, and economic developments? In what ways did it influence them? In what way does this image explain some of the values that lie deep in our tradition: our sense of difference from the European world, our isolationism, our individualism, our respect for the frontier, our belief that we are a frontier people?

In studying the image of the eighteenth-century farmer, one wonders inevitably about its meaning for today. If a generic portrait could be found in an age when most Americans were farmers, could such a portrait be found today? And what would it show? To what extent have the virtues of the farmer's life persisted, to what extent have they been lost? To what extent, for example, is suburbia the homage that an industrial America is paying to the idyl of a lost agrarian world? To what extent has the American now come to identify himself with the European because of the challenge of the non-Western world? Some components of the national portrait are currently being stressed. Its subject is a member of an affluent society, unaware of the other America, the impoverished rural backlands and the miserable central cities; he is being homogenized by mass culture; he is a white racist, passing through the crisis in black and white with prejudice rather than perception, hostility rather than sympathy; he is a conformist, fearful of prophetic minorities and new radicals; his children, dropouts from society, are growing up absurd. This portrait is the joint product of professional sociologists and social psychologists; yet it is fair to ask if they are not also professional Jeremiahs. Are there no redeeming virtues in the American image today?

Ultimately, the question we arrive at is the role of such an image in the national life. The image serves a purpose. It speaks a wish. It expresses a disappointment. It compensates for a sense of inadequacy. It sets a goal. It affords a blending of reality and myth in which the myth intensifies some of the reality and also blurs some of it over. It nominates the national heroes and permits the nation to become heroic by identifying itself with them. It defines what is American in contradistinction to what is foreign. In whatever mirrors we may see it—almanacs, magazines, novels, newspapers, radio, television—the national image is that sufficient reflection of reality which we call truth and by which we live our daily lives. In its changing forms, it sums up the self-consciousness of our changing generations. As such, it is a vital part of the American past.

In recent decades, scholarship has revealed the value of the old farmer's almanac for social and intellectual history. Even a cursory examination of these little books shows how they acted as cultural carriers in the eighteenth century, disseminating knowledge about the new science, the new religion, and the new politics. But since the almanacs were compiled primarily, if not uniquely, for the farmer, the question arises: what knowledge and what ideas did they convey about the farmer and agriculture? It is to the answer of this obvious but hitherto neglected question that the present paper addresses itself.

Quite simply, the answer is that the almanac, a mirror of its time, reflected the American acceptance in the eighteenth century of what I have called elsewhere the freehold concept, a notion that became for the American imagination of the nineteenth century a belief that here in our West was the Garden of the World, a fructifying belief that made of the yeoman farmer the archetypal American and advanced the settlement of western lands. Partly myth and partly fact, the freehold concept rests on holding land in freehold tenure, and includes the propositions that men have a natural right to the land; ownership of it gives them status and a stake in society, as well as social and economic security; agriculture is the most productive form of labor, and it is conducive to moral and physical health; the agrarian way of life stimulates and makes possible individualism and self-reliance; the farmer is the backbone of democracy whom the government must support. This complex of ideas had wide currency among eighteenth century writers; its principal champions were Franklin, Jefferson, and St. Jean de Crèvecoeur. These men, like their contemporaries who shared a belief in the freehold concept, saw in agrarianism a key that would open to them the quality and aspiration of the society about them. Generally speaking, the almanacs accepted the agrarian view of eighteenth century life in America and conveyed it to their readers, thus fulfilling their function as media of popular culture.

Hardly as a matter of an interpretation of society, but simply as a useful practice, the almanacs, one would assume, would be full of practical advice to farmers. This assumption should apply especially to an eighteenth century almanac, published at the dawn of scientific farming when agricultural reformers like Arthur Young and Jared Eliot were beginning to make themselves heard.   Curiously enough, such practical materials appeared only sporadically in the almanacs and obviously had no special importance in the editorial scheme.   The early Leeds almanac is an illuminating example.   In the 1687 issue Daniel Leeds announces that he is a student of agriculture, and he runs a section on "Short Rules in Husbandry."   This appears annually, giving information on such matters as the dates of sowing and harvesting and the making of cider.   But the section is omitted in 1694, and from that date to the end of the almanac's career in the early eighteenth century there are only scattered references to farming.   The student of agriculture had turned to other interests.   Leeds is more typical in this respect than Richard Saunders' *Poor Richard Improved,* which published advice in virtually every issue after 1762 on such subjects as preventing smut, raising silkworms, increasing corn crops, or cultivating vines for wine.   One would guess that pragmatic American editors and readers alike would welcome such aids to improvement, but the evidence in the majority of the almanacs does not support such a conclusion. Strangely enough, in this area the almanacs seem to have disregarded an opportunity to interest and serve the farmer.

Apparently, however, the almanac editor felt his reader would be interested in pastoral poetry, for he published an inordinate amount of it.   It is a paradoxical comment on the American mind of the period that the almanacs should have neglected the practical aspects of farming in favor of verse celebrating rural harvests and rural pleasures.   This poetry, I think it fair to say, constitutes an indirect eulogy of the farmer. It is a means of assuring him of his own importance and good fortune and of the valuable role he plays in society.   These appear to me to have been the self-consciously agrarian motives of the almanac makers in using pastoral verse.   Furthermore, such verse incorporated several typically agrarian themes.   Primitivism is one of the fundamental assumptions in these pastorals, as it is in all agrarianism.   The poets insisted on singing of the rustic youth "brown with meridian toil,/ Healthful and strong"; or pointing out the virtues of sweating in the field while making hay.   They enumerated the pleasures of country life, "void of care" where "Woods, and op'ning Fields,/With purling Streams to harmless Joys invite"; rural pastimes are invariably innocent. Another theme is domestic felicity, which distinguishes the countryman from the great men whose minds are filled with "anxious Pain":

> The Farmer in his Cot enjoys more Bliss,
> With's little Children climbing for a Kiss.

Of course the idyllic note is frequently sounded; here it is in a poem of provincial pride celebrating the development of New England.

From Savage Deserts rise our green Retreats
. . . . .
Great Britain's Glory buds and blossoms here:
Ye Gods in *Rome,* what have ye more to do?
Elysium in *New England* waits for you.

The final paragraph, in a kind of prose poem on "Spring," published in 1799, summarizes the whole pastoral spirit in associating agricultural life with the golden age that must have existed before the fall of man.

> The industrious tiller of the ground now rises to behold the beauties of the morn—to breathe the fragrance of nature, and to be entertained by the airy choirs, which, in animated strains, sing their morning hymns. With the enlivening sun he begins his pleasing task—unwrecked with care, and unperplexed with doubt, he joins his simple song to the varied music of the day. Let none consider the culture of the ground as an ignoble employment: It was the business originally assigned to man: It was his business, and his pleasure, when all his passions were harmonious, and every wish was innocent.

Most often encountered in the pastoral verse is the cornucopia theme, which displays an intense preoccupation with the abundance of the crops. Not only is there a constant reiteration of the idea of plenty, but also this theme is presented to the almost inevitable accompaniment of the chuckling sense of triumph that signalizes man's victory over nature. The great enemy is winter, for it brings the possibility of freezing and starving. The desideratum is security: warmth and sufficient food. The pastoral is not only an expression of exultation but a paean to the farmer whose success in the art of cultivation has forced the fear of want farther and farther into the distance. The farmer becomes in this context the founder and carrier of civilization; Prometheus joins hands with Ceres. The importance of these pastoral themes for America lies in the fact that the conflict described was intensely felt in America, a relatively new country, and the significant role of the farmer in it was immediately discernible.

These considerations, then, lend an authoritative ring of conviction to the poet's statement that there is no "greater heaven on earth" than watching the last load of the harvest come home. They give us real sympathy with the satisfaction of the full barn:

> Now Ceres crowns the barns with plenty;
> Joyful farmers view their store:
> Be happy men, let this content ye,
> Nor dread the winter [storms] no more.

The same sentiment is found in "The Joys of Harvest," which tells how the damsels and swains celebrate the end of their harvest toils with a dance. The swain, as if carried away in some pagan rite, always turns his eyes in rapture toward the harvest, the reward that crowns all his toil.

When we turn to other aspects of agrarianism in the almanacs, we find some support for the foregoing view of the pastorals. Agriculture is regarded as the basis for all society and the source of all progress, and it is the one indispensable industry. No almanacs I have examined contradict this view. Although not all almanacs are concerned with these matters, many of them contain relevant evidence; a sampling will reveal the general pattern. Note, then, this couplet which Eben W. Judd used:

> HAIL agriculture! by whose parent aid,
> The deep foundations of our states are laid. . . .

In 1786 Judd had published a brief essay, "Agriculture," which touched upon many of the most significant aspects of the freehold concept:

> Nothing can more fully prove the ingratitude of mankind (a crime often charged upon them, and often denied) than the little regard which the disposers of honorary rewards have paid to *Agriculture;* which is treated as a subject so remote from common life, by all those who do not immediately hold the plough, or give fodder to the ox, that there is room to question, whether a great part of mankind has yet been informed that life is sustained by the fruits of the earth.
>
> Agriculture not only gives riches to a nation, but the only riches we can call our own, and of which we need not fear either deprivation or diminution.
>
> Of nations, as of individuals, the first blessing is independence. Neither the man nor the people can be happy, to whom any human power can deny the necessaries, or conveniencies of life. There is no way of living without foreign assistance, *but by the product of our own land improved by our own labour.* Every other source of plenty is perishable or casual.

Here the central position of agriculture in the national life and in the economy is affirmed by arguments similar to those used by the Physiocrats in France. Another Physiocratic notion—that agriculture is the only source of wealth—is also suggested. The democratic ideas of political and economic independence are linked to agriculture, while the traditional atomistic and isolationist attitude, which has since the eighteenth century been associated with agricultural areas in this country, also emerges in this passage.

Nathaniel Ames, maker of perhaps the most distinguished almanac of his time, also devoted thought to agrarianism. In 1761 he printed this Physiocratic aphorism: "Husbandry is the Philosopher's Stone which turns Trees, Fruits, Earth, Iron & Water into Gold." A few years later in the introductory paragraph to a discussion of the use of marl as a fertilizer, Ames underlines some of the ideas Judd had used. ". . . the Kingdoms of the Earth, and the Glory of the World will be transplanted into AMERICA: But the Study and Practice of Agriculture must go Hand in Hand with our Increase. . . ." R. B. Thomas, who issued *The Farmer's Almanack,* displayed more consistent interest in the freehold concept than any other almanac maker of the century. He too should be heard on this score: "The cultivation of the earth`. . . [is] the most useful and necessary employment in life." Agriculture is "the art which supports, supplies, and maintains all the rest." And Richard Saunders developed all these ideas in an essay "On Husbandry," preceded by this quatrain:

> To render service, and perfection give
> To this great *Art,* by which all others live:
> To twine the laurel round the farmer's brow,
> And learn to *use*—to *venerate* the PLOUGH.

No employment is more beneficial than agriculture, Saunders tells us. Poets have celebrated it; the leaders of antiquity have followed it. He relates the story of Cincinnatus and exalts Washington as the modern counterpart. Furthermore, husbandry is advantageous because it converts a barren desert into an area of "smiling meads, fertile fields, and numerous flocks and herds." We cannot praise too highly, Saunders concludes, those enterprising farmers who, blest with liberty, brought civilization to this country and set it on the road to glory.

Many of these grandiose generalizations about the role of agriculture in society reveal the spirit of agrarian nationalism that was widespread in America; it is this manifestation of the freehold concept that we may now specifically consider. Patriotic pride could be readily expressed in agricultural terms, since two factors, the availability of land and farming under freehold tenure, gave attractive opportunity to those who were denied it in Europe. Furthermore, the social and political tone of colonial, and later democratic, America was conducive to a more independent and free rural life than could be enjoyed anywhere else. In fact, that freehold tenure which evokes so much praise from Americans and visiting foreigners alike seems to have nourished those qualities of independence, individualism, and love of freedom which constitute the democratic manner and were eventually written into the democratic dogma.

Early expressions of agrarian nationalism appear in the almanacs before one can legitimately talk about American nationalism, but they reflect even well before the Revolution a consciousness of the differences between America and Europe that indicates a conviction of the superiority of American place and custom. In his *Almanack for . . . 1693,* Daniel Leeds has a few lines voicing the confident hope that the produce of American farms will not be the victim of those twins of Old World tyranny, the church and the military.

> Winter we now forget, green Grass we see,
> In Woods and Fields, and Leaves on every Tree.
> The Planters Hopes nor thrifty Husbands Tillage
> Becomes not here the Priest nor Souldiers Pillage.

Fifty years later Titan Leeds glories in the freedom from oppression that marks the American farmer who is happy because bounteous Providence allows him "With his own hands Paternal Grounds to Plow"; he is secure from the "Cheats of Law," "Nor does [he] the Affronts of Palaces endure." In a poem "On Publick Spirit" that runs throughout the 1752 issue of *Poor Richard Improved,* Franklin predicts that America will develop into a great country. Contributing to its growth will be those "Sons of Mis'ry" from Europe who come here to populate the land and enjoy its blessings, where

> Allotted Acres (no reluctant Soil)
> Shall prompt their Industry and pay their Toil.

Characteristic of agrarian nationalism is the open invitation to share the bounty of a fruitful earth and a desire to impugn the social institutions of Europe as they affect the agricultural classes. Thus Judd quotes David Humphreys, who tells us that love of independence prompts the European pilgrim to labor in the soil; having escaped "vassall'd woes," he will find a quiet farm home here. It was obvious that the freehold was superior to serfdom.

For the freehold meant independence, which was another source of nationalistic pride and also a positive good in itself. The almanac makers recognized that the farmer embodied more completely than any other class of citizens in the New World the democratic virtues of independence and equality, and that he loved liberty and was able to live more freely than others. "The Contented Farmers" in Ames' Almanac for 1761 says,

> I eat, drink, and sleep, and do what I please,
> The King in his Palace can only do these.

This freedom and this rather aggressive egalitarianism are hallmarks of the freehold concept. The farm was recognized in explicit terms as a source of "independence and affluence" by Richard Saunders. The same author published a vigorous and a self-conscious agrarian statement on liberty in his *Poor Richard Improved . . . 1771:*

> Who'd know the Sweets of Liberty?
> 'Tis to climb the Mountain's Brow,
> Thence to discern rough Industry,

At the Harrow or the Plough;
'Tis where my Sons their Crops have sown,
Calling the Harvest all their own,
'Tis where the Heart to Truth allied,
Never felt unmanly Fear;
'Tis where the Eye, with milder Pride,
Nobly sheds sweet Pity's Tear,
Such as AMERICA yet shall see,
These are the sweets of Liberty.

Much earlier Franklin had praised the farmer's lot in a poem called, appropriately, "The Farmer."

O happy he! happiest of mortal Men!
Who far remov'd from Slavery, as from Pride,
Fears no Man's Frown, nor cringing waits to catch
The gracious Nothing of a great Man's Nod;
. . . . .
Tempted nor with the Pride nor Pomp of Power,
Nor Pageants of Ambition, nor the Mines
Of grasping Av'rice, nor the poison'd Sweets
Of pamper'd Luxury, he plants his Foot
With Firmness on his old paternal Fields,
And stands unshaken.

The dignity of man, in which Franklin takes a justifiable pride, is guaranteed by the security of the freehold.

Full ownership of the paternal fields was ever a theme emphasized and enjoyed by Americans who cherished their liberties. Land was always available in America; after the French and Indian war, Ames thought, it might be had for nothing in some areas. Free land offered the farmer wonderful opportunity but just as important was the nature of the tenure: "We hold our Lands under no other Lord but He who gave the Land of *Canaan* to *Abraham*. . . ." In a long address to the Husbandmen of America, written a few years later, Ames is discussing the practical aspects of farming; he points out that we must raise crops for export in order to increase our wealth. "We are not tenants but *lords* of the soil, and may live as genteel, tho' not in such splendour, as lords . . ." by increasing our trade, diligence, and industry.

These prideful sentiments have an obvious corollary: the independent farmer should be the master of his political destiny. Ames asserts the responsibility of the farmer to participate in government, and suggests that he become, in a sense, a politician. But strangely enough, he is alone in this opinion. Other almanacs feel that the farmer should stick to his plough. This is a significant deviation from the general pattern of eighteenth century agrarianism in the almanacs.

It should be added that the only other idea in the freehold concept that does not appear is the notion that men have a natural right to the land.

These two deficiencies in the almanac's total coverage of the freehold concept are in reality the exceptions that prove the validity of the thesis here, namely, that the almanac reflected the American acceptance of the concept. For while it is indeed curious that there was not a more vigorous and original contribution to agrarian thought in the almanacs, it is nevertheless clear that the bulk of the propositions that make up the freehold concept were cordially received and advanced by almanac makers. Their championship of this concept reveals them as spokesmen for the farmer and prophets of the agricultural wealth and destiny of our nation.

9

One Hundred Years of Urban Growth
CARL BRIDENBAUGH

What has been the role of the city in directing the course of American history? Our culture is so largely urban today that it is hard to realize that during the greater part of our history we were a rural people, and that most of human history has been lived in the village and the farm rather than in the city. Figures on the distribution of population between city and country do not tell the whole story, however. The metropolis has throughout the course of history exercised an impact on the polity of states that is out of all proportion to the actual numbers of its inhabitants. It is an impact that can be traced in a variety of examples: Athens in the Periclean Age, Rome under the emperors, Florence in the age of the Medici, Madrid under the Habsburgs, Paris under the Bourbons, London in the Victorian Age, New York in the twentieth century.

SOURCE: Carl Bridenbaugh, *Cities in the Wilderness* (New York: Alfred A. Knopf, Inc., 1955), pp. 467–481. Copyright 1938 by Carl Bridenbaugh. Reprinted by permission of the publisher.

It would be a misunderstanding of our colonial history, suggests Pro-
fessor Carl Bridenbaugh of Brown University, to minimize the importance
of the urban centers that flourished before the Revolution, despite, again,
their relatively small percentage of total population. Bringing the urban
aspect of early American history into proper perspective has, indeed, been
the particular contribution of Professor Bridenbaugh in his two most
significant works: Cities in the Wilderness *(1938, 1955) and* Cities in
Revolt *(1955). Professor Bridenbaugh has extended our knowledge of the*
dimensions of colonial society through his other works as well, including
Rebels and Gentlemen: Philadelphia in the Age of Franklin *(1942),*
The Colonial Craftsman *(1950),* Myths and Realities: Societies of the
Colonial South *(1952),* Mitre and Sceptre: Transatlantic Faiths, Ideas,
Personalities, and Politics, 1689–1775 *(1962), and* Vexed and Troubled
Englishmen, 1590–1642 *(1968).*

The essay that follows is the final chapter of Cities in the Wilderness.
Professor Bridenbaugh's portrait of the major urban centers of the colonial
period—Boston, Newport, New York, Philadelphia, and Charles Town—
highlights four significant aspects of their history: their physical growth,
their economic activities, their handling of social problems, and their cul-
tural traits and attainments.

Studying the five colonial cities in the framework of a larger perspective,
Professor Bridenbaugh comes up with several challenging observations.
Commercial wealth, more than any other factor, determined why and how
the towns grew. The problems they faced were generally similar and so too
were the ways in which they solved them. The American cities based their
solutions upon European examples, adapting the examples to fit in with
American circumstances. The transcending importance of the colonial
cities was that they "were centers of the transit of civilization from the Old
World to the New." They represented a distinct aspect of American life,
different at once from the rural hinterlands of the tidewater regions and from
the primitive pioneering thrusts of the frontier. The five urban centers
played a major role in the political, social, and intellectual activities of the
colonial period and particularly in the tense drama which reached its climax
in the American Revolution.

Professor Bridenbaugh's observations invite further thought. How far,
for example, may one argue an urban interpretation of the American past
as a counterpoise to the long-familiar frontier interpretation? The writings
of such historians as Constance Green, Bessie L. Pierce, Arthur M.
Schlesinger, Bayrd Still, and Richard Wade, to cite some examples, would
suggest that cities have profoundly affected the entire course of our history.
What factors were responsible for the growth of cities after the colonial
period? What problems did cities face and how did they meet them? How
much did the problems they faced and the ways they solved them differ
from those of urban centers in other areas of the Western world?

Living in the age of the megalopolis, the super-city, with its teeming millions and its sprawling suburban empire, we are naturally concerned with understanding the nature of our own urban culture. We are concerned to know the patterns and problems of the exploding metropolis—how it is housing its citizens, weaving its transportation network, relieving the growing tensions of its central city, removing the causes of its racial conflicts and civil disorders, renovating its slums, cleaning up its politics, entertaining its masses, educating its children, relating itself to the problems of the state, the nation, and the world. With the preponderant majority of America's population of over 200,000,000 concentrated in the great metropolitan areas, these are matters well worth our concern and our investigation.

The first hundred years of town history on the American continent witnessed the foundation and gradual development of a truly urban society. The story of American life is customarily regarded as a compound of sectional histories, and in the early colonial period two sections are commonly considered—the tidewater and the frontier. Yet the tidewater was itself divided, and if we consider the sections as social and psychological rather than as purely geographical entities, it is possible to distinguish three of them—the rural, agricultural society of the countryside; the restless, advancing society of the frontier; and the urban, commercial society of the larger seaports. Beginning as small specks in the wilderness, the five communities grew from tiny villages into towns, and finally attained the status of small cities. With other village communities of similar interests and outlook which multiplied and grew in the eighteenth century, they emerged as a social and economic "section" extending the length of the Atlantic seaboard, and exhibiting definite urban characteristics in striking contrast to rural farming districts and wilder regions of the frontier. Life in urban areas produced its own peculiar problems to be faced, and the urban viewpoint, based upon continuous close contacts with Europe, derived less from agriculture than from trade. Commercially minded town society looked to the East rather than the West, and was destined from the first to serve as the connecting link between colonial America and its Old World parents.

The future of the colonial towns became immediately evident from the conditions surrounding their birth. Designed as trading communities, they were established on sites most favorable for the pursuit of commerce. They were the western outposts of European commercial expansion in the seventeenth century. City-dwellers from the Old World formed the larger proportion of early town populations, and from the start commercial relations with England or Holland were maintained. Most significantly, the founding process occurred at a time when western Europe, under Dutch and English leadership, was gradually outgrowing and casting off the limitations of medieval feudal economy. Colonial towns grew to maturity in the era of world expansion attending the emergence of modern capitalism, and being new communities, with few irrevocably established customs or traditions, they frequently adapted themselves to the economic drift with more ease and readiness than did the older cities of England. Moreover, the colonizing movement was itself an expression of early capitalistic activity. It called forth organized rather than individual efforts and resources, created new and wider markets for economic development, and opened up seemingly unlimited territories for imperialistic exploitation. It thus produced a marked effect upon Old World economy, accelerating the breakdown of local units of business, and facilitating the formation of larger and more complex organizations of commerce and finance.

The problems which confronted town-dwellers in America were not only those of urban communities, but of a pioneer society as well. Urban development depends largely upon community wealth, and upon the willingness of the group to devote portions of it to projects for civic betterment, or to consent to taxation for this purpose. To a considerable extent the nature of town governments and the extent of authority vested in them conditioned the expenditure of town wealth for community enterprises. Here the colonists were hampered by the traditional nature of the charters of medieval English municipal corporations, whose limitations ill accorded with circumstances in seventeenth and eighteenth century America, especially with the imperious demands for expansion and immediate activity in the New World. In New England towns a new political organization, the town meeting, developed, which exhibited considerable efficiency in the handling of urban problems. This institution was more immediately susceptible to social wants and requirements than were the aristocratic, self-perpetuating corporations founded in America after the example of English municipal governments. Its greater powers of local taxation, and the fact that it placed the spending of public moneys and the enactment of civic ordinances in the hands of those directly affected by these operations, made it a far more effective form of government for dealing with community problems. These problems were the greater, because in the first century of their history the five colonial seaports enjoyed a much more rapid physical growth than did the cities of contemporary Europe. The individual enterprise of American town-dwellers, and the commercial expansion and prosperity they achieved, aided in the solution of these problems of town living, but much of the efficiency and success which attended their efforts may be attributed to the emergence in the New World of a relatively high sense of civic responsibility in the early eighteenth century, at a time when public consciousness in Europe had receded to an extremely low ebb.

The towns were primarily commercial communities seeking treasure by foreign trade, and their economic vitality and commercial demands led to their early breaking the narrow bonds of medieval economic practice to forge ahead on uncharted but highly profitable commercial adventures. All five, during the first century, developed from simple manorial organizations, completely dependent upon European connections, into full-fledged commercial centers, only partially tied to England, and in many cases competing with British cities for a share of imperial traffic. Boston entered early into the West Indian provision trade, thereby setting an example for other American commercial communities. Soon Massachusetts mariners were seeking to monopolize the colonial carrying traffic in ships of their own building, and the profits of carrier and middleman became the basis of the Bay town's prosperity. Her priority in this field gave her an advantage which other seaports did not begin to overcome until the fourth decade of the eighteenth century. A further foundation for urban economic prosperity lay in the existence of an expanding frontier society with its great need for manufactured products. This made possible an earlier development of the towns as distributing centers for a wide hinterland than was the case with English cities like Bristol, Norwich and Exeter, and became in this first century as important a factor in the economic growth of New York, Philadelphia and Charles Town as in that of the New England metropolis. As a producer of staple goods for exchange in trade, Boston, with its limited back country, was at a disadvantage. More fortunate were New York with its flour and furs, Philadelphia, with its great staples of wheat, meat and lumber, and Charles Town, which after 1710 found prosperity in the important South Carolina crops of rice and indigo. Eventually the communities enjoying this sound economic backing rose to threaten the supremacy of Boston in colonial trade, while Newport and Philadelphia cut heavily into the Bay town's West India commerce. In the eighteenth century also Newport attained importance in shipbuilding and the slave trade. By 1742 Boston merchants were facing a period of relative decline, while their competitors in other colonial towns found the volume and profits of their traffic steadily mounting.

Continual increase in the volume of colonial trade and enlargement of the territory served by the towns led to a greater complexity in commercial relations. In the early years merchants performed all types of business, but toward 1700 their functions began to be more specialized. Retail merchandising having definitely emerged by 1700, the great merchant now dealt chiefly with larger operations of exporting, importing and wholesaling, leaving much of the small trade to the shopkeeper. Demands of trade had by 1710 necessitated the issuance of paper currency in most of the colonies, and the establishment of the colonial post office to serve intercolonial communication. Growing business further led to the creation of insurance offices and some extension of credit facilities. Profits from trade, originally completely absorbed in shipbuilding ventures and industries subsidiary to shipping, now began to create a surplus which sought investment in land, or, in some communities, in the development of certain forms of manufacturing.

Economic prosperity thus made possible the rise of colonial cities. It led to physical expansion of town boundaries, and facilitated dealing with urban problems by corporate effort. Wealth wrung from trade, more than any other single factor, determined the growth of a town society, in which urban amusements and a colonial culture might thrive. This is not, however, to force the history of urban America within the narrow bounds of an exclusively economic interpretation. Social and intellectual development are dependent upon and conditioned by economic progress, but they are not its necessary and inevitable result. They are altered, encouraged or stifled by the action and influence of material forces, but they are not necessarily caused or even initiated solely by economic factors.

When we consider American urban society, apart from its economic aspects, we find it characterized by certain problems affecting it as a unit, and with which as a unit it had to deal. Such problems in general, or collective attempts for their control and regulation, are either absent from or unimportant in rural or frontier societies, but in the case of our urban section they are present, in rudimentary form at least, from its inception. They persist and grow with the maturing of that section, and the means taken for dealing with them further differentiate the urban from other types of society.

Logically, the first of these problems to appear are the physical, and of these the most immediate was housing. As in rural regions this remained for the most part an individual problem, and there are only a few cases on record where even indirectly, by sale or subdivision of land or by encouragement of artisans, the community stepped in to relieve a housing shortage. On the other hand, the laying out and maintaining of a highway system constituted a problem, perhaps the first, which transcended private initiative. Not that the community at any time scorned the assistance of private enterprise; a favorite device, at Boston and elsewhere, throughout the colonial era, was by remission of taxes or grant of other privileges to encourage individuals to open up streets and undertake paving operations for public use at their own charge. But from the beginning public authorities indicated the location of roads, supervised the opening up of new ones, ordered their clearing or partial paving by abutters, and strove to prevent encroach-ments upon them.   At Philadelphia and Charles Town, where some prior power had surveyed and planned the thoroughfares, the first task of local authorities was light; it was more arduous in other commu-nities, where there was no preliminary plan, and where the design had constantly to be expanded and altered to keep pace with town growth. The problems accompanying the mere existence of a highway system,—paving, cleaning and upkeep,—called for full exercise of municipal authority.   Sometimes the community exacted from each inhabitant a yearly amount of labor on the streets; in other cases it hired this labor and paid for it outright.   In either case it had to levy special taxes, for materials or labor or both.   To insure some cleanliness in the streets, it passed mandatory ordinances restricting the conduct of townsmen, impressed the services of carters, and employed public funds for the hire of scavengers.   Further to protect the public ways, it restricted and regulated the traffic upon them, especially the weight of cart loads and the width of their wheels.   Less necessary but desirable improvements in the highways, like the construction of drains, first came about through private demand and initiative, but as the civic power matured and public funds became available, these too became public functions and responsibilities.   In either the municipal or the individual approach to highway problems the towns had good precedent in the Mother Country.   In actual execution, especially with regard to refinements like paving and drainage, they seem in some cases to have gone beyond contemporary English cities.   With a few exceptions, this generalization does not apply to the corporation governed towns, or to the unfortunately ungoverned metropolis of South Carolina.

Highways may be said to constitute the most rudimentary of public utilities, but there were others,—bridges, wharves, and engineering projects,—of which colonial townsfolk almost immediately felt the need.   In the beginning, while municipal authority was politically and financially feeble, these were almost solely the product of private enter-prise, but with the gradual tendency of town development they became increasingly matters of public concern.   Following Old World precedent, bridges were conceived as parts of the highway system, and hence un-doubtedly under public control, but they were usually constructed and operated by private persons or companies, under grant from local or provincial authorities.   As the century progressed, in a few cases, notably at Philadelphia and Boston, town governments directly managed the operation and upkeep of bridges.   Land reclamation projects, and harbor facilities like lighthouses, pursued a similar his-tory.   In the case of wharves, they were either a municipal or a private concern.   Most towns maintained a minimum of public docking facilities, while more ambitious wharf projects, like the Long Wharves of Boston and Newport, were only within the capacity of private capital. At Philadelphia public docking facilities were so excellent as to discourage employment of private capital in their erection; at New York, so poor as to require it. Toward the end of the era, when the demands of trade began to make regular transportation between communities desirable, stage and freight routes, too, were operated by private capital, under license, usually from the provincial government.

Fire constitutes a threat especially dangerous to urban communities, and as buildings in colonial towns were from the beginning placed close together, its imminence was immediately felt. The combatting and prevention of fire called forth more than individual efforts from the start. Municipal ordinances required the keeping of fire fighting equipment by all townsmen, regulated their chimneys, forbade bonfires, fireworks, and the housing of explosives in crowded areas. Public authorities had also to make direct outlays for fire fighting equipment of their own, and hire companies for its care and operation. In Boston, Philadelphia and Newport private societies for the protection of property during fires were organized to supplement public agencies. Similarly, water supply for fire uses was a matter of public concern and regulation. Boston, with its crowded streets and buildings of inflammable construction, and its willingness to spend public money and energy for public welfare, was in general far in the forefront with regard to its fire defenses, but by the end of the first century all towns possessed fire engines of the latest European model, and fire fighting regulations equal or superior to those of the average English town.

A distinctive urban function grew in part out of the fire hazards of crowded sections,—the enactment of building regulations. Only public authority could specify the nature of legal building materials as did Boston after the fire of 1679 and the South Carolina Assembly after the Charles Town fire of 1740. Exercise of municipal powers was also necessary to prevent imperfect construction and dangerous neglect of town chimneys and hearths. In addition, conditions of urban congestion led to party-wall regulations like those of Boston and Philadelphia.

Another, more subtle class of problems, those which involved the personal relationships of inhabitants, affected town society from its inception. Intensified by the peculiar conditions of urban life, they required collective rather than individual efforts and powers for their control. Old World experience had taught town-dwellers the immediate need for means of preserving the public peace in settled communities, and the early appearance of constables in all towns supplied the traditional response to that need. For their security after nightfall the towns appointed bellmen or watchmen of varying degrees of efficiency. New York, after developing a highly effective nocturnal police in the seventeenth century, allowed this institution to languish from unwillingness to devote the necessary public funds thereto; other towns were slower in supplying the need, though somewhat more successful by the end of the first century. Efficiency of the watch was in direct ratio to the availability of public funds for its support,—impressment of a citizen's watch having revealed its inadequacy by the turn of the century,—and here the New England towns, with their powers of local taxation, were at a distinct advantage. There are numerous instances, during periods of unusual danger or disturbance like wars or epidemics, when the towns entirely failed in their efforts to preserve nocturnal peace, and their functions had to be taken over by the military arm of the provincial government.

Existence of crime and disorder early became a community concern in urban settlements. Here invitations to lawbreaking existed in the inequalities of wealth and opportunity, and materials for its perpetration in the diverse and unruly elements of town and seaport society. The concentration of people, many of them hardworked and underprivileged, also made for mob disorders, which increased in violence and frequency with the growth of the towns. Presence of sailors, blacks, foreigners, paupers, unpopular religious sects, interlopers in trade, profiteers, and rival political factions, all provided increasing incentives for disorder and violence as the period progressed. Town society clearly soon passed beyond the stage where individual efforts or the force of public opinion could deal with this problem; rather it required the sanctions of the law. Provincial governments passed legislation, and municipal authorities enacted ordinances outlawing offenses against society. Riot acts were drawn up by colonial assemblies, and the local constabulary did its best to round up and confine the perpetrators of disorder and violence. In general, the towns could do little to remove the causes of criminality, and the solution of this peculiarly vexing problem of city life remained as remote in the seventeenth and eighteenth centuries as today.

For punishments, colonial authorities followed a number of Old World precedents, favoring especially the speediest and least expensive methods,—fines, floggings, public humiliation, restitution of stolen goods, and, occasionally, mutilation. In general, their criminal codes were less brutal than those of contemporary Europe. Efforts to make the whole community a partner in the work of law enforcement appeared in the division with informers of the proceeds from fines. Prisons were still generally places of detention for those awaiting trial, though imprisonment as punishment for crime seems to have become more widespread as the period advanced, and save in the case of debtors was probably somewhat more in use in the colonies than in the Old World. The frequency of jail breaks indicates the inefficiency of all colonial prisons, and their inadequacy suggests the absence of more vicious criminal types that troubled older societies. Yet colonial prisons were probably no more inadequate than those of contemporary England, and certainly far less squalid and brutal. Save in the case of Philadelphia in the eighteenth century, the rudimentary penology of the times made no distinction between various classes of offenders, and absence of prison facilities led to frequent misuse of alms and workhouses, wherein pauper and lawbreaker were housed together.

Offenses against the moral and ethical standards which society imposes appear more flagrant in the comparative populousness and congestion of urban environments, and early forced themselves upon the attention of colonial communities. In addition, the psychology of the times made many aspects of the regulations of conduct, manners and dress a legitimate province for the public authority. Early appearance of prostitution in the towns shocked authorities into decreeing harsh penalties for it and similar offenses. With its increasing prevalence in a society which included growingly diverse and uncontrollable elements, they seem everywhere to have become less concerned with the actual offense than with the fear lest the illegitimate offspring become charges to the community. Drunkenness was a prevailing vice, and in all towns the authorities and the better elements fought to eradicate it. Excellent tavern legislation in several of the towns reduced this offense to a minimum, but illegal sale of liquor, and misuse of the legitimate product, continued to baffle municipal authority throughout the period. Sabbath legislation in every town,—as strict in the Anglican South as in Puritan New England,—attempted to insure the sacred character of the Lord's Day. Gambling, card-playing, loitering, idleness, extravagance in dress and behavior, and evidence of frivolity came under the ban of public regulation, either through colony or municipal authority, or as at Philadelphia through the dominant religious group. Especially at Boston and Philadelphia many seemingly innocent amusements suffered from the disapproval of a stern and narrow religion, which served as a powerful and useful supplement to the civic power.

The existence and effects of crime and immorality are intensified in urban communities; so, too, the problem of pauperism. Reports of travelers as to the absence of poverty from colonial towns can only be regarded as comparatively true, for in each town numbers of those unable to care for themselves soon constituted a problem of which the community had to take cognizance. The generally excellent methods with which the towns met this problem indicate a considerable sense of civic maturity and responsibility. New York and Charles Town favored the out-relief method through most of the period, but Boston and Philadelphia had by the end of the century well-regulated and practically self-supporting workhouses, and Newport maintained an adequate almshouse.   Considerable direct relief had to be granted, especially at Boston, and in all towns save New York private or religious organizations supplemented the public work of poor relief. Methods to forestall the growth of poverty were devised, such as compulsory apprenticeship of poor children, exclusion of strangers without obvious means of livelihood, and, especially in the New England towns, restriction of immigration. In times of particular stress special devices had to be resorted to, as the distribution of corn or firewood, or a temporary embargo on export of necessary commodities. At Boston, where the problem of poverty became acute in the 1670's and was never thereafter absent, careful registration of all aliens and dependents prevailed, and a public granary was maintained.

The general health, which in rural regions may be privately cared for, early became in urban communities a matter for public concern, and municipal ordinances soon restricted the conduct of inhabitants in matters which might affect the general well-being. Location of wells and privies, and of slaughterhouses and tan pits which might become public nuisances, removal of dumps and disposal of refuse were all subjects of municipal regulation. Similarly, public authorities directed inhabitants in their behavior during epidemics, and enacted quarantine regulations in an attempt to prevent visitations of infectious disease. Toward the end of the century excellent isolation hospitals appeared in several of the towns, erected and operated by the municipality. Despite failure in this period of all attempts to regulate the practice of medicine by town or colony, the medical profession in the towns attained a relatively high development for the times.

In their approach to the physical and social problems of urban life the towns were imitators, not originators. The townsmen came to America with a fund of European experience from which they seldom deviated, and new methods as they employed them had usually first to cross the Atlantic. Poor relief and tavern legislation were directly imported from Great Britain, and the towns might conceivably have done better with their police problem had not Old World precedent served them so exclusively as a guide. Yet it may be said that in several cases there are distinct improvements in the thoroughness with which old methods were employed, and which may usually be traced to the individual civic pride of townsmen, reflected in their municipal governments. This is especially true of communities which enjoyed the town meeting form of government, where, as we have seen, the direct demands of townspeople could effect greater thoroughness and efficiency in dealing with town business, but even in the corporation governments of America there is less indifference to the public welfare than may be noted in contemporary England or Europe. Visitors were impressed with the excellence of poor relief at Boston and Philadelphia, and with Philadelphia's model prison. Fire defences in the towns were a combination of English and Dutch examples, and, especially at Boston, probably unsurpassed for their time. Solution of urban problems in colonial towns was continually hampered by lack of public funds or of necessary authority for obtaining them,—the sad decline of New York's excellent watch is an illustration,—but it was assisted, where public power failed, either politically or financially, by an encouraging growth of civic consciousness among private individuals and non-political organizations. Establishment of private agencies for charity, education, fire protection, improvement of morals, and the like, and the appearance of individual benefactors to the public welfare of the community, in an age not distinguished for civic virtue or interest, is a remarkable and significant accomplishment of town society in colonial America.

Having as they all did a common model and experience, colonial towns exhibit a remarkable similarity in the solution of their urban problems. There are many instances of the failure of a community to provide the usual and accepted necessary solution, but, with the possible exception of Philadelphia's eighteenth century prison, hardly a single example of the development by one town of a unique institution. By the time that local divergences from the original plan might have been expected to appear, communication had sufficiently improved to permit of one town's borrowing from the successful experience of another. The same holds true for privately initiated supplements of municipal endeavor. The Scot's Charitable Society and the Fire Society appear in Boston, copied from European models, and at a later date are further copied by other American towns. In the eighteenth century, because of its long experience in dealing with urban problems, the greater efficiency of its form of government, and its willingness to spend public money for the public good, Boston became the great example, with respect to municipal institutions, for other towns on the continent, but it enjoyed no monopoly of this function. New Yorkers had the fire defences of Philadelphia held up to them as a model, Bostonians were shamed by the excellence of Philadelphia's market, while Charlestonians tried to fashion their city government after the example of the corporation of New York. By the end of the period under review this inter-city exchange of experience had resulted in a striking similarity in municipal institutions, as well as a fairly uniform level of their development. Boston, for the reasons enumerated above, was probably still somewhat in advancé in matters of social and material concern, though with its humanitarian agencies Philadelphia was running a close second. Charles Town, within the limits of its governmental incapacity, dealt in fairly efficient fashion with its problems; at Newport, a lesser development of these problems had not yet necessitated any great display of urban consciousness. Even at

New York, where political factionalism, a selfish corporation, and the difficulty of amalgamating two languages and nationalities prevented a consistent and devoted attempt to solve the problems of urban living, a comparison of its municipal life with that of older provincial cities of the British Empire would not have resulted in discredit to the former.

The accumulation of economic resources and their concentration in urban units, their direction in commercial ventures which attracted and supported large populations within these units, and the problems of providing for the physical and social well-being of those who thus became city-dwellers, all these aspects of urban development succeeded in bringing forth in America a distinctive society. In constitution, spiritual life, recreational activities, and intellectual pursuits it differed from types of society to be found in other sections of the continent. In respect neither to national origins nor to economic status of their inhabitants did the towns long remain homogeneous. Settled originally by people of the same nation, usually of the same locality, they soon came to include children of other European countries and of another race. Early in their history there could be found small groups of Scots in Boston, French Huguenots in Boston, New York and Charles Town, Welsh in Philadelphia, and a few Jews in every town. Many Germans settled in the 1680's in the environs of Philadelphia, and New York from the time of the first English occupation presented the problem of two peoples, each with their own language, schools and churches, living side by side under government by the numerically weaker group. This incipient cosmopolitanism flowered with the renewed immigration of the early eighteenth century, when all towns received numbers of Scotch-Irish, and the middle and southern cities, especially Philadelphia, large accessions of German exiles. For the most part these strangers were allowed to settle peaceably in colonial towns, whose economic expansion enabled them easily to absorb the newcomers, and though recent arrivals seldom attained social recognition or overcame the barrier of language where it existed, still there was little nativism and small emphasis on the superior advantages of Anglo-Saxon nativity. Such bountiful immigration did, however, lead to many restrictions, especially in the north, where the labor market was well supplied and the poor rates overburdened, to establishment of special churches and social organizations, and in Philadelphia, at least, to common use of the German language in business transactions. By far the greater problem was created by the presence of African Negroes in all towns. In Boston and Newport, where they were used mainly as house servants, and where many of them were free, the problem was negligible. They were subject to various discriminatory rules, such as those which required them to work out their obligations to the community in menial labor rather than by watch or militia duty. But at New York and Charles Town their greater numbers kept constantly present the fear of servile insurrection. At the former town they were the unfortunate objects of such waves of hysteria as the Negro Conspiracy of 1741, and at Charles Town, where they at times equalled the white population in numbers, a severe slave code kept them in subjection.

Social stratification further differentiated urban society from the easy democracy of the back country, where any man might own land and all must work with their hands. Distinctions between the well-to-do and the not-so-rich were perhaps relatively unimportant in the beginning, when society was still so fluid that luck or diligence might elevate a man above his fellows in a short time, but with the accumulation of wealth and economic power in the hands of a few, and the coming in of numbers of artisans, indentured servants and immigrant laborers, class lines tightened and society crystallized into easily recognizable categories of better, middling, and poorer sorts. In all towns native aristocracies were commerical in origin, even at Charles Town where they later sought land as a basis for social distinction. They consolidated their position by means of wealth from successful trading ventures, collecting thereby social prestige and political influence. They lived grandly, dressed gaily, kept horses and coaches, and employed the labor of the less fortunate. The commercial, political and social leadership of the towns was in their hands. Later, as urban life became more sophisticated, they contributed to the development of secular amusements and to the relaxation of earlier strict moral codes. They gained further brilliance by alliance with representatives of British officialdom in America. Below them the middle class, professional people, tradesmen and artisans, lived comfortably but more plainly, enjoying in prosperous times many of the good things of life, but in hard times feeling the pinch far more than did their wealthy neighbors. Steady laborers might know periods of prosperity, but many of them could be squeezed out by the vicissitudes of the economic cycle. They performed the menial labor of the towns, enlisted as common seamen, and constituted a group from which much urban poverty and disorder were recruited. Negro and Indian slaves, mere unprivileged pieces of property, rounded out the caste system as it developed itself in metropolitan America.

Save Newport, each of the towns had originally been dedicated to a dominant Protestant religious organization, but after a century of growth diversity, indifference and actual unbelief came to characterize the religious scene. The complexities of town society were in large measure responsible for this development, for different national or social groups soon evolved their favored sects and denominations.

When the ministry could no longer speak with one voice to all elements of town populations, it lost much of its influence, both social and clerical, and the appearance of agnosticism and irreverence was rapid. In general, at the end of the first century, Anglicanism was in all towns the religion of officials and aristocrats; Quakerism and Congregationalism, which had once in their own localities enjoyed this favored position, had joined the ranks of middle class religions, which further included Baptists and Presbyterians; while for the common man a religious refuge was just appearing in the enthusiastic, emotional revivalism of Whitefield. Absence of devotion penetrated all classes; the poorer sort were largely indifferent to the attractions of religion, freethinking characterized such middle class groups as Franklin's Junto, and aristocrats indulged a fashionable Deism. In contrast, a stern and uniform religious fundamentalism for a much longer time characterized the rural communities of the countryside.

Much of their power the quasi-established churches had attained in an age when religious concerns so dominated men's thoughts as to exclude many other aspects of life. But the commercial success of colonial towns altered this singleness of outlook by acquainting townsmen with the delights of secular grandeurs and providing money for their enjoyment. As the age advanced the church step by step gave way before the institution of more attractive secular recreations. Most successful of these, appearing very early and appealing to all classes, was the tavern. Instituted originally as a necessary convenience for strangers and travelers, it soon showed itself to be the resort of all classes of townsmen, the place where they conducted much of their business and where much of their social life was passed. In the eighteenth century coffee houses became as in England the rendezvous of business men and the scene of many commercial transactions. Taverns served not only as places of casual conviviality, but as headquarters for the multifarious clubs into which town social life gradually organized itself. They also offered opportunities for cards, billiards and games of chance, and housed the many traveling shows and exhibitions which the better transportation of the eighteenth century made possible.

Games, contests, tavern recreations, and public celebration of holidays constituted the entertainment of the common man, but for the aristocrats mounting wealth and sophistication were creating more elaborate forms of amusement. To the hearty private dinners and occasional excursions of early days succeeded great public banquets, dances and balls, musical entertainments, and finally, in two of the towns, dramatic presentations. Gradually the commercial aristocracy of the towns, combining with royal officials, evolved a society whose entertainments were artificial, costly, sophisticated and exclusive. But for aristocrat or common man, the vicarious amusements that money could buy, and their variety and attractiveness, differentiated town society from that of the countryside with its simpler, spontaneous pleasures, and tended to draw town-dwellers away from a strict and narrow conception of life as a duty and a task. Copied as they were from the recreations of English society, they also tended to make social life in the towns more like that of the metropolis.

A final characteristic of town society was that it offered to its members a wider intellectual opportunity and challenge than was possible to the man whose life was bounded by his fields or by the hard necessity of clearing away the forest. From earliest childhood opportunities for education, free or otherwise, were open to the town-dweller. Especially was this true of the poor, whose educational needs were largely cared for by religious societies, charity schools, or compulsory apprenticeship. This last system enabled youth of the poorer classes to equip themselves for a trade. In other strata of society young men might fit themselves for business at private vocational schools, for a place in society with private masters, or for higher education for a learned profession at public or private Latin schools or with a private tutor. Young women, too, in the towns might purchase instruction in various fields of learning or merely in the polite arts of feminine society. Also, in the northern English towns, Boston, Newport and Philadelphia, there was from the start a tradition of scholarliness and of respect for intellectual achievement. It followed that a society so trained, constantly in contact by ship with Europe, was alive and ready to adopt the intellectual fashions of the age. Hence, in this first century of American life, most of the intellectual activity, in science, literature and the arts, and what intellectual progress there was, took place in the towns. Only there were there material and opportunity for such activity. And rather than regard the results of that progress with condescension, we should, with James Franklin's subscriber, wonder at the contrary. In comparison with the Augustan Age of eighteenth century London, intellectual and social life in the colonies may seem bare and sterile, but in comparison with the intellectual barrenness of provincial life in England itself, its cultivation and sophistication appear revealed. Urban culture in the eighteenth century was provincial culture at its best, nourished during this period of faltering imitation, which had to precede that of native accomplishment, by constant contact with the vital intellectual currents of England and Europe.

In these various ways the developments of a hundred years of life under relatively urban conditions created a society at once distinct from that of rural regions, whether tidewater or back country, and even further removed from that of the westward reaching frontier. The communal attitude toward the solution of the physical and social problems of diversified populations dwelling together in close propinquity, and the constantly widening outlook which material progress, commercial expansion, and contact with the larger world of affairs made possible, were its distinguishing characteristics. In general, this society was more cooperative and social, less individualistic in its outlook toward problems of daily life, far more susceptible to outside influences and examples, less aggressively independent than the society of frontier America. At the same time it was more polished, urbane, and sophisticated, more aware of fashion and change, more sure of itself and proud of its achievements, more able to meet representatives from the outside world as equals without bluster or apology than the rural society of the colonial back country. Because its outlook was eastward rather than westward, it was more nearly a European society in an American setting. It had appropriated various points on the American continent and transformed them as nearly as possible into likenesses of what it had known at home. It was itself less transformed in the process than might have been expected, because the contact with the homeland never ceased, but rather increased with the passage of years. Its importance to American life as a whole was therefore great. Here were centers of the transit of civilization from Old World to New,—five points at the least through which currents of world thought and endeavor might enter, to be like other commodities assimilated and redistributed throughout the countryside. It was well for the future of national America that its society should not remain completely rural and agricultural, isolated and self-sufficient, ignorant of outside developments and distrustful of new ideas from abroad, as it might well have done had there been no cities. Instead, the five towns provided the nucleus for a wider and more gracious living in the New World.

Society and the Great Awakening in New England

EDWIN S. GAUSTAD

Of the sequence of dramas which make up human history none is perhaps more dramatic than that of man's faith and its periodic renewal. The way in which it is renewed is never the same, nor are the causes and consequences of its renewal. It is the need for understanding the various ways in which man has pursued the same goal of seeking his God and revitalizing his faith which challenges and interests the student of history. There are many questions to be answered. Each touches ultimately upon times that try men's souls.

Such times of trial, certainly, were the 1740's when the deep and wide revival known as the Great Awakening swept through the American colonies. Appealing to a primitive sense of faith and salvation, evangelical in its fervor and doctrine, capturing the hearts and minds of tens of thousands, bypassing if not quite undoing formal religions and established orthodoxies, it was clearly the most important movement of its kind in the colonial period. Inevitably, therefore, the Great Awakening has become a focus of attention for historians. Inevitably, too, it has been variously understood as the patterns of historical understanding have themselves varied.

Here are two reasons for the value of the following essay by Edwin Scott Gaustad, professor of history at the University of California, Riverside, and author of A Religious History of America *(1966). The essay is, for one thing, an illuminating analysis of the Great Awakening itself, which Professor Gaustad studied at greater length in his noteworthy monograph,* The Great Awakening in New England *(1957). Secondly, the essay is a revealing commentary on the historical writings about the movement. Professor Gaustad takes exception to the view that the Great Awakening was limited to certain social classes and to certain geographical areas. In this respect, what he is saying is part of a wider rejection of the school of Beard and Turner, a school that has until recently exercised considerable*

SOURCE: *The William and Mary Quarterly*, Third Series, XI (October, 1954), 566–577. Reprinted by permission of the author and publisher.

influence upon American historical writing. His rejection can be properly understood, therefore, if it is related to the critical reconsiderations of the colonial and early national periods, that have been made in recent years by such historians as Robert E. Brown, Edmund S. Morgan, Douglass Adair, Cecelia M. Kenyon, and Richard B. Morris.

The exciting phenomenon of the Great Awakening will suggest questions to the critical inquirer that relate both to its uniqueness and to its similarity to other religious outpourings. What factors have been responsible for spiritual resurgence in any age, and what were they for the Great Awakening in particular? What developments had produced the decline in religious feeling that preceded the Great Awakening? To what extent was it the product of great leaders, to what extent did the latter no more than tap deeper currents that had been welling up? What relevance did the Great Awakening have to the larger political, economic, and social developments of its times? What impact did it have upon subsequent developments, not merely of a religious nature, but also political, social, and economic? To what degree was it not a single revival, but a whole complex of related revivals? If it was the latter, what were its various causes, courses, and consequences?

Beyond the many questions of this sort lies the deeper one of man's faith. What is the nature of faith, what are its sources? To what degree is it consonant with science, to what degree is it antagonistic? Is man more prone to seek God in times of troubles? If so, what is he seeking, what are the troubles that are besetting him, who is the God he seeks? The student of history will have more than superficial interest in answering these questions. They are important for an understanding of earlier ages. They are central to an understanding of our own.

Contemporaries of the turbulent religious upheaval which took place in New England in the years 1740 to 1742 described it as a "great and general awakening." Later historians, less ready to admit either its greatness or its generality, have in concert described the revival as limited to this area or that, to this social class exclusive of that, and as brought about by this or that socio-economic force. We have come a long way from "the economic interpretation of religion," when all felt obliged to excuse the obtrusion of churches and pious sentiments by explaining that this sheep's clothing of religion concealed an economic wolf within. Yet the phenomenon known as the Great Awakening is of such proportions as to lead to its interpretation as something other than a religious movement.

It would be folly to suggest that the Awakening was completely divorced from the culture of eighteenth-century New England, from the shortage of specie, from the growth of trade, from the greater leisure and less crudity of life, from the vigilant struggles for popular representation and the increasing degree of political independence. To admit its connection with these secular developments is, however, vastly different from cataloguing the revival as a "deep-rooted social movement," as a lower-class uprising, or as "a revolt of the backcountry producers." John Chester Miller viewed the movement as riding on the wave of hostility between rich and poor created by the Land Bank uproar, and producing a full and permanent cleavage between the social classes. The uninhibited and fervent James Davenport, according to Miller, divided the

> social classes much as during the Land Bank fervor. The Opposers were joined by more and more of the wealthy and educated as Davenport carried the Great Awakening down to a lower stratum and preached the gospel of discontent and levellism. . . . This conviction among the common people that they had been singled out by God for salvation and that the Opposers— the upper classes—were for the most part damned gave class feeling a new twist in Massachusetts.

Though this theory probably serves as a useful counterweight to that other tenacious myth that "the elect" and "the élite" were synonymous terms in colonial New England, it does not do justice to the historical evidence concerning the revival itself. Indeed, John Miller begins his discussion with a question that begs the question: "What caused the Great Awakening to split up the Congregational church and cut a swath between rich and poor, stimulating the hostility that already divided them?" This identification of the anti-revivalists with the upper classes is made by Perry Miller, who declares the list of subscribers to Chauncy's *Seasonable Thoughts* to be "a roster of antirevivalists and also a social register." Eugene E. White writes of the revival as one of the "deep-rooted social movements," a "social phenomenon," "confined to the cities and the settled areas of the East." More recently, Richard D. Mosier views it as an affair not of the cities, but of the rural areas, "a revolt of the backcountry producers from the stringent controls of the mercantile aristocracy which ruled from afar"; the Awakening was also anti-clerical and anarchical, "the first step in a movement which culminates in the American Revolution." And Clinton Rossiter, speaking of the Great Awakening in all the colonies, writes as follows: "It appealed primarily to the poor and despised; it revolted the well-born, well-educated, and well-to-do." These are statements of faith.

There is, on the contrary, abundant evidence that this religious turmoil was in fact "great and general," that it knew no boundaries, social or geographical, that it was both urban and rural, that it reached both lower and upper class. The geographical non-particularity of the Great Awakening is readily established, though it is necessary to distinguish it from the earlier series of revivals emanating from Northampton. Beginning in 1734 and continuing for two or three years, these revivals were largely a frontier phenomenon, concentrated along the banks of the Connecticut River from Northfield to Saybrook Point. They arose under the influence of Jonathan Edwards and the "surprising conversions" which took place in Northampton. To them, but only to them, the term "frontier revivalism" can with propriety be applied, and not to the Great Awakening, which began after the earlier revivals were "very much at a Stop" and the initial phase of which occurred rather in the coastal than in the inland area. Edwards regarded the two movements as quite distinct, speaking of the revivalism early in 1741 as "the beginning of that extraordinary religious commotion, through the land. . . ." In the frontier revivals, no churches were split, no clergy were offended, no flagrant itineracy occurred, no elaborate apologetic was necessary, no legislation was provoked, and no vast array of abusive epithets came into use.

The Awakening itself began when, on September 14, 1740, the proud, portly, and pompous George Whitefield arrived at Newport to preach (he tells us) with "much Flame, Clearness and Power. . . . The People were exceedingly attentive. Tears trickled down their Cheeks. . . ." His arrogance passed for conviction, his sentiment for piety, his superficiality for simplicity, and his moving rhetoric for inspiration. And wherever the youthful Anglican went, so did the Awakening. It spread from Newport to Bristol to Boston, and northeast to Roxbury, Marblehead, Ipswich, Newbury, Hampton, Portsmouth, and York. It moved west of Boston into Concord, Sudbury, Worcester, Leicester, Brookfield, and Northampton; thence south, through Springfield, Suffield, Windsor, Hartford, and New Haven; and southwest, through Milford, Stratford, Fairfield, and Stamford. In less than two months, the tour of New England by "the Grand Itinerant" was over. From the many areas left shaking, tremors reached out to meet each other, and to move all that lay between.

At the small town of Harvard, about forty miles west of Boston, "God was pleased . . . to rouze and awaken sleepy Sinners," this being done without the intervention of any itinerants or "Strangers." On November 23, 1741, all heaven broke loose in Middleborough, Massachusetts. "I have written Accounts of seventy-six that Day struck, and bro't first to inquire what they should do to escape condemnation." Their joyful pastor, Peter Thacher, further notes that from that time on, there was "an uncommon Teachableness among my People." In Wethersfield, Connecticut, Eleazar Wheelock reported late in 1741 that "the Lord bowed the heavens and Came Down upon a Large assembly in one of the Parishes of the town the Whole assembly Seam'd alive with Distress. . . ." Gilbert Tennent, who followed Whitefield in a tour of New England, observed that at Charlestown "multitudes were awakened, and several had received great consolation, especially among the young people, children and Negroes." He recorded also a general "shaking among the dry bones" at Harvard College, while in New Haven the concern was considerable and "about thirty students came on foot ten miles to hear the word of God." In brief, it is simply not possible to draw any meaningful lines on a map of New England in order to distinguish where in 1741 the revival was and where it was not. It was a phenomenon not alone of the back country or exclusively of the cities, of the coast or of the frontier. From Stamford, Connecticut, to York, Maine, from Danbury to Northfield (the New England Dan to Beersheba), there had been a great and general awakening.

In 1742, six Boston ministers testified that these "uncommon religious Appearances" were found "among Persons of all Ages and Characters." Another Boston clergyman, the fiery Presbyterian John Moorhead, extolled "the wonderful things which God is adoing, and has already Manifested amongst Indians, Negros, Papists and Protestants of all Denominations." Though somewhat extreme, Moorhead's observation points to the truly universal character of the Awakening. If it reached Indians, Negroes, and even Quakers, is it possible that it extended also to the upper classes?

It has never seemed urgently necessary to offer proof of lower-class participation in the revival, perhaps because of the finality of such a quotation as the following, which describes James Davenport and his Boston listeners:

> Were you to see him in his most violent agitations, you would be apt to think, that he was a Madman just broke from his Chains: But especially had you seen him returning from the Common after his first preaching, with a large Mob at his Heels, singing all the Way thro' the Streets . . . attended with so much Disorder, that they look'd more like a Company of Bacchanalians after a mad Frolick, than sober Christians who had been worshipping God. . . .

A strong image such as this lingers long in the imagination, causing Davenport and his large mob, in retrospect, to seem the epitome of the Awakening. Even in those surveys of New England's revival where Davenport is not regarded as its personification, he is given disproportionate emphasis. There was no Davenport party. By the ardent supporters of the revival he was judged, in the middle of 1742, to be "deeply tinctur'd with a Spirit of Enthusiasm," and unworthy to be invited "into our Places of publick Worship"—this from the ministers who diligently worked in behalf of the "great and glorious work of God." Indeed, the friends of the Awakening feared him more than its foes, for they recognized in him the potential for discrediting the entire movement. Thomas Prince, joyfully describing the successes of the revival in Boston, tells of Davenport's coming in these words: "And then through the providence of the sovereign God, the wisdom of whose ways are past finding out, we unexpectedly came to an unhappy period, which it exceedingly grieves me now to write of. . . ." His fellow Presbyterian, Gilbert Tennent, himself repeatedly condemned for going to rash and intemperate extremes, denounced Davenport's technique as "enthusiastical, proud, and schismatical." Further, in the summer of 1742, a Connecticut court found Davenport "disturbed in the rational Faculties of his Mind," while a Massachusetts court declared him *non compos mentis.* To be sure, if Davenport represented anything at all, it would be of a lower order. The point is, however, that he was the spokesman for no class or party, and least of all is he a symbol of the Great Awakening as a whole.

When Whitefield departed from Boston on his first New England tour, the *Evening-Post* editorialized that "the Town is in a hopeful way of being restor'd to its former State of Order, Peace and Industry." Three days later, a letter, appearing in the *News-Letter,* deplored this attitude, affirming that "the Generality of sober and serious Persons, of all Denominations among us (who perhaps are as much for maintaining Order, Peace and Industry as Mr. Evening-Post and Company) have been greatly Affected with Mr. Whitefield's Plain, Powerful, and Awakening Preaching. . . ." Were the "sober and serious" actually reached by the revival? Benjamin Colman, of the Brattle Street Church, wrote Whitefield that after Tennent's visit to Boston "great Additions are made to our Churches. . . . Many of them among the Rich and Polite of our Sons and Daughters. This week the overseers of our Colleges have appointed a Day of Prayer and Humiliation with thanksgiving, for the Effusion of the Spirit of God. . . ." The phrase, "especially among young people," often occurs in contemporary accounts of the revival, suggesting a greater concentration of "concern" in that generation. But that the movement followed class lines, there is no indication.

With reference to the colleges, of which Colman spoke and of whose social standing there can be little question, their sympathies would have remained with the Awakening had not Whitefield heedlessly insulted them. Yale and Harvard both cheerfully heard the leading exponents of the movement, and some of the instructional staff left their posts to carry the word. An effective deterrent to their support was this remark, published in Whitefield's *Journal:* "As for the Universities, I believe it may be said, their Light is become Darkness, Darkness that may be felt, and is complained of by the most godly Ministers." Whitefield sought to mitigate the effect of this unwarranted affront by writing a letter in July, 1741, "To the Students, &c. under convictions at the colleges of Cambridge and New-Haven," declaring that "It was no small grief to me, that I was obliged to say of your college, that 'your light was become darkness;' yet are ye now become light in the Lord." The damage had already been done; nevertheless, not until 1744 did Harvard issue a formal testimony against Whitefield, Yale following suit in 1745. Even then, it must be noted, the testimony was "Against the Reverend Mr. George Whitefield, And his Conduct" and not against the revival in general. Yale and Harvard graduates alike continued to bear the main responsibility in furthering the "extraordinary Work of God."

Pro-revivalism was in no way the equivalent of social egalitarianism. One of the sins for which Jonathan Edwards reproved his young people was their spending much time in "frolicks," without having "any regard to order in the families they belonged to. . . ." There was a large measure of social consciousness in Edwards's Northampton parish, as later events even more clearly revealed; yet the church could hardly be regarded as outside the scope of the Awakening. Ebenezer Parkman of Westborough, a peerless social conservative, was fully sympathetic with the revival at the same time that he complained in horror that the young men of the lower classes had the presumption to adorn themselves with "Velvet Whoods." Gilbert Tennent, often represented as a leveller and "a Man of no great Parts or Learning," had in fact received from his father no mean education in Hebrew, the classics, and theology, and could move easily in any stratum of society.

In Boston, then if not now, the upper reaches of New England society were concentrated. And that city's support of the revival was an effective force in the entire movement. When Whitefield first came to town, he was "met on the Road and conducted to Town by several Gentlemen." Later in the week, he dined with the governor, Jonathan Belcher, with whom he enjoyed a most cordial relationship. Of Boston's four newspapers, three were either favorable to the Awakening or successfully maintained some degree of neutrality. Only Timothy Fleet's rather coarse *Evening-Post* was openly opposed to the revival, and even this paper did not dare to swim against the tide of public feeling until near the end of 1742, when the movement had already begun to ebb.

The established clergy of New England's capital were preponderantly pro-revivalist or New Light: the proportion was three to one. Of the three divines hostile to the Great Awakening, only Charles Chauncy was open and active in his opposition, and he did not begin a deliberate refutation of the revival until 1743. Throughout 1741, Chauncy allowed himself to be carried along in the main current of the movement, even to the point of telling sinners that they "hang, as it were, over the bottomless pit, by the slender thread of life, and the moment that snaps asunder, you sink down into perdition. . . ." As late as May of 1742,

Chauncy declared, "There are, I doubt not, a number in this land, upon whom God has graciously shed the influence of his blessed Spirit. . . ." So that during the height of the Awakening, 1740 to 1742, its most able and prodigious opponent sounded much like Jonathan Edwards himself. The two remaining Old Lights or "Opposers" among Boston's established clergy, both of the Mather family, published nothing concerning the religious excitement, though they privately expressed their disdain of the affair. Samuel Mather, son of Cotton, was dismissed from Second Church in 1741 because, among other reasons, of his negative attitude toward the Awakening and his reluctance to participate in it. In a vain attempt at reconciliation, Mather promised "to beware of any thing in my sermons or conversation which may tend to discourage the work of conviction and conversion among us." Mather Byles, grandson of Increase and first pastor of the Hollis Street Church, succeeded in avoiding any public controversy over the revival. Though publishing a sermon in 1741 on *Repentance and Faith The Great Doctrine of the Gospel of Universal Concernment,* Byles' position—religious and political—was unalterably conservative, and his sympathies were thoroughly Old Light.

Except for three wavering neutrals, the other Boston ministers vigorously, tirelessly, promoted the revival. The city's senior pastor at this time was Benjamin Colman, of Brattle Street Church. A great friend to institutions of higher learning and widely respected abroad as well as at home for his erudition, Colman received the degree of Doctor of Divinity in 1731 from the University of Glasgow. Liberal and learned, he did not hesitate to "play the Artillery of Heaven against the hardy Sons of Vice," and in 1741 he happily reported that "The Work of God with us goes on greatly . . . our crowded serious Assemblies continue, and great Additions are made to our Churches." Following Whitefield's initial visit, Colman spoke at Boston's first evening lecture of the pleasure it gave the ministers to see "in the Weeks past, Old and Young, Parents and Children, Masters and Servants, high and low, rich and poor together, gathering . . . to the Doors and Windows of our Places of Worship. . . ." Benjamin Colman is certainly to be regarded as a constant friend of the Awakening—though, just as certainly, he is to be distinguished from such fanatics as James Davenport and Andrew Croswell. His position, however, was rather one of discrimination than of moderation. He had even shown great interest in the earlier Northampton revival, corresponding with Edwards and others connected with it, passing on to his friends abroad news of religious awakenings in the colonies, and urging Edwards to write the *Faithful Narrative of Surprising Conversions.* The first minister of New England to correspond with Whitefield, he was instrumental in bringing the latter to that area. With much zeal and sincere concern, he favored and furthered the revival to the very end, seeking, like Edwards, to discourage the excesses and abnormalities as no proper part of the true display of God's grace.

William Cooper, Colman's associate since 1715, joined with his colleague in praising "the remarkable Work of Grace begun, and I hope going on amongst us; the eminent Success which God has been pleas'd to give to his preached Gospel of late; the surprizing Effusion of the Holy Spirit, as a Spirit of Conversion to a blessed Number. . . ." At First Church, there was no such harmony. Chauncy's opposition was offset by the approbation of his associate, Thomas Foxcroft, of what he called the "Pauline Spirit and Doctrine remarkably exemplify'd among us." Thomas Prince and Joseph Sewall of Old South Church were eminently successful in making that church a vital center of revival activity. Prince, Boston's foremost reporter of the Awakening, was largely responsible for the creation of the disorganized but important *Christian History,* the first specifically religious magazine in the colonies, the purpose of which was to give accounts of the "surprizing and . . . extensive Revivals." Although it was ostensibly edited by Thomas Prince, Junior, the magazine's enemies were probably correct in declaring the elder Prince to be the power behind the pen. Joseph Sewall, who looked upon the revival as itself a means or channel of grace, inveighed against "every Thing that hath a Tendency to quench his [God's] Spirit, and obstruct the Progress and Success of his good Work." John Webb, senior minister at New North Church, vividly portrayed Christ entreating reluctant sinners in this time of concern to seek and receive the saving grace. His colleague, Andrew Eliot, in 1743 signed a testimony favoring the Great Awakening, noting only that itineracy had not been sufficiently protested against. Samuel Checkley of New South Church, who in 1741 preached on the topic "Little children brought to Christ," was among the same group of signers. And Joshua Gee of Second Church, having reproved the cool indifference of his associate, Samuel Mather, exploded with bitterness when in 1743 a group of ministers issued a testimony against errors and disorders in the Awakening without making "an open Acknowledgment of the late remarkable Effects of a gracious Divine Influence in many of our Churches." Gee succeeded in calling a gathering of ninety New England ministers who were "persuaded there has of late been a happy Revival of Religion," and in issuing a favorable witness to the revival signed by sixty-eight divines and attested to by forty-three others unable to attend the meeting.

The division of Boston's Congregational clergy in this turbulent period is, therefore, as follows: nine New Light, three Old Light, three neutral. Five churches were pro-revivalist (Brattle Street, Old South, Second, New North, and New South); New Brick and West were neutral; Hollis Street was anti-revivalist; and First was divided. The city's one Presbyterian church, with John Moorhead as pastor, was as determined in its support of the Awakening as the one Baptist church was in its opposition. One segment of Boston society did hold aloof: namely, that which attended the city's three Anglican churches. But respectability, in eighteenth-century New England at least, was not wholly identified with Anglicanism. Even as it is impossible to fix any meaningful geographical boundaries to the sweep of the Awakening, so the attempt to limit its sway or ascribe its rise to any single social class proves misleading.

As the revival declined and the "distinguishing names of reproach" came to be employed more freely and less gently, theological and ec-clesiastical factions hardened, sometimes producing divisions that were social—in Connecticut, even political. With the increase in ani-mosities, reports of revivalism were dismissed as "stupid Bombast Stuff," and Ezra Stiles in 1760 described the period of the revival as a time when "Multitudes were seriously, soberly and solemnly out of their wits."   A Connecticut divine summarized the effects of the movement as follows:

> Antinomian Principles are advanc'd, preach'd up and printed;—Christian Brethren have their Affections widely alienated;—Unchristian Censorious-ness and hard judging abounds, Love stands afar of, and Charity cannot enter;—Many Churches and Societies are broken and divided. . . . Numbers of illiterate Exhorters swarm about as Locusts from the Bottomless Pit. . . .

As such reports came to abound, it seemed plausible, if not desirable, to describe the revival as socially suspect from the beginning, as carried along by a disinherited, rural debtor class. It is, however, tendentious history that sees New England's religious upheaval of 1740 to 1742 as something less than "a great and general awakening."

THE AMERICAN REVOLUTION

11

Political Experience and Enlightenment Ideas in Eighteenth-Century America
BERNARD BAILYN

The American Revolution was a secession of the American colonies from the eighteenth-century British empire, a war of independence from European control. To define the revolution one must define America's place within the larger context of British and European ideas and institutions. The age of the American Revolution was also the age of the European Enlightenment and it is fair enough to ask how far both were related. Did the Revolution realize the program of the Enlightenment, and were the European revolutions then modeled on ours? What did America and Europe signify for each other? Were the colonies the pays raisonné *of the* philosophes, *Europe's "last best hope" under the* ancien régime, *a city upon a hill to serve as an example for Western reformation? Was America an already enlightened polity, and if it was, what did the Revolution achieve?*

It is the reciprocal significance of eighteenth-century Europe and America which Professor Bernard Bailyn of Harvard University seeks to explore in the following essay. Professor Bailyn, whom we have already met, is editor of Pamphlets of the American Revolution, 1750–1776 *(the first of four projected volumes appeared in 1965) and author of* The Ideological Origins of the American Revolution *(1967), for which he won several awards, including the Pulitzer Prize and the Bancroft Prize. In the essay below, he*

SOURCE: *The American Historical Review,* LXVII (January, 1962), 339–351. Reprinted by permission of the author.

undertakes to answer three salient questions: 1) What are the older and the newer interpretations of the American Revolution? 2) In what ways did an enlightened society emerge in later colonial America, not as a result of the ideas of the Enlightenment, but spontaneously and "by the mundane exigencies of the situation. . . . ?" 3) What was the relevance of the European Enlightenment to the American Revolution?

Professor Bailyn's answers to these questions are fresh and imaginative; yet they invite a further series of questions. Does Bailyn really prove his central paradox: that the eighteenth-century American polity was enlightened in practice before it became enlightened in theory? To ask this is not necessarily to maintain that our institutions owed nothing to the Enlightenment theory; but the question does compel us to indicate clearly what we mean by the Enlightenment and when we presume it to have been a significant force in Western life, two points about which Bailyn says nothing. If we suggest that the political community the English had achieved during the course of the seventeenth century was the model for the European Enlightenment, and if we note that English experience had been central and immediate to that of their colonies, then may we not argue that colonial America built enlightened institutions to the specification of enlightened theory? To Bailyn's way of looking at it, Europe thought, America acted; and indeed America had pretty much acted before Europe had thought. The division is too neat, too pat. Without denying the response of the Americans to the conditions of their local environment, may we not properly see them acting within the larger European environment of ideas and institutions in which they belonged, of which they were part? That American life might be unrelated to the dominant tendency in contemporary European thought is too improbable a thesis to accept. Even the most conservative members of the American community lived by the premises of enlightened thought; even Cotton Mather accepted Sir Isaac Newton, even Jonathan Edwards embraced John Locke.

In dismissing Enlightenment theory as the source of eighteenth-century American political institutions, Bailyn thus leaves unanswered some basic questions about both the Enlightenment and theory. Indeed, even if we should yield the point, and agree that Enlightenment theory did not influence American institutions, would we be correct in concluding that no theory did—that, as Bailyn insists, our institutions grew, if not like Topsy, then merely "spontaneously," "naturally," responding to "exigencies," and as "matters of fact"? But is not the spontaneity only apparent, and not really so artless, patternless, unrelated to larger Western developments as it may at first seem? Was not the natural world of America inhabited by European values? Were not the matters of fact also matters of premises and a larger orientation? Was American life at this stage of its evolution merely a corpus *without a* mens; *and if it was not mindless or thoughtless, then what were the framework of its mind and the architecture of its thought?*

Arguing that Enlightenment ideas had already been realized in early eighteenth-century America, Bailyn is left with the obvious problem of having to explain why there was an American Revolution and just what it signified; and it is at this point that he introduces the European Enlightenment as a palpable, vital force in American life. But is he not letting in through the back door what he ejected through the front? And in his argument for the role that the Enlightenment played in the Revolution, is he not in effect introducing into American life the tension and conflict he had earlier denied?

That Bailyn's thesis evokes so many questions testifies surely to its originality and challenge. It testifies too to the sustained interest that the Revolution holds for us. Both the thesis and the questions concern the relevance of European experience to our own, and the axiom that American history cannot be properly understood without reference to the history of Europe. If a nation's history expresses its identity, its changing perspective on the past expresses its changing sense of what it is and where it is going. Today's newer interpretations of our revolutionary origins are significant clues as to where we think we now stand vis-à-vis Europe, the mother continent, and indeed vis-à-vis the world. The emergence of the American nation—its circumstances and ideology—will be the subject of continual redefinition as we go on redefining our role in the world of nations.

The political and social ideas of the European Enlightenment have had a peculiar importance in American history. More universally accepted in eighteenth-century America than in Europe, they were more completely and more permanently embodied in the formal arrangements of state and society; and, less controverted, less subject to criticism and dispute, they have lived on more vigorously into later periods, more continuous and more intact. The peculiar force of these ideas in America resulted from many causes. But originally, and basically, it resulted from the circumstances of the prerevolutionary period and from the bearing of these ideas on the political experience of the American colonists.

What this bearing was—the nature of the relationship between Enlightenment ideas and early American political experience—is a matter of particular interest at the present time because it is centrally involved in what amounts to a fundamental revision of early American history now under way. By implication if not direct evidence and argument, a number of recent writings have undermined much of the structure of historical thought by which, for a generation or more, we have understood our eighteenth-century origins, and in particular have placed new and insupportable pressures on its central assumption concerning the political significance of Enlightenment thought. Yet the need for rather extensive rebuilding has not been felt, in part because the architecture has not commonly been seen as a whole—as a unit, that is, of mutually dependent parts related to a central premise —in part because the damage has been piecemeal and uncoordinated: here a beam destroyed, there a stone dislodged, the inner supports only slowly weakened and the balance only gradually thrown off. The edifice still stands, mainly, it seems, by habit and by the force of inertia. A brief consideration of the whole, consequently, a survey from a position far enough above the details to see the outlines of the overall architecture, and an attempt, however tentative, to sketch a line—a principle—of reconstruction would seem to be in order.

A basic, organizing assumption of the group of ideas that dominated the earlier interpretation of eighteenth-century American history is the belief that previous to the Revolution the political experience of the colonial Americans had been roughly analogous to that of the English. Control of public authority had been firmly held by a native aristocracy —merchants and landlords in the North, planters in the South—allied, commonly, with British officialdom. By restricting representation in the provincial assemblies, limiting the franchise, and invoking the restrictive power of the English state, this aristocracy had dominated the governmental machinery of the mainland colonies. Their political control, together with legal devices such as primogeniture and entail, had allowed them to dominate the economy as well. Not only were they successful in engrossing landed estates and mercantile fortunes, but they were for the most part able also to fight off the clamor of yeoman debtors for cheap paper currency, and of depressed tenants for freehold property. But the control of this colonial counterpart of a traditional aristocracy, with its Old World ideas of privilege and hierarchy, orthodoxy in religious establishment, and economic inequality, was progressively threatened by the growing strength of a native, frontier-bred democracy that expressed itself most forcefully in the lower houses of the "rising" provincial assemblies. A conflict between the two groups and ways of life was building up, and it broke out in fury after 1765.

The outbreak of the Revolution, the argument runs, fundamentally altered the old regime. The Revolution destroyed the power of this traditional aristocracy, for the movement of opposition to parliamentary taxation, 1760–1766, originally controlled by conservative elements, had been taken over by extremists nourished on Enlightenment radicalism, and the once dominant conservative groups had gradually been alienated. The break with England over the question of home rule was part of a general struggle, as Carl Becker put it, over who shall rule at home. Independence gave control to the radicals, who, imposing their advanced doctrines on a traditional society, transformed a rebellious secession into a social revolution. They created a new regime, a reformed society, based on enlightened political and social theory.

But that is not the end of the story; the sequel is important. The success of the enlightened radicals during the early years of the Revolution was notable; but, the argument continues, it was not wholly unqualified. The remnants of the earlier aristocracy, though defeated, had not been eliminated: they were able to reassert themselves in the postwar years. In the 1780's they gradually regained power until, in what amounted to a counterrevolution, they impressed their views indelibly on history in the new federal Constitution, in the revocation of some of the more enthusiastic actions of the earlier revolutionary period, and in the Hamiltonian program for the new government. This was not, of course, merely the old regime resurrected. In a new age whose institutions and ideals had been born of revolutionary radicalism, the old conservative elements made adjustments and concessions by which to survive and periodically to flourish as a force in American life.

The importance of this formulation derived not merely from its usefulness in interpreting eighteenth-century history. It provided a key also for understanding the entire course of American politics. By its light, politics in America, from the very beginning, could be seen to have been a dialectical process in which an aristocracy of wealth and power struggled with the People, who, ordinarily ill-organized and inarticulate, rose upon provocation armed with powerful institutional and ideological weapons, to reform a periodically corrupt and oppressive polity.

In all of this the underlying assumption is the belief that Enlightenment thought—the reforming ideas of advanced thinkers in eighteenth-century England and on the Continent—had been the effective lever by which native American radicals had turned a dispute on imperial relations into a sweeping reformation of public institutions and thereby laid the basis for American democracy.

For some time now, and particularly during the last decade, this interpretation has been fundamentally weakened by the work of many scholars working from different approaches and on different problems. Almost every important point has been challenged in one way or another. All arguments concerning politics during the prerevolutionary years have been affected by an exhaustive demonstration for one colony, which might well be duplicated for others, that the franchise, far from having been restricted in behalf of a borough-mongering aristocracy, was widely available for popular use. Indeed, it was more widespread than the desire to use it—a fact which in itself calls into question a whole range of traditional arguments and assumptions. Similarly, the Populist terms in which economic elements of prerevolutionary history have most often been discussed may no longer be used with the same confidence. For it has been shown that paper money, long believed to have been the inflationary instrument of a depressed and desperate debtor yeomanry, was in general a fiscally sound and successful means—whether issued directly by the governments or through land banks—not only of providing a medium of exchange but also of creating sources of credit necessary for the growth of an underdeveloped economy and a stable system of public finance for otherwise resourceless governments.   Merchants and creditors commonly supported the issuance of paper, and many of the debtors who did so turn out to have been substantial property owners.

Equally, the key writings extending the interpretation into the revolutionary years have come under question.   The first and still classic monograph detailing the inner social struggle of the decade before 1776—Carl Becker's *History of Political Parties in the Province of New York, 1760–1776* (1909)—has been subjected to sharp criticism on points of validation and consistency.   And, because Becker's book, like other studies of the movement toward revolution, rests upon a belief in the continuity of "radical" and "conservative" groupings, it has been weakened by an analysis proving such terminology to be deceptive in that it fails to define consistently identifiable groups of people.   Similarly, the "class" characteristic of the merchant group in the northern colonies, a presupposition of important studies of the merchants in the revolutionary movement, has been questioned, and along with it the belief that there was an economic or occupational basis for positions taken on the revolutionary controversy.   More important, a recent survey of the writings following up J. F. Jameson's classic essay, *The American Revolution Considered as a Social Movement* (1926), has shown how little has been written in the last twenty-five years to substantiate that famous statement of the Revolution as a movement of social reform.   Most dramatic of all has been the demolition of Charles Beard's *Economic Interpretation of the Constitution* (1913), which stood solidly for over forty years as the central pillar of the counterrevolution argument: the idea, that is, that the Constitution was a "conservative" document, the polar opposite of the "radical" Articles of Confederation, embodying the interests and desires of public creditors and other moneyed conservatives, and marking the Thermidorian conclusion to the enlightened radicalism of the early revolutionary years.

Finally, there are arguments of another sort, assertions to the effect that not only did Enlightenment ideas not provoke native American radicals to undertake serious reform during the Revolution, but that ideas have never played an important role in American public life, in the eighteenth century or after, and that the political "genius" of the American people, during the Revolution as later, has lain in their brute pragmatism, their successful resistance to the "distant example and teachings of the European Enlightenment," the maunderings of "garret-spawned European illuminati."

Thus from several directions at once have come evidence and arguments that cloud if they do not totally obscure the picture of eighteenth-century American history composed by a generation of scholars. These recent critical writings are of course of unequal weight and validity; but few of them are totally unsubstantiated, almost all of them have some point and substance, and taken together they are sufficient to raise serious doubts about the organization of thought within which we have become accustomed to view the eighteenth century. A full reconsideration of the problems raised by these findings and ideas would of course be out of the question here even if sufficient facts were now available. But one might make at least an approach to the task and a first approximation to some answers to the problems by isolating the central premise concerning the relationship between Enlightenment ideas and political experience and reconsidering it in view of the evidence that is now available.

Considering the material at hand, old and new, that bears on this question, one discovers an apparent paradox. There appear to be two primary and contradictory sets of facts. The first and more obvious is the undeniable evidence of the seriousness with which colonial and revolutionary leaders took ideas, and the deliberateness of their efforts during the Revolution to reshape institutions in their pattern. The more we know about these American provincials the clearer it is that among them were remarkably well-informed students of contemporary social and political theory. There never was a dark age that destroyed the cultural contacts between Europe and America. The sources of transmission had been numerous in the seventeenth century; they increased in the eighteenth. There were not only the impersonal agencies of newspapers, books, and pamphlets, but also continuous personal contact through travel and correspondence. Above all, there were Pan-Atlantic, mainly Anglo-American, interest groups that occasioned a continuous flow of fresh information and ideas between Europe and the mainland colonies in America. Of these, the most important were the English dissenters and their numerous codenominationalists in America. Located perforce on the left of the English political spectrum, acutely alive to ideas of reform that might increase their security in England, they were, for the almost endemically nonconformist colonists, a rich source of political and social theory. It was largely through nonconformist connections, as Caroline Robbins' recent book, *The Eighteenth-Century Commonwealthman* (1959) suggests, that the commonwealth radicalism of seventeenth-century England continued to flow to the colonists, blending, ultimately, with other strains of thought to form a common body of advanced theory.

In every colony and in every legislature there were people who knew Locke and Beccaria, Montesquieu and Voltaire; but perhaps more important, there was in every village of every colony someone who knew such transmitters of English nonconformist thought as Watts, Neal, and Burgh; later Priestly and Price—lesser writers, no doubt, but staunch opponents of traditional authority, and they spoke in a familiar idiom. In the bitterly contentious pamphlet literature of mid-eighteenth-century American politics, the most frequently cited authority on matters of principle and theory was not Locke or Montesquieu but *Cato's Letters,* a series of radically libertarian essays written in London in 1720–1723 by two supporters of the dissenting interest, John Trenchard and Thomas Gordon. Through such writers, as well as through the major authors, leading colonists kept contact with a powerful tradition of enlightened thought.

This body of doctrine fell naturally into play in the controversy over the power of the imperial government. For the revolutionary leaders it supplied a common vocabulary and a common pattern of thought, and, when the time came, common principles of political reform. That reform was sought and seriously if unevenly undertaken, there can be no doubt. Institutions were remodeled, laws altered, practices questioned all in accordance with advanced doctrine on the nature of liberty and of the institutions needed to achieve it. The Americans were acutely aware of being innovators, of bringing mankind a long step forward. They believed that they had so far succeeded in their effort to reshape circumstances to conform to enlightened ideas and ideals that they had introduced a new era in human affairs. And they were supported in this by the opinion of informed thinkers in Europe. The contemporary image of the American Revolution at home and abroad was complex; but no one doubted that a revolution that threatened the existing order and portended new social and political arrangements had been made, and made in the name of reason.

Thus, throughout the eighteenth century there were prominent, politically active Americans who were well aware of the development of European thinking, took ideas seriously, and during the Revolution deliberately used them in an effort to reform the institutional basis of society. This much seems obvious. But, paradoxically, and less obviously, it is equally true that many, indeed most, of what these leaders considered to be their greatest achievements during the Revolution—reforms that made America seem to half the world like the veritable heavenly city of the eighteenth-century philosophers—had been matters of fact before they were matters of theory and revolutionary doctrine.

No reform in the entire Revolution appeared of greater importance to Jefferson than the Virginia acts abolishing primogeniture and entail. This action, he later wrote, was part of "a system by which every fibre would be eradicated of antient or future aristocracy; and a foundation laid for a government truly republican." But primogeniture and entail had never taken deep roots in America, not even in tidewater Virginia. Where land was cheap and easily available such legal restrictions proved to be encumbrances profiting few. Often they tended to threaten rather than secure the survival of the family, as Jefferson himself realized when in 1774 he petitioned the Assembly to break an entail on his wife's estate on the very practical, untheoretical, and common ground that to do so would be "greatly to their [the petitioners'] Interest and that of their Families." The legal abolition of primogeniture and entail during and after the Revolution was of little material consequence. Their demise had been effectively decreed years before by the circumstances of life in a wilderness environment.

Similarly, the disestablishment of religion—a major goal of revolutionary reform—was carried out, to the extent that it was, in circumstances so favorable to it that one wonders not how it was done but why it was not done more thoroughly. There is no more eloquent, moving testimony to revolutionary idealism than the Virginia Act for Establishing Religious Freedom: it is the essence of Enlightenment faith. But what did it, and the disestablishment legislation that had preceded it, reform? What had the establishment of religion meant in prerevolutionary Virginia? The Church of England was the state church, but dissent was tolerated well beyond the limits of the English Acts of Toleration. The law required nonconformist organizations to be licensed by the government, but dissenters were not barred from their own worship nor penalized for failure to attend the Anglican communion, and they were commonly exempted from parish taxes. Nonconformity excluded no one from voting and only the very few Catholics from enjoying public office. And when the itineracy of revivalist preachers led the establishment to contemplate more restrictive measures, the Baptists and Presbyterians advanced to the point of arguing publicly, and pragmatically, that the toleration they had so far enjoyed was an encumbrance, and that the only proper solution was total liberty: in effect, disestablishment.

Virginia was if anything more conservative than most colonies. The legal establishment of the Church of England was in fact no more rigorous in South Carolina and Georgia: it was considerably weaker in North Carolina. It hardly existed at all in the middle colonies (there was of course no vestige of it in Pennsylvania), and where it did, as in four counties of New York, it was either ignored or had become embattled by violent opposition well before the Revolution. And in Massa-

chusetts and Connecticut, where the establishment, being nonconformist according to English law, was legally tenuous to begin with,
tolerance in worship and relief from church taxation had been extended
to the major dissenting groups early in the century, resulting well
before the Revolution in what was, in effect if not in law, a multiple
establishment. And this had been further weakened by the splintering
effect of the Great Awakening. Almost everywhere the Church of
England, the established church of the highest state authority, was
embattled and defensive—driven to rely more and more on its missionary arm, the Society for the Propagation of the Gospel, to sustain it
against the cohorts of dissent.

None of this had resulted from Enlightenment theory. It had been
created by the mundane exigencies of the situation: by the distance that
separated Americans from ecclesiastical centers in England and the
Continent; by the never-ending need to encourage immigration to the
colonies; by the variety, the mere numbers, of religious groups, each by
itself a minority, forced to live together; and by the weakness of the
coercive powers of the state, its inability to control the social forces
within it.

Even more gradual and less contested had been the process by which
government in the colonies had become government by the consent of
the governed. What has been proved about the franchise in early
Massachusetts—that it was open for practically the entire free adult
male population—can be proved to a lesser or greater extent for all the
colonies. But the extraordinary breadth of the franchise in the American colonies had not resulted from popular demands: there had been
no cries for universal manhood suffrage, nor were there popular
theories claiming, or even justifying, general participation in politics.
Nowhere in eighteenth-century America was there "democracy"—
middle-class or otherwise—as we use the term. The main reason for
the wide franchise was that the traditional English laws limiting
suffrage to freeholders of certain competences proved in the colonies,
where freehold property was almost universal, to be not restrictive but
widely permissive.

Representation would seem to be different, since before the Revolution complaints had been voiced against the inequity of its apportion-
ing, especially in the Pennsylvania and North Carolina assemblies. But
these complaints were based on an assumption that would have seemed
natural and reasonable almost nowhere else in the Western world; the
assumption that representation in governing assemblages was a proper
and rightful attribute of people as such—of regular units of population,
or of populated land—rather than the privilege of particular groups,
institutions, or regions. Complaints there were, bitter ones. But they

were complaints claiming injury and deprivation, not abstract ideals or unfamiliar desires. They assumed from common experience the normalcy of regular and systematic representation. And how should it have been otherwise? The colonial assemblies had not, like ancient parliaments, grown to satisfy a monarch's need for the support of particular groups or individuals or to protect the interests of a social order, and they had not developed insensibly from precedent to precedent. They had been created at a stroke, and they were in their composition necessarily regular and systematic. Nor did the process, the character, of representation as it was known in the colonies derive from theory. For colonial Americans, representation had none of the symbolic and little of the purely deliberative qualities which, as a result of the revolutionary debates and of Burke's speeches, would become celebrated as "virtual." To the colonists it was direct and actual: it was, most often, a kind of agency, a delegation of powers, to individuals commonly required to be residents of their constituencies and, often, bound by instructions from them—with the result that eighteenth-century American legislatures frequently resembled, in spirit if not otherwise, those "ancient assemblies" of New York, composed, the contemporary historian William Smith wrote, "of plain, illiterate husbandmen, whose views seldom extended farther than to the regulation of highways, the destruction of wolves, wild cats, and foxes, and the advancement of the other little interests of the particular counties which they were chosen to represent." There was no theoretical basis for such direct and actual representation. It had been created and was continuously reinforced by the pressure of local politics in the colonies and by the political circumstances in England, to which the colonists had found it necessary to send closely instructed, paid representatives —agents, so called—from the very beginning.

But franchise and representation are mere mechanisms of government by consent. At its heart lies freedom from executive power, from the independent action of state authority, and the concentration of power in representative bodies and elected officials. The greatest achievement of the Revolution was of course the repudiation of just such state authority and the transfer of power to popular legislatures. No one will deny that this action was taken in accordance with the highest principles of Enlightenment theory. But the way had been paved by fifty years of grinding factionalism in colonial politics. In the details of prerevolutionary American politics, in the complicated maneuverings of provincial politicians seeking the benefits of government, in the patterns of local patronage and the forms of factional groupings, there lies a history of progressive alienation from the state which resulted, at least by the 1750's, in what Professor Robert Palmer has lucidly described as a revolutionary situation: a condition

> ... in which confidence in the justice or reasonableness of existing authority is undermined, where old loyalties fade, obligations are felt as impositions, law seems arbitrary, and respect for superiors is felt as a form of humiliation; where existing sources of prestige seem undeserved ... and government is sensed as distant, apart from the governed and not really "representing" them.

Such a situation had developed in mid-eighteenth-century America, not from theories of government or Enlightenment ideas but from the factional opposition that had grown up against a succession of legally powerful, but often cynically self-seeking, inept, and above all politically weak officers of state.

Surrounding all of these circumstances and in various ways controlling them is the fact that that great goal of the European revolutions of the late eighteenth century, equality of status before the law—the abolition of legal privilege—had been reached almost everywhere in the American colonies at least by the early years of the eighteenth century. Analogies between the upper strata of colonial society and the European aristocracies are misleading. Social stratification existed, of course; but the differences between aristocracies in eighteenth-century Europe and in America are more important than the similarities. So far was legal privilege, or even distinction, absent in the colonies that where it existed it was an open sore of festering discontent, leading not merely, as in the case of the Penn family's hereditary claims to tax exemption, to formal protests, but, as in the case of the powers enjoyed by the Hudson River land magnates, to violent opposition as well. More important, the colonial aristocracy, such as it was, had no formal, institutional role in government. No public office or function was legally a prerogative of birth. As there were no social orders in the eyes of the law, so there were no governmental bodies to represent them. The only claim that has been made to the contrary is that, in effect, the governors' Councils constituted political institutions in the service of the aristocracy. But this claim—of dubious value in any case because of the steadily declining political importance of the Councils in the eighteenth century—cannot be substantiated. It is true that certain families tended to dominate the Councils, but they had less legal claim to places in those bodies than certain royal officials who, though hardly members of an American aristocracy, sat on the Councils by virtue of their office. Councilors could be and were removed by simple political maneuver. Council seats were filled either by appointment or election: when appointive, they were vulnerable to political pressure in England; when elective, to the vagaries of public opinion at home. Thus on the one hand it took William Byrd II three years of maneuvering in London to get himself appointed to the seat on the Virginia Council vacated by his father's death in 1704, and on the other, when in 1766 the Hutchinson faction's control of the Massachusetts Council proved unpopular, it was simply removed wholesale by being voted out of office at the next election. As there were no special privileges, no peculiar group possessions, manners, or attitudes to distinguish councilors from other affluent Americans, so there were no separate political interests expressed in the Councils as such. Councilors joined as directly as others in the factional disputes of the time, associating with groups of all sorts, from minute and transient American opposition parties to massive English-centered political syndicates. A century before the Revolution and not as the result of anti-aristocratic ideas, the colonial aristocracy had become a vaguely defined, fluid group whose power—in no way guaranteed, buttressed, or even recognized in law—was competitively maintained and dependent on continuous, popular support.

Other examples could be given. Were written constitutions felt to be particular guarantees of liberty in enlightened states? Americans had known them in the form of colonial charters and governors' instructions for a century before the Revolution; and after 1763, seeking a basis for their claims against the constitutionality of specific acts of Parliament, they had been driven, out of sheer logical necessity and not out of principle, to generalize that experience. But the point is perhaps clear enough. Major attributes of enlightened polities had developed naturally, spontaneously, early in the history of the American colonies, and they existed as simple matters of social and political fact on the eve of the Revolution.

But if all this is true, what did the Revolution accomplish? Of what real significance were the ideals and ideas? What was the bearing of Enlightenment thought on the political experience of eighteenth-century Americans?

Perhaps this much may be said. What had evolved spontaneously from the demands of place and time was not self-justifying, nor was it universally welcomed. New developments, however gradual, were suspect by some, resisted in part, and confined in their effects. If it was true that the establishment of religion was everywhere weak in the colonies and that in some places it was even difficult to know what was orthodoxy and what was not, it was nevertheless also true that faith in the idea of orthodoxy persisted and with it belief in the propriety of a privileged state religion. If, as a matter of fact, the spread of freehold tenure qualified large populations for voting, it did not create new reasons for using that power nor make the victims of its use content with what, in terms of the dominant ideal of balance in the state, seemed a disproportionate influence of "the democracy." If many colonists came naturally to assume that representation should be direct and actual, growing with the population and bearing some relation to its distribution, crown officials did not, and they had the weight of precedent and theory as well as of authority with them and hence justification for resistance. If state authority was seen increasingly as alien and hostile and was forced to fight for survival within an abrasive, kaleidoscopic factionalism, the traditional idea nevertheless persisted that the common good was somehow defined by the state and that political parties or factions—organized opposition to established government—were seditious. A traditional aristocracy did not in fact exist; but the assumption that superiority was indivisible, that social eminence and political influence had a natural affinity to each other, did. The colonists instinctively conceded to the claims of the well-born and rich to exercise public office, and in this sense politics remained aristocratic. Behavior had changed—had had to change—with the circumstances of everyday life; but habits of mind and the sense of rightness lagged behind. Many felt the changes to be *away from,* not *toward,* something: that they represented deviance; that they lacked, in a word, legitimacy.

This divergence between habits of mind and belief on the one hand and experience and behavior on the other was ended at the Revolution. A rebellion that destroyed the traditional sources of public authority called forth the full range of advanced ideas. Long-settled attitudes were jolted and loosened. The grounds of legitimacy suddenly shifted. What had happened was seen to have been good and proper, steps in the right direction. The glass was half full, not half empty; and to complete the work of fate and nature, further thought must be taken, theories tested, ideas applied. Precisely because so many social and institutional reforms had already taken place in America, the revolutionary movement there, more than elsewhere, was a matter of doctrine, ideas, and comprehension.

And so it remained. Social change and social conflict of course took place during the revolutionary years; but the essential developments of the period lay elsewhere, in the effort to think through and to apply under the most favorable, permissive circumstances enlightened ideas of government and society. The problems were many, often unexpected and difficult; some were only gradually perceived. Social and personal privilege, for example, could easily be eliminated—it hardly existed; but what of the impersonal privileges of corporate bodies? Legal orders and ranks within society could be outlawed without creating the slightest tremor, and executive power with equal ease subordinated to the legislative: but how was balance within a polity to be achieved? What were the elements to be balanced and how were they to be separated? It was not even necessary formally to abolish the interest of state as a symbol and determinant of the common good; it was simply dissolved: but what was left to keep clashing factions from tearing a government apart? The problems were pressing, and the efforts to solve them mark the stages of revolutionary history.

In behalf of Enlightenment liberalism the revolutionary leaders undertook to complete, formalize, systematize, and symbolize what previously had been only partially realized, confused, and disputed matters of fact. Enlightenment ideas were not instruments of a particular social group, nor did they destroy a social order. They did not create new social and political forces in America. They released those that had long existed, and vastly increased their power. This completion, this rationalization, this symbolization, this lifting into consciousness and endowing with high moral purpose inchoate, confused elements of social and political change—this was the American Revolution.

12

The American Revolution as an Aftermath of the Great War for the Empire, 1754–1765

LAWRENCE HENRY GIPSON

When did the American Revolution begin? To set a date is at once to explain its nature and suggest its causes. It is clear enough that hostilities between the mother country and her mainland colonies became overt and very sharp after the Treaty of Paris in 1763. But what did this state of affairs signify? Were these hostilities the outcropping of tensions that had been long in growth and that were deeply imbedded in British colonial policy? Or were they more immediately the product of the peace concluded by Britain and France and of the war that had preceded it? Just what had been the nature of that war? Each of these questions relates closely to the larger one of what the Revolution was all about.

SOURCE: *The Political Science Quarterly*, LXV, 1 (March, 1950), 86–104. Reprinted by permission of the author and publisher.

The answer given by Professor Lawrence Henry Gipson of Lehigh University is certainly one of the most impressive of our age. Professor Gipson's thirteen volumes on The British Empire before the American Revolution *(1936–65) establish him as the scholar par excellence of the late colonial period. While his subject is broad and his interests manifold, he is concerned in particular with explaining the changing conditions within the great British Empire of the mid-century and the ways in which these led to the first successful colonial revolution of modern times. The explanation is absorbing, deriving as it does from Professor Gipson's considered opinion that, for the larger part, imperial conditions had been favorable to the colonies.*

In the following essay, Professor Gipson presents some of the challenging conclusions to which his long researches have led him. He shows that the French and Indian War was in fact part of a great imperial war. He explores at close range the origins of the war and, in particular, the desire of the British to secure and protect their North American colonies. He indicates how problems born in war grew immensely in peace. And he stresses above all that the terms of peace played no small part in precipitating a revolt that might otherwise not have come.

Professor Gipson belongs to a school of historians that has argued for a thorough hearing of the British cause during the American Revolution and that has found the cause to have had considerable merit. Moreover, in raising doubts about the cause of the revolutionaries, these historians have put a different light upon the nature and meaning of the Revolution. Belonging ourselves to the conservative order of the modern age, when the colonial system throughout the world is in revolt and new nations are emerging rapidly and in abundance, we would do well to ponder the suggestions of Professor Gipson concerning that earlier age when we revolted against our own colonial status and struck out for national independence.

Great wars in modern times have too frequently been the breeders of revolution. The exhausting armed struggles in which France became engaged in the latter half of the eighteenth century led as directly to the French Revolution as did the First World War to the Russian Revolution; it may be said as truly that the American Revolution was an aftermath of the Anglo-French conflict in the New World carried on between 1754 and 1763. This is by no means to deny that other factors were involved in the launching of these revolutionary movements. Before proceeding with an analysis of the theme of this paper, however, it would be well to consider the wording of the title given to it.

Words may be used either to disguise or to distort facts as well as to clarify them, but the chief task of the historian is to illuminate the past. He is faced, therefore, with the responsibility of using only such words as will achieve this broad objective of his calling and to reject those that obscure or defeat it. For this reason "the French and Indian War," as a term descriptive of the conflict to which we have just referred, has been avoided in this essay as well as in the writer's series on the *British Empire before the American Revolution.* This has been done in spite of the fact that it has been employed by most Americans ever since the early days of our Republic and therefore has the sanction of long usage as well as the sanction of American national tradition assigning, as does the latter, to the Revolutionary War a position of such command- ing importance as to make all other events in American history, preceding as well as following it, quite subordinate to it. In contrast to this traditional interpretation of our history one may affirm that the Anglo-French conflict settled nothing less than the incomparably vital question as to what civilization—what complex cultural patterns, what political institutions—would arise in the great Mississippi basin and the valleys of the rivers draining it, a civilization, whatever it might be, surely destined to expand to the Pacific seaboard and finally to domi- nate the North American continent. The determination of this crucial issue is perhaps the most momentous event in the life of the English- speaking people in the New World and quite overshadows in im- portance both the Revolutionary War and the later Civil War, events which, it is quite clear, were each contingent upon the outcome of the earlier crisis.

A struggle of such proportions, involving tremendous stakes, deserves a name accurately descriptive of its place in the history of the English-speaking people, and the title "the French and Indian War," as suggested, in no way fulfills this need. For the war was not, as the name would seem to imply, a conflict largely between English and French New World colonials and their Indian allies, nor was it localized in North America to the extent that the name would appear to indicate. In contrast, it was waged both before and after an open declaration of war by the British and French nations with all their resources for nine years on three oceans, and much of the land washed by the waters of them, and it ultimately brought in both Spain, allied to France, and Portugal, allied to Great Britain. While it involved, it is true, as the name would connote, wilderness fighting, yet of equal, if not of greater, importance in assessing its final outcome was the pouring forth of Britain's financial resources in a vast program of shipbuilding, in the equipment and support of the British and colonial armies and the royal navy, and in the subsidization both of allies on the European continent and of the colonies in America. If it also involved the reduction of the fortress of Louisbourg, Fort Niagara, Fort Duquesne, Quebec and Montreal in North America, each in turn to fall to British regulars aided by American provincial troops, these successes, of great significance, were, in fact, really contingent upon the resounding British naval victories in the Mediterranean, off the Strait of Gibraltar, in the Bay of Biscay, and elsewhere, that brought about the virtual extinction of the French navy and merchant marine and thereby presented to France —seeking to supply her forces in Canada and elsewhere with adequate reinforcements and matériel—a logistical problem so insoluble as to spell the doom of her North American empire and of her possessions in India and elsewhere.

If the term "the French and Indian War" meets none of the requirements of accurate historical nomenclature, neither does the term "the Seven Years' War"—a name appropriately enough employed by historians to designate the mighty conflict that raged for seven years in Germany before its conclusion in the Treaty of Hubertusburg in 1763. The principals in this war were Prussia, allied with Great Britain, Hanover, Brunswick and Hesse, facing Austria, most of the Holy Roman Empire, Russia and Sweden, all allied with France and receiving subsidies from her. Although George II, as King of Great Britain and Elector of Hanover, in the treaty of 1758 with Frederick of Prussia, promised not to conclude peace without mutual agreement with the latter, and although large subsidies were annually paid to Prussia as well as to the other continental allies out of the British treasury and troops were also sent to Germany, it must be emphasized that these aids were designed primarily for the protection of the King's German Electorate. In other words, the British alliance in no way supported the objectives of the Prussian King, when he suddenly began the German war in 1756 by invading Saxony—two years after the beginning of the Anglo-French war. In this connection it should be borne in mind that throughout the Seven Years' War in Germany Great Britain remained at peace with both Russia and Sweden and refused therefore to send a fleet into the Baltic in spite of the demands of Frederick that this be done; nor were British land troops permitted to assist him against Austria, but only to help form a protective shield for Hanover against the thrusts of the French armies. For the latter were determined not only to overrun the Electorate—something that they succeeded in doing—but to hold it as a bargaining point to be used at the conclusion of hostilities with Great Britain, a feat, however, beyond their power of accomplishment. Closely related and intertwined as were the two wars, they were, nevertheless, distinct in their beginning and distinct in their termination.

Indeed, while British historians at length were led to adopt the nomenclature applied by German and other continental historians to all hostilities that took place between 1754 and 1763 in both the Old and New Worlds, American historians, by and large in the past, have rejected, and rightly so, it seems, the name "the Seven Years' War" to designate specifically the struggle during these years in North America with the fate of that continent at stake; so likewise many of them have rejected, as equally inadmissible, the name "the French and Indian War." Instead, the late Professor Osgood employed the title "the Fourth Intercolonial War," surely not a good one; George Bancroft called the war "the American Revolution: First Phase," still more inaccurate in some respects than the names he sought to avoid; Francis Parkman, with the flare of a romanticist, was at first inclined to call it "the Old French War" but finally, under the influence of the great-man-in-history thesis, gave to his two remarkable volumes concerned with it the totally misleading name, *Montcalm and Wolfe*; finally, John Fiske, the philosopher-historian, as luminous in his views as he was apt to be careless in the details of historical scholarship, happily fastened upon the name "the Great War." In the series on the *British Empire before the American Revolution* the writer has built upon Fiske's title and has called it "the Great War for the Empire" in order to emphasize not only the fact that the war was a very great conflict both in its scope and in its lasting effects, as Fiske saw it with clearness, but also, as a war entered into specifically for the defense of the British Empire, that it was by far the most important ever waged by Great Britain to this end.

It may be pointed out that later charges, especially by American writers, that the war was begun by Great Britain with less worthy motives in mind, are not supported by the great mass of state papers and the private correspondence of British statesmen responsible for making the weighty decisions at the time—materials now available to the student which the writer has attempted to analyze in detail in the two volumes of his series that appeared under the title of *Zones of International Friction, 1748–1754*. In other words, the idea that the war was started as the result of European balance-of-power politics or by British mercantilists for the purpose of destroying a commercial rival and for conquering Canada and the French West Indies, and for expelling the French from India, rather than for the much more limited and legitimate objective of affording the colonies and particularly the new province of Nova Scotia and the Old Dominion of Virginia protection against the aggressive aims of France, must be dismissed by students brought face to face with impressive evidence to the contrary.

The development of the war into one for the military mastery of the North American continent came with the growing conviction on the part of the British ministers that nothing short of this drastic step would realize the primary aims of the government in arriving at the determination, as the result of appeals from the colonies for assistance, to challenge the right of French troops to be planted well within the borders of the Nova Scotia peninsula and at the forks of the Ohio. One may go as far as to state that the acquisition of Canada—as an objective

sought by mercantilists to contribute to the wealth of Great Britain—
would have seemed fantastic to any contemporary who had the slightest knowledge of the tremendous financial drain that that great possession had been on the treasury of the French King for over a century
before 1754. Moreover, the motives that ultimately led, after much
searching of heart, to its retention after its conquest by Great Britain
were not commercial but strategic and had primarily in view the
security and welfare generally of the older American colonies.

In view of these facts, not to be confused with surmises, the name
"the Great War for the Empire" seems to the writer not only not inappropriate but among all the names heretofore applied to the war in
question by far the most suitable that can be used by one concerned
with the history of the old British Empire, who seeks earnestly to maintain that standard of exactness in terminology, as well as in other
respects, which the public has a right to demand of him.

The description just given of the motives that led to the Great War
for the Empire, nevertheless, runs counter, as suggested, to American
national tradition and most history that has been written by American
historians in harmony with it. This tradition had a curious beginning.
It arose partly out of Pitt's zealous efforts to energize the colonies to
prosecute the war most actively; but there also was another potent
factor involved in its creation. Before the conclusion of hostilities in
1763 certain powerful commercial interests—centered particularly at
Newport, Rhode Island, Boston, New York City, and to a lesser extent
in Philadelphia—in a desire to continue an enormously lucrative trade
with the French West Indies, and therefore with the enemy, all in the
face of Pitt's determination to keep supplies from the French armed
forces operating in the New World, began to express themselves in
terms that implied that the war was peculiarly Great Britain's war and
only incidentally one that concerned her colonies and that the French,
really friendly to the aspirations of British colonials, were opposed only
to the mercantilistic ambitions of the mother country. By 1766—just
twelve years after the beginning of the war and three years after its
termination—this extraordinary tradition had become so well established that Benjamin Franklin, astonishingly enough, could actually
assert in his examination before a committee of the House of Commons:

> I know the last war is commonly spoke of here as entered into for the
> defence, or for the sake of the people of America; I think it is quite mis-
> understood. It began about the limits between Canada and Nova Scotia,
> about territories to which the crown indeed laid claim, but were not claimed
> by any British colony. . . . We had therefore no particular concern or interest
> in that dispute. As to the Ohio, the contest there began about your right
> of trading in the Indian country, a right you had by the Treaty of Utrecht,

which the French infringed . . . they took a fort which a company of your merchants, and their factors and correspondents, had erected there to secure that trade. Braddock was sent with an army to retake that fort . . . and to protect your trade. It was not until after his defeat that the colonies were attacked. They were before in perfect peace with both French and Indians. . . .

By the beginning of 1768 the tradition had been so extended that John Dickinson—voicing the popular American view in his highly important *Letters from a Farmer in Pennsylvania,* No. VIII—felt that he not only could affirm, as did Franklin, that the war was strictly Britain's war and fought for selfish purposes, but could even insist that the acquisition of territory in North America as the result of it "is greatly injurious to these colonies" and that they therefore were "not under the slightest obligation to the mother country.

But to return to the last phases of the Great War for the Empire. The British customs officials—spurred into unusual activity in the face of Pitt's demand for the strict enforcement of the Trade and Navigation Acts in order to break up the pernicious practice of bringing aid and comfort to the enemy—were led to employ writs of assistance for the purpose of laying their hands upon goods landed in American ports and secured in exchange for American provisions sent for the most part either directly or indirectly to the French West Indies. Although in the midst of hostilities, most of the merchants in Boston showed bitter opposition to the writs and equally ardent support of James Otis' declaration made in open court in 1761 that Parliament, acting within the limits of the constitution, was powerless to extend the use of these writs to America, whatever its authority might be in Great Britain. The importance of this declaration lies not so much in its immediate effect but rather in the fact that it was indicative of the line of attack that not only Otis would subsequently follow but also the Adamses, Hawley, Hancock, and other popular leaders in the Bay colony during the developing crisis, in the laying down of constitutional restrictions upon the power of Parliament to legislate for America. Further, it is clear that, even before the Great War for the Empire had been terminated, there were those in the province who had begun to view Great Britain as the real enemy rather than France.

Just as definitely as was the issue over writs of assistance related to the war under consideration was that growing out of the twopenny acts of the Virginia Assembly. In search of funds for maintaining the frontier defensive forces under the command of Colonel George Washington, the Assembly was led to pass in 1755 and 1758 those highly questionable laws as favorable to the tobacco planters as they were indefensively unjust to the clergy. Even assuming the fact that these laws were war measures, and therefore in a sense emergency measures, it was inconceivable that the Privy Council would permit so palpable a violation of contractual relations as they involved.   The royal disallowance of the laws in question opened the way for Patrick Henry, the year that hostilities were terminated by the Peace of Paris, not only to challenge in the Louisa County courthouse the right of the King in Council to refuse to approve any law that a colony might pass that in its judgment was a good law, but to affirm that such refusal was nothing less than an act of tyranny on the part of the King. It was thus resentment at the overturning of Virginia war legislation that led to this attack upon the judicial authority of review by the Crown—an authority exercised previously without serious protest for over a century.   It should also be noted that the Henry thesis helped to lay the foundation for the theory of the equality of colonial laws with those passed by Parliament, a theory of the constitution of the empire that most American leaders in 1774 had come to accept in arguing that if the King could no longer exercise a veto over the acts of the legislature of Great Britain, it was unjust that he should do so over those of the colonial assemblies.

But the most fateful aftermath of the Great War for the Empire, with respect to the maintenance of the historic connection between the mother country and the colonies, grew out of the problem of the control and support not only of the vast trans-Appalachian interior, the right to which was now confirmed by treaty to Great Britain, but of the new acquisitions in North America secured from France and Spain. Under the terms of the royal Proclamation of 1763, French Canada to the east of the Great Lakes was organized as the Province of Quebec; most of old Spanish Florida became the Province of East Florida; and those areas, previously held by Spain as well as by France to the west of the Apalachicola and to the east of New Orleans and its immediate environs, became the Province of West Florida. The Proclamation indicated that proper inducements would be offered British and other Protestants to establish themselves in these new provinces. With respect to the trans-Appalachian region, however, it created there a temporary but vast Indian reserve by laying down as a barrier the crest of the mountains beyond which there should be no white settlement except by specific permission of the Crown.

The Proclamation has been represented not only as a blunder, the result largely of carelessness and ignorance on the part of those responsible for it, but also as a cynical attempt by the British ministry to embody mercantilistic principles in an American land policy that in itself ran counter to the charter limits of many of the colonies and the interests in general of the colonials.   Nevertheless, this view of the Proclamation fails to take into account the fact that it was the offspring of the war and that the trans-Appalachian aspects of it were an almost inevitable result of promises made during the progress of hostilities.

For both in the Treaty of Easton in 1758 with the Ohio Valley Indians, a treaty ratified by the Crown, and in the asseverations of such military leaders as Colonel Bouquet, these Indians were assured that they would be secure in their trans-Appalachian lands as a reward for deserting their allies, the French. As a sign of good faith, the lands lying within the bounds of Pennsylvania to the west of the mountains, purchased by the Proprietors from the Six Nations in 1754, were solemnly released. Thus committed in honor in the course of the war, what could the Cabinet Council at its termination do other than it finally did in the Proclamation of 1763? But this step not only was in opposition to the interests of such groups of land speculators as, for example, the Patrick Henry group in Virginia and the Richard Henderson group in North Carolina, both of whom boldly ignored the Proclamation in negotiating with the Cherokee Indians for land grants, but also led to open defiance of this imperial regulation by frontiersmen who, moving beyond the mountains by the thousands, proceeded to settle within the Indian reserve—some on lands previously occupied before the beginning of the late war or before the great Indian revolt in 1763, and others on new lands.

The Proclamation line of 1763 might have become an issue, indeed a most formidable one, between the government of Great Britain and the colonials, had not the former acquiesced in the inevitable and con-firmed certain Indian treaties that provided for the transfer of much of the land which had been the particular object of quest on the part of speculators and of those moving westward from the settled areas to establish new homes. Such were the treaties of Hard Labor, Fort Stan-wix, Lochaber, and the modification of the last-named by the Donelson agreement with the Cherokees in 1771. Nor did the regulation of the trans-Appalachian Indian trade create serious colonial irritation, especially in view of the failure of the government to implement the elaborate Board of Trade plan drawn up in 1764. The same, however, cannot be said of the program put forward by the ministry and accepted by Parliament for securing the means to maintain order and provide protection for this vast area and the new acquisitions to the north and south of it.

Theoretically, it would have been possible for the government of Great Britain to have dropped onto the lap of the old continental colonies the entire responsibility for maintaining garrisons at various strategic points in North America—in Canada, about the Great Lakes, in the Ohio and Mississippi valleys, and in East and West Florida. In spite, however, of assertions made by some prominent colonials, such as Franklin, in 1765 and 1766, that the colonies would be able and were willing to take up the burden of providing for the defense of America, this, under the circumstances, was utterly chimerical, involving, as it would have, not only a vast expenditure of funds but highly complicated inter-colonial arrangements, even in the face of the most serious inter-colonial rivalry such as that between Pennsylvania and Virginia respecting the control of the upper Ohio Valley. The very proportions of the task were an insuperable obstacle to leaving it to the colonies; and the colonies, moreover, would have been faced by another impediment almost as difficult to surmount—the utter aversion of Americans of the eighteenth century, by and large, to the dull routine of garrison duty. This was emphasized by the Massachusetts Bay Assembly in 1755 in its appeal to the government of Great Britain after Braddock's defeat to send regulars to man the frontier forts of that province; the dispatches of Colonel George Washington in 1756 and in 1757 respecting the shameful desertion of militiamen, ordered to hold the chain of posts on the western frontier of Virginia in order to check the frightful French and Indian raids, support this position, as does the testimony in 1757 of Governor Lyttelton of South Carolina, who made clear that the inhabitants of that colony were not at all adapted to this type of work. The post-war task of garrison duty was clearly one to be assumed by regulars held to their duty under firm discipline and capable of being shifted from one strategic point to another as circumstances might require. Further, to be effective, any plan for the defense of the new possessions and the trans-Appalachian region demanded unity of command, something the colonies could not provide. Manifestly this could be done only through the instrumentalities of the mother country.

The British ministry, thus confronted with the problem of guaranteeing the necessary security for the extended empire in North America, which it was estimated would involve the annual expenditure of from three to four hundred thousand pounds for the maintenance of ten thousand troops—according to various estimates made by General Amherst and others in 1764 and to be found among the Shelburne Papers—was impelled to raise the question: Should not the colonials be expected to assume some definite part of the cost of this? In view of the fact that it was felt not only that they were in a position to do so but that the stability of these outlying possessions was a matter of greater concern and importance generally to them, by reason of their proximity, than to the people of the mother country three thousand miles away, the answer was in the affirmative. The reason for this is not hard to fathom. The nine years of war had involved Britons in tremendous expenditures. In spite of very heavy taxation during these years, the people were left saddled at the termination of hostilities with a national debt of unprecedented proportions for that day and age of over one hundred and forty million pounds. It was necessary not only to service and to retire this debt, in so far as was possible, but also to meet the ordinary demands of the civil government and to maintain the navy at a point of strength that would offer some assurance that France and Spain would have no desire in the future to plan a war to recover their territorial losses. In addition to all this, there was now the problem of meeting the charges necessary for keeping the new possessions in North America under firm military control for their internal good order and for protection from outside interference.

It may be noted that before the war the British budget had called for average annual expenditures of six and a half million pounds; between the years 1756 and 1766 these expenditures mounted to fourteen and a half million pounds a year on the average and from the latter date to 1775 ranged close to ten million pounds. As a result, the annual per capita tax in Great Britain, from 1763 to 1775, without considering local rates, was many times the average annual per capita tax in even those American colonies that made the greatest contribution to the Great War for the Empire, such as Massachusetts Bay and Connecticut—without reference to those colonies that had done little or nothing in this conflict, and therefore had accumulated little in the way of a war debt, such as Maryland and Georgia. The student of the history of the old British Empire, in fact, should accept with great reserve statements to the contrary—some of them quite irresponsible in nature—made by Americans during the heat of the controversy, with respect to the nature of the public burdens they were obliged to carry in the years pre-ceding the outbreak of the Revolutionary War. In this connection a study of parliamentary reimbursement of colonial war expenses from 1756 to 1763 in its relation to public debts in America between the years 1763 and 1775 is most revealing. As to American public finance, all that space will here permit is to state that there is abundant evidence to indicate that, during the five-year period preceding the outbreak of the Revolutionary War, had the inhabitants of any of the thirteen colonies, which therefore included those of Massachusetts Bay and Virginia, been taxed in one of these years at the average high per capita rate that the British people were taxed from 1760 to 1775, the proceeds of that one year's tax not only would have taken care of the ordinary expenditures of the colony in question for that year but also would have quite liquidated its war debt, so little of which remained in any of the colonies by 1770. Well may John Adams have admitted in 1780 what was equally true in 1770: "America is not used to great taxes, and the people there are not yet disciplined to such enormous taxation as in England."

Assuming, as did the Grenville ministry in 1764, the justice of ex-pecting the Americans to share the cost of policing the new possessions in North America, the simplest and most obvious way, it might appear, to secure this contribution to a common end so important to both

Americans and Britons was to request the colonial governments to make definite grants of funds. This was the requisition or quota system that had been employed in the course of the recent war. But the most obvious objections to it were voiced that same year by Benjamin Franklin, who, incidentally, was to reverse himself the following year in conferring with Grenville as the Pennsylvania London agent. In expressing confidentially his personal, rather than any official, views to his friend Richard Jackson on June 25, 1764 he declared: "Quota's would be difficult to settle at first with Equality, and would, if they could be made equal at first, soon become unequal, and never would be satisfactory." Indeed, experience with this system in practice, as a settled method of guaranteeing even the minimum essential resources for the end in view, had shown its weakness and utter unfairness. If it could not work equitably even in war time, could it be expected to work in peace? It is, therefore, not surprising that this method of securing even a portion of the funds required for North American security should have been rejected in favor of some plan that presented better prospects of a definite American revenue.

The plan of last resort to the ministry was therefore to ask Parliament to act. That Grenville, however, was aware that serious objections might be raised against any direct taxation of the colonials by the government of Great Britain is indicated by the caution with which he approached the solution of the problem of securing from America about a third of the total cost of its defense. The so-called Sugar Act first of all was passed at his request. This provided for import duties on certain West Indian and other products. Colonial import duties imposed by Parliament, at least since 1733, were no innovation. But the anticipated yield of these duties fell far short of the desired one hundred thousand pounds. He therefore, in introducing the bill for the above Act, raised the question of a stamp duty but requested postponement of parliamentary action until the colonial governments had been consulted. The latter were thereupon requested to make any suggestions for ways of raising an American fund that might seem more proper to the people than such a tax. Further, it would appear—at least, according to various London advices published in Franklin and Hall's *Pennsylvania Gazette* —that proposals were seriously considered by the Cabinet Council during the fall of 1764 for extending to the colonies representation in Parliament through the election of members to the House of Commons by various colonial assemblies. However, it is quite clear that by the beginning of 1765 any such proposals, as seem to have been under deliberation by the ministry, had been put aside when Grenville at length had become convinced that representation in Parliament was neither actively sought nor even desired by Americans. For the South Carolina Commons House of Assembly went strongly on record against this idea in September 1764 and was followed by the Virginia House of Burgesses in December. In fact, when in the presence of the London colonial agents the minister had outlined the objections raised by Americans to the idea of such representation, no one of them, including Franklin, was prepared to deny the validity of these objections. That he was not mistaken in the opposition of Americans at large to sending members to Parliament, in spite of the advocacy of this by James Otis, is clear in the resolutions passed both by other colonial assemblies than the ones to which reference has been made and by the Stamp Act Congress in 1765. Indeed, in 1768 the House of Representatives of Massachusetts Bay went so far in its famous Circular Letter framed in opposition to the Townshend duties as to make clear that the people of that colony actually preferred taxation by Parliament without representation to such taxation with representation.

When—in view of the failure of the colonial governments to suggest any practicable, alternate plan for making some contribution to the postwar defensive program in North America—Grenville finally urged in Parliament the passage of an American stamp bill, he acted on an unwarranted assumption. This assumption was—in paraphrasing the minister's remarks to the colonial agents in 1765—that opposition to stamp taxes, for the specific purpose in mind, would disappear in America both in light of the benefits such provision would bring to colonials in general and by reason of the plain justice of the measure itself; and that, in place of opposition, an atmosphere of mutual goodwill would be generated by a growing recognition on the part of Americans that they could trust the benevolence of the mother country to act with fairness to all within the empire. Instead, with the news of the passage of the act, cries of British tyranny and impending slavery soon resounded throughout the entire eastern Atlantic American seaboard. What would have been the fate of the empire had Grenville remained in office to attempt to enforce the act, no one can say. But as members of the opposition to the Rockingham ministry, he and his brother, Earl Temple, raised their voices—one as a commoner, the other as a peer—in warning that the American colonies would inevitably be lost to the empire should Parliament be led to repeal the act in the face of colonial resistance and the pressure of British merchants. Had Parliament determined, in spite of violence and threats of violence, to enforce the act, it might have meant open rebellion and civil war, ten years before it actually occurred. Instead, this body decided to yield and, in spite of the passing of the so-called Declaratory Act setting forth its fundamental powers to legislate on all matters relating to the empire, suffered a loss of prestige in the New World that was never to be regained.

But the Stamp Act was not the sole object of attack by colonials. To many of them not only the Sugar Act of 1764 but the whole English prewar trade and navigation system was equally, if not actually more, obnoxious. Indeed, the unusual energy displayed by the navy and the customs officials, spurred into action by Pitt during the latter years of the war—bringing with it the condemnation in courts of vice-admiralty of many American vessels whose owners were guilty of serious trade violations, if not greater cimes—generated a degree of antagonism against the whole body of late seventeenth- and early eighteenth-century restrictions on commercial intercourse such as never had previously existed. It is not without significance that the greatest acts of terrorism and destruction during the great riot of August 1765 in Boston were directed not against the Massachusetts Bay stamp distributor but against those officials responsible for encouraging and supporting the enforcement, during the late war, of the various trade acts passed long before its beginning in 1754. The hatred also of the Rhode Island merchants, as a group, against the restrictions of the navigation system as well as against the Sugar Act of 1764, remained constant. Moreover, in December 1766 most of the New York merchants, over two hundred in number, showed their repugnance to the way that this system was functioning by a strongly worded petition to the House of Commons in which they enumerated an impressive list of grievances that they asked to be redressed. Even Chatham, the great friend of America, regarded their petition "highly improper: in point of time most absurd, in the extent of their pretensions, most excessive; and in the reasoning, most grossly fallacious and offensive." In fact, all the leading men in Great Britain supported the system of trade restrictions.

Nevertheless, the determination of the government—in view especially of the great financial burdens that the late war had placed upon the mother country—to enforce it now much more effectively than had been done before 1754, and to that end in 1767 to pass appropriate legislation in order to secure funds from the colonies by way of import duties so that public officials in America might be held to greater accountability when paid their salaries by the Crown, could have only one result: the combined resistance of those, on the one hand, opposed to any type of taxation that Parliament might apply to America and to those, on the other, desiring to free the colonies of hampering trade restrictions.

The suggestion on the part of the Continental Congress in 1774 that Americans would uphold the British navigation system, if exempted from parliamentary taxation, while a shrewd gesture to win support in England, had really, it would seem, no other significance. For it is utterly inconceivable that the Congress itself, or the individual colonial governments, could have set up machinery capable of preventing violations of the system at will on the part of those whose financial interests were adversely affected by its operation. Moreover, it is obvious that, by the time the news had reached America that Lord North's ministry had secured the passage of the coercive acts—for the most part directed against Massachusetts Bay for the defiant destruction of the East India Company's tea—leading colonials, among them Franklin, had arrived at the conclusion that Parliament possessed powers so very limited with respect to the empire that without the consent of the local assemblies it could pass neither constitutional nor fiscal legislation that affected Americans and the framework of their governments. It is equally obvious that this represented a most revolutionary position when contrasted with that held by Franklin and the other delegates to the Albany Congress twenty years earlier. For it was in 1754 that the famous Plan of Union was drawn up there and approved by the Congress—a plan based upon the view that Parliament, and not the Crown, had supreme authority within the empire, an authority that alone was adequate in view of framers of the Plan to bring about fundamental changes in the constitutions of the colonies in order legally to clothe the proposed union government with adequate fiscal as well as other powers.

In accounting for the radical change in attitude of many leading colonials between the years 1754 and 1774 respecting the nature of the constitution of the empire, surely among the factors that must be weighed was the truly overwhelming victory achieved in the Great War for the Empire. This victory not only freed colonials for the first time in the history of the English-speaking people in the New World from dread of the French, their Indian allies, and the Spaniards, but, what is of equal significance, opened up to them the prospect, if given freedom of action, of a vast growth of power and wealth with an amazing westward expansion. Indeed, it is abundantly clear that a continued subordination of the colonies to the government of Great Britain was no longer considered an asset in the eyes of many Americans by 1774, as it had been so judged by them to be in 1754, but rather an onerous liability. What, pray tell, had the debt-ridden mother country to offer in 1774 to the now geographically secure, politically mature, prosperous, dynamic, and self-reliant offspring along the Atlantic seaboard, except the dubious opportunity of accepting new, as well as retaining old, burdens? And these burdens would have to be borne in order to lighten somewhat the great financial load that the taxpayers of Great Britain were forced to carry by reason of obligations the nation had assumed both in the course of the late war and at its termination. If many Americans thought they had a perfect right to profit personally by trading with the enemy in time of war, how much more deeply must they have resented in time of peace the serious efforts made by the home government to enforce the elaborate restrictions on commercial intercourse? Again, if, even after the defeat of Colonel Washington at Great Meadows in 1754, colonials such as Franklin were opposed to paying any tax levied by Parliament for establishing a fund for the defense of North America, how much more must they have been inclined to oppose such taxation to that end with the passing in 1763 of the great international crisis?

At this point the question must be frankly faced: If France had won the war decisively and thereby consolidated her position and perfected her claims in Nova Scotia, as well as to the southward of the St. Lawrence, in the Great Lakes region, and in the Ohio and Mississippi valleys, is it at all likely that colonials would have made so fundamental a constitutional issue of the extension to them of the principle of the British stamp tax? Would they have resisted such a tax had Parliament imposed it in order to provide on an equitable basis the maximum resources for guaranteeing their safety, at a time when they were faced on their highly restricted borders by a militant, victorious enemy having at its command thousands of ferocious redskins? Again, accepting the fact of Britain's victory, is it not reasonable to believe that, had Great Britain at the close of the triumphant war left Canada to France and carefully limited her territorial demands in North America to those comparatively modest objectives that she had in mind at its beginning, there would have been no very powerful movement within the foreseeable future toward complete colonial autonomy—not to mention American independence? Would not Americans have continued to feel the need as in the past to rely for their safety and welfare upon British sea power and British land power, as well as upon British resources generally? In other words, was Governor Thomas Hutchinson of Massachusetts Bay far mistaken when, in analyzing the American situation late in 1773, he affirmed in writing to the Earl of Dartmouth:

> Before the peace [of 1763] I thought nothing so much to be desired as the cession of Canada. I am now convinced that if it had remained to the French none of the spirit of opposition to the Mother Country would have yet appeared & I think the effects of it [that is, the cession of Canada] worse than all we had to fear from the French or Indians.

In conclusion, it may be said that it would be idle to deny that most colonials in the eighteenth century at one time or another felt strongly the desire for freedom of action in a wider variety of ways than was legally permitted before 1754. Indeed, one can readily uncover these strong impulses even in the early part of the seventeenth century. Yet Americans were, by and large, realists, as were the British, and under the functioning of the imperial system from, let us say, 1650 to 1750 great mutual advantages were enjoyed, with a fair division, taking everything into consideration, of the financial burdens necessary to support the system. However, the mounting Anglo-French rivalry in North America from 1750 onward, the outbreak of hostilities in 1754, and the subsequent nine years of fighting destroyed the old equilibrium, leaving the colonials after 1760 in a highly favored position in comparison with the taxpayers of Great Britain. Attempts on the part of the Crown and Parliament to restore by statute the old balance led directly to the American constitutional crisis, out of which came the Revolutionary War and the establishment of American independence. Such, ironically, was the aftermath of the Great War for the Empire, a war that Britons believed, as the Earl of Shelburne affirmed in 1762 in Parliament, was begun for the "security of the British colonies in N. America. . . ."

13

The American Revolution: Revisions in Need of Revising
EDMUND S. MORGAN

The American Revolution is central to our national ideal. The image which the nation has of itself at once defines and is defined by the way it came into existence. But the image is a changing one. The birth of the American nation is variously seen, and what is seen is in no small measure a reflection of the problems and prepossessions of the present. One age has construed the Revolution as a struggle for liberty, another as a defense of property, and still a third as a somewhat regrettable explosion brought on by extremists on both sides. The concerns of the present have been turning the kaleidoscope of our revolutionary past.

It is this matter of changing interpretations of the American Revolution which concerns Professor Edmund Sears Morgan of Yale University. Professor Morgan, who has written several admirable books on different aspects of Puritanism in colonial America, established himself as an authority

SOURCE: *The William and Mary Quarterly,* Third Series, XIV (January, 1957), 3–15. Reprinted by permission of the author and publisher.

on the revolutionary period in The Stamp Act Crisis: Prologue to Revolution *(1953), which he wrote in collaboration with his wife, Helen M. Morgan. He has canvassed the whole period in* The Birth of the Republic *(1956), a volume that is excellent for its brevity, its wit, its clarity, and its viewpoint. In it Morgan addresses himself squarely to the basic questions about the Revolution: What was its nature? What were its causes? To what extent was it justified?*

His answer has in effect marked the return of the Whig or patriotic approach to American historical writing. This approach found its greatest expression in the writings of George Bancroft during the middle and latter decades of the nineteenth century. For the last half-century or more historians have put the American cause to the most severe questioning, abjuring patriotism as the last refuge of the scholar. With Morgan, however, the Revolution has again become a struggle for freedom from British tyranny, a search for principles, indeed, a "people's war." The Americans of that generation he tends to see as uniformly patriotic, and the motives impelling them as uniformly lofty.

How does Morgan's interpretation reflect the problems and prepossessions of our own times? Perhaps a clue may be found in the fact that the ultimate concern of our nation today is that ideal of freedom which it is seeking to retain and defend in a world increasingly unfree. The liberal ideal is central to our institutions, and an age in which its survival is being challenged is also one which will contemplate and applaud its early struggles.

In the essay below, Professor Morgan challenges each of the major interpretations of the American Revolution that have been current during the past half-century. How valid, he asks, are the views of those who found that the First British Empire was run fairly and benevolently? How accurate is the social and economic interpretation, in the light of which the Fathers were founding fortunes rather than liberty? And what is to be said of Sir Lewis B. Namier's approach, which sees English politics in local and personal terms and has the effect of damning the Whigs and faintly praising George III? All these interpretations, insists Professor Morgan, have failed to answer basic questions about the Revolution. More than that, they raise difficult questions for each other.

But Professor Morgan raises questions for himself no less than for others. Is he being fair, for example, to say that historians who saw the old colonial system as essentially non-oppressive of the Americans before 1763 would necessarily condone its operation after that date? Is Morgan fair in denying that different social and economic interests were factors in causing different American attitudes toward the British program and toward each other? To what extent is he correct in suggesting that Americans were united in principle and action? To what extent is he correct in suggesting that unless we explain the minds of the great leaders like Washington, Adams, Jefferson, and Franklin, we explain nothing of the nature and causes of the Revolution?

Is it valid to identify all of the Revolution with them? Is it fair to presume that, if any one of the interpretations which Morgan questions does not entirely explain the Revolution, then it does not do so at least in part? May not one believe that Professor Morgan's views and those he criticizes are not mutually exclusive, but rather supplementary in explaining a highly complex series of developments?

The interpretation we settle on is a matter of great importance, for in our view of the nature and causes of the American Revolution we are defining something more than the birth of a nation. We are defining as well what has become of the nation since its birth and what it is today.

During the past fifty years three ideas have inspired research into the history of the eighteenth century in America and England. The earliest of these to appear, and the most fruitful of results, was the idea that American colonial history must be seen in the setting of the British Empire as a whole. We are all familiar today with the new insights and new discoveries that have grown out of this view: the great works of George Louis Beer and Charles McLean Andrews, the monumental synthesis of Professor Lawrence Gipson, which now approaches its culmination. This has been a great idea, and it has done more than any other to shape our understanding of the colonial past.

A second idea, which has affected in one way or another most of us who study colonial history, is that the social and economic divisions of a people will profoundly influence the course of their history. This idea received early application to American history in Carl Becker's study of New York politics on the eve of the Revolution and in Charles Beard's *An Economic Interpretation of the Constitution.* New York politics before the Revolution, Becker said, revolved around two questions, equally important, the question of home rule and that of who should rule at home.[1] Subsequent historians have found in Becker's aphorism a good description of the Revolutionary period as a whole. The conflict between different social groups now looms as large in our histories of the Revolution as the struggle against England. Like all seminal ideas, this one has sometimes been used as a substitute for research instead of a stimulus to it. Historians have been so convinced of the importance of social and economic divisions that they have uttered the wildest kind of nonsense, for example, about the social and economic basis of a religious movement like the Great Awakening of the 1740's. The view has nevertheless been productive of important new insights and new information.

The third idea, although it has had scarcely any effect as yet on the study of American history, has furnished the principal impetus to

---

[1] Carl Becker, *The History of Political Parties in the Province of New York, 1760–1776* (Madison, Wis., 1909), p. 22.

recent research in British history. It is a more complex idea, growing out of the discoveries of Sir Lewis Namier. The effect of these discoveries has been to attach a new importance to local as opposed to national forces. "It has been the greatest of Sir Lewis Namier's achievements," says Richard Pares, "to exhibit the personal and local nature of political issues and political power at this time."[2] Namier and his disciples, of whom Pares is the most notable, have destroyed the traditional picture of British politics in the age of the American Revolution. During this period, they tell us, there were no political parties in the modern sense, nor were there any political factions or associations with any principle or belief beyond that of serving selfish or local interests. The Rockingham Whigs, who made such a display of their opposition to the repressive measures against the colonies, were no different from the other squabbling factions except in their hypocritical pretense of standing for broader principles.   And George III owed his control over Parliament not to bribery and corruption but simply to his constitutional position in the government and to his skill as a politician during a time when the House of Commons lacked effective leaders of its own.

Each of these three ideas, the imperial, the social or economic, and the Namierist, has had a somewhat similar effect on our understanding of the American Revolution. That effect has been to discredit, in different ways, the old Whig interpretation. The imperial historians have examined the running of the empire before the Revolution and pronounced it fair. The Navigation Acts, they have shown, were no cause for complaint. The Board of Trade did as good a job as could be expected. The Admiralty Courts were a useful means of maintaining fair play and fair trade on the high seas. Indeed, Professor Gipson tells us, the old colonial system "may not unfairly be compared to modern systems of state interference with the liberty of the subject in matters involving industry and trade, accepting the differences involved in the nature of the regulations respectively.   In each case, individuals or groups within the state are forbidden to follow out lines of action that, while highly beneficial to those locally or personally concerned, are considered inimical to the larger national objectives."[3] In the light of such imperial benevolence and farsightedness, the unwillingness of the Americans to pay the trifling contribution demanded of them in the sixties and seventies becomes small and mean, and the resounding rhetoric of a Henry or an Otis or an Adams turns into the bombast of a demagogue.

---

[2] Richard Pares, *King George III and the Politicians* (Oxford, 1953), p. 2.

[3] Lawrence H. Gipson, *The British Empire before the American Revolution,* III (Caldwell, Idaho, 1936), 287.

The social and economic interpretation does nothing to redeem the fallen Revolutionary patriots but rather shows them up as hypocrites pursuing selfish interests while they mouth platitudes about democracy and freedom. Their objections to parliamentary taxation are reduced to mere tax evasion, with the arguments shifting as the character of the taxes shifted. Their insistence on freedom and equality is shown to be insincere, because in setting up their own governments they failed to establish universal suffrage or proportional representation. They were, it would appear, eager to keep one foot on the lower classes while they kicked the British with the other.

Namier and his followers have little to say about the American revolutionists but devote themselves to scolding the English Whigs. Though the Namierists generally achieve a sophisticated objectivity with regard to persons and parties, they sometimes seem fond of beating the Whigs in order—one suspects—to displease the Whig historians. For example, the unflattering portrait of Charles James Fox that emerges from Richard Pares's brilliant study must surely be read in part as a rebuke to Sir George Otto Trevelyan, or rather to those who have accepted Trevelyan's estimate of Fox. This deflation of Fox and Burke and the other Rockingham Whigs, while accomplished with scarcely a glance in the direction of the colonies, nevertheless deprives the American revolutionists of a group of allies whose high-minded sympathy had been relied upon by earlier historians to help demonstrate the justice of the American cause.

By the same token the righteousness of the Americans is somewhat diminished through the loss of the principal villain in the contest. George III is no longer the foe of liberty, seeking to subvert the British constitution, but an earnest and responsible monarch, doing his job to the best of his abilities. And those abilities, we are told, while not of the highest order, were not small either. George, in fact, becomes a sympathetic figure, and one can scarcely escape the feeling that the Americans were rather beastly to have made things so hard for him.

While the imperial, the economic, and the Namierist approaches have thus contributed in different ways to diminish the prestige of the American Revolution and its promoters, it is a curious fact that none of the ideas has produced any full-scale examination of the Revolution itself or of how it came about. The imperial historians have hitherto been occupied primarily in dissecting the workings of the empire as it existed before the Revolutionary troubles. Although their works have necessarily squinted at the Revolution in every sentence, the only direct confrontations have been brief and inconclusive.

The social and economic interpretation has been applied more extensively to different aspects of the Revolution, but surprisingly enough we still know very little about what the social and economic divisions actually were in most of the colonies and states at the time of the Revolution. Professor Schlesinger's analysis of the role of the merchant class[4] remains a fixed point of knowledge at the opening of the period, and Charles Beard's *Economic Interpretation of the Constitution* is a somewhat shakier foundation at the close of it, reinforced, however, by the work of Merrill Jensen.[5] Historians have bridged the gap between these two points with more assurance than information. There are, it is true, several illuminating studies of local divisions but not enough to warrant any firm conclusions about the role of economic and social forces in the Revolution as a whole. After thirty years we are only a little closer to the materials needed for such conclusions than J. Franklin Jameson was in 1926.

The Namierist approach, as already indicated, has been confined to events in England rather than America. Though the effect of such investigations has been to exonerate George III and discredit the English Whigs, the Revolution has not been a primary issue for Namier or Pares. One student of Professor Namier's, Eric Robson, made a preliminary excursion into the subject but confined his discussion primarily to military history.[6] And while Professor Charles Ritcheson has treated the place of the Revolution in British politics,[7] the implications of Namier's discoveries for developments on this side of the water remain unexplored.

Thus while the new ideas and new discoveries have altered our attitudes toward the American Revolution, they have done so for the most part indirectly, almost surreptitiously, without coming up against the Revolution itself. There is need for intensive and direct examination of all phases of the Revolution in the light of each of these ideas, and we may expect that in the next few years such examinations will be made. Professor Gipson has already begun. I should like to suggest, however, that we need not only to examine the Revolution in the light of the ideas but also to re-examine the ideas in the light of the Revolution; and in doing so we need also to examine them in relation to each other.

The Revolution is one of those brute facts which historians must account for, and it is a fact of central importance for ascertaining the

---

[4] Arthur M. Schlesinger, *The Colonial Merchants and the American Revolution* (New York, 1918).

[5] Merrill Jensen, *The Articles of Confederation* (Madison, Wis., 1940); *The New Nation* (New York, 1950).

[6] Eric Robson, *The American Revolution in its Political and Military Aspects* (London, 1955).

[7] Charles Ritcheson, *British Politics and the American Revolution* (Norman, Okla., 1954).

meaning and limits of the three ideas we are discussing. I believe that each of the three needs revisions and will take them up in order.

While everyone will acknowledge the importance of the imperial idea and of the discoveries made under its influence, the net effect of that idea has been to emphasize the justice and beneficence of the British imperial system as it existed before the Revolution. May we not therefore pose a question to the imperial historians: if the empire was as fairly administered as you show it to have been, how could the Revolution have happened at all? In their preliminary skirmishes with this problem, imperial historians have frequently implied that the American revolutionists were moved, in part at least, by narrow or selfish views and stirred up by evil-minded agitators. But if historians are to sustain such a view in any full-scale consideration of the Revolution, they face a very difficult task: they must explain men like George Washington, John Adams, Thomas Jefferson, and Benjamin Franklin as agitators or as the dupes of agitators, or as narrow-minded men without the vision to see beyond provincial borders. After all due allowance is made for patriotic myopia, this still seems to me to be an impossible undertaking. Anyone who studies the Revolution can scarcely emerge without some degree of admiration for the breadth of vision that moved these men. In twenty-five years they created a new nation and endowed it with a government that still survives and now has the longest continuous history of any government in existence outside of England. The idea that they were narrow-minded simply will not wash. Nor is it possible to see them as the dupes of their intellectual inferiors. Samuel Adams, Patrick Henry, and James Otis may perhaps be cast as demagogues without seeming out of place, but not the giants of the period. If the British government could not run the empire without bringing on evils that appeared insufferable to men like Washington, Jefferson, John Adams, and Franklin, then the burden of proof would seem to be on those who maintain that it was fit to run an empire.

When the imperial historians are ready to attempt the proof, they must face a second task: they must explain away the character which the Namierist historians have given to the British statesmen of the period. The Namierists, as already indicated, have emphasized the parochial character of English politics in this period. They have cut the Whigs down to size, but they have cut down everyone else on the British political scene likewise. If Parliament was dominated by local interests, what becomes of imperial beneficence and farsightedness?

The whole effect of the Namierist discoveries, so far as the colonies are concerned, must be to show that British statesmen in the 1760's and 1770's, whether in Parliament or in the Privy Council, were too dominated by local interests to be able to run an empire. There was no institution, no party, no organization through which imperial interests, as opposed to strictly British interests, could find adequate expression. In fact the Namierist view and the view of the imperial historians are directly at odds here: though neither group seems as yet to be aware of the conflict, they cannot both be wholly right, and the coming of the Revolution would seem to confirm the Namierist view and to cast doubt on the imperialist one. The achievements of the revolutionists and the failures of the British statesmen suggest in the strongest possible terms that it was the Americans who saw things in the large and the British who wore the blinders. If this is so, may it not be that the case for the beneficence and justice of the British Empire before the Revolution has been overstated?

In response to our argument *ad hominem* the imperialists may summon the aid of the economic interpretation to show that the Americans, however high-toned their arguments, were really moved by economic considerations of the basest kind. We may, however, call these considerations basic rather than base and offer our previous character witnesses against the economists too. There is no time to plead to every indictment here, but one may perhaps answer briefly the strongest yet offered, that of Charles Beard, and then suggest how the economic interpretation needs revision. Though Beard expressly disclaimed that his economic interpretation was the whole story, he gave not merely a one-sided view but a false one. All the evidence that Beard extracted from the records of the Constitutional Convention points toward the sordid conclusion that the delegates who held public securities also held undemocratic political views, motivated consciously or unconsciously by the desire to protect their investments. Beard consistently overlooked contradictory evidence. I will cite only two examples.

The first is his treatment of Roger Sherman, the delegate to the Constitutional Convention from Connecticut. Sherman, he notes, had risen from poverty to affluence and held nearly eight thousand dollars worth of public securities. Sherman's corresponding political philosophy he represents by the following statement: "Roger Sherman believed in reducing the popular influence in the new government to the minimum. When it was proposed that the members of the first branch of the national legislature should be elected, Sherman said that he was 'opposed to the election by the people, insisting that it ought to be by the state legislatures. The people, he said, immediately should have as little to do as may be about the government. They want information and are constantly liable to be misled.' "[8]

---

[8] Charles Beard, *An Economic Interpretation of the Constitution of the United States* (New York, 1913), pp. 213–214.

The quotation certainly supports Beard's view, but Beard failed to indicate what Sherman said at other times in the convention. On June 4, four days after the speech Beard quotes, Sherman was against giving the President a veto power, because he "was against enabling any one man to stop the will of the whole. No one man could be found so far above all the rest in wisdom." On June 21 he argued again for election of the House of Representatives by the state legislatures, but after election by the people had been decided upon, spoke for annual elections as against triennial, because "He thought the representatives ought to return home and mix with the people." On August 14 he was in favor of substantial pay for congressmen, because otherwise "men ever so fit could not serve unless they were at the same time rich."[9] Whatever explanation may be offered for these views, they suggest a much broader confidence in the people than might be inferred from the single remark by which Beard characterized the man.

It cannot be said that the statements which Beard neglected are concerned with an aspect of Sherman's views not relevant to the problem Beard was examining: they are certainly as relevant as the statement he did quote. His treatment of Pierce Butler, the delegate from South Carolina, is similar. Beard notes that Butler held public securities and that he argued for apportionment of representation according to wealth.[10] He neglects to mention that Butler, in spite of his security holdings, opposed full payments of the public debt, "lest it should compel payment as well to the Blood-suckers who had speculated on the distresses of others, as to those who had fought and bled for their country."[11] The statement is relevant, but directly opposed, to Beard's thesis.

It requires only a reading of the Convention debates to see that Beard's study needs revision.[12] But the trouble with the economic interpretation, as currently applied to the whole Revolutionary period, goes deeper. The trouble lies in the assumption that a conflict between property rights and human rights has been the persistent theme of American history from the beginning. It was undoubtedly the great theme of Beard's day, and Beard was on the side of human rights, where decent men belong in such a conflict. From the vantage point of

---

[9] *Records of the Federal Convention of 1787,* ed. Max Farrand (New Haven, 1911–37), I, 99, 362; II, 291.

[10] Beard, *Economic Interpretation,* pp. 81–82, 192.

[11] Farrand, *Records,* II, 392.

[12] Robert E. Brown's *Charles Beard and the Constitution* (Princeton, 1956) appeared too late to be of use in preparation of this paper, but the reader will find in it abundant additional evidence of deficiencies in Beard's use of the Convention records.

twentieth-century Progressivism, he lined up the members of the Constitutional Convention, found their pockets stuffed with public securities, and concluded that they were on the wrong side.

It was a daring piece of work, and it fired the imagination of Beard's fellow progressives.[13]   Vernon L. Parrington has recorded how it "struck home like a submarine torpedo—the discovery that the drift toward plutocracy was not a drift away from the spirit of the Constitution, but an inevitable unfolding from its premises." As a result of Beard's work, Parrington was able to see that "From the beginning . . . democracy and property had been at bitter odds."[14]

Parrington went on to construct his own image of American history in these terms, and he too had a powerful influence. Together he and Beard virtually captured the American past for Progressivism, a performance all the more remarkable when we consider that they did not enlist the revered founding fathers of the Constitution on their side.

It is time, however, that we had another look at the conflict between human rights and property rights; and the Revolutionary period is a good place to begin, for however strong the conflict may later have become, it was not a dominant one then. Anyone who studies the Revolution must notice at once the attachment of all articulate Americans to property. "Liberty and Property" was their cry, not "Liberty and Democracy." In the face of the modern dissociation of property from liberty, historians have often felt that this concern of the revolutionists for property was a rather shabby thing, and that the constitutional principles so much talked of, before 1776 as well as afterward, were invented to hide it under a more attractive cloak. But the Americans were actually quite shameless about their concern for property and made no effort to hide it, because it did not seem at all shabby to them. The colonial protests against taxation frankly and openly, indeed passionately, affirm the sanctity of property. And the passion is not the simple and unlovely passion of greed. For eighteenth-century Americans, property and liberty were one and inseparable, because property was the only foundation yet conceived for security of life and liberty: without security for his property, it was thought, no man could live or be free except at the mercy of another.

The revolutionists' coupling of property with life and liberty was not an attempt to lend respectability to property rights, nor was it an attempt to enlist the masses in a struggle for the special privileges of a small wealthy class. Property in eighteenth-century America was not

---

[13] See Douglass Adair, "The Tenth Federalist Revisited," *William and Mary Quarterly*, 3d Ser., VIII (1951), 48–67; Richard Hofstadter, "Beard and the Constitution: The History of an Idea," *American Quarterly*, II (1950), 195–213.

[14] Vernon L. Parrington, *Main Currents in American Thought* (New York, 1927–30), III, 410.

associated with special privilege, as it came to be for later generations. Land was widely owned. A recent investigation has demonstrated that in Massachusetts, a key state in the Revolution, nearly every adult male could meet the property qualifications for the franchise.[15] We hear much from modern historians about the propertyless masses of the Revolutionary period, but it is altogether improbable that the mass of Americans were without property.

The Americans fought England because Parliament threatened the security of property. They established state constitutions with property qualifications for voting and officeholding in order to protect the security of property. And when the state governments seemed inadequate to the task, they set up the Federal government for the same purpose. The economic motive was present in all these actions, but it was present as the friend of universal liberty. Devotion to security of property was not the attitude of a privileged few but the fundamental principle of the many, inseparable from everything that went by the name of freedom and adhered to the more fervently precisely because it did affect most people so intimately.

What we have done in our social and economic interpretations of the Revolution is to project into eighteenth-century America a situation which existed in the nineteenth and early twentieth centuries, when property and the means of production became concentrated in the hands of a few, when liberty if it was to exist at all had to get along not only without the aid of property but in opposition to it. We seem now to be approaching a period when property, in another form, may again be widely distributed and may again become the friend rather than the enemy of liberty. Whether such is the case or not, as historians we should stop projecting into the eighteenth century the particular economic and social antagonisms that we have found in later generations. We may still believe that the American Revolution was in part a contest about who should rule at home, but we should beware of assuming that people took sides in that contest according to whether or not they owned property. And we should totally abandon the assumption that those who showed the greatest concern for property rights were not devoted to human rights.

The challenge of the Revolution to the Namier school of historians is less direct and less crucial, but it does pose one or two questions which these historians seem not to have confronted. The first is whether the new judgment of George III has not raised that monarch's reputation a little too high. Granted that George was neither the fool nor the knave he has hitherto been thought, granted that he was moved

---

[15] Robert E. Brown, *Middle-Class Democracy and the Revolution in Massachusetts, 1691–1780* (Ithaca, N.Y., 1955).

by a desire to maintain parliamentary supremacy rather than regal supremacy, it is nevertheless true that under his leadership England lost an important, if not the most important, part of her empire. The loss was not inevitable. All the objectives of the Americans before 1776 could have been attained within the empire, and would have cost the mother country little or nothing. George undoubtedly received a good deal of assistance from other politicians in losing the colonies, but the contention of the Namierists has been that the King still held a position of central responsibility in the British government in the 1760's and 1770's, a responsibility which they have shown that he shouldered and carried. If he was responsible then he must be held responsible. He must bear most of the praise or blame for the series of measures that alienated and lost the colonies, and it is hard to see how there can be much praise.

The other question that the Revolution poses for the Namierists may be more fundamental. Virtually no one in British politics, they argue, had any political principles that reached beyond local or factional interests. The argument, though convincingly presented, presumes a consistent hypocrisy or delusion on the part of the Whig opposition. It may be that the Whigs were hypocritical in their attack on George III and their support of the Americans. But if so why were they hypocritical in just the way they were? Why did they appeal to principles of government that later won acceptance? Can we be sure that it was only in order to attack their opponents? Can we be sure they were on the right side for the wrong reasons? I do not pretend to know the answers to these questions, but I am not quite comfortable about judgments of history in which people are condemned for being prematurely antimonarchical.

What I would suggest in conclusion is that the Whig interpretation of the American Revolution may not be as dead as some historians would have us believe, that George Bancroft may not have been so far from the mark as we have often assumed. Is it not time to ask again a few of the old questions that he was trying to answer? Let us grant that local interests were the keynote of British politics; we must still ask: how did the Americans, living on the edge of empire, develop the breadth of vision and the attachment to principle which they displayed in that remarkable period from 1763 to 1789? While English politics remained parochial and the empire was dissolving for lack of vision, how did the Americans generate the forces that carried them into a new nationality and a new human liberty?

The answer, I think, may lie in a comparatively neglected field of American scholarship. During the past fifty years our investigations of the colonial period have been directed primarily by the imperial idea and the social and economic one. We have seen the colonists as part of the empire or else we have seen them as the pawns of sweeping economic and social forces. What we have neglected is the very thing that the English have been pursuing in the study of their institutions. We have neglected, comparatively speaking at least, the study of local institutions, and it is in such a study that we may perhaps discover the answer to the fundamental question that moved Bancroft, the question of how a great nation with great principles of freedom was forged from thirteen quarrelsome colonies. What kind of institutions produced a Jefferson, a Madison, a Washington, a John Adams? Not imperial institutions certainly. The imperial machinery had no place for Americans except in performing local services. No American ever sat on the Board of Trade or the Privy Council. Few Americans ever came in contact with imperial officers. It was in local American institutions that these men gained their political experience.

Two generations ago Herbert Baxter Adams thought he had the clue to the question of where American liberty began, and he put a host of graduate students to work studying the local institutions of the colonies. As we all know, they did not find precisely what Adams was looking for, but they produced a prodigious number of studies, which are still the principal source of historical information about many colonial institutions. Some have been superseded by more recent scholarship, but we need more new studies of this kind, which will take advantage of what we have learned since Adams's time about the imperial setting and about social and economic forces.

We need to know how the individual's picture of society was formed. We need to study the social groupings in every colony: towns, plantations, counties, churches, schools, clubs, and other groups which occupied the social horizons of the individual colonist. We need to study political parties and factions in every colony. We need to study the way government worked at the local level. We need to study the county courts and the justices of the peace. We need to study the distribution of land and other forms of wealth from decade to decade and from place to place. We need to know so elementary a thing as the history of representation and the history of taxation in every colony. We have always known that the Revolution had something to do with the phrase, "no taxation without representation," and yet, after two generations of modern scholarship, how many scholars have studied the history of taxation in the colonies? Who really knows anything about the history of representation?

Without abandoning what we have gained from the imperial idea and from economic interpretations, we must dissect the local institutions which produced the American Revolution, the institutions from which were distilled the ideas that enabled men of that age to stand as the architects of modern liberty. The task has not been wholly neglected. A number of scholars have been quietly working at it. I will not attempt to name them here, but their discoveries are sufficient to show that this is the direction which scholarship in colonial history should now take and that the rewards will not be small.

14

The Diplomats and the Mythmakers
RICHARD B. MORRIS

American independence has long had the appearance not only of a truth self-evident, but also of a fact inevitable. We are so much concerned with what the American Revolution meant that we little consider that our War of Independence might have failed or that we might not have achieved the conditions of peace, and therefore the conditions of the nation's existence, that we actually did achieve in the Treaty of Paris. The diplomacy of the Revolution, in particular, has not commanded our attention, and one of the reasons may be that the history of a democracy is written in terms of grand movements and the action of the demos, not in terms of particular men and covert acts. The style of democracy requires grand open covenants, openly arrived at. The details, maneuverings, and secrecy of diplomacy would seem to bespeak the style of aristocracy.

No single book has, in recent years, contributed more to our understanding of American diplomacy during the Revolutionary War than Richard B. Morris's The Peacemakers: The Great Powers and American Independence *(1965). For it, Morris received the Bancroft Prize in 1966. He is Gouverneur Morris Professor of History at Columbia University, the author of many notable books on early American history and the history of American government and law, and co-editor (with Henry Steele Commager) of the multi-volume* New American Nation *series. The following essay*

SOURCE: Richard B. Morris, *The American Revolution Reconsidered* (New York: Harper and Row, 1967), pp. 92–125. Copyright © 1967 by Richard B. Morris. Reprinted by permission of the author and the publisher.

is one of a series of public lectures that Professor Morris gave in 1966 at New York University. Addressing himself to the subject of the myths that have enveloped the history of our diplomacy during the Revolutionary War, he undertakes to answer several questions. How have scholars, here and abroad, contributed to the making of these myths? In what ways did material French aid and the Franco-American alliance of 1778 support the American cause? How far was the alliance essential to the winning of American independence? How faithful was France to the alliance, and what in particular were the program and actions of Vergennes? And finally, in achieving the independence of the United States, what were the respective contributions of the four American peace commissioners in Paris, and what was the special contribution of John Jay?

In the following essay, Professor Morris offers us not merely significant instruction but also instruction in significance. He reminds us that myths have their own vitality in national history, that they are indeed their own facts. He demonstrates effectively that what particular individuals do in history is of transcendent importance and that, however subject history is to the sway of great forces and deep tendencies, it turns widely on the decisions of men who stand in key places at critical times. Professor Morris also underscores the influence of diplomacy on the conduct of national affairs, making us aware that a nation's diplomacy is more than a function of its temper; it is also its determinant. He recalls in particular how the American peacemakers of 1782, by an adroitness that surely equaled that of their Old World counterparts, advanced our nation's interest and brought us victory, peace, nationhood, territory, resources, and a wide area for the play of our aspirations. He concludes by noting the relevance of our earlier diplomacy to today's. We would do well to consider whether our recent conduct of foreign affairs has been governed, in Senator Fulbright's phrase, by an arrogance of power. We would also do well to estimate how far the rhetoric of moral absolutism has supplanted the art of flexibility and compromise that was so skillfully practiced by our nation's earliest diplomats, the peacemakers of 1782.

A recent Broadway musical extravaganza reflects the romantic notions many Americans still entertain about the diplomacy of the American Revolution. According to this popular conception, America was so fortunate as to have a shrewd and benevolent sage in France to safeguard and promote her interests, a master diplomat whose democratic garb, severe Quaker black and beaver hat, made him stand out strikingly among the peacocks at Versailles, a man who could exploit flirtation to the advantage of patriotism, who could confound the most devious statesman in direct confrontation, and was able almost single-handedly to persuade La Belle France to come to the rescue of American liberty for purposes largely altruistic.

A roseate hue has always colored our vision of that military marriage of France and America contracted during the War for Independence. For long it was felt that somehow the debt that America owed France remained unpaid. Was not General Pershing reputed to have declared before the tomb of a Revolutionary war hero, "Lafayette, we are here!" Some toiler in historical pastures has unearthed the fact that it was not Pershing but Colonel Charles E. Staunton, a quartermaster officer, who said it, but his words destined for immortality voice the sentiment of a warmhearted and grateful American people.

About their historical relationship Americans and Frenchmen today share mutual disillusionment. To that disillusionment about a shared past much of the credit must go to a charismatic French leader, for *le Général* stands as the best recent exemplar of the truism that in diplomacy "the still small voice of gratitude" is not only small but generally still. Despite the more objective, even acerbic, note that marks exchanges between the First American and the Fifth French Republic, the mythmakers of past generations have done their work so well that the legend of France's disinterested support for the Revolutionary cause has died hard.

One would have expected the sensible views of the diplomats who argued America's cause abroad to prevail, but such expectations fail to discount the depth of anti-British sentiment in America in the generation or two following the American Revolution, and the widespread tendency to regard the enemies of England as the friends of America. Nor should one underestimate the role played by editors in the publication of official documents. This was notably the case in the publication of the diplomatic archives of the American Revolution. Jared Sparks, a member of the intellectual Establishment of his day, president of Harvard College, and confidant of the great and near great, was the first to edit on an extensive scale the diplomatic correspondence of the American Revolution. Sparks set himself up as prosecutor and judge of the actors whose papers he edited and published in garbled versions. Quite rightly did John Quincy Adams, who as a very young man played a small role in the diplomacy of the Revolution abroad, discount the credibility of Sparks' notes by which, he remarked, the record was "impoverished from the hand of the editor." A later and far more objective editor of America's Revolutionary diplomatic documents, Francis Wharton, left out portions of letters he was unable to decipher, often the real meat of the dispatch, and frequently did so without even troubling to inform the reader of the omission. He started out with a pro-French bias that led him to brand as a forgery Barbé-Marbois's notorious dispatch critical of the American claims to the fisheries, although that letter innocently reposes in its proper file in the Quai d'Orsay. In his anxiety to protect the reputation of Franklin, he also felt impelled to exonerate all Franklin's associates from wrongdoing. Thus, he was too gentle with Silas Deane, the American diplomat who finally denounced his own country, and he protested against the recurring innuendoes that Edward Bancroft was a traitor and a spy. Unluckily for Wharton, not too long after his edition was published the Auckland Manuscripts uncovered Bancroft's extraordinary career as a double agent.

Today a substantial portion of the American diplomatic documents have been published, but those of the other belligerents have been largely neglected. Save for fragments, neither the British nor the Spanish documents appear in print, and where, as in the case of France, they have been published, they have been selected and interpreted from a French national viewpoint. The most apt example, the French edition of the dispatches of the Comte de Vergennes, France's magisterial foreign minister, is massive in bulk and conveys an illusion of objective scholarship. In his selective editing and slanted interpretation, Henri Doniol set back the writing of an objective diplomatic history of the American Revolution by several generations. Even where Doniol published a document in full, he accepted the Comte's professions at their face value. As that dean of American diplomatic historians, Samuel Flagg Bemis, has remarked, the Comte put into his dispatches what he wanted his diplomats to say. Like other di)lomats he selected, colored, and even invented facts and arguments w ich he wished to instill. This caution about the Comte's dispatches may fairly be applied to diplomatic dispatches in general for this period. In the first place, they served two levels of government—the responsible officialdom charged with conducting foreign affairs and the secret operatives of the invisible governments. Secondly, while such dispatches can and often do contain extremely frank revelations, they are quite as likely to constitute pieces of special pleading to mask a diplomat's indiscretion or poor judgment.

The obstacles to achieving a sane and thorough appraisal of the diplomacy of the War of the Revolution are no longer so formidable as they were even a generation ago. It may indeed be said that, save for accident or deliberate destruction, the diplomatic records in totality are more fully available to the investigator than at any time since 1783. Prodigies of editorial labors have been expended to assemble the papers of the Founding Fathers and to edit and publish them according to modern standards of historical scholarship. One need only mention the projects now well under way for gathering and publishing the papers of the four American peace commissioners in Paris, Benjamin Franklin, John Adams, John Jay, and Henry Laurens, and the availability in microfilm edition of the massive Papers of the Continental Congress, a rich ore for diplomatic history. New and inexpensive means of photo enlargement have facilitated the task of assembling, organizing, and studying the huge masses of relevant documents that have been gathering dust in distant chancelleries.

Having amassed so huge an inventory, it is perhaps time to take stock. We may well ask whether this fuller documentation has revised our thinking about the diplomacy of the American Revolution, about the nature and course of Franco-American relations and the negotiations to end the war. To what extent must we alter the traditional stereotype?

At the start it might be well to bear in mind that the fuzzy thinking that characterizes the treatment of the Franco-American alliance stems largely from the failure to distinguish between French aid and the formal military pact entered into in 1778. So recently as 1966 a diplomatic historian has asserted, "Without France the Americans were completely helpless." Such indiscriminate confusion, even on the part of reputable scholars, between French aid and France's overt military assistance was not shared by Revolutionary Patriots.

Very early in the conflict, in fact considerably before the Declaration of Independence, American statesmen recognized the importance, even the necessity, of foreign aid if their cause was to meet with success. In July of 1775 Congress, in a Declaration on the Causes and Necessity of Taking Up Arms, a document which we now know Jefferson and John Dickinson composed together, made the point that not only were America's internal resources great but that, *if necessary*, foreign assistance was "undoubtedly attainable." Still Jefferson himself was not yet entirely reconciled to foreign aid. He felt that it might not be obtainable "but in a condition of everlasting revulsion from Great Britain," "a hard condition" indeed, Jefferson added, "to those who still wish for reunion with their parent country."

It is clear that, as the path to reconciliation ended in a thicket, the leading Patriots put their minds to first things first—that is, to foreign aid rather than foreign alliance. No man was more farsighted or outspoken on this score than John Adams. Beyond a commercial alliance with France, Adams was not prepared to go. He suspected the French Court and took a jaundiced view of the way diplomatic operations were conducted at Versailles. An American minister to France might, he ventured in October, 1775, "possibly, if well skill'd in intrigue, his pockets well filled with money and his person robust and elegant enough, get introduced to some of the Misses and Courtesans in keeping of the statesmen of France," but Adams could see no other benefits. Arguing at this time that France was bound to come into the war anyhow, Adams warned that America must avoid alliances which would entangle her in future European wars. This isolationist note was also sounded by Tom Paine, who in *Common Sense* insisted that independence would free the former colonies from being dragged at the heels of England into European wars that were no concern of theirs. Even Benjamin Franklin, often credited, with more generosity than accuracy, with being the architect of the Franco-American alliance, had in the pre-Revolutionary period commented on the disastrous consequences of "our romantick European Continental Connections." When men like Adams and Franklin spoke in these early years about "alliances" they were referring to commercial treaties, not military alliances. In fact, it is quite clear from all the evidence of Franklin's thought and action on the eve of Saratoga that he did not favor pressing France for a military alliance. Not only did he consider it inadvisable to negotiate from weakness, but he still insisted that America could maintain the contest without direct European intervention.

France's aid to America was not impelled by enthusiasm for revolutions against monarchs, but rather was it prompted by a sense of deliberate calculation that such support short of war would enhance her own national interest. France found it opportune to take steps which, while avoiding an open confrontation with her ancient foe, would serve to redress the balance of power against England. That balance, upset by the peace of 1763, might indeed be redressed should England be weakened in a protracted war with her rebellious colonies. The Comte de Vergennes, France's foreign minister, whose caution was legendary, saw to it that the aid should be kept secret and within bounds. So stupendous a secret could not be kept for long, especially since some of those who were privy to it were not noted for their discretion. Not only Silas Deane, who negotiated the original contracts with France, but also the British financier Thomas Walpole, an intimate of Franklin, and the double agent Bancroft, were closely posted on the details of this thinly camouflaged operation. Soon Lord Stormont, Britain's ambassador at Versailles, was to besiege his superiors at home with an unending stream of charges documenting the shipment of arms to America in French armed vessels, legally disguised as privately owned ships. At the start the French provided gunpowder and saltpeter, but as the war intensified and lengthened they shipped heavy guns and mortars, muskets, clothing, blankets, and, most important, substantial sums of hard cash.

Without this French aid, to which the Spaniards initially contributed their mite, the Patriots could not have sustained their military effort, kept their armies in the field, carried out their Fabian tactics, or confronted and conquered the Redcoats and Hessians at Saratoga. It can scarcely be denied, then, that from every point of view *French aid was essential to victory.*

There is another side to the coin, however. Was the French military alliance equally indispensable to the winning of independence? Almost every piece of evidence that is pertinent suggests that it was not. Take, for example, the period of unofficial military assistance prior to the formal alliance when a host of European officers volunteered for the American service. Silas Deane and, later, Benjamin Franklin were overwhelmed in Paris with applications from Frenchmen and other foreigners for high commands in the American army. Most of these officers added very little. Quite a few even contributed to the deterioration of Patriot military morale. Deane conceded that he was "harassed to death" with applications; Robert Morris complained that French officers were flocking over in such numbers that "I don't know what we shall do with them."

Alexander Hamilton, whose pro-French stance during the American Revolution contrasts sharply with his later views, made this measured comment in a letter written from Washington's Morristown headquarters in May, 1777:

> We are already greatly embarrassed with the Frenchmen among us, and from the genius of the people, shall continue to be so. It were to be wished that our agents in France, instead of courting them to come out, were instructed to give no encouragement but where they could not help it; that is, where applications were made to them by persons, countenanced and supported by great men, whom it would be impolitic to disoblige. Be assured, sir, we shall never be able to satisfy them; and they can be of no use to us, at least for some time. Their ignorance of our language, of the disposition of the people, the resources and deficiencies of the country— their own habits and tempers; all these are disqualifications that put it out of their power to be of any real use or service to us. You will consider what I have said entirely as my own sentiments.

Washington, indubitably the best informed of all Americans on the question of army morale and the competence of his officers, complained to Gouverneur Morris in a letter dated White Plains, July 24, 1778, significantly months after the news of the French alliance had reached him. Since the correct text of the Washington original has never been published, it is worth reproducing it in entirety:

24 July 1778, White Plains
DEAR SIR:

Whether you are indebted to me, or I to you, for a Letter, I know not, nor is it a matter of much moment. The design of this is to touch, cursorily, upon a Subject of very great importance to the well-being of these States; much more so than will appear at first view. I mean the appointment of so many to offices of high rank and trust in our service.

The lavish manner in which Rank has hitherto been bestowed on these Gentlemen, will certainly be productive of one, or the other of these two evils, either, to make it despicable in the eyes of Europe, or, become a mean of pouring them in upon you like a torrent, and adding to your present burthen—but it is neither the expence nor trouble of them I most dread—there is an evil more extensive in its nature, and fatal in its consequences to be apprehended, and that is, the driving all your own officers out of the Service, and throwing not only your Arms, but your Military Councils, entirely in the hands of Foreigners.

The Officers, my dear Sir, on whom you must depend for defence of this cause, and who from length of Service—their connexions—property—and (in behalf of many) I may add, military merit, will not submit much, if any longer, to the unnatural promotion of men over them, who have nothing more than a little plausibility—unbounded pride and ambition —and a perseverance in application, which is not to be resisted but by uncommon firmness, to support their pretensions—Men, who in the first instance tell you, that they wish for nothing more than the honour of serving in so glorious a cause, as Volunteers—The next day sollicit Rank without pay—the day following want money advanced them—and in the course of a Week want further promotion, and are not satisfied with any thing you can do for them.

When I speak of Officers not submitting to these appointments, let me be understood to mean, that they have no more doubt of their right to resign (when they think themselves aggrieved), than they have of a power in Congress to appoint—both being granted then, the expedience, & the policy of the measure remain to be considered; & whether, it is consistent with justice, or prudence, to promote these military fortune hunters at the hazard of your Army—especially as I think they may be denominated into three classes—to wit mere adventurers without recommendation or recommended by persons who do not know how else to dispose of, or provide for them—Men of great ambition, who would sacrifice every thing to promote their own personal glory—or, mere spies, who are sent here to obtain a thorough knowledge of our situation, circumstances etc.; in the executing of which, I am persuaded, some of them are faithful emissaries, as I do not believe a single matter escapes unnoticed, or unadvised, at a foreign Court.

I could say a great deal on this subject, but will add no more at present. I am led to give you this trouble at this time, by a *very handsome* certificate shewed me yesterday in favor of M. Neville, written (I believe) by himself; and subscribed by General Parsons, designed, as I am informed, for a foundation of the superstructure of a Brigadiership.

Baron Steuben I now find is also wanting to quit his Inspectorship for a command in the line, this will also be productive of much discontent to the Brigadiers. In a word, altho I think the Baron an excellent Officer, I do most devoutly wish that we had not a single Foreigner among us, except the Marquis de la Fayette, who acts upon very different principles than those which govern the rest. Adieu. I am most sincerely yours,

GEORGE WASHINGTON

P.S. This Letter, as you will perceive, is written with the freedom of a friend do not therefore make me enemys by publishing what is intended for your own information & that of particular friends.

Whether the French were induced to align themselves openly on America's side out of conviction, following news of the victory at Saratoga, that the Americans could win, or whether, as a recent diplomatic historian has argued, the French and Spaniards, to judge from the formidable naval power they had amassed in the West Indies by the fall of '77, had planned an overt intervention even before news reached Europe of Burgoyne's surrender seems beside the point. What triggered the French alliance was the desperate fear that gripped the French Ministry that the British were about to come to terms with America. It is not by coincidence that the alliance came on the eve of Parliament's authorization of what proved to be the ill-fated Carlisle Peace Mission to America, a mission that was prepared to offer everything to America that would have prevented conflict in 1775, but too little now and too late.

It has been tediously repeated time on end that without the assistance of French naval and military forces in the Chesapeake area the Patriots could not have prevailed at Yorktown. How can one deny one of the most venerated of all historical clichés? The fortuitous presence of de Grasse's fleet, sealing off rescue or reinforcements for the hardpressed Cornwallis, and the sizable and effective French land force under Rochambeau were essential factors in Washington's victory.

One might well speculate, though, whether the war might have been ended on terms favorable to the Patriots long before Yorktown had it not been for the French alliance. In estimating the effectiveness of French military intervention one must bear in mind that it took the French almost three and a half years to mount an offensive land and sea force that could work in cooperation with the Americans. All previous efforts were fiascoes. The first fleet under d'Estaing, which entered Delaware Bay in July of 1778 to find that the British had already departed, comprised ships too large to get past the bar at Sandy Hook. Instead of bottling up the inferior British fleet in New York Harbor, d'Estaing moved his ships to Rhode Island, only to infuriate the Patriot General Sullivan by refusing to cooperate in capturing the British garrison at Newport. Moved on to Boston, d'Estaing's men outraged the inhabitants, with whom they had armed clashes. In effect, d'Estaing's inept performance induced men as different in personality but as ardent in their patriotism as Jefferson and Lee to reflect on the possibility of an advantageous peace with Britain. But that was not to be the last of d'Estaing. In the early fall of '79 he besieged Britishheld Savannah, where he was joined by General Lincoln. Although the Franco-American amphibious force outnumbered the British defenders by almost two to one, the former were repulsed with casualties more than five times those of the Redcoats.

Indeed, the year 1779 was a disastrous one for the French on all fronts. That year Spain secretly joined the war as a cobelligerent of

France but not as an ally of the insurgent Americans. The two Continental allies, without confiding in the Americans, embarked upon a
daring combined operation to invade England, an operation comparable in magnitude to the great armada of two centuries earlier.
Yet the Franco-Spanish allies let a golden opportunity slip through
their fingers. The dismal motions of the combined fleets in Channel
waters made clear to the French just what they might expect from the
Spanish pact. In turn, the Spaniards became increasingly pessimistic
in their estimates of France's ability to prosecute the war. With the
year 1779 ending in a deadly stalemate on both the military and diplomatic fronts, peace held more appeal to the Bourbon partners than it
had back in the spring. Spain's principal minister, the Conde de
Floridablanca, now bent his mind to ways of quitting the war with
both honor and profit, and in France disillusionment and division encouraged the appeasers. In short, a strong case could be made to
support the argument that, barring Yorktown, an event which caught
France and Spain completely by surprise, the Franco-Spanish belligerents might have brought pressure on America to accept a peace short
of full independence, and that such pressure might well have proved
irresistible.

Apart from the hapless Dutch, who entered the war very late and
hardly of their own volition, the addition of France and Spain as
belligerents complicated and tangled the war aims of the coalition
arrayed against Great Britain. It is hardly news at this late date that the
war aims of Spain and France differed from those of America and even
conflicted at various points. Spain's insistence on continuing the war
until Gibraltar was regained, a point to which France agreed, threatened
to lengthen the conflict for objectives to which the Americans had not
committed themselves in their treaty of alliance with France. Regardless of the justice of the rival claims, Spain opposed America's westward
ambitions as threatening her own colonial empire and France sedulously and systematically discouraged America from mounting a second
invasion of Canada, which she did not mean to see added as a Fourteenth State. Nor was France at all happy about America's claim to fishing rights off the Grand Bank which New Englanders had so profitably
enjoyed as British colonists but had seemingly forfeited as rebels.

Finally, regardless of the estimate one places on French military
intervention down to the summer of 1781, there is no question but that
France's overt entry into the war prevented the overthrow of the North
Ministry in 1778 and delayed that turnover until after Yorktown. It
was a body blow to the appeasers among the Whigs, who, of course,
were traditionally anti-French, and thus succeeded in uniting a divided
England against an ancient foe as it had not previously been united in
its war against the Americans. It made a detested war respectable and
patriotic, and for a brief time at least enormously strengthened the

hands of both the North Ministry and the King. When one of the British peace commissioners was informed by a rebel leader that France was sure to join the war, he replied: "We must consider you then as Frenchmen; the contest has changed; and so we must prosecute the war."

If, then, the French military alliance was at least as much a liability as it was an asset to the ultimate American military victory, how must we evaluate the impact of the alliance on the chief ends of American diplomacy? In answering that question we are confronted with one of the most sedulously cultivated myths of the American Revolution. Concocted and perpetuated by partisan diplomatic historians and biographers, the myth piously affirms that France was faithful to her alliance of 1778 with the United States, and that the American commissioners demonstrated an unwarranted distrust of the Comte de Vergennes when, in a moment of disloyalty, they negotiated a separate Preliminary Peace with England.

Numerous facets of this controversy have been dealt with at considerable length in *The Peacemakers*, and no capsule summary can do justice either to the participants in the diplomacy of those years or to the issues with which they came to grips. Without doing violence to essential detail, one can, however, establish a few basic points briefly. First, it should be pointed out that within a year after she had made her alliance with the United States, France broke the spirit if not the letter of her two treaties with America. The secret pact of Aranjuez she entered into with Spain violated France's treaty of commerce with the United States in the stipulation therein made to share the fishery *only* with Spain provided she could drive the British from Newfoundland. The French commitment to continue the war until Gibraltar should be taken amounted to a unilateral change in the terms of the treaty between France and America.

The American commissioners should have trusted Vergennes. From Jared Sparks to Orville Murphy critics have so contended, implying that the commissioners were guilty of disloyalty to France by having signed the Preliminaries separately and negotiated them secretly. Their arguments, it must be answered, seem fallacious on several scores. In the first place, the critics of the commissioners assume that the government of France had but a single voice on foreign policy, and that the voice of the Comte de Vergennes. It would be equally as unrealistic to assume that the foreign policy of Secretary of State Jefferson mirrored the position of President Washington or that the foreign policy of Charles James Fox reflected fully the Rockingham-Shelburne Ministry. Thanks to Julian Boyd, we now know how Alexander Hamilton, as self-constituted prime minister in Washington's administration, tried to push his own foreign policy, and passed on to the

British agent Beckwith as administrative views ideas which were very personal to him. He did not neglect to do the same at the time of Jay's Treaty, as we have long known. Likewise it should be noted that the French Ministry was riddled by faction, court politics, and intrigue, and that others in that Ministry failed to see eye to eye with Vergennes, specifically as regards the goal of American independence. Feeling strongly that Vergennes's policies would lead to ruin, they took it upon themselves to initiate their own negotiations with the enemy, negotiations which, if consummated, would have been damaging if not fatal to American independence.

A real push toward peace got under way during the summer of 1780 from inside the French Court but without the knowledge of its foreign minister. The fall of Charleston to the British shook French confidence in America's will to win; the plan to redeem paper at a 40-to-1 ratio evoked shrieks of anguish from Parisian bankers, war contractors, and speculators, and caused still another contretemps between John Adams and Vergennes. Joseph II had gone off to Mogilev to talk with Catherine for reasons that were not clear to Vergennes, but which boded ill for France's aspirations as the arbiter of Europe. At San Ildefonso Floridablanca was toying with the British emissary, Richard Cumberland, and implanting deep suspicions among French diplomats that Spain was ready to quit the war.

Troubles were even closer to home. At Versailles Jacques Necker, director general of the Treasury and of finances, submitted the Treasury accounts to a fresh audit. During the late summer of 1780 he informed Comte Maurepas, the ailing octogenarian first minister, that he had discovered a serious discrepancy in those accounts. "A blow of a bomb," he called it, "as unexpected as it is unbelievable." Estimated taxes would not make up this deficiency, and another huge war loan would sit perilously atop the vast debt already accumulated, the Swiss banker warned. The only sensible course, Necker urged, was to come to terms with the enemy.

Maurepas was now ready to desert the war, and the King himself was perilously poised. Vergennes managed to persuade Louis XVI to continue the war effort, and even wrung from Maurepas his reluctant consent to the fateful third campaign in America, the one that would prove decisive. At the same time France's foreign minister now turned to the idea of outside mediation, as a more suitable alternative to self-abasement.

What Vergennes does not seem to have realized was that earlier that summer, doubtless under pressure from Necker, Comte Maurepas had sent out a peace feeler to Lord North, using as an intermediary a dissolute, loose-tongued Englishman named Nathaniel Parker Forth, who had served in the past as an agent of the British government in

France. Since the North Ministry had another iron in the fire, the Cumberland-Floridablanca negotiations at San Ildefonso, which from a distance still held some promise, it was disinclined to become too heavily involved with the French at this time, and clearly would not be rushed. Judging from papers later turned over to Lord Shelburne, it appears that Maurepas on this occasion, and perhaps as early as the late fall of 1779, was prepared to accept an armistice, which would allow the British to keep possession of what they then held in America, and a restitution of any conquests made by France, Spain, or Great Britain since the treaty of Fontainebleau of 1762.

This was not the last we are to hear of the fatal truce proposal. In the early fall of 1780 Thomas Walpole, a London banker and a close associate of Necker, proposed to Maurepas's intimate friend, the Abbé Véri, that a truce would resolve the difficulty posed by American independence, and on the basis of such encouragement as Véri could offer him after talking to Maurepas, Walpole dispatched a letter to North with a truce proposal. George III turned it down not only because he found Walpole politically unpalatable but also because he would not enter into negotiations with France so long as American independence was "an article of their propositions."

Meantime in France the crisis was drawing nearer. Maurepas was laid low by illness; Sartine and Montbarrey, the ministers of marine and war, were dropped as a result of Necker's agitation. Now Necker's star was in the ascendant, and it seemed doubtful that Vergennes could hold on much longer. While he had not yet managed to supplant Vergennes, Necker assumed some of the foreign minister's functions and put out peace feelers on his own, using as intermediary his former tutor, Paul-Henri Mallet, a Swiss professor and historian. By chance Mallet also had been a tutor and companion to Viscount Mountstuart, the British ambassador to Turin, who possessed some of the theatricality that his father, Lord Bute, had once abundantly demonstrated. Mountstuart, taking a summer vacation in Geneva, conferred with Mallet, the latter having only just returned from a long stay in Paris, where he had talked freely with his former pupil, M. Necker. The essence of Necker's conversation was that France needed peace desperately, that the only thing that was holding up that peace for a single minute was the American rebellion. A notorious Anglophile, Necker was quoted by Mallet as expressing the fervent hope "in God the English would be able to maintain their ground a little better this campaign." In a search for a formula Mallet proposed to Necker that "some one province," say New England, be declared independent, "and the others obliged to return to their former allegiance." Necker's response was favorable, but he talked in general terms, avoiding specific details.

Mallet carried on a number of talks with Mountstuart along these lines and agreed to go to Paris to ascertain whether the French Ministry was serious about terms of peace. From Geneva the British ambassador rushed by a personal servant a report of these conversations to Hillsborough, England's obtuse secretary of state. Even before he had heard from home, Mountstuart was the recipient of a series of letters sent by Mallet concerning his proposed Paris mission. Mountstuart then wrote again to Hillsborough proposing to join Mallet in Paris, using some pretext, such as poor health, to necessitate his trip.

The official answer finally arrived. On November 21st Hillsborough wrote Mountstuart that he had laid his communications before the King, who, in accordance with his rigid formula, refused to discuss terms with France so long as she continued to aid and abet the rebellion in America. In a rather stinging rebuke Hillsborough made the point that such unavowed and private talks were unauthorized and that it would be improper for the British ambassador to go to Paris.

How heavily Necker counted upon the Mallet-Mountstuart conversations we perhaps will never know, but as winter was approaching and the British envoy from Turin failed to appear in Paris, Necker became increasingly restive. Peace, no matter of what kind, was essential if war prospects did not improve, Necker was quoted by Austria's ambassador as having remarked. He was prepared to go behind Vergennes's back and effect a peace without satisfying even the minimum goals of France's two allies and without regard to Louis XVI's own honored commitments.

On December 1st Necker, in the full assurance of his growing power, dispatched a secret message to Lord North, "for you alone, my Lord," in which he proposed a truce "more or less long," during which the belligerent parties in America could hold "in a sovereign manner" the territory they now possessed there. North passed the letter on to George III, who, with his habitual promptness, gave the customary answer—a truce is another form of independence, and until France gave up that objective peace was out of the question. The next day North sent off to Necker, "in a feigned Italian hand" and under conditions of secrecy, a note incorporating the substance of the King's response and repulsing the Director-General's personal peace move.

One might well speculate on what the subsequent course of world history might have been had George III encouraged Necker's desperate intervention to halt the war. The Director-General's idea of a truce of varying duration was only an echo of an idea that Floridablanca had thrown out as far back as April, 1779, when the Spanish minister proposed the *uti possidetis* for the United States, and that proposition was to be warmed over and served up from time to time by Russian and Austrian mediators. That a settlement in the early winter of 1780–81 on the basis of territories then effectively controlled by each side would have chopped up the Thirteen United States into little pieces and prevented the establishment of a viable nation did not appear to perturb

Necker. Having first thought quite seriously about a tiny northeastern federation of quasi-independent states, he was now prepared to settle for a nation comprising New England, the Middle States without the port of New York, and a fractured and blighted Southland lacking all access to the sea.

Time, however, was running out for Necker. With the *compte rendu* he shot his bolt, and his enemies marshaled their forces to smash the power-hungry Director-General and the formidable peace party he headed. Though master of the Ministry following Necker's forced resignation on May 19, 1781, Vergennes was visibly shaken by the struggle. The combined dosage of appeasement administered through the separate efforts of Floridablanca and Necker now predisposed him to consider a truce on terms not too far removed from his adversaries'. The only difference was that the Foreign Minister would not accept so unpalatable a prescription from any physician other than outside mediators. Vergennes's approach to a truce, as we shall see, had a subtle difference from Necker's, to be sure, but the consequences could have been equally ruinous to the young republic across the Atlantic.

Mountstuart merely licked his wounds and bided his time for another foray into the diplomatic jungle, and in the spring of 1782, with Charles James Fox's encouragement, he sought to reopen negotiations with the French through Mallet, only to learn how low Necker's stock had fallen. Whether inadvertently or not, the new British administration found a role for Mountstuart to play in the peacemaking, and at a strategic moment. Granted leave to return home, he reached Paris on December 18, 1782, a little over a fortnight after the Americans signed the preliminary peace but before France and Spain had completed their own preliminaries. On December 22nd he dined with Richard Oswald, Britain's negotiator with the Americans. That same evening John Jay made a social call upon the British peace commissioner. Oswald, as Jay recorded in his diary, told him that Lord Mountstuart, who "execrated the American War," had brought along his letterbooks, "which he did not chuse to leave with his chargé d'affaires." Oswald was permitted to read the correspondence with Hillsborough, beginning in September, 1780, reporting the overtures made by Necker through Mallet as intermediary, reputedly "about putting an end to the war by dividing America between Britain and France, the latter to have the eastern part." To hammer the point home, Mountstuart read Oswald from his letterbook of French letters the Mallet correspondence, revealing, as Jay summarized it, Necker's concern that the expenses of the war would disarray his financing and perhaps bring about his disgrace. Jay was also informed "that the overtures about America were conducted with a variety of precautions for secrecy and with a stipulation or condition that both parties, in case they did not agree, should be at liberty to deny all that passed." Mountstuart conceded that Hillsborough had told him that "the subject was out of his line." Of course, the Mallet correspondence never explicitly proposed such a division between France and England, although the formula for a settlement was left purposely vague, and much else might have been suggested in the Mallet-Mountstuart talks that was never recorded.

By coincidence the identical terms were allegedly offered by Vergennes to a British visitor, on the word of Sir William Pulteney, who several years before had secretly offered Benjamin Franklin what the British then considered liberal peace terms. Oswald had previously relayed to Jay and Adams Pulteney's completely undocumented assertion that Vergennes had offered to end the war by dividing America with Britain, "and in case the latter agreed to the partition, that the force of France and Britain should be used to reduce it to the obedience of the respective sovereigns." Pulteney's story was somebody's baseless concoction—"Whispers which should not be credited to us," Adams put it—but the Turin letterbooks of Mountstuart provided Oswald with just enough corroboration to hammer home the point that America's ally was prepared to sell her out at any time. Jay passed the "extraordinary story" on to Adams. Whether or not Jay was taken in, his liveliest suspicions had already been aroused, not only by his long exposure to double-dealing in Spain but more recently by the secret peace mission that Vergennes's undersecretary Rayneval undertook to England in the fall of '82.

Years later Edmond Genêt took it upon himself to deny that the Necker-Mallet-Mountstuart negotiations had ever taken place. He managed to do this by mistaking the time of the negotiations for 1782, when Necker was out of office, instead of 1780, when the banker was at the height of his power, and by blandly asserting that Necker had never interfered in the concerns of the department of foreign affairs. His error was compounded, for at the date in question Genêt's father, Edmé Jacques Genêt, was *premier commis* of the Bureau of Interpretation, and Genêt was a chargé in Vienna. Edmé held the post until September, 1781, when on his death his precocious son, then a minor functionary, succeeded him. By that date Necker was no longer in office but he had seen to it that his negotiations looking toward a peace were carefully concealed from Vergennes and his subordinates. We know now what really happened despite the weak disclaimer of a petty functionary, long removed in time and place from the feverish events he was describing.

From our vantage point it seems transparently clear that a truce on the basis of the ground possessed would almost any time before Yorktown, and even possibly thereafter, have been admitting the wolf into the sheepfold and have imperiled the very independence for which the Thirteen States were battling. Yet by February, 1781, as Samuel Flagg Bemis has made clear, the Comte de Vergennes was prepared to be persuaded by the mediating powers, Russia and Austria, of the virtues of ending the war on the basis of such a formula, only excepting New York, which the British would have to evacuate. American attendance at a peace congress determined by such a formula would have resolved a dilemma posed by the new Revolutionary nation, even though the independence of the United States might have been sacrificed as a result thereof.

The credit for concocting this subtle evasion of the pledge not to end the war until American independence was obtained must be shared by diplomats of several nations. It was the brainchild of several chancelleries. First, the initial formula was the invention of Count Panin, Russia's chancellor. In the late summer of 1780 he proposed to the Comte de Vérac, France's ambassador at St. Petersburg, that during the proposed armistice the King of France could require *each* of the Thirteen States to declare its intention; thereafter he would only be obliged to maintain the independence of those states who wished to keep it. If some, for example, the two Carolinas, preferred the path of submission, then the "point of honor" of France would be satisfied, as the engagement toward them would be annulled. Vergennes immediately perceived how this formula would resolve the great issue of American independence by cutting what the diplomats loved to call "the Gordian knot of the present war." Vergennes, who privately believed that a separate polling, colony by colony as Panin advised, would have resulted in a vote for partition, now came out for an immediate armistice of at least four or five years and separate consultations with each of the states regarding their wish to maintain their independence. As of that date, the Comte was prepared to turn back to the British the whole of the Lower South, which was what Panin's shrewd formula would have meant.

Panin's second proposal was that *each* of the "united colonies of America" send delegates to a European peace Congress, delegates who would be accountable to their respective assemblies and not to Congress. In fact, that federal body was to remain suspended until each province had ruled on its fate.

At this point the British, with their skill at diplomatic maneuver, fearful that Panin was biased against them, brought Austria in as a comediator, and in effect the notion of a peace congress was transferred to Vienna, with the Austrian Chancellor, Prince von Kaunitz, rather than Panin, holding the center of the stage. Kaunitz pounced upon the Panin plan and proposed that each state send a deputy to the Congress to treat separately of its affairs with England. Not being privy to the Panin-Vérac-Vergennes correspondence, the French ambassador to Vienna, Baron de Breteuil, insisted that the American negotiations be confined to "as few hands as possible." To his amazement, he was immediately repudiated. Vergennes instructed him to accept Kaunitz's proposal, and specifically endorsed the Panin-Kaunitz plan of having the separate state legislatures choose their own peace deputies. Perhaps a little bewildered by his new instructions, Breteuil was unable to obtain from Kaunitz a clarification of the notion of thirteen American deputies instead of a solitary delegate before the mediators adopted a series of preliminary points to serve as a basis of negotiations. These points included a one-year armistice during which everything should remain *in statu quo.*

Although Great Britain was teetering on the brink of one of the great military defeats of her history, her Ministry was not prepared to make the concessions that these preliminary bases required of her. As Graf von Belgiojoso, Austria's envoy to London, reported, the British still refused to negotiate with the rebels. They would consider nothing less than their submission, and had no intention of treating with the Americans at Vienna. Indeed, a strange complacency gripped the British Ministry. Only a few days before news reached London of the surrender of Cornwallis, Lord Stormont, Britain's secretary of state, told Russian Ambassador Simolin that England would not recognize the independence of America until the French took the Tower of London, and that she would exchange Gibraltar only for Madrid. France reacted to the turn in the military tide by viewing with a jaundiced eye the one-year armistice and the provision for the *status quo,* both of which Undersecretary Gérard de Rayneval pointed out might well be objected to by the Americans. Vergennes now told Vérac that France had no right to stipulate for the United States, and if she did she would run the risk of being disavowed.

Behind Vergennes's sudden caution about America lay an important interview with John Adams. The New Englander warned Vergennes that any truce would be productive of "another long and bloody war at the termination of it" and a short truce would be especially dangerous. Vergennes was affrighted at the thought of the incorrigible New Englander's scurrying off to Vienna to run the show his own way. Any day now the Comte was expecting word that Adams had been supplanted by Congress or that a plural peace mission in which Adams had but one voice would assume his duties. Somehow Adams had gotten wind of the Panin-Kaunitz scheme of separate consultations with each of the Thirteen States and in his most didactic vein he proceeded to lecture Vergennes on the Articles of Confederation and to point out that the power to negotiate with foreign nations was expressly delegated therein to Congress. Vergennes dared not disregard

Adams' stern warning. In the winter of '81 the French foreign minister had seriously considered a partition of America. In the late spring he had revitalized the notion of negotiating a settlement with the deputies from each of the Thirteen States. After Adams' summer interlude in Paris, Vergennes was less inclined to speak for America, as regards both the terms of an armistice and the question of representation at the proposed Congress. Truly, Mr. Adams had put a spoke in the wheel, and the mediation, to America's gain, soon ground to a halt. So much, then, for the notion that America should trust Vergennes.

Another myth of the peacemaking sedulously cultivated by diplomatic historians writing within the old French-alliance frame of reference is the charge that John Jay, the American peace commissioner who joined Franklin in Paris in the late spring of 1782, was of an inordinately suspicious nature and allowed his overstrained views of national dignity to jeopardize the peace negotiations up to then in the capable hands of Benjamin Franklin. The hackneyed charges against Mr. Jay include the count that the New Yorker, by his insistence on making the recognition of the United States a precondition to entering upon negotiations, held up the Preliminaries, with the result that the United States obtained less in November of 1782 than it could have won in August or September. In *The Peacemakers,* Lord Shelburne has been closely pursued in the zigzag course he followed during these months. Therein it has been shown that not only was the Earl's position equivocal, even vis-à-vis his own intimate associates, but that there was a point beyond which he could not go if (1) he wished to retain the support of the King and (2) he expected to maintain his slim and rapidly diminishing hold upon Parliament.

What are at issue are not the bases of Jay's suspicions of the British government, suspicions incontrovertibly corroborated by the evidence now available, but rather whether there was any substance to Jay's fears about the course France was pursuing. The New Yorker has been castigated for acting upon his conviction that the French were about to double-cross their American ally either by making a separate deal with England apart from the Thirteen States or by delaying an American settlement until the Spaniards could recapture Gibraltar, a delusive hope as it turned out. Here the timetable of negotiations takes on special significance. On August 10, 1782, Franklin and Jay journeyed to Versailles, and were told by the Comte de Vergennes that there was no point in America's insisting upon explicit recognition in advance, that an exchange of commissions would serve the purpose of formal recognition. Franklin, who for months had opposed entering upon negotiations with the British without securing such explicit recognition in advance, now meekly conceded that it "would do." Contrariwise, Jay let Vergennes know that the formula did not satisfy him and that he deemed it best to proceed cautiously. To Lafayette Vergennes dictated a formula providing for the complete renunciation of sovereignty by the first article of the treaty. At that same meeting Rayneval frankly told the Americans that, so far as the West was concerned, they claimed more than they had a right to.

On their way home Jay turned to Franklin and denounced France for wanting America to remain under her direction "until not only their and our objects are attained" but also until Spain should be gratified in her demand to exclude everybody from the Gulf and the Mississippi. The secret documents now available to historians prove that Jay was correct in his appraisal of the situation, that since the beginning of July Floridablanca had been pressing Vergennes to defer recognition of the insurgents until a general peace. Otherwise the Americans, once content, he argued, might drop out of the war before Gibraltar was secured.

Thus, more than a quibble was involved. Shelburne and the Cabinet for bargaining reasons would not concede independence in advance; Vergennes was concerned lest the Americans drop out of the war should they attain their objective. So shrewd an observer of the international scene as the Comte Mercy d'Argenteau, Austria's ambassador to Versailles, felt that the English Cabinet, by raising the legal issue of the King's power to concede independence, were giving themselves a loophole to cut off negotiations. Jay wanted this hole plugged before going ahead.

So far as France was concerned, the formula proposed by Vergennes to the American was devised for the very purpose of having Great Britain put off recognizing the Americans until the final peace. The Foreign Minister of France made that clear himself. Not long after his August 10th conference with Jay and Franklin he remarked to the British envoy, Alleyne Fitzherbert, that he had advised the Americans to defer their insistence on actual recognition by Great Britain until the final peace rather than seek it as a preliminary to negotiating. Vergennes's amazing indiscretion revealed the split between the allies on a burning issue and confirmed the suspicions of the British Foreign Secretary Lord Grantham that "the granting Independency to America as a previous measure is a point which the French have no means at heart, and perhaps are entirely averse from." The British, as one might expect, made sure that Jay was told how Vergennes had crossed him behind his back. Small wonder that John Jay concluded the policy of the Comte de Vergennes was "to keep America in leading strings." Indeed, massive evidence reposing in the Archives of the Quai d'Orsay provides solid and overwhelming refutation of the contention of the

French Foreign Office that the opinions on the fisheries or the West attributed to subordinates were purely personal to them and did not reflect the official policy of the French Court.

On August 29th the British Cabinet secretly decided to agree to Franklin's terms, which provided a more generous northern boundary than the United States finally was forced to accept. That the decision could have served as the basis for the round of preliminary talks still ahead is highly dubious, however. It is hardly conceivable that a Cabinet decision that ignored the issue of compensating the Tories and guaranteeing debts due the British creditors would have been ratified by Parliament even if the British Ministry had committed itself to the Americans on the basis of the August 29th understanding. The fact is that the Ministry did no such thing. It kept the decision secret and continued to withhold information from John Jay about its intentions. Why should the British Ministry have followed so devious a course? The explanation seems ready at hand. The British government was well aware of Vergennes's anxiety that the concession on independence be deferred until the treaty itself. Furthermore, they were also aware, apparently through information provided by the turncoat Edward Bancroft, that John Jay was prepared to hold the Comte de Vergennes responsible for any delays on the part of London.

Three circumstances now impelled John Jay to take the initiative. Around this time the British placed in Jay's hand an intercepted letter from the French Secretary of Legation in America in which the indiscreet Barbé-Marbois back in March of 1782 had expressed his hostility to the claims of America to a share in the Newfoundland fisheries and cautioned his government against New England's current outcry, "No peace without the fisheries." Almost coincidentally with the revelations contained in the fisheries' letter, Gérard de Rayneval, French Undersecretary of Foreign Affairs, had turned over to Jay a memorandum supporting in substance Spain's claims to a substantial share of the territory west of the Appalachians claimed by America for her own. This memorandum, whose general lines had been forecast in numerous conversations between Jay and Rayneval, convinced the American that the French Foreign Ministry was hardly neutral in the dispute raging behind the scenes between Spain and America over the western boundaries.

What triggered Jay's extraordinary response, however, was the revelation that on September 7th Rayneval had taken off for England incognito. Like so many other well-guarded diplomatic secrets, Rayneval's absence was bruited about almost at once and caused a buzz of speculation. Vergennes, while notifying the Spaniards of the mission, did not trouble to inform the Americans. To Jay the gossip about the Undersecretary's pseudo-secret mission sounded an alarm bell in the night. Later critics of John Jay who were not privy to the negotiations have relied heavily on Rayneval's formal instructions which contained nothing about America's claims, but Rayneval's own report of his conversations belies the assertions that he did not advert to America. First of all, Rayneval told Shelburne that the "King would never support an unjust demand" as regards America's claims to the fisheries. A week earlier Shelburne's own Cabinet had decided to concede the Americans a share in the fisheries. Now Rayneval told Shelburne: "We do not want the Americans to share in the fisheries." This was enough to stiffen British counterdemands on that score. As regards the boundaries, Rayneval in his first visit assured Shelburne that it was the King's intention to "contain the Americans within the bounds of justice and reason." He even talked about the 1754 negotiations relative to the Ohio, a point which he had also made in the memoir he had left in Jay's hands before his hurried departure for London. The application of the rule of 1754, as Rayneval interpreted it, would have barred America from the Old Northwest.

Emboldened by the support of the French Court implied in Rayneval's remarks, as well as by the heartening news to come of the successful defense of Gibraltar, Shelburne was to renege the Cabinet offer of August 29th and to put up one more desperate stand along the Ohio. According to Shelburne's own account, Rayneval gave him to understand that, once independence was granted, the French "were disposed to assist us as to the Boundaries."

Quick to perceive the peril to American interests at the peacemaking should France and England arrive at a secret understanding, Jay took the most audacious step of his career. He dispatched a pro-American intermediary, Benjamin Vaughan, a quasi agent of Shelburne's, to England on a mission so secret that neither Vergennes nor Franklin was apprised of it. Vaughan was given a compromise proposal for recognition, and on his arrival in England the Cabinet voted to concede Jay's point and to issue a new commission to Richard Oswald empowering him to treat and conclude "with any Commission or person vested with equal power by and on the part of the Thirteen United States of America." At long last the rebellious states had been recognized by the mother country, and the peacemaking could now proceed to its successful conclusion.

The diplomacy of the American Revolution suggests all sorts of tantalizing analogies to the recent past and the troubled present. One may see striking parallels between the negotiations of 1782–1783 involving the Great Powers and the American colonists and the long and protracted parleys some years back between the French government and the Algerian rebels. The American Commissioners, it must be remembered, sought not only independence but territorial integrity and elbow room. One might compare their insistence upon the inclusion of the trans-Appalachian West with the demands pressed by the Algerian nationalists to the French Sahara. America's case was perhaps no stronger, either juridically or morally, for it rested its claims to the West upon vague charter provisions conferred by the English Crown which it had repudiated, and these claims, like the Algerian, were not bolstered by effective military occupation. It must be borne in mind that the bulk of the territory George Rogers Clark had conquered in the Northwest had largely slipped from America's grip by the close of the war. All the Great Powers opposed America's obtaining the West, and indubitably the claims of both Spain and England to that region were strong ones. But after a partition of the American continent, which everybody but America wanted, the new republic would not have been left with a durable fragment. Similarly, the partition of Algeria according to the myriad plans that were put forth would not have assured the FLN a viable state, nor would the secession of Katanga or Oriente province have allowed the Congo the wherewithal to survive and prosper.

The Algerian negotiations suggest a still further analogy to the American Revolutionary settlement. In both sets of negotiations the Loyalists posed a thorny problem. The latter comprised the American Tories, the former the large European community in Algeria. In both cases the rights and grievances of this substantial segment of the population loyal to the mother country posed formidable obstacles to concluding any agreement. Neither settlement effectively protected the Loyalists in fact and both were followed by mass Loyalist emigrations.

Even more tantalizing is the analogy between King George III's obstinate course in refusing to recognize the insurgent Americans who held part but not all of the Thirteen States and the refusal of the United States to deal directly with the Viet Cong who held part if not all of Vietnam. Obviously there are limits to which the latter analogy can be pressed, as the United States was never a colonial power in Indo-China. Unlike the British in 1776, the Americans in Vietnam are ostensibly fighting for the principle of self-determination by a former colonial people beset by internal subversion and foreign aggression. Regrettably, there has been a corroding confusion about the objectives of America's intervention, objectives which critics put under the rubric of "neo-colonialism." But then "neo-colonialism" as it is used in the Asiatic world is a pejorative word, and many Asiatics, perhaps unfairly, regard America as assuming the mantle of France in Southeast Asia. Finally, the point might be made that during the American Revolution, though Congress first demanded that, as a precondition to entering upon negotiations, the British army leave the Thirteen Colonies, our peacemakers did not lay down such preconditions. They were too realistic to insist on conditions that would be insupportable to the pride of a Great Power or that they were in fact unable to effectuate.

In his Godkin Lectures the late Adlai Stevenson pointed out that "we shall have to learn" that "we cannot deal with questions of foreign policy in terms of moral absolutes." Stevenson went on to observe: "Compromise is not immoral or treasonable. It is the objective of negotiation and negotiation is the means of resolving conflict peacefully. But when we negotiate we have to have something to negotiate with as well as for. If rigidity and absolutist attitudes relieve our representatives of anything to negotiate with, then there is nothing they can negotiate for."

To be sure, the hand of the Americans in Paris was strengthened by the results of Yorktown, after which they could negotiate from victory, because an obdurate enemy will enter into negotiations only when it recognizes that it can no longer win. What was especially distinctive about our American diplomats in Paris in 1782–1783, aside from their effectiveness, was their style. With skill and audacity they wielded the weapons of Revolutionary diplomacy, confident in the strength and promise of the new nation they represented. This confidence in America's future was by no means shared by European statesmen. Rather, they expected America to suffer the lethargy of other republics, a lethargy compounded by sectional rivalries. Almost gleefully did they anticipate division and secession, hopefully expecting some day that the Great Powers would come in and pick up the pieces.

In that great confrontation of the Old Order and the New which the negotiations between the diplomats of the Great Powers and the American commissioners epitomized, the Americans demonstrated the art of compromise, but what they yielded was trivial while they remained adamant on the crucial issues—obtaining absolute independence and a continental domain for thirteen littoral states. For a perspicuity spiced with audacity, for a tenacity tempered by flexibility, a free people is eternally in their debt.

Part 3

NATIONAL GROWTH AND CIVIL WAR, 1783–1877

15

The Founding Fathers: Young Men of the Revolution

STANLEY ELKINS AND ERIC McKITRICK

16

The Anti-Federalists, 1781–1789

FORREST McDONALD

If the American genius is politics, its masterpiece is the Constitution. As the most important document in the history of the United States, the Constitution challenges historians with problems of interpretation. Inevitably it raises questions about its significance in the world of the 1780's, its relevance to the American Revolution, its meaning for the nations of the Western world which were then alive with reform movements, and the purposes and interests which guided the founding fathers in framing it. It is fair enough to say that the American Constitution was the product of an age of revolution, and that it served as an example to other communities in the Western world that were also experiencing revolutionary change. But in what ways? To what degree are the great revolutions of the Western world similar, in terms of both their aims and their dynamics? How far were these revolutions— the English, the American, the French, and the Russian—liberal and bourgeois in nature? How far, in effect, did they compass the goal of disestablishing the monarchical-aristocratic order, of replacing an order of groups and the distinctions of privilege with one of individuals and the distinctions of wealth?

And what have been the dynamics of each of the revolutions? May one not discern among them certain uniformities? In The Anatomy of Revolution *(1938, 1952), Crane Brinton perceived regularities of program and progress in all the revolutions: each challenged an old regime, passed through a period of accommodation—a "honeymoon" stage, moved into a rule by moderates, then into a rule by extremists and a reign of terror and virtue, and ultimately into a Thermidor, that is, a reaction against revolutionary excess and tension. To understand each phase of revolutionary development poses its particular problem. What factors created a potential for revolution? What factors actualized the potential? To what degree did the revolution involve a radicalizing of its aims and means, and how far did this development express the increasingly radical class interests of successive groups of revolutionary leaders?*

Some further questions. What is the significance of a written constitution? In what particular way does it state social ideals? How do the forms of government set up by the constitution also express the purposes of that government? Why did the liberal bourgeois revolution seek to articulate its social ideals in a written constitution? Why was the American Constitution the exemplar for Western revolutionary movements during the nineteenth century?

The essays that are reprinted below concern the leaders of the movements for and against the American Constitution of 1787, and the relevance of these movements to the whole course of the revolutionary era. Both essays reflect the essentially favorable attitude toward the founding fathers that has characterized recent American historiography. Stanley Elkins and Eric McKitrick see them as younger men, whose careers and views were tied to the emerging national polity, and who were staging a "continental" revolution of energy and initiative. Forrest McDonald sees them as "giants in the earth," and their adversaries as "knaves and fools." The fact is that the veneration of the founding fathers has come full circle in our day. A century ago they had been demigods; in the progressive era they were brought rudely down to earth. In recent years historians have taken them out of the pillory. They are no longer men of questionable democracy, psychology, or class interests. They are now libertarians, men of vision, beginners of the American experiment. As such they have been the subject of many sympathetic biographies. And their collected writings are being published in immense, exhaustive, expensive editions.

The authors of the following essays are scholars of eminence. Stanley Elkins and Eric McKitrick have jointly written a number of articles whose hallmark is their imagination, excellent prose, and exploration of insights afforded by social science. Both Elkins and McKitrick are respectively authors of highly significant monographs as well. The former, who teaches at Smith College, has written **Slavery: A Problem in American Institutional and Intellectual Life** *(1959); the latter, who teaches at Columbia University, has written* **Andrew Johnson and Reconstruction** *(1960). Forrest McDonald, who is presently at Wayne State University, is interested in American industrial history and in the revolutionary period. His writings* *include:* Let There Be Light: The Electric Industry in Wisconsin, 1881–1955 *(1957);* We The People: The Economic Origins of the Constitution *(1958);* Insull *(1962); and* E Pluribus Unum: The Formation of the American Republic, 1776–1790 *(1965).*

The essays attempt to answer some significant questions about the making of the American Constitution. To begin with: Who were its protagonists, who were its antagonists, and where did each group stand on the major problems then confronting the new nation? Were the founding fathers democrats or aristocrats, and did they consummate the Revolution or negate it? How much was the difference between them one of premises, how much one of procedure? What contributions to understanding the conflict over the Constitution have been made by the principal historians who have studied it during the past century: George Bancroft, John Fiske, and other members of the "patriotic" school; Charles A. Beard and his latter-day successors, including Merrill Jensen and Jackson Turner Main, who have seen the conflict as essentially one over economic interests; and scholars such as Robert E. Brown, Edmund Morgan, Henry Steele Commager, and Forrest McDonald, who have, in the course of the past decade or so, rejected the Beardian interpretation and espoused one that is neo-patriotic or nationalist? However much they may differ among themselves, do these different schools of interpretation yet share essential premises, or find that their respective protagonists in the revolutionary generation shared essential premises? Why has the scholarly view of the Federalists and of the anti-Federalists undergone revision from one generation to the next? If historical writing expresses a larger social outlook, what do current views of the founding fathers say about our own generation's ideas?

In what respect do the data that Forrest McDonald presents reveal the anti-Federalists to have been "knaves and fools"? What are we to make of his unfavorable estimate of them in the light of the decidedly favorable one offered by Jackson Turner Main? The latter's neo-Beardian interpretation of the struggle over the Constitution was presented in his monograph, The Antifederalists *(1961), in which he argued that it "was primarily a contest between the commercial and non-commercial elements in the population." Unlike their opponents, Main submitted, the rank and file of the anti-Federalists "were men of moderate means, with little social prestige, farmers often in debt, obscure men for the most part." Anti-Federalism was, to his way of thinking, essentially democratic in outlook; it emphasized local rule and the people's retention of power; "it was fundamentally anti-aristocratic . . . always more congenial to the many than the few."*

If a revolution is the precipitate from a solution of potentiality, the student, in analyzing its chemistry, will gain much from trying to understand the forces that account for such a precipitation. In contrasting our own revolution with that of other polities, he will learn much about revolutionary leadership, its nature, its composition and psychology, its mode of action, the purposes and ideology which inform it, and its role vis-à-vis established authority and other social groups. In a very profound sense, the Constitution of 1787 has defined the course of American experience. It will well reward us to study its making closely.

STANLEY ELKINS AND ERIC McKITRICK

The intelligent American of today may know a great deal about his history, but the chances are that he feels none too secure about the Founding Fathers and the framing and ratification of the Federal Constitution. He is no longer certain what the "enlightened" version of that story is, or even whether there is one. This is because, in the century and three quarters since the Constitution was written, our best thinking on that subject has gone through two dramatically different phases and is at this moment about to enter a third.

Americans in the nineteenth century, whenever they reviewed the events of the founding, made reference to an Olympian gathering of wise and virtuous men who stood splendidly above all faction, ignored petty self-interest, and concerned themselves only with the freedom and well-being of their fellow-countrymen. This attitude toward the Fathers has actually never died out; it still tends to prevail in American history curricula right up through most of the secondary schools. But bright young people arriving at college have been regularly discovering, for nearly the last fifty years, that in the innermost circle this was regarded as an old-fashioned, immensely oversimplified, and rather dewy-eyed view of the Founding Fathers and their work. Ever since J. Allen Smith and Charles Beard wrote in the early years of the twentieth century, the "educated" picture of the Fathers has been that of a group not of disinterested patriots but of hard-fisted conservatives who were looking out for their own interests and those of their class. According to this worldlier view, the document which they wrote—and in which they embodied these interests—was hardly intended as a thrust toward popular and democratic government. On the contrary, its centralizing tendencies all reflected the Fathers' distrust of the local and popular rule which had been too little restrained under the Articles of Confederation. The authors of the Constitution represented the privileged part of society. Naturally, then, their desire for a strong central government was, among other things, an effort to achieve solid national guarantees for the rights of property—rights not adequately protected under the Articles—and to obtain for the propertied class (their own) a favored position under the new government.

SOURCE: *The Political Science Quarterly*, LXXVI (June, 1961), 181–216. Reprinted by permission of the authors.

This "revisionist" point of view—that of the Founding Fathers as self-interested conservatives—has had immeasurable influence in the upper reaches of American historical thought. Much of what at first seemed audacious to the point of lèse majesté came ultimately to be taken as commonplace. The Tory-like, almost backward-turning quality which this approach has imparted to the picture of constitution-making even renders it plausible to think of the Philadelphia Convention of 1787 as a counterrevolutionary conspiracy, which is just the way a number of writers have actually described it. That is, since the Articles of Confederation were the product of the Revolution, to overthrow the Articles was—at least symbolically—to repudiate the Revolution. The Declaration of Independence and the Constitution represented two very different, and in some ways opposing, sets of aspirations; and (so the reasoning goes) the Philadelphia Convention was thus a significant turning-away from, rather than an adherence to, the spirit of the Declaration.

In very recent years, however, a whole new cycle of writing and thinking and research has been under way; the revisionists of the previous generation are themselves being revised. The economic ideas of the late Professor Beard, which dominated this field for so long, have been partially if not wholly discredited. And yet many of the old impressions, intermingled with still older ones, persist. Much of the new work, moreover, though excellent and systematic, is still in progress. Consequently the entire subject of the Constitution and its creation has become a little murky; new notions having the clarity and assuredness of the old have not as yet fully emerged; and meanwhile one is not altogether certain what to think.

Before the significance of all this new work can be justly assessed, and before consistent themes in it may be identified with any assurance, an effort should be made to retrace somewhat the psychology of previous conceptions. At the same time, it should be recognized that any amount of fresh writing on this subject will continue to lack something until it can present us with a clear new symbolic image of the Fathers themselves. The importance of this point lies in the function that symbols have for organizing the historical imagination, and the old ones are a little tired. The "father" image is well and good, and so also in certain respects is the "conservative" one. But we may suppose that these men saw themselves at the time as playing other rôles too, rôles that did not partake so much of retrospection, age, and restraint as those which would come to be assigned to them in after years. The Republic is now very old, as republics go, yet it *was* young once, and so were its founders. With youth goes energy, and the "energy" principle may be more suggestive now, in reviewing the experience of the founding, than the principle of paternal conservatism.

I

Charles A. Beard, who in 1913 published *An Economic Interpretation of the Constitution of the United States,* did more than any single figure to make of the Constitution something other than a topic for ceremonial praise. By calling it a product of economic forces, Beard established an alternative position and enabled the entire subject to become one for serious historical debate. He thus created the first real dialectic on the Constitution and Founding Fathers, and for that reason Beard's work must still be taken as the point of departure for any historical treatment of that subject.

For Beard, the reality behind the movement for a constitution in the 1780's was economic interest. The animating surge came from holders of depreciated Continental securities who were demanding that their bonds be paid at par, and from conservative elements throughout the Confederation who wanted a national bulwark against agrarian-debtor radicalism. Beard thus identified the Federalists as those who wanted protection for property, especially personal property. The Anti-Federalists, on the other hand, were the great mass of agrarian debtors agitating for schemes of confiscation and paper money inflation in the state legislatures. Their hard-earned taxes would go to support any new bonds that a stronger United States government might issue; conversely, further fiscal experimentation on their part would be checked by national power. The Anti-Federalists, those who opposed a new constitution, were therefore the radicals; the Federalists, who favored it, were the conservatives.

Beard's argument was immediately challenged and kept on being challenged, which helped it to retain the fresh attractiveness of an avant-garde position for many years. But the man's influence grew, and his work played a vital part in historical thinking until well after the Second World War. Historical thinking, however, has its own historical setting. Why should such a statement as Beard's not have been made until the twentieth century, more than 125 years after the event?

In the nineteenth century the American Constitution had operated as the central myth of an entire political culture. While that culture was still in the tentative stages of its growth, still subject to all manner of unforeseen menaces, and with very little that was nationally sacred, there reigned everywhere the tacit understanding that here was the one unifying abstraction, the one symbol that might command all loyalties and survive all strife. The Constitution thus served multiple functions for a society that lacked tradition, folk-memory, a sovereign, and a body of legend. The need to keep the symbol inviolate seems to have been felt more instinctively during its earlier history than later on. Public controversy of the bitterest kind might occur over the charter's true meaning; enemies might accuse each other of misconstruing the document; but one did not challenge the myth itself. Americans even fought a civil war with both sides claiming to be the true upholders of the Constitution. Thus it was natural that when the historians of the nineteenth century—Bancroft, Hildreth, Frothingham, Fiske, McMaster —came to describe the origins of the Constitution, they should reach for the non-controversial idiom and imagery of a Golden Age. The Supreme Law had been fashioned and given to the people by a race of classic heroes.[1]

America's veneration for its Constitution became steadily more intense in the years that followed the Civil War. Now it was the symbol not only of the Union, for which that generation had made such heavy sacrifices, but also of the unfettered capitalism which was turning the United States into one of the richest and most powerful nations in the world. The new material order—wasteful, disorderly, already acquainted with labor disturbances, yet immensely productive—was watched over by the benevolent and solicitous eye of the Constitution.

In 1888, in a setting darkened by portents of industrial warfare, John Fiske published *The Critical Period of American History,* an account of the events leading to the Philadelphia Convention of 1787. It was an instant success; the notion of the Confederation interlude as a "critical period" was dramatically perfect. A time of trouble, political drift, threatening disunity, and irresponsible agitation provided the occasion at Philadelphia for a supreme act of disinterested statesmanship. There, an intrepid conclave of Old Romans rose above personal and local concerns and presented their countrymen with an instrument of vigorous and effective government.

By the opening of the twentieth century, the state of mind in which men could uncritically ascribe a sort of immaculateness to their political and legal arrangements had altered sharply. By then a profound economic and social crisis had been met and overcome, but with remnants of psychological crisis left unresolved in its wake. The ending of the depression and hard times of the 1890's, the defeat of Populism and Bryanism, the election of McKinley and return of Republican rule —these things were not enough to restore the old complacent innocence. The American public, now full of guilty misgivings, had begun to ask itself searching questions about the evils of the existing order

---

[1] Richard B. Morris has pointed out that in Henry Dawson there was at least one exception to this universal veneration for the Constitution. Dawson in 1871 published an article wherein he deplored the ancestor-worship which already wreathed the Fathers and their work. See Morris, "The Confederation and the American Historian," *William and Mary Quarterly,* XIII, 3rd ser. (April 1956), pp. 139–56; Dawson, "The Motley Letter," *Historical Magazine,* IX, 2nd ser. (March 1871), pp. 157 *et seq.*

and about the price it had allowed itself to pay for material progress. The answer which was hit upon by publicists and civic spokesmen was *vested interest.* The formula was not exactly new, but after the experience of the 1890's, when public rhetoric had abounded in sinister allusions to "Wall Street" and "the monopolies," it was no more than natural that the "vested interest" concept should have taken on an immensely new and widened range of application. The "interests" were the shadowy powers that manipulated things and made them run the way they did. Thus vested interest came to be seen in the Progressive Era—those years roughly from the turn of the century through the First World War—as the ultimate reality behind the life of affairs.

It was in that era, moreover, that "reality" itself first came to be a synonym for all the equivocal, seamy, and downright evil facts of life from which innocent and respectable people are normally sheltered. Few periods in American history have been so strikingly noted for civic awareness and the reforming spirit—and reform meant getting to the bottom of things. The most efficacious step in exorcising an evil was exposing it. Thus the literature of exposure, which claimed an enormous amount of journalistic and literary energy, did much to whet and sustain that generation's relish for reform. "Muckraking" meant dredging up heaps of grubby "reality" for all to behold. "Reality," as Richard Hofstadter has said,

> was the bribe, the rebate, the bought franchise, the sale of adulterated food. It was what one found in *The Jungle, The Octopus, Wealth against Commonwealth,* or *The Shame of the Cities.* . . . Reality was a series of unspeakable plots, personal iniquities, moral failures, which, in their totality, had come to govern American society. . . .

The sheer excitement of discovery tended to leave people's perceptions of appearance and reality somewhat unbalanced. It is perhaps too much to say that anything hidden was taken as bad (though there were certainly strong presumptions); yet one of the great unspoken dogmas of American thought, implanted in this period, was that the "facts of life" had to be hidden in order to qualify as "real."

In academic precincts, meanwhile, such thinkers as Roscoe Pound, John Dewey, Thorstein Veblen, Arthur Bentley, and J. Allen Smith had begun to challenge the older static and formalist theories of law, philosophy, economics, and government. They were no longer so interested in the formal outlines which enclosed, say, government or the law; they were much more concerned to locate the dynamic forces inside these realms—to identify the powers that made them really work. Thus "economic interest" as a kind of *élan vital,* a basic prime mover, came to be given greater and greater emphasis. "Wherever we turn," wrote E. R. A. Seligman as early as 1902, ". . . we are confronted by the overwhelming importance attached by the younger and abler scholars to the economic factor in political and social progress." Here was "reality" being given an intellectual and scholarly sanction.

In view of this mounting preoccupation with "interests," one might be led to conclude that significant numbers of intelligent people were approaching a "class" theory of society not unlike that of Marx—a theory in which classes and class interests contended more or less frankly with each other for advantage. Yet by and large this did not happen; these were not the terms in which most people thought about society. For one reason, there was very little evidence to support such a theory. But a more important reason was that, to a people saturated in democratic prejudices, "class" habits of thought were fantastically difficult to understand, let alone imitate. To the Progressive mind, the way vested interest worked was not so much through class as through *conspiracy*.

Vested interest and conspiracy were concepts so closely related that they were almost synonymous. The interests worked in secret; their power rested on stealthy understandings and was exercised through the pulling of invisible strings. Hidden from view, they might freely circumvent the law and gain their ends by corrupting and manipulating the agencies of government. The Marxian view that a man openly and automatically reflected the interests of his class, doing this even in the name of ideals and justice, was incomprehensible to most Americans. The mediating term between economic interest and political action had to be something both simpler and more disreputable, and the techniques such as could not bear daylight. One important source of this attitude was the Progressive faith in the essential honesty of the people. Only the few, acting in secret, would set their interests against those of the nation. They achieved their aims not by consulting the majority will but by thwarting and evading it. Thus when writers of the Progressive period tried to weigh the importance of economic factors in any political development, the imagery they slipped into was almost invariably that of a conspiracy against the people. Such a mode of conceiving reality would even be brought to bear upon the origins of the United States Constitution.

Two of Charles Beard's immediate precursors in that realm were J. Allen Smith and Algie Simons. They were, for their own purposes, innovators; yet in a broader sense their minds followed a typical Progressive pattern. In J. Allen Smith's *Spirit of American Government, A Study of the Constitution* (1907), the myth of the Philadelphia convention as a forum of disinterested statesmen came under sharp attack. Claiming that "it was the property-owning class that framed and secured the adoption of the Constitution," Smith seemed to be feeling his way toward an economic interpretation based on class. But this tentative theme was quickly overshadowed by the central idea, that of a conspiracy against democratic rule:

> Democracy . . . was not the object which the framers of the American Constitution had in view, but the very thing they wished to avoid. . . . Accordingly the efforts of the Constitutional Convention were directed to the task of devising a system of government which was just popular enough not to excite popular opposition and which at the same time gave the people as little as possible of the substance of political power.

Algie Simons, who was a convinced socialist and should therefore have hewed more consistently to the doctrine of class interest, fell into much the same sort of reasoning. In *Social Forces in American History* (1912), Simons' words seemed at first full of cool detachment when he said that it was not necessarily bad for the Constitutional Convention to have been virtually a committee of the propertied class, because that class "represented progress." But the lures of "conspiracy" in the end proved too much for him. Simons' closing rhetoric almost sweats with rural superstition as he tells his readers that

> the organic law of this nation was formulated in secret session by a body called into existence through a conspiratory trick, and was forced upon a disfranchised people by means of dishonest apportionment in order that the interests of a small body of wealthy rulers might be served.

But it was Charles A. Beard, taking up the "class interest" formula in his famous *Economic Interpretation* the following year, who succeeded to all intents and purposes in making it stick. Whereas neither Smith nor Simons had made any secret of their reforming passions (they denied that the Constitution was a sacred document, so their fellow-citizens should feel free to change it if they wished), Beard disclaimed any intention of writing a political tract. He would simply be the observer of historical events, impassively examining the facts. All he wanted to do was discover whether in fact economic forces had played a significant part in the drafting and ratification of the Constitution. Early in his book Beard insisted that it was not his purpose "to show that the Constitution was made for the personal benefit of the members of the Convention," but merely to determine whether the Fathers represented "distinct groups whose economic interests they understood and felt in concrete, definite form, through their own personal experience with identical property rights. . . ." Then, setting in motion an impressive system of scholarly apparatus, he proceeded to answer his own questions.

Beard's ostensible argument—that the Fathers were pursuing class rather than personal interests and that there was a real distinction between them—had a certain Marxian subtlety, but he would not have made his case with very many Progressive readers if he had actually stuck to it. Instead, in the course of his book that side of the case, the "class" side, slipped entirely out of sight while the personal side, the one that really engaged Beard's mind, just grew and grew. The distinction was impossible to maintain; even to him it was probably not very serious. At any rate, the reason he was able to create his sensation was that the things he showed the Fathers doing were of exactly the sort that the muckraking magazines had, in other connections, made all too familiar.

Beard's basic research materials were a batch of old Treasury records which had never previously been opened ("reality"), and in them he found the names of a number of the Federalist leaders, members of the Philadelphia Convention as well as delegates to ratifying conventions in the various states. These men held substantial amounts of Continental securities which—Beard reasoned from later developments—would rise sharply in value with the establishment of a strong central government. This seemed to explain the energy with which they worked to bring such a government into being, and this was just the sort of evidence that impressed Beard's contemporaries most. Beard himself, for all his disclaimers, sums up his argument in language whose dominant theme is *direct personal interest*. Here, three of his thirteen conclusions are quite explicit:

(1) The first firm steps toward the formation of the Constitution were taken by a small and active group of men immediately interested through their personal possessions in the outcome of their labors.

(2) The members of the Philadelphia Convention who drafted the Constitution were, with a few exceptions, immediately, directly, and personally interested in, and derived economic advantages from, the establishment of the new system.

(3) The leaders who supported the Constitution in the ratifying conventions represented the same economic groups as the members of the Philadelphia Convention; and in a large number of instances they were also directly and personally interested in the outcome of their efforts.

Accompanying the principal theme of personal interest were several sub-themes:

(1) The Constitution was essentially an economic document based upon the concept that the fundamental private rights of property are anterior to government and morally beyond the reach of popular majorities.

(2) [The entire process, from the calling of the Philadelphia Convention to the ratifying of the Constitution, was unrepresentative and undemocratic; there was no popular vote on calling the convention; a large propertyless (and therefore disfranchised) mass was not represented at Philadelphia;

and only a small minority in each state voted for delegates to the ratifying conventions.][2]

(3) [Where battles did occur over ratification], the line of cleavage . . . was between substantial personalty interests on the one hand and the small farmers and debtor interests on the other.

Beard thus managed in the end to have it both ways; he charged the Fathers, as members of a class, with things of which he had said he was not going to accuse them as individuals.   But the distinction was too fine to matter a great deal; the response to the book, both favorable and hostile, was based on the secrets Beard had unearthed about the Fathers as individuals.   Few of his readers had paid much attention to the subtle relationship which he had tried to establish between class interest and political ideology, so few could have noticed when the relationship began to dissolve.   Actually, few had had any real quarrel with capitalism in the first place; the Progressive mentality was simply frightened by *big* capitalism—that is, by the vested interests.   Beard himself was nothing if not a Progressive, fully immersed in his times. It was the interests and their inside doings that caught the Progressive imagination; it was this that the Progressives longed to befool and discomfit by public exposure.   If Beard was to show that the Federal Constitution was not a product of abstract political theory but of concrete economic drives, there was no happier way of doing it than to paint the Founding Fathers in the familiar image of the vested interests—the small group of wealthy conspirators hostile to, even contemptuous of, the majority will, and acting for clear, "practical" reasons such as rigging the value of public securities.

Despite the bursts of pained protests which *An Economic Interpretation* initially drew from many older academics (who either thought that Beard could comprehend no motives other than base ones, or else concluded that he must be a socialist), it also drew plenty of praise from academic as well as non-academic quarters.   Not only did the book do well for a scholarly monograph, it did better and better as time went on.   In the 1920's the reforming side of Progressivism had lost its popularity, but this was not true of the debunking side.   Meanwhile the success of Vernon L. Parrington's *Main Currents in American Thought* (which owed much to Beardian influences), as well as of Beard's own *Rise of American Civilization,* served to keep Beard's views before the public.

The *Economic Interpretation* came fully into its own in the New Deal era.   The times by then required a conception of the Constitution that

---

[2] Not a direct quotation but a summary of four of the thirteen conclusions.

would stress the flexible, rather than the rigid and immutable aspects of the document. Former President Hoover, and even the Supreme Court, were apparently insisting in the face of all enlightened opinion that social and economic experimentation of any kind was ruled out by the spirit of the Constitution. Yet it would be reasonable enough to expect that the Constitution should respond to the economic needs of the present, if there were convincing historical proof that its very birth had been in response to the economic needs of its framers. American intellectuals, moreover, had by this time become a good deal more accustomed to ideas of class conflict than formerly. To significant numbers of them the image of class struggle was now appealing enough that they had begun applying it in the spirit of experimentation to a great variety of problems. Business groups of every sort had fallen into bad odor. This was the setting in which prophetic insights came to be ascribed to the writings of Charles A. Beard. Those writings by the late 1930's had become voluminous, and the Master had acquired a legion of followers.

And the Master himself could still have it both ways. Marxist and quasi-Marxist interpretations of society could, and did for a season, draw much historical sanction from his pages. At the same time Beard had bequeathed to American historical method something far more pervasive, a technique of explanation which could take "class" interpretations or leave them alone. This was the "reality" technique, which assumes that the most significant aspects of any event are those concealed from the eye. Men's true intentions are to be judged neither from the words we hear them speak nor the deeds we see them do, and the "real" forces behind historical change will turn out, more often than not, to be those of conspiracy.

II

In 1940 certain new and interesting corollaries were added to the mode of approach which, due so largely to Beard's example, had come to influence historical thinking on the formation of the Constitution. In that year Merrill Jensen published *The Articles of Confederation: An Interpretation of the Social-Constitutional History of the American Revolution, 1774–1781.* Jensen's own approach was consistent with most of the general principles which had been laid down by Beard. But whereas Beard's primary interest had been with the Federalists—the men who led and supported the campaign for a new constitution— Jensen turned his attention to the Anti-Federalists, those who had opposed the constitutional movement. What, he asked, was the nature of the political system which the Constitution displaced, and what were the aims and intentions of the men who had created that system?

In the face of most prior opinion to the contrary, Jensen found in the Confederation just the sort of loose arrangement most favorable to democratic self-rule on the local and state level, inasmuch as the primary authority was located in the state legislatures. It was for achieving exactly this object, he thought, that the Confederation's strongest supporters—such leaders as Samuel Adams, Patrick Henry, Thomas Burke, and Richard Henry Lee—had pushed the Colonies into the Revolution in the first place. Conversely, those who opposed the Confederation were the men who had at first been reluctant to support the Revolution. They had feared the consequences of a break with England because that would remove the one central power strong enough to restrain the forces of local democracy. These men did, to be sure, join the Patriot forces after the break had become inevitable. Yet almost at once they began working for a continental government which might supply the stabilizing and conservative force previously maintained by the Crown. Their eventual triumph would come, of course, at Philadelphia in 1787.

In a second book, *The New Nation* (1950), Jensen considered the accomplishments of the Confederation, together with the social and economic conditions of the period from 1781 to 1789. He concluded that the "critical period" was really not so critical after all. American ships were not excluded from many foreign ports; tariff wars between states were the exception rather than the rule; the Confederation government had solved the problem of western lands and was well on the way to settling the outstanding boundary disputes. By 1786 the economic depression which had struck the country in 1784 was coming to an end. Even the problem of national credit was not so serious as the Federalists wanted people to believe, since a number of the states had assumed responsibility for portions of the Continental debt held by their own citizens. Had the states been brought to accept a national impost—a tariff duty on incoming foreign goods levied solely and exclusively by Congress, the revenue of which would be reserved for the support of the government—the Confederation would have been fully capable of surviving and functioning as a true federal establishment.

The collapse of the Confederation, Jensen argued, was not the logical outcome of weakness or inefficiency. It was the result of a determined effort by a small but tightly-organized group of nationalists to impose a centralized government upon the entire country despite the contrary desires of great majorities everywhere:

> Most of these men were by temperament or economic interest believers in executive and judicial rather than legislative control of state and central governments, in the rigorous collection of taxes, and, as creditors, in strict

payment of public and private debts. . . . They deplored the fact that there was no check upon the actions of majorities in state legislatures; that there was no central government to which minorities could appeal from the decisions of such majorities, as they had done before the Revolution.

These were the men who conspired to overthrow the Confederation and who masterminded the triumph of the Constitution.

There were points at which Jensen had not seen eye to eye with Beard. He was more impressed, for instance, by the Fathers' general outlook and ideology than by their property holdings; unlike Beard, moreover, he denied that the Confederation era was a time of serious economic difficulty. Yet he had actually strengthened the Beardian logic at more than one point, and the differences were minor in the light of the convictions which united the two in spirit and intention. The work of Merrill Jensen, like that of Beard and Parrington and J. Allen Smith before him, still balanced on the assumption that the energy behind the American Constitution was conspiratorial energy, and that the Constitution came into being by means of a *coup d'état*—through the plotting of a well-disciplined Toryish few against the interests of an unvigilant democratic majority.

Indeed, Merrill Jensen's *The New Nation*—published two years after the death of Charles Beard—was the last major piece of Constitution scholarship to be done in the Progressive tradition, and represented the end of an era. By that time, 1950, Beard's own notions had begun to arouse not the admiration, but the suspicion, of a new generation of postwar intellectuals.

III

A few modest little articles, case studies of ratifying conventions held in individual states in 1788, had begun appearing here and there in the regional quarterlies. In 1947 there was one by Philip Crowl on Maryland, another on North Carolina by William Pool in 1950, still another on Virginia by Robert Thomas in 1953. Such fragments, of course, could not be expected to cause much immediate stir. But these studies carried implications, similar in each case, that would prove in the long run profoundly damaging to the whole structure of Beardian scholarship and Beardian reasoning.

A major item in that reasoning had been Beard's assumption that the principle which differentiated Federalists from Anti-Federalists was the principle of class and property interests—that the Federalists as a group were upholding one kind of class interest and defending one form of property while the Anti-Federalists, presumably, represented something else, something basically opposed. For some reason, Beard had never taken the trouble to check the Anti-Federalist side of his equation. Thomas, in his study of the delegates to the Virginia ratifying convention (where the fight had been unusually bitter), discovered that the members of both sides held property of essentially the same kind, in approximately the same amounts, and represented the same social class—the planting gentry. The other studies showed a similar pattern. In short, the conflict over ratification was apparently fought out not between classes, but between cliques of the same ruling class within these states, and whatever the conflict's "real" basis, it was not a struggle over property rights as such. Beard's "class" and "property" formula was simply indeterminate; the story had to be found elsewhere.

By 1956, Beard's *Economic Interpretation* had been set up for the *coup de grâce*. The executioner was Robert E. Brown, a professor at Michigan State who had been at work for some time implacably compiling a catalogue of the Master's offenses. In his *Charles Beard and the Constitution*, published that year, Brown tracked Beard through every page of the latter's masterpiece and laid the ax to virtually every statement of importance that Beard had made in it. There was absolutely no correlation between the Philadelphia delegates' property holdings and the way they behaved on the question of a constitution. It was not true that large numbers of adult males were disfranchised; the suffrage was remarkably liberal everywhere. Farmers as a class were by no means chronically debtors; many were creditors and many others were both. The supporters of Shays' Rebellion (the debtors' uprising in western Massachusetts which occurred during the fall and winter of 1786–1787) were certainly not united against the Constitution; if they had been, it could never have been ratified, since the Shaysites had a clear majority at the time of the Massachusetts convention. Nor did the Philadelphia delegates know that the Continental debt would be funded at par. If they had, the banker Robert Morris, for one, would never have speculated in western lands with the thought of paying for them in depreciated Continental paper.

Not only was Beard's evidence inconclusive at all points, Brown insisted, but there were even occasions when the Master had not been above doctoring it. He edited Madison's Federalist No. 10 to eliminate all but its economic emphasis; he quoted only those passages of the Philadelphia debates that made the Fathers look least democratic; he arranged his treatment of the ratification process in an order that violated chronology, centered unjustified attention on states where hard struggles did occur, overlooked the ease with which ratification was achieved in other states, and thus created a wildly exaggerated picture of the opposition at large.

Brown's book was respectfully received; there was little inclination to dispute his arguments; no champions arose to do serious battle for the departed Beard. Some of the reviewers were a little dismayed at Brown's tone; they thought it need not have been quite so ferocious. And the book did seem to bear out the principle that any work of destruction in the realm of discourse, however necessary, must be executed within restrictions that make for a certain stultification. Richard Hofstadter remarked in this connection that Brown was "locked in such intimate embrace with his adversary that his categories are entirely dictated by Beard's assertions." Even Brown, in his way, had toyed with the "reality" theme. He had exonerated the Fathers of conspiratorial intentions but convicted Charles Beard in their place: Beard had cooked the evidence, had conspired to hide the truth.

The first effort in recent years to view the Constitution all over again in a major way, shaking off the Beardian categories and starting as it were from scratch, has been undertaken by Forrest McDonald. *We The People,* published in 1958, was the first of a planned trilogy whose design was to survey anew the entire story of how the Constitution was brought into existence. Although McDonald, like Brown, felt it necessary to show the inadequacy of Beard's conclusions, his strategy was quite different from Brown's; it was undertaken less to discredit Beard than to clear the way for his own projected treatment of the great subject. In the *Economic Interpretation,* Beard had made a number of proposals for research which he himself had not performed—and never did perform—but which would, Beard felt, further corroborate his own "frankly fragmentary" work. McDonald began by undertaking the very research which Beard had suggested, and its results convinced him that Beard had simply asked all the wrong questions.

One of the things McDonald investigated in *We The People* was an assumption upon which Beard had put a great deal of stress, the notion of a fundamental antagonism between "personalty" and "realty" interests at the time of the Philadelphia Convention. ("Personalty" was wealth based on securities, money, commerce, or manufacturing; "realty" was landed property whose owners' outlook tended to be primarily agrarian.) He found that there was no such split in the Convention. The seven men who either walked out of the Convention or else refused to sign the completed document were among the heaviest security-holders there, and represented "an all-star team of personalty interest." In state after state, moreover, there was no appreciable difference between the property holdings of Federalists and Anti-Federalists. Finally, the three states that ratified the Constitution unanimously—Delaware, New Jersey, and Georgia—were overwhelmingly dominated by agrarian interests.

Unlike Brown, McDonald was quite unwilling to write off the possibility of an economic analysis (his book's subtitle was *The Economic Origins of the Constitution*); it was just that Beard's particular economic categories led nowhere. Beard's sweeping "personalty" and "realty" classifications were meaningless, and he had deceived himself profoundly in supposing that the Federalists' property interests "knew no state boundaries" but were "truly national in scope." On these two points of difference McDonald set up an entirely new and original research scheme, and in so doing effected a really impressive conceptual maneuver. He was quite ready, in the first place, to find "economic forces" behind the movement for a constitution, but these must be sought not in "classes" or in broad categories of property but rather in the specific business interests of specific groups in specific places. The other organizing category would be the individual states themselves. The political framework within which any group had to operate was still that imposed by the state; the states were, after all, still sovereign units, and the precise relationship between economic forces and political action depended almost entirely on the special conditions within those states, conditions which varied from one to the other.

By abandoning Beard's "national" framework and recasting the entire problem on a state-by-state basis, McDonald made it possible to see with a sudden clarity things which ought to have been obvious all along. The states where ratification was achieved most readily were those that were convinced, for one reason or another, that they could not survive and prosper as independent entities; those holding out the longest were the ones most convinced that they could go it alone. The reasons for supporting ratification might vary considerably from state to state. For Georgia, an impending Indian war and the need for military protection could transcend any possible economic issue; New York, at one time imagining for itself an independent political and economic future, would finally ratify for fear of being isolated from a system which already included ten states and which might soon be joined by a seceded New York City.

The single problem of the Continental debt took different forms in different states. New Jersey, Massachusetts, and New York had each assumed portions of the debt held by their own citizens, but New Jersey and Massachusetts found their obligations intolerably burdensome while New York did not. Massachusetts had put an excessively heavy load on its direct property and poll-tax system; thus any possibility of the debt's being funded by a new Federal government should have found both the Boston security-holder and the Shaysite debtor more than willing to support such a government—and this, it appears, is about what happened. In New York and New Jersey an additional key to the debt issue was the question of a national tariff. New York had a state tariff, which was part of a financial system worked out to service the debt, and for that reason the state had been reluctant to accept a national impost in 1786. New Jersey, on the other hand, with no ocean trade of any account and having to receive most of its imports through New York, had no such revenue, was hard pressed to maintain interest payments on its debt, and thus had everything to gain from both a national impost and a national funding system. New Jersey was one of the first to ratify, and did so unanimously.

Recognizing the importance of specific location made it also easier and more natural to appreciate the way in which particular interests in particular places might be affected by the question of a stronger national government. Boston shipping interests, for example, seem to have been less concerned in the 1780's over class ideology or general economic philosophy than over those conditions of the times which were especially bad for business. The British would not let them into the West Indies, the French were excluding their fish, and their large vessels were no longer profitable. A strong national government could create a navy whose very existence would reduce high insurance rates; it could guarantee an orderly tariff system that would remove all pressure for higher and higher state tariffs; and it could counter British and French discrimination by means of an effective navigation act. Manufacturing interests would also tend to favor the Constitution, though not necessarily on principle; the vigor of their support would depend on the size of their establishments and the extent to which they competed with England. Support from Pennsylvania iron and Connecticut textiles would be particularly energetic. So also with the wheat and tobacco farmers of the Connecticut Valley, though not for the same reason. They had to pay import taxes to New York for the goods they bought (their crops were sold there); they were heavily taxed, at the same time, to support a state-funded debt which they would be only too glad to see removed by a central government. Farmers in the Kentucky area, on the other hand, could be very suspicious of a Constitution under which northeastern shipping interests might influence the government to surrender free navigation on the Mississippi in return for a favorable trade treaty with Spain.

Forrest McDonald's work, according to him, has only just begun; years of it still lie ahead. But already a remarkable precision of detail has been brought to the subject, together with a degree of sophistication which makes the older economic approach—"tough-minded" as it once imagined itself—seem now a little wan and misty. The special internal conditions of the several states now seem fully valid as clues to the ratification policies of those states, each in its separate turn. And there is a credibility about the immediate needs and aspirations of particular groups, and the way they varied from place to place, that Beard's "interests" never quite possessed—or if they did, they had long since lost their hold on the modern mind.

And yet there are overtones in McDonald's work—for all its precise excellence, perhaps partly because of it—that have already succeeded in creating a new kind of "reality" spell. McDonald is very open-minded about all the manifold and complex and contradictory forces that converged upon the movement for a constitution. But somehow the ones he takes most seriously—the "real" forces behind the move-ment—were specific, particular, circumscribed, hard, and immediate. They were to be looked for mostly on the local level, because that is where one really finds things. A state—the largest permissible "reality" unit—was an agglomeration of specific, particular, immediate localities. There were interests to be served, political or economic, and they were *hard*. They were pursued rationally and without sentimentality; men came down where they did because their hard, immediate, specific interests brought them there. But are we prepared to say that the final result was just the sum—or extension—of these interests?

No doubt large enough numbers of people were convinced of the economic advantages they would gain under a new federal government that we may, thanks to Professor McDonald, account for a considerable measure of the support which the Constitution received. In places where there was a balance to tip, we have a much better idea of just how it happened. Still, Merrill Jensen pointed out some time ago that the economic situation was already somewhat on the mend by 1786. There were, moreover, certain powerful states such as Virginia and New York that might very well have thrived either as independent units or in coalitions with their immediate neighbors. And conditions in general could not have been so desperate that a national government was absolutely required for solving economic problems, let alone for staving off economic collapse. The steps actually taken were not the only ones possible; there were certainly alternatives, and it is hard to believe that they would all have led to disaster.

The new approach is extremely enlightening and useful. But has it yet taken on life? When will it fully engage the question of initiative and energy? How do we account for the dedication, the force and éclat, of Federalist leadership? When all is said and done, we do not exactly refer to the "interests" of a James Madison. We wonder, instead, about the terms in which he conceives of personal fulfillment, which is not at all the same. What animates him? The nationalist movement *did* have a mystique that somehow transfigured a substantial number of its leaders. What was it like, what were its origins?

IV

The work of Merrill Jensen, done in the 1930's and 1940's, has suffered somewhat in reputation due to the sweep and vehemence of the anti-

Beardian reaction. Yet that work contains perceptions which ought not to be written off in the general shuffle. They derive not so much from the over-all Beardian traditions and influences amid which Jensen wrote, as from that particular sector of the subject which he marked off and preëmpted for his own. Simply by committing himself—alone among Beardians and non-Beardians—to presenting the Confederation era as a legitimate phase of American history, entitled to be taken seriously like any other and having a positive side as well as a negative one, he has forced upon us a peculiar point of view which, by the same token, yields its own special budget of insights. For example, Jensen has been profoundly impressed by the sheer force, determination, and drive of such nationalist leaders as Hamilton, Madison, Jay, Knox, and the Morrises. This energy, he feels, created the central problem of the Confederation and was the major cause of its collapse. He deplores this, seeing in the Confederation "democratic" virtues which it probably never had, finding in the Federalists an "aristocratic" character which in actual fact was as much or more to be found in the Anti-Federalists, smelling plots everywhere, and in general shaping his nomenclature to fit his own values and preferences. But if Professor Jensen seems to have called everything by the wrong name, it is well to remember that nomenclature is not everything. The important thing—what does ring true—is that this driving "nationalist" energy was, in all probability, central to the movement that gave the United States a new government.

The other side of the picture, which does not seem to have engaged Jensen's mind half so much, was the peculiar sloth and inertia of the Anti-Federalists. Cecelia Kenyon, in a brilliant essay on these men,[3] has shown them as an amazingly reactionary lot. They were transfixed by the specter of power. It was not the power of the aristocracy that they feared, but power of any kind, democratic or otherwise, that they could not control for themselves. Their chief concern was to keep governments as limited and as closely tied to local interests as possible. Their minds could not embrace the concept of a national interest which they themselves might share and which could transcend their own parochial concerns. Republican government that went beyond the compass of state boundaries was something they could not imagine. Thus the chief difference between Federalists and Anti-Federalists had little to do with "democracy" (George Clinton and Patrick Henry were no more willing than Gouverneur Morris to trust the innate virtue of the people), but rather in the Federalists' conviction that there was such a thing as national interest and that a government could be established

---

[3] "Men of Little Faith: The Anti-Federalists on the Nature of Representative Government," *William and Mary Quarterly*, XII, 3rd ser. (January 1955), pp. 3–43.

to care for it which was fully in keeping with republican principles. To the Federalists this was not only possible but absolutely necessary, if the nation was to avoid a future of political impotence, internal discord, and in the end foreign intervention. So far so good. But still, exactly how did such convictions get themselves generated?

Merrill Jensen has argued that the Federalists, by and large, were reluctant revolutionaries who had feared the consequences of a break with England and had joined the Revolution only when it was clear that independence was inevitable. The argument is plausible; few of the men most prominent later on as Federalists had been quite so hot for revolution in the very beginning as Patrick Henry and Samuel Adams. But this may not be altogether fair; Adams and Henry were already veteran political campaigners at the outbreak of hostilities, while the most vigorous of the future Federalists were still mere youngsters. The argument, indeed, could be turned entirely around: the source of Federalist, or nationalist, energy was not any "distaste" for the Revolution on these men's part, but rather their profound and growing involvement in it.

Much depends here on the way one pictures the Revolution. In the beginning it simply consisted of a number of state revolts loosely directed by the Continental Congress; and for many men, absorbed in their effort to preserve the independence of their own states, it never progressed much beyond that stage even in the face of invasion. But the Revolution had another aspect, one which developed with time and left a deep imprint on those connected with it, and this was its character as a continental war effort. If there is any one feature that most unites the future leading supporters of the Constitution, it was their close engagement with this continental aspect of the Revolution. A remarkably large number of these someday Federalists were in the Continental Army, served as diplomats or key administrative officers of the Confederation government, or, as members of Congress, played leading rôles on those committees primarily responsible for the conduct of the war.

Merrill Jensen has compiled two lists, with nine names in each, of the men whom he considers to have been the leading spirits of the Federalists and Anti-Federalists respectively. It would be well to have a good look at this sample. The Federalists—Jensen calls them "nationalists"—were Robert Morris, John Jay, James Wilson, Alexander Hamilton, Henry Knox, James Duane, George Washington, James Madison, and Gouverneur Morris. Washington, Knox, and Hamilton were deeply involved in Continental military affairs; Robert Morris was Superintendent of Finance; Jay was president of the Continental Congress and minister plenipotentiary to Spain (he would later be appointed Secretary for Foreign Affairs); Wilson, Duane, and Gouverneur Morris were members of Congress, all three being active members of the war committees. The Anti-Federalist group presents a very different picture. It consisted of Samuel Adams, Patrick Henry, Richard Henry Lee, George Clinton, James Warren, Samuel Bryan, George Bryan, George Mason, and Elbridge Gerry. Only three of these—Gerry, Lee, and Adams—served in Congress, and the latter two fought consistently against any effort to give Congress executive powers. Their constant preoccupation was state sovereignty rather than national efficiency. Henry and Clinton were active war governors, concerned primarily with state rather than national problems, while Warren, Mason, and the two Bryans were essentially state politicians.

The age difference between these two groups is especially striking. The Federalists were on the average ten to twelve years younger than the Anti-Federalists. At the outbreak of the Revolution George Washington, at 44, was the oldest of the lot; six were under 35 and four were in their twenties. Of the Anti-Federalists, only three were under 40 in 1776, and one of these, Samuel Bryan, the son of George Bryan, was a boy of 16.

This age differential takes on a special significance when it is related to the career profiles of the men concerned. Nearly half of the Federalist group—Gouverneur Morris, Madison, Hamilton, and Knox —quite literally saw their careers launched in the Revolution. The remaining five—Washington, Jay, Duane, Wilson, and Robert Morris —though established in public affairs beforehand, became nationally known after 1776 and the wide public recognition which they subsequently achieved came first and foremost through their identification with the continental war effort. All of them had been united in an experience, and had formed commitments, which dissolved provincial boundaries; they had come to full public maturity in a setting which enabled ambition, public service, leadership, and self-fulfillment to be conceived, for each in his way, with a grandeur of scope unknown to any previous generation. The careers of the Anti-Federalists, on the other hand, were not only state-centered but—aside from those of Clinton, Gerry, and the young Bryan—rested heavily on events that preceded rather than followed 1776.

As exemplars of nationalist energy, two names in Professor Jensen's sample that come most readily to mind are those of Madison and Hamilton. The story of each shows a wonderfully pure line of consistency. James Madison, of an influential Virginia family but with no apparent career plans prior to 1774, assumed his first public rôle as a member of the Orange County Revolutionary Committee, of which his father was chairman. As a delegate from Orange County he went to the Virginia convention in 1776 and served on the committee that drafted Virginia's new constitution and bill of rights. He served in the

Virginia Assembly in 1776 and 1777 but failed of re-election partly because he refused to treat his constituents to whisky. (He obviously did not have the right talents for a state politician.) In recognition of Madison's services, however, the Assembly elected him to the Governor's Council, where he served from 1778 to 1780. Patrick Henry was then Governor; the two men did not get on well and in time became bitter political enemies. At this period Madison's primary concern was with supplying and equipping the Continental Army, a concern not shared to his satisfaction by enough of his colleagues. It was then, too, that he had his first experience with finance and the problems of paper money. He was elected to the Continental Congress in 1780, and as a member of the Southern Committee was constantly preoccupied with the military operations of Nathanael Greene. The inefficiency and impotence of Congress pained him unbearably. The Virginia Assembly took a strong stand against federal taxation which Madison ignored, joining Hamilton in the unsuccessful effort to persuade the states to accept the impost of 1783. From the day he entered politics up to that time, the energies of James Madison were involved in continental rather than state problems—problems of supply, enlistment, and finance—and at every point his chief difficulties came from state parochialism, selfishness, and lack of imagination. His nationalism was hardly accidental.

The career line of Alexander Hamilton, *mutatis mutandis,* is functionally interchangeable with that of James Madison. Ambitious, full of ability, but a young man of no family and no money, Hamilton arrived in New York from the provinces at the age of 17 and in only two years would be catapulted into a brilliant career by the Revolution. At 19 he became a highly effective pamphleteer while still a student at King's College, was a captain of an artillery company at 21, serving with distinction in the New York and New Jersey campaigns, and in 1777 was invited to join Washington's staff as a lieutenant-colonel. He was quickly accepted by as brilliant and aristocratic a set of youths as could be found in the country. As a staff officer he became all too familiar with the endless difficulties of keeping the Continental Army in the field from 1777 to 1780. With his marriage to Elizabeth Schuyler in 1780 he was delightedly welcomed into one of New York's leading families, and his sage advice to his father-in-law and Robert Morris on matters of finance and paper money won him the reputation of a financial expert with men who knew an expert when they saw one. He had an independent command at Yorktown. He became Treasury representative in New York in 1781, was elected to Congress in 1782, and worked closely with Madison in the fruitless and discouraging effort to create a national revenue in the face of state particularism. In the summer of 1783 he quit in despair and went back to New York.

Never once throughout all this period had Alexander Hamilton been involved in purely state affairs. His career had been a continental one, and as long as the state-centered George Clinton remained a power in New York, it was clear that this was the only kind that could have any real meaning for him. As with James Madison, Hamilton's nationalism was fully consistent with all the experience he had ever had in public life, experience whose sole meaning had been derived from the Revolution. The experience of the others—for instance that of John Jay and Henry Knox—had had much the same quality; Knox had moved from his bookstore to the command of Washington's artillery in little more than a year, while Jay's public career began with the agitation just prior to the Revolution and was a story of steady advancement in continental affairs from that time forward.

The logic of these careers, then, was in large measure tied to a chronology which did not apply in the same way to all the men in public life during the two decades of the 1770's and 1780's. A significant proportion of relative newcomers, with prospects initially modest, happened to have their careers opened up at a particular time and in such a way that their very public personalities came to be staked upon the national quality of the experience which had formed them. In a number of outstanding cases energy, initiative, talent, and ambition had combined with a conception of affairs which had grown immense in scope and promise by the close of the Revolution. There is every reason to think that a contraction of this scope, in the years that immediately followed, operated as a powerful challenge.

V

The stages through which the constitutional movement proceeded in the 1780's add up to a fascinating story in political management, marked by no little élan and dash. That movement, viewed in the light of the Federalist leaders' commitment to the Revolution, raises some nice points as to who were the "conservatives" and who were the "radicals." The spirit of unity generated by the struggle for independence had, in the eyes of those most closely involved in coordinating the effort, lapsed; provincial factions were reverting to the old provincial ways. The impulse to arrest disorder and to revive the flame of revolutionary unity may be pictured in "conservative" terms, but this becomes quite awkward when we look for terms with which to picture the other impulse, so different in nature: the urge to rest, to drift, to turn back the clock.

Various writers have said that the activities of the Federalists during this period had in them a clear element of the conspiratorial. Insofar as this refers to a strong line of political strategy, it correctly locates a key element in the movement. Yet without a growing base of popular dis-satisfaction with the status quo, the Federalists could have skulked and plotted forever without accomplishing anything. We now know, thanks to recent scholarship, that numerous elements of the public were only too ripe for change. But the work of organizing such a sentiment was quite another matter; it took an immense effort of will just to get it off the ground. Though it would be wrong to think of the Constitution as something that had to be carried in the face of deep and basic popular opposition, it certainly required a series of brilliant maneuvers to escape the deadening clutch of particularism and inertia. An Anti-Federalist "no" could register on exactly the same plane as a Federalist "yes" while requiring a fraction of the energy. It was for this reason that the Federalists, even though they cannot be said to have circum-vented the popular will, did have to use techniques which in their sustained drive, tactical mobility, and risk-taking smacked more than a little of the revolutionary.

By 1781, nearly five years of intimate experience with the war effort had already convinced such men as Washington, Madison, Hamilton, Duane, and Wilson that something had to be done to strengthen the Continental government, at least to the point of pro-viding it with an independent income. The ratification of the Articles of Confederation early in the year (before Yorktown) seemed to offer a new chance, and several promising steps were taken at that time. Congress organized executive departments of war, foreign affairs, and finance to replace unwieldy and inefficient committees; Robert Morris was appointed Superintendent of Finance; and a 5 per cent impost was passed which Congress urged the states to accept.

By the fall of 1782, however, the surge for increased efficiency had lost the greater part of its momentum. Virginia had changed its mind about accepting the impost, Rhode Island having been flatly opposed all along, and it became apparent that as soon as the treaty with England (then being completed) was ratified, the sense of common purpose which the war had created would be drained of its urgency. At this point Hamilton and the Morrises, desperate for a solution, would have been quite willing to use the discontent of an unpaid army as a threat to coerce the states out of their obstructionism, had not Washington refused to lend himself to any such scheme. Madison and Hamilton thereupon joined forces in Congress to work out a revenue bill whose subsidiary benefits would be sufficiently diffuse to gain it general support among the states. But in the end the best that could be managed was a new plan for a 5 per cent impost, the revenues of which would be collected by state-appointed officials. Once more an appeal, drafted by Madison, was sent to the states urging them to accept the new impost, and Washington wrote a circular in support of it. The effort was in vain. The army, given one month's pay in cash and three in certificates, reluctantly dispersed, and the Confederation government, with no sanctions of coercion and no assured revenues, now reached a new level of impotence. In June, 1783, Alexander Hamilton, preparing to leave Congress to go back to private life, wrote in discouragement and humiliation to Nathanael Greene:

> There is so little disposition either in or out of Congress to give solidity to our national system that there is no motive to a man to lose his time in the public service, who has no other view than to promote its welfare. Experience must convince us that our present establishments are Utopian before we shall be ready to part with them for better.

Whether or not the years between 1783 and 1786 should be viewed as a "critical period" depends very much on whose angle they are viewed from. Although it was a time of economic depression, the depressed conditions were not felt in all areas of economic life with the same force, nor were they nearly as damaging in some localities as in others; the interdependence of economic enterprise was not then what it would become later on, and a depression in Massachusetts did not necessarily imply one in Virginia, or even in New York. Moreover, there were definite signs of improvement by 1786. Nor can it necessarily be said that government on the state level lacked vitality. Most of the states were addressing their problems with energy and decision. There were problems everywhere, of course, many of them very grave, and in some cases (those of New Jersey and Connecticut in particular) solutions seemed almost beyond the individual state's resources. Yet it would be wrong, as Merrill Jensen points out, to assume that no solutions were possible within the framework which then existed. It is especially important to remember that when most people thought of "the government" they were not thinking of Congress at all, but of their own state legislature. For them, therefore, it was by no means self-evident that the period through which they were living was one of drift and governmental impotence.

But through the eyes of men who had come to view the states collectively as a "country" and to think in continental terms, things looked altogether different. From their viewpoint the Confederation was fast approaching the point of ruin. Fewer and fewer states were meeting their requisition payments, and Congress could not even pay its bills. The states refused to accept any impost which they themselves could not control, and even if all the rest accepted, the continued refusal of New York (which was not likely to change) would render any impost all but valueless. Local fears and jealousies blocked all efforts to establish uniform regulation of commerce, even though some such regulation seemed indispensable. A number of the states, New York in particular, openly ignored the peace treaty with England and passed discriminatory legislation against former Loyalists; consequently England, using as a pretext Congress' inability to enforce the treaty, refused to surrender the northwest posts. Morale in Congress was very low as members complained that lack of a quorum prevented them most of the time from transacting any business; even when a quorum was present, a few negative votes could block important legislation indefinitely. Any significant change, or any substantial increase in the power of Congress, required unanimous approval by the states, and as things then stood this had become very remote. Finally, major states such as New York and Virginia were simply paying less and less attention to Congress. The danger was not so much that of a split with the Confederation—Congress lacked the strength that would make any such "split" seem very urgent—but rather a policy of neglect that would just allow Congress to wither away from inactivity.

These were the conditions that set the stage for a fresh effort—the Annapolis Convention of 1786—to strengthen the continental government. The year before, Madison had arranged a conference between Maryland and Virginia for the regulation of commerce on the Potomac, and its success had led John Tyler and Madison to propose a measure in the Virginia Assembly that would give Congress power to regulate commerce throughout the Confederation. Though nothing came of it, a plan was devised in its place whereby the several states would be invited to take part in a convention to be held at Annapolis in September, 1786, for the purpose of discussing commercial problems. The snapping-point came when delegates from only five states appeared. The rest either distrusted one another's intentions (the northeastern states doubted the southerners' interest in commerce) or else suspected a trick to strengthen the Confederation government at their expense. It was apparent that no serious action could be taken at that time. But the dozen delegates who did come (Hamilton and Madison being in their forefront) were by definition those most concerned over the state of the national government, and they soon concluded that their only hope of saving it lay in some audacious plenary gesture. It was at this meeting, amid the mortification of still another failure, that they planned the Philadelphia Convention.

The revolutionary character of this move—though some writers have correctly perceived it—has been obscured both by the stateliness of historical retrospection and by certain legal peculiarities which allowed the proceeding to appear a good deal less subversive than it actually was. The "report" of the Annapolis meeting was actually a call, drafted by Hamilton and carefully edited by Madison, for delegates of all the states to meet in convention at Philadelphia the following

May for the purpose of revising the Articles of Confederation. Congress itself transmitted the call, and in so doing was in effect being brought to by-pass its own constituted limits. On the one hand, any effort to change the government within the rules laid down by the Articles would have required a unanimous approval which could never be obtained. But on the other hand, the very helplessness which the several states had imposed upon the central government meant in practice that the states were sovereign and could do anything they pleased with it. It was precisely this that the nationalists now prepared to exploit: this legal paradox had hitherto prevented the growth of strong loyalty to the existing Confederation and could presently allow that same Confederation, through the action of the states, to be undermined in the deceptive odor of legitimacy. Thus the Beardian school of constitutional thought, for all its errors of economic analysis and its transposing of ideological semantics, has called attention to one element—the element of subversion—that is actually entitled to some consideration.

But if the movement had its plotters, balance requires us to add that the "plot" now had a considerable measure of potential support, and that the authority against which the plot was aimed had become little more than a husk. Up to this time every nationalist move, including the Annapolis Convention, had been easily blocked. But things were now happening in such a way as to tip the balance and to offer the nationalists for the first time a better-than-even chance of success. There had been a marked improvement in business, but shippers in Boston, New York, and Philadelphia were still in serious trouble. Retaliatory measures against Great Britain through state legislation had proved ineffective and useless; there was danger, at the same time, that local manufacturing interests might be successful in pushing through high state tariffs. In the second place, New York's refusal to reconsider a national impost, except on terms that would have removed its effectiveness, cut the ground from under the moderates who had argued that, given only a little time, everything could be worked out. This did not leave much alternative to a major revision of the national government. Then there were Rhode Island's difficulties with inflationary paper money. Although that state's financial schemes actually made a certain amount of sense, they provided the nationalists with wonderful propaganda and helped to create an image of parochial irresponsibility.

The most decisive event of all was Shay's Rebellion in the fall and winter of 1786–1787. It was this uprising of hard-pressed rural debtors in western Massachusetts that frightened moderate people everywhere and convinced them of the need for drastic remedies against what looked like anarchy. The important thing was not so much the facts of the case as the impression which it created outside Massachusetts. The Shaysites had no intention of destroying legitimate government or of redistributing property, but the fact that large numbers of people could very well imagine them doing such things added a note of crisis which was all to the Federalists' advantage. Even the level-headed Washington was disturbed, and his apprehensions were played upon quite knowingly by Madison, Hamilton, and Knox in persuading him to attend the Philadelphia Convention. Actually the Federalists and the Shaysites had been driven to action by much the same conditions; in Massachusetts their concern with the depressed state of trade and the tax burden placed them for all practical purposes on the same side, and there they remained from first to last.

Once the balance had been tipped in enough states, to the point of a working consensus on the desirability of change, a second principle came into effect. Unless a state were absolutely opposed—as in the extreme case of Rhode Island—to any change in the Articles of Confederation, it was difficult to ignore the approaching Philadelphia Convention as had been done with the Annapolis Convention: the occasion was taking on too much importance. There was thus the danger, for such a state, of seeing significant decisions made without having its interests consulted. New York, with strong Anti-Federalist biases but also with a strong nationalist undercurrent, was not quite willing to boycott the convention. Governor Clinton's solution was to send as delegates two rigid state particularists, John Yates and Robert Lansing, along with the nationalist Hamilton, to make sure that Hamilton would not accomplish anything.

We have already seen that nineteenth century habits of thought created a ponderous array of stereotypes around the historic Philadelphia conclave of 1787. Twentieth century thought and scholarship, on the other hand, had the task of breaking free from them, and to have done so is a noteworthy achievement. And yet one must return to the point that stereotypes themselves require some form of explanation. The legend of a transcendent effort of statesmanship, issuing forth in a miraculously perfect instrument of government, emerges again and again despite all efforts either to conjure it out of existence or to give it some sort of rational linkage with mortal affairs. Why should the legend be so extraordinarily durable, and was there anything so special about the circumstances that set it on its way so unerringly and so soon?

The circumstances *were*, in fact, special; given a set of delegates of well over average ability, the Philadelphia meeting provides a really classic study in the sociology of intellect. Divine accident, though in some measure present in men's doings always, is not required as a part of this particular equation. The key conditions were all present in a pattern that virtually guaranteed for the meeting an optimum of effectiveness. A sufficient number of states were represented so that the delegates could, without strain, realistically picture themselves as thinking, acting, and making decisions in the name of the entire nation. They themselves, moreover, represented interests throughout the country that were diverse enough, and they had enough personal prestige at home, that they could act in the assurance of having their decisions treated at least with respectful attention. There had also been at work a remarkably effective process of self-selection, as to both men and states. Rhode Island ignored the convention, and as a result its position was not even considered there. There were leading state particularists such as Patrick Henry and Richard Henry Lee who were elected as delegates but refused to serve. The Anti-Federalist position, indeed, was hardly represented at all, and the few men who did represent it had surprisingly little to say. Yates and Lansing simply left before the convention was over. Thus a group already predisposed in a national direction could proceed unhampered by the friction of basic opposition in its midst.

This made it possible for the delegates to "try on" various alternatives without having to remain accountable for everything they said. At the same time, being relieved from all outside pressures meant that the only way a man could expect to make a real difference in the convention's deliberations was to reach, through main persuasion, other men of considerable ability and experience. Participants and audience were therefore one, and this in itself imposed standards of debate which were quite exacting. In such a setting the best minds in the convention were accorded an authority which they would not have had in political debates aimed at an indiscriminate public.

Thus the elements of secrecy, the general inclination for a national government, and the process whereby the delegates came to terms with their colleagues—appreciating their requirements and adjusting to their interests—all combined to produce a growing esprit de corps. As initial agreements were worked out, it became exceedingly difficult for the Philadelphia delegates not to grow more and more committed to the product of their joint efforts. Indeed, this was in all likelihood the key mechanism, more important than any other in explaining not only the peculiar genius of the main compromises but also the general fitness of the document as a whole. That is, a group of two or more intelligent men who are subject to no cross-pressures and whose principal commitment is to the success of an idea, are perfectly capable—as in our scientific communities of today—of performing what appear to be prodigies of intellect. Moving, as it were, in the same direction with a specific purpose, they can function at maximum efficiency. It was this that the historians of the nineteenth century did in their way see, and celebrated with sweeping rhetorical flourishes, when they took for granted that if an occasion of this sort could not call forth the highest level of statesmanship available, then it was impossible to imagine another that could.

Once the Philadelphia Convention had been allowed to meet and the delegates had managed, after more than three months of work, to hammer out a document that the great majority of them could sign, the political position of the Federalists changed dramatically. Despite the major battles still impending, for practical purposes they now had the initiative. The principal weapon of the Anti-Federalists—inertia—had greatly declined in effectiveness, for with the new program in motion it was no longer enough simply to argue that a new federal government was unnecessary. They would have to take positive steps in blocking it; they would have to arouse the people and convince them that the Constitution represented a positive danger.

Moreover, the Federalists had set the terms of ratification in such a way as to give the maximum advantage to energy and purpose; the key choices, this time, had been so arranged that they would fall right. Only nine states had to ratify before the Constitution would go into effect. Not only would this rule out the possibility of one or two states holding up the entire effort, but it meant that the Confederation would be automatically destroyed as an alternative before the difficult battles in New York and Virginia had to be faced. (By then, Patrick Henry in Virginia would have nothing but a vague alliance with North Carolina to offer as a counter-choice.) Besides, there was good reason to believe that at least four or five states, and possibly as many as seven, could be counted as safe, which meant that serious fighting in the first phase would be limited to two or three states. And finally, conditions were so set that the "snowball" principle would at each successive point favor the Federalists.

As for the actual process of acceptance, ratification would be done through state conventions elected for the purpose. Not only would this circumvent the vested interests of the legislatures and the ruling coteries that frequented the state capitals, but it gave the Federalists two separate chances to make their case—once to the people and once to the conventions. If the elected delegates were not initially disposed to do the desired thing, there was still a chance, after the convention met, of persuading them. Due partly to the hampering factor of transportation and distance, delegates had to have considerable leeway of choice and what amounted to quasi-plenipotentiary powers. Thus there could be no such thing as a fully "instructed" delegation, and members might meanwhile remain susceptible to argument and conversion. The convention device, moreover, enabled the Federalists to run as delegates men who would not normally take part in state politics.

The revolutionary verve and ardor of the Federalists, their resources of will and energy, their willingness to scheme tirelessly, campaign everywhere, and sweat and agonize over every vote meant in effect that despite all the hairbreadth squeezes and rigors of the struggle, the Anti-Federalists would lose every crucial test. There was, to be sure, an Anti-Federalist effort. But with no program, no really viable commitments, and little purposeful organization, the Anti-Federalists somehow always managed to move too late and with too little. They would sit and watch their great stronghold, New York, being snatched away from them despite a two-to-one Anti-Federalists majority in a convention presided over by their own chief, George Clinton. To them, the New York Federalists must have seemed possessed of the devil. The Federalists' convention men included Alexander Hamilton, James Duane, John Jay, and Robert Livingston—who knew, as did everyone else, that the new government was doomed unless Virginia and New York joined it. They insisted on debating the Constitution section by section instead of as a whole, which meant that they could out-argue the Anti-Federalists on every substantive issue and meanwhile delay the vote until New Hampshire and Virginia had had a chance to ratify. (Madison and Hamilton had a horse relay system in readiness to rush the Virginia news northward as quickly as possible.) By the time the New York convention was ready to act, ten others had ratified, and at the final moment Hamilton and his allies spread the chilling rumor that New York City was about to secede from the state. The Anti-Federalists, who had had enough, directed a chosen number of their delegates to cross over, and solemnly capitulated.

In the end, of course, everyone "crossed over." The speed with which this occurred once the continental revolutionists had made their point, and the ease with which the Constitution so soon became an object of universal veneration, still stands as one of the minor marvels of American history. But the document did contain certain implications, of a quasi-philosophical nature, that make the reasons for this ready consensus not so very difficult to find. It established a national government whose basic outlines were sufficiently congenial to the underlying commitments of the whole culture—republicanism and capitalism—that the likelihood of its being the subject of a true ideological clash was never very real. That the Constitution should mount guard over the rights of property—"realty," "personalty," or any other kind—was questioned by nobody. There had certainly been a struggle, a long and exhausting one, but we should not be deceived as to its nature. It was not fought on economic grounds; it was not a matter of ideology; it was not, in the fullest and most fundamental sense, even a struggle between nationalism and localism. The key struggle was between inertia and energy; with inertia overcome, everything changed.

There were, of course, lingering objections and misgivings; many of the problems involved had been genuinely puzzling and difficult; and there remained doubters who had to be converted. But then the perfect bridge whereby all could become Federalists within a year was the addition of a Bill of Rights. After the French Revolution, anti-constitutionalism in France would be a burning issue for generations; in America, an anti-constitutional party was undreamed of after 1789. With the Bill of Rights, the remaining opponents of the new system could say that, ever watchful of tyranny, they had now got what they wanted. Moreover, the Young Men of the Revolution might at last imagine, after a dozen years of anxiety, that *their* Revolution had been a success.

FORREST McDONALD

The term anti-Federalists[1] means those persons who opposed the establishment of a national government under the Constitution. Anti-Federalists did not use the term to designate themselves; it was coined by Federalists as a term of opprobrium, and was used much as one might today denounce a conservative by calling him a reactionary or a fascist, or denounce a liberal as a radical left-winger or communist. Because the label stuck, however, it can be used here as a convenient term for purposes of communication, without conveying disapproval, at least not in the sense in which it originally conveyed disapproval.

Indeed, the most important point to be made about the anti-Federalists is that they were not, as they were sometimes depicted by the Federalists, uniformly unintelligent, uninformed, and unprincipled; and neither were they the downtrodden masses, the exploited farmers,

---

[1] Spellings of the term vary. Mr. Jackson T. Main, in his book *The Antifederalists* (Chapel Hill, 1961), uses a single, unhyphenated word with a capital "A": Antifederalists. This and "Antifœderalists" were as commonly used by Federalist writers as were "Anti-federalists" and "anti-Federalists" and their variants with the "œ" character. Historians have used all these spellings. The single capitalized word, Antifederalists, suggests that the writers of the term had something positive in common that would justify thinking of them as a group—in general, cohesiveness, organization, self-consciousness, and some existence pre-dating the contest over the Constitution. The term anti-Federalists has a different connotation: it only designates those persons who, on the single issue of the ratification of the Constitution, opposed the persons calling themselves Federalists. It is thus the more neutral term and in my judgment, the preferable term.

SOURCE: *The Wisconsin Magazine of History*, XLVI (Spring, 1963), 206–214. All but two of the original footnotes have been omitted. Reprinted by permission of the publisher.

or the debtor class; nor yet the "agrarian-minded," the old Whigs, or the radicals, as they have been depicted by various twentieth-century historians. Their leadership matched that of the Federalists for intelligence, education, experience, and political savoir faire, and they comprehended a similar assortment of rich men, poor men, virtuous men and thieves. In short, they can not be ordered with any rigid or simple system of classification.

Answering the question, Who were the anti-Federalists and how did they come to be that way? involves answering, in large measure, the same question about their opposite number, the Federalists, and neither is an easy undertaking. A suitable point of departure, I think, is a comment made by Edmund Morgan: "The most radical change produced in Americans by the Revolution was in fact not a division at all"—for they began divided—"but the union of three million cantankerous colonists into a new nation." It is explaining why so many people espoused more perfect union through the Constitution, and not why so many people opposed it, that is the difficult task.

This point will be illustrated, and the first basis of division established, by recalling certain facts of life, as life was lived in the eighteenth century, that are so obvious as to be almost invisible. Given the existing technology of communication and transportation—which dictated that these functions be synonymous, and that travel by water was far easier and faster than travel by land—it took about the same amount of time to move men, goods, money, or ideas and information from Portsmouth, New Hampshire, to Liverpool as it did to move them to, say, Augusta, Georgia. Similarly, in point of time Philadelphia— possibly the second largest English-speaking city in the world—was little further from London, the largest, than it was from Pittsburgh, and it was closer to London than was Vienna. Norfolk was closer to the Azores than to the furthermost Virginia town; Charleston was closer to any island in the British West Indies than it was to Raleigh.

It was thus far more natural for most Americans to think in local terms than in national terms, and, when they thought about it at all, to prefer local authority to national authority. If distance made unreasonable the notion that the thirteen colonies could be well governed from London, distance made almost equally far-fetched the notion that the thirteen states could be well governed by a single national government. In short, for most people the natural thing to be was an anti-Federalist, and it took something special to make them think otherwise. Too, simply by virtue of living in one place instead of another, Americans were less or more prone to think nationally: to be aware of the existence of national problems, and to think of themselves as Americans before thinking of themselves as citizens of their states or towns. An inhabitant of, say, Jaffrey, New Hampshire, would normally not have direct contact with the government of the United States from one year to the next, would deal with his state government only through the annual visit of the tax collector, and would come into direct contact with information, ideas, or people from the outside world only two or three times a year. On the other hand, in the normal course of events an inhabitant of Philadelphia would, irrespective of his occupation, wealth, education, or station in life, come into daily contact with persons and news and ideas from the other states and, indeed, from Europe as well.

These were the first and most important factors predisposing Americans towards national or provincial loyalties during the post-war decade, and towards corresponding loyalties during the contest over ratification—and their preponderating weight was on the side of localism. Several other sets of predisposing factors worked the other way: particularly, the wartime experience of some people, the peacetime experience of others, and the economic interests of still others.

Among those who became devoted to the national cause as a result of the war, three groups are most important. First, those who learned at first-hand the idiocy of attempting to wage a war without a government, which would include particularly members of Congress and important administrative officials who served between 1778 and 1782.[2] Second, those who fought in the war, particularly those in the continental line and most particularly those officers who served close to Washington. Third, those who inhabited areas which suffered great devastation or long occupation at the hands of the British during the war.

The peacetime experience (1783–1787) likewise convinced some that a national government was necessary, but its effect was upon whole populations of whole states—that is, on those states in which the experiments in independence convinced most people that their states could not make a go of it alone. Making a go of it appeared impossible for a variety of reasons: in Connecticut because of a hopelessly ensnarled fiscal system that blocked the successful working of both government and economy; in Maryland because of a political movement that portended great social upheaval; in Georgia because of an Indian uprising that threatened the very survival of the inhabitants; and so on.

As to the role of economic interests, I have previously devoted 435 pages of a book to an effort to delineate how these worked in winning

---

[2] This generalization, like all generalizations made here, is only partially valid; an effort will be made later to account for the exceptions. The striking exception to the generalization about Congress is the members of the so-called Lee-Adams Junto—delegates from Virginia and Massachusetts and certain of their allies, especially in New England—who were in Congress for part of the years cited, and some of whom later opposed the Constitution.

friends for the Constitution, and apart from repeating that they were complex, subtle, and variable, I shall not reiterate the effort here. But I shall return to economic interests that worked for anti-Federalism in a moment.

Now, if one applies to the contest over ratification the several considerations just mentioned, one comes up with a remarkable picture of it. I invite you to try it. Begin with an outline map of the United States, vintage 1787, with counties and towns indicated. Then color in red (for Federalist) all places which had regular intercourse with other states, and color the remainder blue (for anti-Federalist). Then erase and change from blue to red all areas which were occupied by British armies for more than a year, or in which the ascertainable destruction from warfare exceeded, say, 25 per cent of the total value of property other than land. Then repeat the operation for places which furnished members of Congress between 1778 and 1782, and men who served in the continental line with the rank of lieutenant colonel or higher; and do so again for places in which the place itself or three of its half-dozen richest inhabitants stood to profit directly by the adoption of the Constitution. Finally, repeat the operation for the entirety of the five states which, given the objective conditions prevailing under the Articles of Confederation, considered themselves the weakest: Connecticut, New Jersey, Maryland, Delaware, and Georgia. The map you end up with will, at a glance, seem scarcely distinguishable from Orin G. Libby's maps showing the geographical distribution of the vote on the ratification of the Constitution.

But only at a glance. Closer inspection will reveal discrepancies, e.g., that thirteen of the fourteen delegates from counties in the Trans-Alleghany region of Virginia, which you have as blue (anti-Federalist) actually voted for ratification; or that the Connecticut Valley and Cape Cod come out as checkerboards, whereas you have them definitely one way or the other. In all, perhaps a fourth or a fifth of the votes are as yet unaccounted for.

And that is as far as a general analysis of the contest can go. For the remainder of the analysis, one must look to individuals and to vested interests in local politics. When the microscope is thus applied, the leaders of anti-Federalism, as well as the most important dynamic elements in their opposition to the Constitution, stand revealed.

Individuals first. For one kind of person, at least, it was possible to be well educated, well informed, disinterested, and genuinely concerned over the national welfare, and yet opposed to ratification. This was the ideologue, the doctrinaire republican in the classical sense, who could oppose the Constitution on the grounds that it contained many imperfections from the point of view of republican principles of political theory. Now, what makes a man a doctrinaire—republican or any other kind—I can not say, but who these men were and what they believed and how they behaved is easily enough pointed out. In the Constitutional Convention, they were Elbridge Gerry, Edmund Randolph, John Francis Mercer, George Mason, and perhaps others; in the country at large, they were such prominent anti-Federalists as Joshua Atherton of New Hampshire, Rawling Lowndes of South Carolina, George Bryan of Pennsylvania, Timothy Bloodworth of North Carolina, and a host of Virginians. They were men in the rationalist tradition, men who reasoned from principles to particulars, men whose views were the precise opposite of that so well expressed by John Dickinson in the Constitutional Convention: "Experience," said Dickinson, "must be our only guide. Reason may mislead us." Such men viewed Harrington, Locke, and Montesquieu much as a fundamentalist views the Holy Bible; to them, political salvation lay in the difficult but possible task of devising a perfect system. Inasmuch as reason would show that any imperfect form (whether democratic, aristocratic, or monarchistic) would inevitably degenerate into tyranny, it was better to make do without a national government than to create an imperfect one.

With the ideologues the Federalists could argue, through the facile pens and dexterous wits of such skilled theoreticians as Hamilton, Madison, Wilson, Coxe, and Webster. Vested interest groups were another matter, and Federalists could cope with them only by hurling derisive epithets—"pretended patriots," "ambitious and interested men," "artful and designing men," "anti-Federalists"—or by attempting to offer contrary interests. A part of the opposition to the Constitution by vested interest groups has long since been recognized: in the very first number of *The Federalist,* Hamilton predicted that "men in every State" would "resist all changes which may hazard a diminution of the power, emolument and consequence of the offices they hold under the State-establishments"; and in 1924 Allan Nevins made it clear that holders of important state offices generally were, in fact, anti-Federalists. But we are dealing here with a much larger field. Lucrative and prestigious state offices were few, and men with vested interests in state primacy were legion.

It is impossible to delineate all such vested interest groups here, but it is possible to draw lines around enough of them to afford abundant illustration of the point. New York offers a prime example. Governor George Clinton, aspiring to make his the Empire State and to establish a dynasty to rule it, had the good sense to realize that doing so involved the use of political power both to govern well and to buy the loyalties of people through their ambition or avarice.

This was not a simple task, and should not be regarded as such. That is, most modern devices which we associate with the welding of political organizations were not available to Clinton. The functions of government were yet too limited to permit building power through patronage; public works were too few to permit building power through graft in the construction business; and so on. One will search in vain for evidence of modern manifestations of machine politics.

But one can hold to this maxim: wherein lies the profit in dealing with government, there also lies the greatest source of power. In New York, as in most states, profit in dealing with government lay in public lands and the public debt. Salable public lands in New York consisted primarily of confiscated loyalist estates, the total market value of which was some £750,000 New York current, or almost $2,000,000. The unimaginative stirrer of these ingredients might have been disposed simply to sell the estates, pay the debts, and be done with it. Not so with Clinton; no dullard was he. On the theory that one wins friends among the well-to-do by making them better-to-do, he arranged, through a series of acts and administrative decisions, that the confiscated estates be disposed of according to a careful design. So as to insure that the field of buyers would not be cluttered with small purchasers, the lands were sold in large blocs at public auction. So as to insure profits to all speculators, it was provided in 1780 that purchases could be made on the installment plan and in certain kinds of public securities, at par. Since these securities had not yet been provided for, they could be bought on the open market at prices which returned handsome profits to purchasers of confiscated estates. In effect, such operators were enabled to buy on the market at prices ranging from three shillings nine pence to four shillings on the pound, and sell to the state (for confiscated estates) at twenty shillings.

The speculative orgy thus engendered lasted from the latter part of the war to 1786, until a number of rich people had become political friends and a larger number of political friends had become rich people. Then it was time for the next step. It was time to do justice to the suffering public creditors. But not quite all of them. Clinton's chief financial advisor, state treasurer Gerard Bancker, first reckoned how much debt could be supported with the income from the state's lucrative import duties, and then combed the lists of security holders and came up with tables of the various combinations of securities in which a minimum expenditure could result in largesse for a maximum number of voters. In what was offered to the public as a generous, responsible, and patriotic action, the Clintonians decided to fund not only all the state debts but about $1,400,000 of continental debts as well. Two forms of continental debts were assumed: Loan Office Certificates and so-called Barber's Notes, certificates issued by the United States for supplies furnished the continental army. Some 5,000 holders of continental securities—about half the number of voters in a normal election—were provided for under this act. As the system was devised, these securities were neither paid off nor funded; they were simply lent to the state, and the state punctually paid interest on them. Note that the system created, in effect, a list of 5,000 pensioners. Note also that the action could hardly have been inspired by either patriotism or responsibility, for $3,600,000 in other kinds of continental debts held in the state, which were politically less potent because they were concentrated in the hands of only a couple of hundred persons, remained unfunded. These scheme was, as one critic charged, "a studied design to divide the interests of the public creditors."

But it was even more than that. It was also a method for doubly rewarding the faithful and punishing those who had been so wicked as to fail to appreciate past favors. The rise in security prices which quickly followed the funding act caught the speculators in confiscated estates as bears in a bull market. That is, they were in effect short sellers, whose profits depended upon keeping the security market low; they were heavily extended for installment delivery of securities against purchases of confiscated estates. When the securities market rose, they found themselves having to pay roughly 300 per cent as much as they had expected to pay for the securities with which to make their payments. Not surprisingly, many of them were broken.

Those who had appreciated Clinton's generosity, however, those who had given him unreserved political support, were protected. They were informed in advance (1) that the funding would take place, (2) the precise securities which would be funded, and (3) when the operations would occur. Accordingly, they were able to cover their positions and even make a tidy sum by going long in appropriate securities.

These were merely among the more spectacular of Clinton's devices. There were others, and they all worked. Small wonder, then, that when the Constitution came along and threatened to undermine Clinton by transferring control of the more lucrative devices from the state to a general government, as well as similarly transferring that great source of revenue, the tariff, Clinton greeted the document with less than enthusiasm. Small wonder, too, that when he vigorously opposed ratification, the people of the state voted against it, 14,000 to 6,500.

Before proceeding with an effort to outline the development of major vested interest groups in other states, it is well to pause and observe that by no means all vested interests created during the period were economic interests. Greed may have been the quickest motive to which politicians could appeal, but lust for prestige and power drove most of the managers themselves and, when properly utilized, could provide a continuing basis of strength among the followers. This is clearly seen in a contrasting view of Clinton himself and of the two Clintonian delegates to the Philadelphia Convention, John Lansing and Robert Yates. Clinton was clearly driven by desire for power, and it does not alter the case that he exercised his power judiciously and, for the most part, in the interest of the state. Lansing, on the other hand, liked money. He was a rich man when he began his association with Clinton, and because he capitalized on the opportunities his party afforded, he became a much richer man. He also became a perpetually loyal party adherent. Yates, on the contrary, was incorruptible—at least, he was not corruptible by the love of money. His biographer, writing soon after his death, gives us a moving picture: "He was often urged to unite with some of his friends in speculating in forfeited estates during the war, by which he might easily have enriched himself and his connections without censure or suspicion—and although such speculations were common, yet he would not consent to become wealthy upon the ruin of others." (The biographer adds a touching footnote: "Chief Justice Yates died poor.")

Nor was Yates particularly ambitious for power. But where avarice and ambition were absent, vanity was abundantly and fatally present. Yates was induced to become a loyal Clintonian by the simple expedient of giving him an extremely prestigious position, albeit one which was neither particularly powerful nor remunerative, that of chief justice of the state supreme court. Interestingly, New York Federalists won him away from Clinton in 1789 by offering him their support for governor in a campaign against Clinton himself.

It should be noted that in regard to noneconomic vested interests the weight of advantages favored the anti-Federalists, but in individual instances of particular strategic importance, the Federalists were invariably in a position to gain. Two well-known examples illustrate this matter. Massachusetts Federalists won the indispensable support of Governor John Hancock by promising him the vice-presidency, a promise they subsequently felt no obligation to fulfill; and Virginia Federalists won the indispensable support of Governor Edmund Randolph by promising him the attorney-generalship, which he was actually awarded.

Now let us return to a survey of the development of vested interests in the states of the Confederation. The most fruitful soil for such development existed when a policy designed for the over-all, best interests of the state as a whole could be combined with policies that worked to the particular advantage of particular individuals. Such was the case with New York, and in this respect the history of Virginia during the period strikingly resembles that of New York, though it was different in every detail. The tangle of interests in Virginia—state, regional, local, and personal—was so involved that any attempt to discuss them in full here would be folly. Let us, then, take notice of such matters as confiscated estates, western lands, navigation of the Mississippi, and the nebulous but vital questions of personal prides and prestiges, but pass over them and focus on but a single aspect of the problem, Virginia's commercial policy.

Virginia had, at least in considerable measure, been moved to join the revolutionary movement as a means of dissolving the credit bands which had bound planters to British and Scotch merchants. The sequestration acts by which prewar private indebtedness, amounting to some £2,000,000, was wiped out are well known. As Isaac Harrell has so well shown, hordes of planters seized the opportunity to pay nominal sums into the state treasury and thereby legally expunge their debts to foreign merchants. What is less known is that Virginia's postwar commercial policy, whose principal architects were Patrick Henry and the Lees, was carefully designed to preserve the economic independence so unscrupulously won.

To oversimplify considerably, that program was as follows. In the view of the framers of the program, merchants had been able to enshackle Virginia planters before the war only because they operated in an artificially created oligopolistic (or semi-monopolistic) marketing system. To prevent the reforging of the chains, all that was necessary was to create, artificially, a system of excessive competition. The method chosen was to develop a Virginia mercantile class to conduct about a third of the tobacco business, and to underwrite it with a system of bounties, drawbacks, and so on, that enabled it to operate far more cheaply than foreigners. This and many nicer refinements of the state's commercial policy produced intense competition between British, Scotch, French, and other American carriers and merchants for a share of the business, for there was not enough business to go around. As a result, in the 1780's, *relative to the prewar years,* credit was easy, money was abundant, freight rates were low, and tobacco prices, despite Robert Morris' efforts to drive them down so as to fill his contract with the French Farmers' General, were high. In short, because of its political independence, Virginia had been able to liberate a vast number of its inhabitants from the clutches of their foreign creditors, and bring about a prosperity rarely matched in the preceding century.

The ensuing vested interests in Virginia's continued sovereignty are thus obvious. Equally obvious is the fact that the Constitution ran directly counter to these interests in every way. Again, the intense opposition to ratification on the part of state leaders, and the near-success of their efforts, are hardly surprising.

While public policy in these states worked to the advantage of the states as well as to that of rapacious individuals, it was not so in all places. In Massachusetts, for example, public creditors loaded an insupportable burden upon the taxpayers when they succeeded in having all their public paper funded at par in 1784. Private advantage here was contrary to public advantage, and the result was first the weakening of a state whose economy had already been totally disrupted, then in increasing popular discontent, and finally a brief civil war. In Pennsylvania the most important public actions that enriched special groups had a neutral effect upon the welfare of the whole, and consequently won only such friends of state sovereignty as could profit directly from it. In 1785, for example, that state's Constitutionalist Party (those who became anti-Federalists) caused the passage of an act simultaneously funding the state debt and that portion of the national debt owned in the state, and issuing £150,000 ($400,000) in paper money. The Bank of North America opposed this action and offered to lend the state $300,000 if it would not go through with the scheme, but the Constitutionalist majority refused. As one writer said of the entire program, "to unravel the code of policy which it contains, requires no small amount of sagacity and Machiavelian shrewdness." The principal elements in the code of policy it contained, however, are clearly visible: a calculated appeal to an existing interest group and a scheme for enriching the politicians who devised the program. The existing interest group was the public creditors, to whom the program was made immediately palatable by the payment of £100,000 of the new money to them for back interest on their holdings of national debt. The remainder of the paper was issued on loan. Constitutionalist insiders borrowed the paper from the state on long-term, easy credit, and invested in the securities being funded. Thus such Constitutionalists as Charles Pettit, William Moore, John Bayard, Frederick Kuhl, William Will, John Steinmetz, and William Irvine, all holders of several thousand pounds of public securities, profited; and such Constitutionalists as Joseph Heister, John Bishop, Nicholas Lotz, John Hanna, William Brown, William Findley, James Martin, and Robert Whitehill, most of them back-country politicians who had not previously owned any securities, suddenly emerged with profits of several thousand dollars apiece from the rise in security prices.

In 1787, Constitutionalist Party leaders formed a strong phalanx against ratification, but, not surprisingly, they were grossly lacking in public support.

If space permitted, similar developments in virtually all other states could be described. In Rhode Island the habit of mixing public policy and private gain was perhaps deepest rooted and highest developed; interestingly, this was also the state that offered the greatest resistance to the Constitution. But the existence of strong vested interest groups in Connecticut, Maryland, and North Carolina—all of whom became anti-Federalists—is abundantly evident, and traces of the phenomenon are visible elsewhere.

I would leave you, not with a summary or a conclusion, but with a question. The foregoing data, all of which are profusely documentable, smack strongly of a knaves-and-fools interpretation of anti-Federalism. Knaves and fools is precisely what Federalists charged their opponents were—the knaves, in their view, being the groups with vested interests in state governments, and the fools being both the ideologues and the uninformed or misinformed. The anti-Federalists, on the other hand, regularly charged that Federalists were knaves, but rarely accused them of being fools. Federalists viewed themselves as friends of the nation; anti-Federalists depicted themselves as friends of the people.

My question is this: if it is true, as I believe it to be, that as a general rule the verdict of history has been the view held by the winner—that of the Patriots over that of the Loyalists, of Jefferson over Hamilton, of Jackson over Biddle, of Franklin Roosevelt over Sam Insull—then how did it happen that historians have, in the main, preferred the anti-Federalists' description of themselves and of their opponents?

17

Party Development and Party Action: The American Origins
WILLIAM NISBET CHAMBERS

Among the most important developments in world history during the latter half of the twentieth century has been the rapid appearance of a great number of new states. When the United Nations was first organized, in October 1945, there were 51 signatories of the charter; by the end of 1966 membership had risen to 120, of which about half consisted of new states created out of former colonial territories in Asia and Africa. The formation of each new state posed a question about the system of politics it would adopt. It also posed the question of how that system would relate to the political ideas and institutions of the major powers: principally, the United States and

SOURCE: *History and Theory,* III, 1, pp. 91–120. Copyright © 1963 by Wesleyan University. Reprinted by permission of Wesleyan University Press.

the Soviet Union. Such a relation involved something more than the advantages, in protection and capital investment, that could accrue to the new nation. It also involved the accrual of advantages to whichever major power could add a new satellite to its constellation of influence, therewith enhancing the viability of its own politics.

The rival appeals by the great powers to the new nations have been part of a conflict between ideological imperialisms. In a century in which the ethos is democratic, the appeals have been to various forms of democracy. And since there is nothing so urgent to a new nation as the organization of its polity, nothing has been so relevant and useful in the ideological conflict among the major powers as the experience by which they themselves became democracies and formed their own political systems. In a world of so many new nations, the object lesson to be drawn from the birth of a great power is obviously full of significance.

This is why American historians have taken a new interest in the making of the American nation, and this too is why their interest has been shared by their confreres in the social sciences. A notable contribution to the study of this subject was made recently by a historian who also specializes in political science, William Nisbet Chambers of Washington University. In Political Parties in a New Nation: The American Experience, 1776–1809 *(1963), Professor Chambers undertook to tell "the story of the genesis of the first modern political parties in the United States as the first modern nation." The story was important, he felt, because "in the process of nation building, the American founders explored many problems generic to the new nations. . . . They were also involved, if most unknowingly, in a general process of political modernization in which parties were at once an element and a catalyst in a broader change from older to newer things."*

Professor Chambers distills the findings of his monograph and projects them upon a wide screen of comparative politics in the essay reprinted below. He is concerned to take the full measure of political experience in the new American republic by contrasting it with parallel experiences in Great Britain. In formulating a concept of party development and action, he considers the relevant suggestions of some noteworthy writers on the subject, viz.: Charles A. Beard, Edgar E. Robinson, Louis Hartz, Avery Leiserson, Wilfred E. Binkley, V. O. Key, Jr., Maurice Duverger, M. I. Ostrogorski and, of course, that very model of a modern major social scientist, Max Weber.

In the process of pursuing his analysis, Professor Chambers seeks to answer the following significant questions. How true is it that modern political parties arose first in Britain and later in the United States? What conceptual differences may one draw between parties and other political formations? In what respects has the concept of party used by some of our principal writers on American and British politics been inadequate? Why may it be said that politics in America in the 1770's and

1780's was premodern or faction politics? How did Hamilton transform a faction into a party? How did the Republican Party take shape? What "generalized comparative distinctions between factions and parties" will define the characteristics of the modern political party? What historical factors explain the course of party development in the United States and Britain? Finally, what is the relevance of party development to the process of modernization and to the emergence of mass or democratic politics in a new state?

It is surely a commendable enterprise for Professor Chambers to use historical facts for formulating broad observations and to apply them to comparable developments in modern times. But it is also fair to inquire whether his observations are entirely accurate and therefore whether his application is entirely valid. Is it not self-contradictory, for example, for Chambers to argue that the modern political party in America was an innovation, a contrivance, an "artificial" creation, but that the founding fathers were unaware, in introducing it, of what they were doing? Is Chambers quite secure in following Louis Hartz's single-factor explanation of the different political systems in Britain and America, and may he not be discounting the degree to which eighteenth-century America was "feudal" and contemporaneous Britain shaped by liberalism and Lockianism? What is particularly absent from Chambers's account of American party development in the 1790's is what recent historians have been stressing a good deal: the psychology of fear, begotten of profound and unavoidable involvement in Europe's revolutionary and Napoleonic wars. How far, then, was the emergence of parties in the United States not so much what Chambers makes it out to be—the "artificial" contrivance of genius, designed to promote the working of a new democracy—as it was a "natural" by-product of mutual fears, by different groups, of what might happen to their respective liberties should control of the new state, in those very critical times, fall into the hands of alien and hostile forces?

Other questions may be asked about Professor Chambers's analysis of politics in the new nation, and indeed are being asked by such recent writers as Morton Borden, Roger Brown, Paul Goodman, Noble Cunningham, and David Hackett Fischer. But the questions are, after all, a tribute to Chambers's enterprise and perception, both for having suggested new approaches to an old and perennially challenging problem and for having opened up new fields to explore. His suggestions will prove fruitful to those studying the early American republic as well as to those studying political modernization in today's teeming world of new nations.

According to much conventional historiography, modern political parties arose first in Great Britain and later in America. A more accurate view would assert the contrary—that parties in the proper sense appeared first in the United States with the Federalists and Jeffersonian

Republicans of the 1790s, and in Great Britain only some decades later with the Whig-Liberal and Tory-Conservative formations of the 1830s and 1840s. The dates themselves are not of great moment; it is rather the issue of when, how, or under what conditions modern parties emerged that is significant. It is an argument of this essay that much about the nature and role of party can be learned from an historical analysis of the origins of party in America. A further argument is that even a brief comparison of American and English experience can further clarify such understanding. The American case is at once "special" and indicative of certain key aspects of party development in general.

The term "proper sense," of course, suggests some conceptual or theoretical distinction between parties and other formations. The point here is that it is of primary importance for the historian or political scientist who is concerned with party development or action to distinguish in a conscious, analytical manner between pre-party political formations or factions on the one hand, and parties on the other. If this distinction is carefully made, much else follows, including clarification which opens the way to historical explanation of the early development of party in the United States, and ultimately of the origin of parties generally. Thus, party is explored here as a modern political phenomenon and indeed as an aspect of political modernization in general. Finally, party is also understood as being associated with some form of *mass* politics, whether actively "democratic" or passively "plebiscitarian."[1] Democracy is construed summarily as popular representation, popular participation or initiative, and popular choice.

The focus of inquiry is on the American experience and literature, against a limited comparison with the English background. Throughout, emphasis is on certain key notions—structure and function, as central defining aspects of party action; and ideology, as a crucial but not sole defining characteristic of party behavior.

I

Studies of party development in the United States, as well as general histories of America and studies of party history in general, surprisingly seldom fix a conception of party sharply.

One may, of course, apply "party" quite loosely. The term has been used in effect to mean any considerable aggregate of men who exhibit parallel action in politics or, alternatively, any set of men who share similar beliefs, perspectives, or attitudes concerning government or policy. The first usage implies a kind of rough structural conception;

---

[1] See Max Weber, "Politics as a Vocation," in *From Max Weber: Essays in Sociology*, edited by H. H. Gerth and C. Wright Mills (New York, 1946), 102–103.

the second an equally rough ideological distinction. Such notions turn out to be the unexamined conceptions of much conventional historiography. Thus, in England, a list of parties may include Court and Country (a demarcation of geography and interest), or Royalists and Parliament Men or Whigs and Tories (loose cleavages of persuasion or outlook), whether they involve divisions in Lords and Commons only, divisions in the population, or both.[2] In America, such conceptions have encompassed Court and Country in the colonies, Patriots and Loyalists in the Revolutionary War of 1775–1783, or above all Federalists and Anti-Federalists in the conflict over the proposed Constitution in 1787–1789. As distinguished a scholar as Charles A. Beard tends thus loosely to use the term "party." He consequently draws clear, dramatic lines of continuity between the pro- and anti-Constitution forces of the 1780s on the one hand, and the Federalists and Republicans of the 1790s on the other.[3]

Several difficulties attend such usage. Conceptually, it provides no differentiation between transient, formless aggregates or alliances such as the so-called Federalists and Anti-Federalists of 1787–1789, and the more durable social formations we call parties today; and it offers no differentiation between parties, interest groups, bodies of opinion, and factions. Empirically, for the American case, such usage fits ill with the fact that the contest over ratification was actually a pluralistic sprawl of innumerable forces in thirteen state arenas rather than a clean dualistic national (much less party) conflict, or with the fact that the Federalists and Republicans of the 1790s were not in truth mere continuations-in-metamorphosis of elements involved in the ratification question.[4] Finally, loose notions of party slur over problems which are important for analytical history and political science. They encourage evasion of distinctions between party and non-party politics, and leave unexposed questions which are basic to a theory of modern party politics.

To be sure, nearer approaches to a conception of party may be found in the historical treatments. One approach is to mark party as *organization*. This concept is contained in the monumental work of Ostrogorski as it refers to both Great Britain and the United States, and it is quite

---

[2] See, e.g., the recent summary history of English parties by Sir Ivor Jennings, *Party Politics: The Growth of Parties* (Cambridge, England, 1961), 6–26.

[3] Charles A. Beard, *An Economic Interpretation of the Constitution of the United States* (New York, 1913); *Economic Origins of Jeffersonian Democracy* (New York, 1915); and his brief history, *The American Party Battle* (New York, 1928).

[4] For the politics of ratification, Forrest McDonald, *We the People: The Economic Origins of the Constitution* (Chicago, 1958), which also offers remarkable coverage of the actual state politics of the time; for the fresh origins of the parties of the 1790s, Joseph Charles, *The Origins of the American Party System* (Williamsburg, Virginia, 1956), which makes the point most effectively.

explicit in the valuable historical summary by Robinson, who stresses for America in the 1790s the existence of two "party organizations" whose "activity" rather than beliefs were of "primary importance." Finally, it is stressed in a comparative analysis by the political scientist Avery Leiserson.[5] Difficulties attend this approach also. Conceptually, it does not distinguish parties from organized interest groups or organized factions; and indeed Leiserson argues that it is probably not important to separate parties from factions. Empirically, for the American instance at least, there is a fatal flaw. The Federalists and Republicans of the 1790s may certainly be thought of as parties before they were organizations, if indeed the Federalists ever accomplished organization in any strict sense.[6] Furthermore, though in Britain organization follows more closely upon origins, Liberals and Conservatives stood as effective parties before they had achieved much in the way of organization.

A third approach to party, derived from Beard and his school of neo-Madisonian interpretation, is emphasized and reiterated by Wilfred E. Binkley in the currently leading (and most substantial) treatise in American party history.[7] He views parties, at least major or majority-bent parties, as broad *combinations* of interest groups—the "grand coalitions" of semi-sophisticated historical writing and popular commentary. This is certainly a useful conception with considerable analytical "bite," yet it too is attended by many difficulties and inadequacies. First, Binkley's conception does not distinguish parties from extended factions, which may also embrace a plurality of interest groups—and, one may add, a plurality of bodies of opinion. Second, his approach does not clarify any conceptual distinction between transient combinations on the one hand and parties as somehow more durable formations on the other. Third, the notion of party as combination of interest groups tends implicitly to locate parties in the

---

[5] M. Ostrogorski, *Democracy and the Organization of Political Parties*, 2 volumes (New York, 1902); Edgar E. Robinson, *The Evolution of American Political Parties: A Sketch of Party Development* (New York, 1924), 69–71; Avery Leiserson, *Parties and Politics: An Institutional and Behavioral Approach* (New York, 1958), 43–44, 48–50. See also the suggestive review of the literature and summary by Neil A. McDonald, *The Study of Political Parties*, Short Studies in Political Science (New York, 1955), 9–36.

[6] Truly durable and significant party organization was established on the American scene only with the advent of the Jacksonian Democrats in the 1820s and 1830s. Cf. Ostrogorski, *op. cit.*, II, 39–79, despite his treatment of earlier patterns of structure or action in the late 1700s as "the germs of . . . organization," *ibid.*, 3–38.

[7] Wilfred E. Binkley, *American Political Parties: Their Natural History*, third edition (New York, 1958).

public and in the electorate—"party-in-the-electorate," in Key's phrase[8]
—thereby slurring over important questions of intra-party relationships and behavior.   Fourth, particularly as Binkley employs it, the
concept emphasizes the role of economic group interest at the expense
of other important aspects of party behavior and politics, particularly
ideology or general perspectives, *élan*, leadership, innovation, and
organization.   Fifth, in consequence, the tendency in combination
analysis is toward a tacit model of party action as a set of mechanical
reflex-responses to the pressures of interest groups in the party
coalition.

Indeed, Binkley himself treats some of these problems.   On the
structural side, he explicitly allows for resolving "differences" among
"the several social groups attracted by common interests into an unplanned [party] association," through "the familiar practice of finding
the formula that ends debate."   He does not, however, make it clear
who "finds" the ultimate party formulas of agreement, or *how*, though
the task is implicitly treated (sometimes at least) as a leadership function.   On the ideological side, he speaks of the Federalist coalition of
1787–1789 becoming "the first of our several national political parties"
when it "coalesced into a permanent combination [and] developed a
consistent ideology" in the 1790s.   He thus at least implies ideas of
durability and distinctively partisan perspectives.   He also juggles
notions of "a cherished tradition, a passionate faith, and sometimes a
crusading spirit" within parties.[9]   Nevertheless it is difficult to see just
where this party mind-stuff or ideology lodges in Binkley's framework
of party as a congeries of economic interest groups.

More cogent suggestions as to the nature of party may be found in
two European observers who share a concern for theory, Max Weber
and Maurice Duverger.   In Weber we find a stress on the relationship
between leaders on the one hand and a party following on the other.
Distinguishing between "politically active and politically passive
elements," he argues that "a relatively small number of men [who] are
primarily interested in political life . . . [will] provide themselves with
a following through free recruitment."   The result is that "active
leadership and their freely-recruited following are the necessary
elements in the life of any party."   The "structure of parties varies,"
however, from "the purely personal followings" of "the 'parties' of
the medieval cities, such as those of the Guelphs and Ghibellines," to

---

[8] The phrase originated with Ralph M. Goldman, but has been given currency by V. O. Key, Jr., *Politics, Parties, and Pressure Groups,* fourth edition
(New York, 1958), 181–182 ff.

[9] Binkley, *op. cit.,* 3, 11, 14, 18, 22, 27–28, 29, 45–46, passim.

highly developed relationships in "the most modern form of party organizations." Without elaborating the suggestive notions of structure, and of leader-follower relationships as that structure, Weber proceeds to his well-known and useful typology: parties of aristocracy, parties of notables, and parties of politicians. These last he sees as "the children of democracy, of mass franchise, of the necessity to woo and organize the masses"—in short, of the need to mobilize a following.[10] Unfortunately, however, Weber does not go on to provide a finished concept of party operating in a political system.

In discussing the genesis of parties, Duverger suggests a recurring pattern which sheds light on the nature of parties. The mode of genesis, he maintains, at least for what he thinks of as "cadre" parties, is "the creation of parliamentary groups," followed by "the appearance of electoral committees," and then by "the establishment of a permanent connection between these two elements." Thus, given "parliamentary groups and electoral committees . . . it is enough that some permanent coordination be established between them and that regular connections unite them for us to find ourselves faced with a true political party." In fact it is not "enough"; a great many problems remain; but at least we are on the way. As parties develop, Duverger notes, and "as a result of an impulse from the centre," electoral committees are created in areas where the party previously had none.[11] This conclusion is drawn largely from an overview of experience in Great Britain, and the American story, as we shall see, is somewhat different. Yet Duverger's point is suggestive, and he himself admits other patterns.

Even so, however, a sense of puzzlement or confusion must persist, for Duverger's concept of party also remains incomplete. Puzzlement is likely to lodge even more strongly in the mind of the serious student who ranges the vast uneven quarry of the literature on American parties. If he wants to make effective use of the material, and certainly if he wants to undertake any measure of comparative or historical explanation, he must feel a need for greater conceptual clarity and firmness. As a means to such ends, it will be useful to review some of the data of politics in the American states in the 1770s and 1780s, and in the new American nation in the 1790s. In particular it should be fruitful to compare patterns of faction politics in the first period with party politics in the second.

---

[10] Weber, *loc. cit.*, 99–102.
[11] Maurice Duverger, *Political Parties: Their Organization and Activity in the Modern State* (New York, 1954), xxiv, xxvii–xxviii, xxix.

II

With only one clear exception, early American state politics was non-party politics. This was true, as noted above, even in the contest (or contests) over ratification in 1787, and it remained true in the initial "national" elections for President and Congress in 1788–1789,[12] when for the first time a potential national electoral arena existed. In the states themselves, politics was a kaleidoscopic flux of interest groupings and opinion aggregates, of free-style individual action, of shifting alignments between notable-leaders, groups, unstable factions, juntos, caucuses, and cliques.

The configurations of the political hurly-burly varied from state to state. So also, as Luetscher pointed out long ago, did the methods of politics, whether in nominations, elections, legislative behavior, or propaganda.[13] Only sophisticated Pennsylvania, with its continuing rivalry between organized Constitutionalists and Republicans (the titles referred to state issues) brewed a state party system. Yet even in Pennsylvania the alignments of leaders and interests between and within the parties were often nearly invisible to any but the practiced eye.[14] In New York, sometimes marked as a state with parties, politics actually continued with the old gruel of personal-family cliques and satellite factions inherited from colonial times. Clintonians were dominant from about 1777 to 1789 against the Delanceys or Schuylerite, Livingstonian, and (ultimately triumphant) Hamiltonian rivals. Methods were sophisticated enough to foreshadow Tammany Hall, but principals like George Clinton or agents like Alexander Hamilton remained the foci of political formations.[15] These formations showed many similarities to the old Whig "connexions" of eighteenth-century England, depending as they did on the leadership and patronage of notables, important personages, or magnates, and resting as they did on

---

[12] Charles O. Paullin, "The First Elections Under the Constitution," *Iowa Journal of History and Politics,* II (1904), 3–33.

[13] George D. Luetscher, *Early Political Machinery in the United States* (Philadelphia, 1903).

[14] See, e.g., portions on early politics in Harry M. Tinkcom, *The Republicans and Federalists in Pennsylvania, 1790–1801: A Study in National Stimulus and Local Response* (Harrisburg, Pennsylvania, 1950), and in Russell J. Ferguson, *Early Western Pennsylvania Politics* (Pittsburgh, 1938); also Forrest McDonald, *op. cit.,* 163–172.

[15] See Dixon Ryan Fox, "The Decline of Aristocracy in the Politics of New York," *Studies in History, Economics and Public Law,* LXXXVI, Columbia University (New York, 1919), and biographies such as E. Wilder Spaulding, *His Excellency George Clinton* (New York, 1938), or Nathan Schachner, *Alexander Hamilton* (New York, 1946); also, Forrest McDonald, *op. cit.,* 283–300.

intricate webs of personal ties. Indeed, Edmund Burke would have found them familiar.[16]

Despite variations, and with the exception of Pennsylvania, this early American state politics may be described most generally as *faction politics*—with the variations lying in personal cliques, the planter-élite "Fifty Families" junto in Maryland, the caucuses of Massachusetts, and the like.

Analysis of these early formations affords some important distinctions. Generally, a *faction* appeared as a portion of an electorate, political élite, or legislature, whose adherents were engaged in parallel action or coordination of some consistency but of limited durability, in conflict with other portions. Innumerable such loose factions characterized the early American scene. A *clique* was a portion whose relationships depended upon a commanding individual, a family, or a close coterie of personal associates; generally, the death or retirement of the focal individual led to the extinction of the clique. A *junto*, as the term was commonly used, meant a portion which operated as a small, often secret, dominant group at a seat of government, whether state, county, or town; this variety of formation was most commonly found in the Southern states. A *caucus* was generally the coordinating nucleus group of a larger faction. None of these formations took on the stature of a party, and such formations were not generally thought of as parties by contemporaries. It is in this sense of its hinging on factions rather than parties that we may speak of early American politics as "faction politics," using the term "faction" to include lesser but similar formations such as cliques, juntos, and caucuses. Except where factions were unusually broad in their range, we might speak of "connexion politics." It is with such patterns of political operation,[17] and their implications, that we shall later contrast party politics.

---

[16] It was Burke, of course, who praised "Honourable connexion[s]" as means by which men could "act in concert," and "act with confidence," because they were "bound together by common opinions, common affections, and common interests," or "practiced friendship and experimented fidelity"—but it was also Burke who defined "party" as "a body of men united, for promoting by their just endeavours the national interest, upon some particular principle in which they are all agreed," and who argued the necessity of party as a "proper means towards . . . the proper ends of government," in "public life" as "a situation of power and energy" (Edmund Burke, *Thoughts on the Cause of the Present Discontents,* ed. F. G. Selby [London, 1902], 78–84). In short, Burke is a transitional figure, familiar in practice with old-style *"connexions,"* but concerned with possibilities of political action which could be realized only in *parties,* and remarkably principled parties at that.

[17] For faction politics in the early American states, cf. Elisha P. Douglas, *Rebels and Democrats: The Struggle for Equal Political Rights and Majority Rule During the American Revolution* (Chapel Hill, North Carolina, 1955); Frederick

Faction politics in America in the 1770s and 1780s was, broadly speaking, premodern. Like English politics in the eighteenth century, it depended heavily on personalities and personal connections, and often on the deference of plain men to "notabilistic" leaders. Again like English politics, it was disorderly, subject to abrupt changes, and semi-invisible—often, for example, the factional ties of candidates or government officials were unknown to the public, or changed without notice from election to election or between elections; and few factions showed much durability. While political methods were frequently sophisticated, they were also highly variable and subject to change according to the impulses of leaders of the moment. Policy-making was, like much policy-making in eighteenth-century England, heavily influenced by shifting factional or bloc combinations in the legislatures, by clique or junto domination, by the plurality of group pressures or opinions at the moment, and by individual caprice. In short, early American faction politics lacked the degrees of order, visible continuity and relative clarity of political formations or positions, and stable rationalization of political methods, which may be counted among the characteristics of modern party politics. Compared with English politics of the same era,[18] however, it was less hierarchical, aristocratic, or élitist, and in this sense may be viewed as a transitional form.

W. Dallinger, *Nominations for Elective Office in the United States* (New York, 1903); Ralph Volney Harlow, *The History of Legislative Methods in the Period Before 1825* (New Haven, 1917); Allan Nevins, *The American State During and After the Revolution* (New York, 1924); Charles Henry Ambler, *Sectionalism in Virginia from 1776 to 1861* (Chicago, 1910); Walter R. Fee, *The Transition from Aristocracy to Democracy in New Jersey* (Somerville, N.J., 1933); Fox, "The Decline of Aristocracy in the Politics of New York," *loc. cit.*; also, Forrest McDonald, *op. cit.*, 113–346.

[18] For the English contrast, and politics, "parties," connexions, and factions in the eighteenth century, cf. Charles B. Realey, *The Early Opposition to Sir Robert Walpole, 1720–1727* (Lawrence, Kansas, 1931); Keith Feiling, *The Second Tory Party, 1714–1832* (London, 1938); Lewis M. Wiggin, *The Faction of Cousins: A Political Account of the Grenvilles, 1733–1763* (New Haven, Connecticut, 1958); L. B. Namier, *The Structure of Politics at the Accession of George III*, second edition (London, 1957), and *England in the Age of the American Revolution* (London, 1930), esp. Chapters II, III; John Brooke, *The Chatham Administration, 1766–1768* (London, 1956), esp. 218–294; Herbert Butterfield, *George III, Lord North and the People, 1779–80* (London, 1949). For recent discussions of the subject, cf. also Namier, "Monarchy and the Party System," in *Personalities and Powers* (London, 1955), and Herbert Butterfield, *George III and the Historians*, revised edition (New York, 1959), esp. 193–299; Jacob M. Price, "Party, Purpose, and Pattern: Sir Lewis Namier and His Critics," *Journal of British Studies*, I (1961), 71–93. The insights of Ostrogorski, *op. cit.*, I, 6–134, into eighteenth-century English politics as a kind of pre-party politics should also be noted.

Such politics also offered differential advantages to persons or groups who stood high on the scale of property, position, and power. Government was broadly republican and a substantial potential electorate existed despite property and tax qualifications. The extreme looseness, semi-invisibility, and confusion of informal politics, however, tended to limit effective popular influence, to the advantage of "well-placed" interests.

III

Although the Constitution of 1787 provided a national electoral arena, obstacles to the formation of national parties remained. The pluralism of American society and early politics—regional dissimilarities, the variety of economic undertakings, the multiplicity of groups and religious sects, varying perspectives across the country—all stood in the way. Individuals resisted being herded, many citizens feared what George Washington called "the baneful effects of the spirit of party generally,"[19] and state leaders and populations clung to special local identities and interests against national "consolidation."

The earliest impetus for party formation came from the new center of national government. Furthermore, as Joseph Charles has argued effectively, party origins sprang from cleavage over significant national issues affecting the shape the new nation would take and over general ideological outlooks, together with critical questions of world politics and foreign policy.[20] Controversies which began at the national capital were carried to the country, and provided the reference points for party development.

The first representative leader in polarizing proto-party forces was Hamilton, whose political style is thus critically relevant. In a new, almost unstructured situation, he stepped forward as a bold advocate determined to create policy innovation, and his controversial five-point

---

[19] Indeed, "this spirit, unfortunately, is inseparable from our nature . . . It exists under different shapes in all governments . . . but in those of the popular form it is seen in its greatest rankness and is truly their worst enemy . . . in governments purely elective, it is a spirit not to be encouraged." (George Washington, "Farewell Address," September 17, 1796, in Henry Steele Commager, ed., *Documents of American History,* third edition [New York, 1946], I, 172). Given Washington's hidden patrician value premises, there are interesting empirical suggestions here—perhaps Hamilton's—about the nature and operations of party, particularly as they may be related to mass or democratic politics and the potential effect of party on differential advantages in power.

[20] Charles, *op. cit.,* 4–53, 74–90. Despite some over-argument and other flaws, Charles' volume remains a provocative treatment of the main themes of early American party development. See also the present writer's study, *Parties in a New Nation: The American Experience, 1776–1809* (New York, 1963).

program for capitalist development was far more than a mere reflex to established views of business interest groups. To innovation Hamilton added a driving, shrewd talent for political management—in the executive branch, in the Senate and House of Representatives, in caucuses, with notable leaders across the country, and with the public. The effects of Hamilton's initial leadership told first on Congressional behavior. From his post as President Washington's Secretary of the Treasury, he worked to establish ties between the separated executive and legislative branches. In doing so, he gathered an entourage of sympathizers in the cabinet and of caucusing followers in Congress, who came soon to constitute a distinct capital faction. In the process he was able to rely on the prestige of Washington's name and generally on Washington's support. By the sessions of 1790 and 1791, the scattered and individualistic activity that had marked the first session in 1789 began to show signs of coordination and policy coherence.[21]

Before long, Hamilton's leadership (and politics in general) also became embroiled in world issues. The French Revolution was at first widely hailed in America; but regicide, the rise of the Jacobins, radical republicanism, and the Terror, followed by France's declaration of war on Great Britain in February, 1793, divided Americans sharply. A lush pamphlet and periodical literature sprang up. Men took sides emotionally as Anglomen (stigmatized by opponents as "Monocrats") or Gallomen (stigmatized in turn as "Jacobins"). Thus issues of domestic interests and outlook were supplemented by ideological reactions to European events and the result was a further consolidation of political forces.

In time, a series of steps led from the Hamiltonian capital *faction* to a national Federalist *party*. The process may be summarized under four headings.

First, linkages of association, parallel action, and finally coordination were extended from the capital into the states, counties, and towns. Correspondents, personal friends, natural sympathizers, business associates, the many individuals whom Hamilton as Secretary of the Treasury had been able to oblige—all were sounded. Active response came particularly from local notables such as former military officers, mercantile magnates in New York, Congregational divines in New England, and many planter-nabobs in the South. National leaders gave

---

[21] Schachner, *op. cit.*; John C. Miller, *Alexander Hamilton; Portrait in Paradox* (New York, 1959), and *The Federalist Era, 1789–1801* (New York, 1960), 33–69, 84–125; also, if it is read constructively for insights into actual Congressional behavior and not simply for its polemic, *The Journal of William Maclay* (New York, 1927), covering the beginnings of Hamilton's ascendency. Despite his capacity for strictures on the *idea* of "the spirit of party," broadly directed against the opposition, Hamilton *in practice* was initiating party action.

cues to local leaders and to lesser party spokesmen and sponsors in the localities, and such men came to form the working vertebrae of the party. Many of them stood as prototypes of a new breed of party politicians, or party "cadre." In short, a firm and distinctive Federalist structure was in the process of forming and of finding a following.

Second, national leaders and local leaders or cadre collaborated to develop increasingly standardized ways of performing certain key political functions. These ranged from managing and connecting (between branches) in government, to nominating candidates, electioneering and mobilizing voters, and shaping opinion in the states and localities. A national factional or party paper under John Fenno, the *Gazette of the United States*, disseminated Federalist perspectives, and local sheets followed its lead.

Third, a substantial combination of interests and opinions was enlisted in the Federalist following. Domestic merchants, exporters, shippers and shipbuilders, holders of public securities, bankers, investors and financiers generally, struggling manufacturers, certain great planters, dependent business and professional men—all could see concrete advantages in Federalist policies. Yet the Federalist combination came also to include many wage-earners, particularly in shipbuilding, and farmers producing commercial and particularly export crops; and thus, contrary to the conception of much of the older historiography, the Federalists possessed a significant mass base—although their Achilles' heel remained an insensitivity to the concerns of agriculture as a whole.[22] The interests of all these groups were not necessarily identical, however, and Hamilton and other leaders in developing policy inevitably performed a function of political brokerage, devising at least tacit formulas of agreement among the varied groups.

Fourth, the emerging Federalist force developed distinctive attitudes and unifying faiths and loyalties—in short, the beginnings of a partisan ideology. At the outset, the charisma of Washington was a key ingredient, and Hamilton remarked years later that "he [Washington] was an *Aegis very essential to me.*"[23] Other items became integral to the Federalist persuasion, such as a stress on "respectability," a concern for national capitalist growth and stability, an emphasis on a national government which was strong and "energetic," an élitist tone. In the backwash of revolutionary Jacobinism, Federalists also saw themselves as a bulwark against a threatening world-revolutionary spirit, of sanity

---

[22] Manning J. Dauer, *The Adams Federalists* (Baltimore, 1953), 3–34, 275–287, contains a systematic treatment of the Federalist power base; see also Binkley, *op. cit.*, 29–51.

[23] Quoted in Charles, *op. cit.*, 39.

against madness, of order against chaos. Thus ties of interest were supplemented by shared outlooks and symbolism. Indeed, it was the development of the emotional *élan* of ideology, more than any other element, which marked the transition of the Federalists from faction to party.

The upshot of all these developments was a new kind of national linkage. It was far more than a "connexion," in the old sense of a shifting set of personal, familial, or clique relationships. It was rather a stable "connection," in the modern spelling and meaning, a structure of men across the nation who not only shared interests, but who were coming together into coordinated rationalized patterns of action around a set of national leaders, on the basis of shared social, economic, political, or moral perspectives. It was, or became by sometime around 1793 or 1794, a modern party in the proper sense—that is to say, a political formation which exhibited *all* of the characteristics which an empirically and theoretically viable conceptual scheme might identify as belonging to party. It marked a progress from faction politics to party politics.

Two observations may be made concerning this development. First, although the Federalist party was in part a combination of groups, it was also *more* than a combination of groups as Beard or Binkley construe the term, in that it was an articulated, semi-independent structure of stable relationships between leaders, cadre, and following, built by the purposeful energies of men, who gave it more in action than they took in reflex reaction to group impulses. Second, the party did not exhibit any significant degree of organization in the strict sense. If we insist on seeing party as organization, as Robinson or Leiserson do, we will have very little to say about America's first national party.

Opposition to the Federalists was soon forthcoming. It also took form at the capital, where James Madison in the House of Representatives played initial antagonist to Hamilton's protagonist—contrary again to much of the conventional historiography, which lists Jefferson as the founder of the Republican party.[24] From the outset, however, the Republican opposition moved in accord with popular stirrings of interest and opinion.

Dissent in the states, counties, and towns was directed at Hamilton's economic program, but it also turned to issues of foreign policy and world-political ideology. After Washington's proclamation of neutrality

---

[24] For the Republican development generally and Madison's and Jefferson's roles, see the leading and thorough monograph, Noble E. Cunningham, Jr., *The Jeffersonian Republicans: The Formation of Party Organization, 1789–1801* (Chapel Hill, North Carolina, 1957); Irving Brant, *James Madison: Father of the Constitution, 1787–1800* (New York, 1950); and Dumas Malone, *Jefferson and the Rights of Man* (Boston, 1951); also, Charles, *op. cit.,* 74–140.

towards warring France and England in 1793, for example, an opposition voice in the western reaches of Pennsylvania cried out that "the cause of France is the cause of man, and neutrality is desertion."[25] In 1794 John Taylor of Virginia published a fat polemical pamphlet, *A Definition of Parties, or the Political Effects of the Paper System Considered*, which gave focus to the domestic and world-political strains of opposition. In 1795 widespread protest against the treaty the Federalist John Jay had negotiated with Great Britain drew divisions over issues of world politics even more sharply. Meanwhile, gaining momentum in 1793 and 1794, several local political associations had sprung up across the country. Called variously Democratic or Republican Societies, they were remarkable for the number of intellectuals in their membership and leadership though, as Eugene Link has shown, they drew on a number of elements in the population.[26] They were also remarkably modern, in that they were open, voluntary assemblages of individual men, and in the degree of formal organization they achieved under democratically adopted constitutions. Their approach originally was largely in terms of ideology, discussion of political philosophy and issues, and propaganda; but they also doled out blessings or censure on members of Congress and endorsed candidates for elections. They began to disappear after Washington, in the wake of the Whisky Insurrection of 1794, denounced them as "self-created societies," presumably all disruptive of public order. Yet, flourishing as they did from Vermont to South Carolina and Kentucky, they were significant while they lasted. The varied voices of dissent and their institutionalization in the Societies indicate the degree to which the Republican opposition was indigenous in nature, and of local and popular origin, rather than simply a product of mobilization by leaders at the center of government. Such coruscations did not, however, make a party. Rather, they constituted a potential *following* for a potential party.

The Republican party found its structure in linkages between the Congressional faction Madison was drawing together at the capital and the groundwork of national opposition. No bold, creative antagonist, Madison began slowly though industriously in the session of 1790 and moved painfully ahead in succeeding sessions, relying particularly on the Virginia men and increasingly on certain members from Pennsylvania. In particular John Beckley of Virginia, Clerk of the House, worked behind the scenes and began to exhibit talents as a national cadre politician that would have been admired by later Van

---

[25] H. H. Brackenridge, frontier philosopher in Pittsburgh, quoted in Marcus Cunliffe, *The Nation Takes Shape, 1789–1837* (Chicago, 1959).

[26] Eugene Perry Link, *Democratic-Republican Societies, 1790–1800* (New York, 1942).

Burens, Hannas, Cannons, or Farleys.[27]   From their base in Congress, Republican leaders reached out to the countryside.   Like the Federalists before them, they gradually established connections in states and localities; encouraged the development of local leaders and cadre; labored to coordinate the choice of candidates, election activities, and propaganda; secured a general following; and worked up a significant group combination.   National leaders made fruitful connections with the Clintonians in New York and with remnants of the old state-Constitutionalists in Pennsylvania, but elsewhere their local elements were generally newly built.   With the founding of the *National Gazette* under the poet-polemicist Philip Freneau in 1791, and an alignment of satellite papers, they established a loose information office which gave impetus to distinctively Republican attitudes and *élan.*

The Republican forces were slower in effecting a clearly party-like structure than the Federalists, however—and again, it was an issue with intensely emotional, symbolic, and ideological overtones that brought them to full party status.   It is probably not proper to speak of a stable Republican *party* nationally earlier than the Jay Treaty controversy of 1795 and Congressional debate of 1796,[28] the assumption by Jefferson of effective party leadership in the latter year, and the intensification of cleavages in political perspectives which contention over the treaty engendered.

---

[27] See Philip M. Marsh, "John Beckley, Mystery Man of the Early Republicans," *Pennsylvania Magazine of History and Biography,* LXXII (1948), 54–69; Noble E. Cunningham, Jr., "John Beckley: An Early American Party Manager," *The William and Mary Quarterly,* Third Series, XIII (1956), 40–52; also, Charles, *op. cit.,* and Cunningham, *op. cit.*

[28] Charles, *op. cit.,* 103–140; Cunningham, *op.cit.,* esp. 76–85; see also discussions and data concerning trends toward party voting in Congress in above, and in Dauer, *op. cit.,* esp. 288–331.   For the consolidation of Republican party structure generally and in the states, see *inter alia* Harry Ammon, "The Formation of the Republican Party in Virginia, 1789–1796," *Journal of Southern History,* XIX (1953), 283–310; Dice Robins Anderson, *William Branch Giles: A Study in the Politics of Virginia and the Nation from 1790 to 1830* (Menasha, Wisconsin, 1914); W. P. Cresson, *James Monroe* (Chapel Hill, North Carolina, 1946); Delbert H. Gilpatrick, *Jeffersonian Democracy in North Carolina, 1789–1816* (New York, 1931); Lewis Leary, *That Rascal Freneau: A Study in Literary Failure* (New Brunswick, New Jersey, 1941); Samuel Eliot Morison, "Squire Ames and Doctor Ames," *New England Quarterly,* I (1928), 5–31; William A. Robinson, *Jeffersonian Democracy In New England* (New Haven, Connecticut, 1916); Nathan Schachner, *Aaron Burr* (New York, 1937); Raymond Walters, Jr., *Albert Gallatin: Jeffersonian Financier and Diplomat* (New York, 1957), and *Alexander James Dallas: Lawyer—Politician—Financier, 1759–1817* (Philadelphia, 1943); Charles Warren, *Jacobin and Junto: or Early American Politics as Viewed in the Diary of Dr. Nathaniel Ames 1758–1822* (Cambridge, Massachusetts, 1931); John H. Wolfe, *Jeffersonian Democracy in South Carolina* (Chapel Hill, North Carolina, 1940); also party monographs previously cited, Notes 14, 15, 17.

As they shaped a party formation, the Republicans exhibited distinctive characteristics in their general attitude toward relations between leaders and followers, and in the character of their party structure. Unlike the tone of the Federalists, which was broadly élitist, the tone of the Republicans was broadly democratic. To Federalist leaders, the purposes of party were to amass and stabilize support in the public and electorate for policies the leaders had already adopted. Their party was overwhelmingly a "party of notables," in Weber's term, despite their significant mass base. Republican leaders, who were in effect evolving a formation which marked a transitional stage between a "party of notables" and a "party of politicians," generally believed that the relationship between leaders and mass following should include responsiveness or responsibility to the wishes and opinions of the following, and that policy should in some degree be shaped accordingly. Thus the Republican ideology embraced a considerable notion of intra-party democracy, in which party following might play a somewhat less "passive" and more "active" role than Weber's abstract formulation suggests. The matter is put aptly if too simply by Robinson, when he speaks of Federalists approaching elections as merely "a test upon [their] policies," while Republicans viewed elections as "a guide to the desires of public opinion."[29] In short, we may conceptualize the Federalists as operating in terms of *plebiscitarian* ideology and action, while the Republicans moved in terms of *democratic* ideology and action. It is thus possible to speak of the Republicans not only as a modern party, but as a *"popular"* party, in the sense of a party grounded in and sensitive to a broad and durable base in the population or electorate. Despite recurring counter-tendencies to oligarchy noted by Michels,[30] this is the form that many modern parties have taken in nation after nation in the last century and a half. Others, however, have pursued the plebiscitarian path.[31]

Furthermore, as compared with the Federalists, Republican development was not only more popular but more complex. The indigenous opposition movement developed sometimes ahead of, and at least partially independently of, the Madisonian capital faction. This was notably the case with the Democratic or Republican Societies. Some

---

[29] E. E. Robinson, *op. cit.*, 73–75.

[30] Robert Michels, *Political Parties: A Sociological Study of the Oligarchical Tendencies of Modern Democracy* (New York, 1915), 21–90, 365–392.

[31] The term "plebiscitarian" is Weber's; it is used here, however, in a restricted sense as indicated above, to connote a politics of mass dependence, mass appeals, limited mass action often through manipulation, and elections as plebiscites—as contrasted with a "democratic" politics of popular representation, active popular initiative or participation, free public opinion, and elections as open choices.

writers have leapt to the conclusion that these associations were integral, organized local units in a national Republican party; actually, however, there was no structural connection between the Madisonian capital faction on the one hand and the Societies on the other. Rather, as Noble E. Cunningham argues persuasively, the associations acted as pressure groups,[32] with a primarily ideological approach. The significance of indigenous Republican sentiment and the Democratic-Republican groups is that they provided pre-existing enclaves of support at the periphery to which Madisonians at the center could reach out. Contrary to Duverger's suggestion that parties of the "cadre" type are typically generated from the center "out," as the Federalists were, they may also emerge in part from the periphery "in," as the Republicans did, in a very complex pattern indeed.

Finally, the Republican party came to include some organization in the strict sense, as a continuing rationalized division of labor and coordination of functions toward shared goals. Indeed, figures like Beckley and Freneau or his press-successor Benjamin Franklin Bache show an obvious kinship with Disraeli's later Taper or Tadpole, who tied up votes or swam in the muddy waters of opinion in Great Britain in the 1830s and 1840s.[33] Organization was spotty, however, and its full development remains a phenomenon of later mature parties of politicians with an enlarged mass electorate to mobilize.

In the development of both the Federalist and the Republican parties, ideology played a catalytic role. As it appeared in this development, it was partial rather than total, consistent with a basic national consensus, and somewhat amorphous—though not so loose as the flaccid ideological outlooks of later American parties have often become. It was also limited in that its "factual assertions about society," to use Birnbaum's terms, were never presented in a form that was wholly comprehensive or even "systematic," and neither were its "evaluations of the distribution of power"—and this circumscribed range of ideology has been typical of the American experience. Yet a sense of identity and direction, patterns of commitment, at least a loose world-view, what Washington called "the spirit of party generally," and consequent cohesion and *élan*, were all essential ingredients in the consolidation of durable linkages of Federalist and Republican party structure and action, and all may be thought of as ideological components. Ideology as it appeared in American party development, furthermore, was more than merely a rationalization of interests, a shadowy variable dependent on economic or other self-oriented group

---

[32] Cunningham, *op. cit.*, 62–66.
[33] Benjamin Disraeli, *Coningsby, or the New Generation* (London, 1844).

concerns, or a figment of the psyche to satisfy inward personal needs. It was rather a positive force which shaped perceptions (or misperceptions) of political reality. It thereby generated faiths and loyalties which might have remained dormant, and prompted effective political action.[34]

The establishment of parties brought a significant degree of order to American politics. Parties operated as continuing bonds between the decision-making processes of government on the one hand, and individuals and groups in the public and electorate on the other. Distinguishable party positions were put forth and Congressional behavior was increasingly bipolarized on partisan lines at the expense of dwindling numbers of center-individualists.[35] Candidates for office ran as Federalists or Republicans, thereby providing voters with a reasonably clear two-way choice. More and more voters identified with party symbols and party ideology. Thus, in the emergence of two-party politics and rivalry, pluralism was harnessed to some degree, the effects of state-by-state fragmentation in politics were reduced, and political methods were increasingly rationalized, standardized, and modernized.

Party politics also reduced the differential advantages in power that had fallen to well-placed individuals and groups. Farmers, small traders, artisans, members of low-status religious groups, many intellectuals, reformers, even aliens found in the Jeffersonian Republican party a representative of their interests, perspectives, opinions, and rights, as against the demands of larger property, ascribed position, high respectability, and established influence. The existence of the two parties in competition provided a meaningful option between Federalist and Republican perspectives, policies, and leaders; and voters quickly learned to make use of the choice the parties put before them. Thus, in an open political system, the first modern political parties brought such important gains in democracy as representation, substantial participation, and choice.[36] In a few short years, the new American nation—decades before its British ancestors—had moved well into a new world-era of politics.

---

[34] See, e.g., Norman Birnbaum, "The Sociological Study of Ideology," *Current Sociology,* IX (1962), 91, 116, *passim*; it may also be noted that my approach here has points in common with the more extended treatment by Michael Walzer, "Puritanism as a Revolutionary Ideology," in the present symposium.

[35] Charles, *op. cit.,* esp. 92–103 ff., and Dauer, *op. cit.,* 288–331.

[36] For a provocative though sometimes provoking recent discussion of democracy as choice, see E. E. Schattschneider, *The Semisovereign People: A Realist's View of Democracy in America* (New York, 1960), 129–142, *passim*.

IV

Some analytical generalizations based on the formative years of American experience may now be offered, as a step toward a model of party.   First some generalized comparative distinctions between factions and parties are in order.   While both have appeared as forma-tions in the conflict of politics, performing functions or activities such as leadership recruitment, contesting for power or office, the conduct of government, or representation of some sort, significant differences as well as resemblances are to be found between them.   Historically, the differences have been matters of degree rather than total dichot-omies of quality, but they are sufficient to sustain some important conceptual distinctions.

Factions have often developed as chance, almost unconscious, *natural* "growths," or "connexions" of men with parallel interests. Parties, by contrast, as more complex formations, appear as *artifacts*, "built" by purposeful effort.   It is misleading to speak, as Binkley does in his subtitle, of a "Natural History" of parties.   Structurally factions have been unstable, generally of short life or life-expectancy, irregular; while parties historically have exhibited greater stability, durability, longevity, and so are clearer to identify.   A faction, for example, may easily coalesce for one election or issue only and then disappear. Parties typically continue or expect to continue from election to election or from issue to issue.[37]

Factions also have not typically offered *stable* procedures for per-forming certain essential political functions.   In American and British history, these have come to include nominating; campaigning or electioneering; formulating opinion; group brokerage, managing in government; and establishing connections between branches or agencies of government.   Unlike factions, parties have generally under-taken or offered to undertake these functions in a regularized, standard-ized, continuing fashion.   It has been said, only half-flippantly, that the purpose of party is "to elect."[38]   In a free society, and in an ultimate sense even in a non-democratic "plebiscitarian" society, if a party is to elect and re-elect its candidates, it must perform the other functions noted here.

Factions have usually generated little in the way of distinct and durable ideological perspectives, while parties have generally evolved

---

[37] Even the short-lived third parties of American history have generally looked forward to continuation, in which case they may be called parties, or, strictly, proto-parties.   Where they have not, they may be written off as quasi-parties.

[38] Thomas H. Eliot, *Governing America: The Politics of a Free People* (New York, 1960), 272.

substantial sets of perspectives. Exceptions may surely be found among factions—in the Royalists and Parliament Men of seventeenth-century England, for example—but more often than not factions do not develop significant identifying symbolisms. In a plural party system, symbolisms or perspectives become durable "we"-"they" perspectives. Partisans see "our" outlooks or positions on issues as "right," and "theirs" as "wrong"; and it thereby becomes important that "we" gain power and not "they." Perhaps, when ideology has reached a stage of flaccid formalism, it is really important only that power and its perquisites be "ours" and not "theirs"; and yet even so party spirit remains among the great cements of politics. As a party acquires a history, it canonizes heroes, develops traditional symbols, exalts present leaders, and relates all this symbolism in some kind of ideology, whether vivid and meaningful or blurred and muddled. Thus, while ideology is not in itself party, it is a critical characteristic *of* party.

Factions have typically scored low and parties high in range and density of following. While factions *may* develop as combinations of a broad range of groups and opinion aggregates, they generally have not done so, whereas parties generally have. There are obvious exceptions, however, and this cannot be a defining, but only a contingent, characteristic of party. Again, factions have not generally achieved or even sought to achieve a high density of following. Parties, on the other hand, have generally done so or sought to do so.

All four of these differences between faction and party were apparent in the emergence of party politics out of faction politics in early America. Furthermore, as we have seen, the transition was significant for the shape of politics. A concept or analytical-historical model of party in terms of structure, function, and ideology may now be formally stated.

A *party* proper or *modern party* may be conceived as a social structure which operates within the political arena, and which is directed toward exercising the power, filling the available offices, and shaping the general policies of government. The structure[39] is distinctive in that it exhibits four defining characteristics and one contingent characteristic:

1) *There is a comparatively stable or durable leader-following relationship; that is, a relationship among party leaders, cadre, and officials-in-*

---

[39] The *specific form* structure takes for any given party at a particular time is conditioned by the total context (social system, political culture, ideology, and situation) in which the party has evolved and acts. Thus, American parties today are not quite the same as the Federalist or Republican parties of the 1790s; parties in Great Britain or France differ from American parties; and party in the U.S.S.R. or Ghana is something else again. Yet—and the point will be argued more fully later—certain broad features will be found in common.

government on the one hand; and with a following, or adherents or identifiers, on the other.

This definiens places stress on Weber's notion of leader-R-following,[40] adding emphasis on *stability* or *durability* as an aspect of structure. "Adherent" indicates individuals who are strongly attached to and may be counted on to support the party, while intensity of attachment declines as we move through "identifiers" to what may be called occasional voters. Structure itself may include *organization* in the strict sense, that is, organization$_1$, a group of persons (particularly cadre and officials) who have an interest separable from other interests in maintaining and perpetuating the party structure, and who thus undertake and conduct organization$_2$, a continuing, regularized pattern of division of labor and coordination of tasks to maintain party structure and perform party functions, which pattern tends to become institutionalized and formalized.

2) *There is communication and coordination of activity (short of, or including, organization proper), between central leaders, cadre, and officials, and local cadre or lesser actives.*

This characteristic does not entail any particular *form* of articulation or organization; thus a given party may be more or less élitist or hierarchical, more or less cohesive or disciplined, and exhibit more or less intra-party democracy.

Strictly speaking, in what may be called after Duverger "cadre" parties, *"the* party" consists of leaders, cadre, officials, and actives who make decisions for the party, conduct party affairs, and appeal to the public as representatives of the party, while adherents or identifiers constitute the following. Where parties have formal membership like the Labor party in Great Britain and stand as what Duverger calls "mass" parties, members may be included in *"the* party," while persons who may vote for the party but are not formal members may be thought of as a following. Even so, the leaders whom Duverger refers to as the *"Inner Circle"*[41] will constitute the core of the party for most practical or functional purposes.

3) *There exist, or are offered as an undertaking, regular procedures for performing functions linking the public or electorate and the governmental decision-making process, thus—*

a) *nominating, campaigning or electioneering, opinion-formulating;*

b) *group-brokerage, managing in government, connecting (branches or agencies of government).*

This definiens, which stresses party-as-function, is dependent on the concept of structure, but the latter is in turn clarified by the concept

---

[40] Weber, *loc. cit.,* 99–104.
[41] Duverger, *op. cit.,* 151–168.

of function. Thus, in terms of actual behavior, those who constitute "*the* party" are those who perform the function of party among the public or electorate. It follows from this functional definiens as well as from the statement of structure that a party is not its leaders *and* following, but rather its structure of leaders, cadre, officials, and actives (or Inner Circle and *active* members), who in turn mobilize a following. If we employ Goldman's or Key's term "*party*-in-the-electorate"[42] without considerable care, we may seem to allude in circular fashion to a party as an aggregate mobilizing that same aggregate, and we are perilously close to the loose notions of party as any aggregate of men engaged in parallel political action or sharing similar political outlooks.

4) *There exists in the party and is shared in the following a set of in-group perspectives, or faiths, loyalties, and commitments, which constitute an ideology.*

This definiens emphasizes the role of ideology as an essential element in party, without however defining party solely as any body of men who may share an ideological view. Perspectives may extend from minimal loyalties and attitudes through emotive symbolism, hagiography, and traditional adherence, to ideological or programmatic commitment. In plural party systems, party perspectives or commitments may be more or less clear and contrasting, thereby providing a greater or less degree of voter choice between parties, or inter-party democracy.

5) *There is attached to the party structure a comparatively durable combination of interests or opinion-aggregates, which the cadre may count on as a power-base.*

In open systems and particularly in two-party systems in multi-group societies, and in certain instances or stages of one-party systems, there is a tendency toward both substantial *range* in interests and aggregates of opinion in the party, and significant *density* (number of persons involved: potential number of persons) in the power-base. Range and density may be promoted through what Binkley calls *formulas of agreement* in the conflict of interests and opinions, by means of brokerage in some situations; or by program mobilization (through opinion-formulation), charismatic leadership, or brokerage in other situations.

These five characteristics, when present in significant degree, may be taken as criteria of party proper. Major parties in modern, mass politics—the American Federalists and Republicans of the 1790s are early instances—may be thought of as exhibiting all of the characteristics of the model in marked degree; minor parties, or closed or élitist ruling parties in one-party systems, may exhibit them in different

---

[42] Key, *op. cit.*, 181–182.

degrees, or for Item 5—the key criterion for Binkley[43]—sometimes hardly at all. Factions or similar formations on the other hand will exhibit few if any of the five characteristics in significant degree, and certainly not all of them to a high degree. This was true of "connexions" and factions in England in the eighteenth century, as well as of factions, cliques, juntos, or caucuses in America before the 1790s. It also appears to be the case that no political formation in Great Britain exhibited the four or five characteristics of party in high degree before the emergence of the Whig-Liberal and Tory-Conservative parties in the nineteenth century. Thus again it may be argued that the advent of the Federalist and Republican parties marked a new phase of political development, which carried the United States significantly beyond the politics of its mother nation.

V

The remarkably early development of political parties in America is worth exploring, particularly as it may illuminate relationships between social structure, national political culture, and ideology on the one hand, and party origins on the other. It is true that the first parties in America survived through only three decades, and that by 1819 or 1820 Federalists and Republicans had ceased to exist as effective structures in the national political arena. Yet their advent reveals most of the generic aspects of American party development, and the successor Democratic and Whig parties of the 1830s trod paths that had already been marked.

American party action, as Weber has noted, "brought the plebiscitarian principle to an especially early and an especially pure expression." It is, however, superficial to argue as Weber does: "That the plebiscitarian 'machine' has developed so early in America is due to the fact that there, and there alone, the executive—this is what mattered— the chief of office-patronage, was a President elected by plebiscite."[44] Patronage and presidency are indeed relevant, but hardly sufficient to explain the early American development. A more general comparative approach should prove more fruitful. It will focus here on a central type of factor or cause in the American situation as contrasted with the British situation; it will then relate this central point to contrasting sets of proximate social conditions, types of factors, or causes. The approach here will thus aim at a kind of immediate or relative historical explanation, partly in terms of a succession of events ("continuous series"), partly in terms of modest, middle-range generalizations (theory). At a

---

[43] Binkley, op. cit., passim.
[44] Weber, loc. cit., 107–108.

later stage, a broader explanation of the rise of parties in modern politics will be offered.[45] Throughout, the assumption is that the problem can best be dealt with by some comparison of American and British development, although the focus remains on the former. Ultimately, of course, such a comparative approach should be deepened, and broadened to include still other societies.[46]

The central point of contrast is the presence in England and the absence in America of a feudal background, and the obverse of this fact—the flowering in America of a "liberal tradition," in a broadly "liberal society," in a highly favorable "material setting." The issue has been argued effectively by Louis Hartz, and the terms are used here basically as he uses them. His analysis, although it deals at once with "the absence of feudalism and the presence of the liberal idea" in America, is basically a single-factor analysis—"in terms of European history itself the abstraction of the feudal force implies the natural development of liberalism, so that for all practical purposes we are dealing with a single factor." The liberal idea or liberal tradition in a non-feudal, atomistic-individualistic, or loosely Lockian sense, is taken as the "significant historical variable" in, among other things, "the early triumph of American democracy" in general.[47]

In the eighteenth century in England, politics operated within a social structure and political culture inherited from a feudal past with its established, fixed estates. Even in the long period of the slow decline of feudalism, a relatively rigid structure of ranks, classes, or established interests emerged. Thus, in the eighteenth and early nineteenth centuries, political representation was effectively representation of such fixed entities, "natural" and/or "virtual," rather than representation of individual voters in geographical districts, or of the open pressures of diverse interest groups in the modern pattern. Thus, organic representation was largely built into the system, as it involved the decision points of Crown, Lords, and Commons. Furthermore, as another part of the feudal heritage, politics was substantially a game for aristocrats, magnates, notable leaders, and their agents. There had developed over the centuries patterns of deference to or reliance on such leadership which, among other consequences, retarded the development of popu-

---

[45] For the vexed problem of historical explanation, I have found particularly interesting Carl Hempel, "The Function of General Laws in History," *Journal of Philosophy*, XXXIX (1942), 35–48; Patrick Gardiner, *The Nature of Historical Explanation* (London, 1952); William Dray, *Laws and Explanation in History* (London, 1957); Maurice Mandelbaum, "Historical Explanation: the Problem of 'Covering Laws,'" *History and Theory*, I (1961), 229–242.

[46] Cf. Leiserson, *op. cit.*, 39–81, *passim.*

[47] Louis Hartz, *The Liberal Tradition in America: An Interpretation of American Political Thought Since the Revolution* (New York, 1955), 3–23, esp. 17, 20, 21, 22.

lar initiative or participation in politics.[48] Moreover, the suffrage was severely limited, up to and even after the bourgeois Reform Bill of 1832.

In the New World, history and its impact on social structure and political culture were different. Social distinctions, "nabobs," pseudo-aristocrats, notables there were in the American colonies and early American states. Habits of deference to such figures of eminence were part of the colonial heritage, along with distinctions between rich and poor or "high" and "low," indentures, and slavery. Nonetheless, most Americans were freeholding farmers; opportunity was broadly open in a new continent; and a high degree of individual freedom and social mobility existed. A liberal ethos readily developed which saw the units of society as free, atomistic, assertive individuals. This ethos took on more and more strongly equalitarian overtones in an ideology or developing political culture of "irrational Lockianism," in Hartz's terms, or perhaps "the Jeffersonian dream." The social impact of the Revolution, "the Spirit of '76," and the liberal decade which followed, were to emphasize and strengthen all of these tendencies, and to speed a process of dissolution of social distinctions and deference patterns, a process which was to culminate in the equalitarian democracy of the Jacksonian era. From the outset, political representation was of necessity representation of individuals choosing more or less freely in geographical districts. There was no Crown, no Establishment, no Lords and therefore no Commons linked in organic relationships—for if a society consists of free individuals and boasts no First and Second Estates, it can hardly have a Third.[49] Finally, the national Constitution of 1787, far from being merely a stratagem of a privileged élite, provided an intricately limited but for the times remarkably democratic frame of government.[50]

---

[48] See, e.g., Samuel H. Beer, "The Representation of Interests in British Government: Historical Background," *American Political Science Review*, LI (1957), 613–650; also his "Great Britain: From Governing Elite to Organized Mass Parties," in Sigmund Neumann, ed., *Modern Political Parties: Approaches to Comparative Politics* (Chicago, 1956), 9–56; and "New Structures of Democracy: Britain and America," in William N. Chambers and Robert H. Salisbury, eds., *Democracy in the Mid-Twentieth Century: Problems and Prospects* (St. Louis, 1960), 30–59. Again, cf. the treatment of English politics in the eighteenth century by Ostrogorski, *op. cit.*, I, 6–134, and the contrast with politics after the Reform Bill of 1832, *passim.*

[49] The almost immediate futility of John Adams' painful efforts to establish Harringtonian mixed government through the "Oceana" constitution of 1780 in Massachusetts underscores the point.

[50] For recent valuable summaries of early American development relating to these points, see Edmund S. Morgan, *The Birth of the Republic, 1763–1789* (Chicago, 1956), and Cunliffe, *op. cit.*; also Hartz, *op. cit.*, 35–96.

All of these matters of fact and faith entailed certain consequences in America which would hardly be expected in the British experience. By giving free play to fluidity, differentiation, and complexity of interests in a developing society, they produced in the first instance an *open, unstructured, complex conflict of interests and opinions as the standard stuff of politics*—the lush, almost uncontrolled pluralism so characteristic of American life.[51] Add to such phenomena the lack of an organic representation built into the political system as in Great Britain, and a second consequence follows in the American context, *if* any group of men was to win power and get the business of governing done; that is, *a need for some mode of political action which would serve as a means of representing, combining, and mobilizing the individuals and variety of interests and opinions in the society.* Third, given this fluid, open situation, it remained only for *men with political vision, ambition, and talent to come forward to meet the need and seize the obvious opportunity.* Such men soon emerged as party leaders, exploring the paths to modern popular parties, building party structures. Furthermore, such men building early American parties in the late eighteenth and early nineteenth centuries did not have to batter down obstacles of the sort they would have faced in Great Britain in the same period—the undergrowth of fixed orders, fixed patterns of organic representation, fixed ways of doing things. Another consequence of the liberal and Revolutionary tradition in America was the development of *a consensus which provided the formal and effective freedom in which parties could take shape, speak out, act, and develop.* Despite early attitudes inimical to the idea of party and of opposition, the American atmosphere was probably considerably freer and more open to party action than that of Great Britain in the same era.

In its more general hypothetical form, the argument here is: where social structure and ideology provide certain types of social and political conditions (an open, pluralistic or atomistic politics characterized by complex conflicts of interest), concomitant needs and opportunities will arise for certain types of political functions and activities (action to represent, combine, and mobilize pluralities of free individuals and interests in order to exercise governmental power); and in the absence of significant obstacles (such as limiting patterns of social and political structure, limitations on freedom of political expression and action, or

---

[51] It is the frank recognition of this free play of pluralism which gives point to Madison's statement that in modern societies a *variety* of interests will "grow up of necessity," where "liberty is to faction what air is to fire," and which differentiates his American conception of politics from Harrington's or Montesquieu's conceptions of a balance of fixed ranks, estates, orders, or classes.

others), these opportunities will attract men with the requisite political ambition and skills, with the consequent development of the indicated modes of political action, which become modern political party action. In terms of this *general* proposition, and in contrast with the English context, the *particular* conditions of the American field in the late eighteenth century seemed both to require and to invite party building and party leadership.[52]

Further aspects of contrast between Great Britain and the United States are relevant. Lacking an Establishment—the Crown, the nobility and the peerage, the Church, their prerogatives and power, their overtones of prestige—the American political system lacked an established center for "court politics." There was no national power-institution of majesty, or array of pomp and circumstance, around which interests, factions, or cliques could seek influence almost without regard to the populace or electorate, and thereby find almost invisible corridors to success in the game of who gets what, when and how. It is significant that, when American advocates of "high-toned" government proposed such panoplies, they were frustrated by what contemporaries called the "republican genius" of the people, or what we may call the democratic aspects of the developing national ideology. To this may be added for the United States the relative absence or steady decline of deference patterns through which aristocrats or notables could count on almost automatic followings, without dependence on free public opinion or a free electorate. The consequence in an increasingly equalitarian, republican political system was *a peculiarly democratic or plebiscitarian imperative, which was the necessity, if individuals or groups were to satisfy their ambitions or interests through politics, to appeal to public opinion and to the electorate for support.* This was the path even the élitist, notabilistic Federalists had to walk, if they were not to lose their objectives.

The American situation and ideology also produced the earliest instances of mass suffrage in the modern world. Tax or property qualifications there were at the outset, but their effect has been greatly overstressed by older historians. More recent research and conclusions are

---

[52] An intra-American comparison is also suggestive here, and "fits." Of all of the American states in the 1780s, Pennsylvania and New York probably exhibited most fully the general conditions noted above as facilitative to party development. They differed, however, in that New York also exhibited some of the factors noted as obstacles, particularly in the old-established patterns of family dominance which sustained an old-style clique and faction politics, whereas these factors had substantially disappeared in Pennsylvania by the 1780s. Thus, Pennsylvania produced state parties early, New York followed (concomitantly with national party development) in the 1790s as the obstacle conditions rapidly broke down, and other states moved still more slowly toward party formations as adjuncts of the national parties.

well expressed by Edmund S. Morgan in his summary of the states after the Revolution—"the vast majority of white Americans could probably meet the property qualifications required of them."[53] The right of suffrage was not always used, yet near the end of the party-building decade of the 1790s voting reached something like 25% or more of all white adult males for important elections. (The exercise of suffrage rose still further, with liberalizations of legal qualifications and the *hoi-polloi* thrust of the Jacksonian era, to 56% of white adult males in Jackson's first election in 1828, and reached a peak of 78% in the "Log Cabin" campaign of 1840 which capped the Jackson period.) The data are striking,[54] particularly if they are contrasted with the limited suffrage of Great Britain, and with the fact that the long agitation for the first Reform Bill finally won suffrage in 1832 for only a few hundred thousand rate payers. Furthermore, democratic attitudes—in the sense of political equalitarianism, notions of popular participation and a popular voice in politics beyond elections, and representative government—became more and more central to American political culture. (These attitudes also began to develop early and were, as Marcus Cunliffe has argued perceptively,[55] by no means just the product of the Age of Equalitarianism which Tocqueville observed, although once again they reached new, *hoi-polloi* heights in the Jacksonian thrust of the 1830s.) The contrast between Great Britain and the United States is once again striking and important. Those who would succeed in American politics *found it necessary—in the face of mass suffrage and general political participation—to deal with, mobilize, and shape into a power-base broad elements of a mass electorate and public.* The task called in effect for party-like structure—for an array of leaders, cadre, and actives who could undertake sustained appeals to public opinion and employ effective campaigning techniques, and for the performance of basic party functions.

The general hypothetical statement of this portion of the argument is: where social structure, ideology, and related socio-political conditions fail to provide, or preclude, some form of closed or limited politics with special accesses to influence (for example, through "court politics," or in an Establishment, or through other closed élites), and preclude or restrict reliance upon established patterns of deference as sources of power (as in the nearly-unchallenged sway of aristocrats or notables, or of other élites of ascribed social status), and where such

---

[53] Morgan, *op. cit.*, 93–94; see also 7–8.

[54] Paullin, *loc. cit.*, 27–31, and Luetscher, *op. cit.*; Bureau of the Census, *Historical Statistics of the United States 1789–1945* (Washington, 1949), esp. 289–290; Richard P. McCormick, "New Perspectives on Jacksonian Politics," *American Historical Review*, LXV (1960), 288–301.

[55] Cunliffe, *op. cit.*, 11–39, 150–180.

conditions produce mass suffrage or regular patterns of mass participation which must be reckoned with in the distribution of power (such
as the American electorate in the 1790s or American mass-participative
attitudes), means to power will be sought by politically active elements
through mobilization of mass public opinion or a mass electorate, with
the consequent development of the most efficient available means
(modern political party action). In particular, where such phenomena
are conditioned by the incidence of active, "democratic" consciousness
and expression of interests, opinion, and ideology within the public
or electorate, the development of modern parties is likely to occur
most rapidly, and to move toward parties of the popular or "democratic" rather than the merely "plebiscitarian" type. Of the four
statements of types of factors stressed above, factors of the first two
types (inhibitive of modern party development) were strongly apparent
in the English situation in the late eighteenth century, and absent or
declining in the American experience; conversely, factors of the second
two types (facilitating party development) were of major significance
for the American experience in the 1790s and after, and of no or limited
significance in English politics until much later. Once again, given
the *general* propositions, the *particular* conditions of American life
appear as especially favorable to party development.

Taken as a whole, the items set forth in this discussion constitute a
proximate explanation for the early rise of parties in America, in terms
first of an inter-related sequence of conditions and events, and second
of two related middle-range generalizations or theoretical formulations.
Methodologically, the theory as it is related to American experience
as against the contrasting background of English experience is mono-
factorial or univariant in its foundations, in that the central variant
isolated is the absence of a feudal past in the United States as contrasted
with Great Britain, stressed by Hartz,[56] with all of the ramifications of
this fact. Insofar as mono-factorial analysis may be questioned, or
univariant comparison may be difficult to verify, the explanation may
be vulnerable. On the other hand, the theory is multi-factorial or
multivariant in its statement of types of social conditions, aspects of
political culture, or ideology, as these conditions may impinge upon
structure and behavior in politics. Insofar as multivariant comparative
analyses are arguable, the explanation may again be vulnerable. Yet
the two lines of analysis might be thought of as substantiating one

---

[56] Noting that his interpretation will be called "a 'single factor' analysis,"
Hartz, *op. cit.*, 20, says that "probably the only way of meeting this charge is to
admit it." The matter may not be so easy, however, in the immediate case or
particularly in the whole panoply of theory or explanation in history or political
science.

another in this instance at least, with the first approach linking many variables into a pattern, while the second specifies in effect consequences or deductions from the larger proposition, which are more readily subject to confirmation or disconfirmation.

Further testing of this relative explanation in American and English history is, of course, in order. It may be reiterated also that the theory itself might be tested more fully if comparisons with still other nations were undertaken, such as France or Germany on the one hand and Canada or Australia on the other.

VI

A more general explanation of the genesis of modern parties may now be offered, as a hypothesis extrapolated from American as contrasted with British experience—a generalization of possible interest to both historians and political scientists, with applications to the present as well as the past.

Parties proper are, apparently, the products of certain types of social-structural conditions and ideological configurations which have come to characterize political modernization as it has taken place in western societies. The relevant social conditions appear to be those which are related to the absence or dissolution of closed, traditionalistic, and hierarchical social structures and modes of conducting politics. The relevant ideologies appear to be those which point to mass or democratic involvement or participation in the political process. In short, parties proper appear to be products of the process of modernization and the emergence of mass or democratic politics, and of democratic or plebiscitarian ideologies—and at the same time to be themselves steps toward political modernization. If the hypothesis is valid, one would expect to find stable parties *if* and *only if,* or *when* but *only when,* the indicated types of social-structural conditions and ideological configurations are present in a society in some significant degree.

Near the center of the argument is the matter of ideology itself. The ideological perspectives which characterized Federalists and Republicans in America in the 1790s were only *particular* ideologies in Mannheim's terms, and as such they were of course conflicting in some measure and representative of the outlooks and interests of particular individuals or groups in the society.[57] Yet each party's ideology was also related to a more general or *total* ideology, or to what we might call, again in Mannheim's terms, a Lockian liberal-democratic "utopia" in the process of becoming the standard American ideology, and one

---

[57] Karl Mannheim, *Ideology and Utopia: An Introduction to the Sociology of Knowledge* (New York, 1954), 64–70.

which stressed the roles of a broad public and a broad electorate in politics. It would of course have been shocking to Hamilton and other "High Federalists" to hear themselves called Lockians, and they were not Lockians in any full sense. Nonetheless, they found it necessary in the American context to construct a political formation and espouse a party ideology which allowed room for popular involvement in politics, although their élitist attitudes led them to perceive such involvement mainly in the mode we have called "plebiscitarian." To Jefferson and his colleagues the Lockian liberal-democratic utopia seemed, as Jefferson himself put it, "the common sense of the subject." The Republicans developed their party structure accordingly and adopted the Lockian ideology with certain adjustments to the immediate American scene as their party ideology, in a form which was fully "democratic." Thus both the Federalist and the Republican particular ideologies partook of the more general developing American total ideology, the first by way of somewhat grudging concession and the second by whole-hearted acceptance.

The working-out of the general hypothesis of party genesis is seen in its earliest and simplest form in the American case. In England the actual phenomena of genesis were bound to be vastly more complex, if the hypothesis is accurate, and to extend through a far longer period of time and through a far more intricate set of transitional stages. In England it took a long, halting process of evolution to break down the feudal past and eighteenth-century patterns of hierarchy, corporatism, virtual representation, "connexions," deference, and the like, and also a tortuous passage through various mixed or intermediate modes of politics, before modern parties stood clearly in the ascendancy. In short, in accord with the explanatory hypothesis, circumstances should be expected to alter cases in their timing, development, and form, but not in their ultimate general result. One of the values of the hypothesis should be heuristic, as it suggests questions of difference as well as of similarity.

Even so, Great Britain in the nineteenth century moved more and more toward patterns of party action which had been explored earlier in the American experience, and certain party practices were thought of, often contemptuously, as "American" methods.[58] Similarly, at least loose parallels to the American party innovation may be discerned in Canada and Australia, with British adaptations, or in the development of parties of the cadre type on the European continent.

---

[58] See, e.g., Jennings on "Joe's Caucus" in Birmingham and related patterns of action, *op. cit.*, 134–143.

However, as Weber has correctly noted, the "structure of parties varies."[59] At least two broad types of later party development may be noted, which differ from the American experience in specific conditions of origin and in resulting specific forms of structure and action. One is represented by the Socialist, Social Democratic, or Labor parties of continental Europe or Great Britain, with variations in later Communist or Fascist developments—in short, the emergence of parties which Duverger has described as departing from the American "cadre" form to assume structures which he calls "mass," "cell," or "militia."[60] By and large such parties at least began as tools for militant social-reformist, social-revolutionary, or social-reactionary purposes, which were expressed in total or near-total rather than particular ideologies or utopias. A second broad type of party development is represented by the new mass nationalist formations in "backward" or "emerging" areas in Asia or Africa—militant parties which have generally been created by alienated intellectuals and others to bring their peoples to nationhood and their new nations up to a par with the already modern nations abroad. Such parties also have had their particular structures and their distinctive ideologies or utopias of modernization, which again, in their utopian beginnings at least, have tended more toward the total than the particular type and also toward extreme intensities of ideological emphasis. These parties have grown not out of indigenous processes of modernization, but rather—in a reversal of western modes—have been created as broad adaptations of alien party prototypes to bring about just such modernization, again on western models.[61]

Yet, in all of these instances of party development, certain common elements which were part of the American experience reappear. All of the instances of party genesis noted here were associated with processes of modernization, or with mimetic ideologies of modernization and consequent mimetic party structures, and all were also associated with mass politics, or patterns of mass mobilization or participation.

---

[59] Weber, loc. cit., 99. In his discussion of the development of American parties as the fullest expression of the "plebiscitarian principle," Weber adumbrates important aspects of the general hypothesis of party origins proposed here, as does Ostrogorski in a different way in his discussion of American and British parties.

[60] Duverger, op. cit., 17–40, 62–71.

[61] See, inter alia, Max F. Millikan and Donald L. M. Blackmer, The Emerging Nations: Their Growth and United States Policy (Boston, 1961); Gabriel A. Almond and James S. Coleman, eds., The Politics of the Developing Areas (Princeton, 1960); John H. Kausky, et. al., Political Change in Underdeveloped Countries: Nationalism and Communism (New York, 1962).

Thus, these general types of factors stand as the apparently irreducible conditions for modern parties, even where the parties assume varying forms of structure or are shaped as reconstructions of foreign models. Some of the European mass parties have approached the problems of mass politics in a manner which is broadly democratic, as cadre parties of the American type generally have, while others such as the Communist or various Fascist formations have been clearly plebiscitarian, with significant consequences in structure and behavior especially when power is attained. In underdeveloped areas, patterns of society and the political backwardness of the masses have not so far been conducive to full democratic development. Thus the new parties of the emerging nations have frequently been mass-mobilizing but not significantly oriented to popular initiative or broad popular participation, and have been keyed to a new structural and ideological élitism of paternal "guidance" by leaders. In consequence, they have tended to be plebiscitarian. Indeed, it follows from the analysis offered here that such parties could not be expected to emerge as fully popular or democratic parties until modernization, social-structural conditions, and ideology in the new nations provided the necessary foundations—and not automatically even then. It would be naive and Procrustean to expect otherwise.[62] However, whether plebiscitarian or democratic, structures of both the broad types distinguished here have performed or offered to perform the central functions of party in mass politics.

In short, the American case as it developed in the eighteenth century stands as only one instance of the general hypothesis of party development, an instance with a strongly democratic bent. For actual historical parties in other situations important differences must be distinguished in purpose, political role, structure, ideological outlook, leadership, organization, style—and the whole general hypothesis is of course subject to review. Yet, basic generic elements discernible in American development appear to remain relevant to the development of parties generally, as instances, in a variety of particular contexts, of party viewed as structure, ideology, and function.

---

[62] Cf. the different comparative analyses by Seymour Martin Lipset, *Political Man: The Social Bases of Politics* (New York, 1960), 45–72, and Harry Eckstein, "A Theory of Stable Democracy," Research Monograph, Center of International Studies (Princeton, 1961), *passim.*

18

Alexander Hamilton as Finance Minister
BROADUS MITCHELL

If there was any central problem among those confronting the new govern-ment, it was the financial one; and if there was any one person acting for the new government, it was the first Secretary of the Treasury, Alexander Hamilton. No one was more conscious than he of the experiment in politics which the new nation was attempting; no one was more aware that the national tree would grow as the institutional twigs were bent by the first administrators of the newly organized republic. The role Hamilton played in defining the dimensions of American government has been surpassed by only a few presidents and perhaps not at all by any other cabinet member since his day.

What that role was has been analyzed by the latest and certainly the most competent of his biographers, Broadus Mitchell. In his long and active career Professor Mitchell has taught at Johns Hopkins, Rutgers, and Hofstra Universities, and has written a number of books dealing mainly with American economic history. His two-volume biography of Alexander Hamilton (1957–62), like the essay below, stresses Hamilton's importance for his own and for later times.

An estimate of Hamilton invariably evokes an estimate of Jefferson, who is generally regarded as his antagonist in the debate over the national purpose and how to pursue it. Yet in their differences regarding the policies to be pursued by the new government, Jefferson and Hamilton are more accurately seen as complementary protagonists of the larger republican and national idea. It should not be forgotten that Hamilton was of the same libertarian philosophy as Jefferson, a spokesman for the rights of minorities and individuals (see Harold C. Syrett, "Alexander Hamilton: History by Stereotype," **The New-York Historical Society Quarterly,** *January, 1959). A political economist in the true sense, Hamilton saw his problem as one of using financial means to achieve national security and growth. His program*

SOURCE: *Proceedings of the American Philosophical Society,* CII (April, 1958), 117–123. Reprinted by permission of the author and publisher.

was a rejection of laissez faire, and it is an error to regard him as a disciple of Adam Smith; national independence, he felt, could be secured only through the active participation of government. In this sense, says Mitchell, he was a collectivist and a mercantilist. Whatever faults he may have had as Secretary of the Treasury, his probity cannot be questioned. He represented not privilege but public good. The course he charted for the role of the national government in public life is the one which, without infringement upon individual liberty, has actually been followed since his day.

In reading Professor Mitchell's essay, one cannot avoid considering the larger questions which hang perennially over the study of American history, some indeed over the study of all history. How much does the individual make the times, how much do the times make the individual? Did the opportunities within a new government create the figure of a Hamilton, or did Hamilton create his own opportunities? What economic policies would the new nation have pursued if Robert Morris, Washington's first choice for the Treasury post, had accepted, thus denying the position to Hamilton, the second choice? To what extent, if at all, should government participate in the development of the national economy? In what way should particular economic interests (in Hamilton's day, the commercial and the agrarian) be related to each other, and what special considerations ought to be extended them? In promoting national economic growth, what should be the roles of the central and local governments respectively?

The answers to these questions reveal the contribution which Alexander Hamilton offers to current thought. His example urges the importance of the experiments in viability being performed by the many new nations of the world today, much as he urged the importance of his own nation's experiment in the 1790's. He summarizes the self-consciousness with which a new state defines both its social philosophy and the way to achieve it.

One is helped in finding his way through the fierce, often bitter controversies of the Federalist period if he has it constantly in mind that Hamilton was, as Wolcott said, "of the first endowments of mind." Some of his contemporaries, acting in the same scenes, possessed more varied knowledge. His formal schooling was compressed into little more than four years. Without patrimony, from boyhood he was thrown largely on his own resources. His relatively short career (cut off at the age of forty-nine) was incessantly occupied with action, most of it not in his private but in the public behalf. Five years of his early twenties, when ideally a thinker would be accumulating diversified informational inventory, he devoted to exacting military service. He never realized his hope of visiting Europe. He had the least opportunity to browse in books, to learn to play a musical instrument, or to lean and loaf at his ease, inviting his soul.

Thus, in the commonly accepted meaning of the term (perhaps denoting mental mellowness) he was not the same philosopher as others to whom we may point. The remarkable feature is that in scraps of time he snatched so much from books, and managed to be so aware of cultural undercurrents. Imagination he was blessed with, a perfect well-spring of optimistic foresight. This *esprit* must ever remain a mystery; is it born of physical vigor, of nervous vitality, of emotional generosity? Does this native verve grow from evidence received, or does it find its own proofs? Dynamism, combined with cheerfulness and good will, does not make a man a sage, but tends in that direction.

Whatever the judgment on the completeness of Hamilton's mental stock, nobody ever denied his acuteness and analytical capacity. Remembering this in surveying his policies as finance minister, one does well to give him the benefit of the doubt on controversial points. He made mistakes of several sorts, more largely personal and political than fiscal, but as a rule his superior wits saved him from following infatuations. Some to which he yielded he afterward forswore with excellent candor and firmness. In the Treasury he did not, could not commit the blunder of supposing that the sinking fund would grow automatically by compounding interest on securities bought up and retired. The fund must expand from revenue alone. Any ambiguity in his language which has induced critics to fancy the reverse should be cancelled by confidence in his good head. The elder Pitt, whose example influenced Hamilton, may be similarly exculpated.

Instances of villains with brains are not wanting. But one feels assured that Hamilton's high intelligence—leave aside his code of honor—would have protected him against improprieties in administration of the country's finances. He knew that he was not in public life for the moment; he had settled purposes that needed time in the nurture. This is ascribing his integrity to the most utilitarian motive. It is easier and juster to lift it to the moral plane. In the heats of party conflict he could not escape the accusation of favoring his friends or, worse, of placating his enemies by betraying his official trust. I may say at once that no evidence of this exists. First, presumption is against it. For the quarter century of his greatest activity he lived in intimacy with Washington, for long periods in daily, almost hourly contact, and he ever enjoyed Washington's approval. He left the Treasury, as even the cynical Talleyrand observed, to make a living for his family. After sitting at the receipt of a nation's customs, and in spite of unremitting industry in his profession, he died insolvent. Congressional investigation, upon which he insisted when it seemed ready to be abandoned by its promoters, cleared him of any wrongdoing. Finally, as is recalled if one knows anything about Hamilton, he proclaimed in print his private lapse in adultery to blast a charge of public malfeasance. We have his letter to Henry Lee, no less friendly than firm, refusing to disclose Treasury information for speculative advantage. He buttressed, if he did not devise, the system of internal checks of one Treasury officer upon another.

This is presumptive evidence. In addition, accusation, busy in his day and since, has not been able to produce from Treasury records or the transactions of businessmen or speculators who stood to profit by privileged knowledge, any proof of the Secretary's complicity. William Constable, as revealed by his letters, in the weeks when Hamilton's first "budget" (Report on the Public Credit, January 9, 1790) was impending, sought opportunities to "be with" Hamilton and also Wolcott. His object was to obtain secret information, but his reports to Andrew Craigie and others show that he came away no wiser than he went, which, however, was tolerably wise, for he was no fool in drawing reasonable inferences from the necessities of the case, and from his experience of Hamilton's prior principles. Indeed, Craigie and his correspondents, some months earlier, seemed to take for granted redemption of the debt in the hands of the holders if Hamilton was appointed Secretary of the Treasury.

Further inquiry may convict Hamilton of passive guilt perhaps in choosing, or more particularly in retaining William Duer as his assistant in the Treasury. Duer was a schemer, and not without success until his enthusiastic indiscretion and secret corruptions caught up with him, landing him in debtor's prison. Before that, and while still outwardly in high feather, he had left the Treasury at his own wish, but with Hamilton's approval. His known machinations, legal if not laudable, do not concern us for themselves. Nor is there room for doubt that in furthering his private engagements, which we have in his own handwriting, he abused, or intended to abuse, his official position. There is no evidence that Hamilton was a partner in these plans to enrich American and European speculators at the expense of unsuspecting sellers and buyers of securities. The question is whether we are to fasten on Hamilton the fault not of complicity but of complacence in the face of Duer's doings.

Here I must apply my own maxim that little escaped Hamilton's notice, and that he was apt in inference from what he knew. The Treasury staff, while larger than that of other departments, was small, and Duer was nominally next to Hamilton in authority and closest to him in association. The suspicious point out that Duer was a relative, by marriage, of Hamilton's wife. Further, Hamilton always befriended Duer—spoke well of him to Robert Morris, the Superintendent of Finance, when Duer was purchasing agent for the army in New York, brought him into the Treasury, later cautioned him against running into speculative disaster, still later solicited his temporary release from jail. All of this looks like too great indulgence of Duer's misdeeds. On the other hand, Duer was recommended by previous experience and character. He had been a patriot in civil and military posts, had been secretary of the Board of Treasury under the Confederation, and was generally credited with financial ingenuity, which presumably would be serviceable in the new national government. Other plausible endorsements might be mentioned.

It is not profitable to conjecture, but in the light of what is now known and which may not be soon or ever amplified, my guess is that Hamilton too far tolerated Duer in the bosom of the Treasury. As Hamilton was responsible for the honorable functioning of the department, he should earlier have prompted Duer's departure, if that is what happened, for the good of the service. On the other hand, not to excuse Hamilton, allowing he was at fault, but to round out the situation, several circumstances may be had in mind. Hamilton was himself excessively occupied in the short period of Duer's tenure, organizing his office, preparing and then defending his momentous first report to Congress. Speculation in public debt was not new; it had been active since 1787, rose conspicuously only when the report was submitted, and not until later, when panic threatened, did Hamilton look on speculation as harmful to the country's credit. Further, it was a period when men who esteemed their own motives had more difficulty than now, and less help from the public conscience, in keeping the line between official trust and private benefit. Members of the old Board of Treasury had been privy to Duer's deviousness while in their midst. Finally, supposing that Hamilton early learned of Duer's duplicity, he may have judged that an open scandal from his exposure would have been more harmful to the public credit—or, if you like, to the administration, though that would have been much the same thing—than handling the case with a little patience. This last gains some credence from the fact that later, when Hamilton received a complaint of Duer's conduct in the Treasury, he explained that Duer had been some time out of office, and let it go at that.

I am not expected, before this Society, to retell the story of Hamilton's fiscal proposals and of his conduct of the Treasury between September, 1789, and January, 1795. I beg your attention to a few features which may be less familiar and to an overall estimate of his aims and services.

It would be a mistake to suppose that Hamilton in his earlier period was political scientist, eager to tighten constitutional bonds, and that after he was installed in the Treasury he became economist, bent upon restoration of the country's credit and advance of its material prosperity. The fact is that there was no alteration in his object to create a strong nation, from the time when he broached plans to James Duane and Robert Morris a decade before for political and economic renovation. Only after assuming charge of the Treasury did he command fiscal and monetary tools with which to rear the structure which the Constitution promised and which he had envisioned all along. In the Treasury his economic devices drew breath from and in turn animated his political purposes. Throughout, he was the political economist in the original and true meaning of the term. He practiced statecraft for the energizing of the economy; he promoted production and exchange of goods and services for the benefit of the body politic. Those who differed with his Treasury policies were quick to perceive and to attack the political design with which he informed his fiscal proposals, for example in the assumption of state debts and establishment of the Bank of the United States. His critics were accurate in their swift recognition of his political incentives, though their broad opposition to his measures and readiness to brand them as of class or party inspiration showed less wisdom. Still, on the whole, we may accept the Secretary of the Treasury at his enemies' estimate.

If anything, Hamilton was more the prophet and practitioner of government than he was the patron of finance, trade and manufactures. In a young country, of enormous potential resources, but sparsely populated, overwhelmingly agricultural and extractive in its pursuits, and fractioned into conflicting political and economic divisions, organization became his dearest object. Public action must come before private. Capital could be secured and varied enterprise stimulated by the fostering care of federal government. He knew that what we call national wealth, in its origin and maintenance, is not material (land, labor, capital, consumption goods), but is exceedingly immaterial. It is capacity for economic processes. This means cooperation under conditions of self-discipline, safety of persons and property, and stability.

Dependence upon government as the engine of economic growth, appropriate in Hamilton's America, had been relaxed and was soon to be abandoned in Europe, notably in Britain of Adam Smith, James Watt, and the Industrial Revolution, and in France of the Physiocrats, *laissez faire,* and the tricolor. I do not need to remind that these had suffered from too much government in economic life—over-regulation, protected monopolies, pestiferous taxation. There the era was ripe for freedom, appeal to natural law, individual self-interest, competition rather than controls. Though these cries rang in Hamilton's ears, he was convinced that America was in the stage to be benefited by governmental promotion and protection. Without these encouragements our business community and citizens generally lacked the capital, confidence, and experience for sure and rapid advance. While he expected that impetus supplied by resourceful central government would raise up private enterprise, so far lessening extension of governmental responsibility in the economy, he can scarcely be described as the apostle of Adam Smith. He understood and was influenced by the *Wealth of Nations,* but considered that America could apply the theory of that work only at some day in the future.

It will be recalled that Hamilton prefaced several of his Treasury reports with persuasive short essays forestalling objections and arguing the merits of his proposals. Particularly in the Report on Manufactures, 1791, he must be circumspect in rearing a rival, as many thought, to the agricultural interest. Almost all property in this country was in land and its appurtenances, including slaves to the southward where lay, besides, the greatest suspicion of central authority. He was obliged to show, tactfully, how industry—protected industry— presented a vigorous claim, not least because it would benefit farmers. But his tenderness toward the extractive economy (which was a way of life too) was induced by inhibitions of most of his hearers, was not his own preference. Appreciating the basic importance of agriculture, he did not yield in his design to produce a quickening variety in activities, which would require public prompting.

So much for his general purpose. What of his practical, institutional means toward equipping a competent nation? Out of disorder, debt, and not a little discouragement flowing from the recent business depression, he must rouse the country to system and progress. He was sustained by his faith that America's advance in union, security, and wealth would be rapid, proliferating in every direction. This sure insight armed him to attack obstacles which others believed were more serious if not insuperable. The debt is the plainest case in point. Seventy-five or eighty millions total (leaving aside the Continental currency which was past rescue) could be promptly discharged once the country addressed itself to the task. Hamilton did better. The debt would be the means of its own payment. He would turn the bane into a blessing.

He had to begin amidst the detritus of Revolution and Confederation. He had to discover what the debt was, and how divided, before he could present it (partly estimated even so) for candid acknowledgment. The debt, including accumulated interest, must be funded, offering a fair option for voluntary conversion. The new securities were to issue to the actual holders of the old. Any discrimination in favor of original holders, who had parted with public paper for however small a fraction of its nominal value, would be fatal to Hamilton's plan. In the debates in the House, genuine solicitude for justice to deserving losers was mixed with a deal of declamation pleading for old soldiers, their widows and orphans, and castigating heartless speculators.

Madison's argument for discrimination was the most thoughtful, perhaps the sincerest.

But Hamilton and his champions could not hearken. Unless the precedent was established of honoring the debt in the hands of the holders, evidences of it would not be certainly transferable. Unless transferable the securities would not serve in a degree as currency, more importantly as the basis for loans which would result in more currency and varied investment. Only so could we mount upon the debt to a higher station. It was charged at the time and has been repeated since that Hamilton, in his insistence, was callous to the cries of suffering and cunningly courted the support of speculators and the wealthy generally. That they were gainers there is no doubt. But their profit was not his purpose.

Mr. Parrington, in his vigorous sketch, has said that it is not necessary to do more than scan Hamilton's writings to know his spirit and aims. One is allowed to suspect that Parrington has followed his own advice. I pause over this admission of partial examination before pronouncing judgment not because this influential critic is the worst offender, for he is not. A thorough reading of Hamilton leaves a different impression from that received by too many. He was not the tactician of privilege, but the advocate of the public good. He was the patriot, not the partisan. In a state of political confusion and economic immaturity, men who commanded means and business talents must in any case play a crucial role. If these were attracted as allies, government would gain in solidity and capacity. So would the capitalists and enterprisers. This was in itself a proper object. But more than that, their efforts would be directed, by government policing as well as promotion, into channels calculated to serve the entire community.

John Adams and Alexander Hamilton were of similar principles but dissimilar personalities. After eyeing each other appraisingly, they worked together uneasily until their hostility became scandalous. Under these circumstances neither would be expected to give a sympathetic report of the other. Adams recorded that Hamilton shouldered his work on associates in the Treasury while he disported himself in society. The remark is worth exploring because the full truth is revealing. In all likelihood Tench Coxe helped Hamilton with the Report on Manufactures. Coxe had the development of industry near his heart, and aided that cause in numerous important ways. Probably he had charge of collecting and afterward cast into form the information on the state of manufactures in the country. That part of the report is distinct from the argumentative prologue. Coxe, deeply imbued with the utility of rounding out the economy by adding factories to fields, may have presented this thesis in outline or more fully for the opening of the document. We shall know only when the body of Coxe's papers, now in private hands, shall become available. Hamilton sought the advice of informed and trusted men on means of restoring the public credit. William Bingham, of Philadelphia, who had unusual knowledge from observation in England and participation in the founding of the Bank of North America, answered Hamilton's inquiry at special length. Some have suggested that Bingham supplied the pattern of Hamilton's funding scheme. Their expedients corresponded at important points, but did not coincide at others. A part of what Bingham urged, Hamilton had advocated earlier. Stephen Higginson, of Boston, was another who offered approximations to Hamilton's devices. We must not forget that the financial program to be broached by the Treasury formed the conversation of business and public men in the autumn of 1789, and that administration policy when announced had been anticipated in main features. Oliver Wolcott, Jr., who was chosen by Hamilton for the Treasury staff because he was expert in accounting matters, theory as well as practice, worked out detailed plans for administration of the funding and conversion operation. We have in his hand his departmental reports to the Secretary which provoke admiration. Besides, much that flowed between Hamilton and his subordinates has left no trace that we can identify. These assignments of the Secretary to his assistants are just what one would expect to find, for everything was to be done in a short space, and Hamilton would not fail to apportion the tasks that required talent as well as the routine demanding industry and accuracy.

If anything, Hamilton took too much of the burden of the Treasury upon himself, detail in addition to foremost policy formations. His manuscripts show this. The main reports are in his hand, sometimes in several drafts which record the elaboration, less frequently the alteration of his ideas. Many particular directions and queries in the administration of the Treasury, likewise in his hand, concern detail but were far from routine. Procedures at the custom houses must be as nearly as possible correct, for what was practiced at that initial stage would set precedents, and unworkable rules would plague the government into the future. For the same reason he referred questions in the interpretation of the laws to Richard Harison, United States Attorney at New York. This was correspondence which Hamilton could not delegate. Hamilton's personal discharge of his duties in the Treasury becomes more remarkable when we remember their variety. He must not only strike out bold plans for the rescue of credit, establishment of a mint, provision of currency, promotion of manufactures, commencement of a military academy, and organization of the coast guard. He must also conduct the day-to-day operation of the most far-flung department of the new federal government. Obstruction of collection of the excise in the western country transcended ordinary administrative vexations, required his preparation of the punitive military expedition to Pittsburgh, which he accompanied, and distracted him in the political controversy which ensued.

This would have been enough, but he engineered his measures through Congress. He was floor leader off the floor. This legislative management, which critics thought unbecoming, was reduced by the competence and loyalty of Federalists in the House, notably Boudinot, Ames, and William Smith. His and their efforts would have been spared in part, by no means entirely, if Hamilton had been allowed to give his reports in person, or had been called in later to answer questions. Much that entered into the protracted and exacerbated debates could have been cleared up and put by. Though Hamilton's power of written statement has hardly ever been exceeded, numerous members were honestly confused by the novelty of the subject matter, particularly in the reports of 1790 on credit and bank, and would have profited by oral exchanges with the Secretary. Of course certain major policy questions, fiscal and constitutional, required legislative discussion. Objections disingenuously raised would have been exploited anyhow. Further, in investigations in the House, 1793–1794, into his official conduct, which were principally party-inspired, Hamilton was obliged to defend himself by prodigious labors. Under pressure of time, which his opponents purposely made exigent, he must summarize and analyze Treasury accounts over a span of years, not to speak of the verbal argument which informed these exhibits. He could have spared himself these pains, at least in part, had he made annual reports on Treasury operations. This he omitted to do, and that is clearly a count against the wisdom of his procedure.

Besides all else, while we are naming over his accumulating occupations, he had to give cabinet counsel. In addition, his enthusiasm (some said aggrandizing meddling) took him into responsibilities which he should have been content to leave in the hands of other ministers. In judging of this, one must be mindful how keenly he felt the opportunity and need for framing good central government policy at the outset. All but nominally, he was the chief minister of state under the President, if only because so much, in the nature of the case, involved the Treasury.

Finally, closing this subject of Hamilton's personal discharge of his Treasury duties, particularly the devising of plans embodied in major reports, it may be mentioned that the day of government ghost writers was not yet. If ghosts penned the lines signed with others' names, often in that spectral company was Hamilton. A variety of instances of his deft service for friends could be given, including Henry Laurens' resignation of the presidency of the Old Congress, Baron von Steuben's plea for reimbursement of his Revolutionary expenses, and, not least, Hamilton's part in Washington's Farewell Address. If he found time to furnish thoughts and words to those who sought his aid, would he have neglected to speak for himself in his closest concerns?

It is recorded of Mrs. Hamilton that she related, at an advanced age, how her husband struck off in a single night his celebrated defense of the constitutionality of the Bank of the United States. President Washington, according to the story, brought the adverse opinions of Jefferson and of Randolph to Hamilton's home, thinking it suitable that he should examine these for his rebuttal. The Secretary of the Treasury retired to his study and did not emerge until his counter-argument was finished. Somewhere along the line, in the memory of Mrs. Hamilton or of her narrator, the composition of this document was too much compressed. For we know from the manuscript itself and from his letters to Washington that the work was spread over a week. Even so, this reduces the impossible to the extraordinary. Allowing that Hamilton had been revolving the project of the bank in his mind for a decade, had broached it anew in one recent report and given it elaborate statement in another, his claim for its constitutionality is one of his finest performances, both in the lesser matter of its vibrant language and the superior one of its bold conception. The idea of implied powers in the Constitution was not entirely new in his own mouth or in the observations of others. But he now applied the doctrine with compelling candor.

We have noticed that in Hamilton's plans and executions as finance minister the political was entangled with the fiscal. The one was imbued with the other. This took on the highest dignity when he declared the supremacy of the central government within its sphere and defined that sphere liberally. The rule for interpretation of the Constitution must be that of reason, beckoned forward by developing social need as well as restrained by the letter of the law. He declared frankly that between illegitimate extension of federal authority and too cautious limitation of it lay a penumbra. Here was room for honest difference of opinion, depending upon information, experience, and what was expected to be useful in federal-state relations. He gave the federal power the benefit of the doubt.

Hamilton himself, besides his agency in inspiring the calling of the Constitutional Convention, had made contribution to the framing of the basic law. He had helped render it ampler in scope than it would have been without his proposals, formally rejected though these were. But nothing that anybody wrote into the document was more enlivening than what he read into it in establishing the propriety of a national bank. This institution that he defended, as handmaiden of the Treasury, as the source of a reliable paper currency, was serviceable, but the principle that supported it, applied through the years, was to make the Constitution a living instrument. Hamilton's generous view of the opportunities and duties of the central power is repeatedly vindicated in the history of America. There have been delays in this constitutional progress, with temporary reversals later repented. But manifestly Hamilton's forecast of our actual national development has been borne out. He feared the centrifugal tendencies, fostered the centripetal forces. Enough have cried that Hamilton did not sufficiently cherish local autonomy, with its friendliness to variety in ways of life and its guarantees of liberty itself. That argument will go on, as I hope it shall, forever. We have it now in an Arkansas guardsman one day, under state orders, barring pupils from a school, and the next day, under national command, ushering them into their classrooms. The proof of Hamilton's forecast is in the event. Hugely growing population, quickened communications, scale and standardization of production have multiplied our common concerns, thereby increasing our reliance on national decisions. Most Americans agree that these, in the secular trend, have not imperiled our freedom, but have enlarged it.

A related subject, imbedded in Hamilton's fiscal policy, is his successful plea for federal assumption of the state Revolutionary debts. In his report, the fiscal reasons prompting this were foremost—simplicity, avoidance of competition between taxing jurisdictions, and consequent larger yield from revenue sources. Federal assumption of the state debts would benefit not only state but federal creditors. There is no occasion for questioning his sincerity in giving precedence to fiscal uniformity and economy. He knew only too intimately the mischiefs of the contest between states and Congress for revenue during the war and under the Confederation. As a member of Congress he had failed in protracted efforts to secure for the central government an independent income from a 5 per cent import duty. In the report he merely hinted at what promptly became the staple of debate, namely, that if all creditors looked to the national authority that would have their loyalty.

Opponents, jealous for state importance, were not to miss the implications of any proposal that tended to magnetize the central power. Having lost on the issue of a discrimination in favor of original holders who had alienated their federal securities, they would make a more determined stand for the rights of states which had met a large part of their own indebtedness or were in the course of doing so. As the controversy waxed, and threatened to go irrevocably against him, Hamilton was bound to accept the dispute in the political terms chosen by his critics. The effectiveness of the federal government, and future viability of the Union as he saw it, hung in the balance.

Hence his saving agreement with Jefferson whereby northern votes would be found to place the capital on the Potomac and southern votes would be changed to carry the assumption. I see no reason to suppose that the exchange was other than genuine and deliberate on the part of both principals. Each must persuade followers to produce the required vote. Their meeting ground was the good of the country under the Constitution. Each sacrificed something for this worthy object. It has regularly been said that Hamilton did not care where the capital was placed geographically, that consequently he made an empty gift for an essential gain. On the other hand, in his last term in the Old Congress, where the placement of the capital obsessed the members, he showed at least a decent regard for the claims of New York or for another northern site which his friends would approve. He had that much local or regional attachment, though it is true that he did not put his heart into the fight with anything like the vehemence shown by Madison on the other side. Jefferson on his part surely understood the unwillingness of his southern compatriots to concede the assumption. The only fault was in the sequel, when Jefferson, after Hamilton's death, represented himself as having been deceived into a measure for which he was blamed.

Seeking to follow the career of Hamilton, I have never seen much profit in pursuing the rancors that developed between him and Jefferson, at least not for their own sake. Numbers of chroniclers, in gleeful partisanship for one champion or the other, have revived these disputes. The bitterness was genuine at the time, and knowledge of its different occasions is illuminating for the historian. Aside from satisfying this curiosity, the quarrels between them are of minor moment compared to the contributions made by both to our national beginnings. A superb combined achievement was in progress. On the one hand, the rights of man, newly proclaimed, were to be nourished. On the other hand, the practicability of these rights was to be tested in the experiment of constructing a firm nation. It was in this second behalf that Hamilton strove. Perhaps the body of the people, as afterward understood, would have found expression and risen to power without Hamilton's preparatory efforts for economic solvency and political unity. What we have is the grateful story as it unfolded.

The Sedition Law, Free Speech, and the
American Political Process
JAMES MORTON SMITH

In the cold war that has dominated our age, the conflict, as we have seen it, is between a free world and a captive one. We see the United States as sharing with its Western allies a legacy of freedom. For us the legacy is clearly defined in the first ten amendments to our Constitution; and of these our most valued possession, perhaps, is the first, which seeks to insure the right of free speech and a free press. In the popular outlook toward the cold war, not too much consideration has been given to the degree to which the free world is captive and the captive world free. Nor, for that matter, has consideration been given to the fact that the United States was not so much conceived in liberty as in the struggle to achieve it. In its early years, indeed, the founders of the republic were sharply divided over the constitutional guarantees of free speech and free press. During the late 1790's, at a time of very strained relations with France, a bitter domestic conflict was fought between the Federalists and the Republicans regarding the nature and applicability of these guarantees. Only as a result of the attempt and failure of the Federalists to enforce their Sedition Law were the concept and practice of free speech and free press amplified to the point of their present importance in the American political process.

*It is this crucial development which is discussed by James Morton Smith, of Cornell University, in the following essay. Professor Smith has edited two significant volumes—*Liberty and Justice: A Historical Record of American Constitutional Development *(1958), which he did jointly with Paul L. Murphy, and* Seventeenth-Century America: Essays in Colonial History *(1959). He is the author of* Freedom's Fetters, *the first of a two-volume appraisal of the Alien and Sedition Laws and the response which they evoked. Professor Smith quite rightly regards his subject as an important phase in the evolution of the American civil-liberties tradition. In*

SOURCE: *The William and Mary Quarterly,* Third Series, IX (October, 1952), 497–511. Reprinted by permission of the author and publisher.

the essay which follows, he assesses the influence of the Sedition Law in shaping the republican process, and in so doing answers several relevant questions. What, to begin, were the provisions of the Sedition Law and the circumstances which occasioned its enactment? What was the English common-law concept of seditious libel and what theory of government did it express? What were the respective views of the Federalists and the Republicans regarding public criticism of officeholders? How was the Sedition Law enforced? To what extent were the theory and practice of the Sedition Law in conflict with the principles of the American Revolution? What was the importance of the election of 1800? What significance did the Sedition Law and its defeat have for the American political process?

No one will deny the importance to that process of establishing the principle that the governed may criticize and control the governors through the instruments of free speech and a free press. It is no less important for us, however, to understand to what extent this principle is practiced today, to what extent it should be practiced, and whether indeed it is a valid one for our times. The extent of its practice would certainly depend on the degree to which our speech and our press are free. One would not have to look very far for evidences of serious limitations upon such freedom in recent times, as during the early 'fifties, when McCarthyism fettered the American mind, and during the middle 'sixties, when the administration questioned the patriotism of those who voiced their criticism of the American war in Vietnam. It is fair to say that a free press is only a press that is free to express and exercise the interests and prerogatives of its publisher. That the citizen has a right to free speech, moreover, does not necessarily mean that he will avail himself of it. And have not Tocqueville and Mill warned us that in a liberal democracy, the forces of democracy—equality and conformity—are a constant threat to the pursuit of liberty?

The principle of the liberty of opinion is constantly being tested. If nations predicated on liberalism have seen it in some measure curtailed, nations predicated on authoritarianism have seen it to no lesser degree asserted. The dialectic of liberalism as a historical force in Europe and America poses challenging questions for the student of the American past. What will become of liberalism in a world that has been transforming itself by authoritarianism? Can the ideas of a liberty-seeking Atlantic community of the eighteenth century serve the needs of the power-seeking revolutionary world of the twentieth? These are the questions we must ask and seek to answer in exploring with Professor Smith that earlier period of our history when the American tradition of civil liberties was first being established.

Popular government rests on the right of the public to choose between opposing views. Since an informed public opinion is vital to republican government, freedom of expression is necessary for the formation of that opinion. If people cannot communicate their thoughts to one another without running the risk of prosecution, no other liberty can be secure because freedom of speech and of the press are essential to any meaning of liberty. The years between 1798 and 1801 afford the first instance under the Constitution in which American political leaders faced the problem of defining the role of public criticism in a representative government. This paper deals with the solution which the Federalists proposed and acted upon and the response of the American people to it.

I

After the revelations of Talleyrand's duplicity in the XYZ affair, President John Adams called for unanimity in framing a defense program against France. When the Jeffersonian Republicans balked at some of the measures that pointed toward war rather than a negotiated settlement, the long-standing Federalist fear of fractional strife led them openly to identify their old political opponents not only as pernicious democrats but also as pro-French traitors. To insure unanimity of action against the French Directory, the Federalists launched a systematic legislative program directed against the opposition party.

The Alien and Sedition Laws have been described as "an effective weapon against what was deemed an especially pernicious and dangerous form of domestic opposition in time of war." Only the Alien Enemy Law, however, was made contingent upon a declaration of war. The rest of these ill-fated acts were designed to deal with domestic political opposition in time of peace. They were political devices which topped the levee erected by the Federalists to withstand the rising tide of Republicanism. Both the Naturalization and the Alien Friends Laws represented a growing distrust not only of aliens but also of the people in general; both acts were designed to restrict the growth of the opposition party. The Sedition Law, aimed directly at the Democratic-Republicans, was the capstone of the internal security program of the Federalist party.

Section one of the statute punished conspiracies and combinations to impede the operation of federal laws and set the penalty at not more than five years in prison and a $5,000 fine. The second section dealt solely with verbal opposition, providing penalties for any person, citizen or alien, making any "false, scandalous and malicious" statements against the President, either house of Congress, or the government with intent to defame them, or to bring them into contempt or disrepute, or to excite against them the hatred of the good people of the United States. The maximum penalty was two years imprisonment and a $2,000 fine.

The law allowed the truth of the critical remarks to stand as an absolute defense against the charge of sedition and specified that the jury, not the judge, should decide whether the words used violated the law. Finally, the law was to expire not at the termination of the diplomatic crisis with France but with the expiration of President Adams' term of office.

II

The view which the law takes of the offense of publishing and uttering seditious words depends upon the attitude held as to the relation of the rulers to the people. Are the people the superiors of the rulers, or are the rulers the superiors of the people? The first view holds that sovereignty resides with the people and not with the government. The so-called rulers are the elected agents and servants of the people, who may discuss questions relating not only to government policy but also to punishment or dismissal of dishonest, inadequate, or unpopular agents. If anyone disagrees with the faultfinding, they may advocate the cause of the agents. The most that can happen is the replacement of the agent with another more to the people's liking.

The criminal law of seditious libel which emerged in England during the seventeenth and eighteenth centuries developed at a time when the accepted view made the rulers the superiors of the people. By virtue of their exalted positions, the rulers were considered the wise and good guides of the country. Authority therefore had to be approached with proper decorum. Mistakes might be pointed out in respectful petitions, but whether the rulers were mistaken or not, no censure could be leveled against them. The people could not make adverse comments in conversation, in clandestine pamphlets, or later in newspapers. The only lawful method of presenting grievances was through their lawful representatives in the legislature, who might be petitioned in an orderly and dignified manner.

This view made words punishable, because to find fault with the government tended to undermine the respect of the people for it and to reduce its dignity and authority. The "bad tendency" test, moreover, presumed that criticism tended to overthrow the state. There was no need to prove any intention on the part of the defendant to produce disaffection or to excite an insurrection; it was enough if he intended to publish the blame. The law of seditious libel was thus the product of the view that the government was master.

III

It was to this English common-law concept that the Federalists turned for their model. Even so, they attempted to adapt the authoritarian practice to the basic realities of popular government by working out a compromise between the rights of the authorities and the rights of the people. An aristocratic party which deplored political democracy, they based their defense of the right of authorities to freedom from public criticism, paradoxically enough, on the fact that the American government rested on the consent of the governed. They contended that the election of officials by the people demonstrated the confidence which the people had in those officers. Once these officials had been elevated by the people to the highest offices in the land, they became the "constituted authorities" who ran things until the next election. Thus, the Federalists exalted the officeholder above the mass of the citizens. It was a greater offense to criticize one of the rulers than it was to criticize one of the people themselves, because the rulers partook of the majesty of the whole people.

The Federalist theory of government, moreover, held that the right of political participation was not the province of all men but the prerogative of a chosen few. As Jay put it, "those who own the country are the most fit persons to participate in the government of it." The Sedition Law was consistent with the Federalist concept of an elite ruling class. Thinking that the stability of American society depended on "the few, the rich, and the well born," they opposed any criticism which might threaten their positions as rulers by undermining public confidence in their administration. Because they had been in power since the adoption of the Constitution, they looked upon themselves as the peculiar guardians of the nation's welfare. By identifying their administration with the government, and the government with the Constitution, the Federalists concluded that criticism of their administration was an attempt to subvert the Constitution and to overthrow the government.

The Republicans agreed that the government of the United States rests on the people, but they widened the concept of "public confidence" to coincide with "public opinion." Elected officials could lose the confidence of the people as well as gain it. To continue to merit public confidence, their measures must meet public approval. Public opinion was not a cyclical phenomenon which appeared every two years to be registered at the polls. It was in the continual process of formulation and could be conveyed constitutionally in speeches or in the press. The people did not vote themselves out of further political participation by the act of voting in elected officials. They were free to examine the conduct of the authorities; they could denounce it as well as praise it. They did not have to wait until election time to withdraw their confidence from an agent whom they decided was unworthy of it.

The Republicans based their arguments against the law on the ground that it destroyed "the responsibility of public servants and public measures to the people." Madison specifically condemned the law, because it exposed the United States, "which acquired the honour of taking the lead among nations towards perfecting political principles," to the disgrace of retreating "towards the exploded doctrine that the administrators of the Government are the masters and not the servants of the people."

IV

Although the Federalists asserted that the Sedition Law was declaratory of the English common law, they also announced that it mitigated the rigors of the law as expounded by Blackstone. It made the intent of the speaker, as well as the tendency of his words, an essential element in the crime of seditious libel. Moreover, it allowed truth as a justification and made the jury the judge of the criminality of the utterances. Of what value to the accused were these three procedural safeguards?

The interpretation which the courts put on the truth provision made it worse than useless as an aid to the defendant. Under the rulings handed down by the judges of the Supreme Court on circuit, this supposed safeguard actually reversed the normal criminal law presumption of innocence. Instead of the government having to prove that the words of the accused were false, scandalous, and malicious, the defendant had to prove that they were true. As Judge Samuel Chase put it, the accused had to prove all of his statements "to the marrow. If he asserts three things and proves but two," the jurist said, "he fails in his defense, for he must prove the whole of his assertions to be true." This is a clear illustration of the doctrine of presumptive guilt; in practice, the courts presumed the defendant guilty until he proved himself innocent.

Moreover, the accused was required not only to prove the truth of every word in every statement but, in some instances, to prove an entire count in an indictment by the same witness. Even though the statement contained more than one point, the defendant could not introduce different witnesses to prove different points. According to Judge Chase, this practice would have been "irregular and subversive of every principle of law."

What was the effect of the clause requiring that bad intent should be proved? In every case, the government prosecutors and the judges presumed the bad intent of the speaker from the bad tendency of the words. Moreover, it was the tendency of the words to find fault with elected officials which was penalized and not the intent to cause violence. The courts narrowed the legal test of criminality to the pre-Revolutionary common-law test; persons were punished if the tendency of their words was to undermine public confidence in the elected officials and thus to render it less likely that they might be re-elected.

Finally, the function of the trial jury was reduced almost to that of a rubber stamp. It is evident from the replies of grand juries to charges from federal judges and from the verdicts of the trial juries that both were Federalist-dominated, if not made up exclusively of Federalists. The strictness with which the trial judges restricted defense challenges of jurors virtually prevented any challenges for political bias, and led to extensive criticism of the courts. Congressman Matthew Lyon, the first victim of the law, claimed that all of his trial jurors were chosen from towns which were hostile to him. The Callender case, however, is the only one in which it can be proved positively that the trial jury was Federalist to a man. Whether the juries were deliberately packed or not, they were usually chosen by the federal marshal, who was a Federalist and who became the keeper of the prisoner upon conviction. In no event can the juries be called impartial. Indeed, Beveridge observes that "the juries were nothing more than machines that registered the will, opinion, or even inclination of the national judges and the United States District Attorneys. In short, in these prosecutions, trial by jury in any real sense was not to be had."

Under the Sedition Law, the jury was to decide on the criminality of the utterance; one of its vital functions was to decide on the intent of the speaker. The proper duty of the court in sedition cases was to aid the jury in reaching a decision, by instructing it on what the law was in one set of circumstances or in another. The judges were given no power to pass on the facts of publication or intent. In practice, however, they determined the intent of the defendant.

In the trial of Thomas Cooper, a leading Republican publicist, Judge Chase ruled that the defendant's effort to prove the truth of his publication demonstrated his bad intent. The defendant's attempt to utilize the legal defense allowed by the Sedition Law, the judge declared, "showed that he intended to dare and defy the Government, and to provoke them, and his subsequent conduct satisfies my mind that such was his disposition. For he justifies the publication, and declares it to be formed in truth. It is proved to be his publication."

Thus the judge ruled, and directed the jury to find, that Cooper had published the words and that he had done so with a wicked intent. "Take this publication in all its parts," he told the jury, "and it is the boldest attempt I have known to poison the minds of the people." It was poison not because it incited the people to force and violence but because it criticized President John Adams in an election year, tending to defeat his campaign against Thomas Jefferson. In short, the instruction of the judges made verdicts of guilty virtually inevitable.

To summarize, then, the clause on truth was nullified by the courts, the right of the jury to decide the criminality of the writing was usurped by the presiding judges, and the test of intent was reduced to the seventeenth-century common-law test of bad tendency. Without these procedural safeguards, the Sedition Law was almost a duplicate of the English common law of seditious libel. Since intent was presumed from tendency, the test of criminality became the same: the tendency of the words to bring rulers into disrepute.

Every man convicted under the Sedition Law was fined and imprisoned for political expressions critical of the administration in power. Indeed, the chief enforcement effort was tied directly to the campaign of 1800. As the contest between Jefferson and Adams approached, Secretary of State Timothy Pickering made systematic plans for action against the leading Republican papers in the United States. The opposition press was led by five papers—the Philadelphia *Aurora*, the Boston *Chronicle*, the New York *Argus*, the Richmond *Examiner*, and the Baltimore *American*. Because of their strategic geographical location and their able editorial direction, these gazettes circulated widely. Nor was their influence confined to their subscription lists. In those days before the communications revolution, the smaller newspapers consisted largely of material reprinted from the important journals. Thus, a blow at any of the "big five" Republican presses would be a severe setback to the Democratic-Republican party in 1800.

In the summer of 1799, Pickering launched a campaign to prosecute every one of the leading Republican papers which either had not been prosecuted under the Sedition Law or which had no cases pending against it. He took personal charge of the proceedings against William Duane, editor of the *Aurora*, and received the approval of President Adams. Since the *Chronicle* had been chastised, the secretary omitted Boston but wrote identical directives to the district attorneys in New York, Richmond, and Baltimore instructing them to scrutinize the Republican papers issued in their cities and to prosecute them for any seditious libels against the President or any federal official.

The timing of these communiqués is important. They were written early in August, 1799, so that the district attorneys would have time to bring indictments at the September or October term of circuit court. Even if the trial had to be postponed until the April or May term in 1800, as was the case against the New York *Argus*, it would still come in time to silence the papers or their editors during the campaign of 1800. As a result of Pickering's efforts, suits were brought against every one of the "big five" Republican journals except the Baltimore *American*. Moreover, four other Republican newspapers of lesser importance were prosecuted, and three were forced out of business.

In every case in which the law was enforced, a political crime was punished for the same reason that all political crimes have ever been punished—for expressions of discontent with the authorities. As Professor Schofield has pointed out, the sedition cases clearly demonstrated "the great danger . . . that men will be fined and imprisoned, under the guise of being punished for their bad motives, or bad intent and ends, simply because the powers that be do not agree with their opinions, and spokesmen of minorities may be terrorized and silenced when they are most needed by the community and most useful to it, and when they stand most in need of the protection of the law against a hostile, arrogant majority."

The evidence is conclusive that the Sedition Law, as enforced, reduced the limits of speech and press in the United States to those set by the English common law in the days before the American Revolution. This was the standard advocated by the Federalists who enacted the law, and it was the standard applied by the Federalist judges who interpreted the law.

V

The basic question, then, is this: is the pre-Revolutionary rule the guide to the liberties protected by the First Amendment? Is the bad tendency test compatible with free and open discussion of public affairs by the people? Formulated in an age of authority, the common-law doctrine of seditious utterances was anti-republican to the core. When Blackstone wrote his *Commentaries,* in 1769, he was trying to describe the law as it then existed. Although prior censorship had expired seventy-five years before he wrote, the government continued to institute numerous sedition prosecutions. Blackstone discussed the importance of a free press in a free state, but he insisted that liberty of the press meant only that no restraints could be laid upon writings prior to their publication.

This definition, however, legalized suppression any time after the moment of publication; the most vital or the most harmless discussion of public policy could be punished if it was obnoxious to the authorities. Common law asserted the right of the state to punish true statements about public magistrates, if they tended to expose them to public hatred, contempt, and ridicule. Sir James Fitzjames Stephen has observed that the practical enforcement of the law of seditious libel in England "was wholly inconsistent with any serious public discussion of political affairs." As long as it was recognized as the law of the land, any political discussion existed only by sufferance of the government.

By following this British precedent, which held that liberty of the press was conferred on the British people by the government when Parliament failed to extend the Licensing Act in 1695, the Federalists subscribed to the authoritarian view that the government is the master, not the servant, of the people.

VI

The American Revolution culminated in the formulation and establishment in the United States of a form of government which rested on the will of the governed. Growing out of the natural-rights philosophy of the seventeenth and eighteenth centuries, this revolutionary theory of government was founded on the principle that governments are instituted to secure, among other things, the liberties of the individual. A written Constitution established a limited government, which was barred from invading these "unalienable-rights."

The meaning of the First Amendment did not crystallize in 1791, when the Bill of Rights was added to the Constitution. Not until the years from 1798 to 1801, when the Sedition Act was debated and enforced, did the limits of liberty of speech and of the press become an issue which focused attention squarely on its definition as a part of the American experiment in self-government. The first thing to be kept in mind in determining the meaning of the First Amendment is that it was added by the people as a further bulwark guarding civil liberties in the United States from governmental interference. Moreover, the liberties protected by the First Amendment were those prevailing not in England but in the United States.

One of the political catalysts of the American Revolution was the effort of the British to subdue the popular press in colonial America. This attempt was twofold. Under the Stamp Act of 1765, a prohibitive tax was placed on the paper used by the press. Had this law been executed, it would have forced out of circulation the inexpensive press, thus suppressing colonial discussion of politics in the popular papers. A second method used to crush colonial opposition to ministerial policies was an accelerated use of the law of seditious libel. Indeed, when George III issued his proclamation of rebellion against the American colonies, he gave as its official title "A Proclamation, By the King, for Suppressing Rebellion and Sedition."

There are several important pronouncements prior to the debates of 1798 which indicate that liberty of the press in the post-Revolutionary United States meant more than the English common-law rule. Many of the colonial publications on political affairs were considered seditious and even treasonable under the common law and its loose administration by the King's judges. That one of the objects of the American Revolution was to abolish the common-law restriction on liberty of the press, especially on political discussion, is illustrated by one of the addresses framed by the first Continental Congress in 1774.

In a letter addressed to the inhabitants of Quebec, Congress enumerated five rights basic to a free government. One of these was liberty of the press. "Besides the advancement of truth, science, morality, and arts in general," its importance consisted "in its diffusion of liberal sentiments on the administration of Government, its ready communication of thought between subjects, and the consequential promotion of union among them, whereby oppressive officers are shamed or intimidated into more honourable and just modes of conducting affairs."

This statement of liberty of the press specifically denies the right of the government to censure remarks because of their tendency to bring magistrates into public shame and contempt. Indeed, it asserts the opposite right of criticizing administrative officials chosen by the "free and full consent" of the governed.

The Declaration of Independence, of course, was the classic repudiation of the idea that the government was the master of the people. The Virginia bill for establishing religious freedom, written by the author of the Declaration, is another Revolutionary document which sets forth a philosophical justification of the right of a person to intellectual freedom. The preamble includes a declaration for individual liberty not only in the field of religion, but also in the field of civil affairs.

> To suffer the civil magistrate to intrude his powers into the field of opinion [it reads] and to restrain the profession or propagation of principles on supposition of their ill tendency, is a dangerous falacy [sic], which at once destroys all religious liberty, because he being of course judge of that tendency, will make his opinions the rule of judgment, and approve or condemn the sentiment of others only as they shall square with or differ from his own; that it is time enough for the rightful purposes of government for its officers to interfere when principles break out into overt acts against peace and good order; and finally, that truth is great and will prevail if left to herself; that she is the proper and sufficient antagonist to error, and has nothing to fear from the conflict unless by human interposition disarmed of her natural weapons, free argument and debate; errors ceasing to be dangerous when it is permitted freely to contradict them.

The basic doctrine of this bill, which Jefferson always ranked next to the Declaration of Independence, was its rejection of the bad tendency test in the field of opinion. It announced the right of an individual to choose his beliefs, religious or political, free from compulsion.

One of the strongest statements made in 1798 on the American meaning of liberty of the press was contained in the reply of the Federalist envoys to France in answer to Talleyrand's protest against remarks in the American press critical of the Directory. "The genius of the Constitution," wrote Marshall, Pinckney, and Gerry, in a passage which their fellow Federalists ignored, "and the opinion of the people of the United States, cannot be overruled by those who administer the Government. Among those principles deemed sacred in America, among those sacred rights considered as forming the bulwark of their liberty, which the Government contemplates with awful reverence and would approach only with the most cautious circumspection, there is no one of which the importance is more deeply impressed on the public mind than the liberty of the press."

All these statements went much farther than the Blackstonian theory which held that liberty of the press prevented only government censorship. Although they all agreed that the absence of censorship was an important part of that freedom, they also asserted the right of the people to participate in free and full discussion of public affairs. They were declarations based on American experience, not on British precedents. They rejected the authoritarian view that the rulers are the superiors of the people.

VII

The Alien and Sedition Laws played a prominent role in shaping the American tradition of civil liberties. Based on the concept that the government was master, these laws provoked a public response which clearly demonstrated that the people occupied that position. The severity of the Sedition Law failed to prevent the "overthrow" of the Adams administration by the Jeffersonian "disorganizers." Indeed, the law furnished a ready text which the Republicans used to incite the American people to legal "insurgency" at the polls; the election resulted in the repudiation of the party which tried to protect itself behind the Sedition Law. The defeat of the Federalists illustrates the common understanding that the First Amendment abolished the English common-law crime of seditious libel, of which the Sedition Law was merely declaratory.

The adherence of the people to the Republicans marked the beginning of a new political era. As John Adams himself pointed out, the election resulted in the "revolution of 1801": the Age of Federalism was at an end. Public opinion had never been without its influence on the conduct of government, but it had been grudgingly acknowledged by the Federalists. It now became the basis of American democratic development. As early as 1794, Madison had stated concisely what has since become the traditional American view: "If we advert to the nature of Republican Government, we shall find that the censorial power is in the people over the Government, and not in the Government over the people."

In his first inaugural address, Jefferson made this his main theme. Referring to the election of 1800 as a "contest of opinion" which had been decided by "the voice of the nation," the new President reasserted the right of the people "to think freely and to speak and to write what they think." Although he stoutly defended the right of the majority to rule, he cautioned that its will "to be rightful must be reasonable. The minority," he declared, "possess their equal rights, which equal law must protect, and to violate would be oppression." In a passage which condemned the Sedition Law without naming it, he restated the fundamental principle of the American experiment in popular government:

> If there be any among us who would wish to dissolve this Union or to change its republican form, let them stand undisturbed as monuments of the safety with which error of opinion may be tolerated where reason is left free to combat it. I know, indeed, that some honest men fear that a republican government can not be strong, that this Government is not strong enough; but would the honest patriot, in the full tide of successful experiment, abandon a government which has so far kept us free and firm on the theoretic and visionary fear that this Government, the world's best hope, may by possibility want energy to preserve itself? I trust not. I believe this, on the contrary, the strongest Government on earth. I believe it the only one where every man, at the call of the law, would fly to the standard of the law, and would meet invasions of the public order as his own personal concern. Sometimes it is said that man can not be trusted with the government of himself. Can he, then, be trusted with the government of others? Or have we found angels in the forms of kings to govern him? Let history answer this question.

20

Western War Aims, 1811–1812
REGINALD HORSMAN

Recent years have witnessed a new interest among historians in the War of 1812. Perhaps the reason is, as Norman K. Risjord of DePauw University suggests, that "the role of the United States today and the complex position of neutral nations in the cold war place in a new perspective the relations between England and the United States 150 years ago." Surely, in looking at the long arc of American development from the achievement of independence to the Civil War, one has perforce to find a place for the War of 1812. There is an imperative connection between knowing what the war was about and knowing what the whole period was about. The one defines the nature and importance of the other.

SOURCE: *Indiana Magazine of History,* LIII (March, 1957), 1–18. Reprinted by permission of author and publisher.

But then what exactly was the War of 1812? By and large, answers to this question have fallen into three broad categories. One view, expressed by Madison in his war message to Congress and widely accepted by historians during the nineteenth century, is that the Americans were fighting to protect their maritime rights and preserve their national honor. A second is that they were agrarian imperialists intent upon acquiring new lands in general and Canada in particular. A third is that they wished to remove the Indian threat to their frontiers and could do it only by defeating Great Britain, who had both befriended and inflamed the Indians. In explaining the War of 1812, we have been better able to understand why Americans should have fought for land and security than for honor and maritime rights, particularly since the shipping interests of the Northeast did not want war at all. For this reason, the prevalent explanation during the past few decades has been that the war sprang from material interests, from the Western desire to protect its frontiers and to add to its domain.

There is of course another possible explanation. There may have been a close connection between Western interests and maritime rights. The connection has been suggested by a few historians but never extensively pursued. It is carefully explored by Reginald Horsman of the University of Wisconsin (at Milwaukee) in a valuable monograph, **The Causes of the War of 1812** (1962), and in the following essay, in which he presents the monograph's principal thesis. In pursuing this thesis, Professor Horsman undertakes to answer several relevant questions. Why may it be argued that the war was a distinctly commercial one? What were the interests of the South and the West in the export trade? To what extent did the Indian policy and the accession of Canada figure in the pro-war speeches of the War Hawks? What connection was there, finally, between the national pocket and the national pride and how could touching the Americans in the first become a sufficient basis for ruffling them in the second?

There was such a dramatic unleashing of forces after the War of 1812 that the relevance of the war to those forces must be understood. By contrast, the quarter-century before 1815 seems to have been hardly as constructive and expansive as that which followed. Why? Perhaps the appearance is somewhat deceiving. Or perhaps the national energy expressed itself in laying foundations and building institutions. Perhaps, too, a nation conceived in liberty and dedicated to the pursuit of happiness could not conceivably be free or happy in an age of global war between Britain and France, a war into which were swept all the states of the Atlantic world.

In itself, the war would not seem, at first sight, to have been of commanding importance. The military and naval battles have neither the primitive heroism of the American Revolution nor the bitter tragedy of the Civil War. When seen in perspective, however, the war stands out as a watershed of profound social and political change. Its nature and causes afford us a significant view of that larger arc of American development from 1776 to 1861.

It is an interesting paradox that a war of such insignificant proportions as that of 1812 should have produced such controversy concerning its causes. Nineteenth century historians, with a unanimity more characteristic of that century than of this, in general accepted the view that the war was essentially a struggle to defend American neutral rights and the national honor against the aggressions of Great Britain. In the present century this unanimity has been shattered. Historian after historian has placed his own particular interpretation on the events preceding the outbreak of war in June, 1812.

Of all the works produced during these years, undoubtedly the most influential has been Julius Pratt's *Expansionists of 1812,* published some thirty years ago.[1] Professor Pratt stated in his introduction that he only intended to examine one set of causes of the war,[2] but this has not prevented later historians from according the work an importance far out of proportion to this statement. Pratt's main thesis was that a factor of primary significance in the causes of the war was the western demand that the British, accused of instigating Indian troubles, should be expelled from Canada. This, he argued, was matched by a southern demand for the Floridas for agrarian, commercial, and strategic reasons. Thus the northern and southern Republicans arrived at an understanding that the acquisition of Canada on the north was to be balanced by the annexation of the Floridas on the south.[3]

Since the publication of Pratt's work in 1925 his ideas have exerted a constant influence upon historians—so much so that two standard works on American diplomatic history, Bemis and Bailey,[4] both base their final conclusions regarding the origins of the war on Professor Pratt's thesis. Samuel F. Bemis, after dealing mainly with maritime questions, concludes that the War of 1812 was finally caused by a western expansionist urge rather than solely by the grievances of neutral rights and impressment, and as authority for this statement

---

[1] Julius W. Pratt, *Expansionists of 1812* (New York, 1925). For earlier attempts to modify the nineteenth century interpretations of the war, see D. R. Anderson, "The Insurgents of 1811," American Historical Association *Annual Report,* 1911 (Washington, 1913), I, 165–176; Howard T. Lewis, "A Re-Analysis of the Causes of the War of 1812," *Americana,* VI (1911), 506–516, 577–585; Christopher B. Coleman, "The Ohio Valley in the Preliminaries of the War of 1812," *Mississippi Valley Historical Review,* VII (1920), 39–50; Louis M. Hacker, "Western Land Hunger and the War of 1812: A Conjecture," *ibid.,* X (1924), 365–395. It was only with the publication of Pratt's work that attempts at a western interpretation of the war achieved general acceptance.

[2] Pratt, *Expansionists of 1812,* 14.

[3] *Ibid.,* 12–13.

[4] Samuel Flagg Bemis, *A Diplomatic History of the United States* (3d ed., New York, 1953); Thomas A. Bailey, *A Diplomatic History of the American People* (4th ed., New York, 1950).

refers to Pratt.[5] Thomas A. Bailey, after a more balanced presentation of the origins of the conflict, states that the presence of Canada probably tipped the scales in favor of war.[6] Nevertheless, in spite of these recent acceptances of Pratt's western expansionist theories, his ideas have not gone unchallenged since 1925.

The most relevant criticisms came in 1931 in two articles by George Rogers Taylor on agricultural conditions in the Mississippi Valley in the years preceding the War of 1812.[7] Taylor argued that the westerners were suffering a commercial depression, and that they had a vital interest in British commercial regulations. He endeavored to show that it was not necessary to seek non-commercial motives to explain the western attitude toward the war. These ideas received remarkably little attention during the remainder of the 1930's, though Bernard Mayo in his excellent study of the young Henry Clay enthusiastically endorsed many of Taylor's views.[8]

It was not until 1941, with the publication of Warren H. Goodman's article on the historiography of the origins of the war, that it was possible to find conveniently summarized the various conflicting theories which had been advanced by historians.[9] In this article, the most significant contribution to the problem in recent years, Goodman surveyed the changing interpretations of the war and reasoned that both the advocates of maritime rights as well as of expansionist theories had been too extreme in their views. In his opinion the importance of the northwestern desire to annex Canada to prevent Indian depredations, and of the southern desire to annex Florida, had been overestimated, and the articles by Taylor on agricultural conditions in the Mississippi Valley deserved more attention.[10]

Goodman's plea for a more balanced viewpoint has not had any marked effect on historians in the years since 1941. The major contribution of this period has been Alfred L. Burt's study of the relations of Britain, her North American colonies, and the United States between

---

[5] Bemis, *Diplomatic History*, 156–157.

[6] Bailey, *Diplomatic History*, 136.

[7] George Rogers Taylor, "Prices in the Mississippi Valley Preceding the War of 1812," *Journal of Economic and Business History*, III (1930), 148–163; Taylor, "Agrarian Discontent in the Mississippi Valley Preceding the War of 1812," *Journal of Political Economy*, XXXIX (1931), 471–505.

[8] Bernard Mayo, *Henry Clay: Spokesman of the New West* (Boston, 1937). This work contains one of the best discussions of the origins of the war, though it has received scant attention from historians.

[9] Warren H. Goodman, "The Origins of the War of 1812: A Survey of Changing Interpretations," *Mississippi Valley Historical Review*, XXVIII (1941), 171–186.

[10] *Ibid.*, 180–185.

1783 and 1818.[11] Professor Burt in this careful study of the diplomacy of the period returned, in some measure, to a nineteenth century view of the war. He argued that the questions of neutral rights and impressment formed the essence of the conflict, and he rejected Pratt's theories concerning peculiarly western aims. Taylor's opinions regarding the depression in the Mississippi Valley were not considered in Burt's arguments, though he briefly pointed out the importance of the commercial depression in the southern states in arousing anger against England.[12] This southern aspect of the origins of the war received more detailed treatment in July, 1956, in an article by Margaret K. Latimer on South Carolina as a protagonist of the conflict.[13] Miss Latimer contended that South Carolina favored the war against England because of the depressed state of her export trade in cotton. She also briefly suggested that the West saw in war the solution of its commercial difficulties.[14]

Professor Pratt has not allowed the various attacks on his theories to go unchallenged. Both in his 1941 review of Burt's volume,[15] and in his general history of American foreign policy, published in 1955,[16] he restated his opinions concerning the importance of particular western demands. He has not, however, offered anything essentially new, though he now acknowledges that depressed agricultural conditions were a factor in American anger.[17] Professor Pratt still stands by the theories which he first produced some thirty years ago.

There still remains, therefore, considerable divergence on this question of the origins of the War of 1812, and of why the West so enthusiastically gave its support to the war measures. The three main streams of opinion, exemplified by the views of Pratt, Taylor, and Burt, in turn show the war-supporters as eager to revenge Indian depredations by the conquest of Canada, desperate and angry owing to the loss of overseas markets for their goods, and burning with patriotic anger at British aggressions, particularly impressment. The tendency of other historians in studying this confused topic is either to list divergent reasons for war without any attempt at division into degrees of importance, or to choose one reason and to relegate the others to a posi-

---

[11] Alfred L. Burt, *The United States, Great Britain, and British North America, from the Revolution to the Establishment of Peace after the War of 1812* (New Haven, 1940).

[12] *Ibid.*, 211–224, 305–310.

[13] Margaret Kinnard Latimer, "South Carolina—A Protagonist of the War of 1812," *American Historical Review*, LXI (1956), 914–929.

[14] *Ibid.*, 928.

[15] *American Historical Review*, XLVII (1941), 87–89.

[16] Julius W. Pratt, *A History of United States Foreign Policy* (New York, 1955).

[17] *American Historical Review*, XLVII (1941), 88.

tion of relative insignificance. Yet, in spite of this confusion, it does seem possible to create some pattern from this jigsaw of neutral rights, agricultural depression, expansionism, and fear of Indian attack, and to assess the relative importance of causes.

The question of overseas markets for American produce is undoubtedly basic to the problem of why the West and the South led America to war in 1812. The factor that originally led historians to seek non-commercial causes for the conflict was that in the vote for war in Congress, the Northeast, the foremost commercial and shipping area, was the section opposed to the conflict.[18] This, however, is not a reason for supposing that non-commercial factors were the primary cause of the war. The fact is that the shippers of New England, engaged in an extensive wartime carrying trade, were able, in spite of British restrictions, to make a considerable profit.[19] They were quite prepared to condone British practices and oppose war with that country as long as these profits were available. They realized that they had much to lose by war. Abstract questions of neutral rights bore little weight with the commercial New Englander waxing rich in spite of all foreign restrictions.

The case was much different in the West and South. These areas harbored the producers, not the carriers. They were not concerned with the vast profits of the carrying trade but with the more marginal question of selling their produce. The South, it is commonly agreed, depended to a great extent on her export of tobacco and cotton, but in the case of the West there has been disagreement. Writers have, on occasion, taken the view that as the West was in a primitive agricultural state it was not concerned with the matter of exporting its produce.[20] It is true that the West was not engaged in an extensive overseas export trade, but the fact that its overseas exports were small made it all the more essential that this trade should not be interrupted. The farmer of the West needed purchasing power for his land, for manufactured articles, and for small luxuries in his home and diet.[21] This fact has been brought out by Taylor in his two articles, and he also shows, by a careful consideration of the prices for western produce at New Orleans, that in the years from 1808 to 1812 the Mississippi Valley was in a period of agricultural depression. At a time when costs were re-

---

[18] See Charles O. Paullin and John K. Wright, *Atlas of the Historical Geography of the United States* (Washington, 1932), 109.

[19] Samuel E. Morison, *The Maritime History of Massachusetts* (Boston, 1941), 191.

[20] See, for example, Hacker, "Western Land Hunger . . .," *Mississippi Valley Historical Review*, X, 366.

[21] Taylor, "Prices in the Mississippi Valley . . .," *Journal of Economic and Business History*, III, 148.

maining stationary or even rising, the prices which farmers could obtain for their produce were falling rapidly.[22]

The important fact, however, is not that there was a depression but that the westerners attributed this depression to British commercial restrictions. Throughout the debates of the Twelfth Congress in 1811 and 1812 it is apparent that westerners and southerners were convinced that the British were ruining the overseas market. Frequently, in works stressing western expansionist urges as the basic cause for war, the words of Henry Clay and Richard M. Johnson of Kentucky, of Peter B. Porter of western New York, and of Felix Grundy of Tennessee, have been quoted. These men have been taken as living proofs of the dominating urge of the West to take Canada and subdue the Indians. A careful consideration of their speeches in Congress shows, however, that though they spoke with feeling and eloquence of the atrocities of the Indians and of taking Canada, the *dominating* themes of their speeches were the questions of maritime rights, especially the right to export American produce.

On December 6, 1811, Peter B. Porter opened the debate on the report of the Foreign Relations Committee,[23] of which he was chairman. He stated: "The committee thought that the Orders in Council, so far as they go to interrupt our direct trade, that is, the carrying of the productions of this country to a market in the ports of friendly nations, and returning with the proceeds of them—ought to be resisted by war."[24] He was maintaining, in no uncertain terms, that the United States should fight for the right to sell her produce. His brother War Hawks gave him full support. The greatest War Hawk of them all, Henry Clay, contended that, "to-day we are asserting our right to the direct trade—the right to export our cotton, tobacco, and other domestic produce to market."[25] Clay was echoing the sentiments of his fellow Kentuckian, Richard M. Johnson, who, as far back as April 16, 1810, had argued that there was no doubt that America had just cause of hostility: "At this moment France and Great Britain have decrees in force, which regulate at their pleasure the exportation of our own produce—the produce of our own soil and labor."[26] This was not a question of the westerners urging war to defend the carrying trade of New England, but the westerners claiming the right to export the

---

[22] *Ibid.*, 154–163.

[23] On the Foreign Relations Committee were a group of ardent war-supporters: John C. Calhoun, Joseph Desha, Felix Grundy, John A. Harper, and Peter B. Porter. The report of the committee was presented on November 29. *Annals of Congress*, 12th Cong., 1st Sess., 373–377.

[24] *Ibid.*, 414.

[25] *Ibid.*, 601, Dec. 31, 1811.

[26] *Ibid.*, 11th Cong., 2d Sess., 1869.

produce of their own area. Felix Grundy of Tennessee, who is regarded as one of the most fervent Indian haters and supporters of the drive for Canada said, on December 9, 1811, that the point of contention between the United States and Great Britain "is the right of exporting the productions of our own soil and industry to foreign markets."[27]

The westerners received full support in this connection from their allies of the South, and it would appear that this unity stemmed from a common interest in the sale of their produce. Robert Wright from Maryland stated on December 11, 1811, after a violent attack on British restrictions on American trade, that "we are to look for the cause of the reduction of the prices of our cotton and tobacco in the political and commercial history of Europe."[28] John C. Calhoun, talking of the people of the South, said that "they see in the low price of the produce, the hand of foreign injustice."[29]

This commercial desire of the war party did not go unnoticed by the opposition. Historians favoring the western expansionist theory have been fascinated by John Randolph of Virginia,[30] who so passionately denounced the westerners for seeking a war of aggression. A favorite quotation is his famous "we have heard but one word—like the whip-poor-will, but one eternal monotonous tone—Canada!   Canada! Canada!"[31]   It is forgotten that in his wandering half-demented diatribes Randolph attributed practically every reason for desiring war to the War Hawks.   Other less vehement, but perhaps more sane, members of the opposition saw other motives behind the desires of the war party.   On December 13, 1811, Adam Boyd of New Jersey stated bluntly: "You go to war for the right to export our surplus produce—tobacco, cotton, flour, with many other articles."[32]   Daniel Sheffey of Virginia, in a long and penetrating speech on January 3, 1812, came to this conclusion: "No! the nominal repeal of the Orders in Council is not your object.   It is the substantial commercial benefit which you conceive will follow that act, that forms the essence of the controversy. The unmolested commerce to France and her dependencies is the boon for which you are going to war.   This is the real object, disguise it as you will."[33]   Such observations of the opposition may of course have been completely unfounded, but it is at least possible to give them as much weight as the exponents of the expansionist theories give to the utterances of Randolph.

---

[27] *Ibid.*, 12th Cong., 1st Sess., 424; see also *ibid.*, 487–503.

[28] *Ibid.*, 470.

[29] *Ibid.*, 482, Dec. 12, 1811; see also *ibid.*, 682.

[30] See, for example, Pratt, *Expansionists of 1812*, 141–144; Hacker, "Western Land Hunger . . .," *Mississippi Valley Historical Review*, X, 376.

[31] *Annals of Congress*, 12th Cong., 1st Sess., 533, Dec. 16, 1811.

[32] *Ibid.*, 521.

[33] *Ibid.*, 623.

In the West itself there seems much evidence that the representatives in Congress were only reflecting the views of their constituents. Bernard Mayo in his biography of Clay states, after an examination of Kentucky newspapers, that "unprecedented hard times" caused by Britain's illegal monopoly was the constant theme of distressed farmers in this period from 1810 to 1812.[34] On December 10, 1811, the *Reporter* of Lexington, Kentucky, stated: "It appears that our government will at last make war, to produce a market for our Tobacco, Flour, and Cotton."[35] A particularly significant series of petitions was presented to Congress from Mississippi Territory in September and November, 1811.[36] There were two petitions from the inhabitants of the territory, and one from the territorial legislature. All the petitions requested that the payment of instalments on the petitioners' land should be deferred until a later date, owing to a lack of specie. The petitioners stated that they were dependent upon foreign commerce for money, and that the price of cotton had been so reduced that they could not discharge the annual expenses of their families, much less pay for their lands. All three petitions attributed this to the destructive effects of foreign restrictions upon American commerce. The petition of November 11 admirably summarized the importance of foreign commercial regulations to this area of the West: "The Severe pressure of the times arising From the unjust Edicts of Foreign Governments, and the unpresedented State of the world . . . the Violation of the legitimate and well Established Rights of neutral Commerce on the high seas, to which the Belligerents of Europe have resorted Are not confin'd in their Destructive consequences to the Commercial enterprize of our Country—But their effects are seen and Felt among the humble Cultivators of the Soil —Who Depend for the reward of their laborious Occupations on an Oppertunity to convey the Surpless Products of their Industry to Those Countries in which they are consumed."[37]

There seems little doubt that the West, through its representatives in Congress and on the frontier itself, had a vital interest in its export market, and that it was attributing the loss of this market and the subsequent decline in prices primarily to British commercial restrictions. It is not surprising then that in Congress in 1811 and 1812 the western representatives spoke vigorously of the need to defend American

---

[34] Mayo, *Henry Clay*, 382–383.

[35] *Reporter* (Lexington, Kentucky), Dec. 10, 1811, quoted in Taylor, "Agrarian Discontent . . .," *Journal of Political Economy*, XXXIX, 500.

[36] Clarence E. Carter (ed.), *The Territorial Papers of the United States*, VI, *The Territory of Mississippi: 1809–1817* (Washington, 1938), 226–227, 238–240, 241–242.

[37] *Ibid.*, 239.

maritime rights—this was not, as the advocates of the expansionist theories would maintain, simply a façade, hiding the real western desire to conquer Canada; it was a genuine feeling that if the West and South were to have a market for their produce British restrictions would have to be resisted.

In reading works such as Pratt it is possible to obtain the impression that the War Hawks talked constantly of Canada and of the Indians, and ignored maritime questions. This was not the case; by far the greater part of the argument of the War Hawks was devoted to attacking British maritime depredations. They had a material interest in doing this, and what is more they had a genuine feeling that American national honor was suffering from British action at sea. Many of these men were young[38] and proud, and were willing to combine the principles of self-interest and honor. They felt anger at the British regulations which they thought had produced the commercial distress, and they felt anger at all the other British infringements of American rights. Only a quarter of a century before, the United States had struggled for independence against a country which now ignored this new-won freedom. The leaders of these War Hawks were young men who had been raised on the traditions of the War of Independence. The older generation, well represented by Jefferson and Madison, were "first generation revolutionaries"—men who had gambled for independence, had won, and were in their later years little inclined to risk their winnings in an uncertain war with England. Henry Clay and his young allies were the "second generation revolutionaries"—young men who were willing to take chances with the hard-won gains of their parents. They had grown to manhood hearing oft-repeated tales of the War of Independence, but they themselves had long been compelled to suffer without retaliation the constant infringement of American rights. The generation of the War Hawks had come of age during a period in which American seamen were being taken from American ships, and in which Britain had attempted to tell America how and what she should export. It is not surprising that when to these acts was added growing agricultural distress there was an ever-increasing cry for war.

The report of the Foreign Relations Committee of November 29, 1811,[39] recommending war preparations for the United States, concerned itself exclusively with maritime matters. This report, which

---

[38] Ages of some of the War Hawks when Congress met: William Lowndes, 29; John C. Calhoun, 29; George M. Troup, 32; Israel Pickens, 31; Henry Clay, 34; Felix Grundy, 34; Langdon Cheves, 36. See James L. Harrison (ed.), *Biographical Directory of the American Congress: 1774–1949* (Washington, 1950).

[39] *Annals of Congress*, 12th Cong., 1st Sess., 373–377.

bluntly stated that the time for submission was at an end, objected bitterly to British commercial regulations and to the practice of impressment. It summarized the essential cause of complaint against Great Britain with the argument that the United States claimed the right to export her products without losing either ships or men.[40] The arguments of the War Hawks in the ensuing debates clearly followed the lines of reasoning laid down in this report. Their leaders agreed that war was necessary against Britain for the defense of American maritime interests and honor. Richard M. Johnson of Kentucky speaking on December 11, 1811, certainly discussed Canada, as quoted by Pratt,[41] but previously he had stated: "Before we relinquish the conflict, I wish to see Great Britain renounce the piratical system of paper blockade; to liberate our captured seamen on board her ships of war; relinquish the practice of impressment on board our merchant vessels; to repeal her Orders in Council; and cease, in every other respect, to violate our neutral rights; to treat us as an independent people."[42]

In speech after speech the War Hawks echoed Johnson's sentiments.[43] Orders in Council, illegal blockades, impressment, and the general terms of neutral rights and national honor dominated their arguments. Clay himself stated on December 31, 1811: "What are we not to lose by peace?—commerce, character, a nation's best treasure, honor!"[44] Clay's whole argument in this speech was for the necessity of war to defend American maritime rights.

The letters of the War Hawks appear to support their public utterances. George W. Campbell, Senator from Tennessee, wrote to Andrew Jackson that it is "difficult to perceve [sic] how war can be avoided, without degrading the national character, still lower. . . . For there is no ground to expect G. Britain will abandon her system of depredation on our commerce, or her habitual violations of the personal rights of our citizens in the impressment of our seamen."[45] George M. Troup of Georgia wrote to Governor David B. Mitchell on February 12, 1812, denouncing all further temporizing or indecision. He wanted either war or an open abandonment of the contest—nothing else would satisfy the just expectations of the southern people, "who have been bearing the brunt of the restrictive system from the beginning."[46] William

[40] *Ibid.,* 376.

[41] Pratt, *Expansionists of 1812,* 52.

[42] *Annals of Congress,* 12th Cong., 1st Sess., 457.

[43] *Ibid.,* 425, 467–475, 483–490, 502, 509, 517–518, 637, 658, 678–691.

[44] *Ibid.,* 599.

[45] Campbell to Jackson, Dec. 24, 1811, John Spencer Bassett (ed.), *The Correspondence of Andrew Jackson* (6 vols., Washington, 1926–1933), I, 212.

[46] Troup to Mitchell, Feb. 12, 1812, Edward J. Harden, *The Life of George M. Troup* (Savannah, 1859), 107.

Lowndes of South Carolina was confident in December, 1811, that unless England repealed her Orders in Council, there would be war before the end of the session.[47] These westerners and southerners were vitally interested in maritime questions, and showed a very real awareness of the long years of British depredations upon American commerce.

Pratt's thesis, that a factor of primary importance in producing the war was the desire of the westerners to prevent Indian troubles by expelling the British from Canada, has exerted such influence that it requires careful investigation. Some writers, notably Louis Hacker in his article on western land hunger, and Burt in his detailed study of this period, have attempted to eliminate the Indian problem as a factor in persuading the westerners to demand war.[48] It would seem from the available evidence that these writers are wrong in completely ignoring the Indian factor. Though it seems likely that the dominant motives of the West were related to British maritime actions, the importance, in certain areas, of the fear of British instigation of the Indians should not be underestimated. It seems likely in fact that, particularly after Tippecanoe, the suspected British backing of Indian depredations was of definite importance in bringing matters to a head, and in convincing the already aroused westerners that some warlike action against Great Britain was needed.

There is no doubt that the presence of hostile Indians on the frontier was of great importance to the westerners. Any careful study of the records of this period inevitably leads one to that conclusion. The debates of the Twelfth Congress and the territorial papers of Indiana, Michigan, and Louisiana-Missouri, have constant references to the Indian problem.[49] One has only to read the letters of Governor William Henry Harrison of Indiana to the War Department to realize the extent to which the thinking of certain areas of the West was dominated by this factor.[50]

Even more important from the point of view of this study is that there was no doubt in the minds of the settlers that the British were

---

[47] Lowndes to his wife, Dec. 7, 1811, Harriott Horry (Rutledge) Ravenel, *Life and Times of William Lowndes of South Carolina* (Boston, 1901), 90.

[48] Hacker, "Western Land Hunger . . .," *Mississippi Valley Historical Review,* X, 372–374; Burt, *United States and Great Britain,* 305–310.

[49] See the debates of the Twelfth Congress *passim,* especially those of December, 1811; also, Carter, *The Territorial Papers of the United States,* VIII, *The Territory of Indiana, 1810–1816* (Washington, 1939); X, *The Territory of Michigan, 1805–1820* (Washington, 1942); XIV, *The Territory of Louisiana-Missouri, 1806–1814* (Washington, 1949).

[50] Logan Esarey (ed.), *Messages and Letters of William Henry Harrison* (2 vols., Indianapolis, 1922); this is Volume VII of the Indiana Historical *Collections.*

instigating the action of the Indians. On July 31, 1811, the citizens of Vincennes, Indiana, adopted a series of resolutions to petition the President regarding the danger from the Indians. The third of these petitions stated: "That we are fully convinced that the formation of this combination headed by the Shawanese prophet, is a British scheme, and that the agents of that power are constantly exciting the Indians to hostility against the United States."[51]

In August the *Kentucky Gazette* stated that "we have in our possession information which proves beyond doubt, the late disturbances in the West to be owing to the too successful intrigues of British emissaries with the Indians."[52] The encounter at Tippecanoe on November 7, 1811, crystallized this western sentiment and convinced the settlers that British intrigues were bringing desolation to the frontier. Whatever the British policy was in reality, the American settlers undoubtedly were convinced that it was inciting the Indians to aggressive warfare.

The fact that the frontiersmen connected the British and the Indians is no reason for supposing that the prevention of this alliance was the *dominating* motive in the vote of Congress for war in 1812. This view fails to take into consideration several relevant facts. In the first place, the core of the feeling against the Indians was in the exposed northwest fronter—in the Indiana, Michigan, and Illinois territories, and it should be remembered that these areas had no vote in Congress. It is true, of course, that the anger against the supposed British inciting of the Indians was felt deeply outside the immediately exposed area— Kentucky was much incensed at the Indian depredations and Kentuckians fought and were killed at Tippecanoe;[53] also Andrew Jackson wrote from Tennessee offering Harrison the use of his forces after that encounter.[54] Yet, it is essential to realize that of the 79 votes for war in the House only a total of nine votes came from the states of Kentucky, Tennessee, and Ohio, while a total of 37 came from the South Atlantic states of Maryland, Virginia, North and South Carolina, and Georgia. Pennsylvania, a state of limited frontier area by this period, alone provided 16 votes for war.[55] There is no doubt that the *leaders* of the movement for war were often westerners, whether from the Ohio

[51] *Ibid.*, 541.

[52] *Kentucky Gazette*, August 27, 1811, quoted in Ellery L. Hall, "Canadian Annexation Sentiment in Kentucky Prior to the War of 1812," *Register of the Kentucky State Historical Society*, XXVIII (1930), 375.

[53] *Annals of Congress*, 12th Cong., 1st Sess., 425–426.

[54] Jackson to William Henry Harrison, Nov. 30, 1811, Bassett, *Correspondence of Andrew Jackson*, I, 210.

[55] See *Annals of Congress*, 12th Cong., 1st Sess., 1637, for list of voters; Paullin and Wright, *Atlas of Historical Geography*, 109, gives an analysis of the vote for war.

Valley, frontier New Hampshire, or western New York, but the actual vote for war depended on non-frontiersmen. The Indian menace undoubtedly influenced frontier areas, and in some was the dominating factor, but it seems unlikely that the large vote for war in non-frontier areas was inspired by a desire to protect the northwest frontier from Indian depredations. The importance of the argument concerning Indians in the Congressional debates of 1811 and 1812 has been greatly overestimated. British encouragement of the Indians was discussed in the war debates but it was discussed in connection with other factors. A reference to the murderous savages urged on by the British provided a fine emotional climax to any speech, but it would appear that the argument which united the 79 representatives of diverse sections to vote for war was the more generally applicable one of the need to sell produce in order to live.

Arising out of the Indian problem is the important question of the demand for Canada. It may well be asked that if the dominant motive for war was not a desire to shatter the Anglo-Indian alliance, how can the fervent demand for the conquest of Canada be explained? The two theses explaining the demand for Canada which have received the most general support are those of Hacker and Pratt. Hacker[56] saw the reason for this, and for war itself, in a desire for Canadian land. Pratt disagreed with him and, in a subsequent article, effectively demonstrated the weaknesses in Hacker's argument.[57] Pratt considered, of course, that the demand for Canada arose from the supposed British instigation of the Indians. This view is worthy of careful consideration. Indeed it appears that in the case of certain areas— particularly the Indiana and Michigan Territories—the desire to quench support for the Indians was probably the dominating wish in the minds of the settlers in 1811 and 1812. Yet, while it is true that much of the debating of the Twelfth Congress was concerned with plans for the conquest of Canada, it would appear that in general these aims were not primarily inspired by a desire to prevent British support of the Indians.

Burt, in his detailed work on Britain, America, and Canada, suggests, without detailed elaboration, that the conquest of Canada was anticipated as the seizure of a hostage rather than as the capture of a prize.[58] It would seem from the debates in Congress that this was indeed the case. The key fact is that almost exclusively in their speeches the War Hawks first considered the *reasons* why war was necessary, and dwelt on maritime grievances, and then, when turning to the

---

[56] See footnote 1.

[57] Julius W. Pratt, "Western Aims in the War of 1812," *Mississippi Valley Historical Review*, XII (1925), 36–50.

[58] Burt, *United States and Great Britain*, 310.

methods of waging war, discussed the question of invading Canada. It is true that the war party saw in the conquest of Canada an opportunity to prevent further Indian depredations, but there seems no reason to believe that this was in itself a sufficient reason for the war party to achieve such general support in 1812. The various sections of the United States were not sufficiently altruistic for the South Atlantic states to demand war and the conquest of Canada for the purpose of relieving the Northwest from Indian attacks. Yet, the demand for Canada entered into the speeches of the southerners as it did into the speeches of the western War Hawks. Pratt explained this away by contending that there was a sectional bargain, by which the South was to obtain Florida, and the West, Canada; but, as Goodman and Burt clearly show,[59] and as is apparent in the debates in Congress, the demand for Florida was a comparatively negligible factor in the actual demand for war. There seems little evidence to support the thesis that the South supported the demand for Canada in return for western support of southern claims to Florida.

Calhoun, the young South Carolinian, clearly stated the reasons for southern support of Canadian conquest, and helped to explain the general attitude of the war party, in a speech on December 12, 1811. In answering Randolph's taunt that the Canadas bore no relation to American shipping and maritime rights he stated: "By his system, if you receive a blow on the breast, you dare not return it on the head; you are obliged to measure and return it on the precise point on which it was received. If you do not proceed with mathematical accuracy, it ceases to be just self-defence; it becomes an unprovoked attack."[60] This gives the essence of the matter. Once the War Hawks had decided they wanted war, they were obliged to face the problem of where they could injure their mighty foe. At sea it seemed that there was little hope. Britain's vast navy, which had swept France from the seas, was to be matched against a handful of American frigates. Apart from the activities of American privateers there seemed little hope of waging effective war against Britain on the sea. The conquest of Canada was the obvious, if not the only method of injuring Britain. Clay's speech of February 22, 1810,[61] has been quoted as one of the first appeals for the conquest of Canada: "The conquest of Canada is in your power" are words of joy to the expansionist historian.[62] Yet these words were said after Clay had discussed British mercantile spoilations, and after

---

[59] Goodman, "Origins of the War of 1812," *Mississippi Valley Historical Review,* XXXIII, 180–181; Burt, *United States and Great Britain,* 306.

[60] *Annals of Congress,* 12th Cong., 1st Sess., 481.

[61] *Ibid.,* 11th Cong., 2d Sess., 579–582.

[62] See Pratt, *Expansionists of 1812,* 40.

he had stated that as peaceful measures had failed it was time for re- sistance by the sword. He then tried to convince the weak and vacil- lating Eleventh Congress that war against Great Britain was practicable, and that injury could be inflicted upon their enemy: "It is said, how- ever, that no object is attainable by war with Great Britain. In its for- tunes, we are to estimate not only the benefit to be derived to ourselves, but the injury to be done the enemy. The conquest of Canada is in your power."[63]

Members of the war party in the Twelfth Congress echoed these words of Clay. Two representatives of North Carolina—Israel Pickens and William R. King—summarized the essential reasoning behind the demand for Canada. King on December 13, 1811, stated that he was not enamored of conquest but that this war had been forced upon America: "We cannot, under existing circumstances, avoid it. To wound our enemy in the most vulnerable part should only be considered."[64] Pickens, less than a month later, answered the opposition that though the contemplated attack on the British Provinces is called a war of offense, "when it is considered as the only mode in our reach, for de- fending rights universally recognised and avowedly violated, its charac- ter is changed."[65] Even calm and honest Nathaniel Macon of North Carolina, whose opinion can surely be given as much weight as the im- passioned and half-mad Randolph, contended that the war which the United States was about to enter was not a war of conquest—"Its object is to obtain the privilege of carrying the produce of our lands to a market"—but he considered that no war could long continue to be merely one of defense.[66] The War Hawks called for attack upon Canada because it was the only certain way they knew of attacking Britain.

Peaceful restriction had apparently failed and the West and South resolved to fight the British in the only area in which she appeared to be vulnerable, her North American provinces. Perhaps the most adequate summary by a westerner of why the West wanted to fight was that given by Andrew Jackson on March 12, 1812, when, as commander of the militia of the western district of Tennessee, he issued a call for volun- teers from this area. In this document, if in no other, one would expect to see reflected the ideas and aspirations of the people of the West; a commander calling for volunteers does not use unpopular arguments. Under the heading, "For what are we going to fight?", Jackson wrote these words: "We are going to fight for the reestablishment of our na- tional charector [sic], misunderstood and vilified at home and abroad;

---

[63] *Annals of Congress,* 11th Cong., 2d Sess., 580.
[64] *Ibid.,* 12th Cong., 1st Sess., 519.
[65] *Ibid.,* 646, Jan. 4, 1812.
[66] *Ibid.,* 663, Jan. 4, 1812.

for the protection of our maritime citizens, impressed on board British ships of war and compelled to fight the battles of our enemies against ourselves; to vindicate our right to a free trade, and open a market for the productions of our soil, now perishing on our hands because the *mistress of the ocean* has forbid us to carry them to any foreign nation; in fine, to seek some indemnity for past injuries, some security against future aggressions, by the conquest of all the British dominions upon the continent of north america."[67]

The coming of war in 1812 was not a sudden event; it was the culmination of a long series of injuries and insults, of checks to American commerce, and of the infringement of American rights. The United States, under the leadership of Jefferson and Madison, repeatedly attempted to defend her rights by peaceful economic coercion. Yet, almost inevitably, a breaking point was reached. The time came when, with national honor at its lowest ebb, and large sections of agricultural America suffering depression, any war seemed preferable to a dishonorable and unprofitable peace. The young War Hawks who urged war in 1811 and 1812 had grown up in this atmosphere of the oppression of American rights, and with apparently nothing to gain by peace, urged America to fight for the right to exist as a fully independent nation. Considering the period through which they had grown to manhood, it is not surprising that they demanded war to preserve American commerce, neutral rights, and honor, and that, in order to revenge themselves upon their enemy, they proposed the invasion of Canada. The suspected British instigation of the Indians was an added irritant, but if Great Britain had pursued a conciliatory maritime policy towards the United States, it seems extremely unlikely that there would have been war between the two countries. The fundamental cause of the War of 1812 was the British maritime policy which hurt both the national pride and the commerce of the United States.

---

[67] Bassett, *Correspondence of Andrew Jackson*, I, 221–222.

21

The Monroe Doctrine[1]

BRADFORD PERKINS

During the past decade or so, a signal contribution to American diplomatic history has been Bradford Perkins's trilogy on Anglo-American relations between 1795 and 1823: The First Rapprochement *(1955),* Prologue to War *(1961), and* Castlereagh and Adams *(1964). In these volumes the author sustains the high standards achieved by his father, Dexter Perkins, who has long been recognized as one of our outstanding writers of American diplomatic history.*

In telling the story of Anglo-American relations during the late eighteenth and early nineteenth centuries, the younger Perkins has proceeded from premises that give his work distinction and achievement: that American independence meant little until England recognized it; that the conduct of our relations with England was therefore a central, urgent condition of the life of the new American republic; that the full measure of this diplomacy could hardly be taken unless the English side of the story—to be found in as yet inadequately explored English archives and journals—were fully presented; and that diplomatic history, having to take a wider view than

---

[1] This entire chapter owes a great deal to the information and particularly the insights provided by Dexter Perkins, *The Monroe Doctrine, 1823–1826* (Cambridge, Mass., 1927); Arthur P. Whitaker, *The United States and the Independence of Latin America, 1800–1830* (Baltimore, 1941); and Samuel F. Bemis, *John Quincy Adams and the Foundations of American Foreign Policy* (New York, 1949).

SOURCE: Bradford Perkins, *Castlereagh and Adams: England and the United States, 1812–1823* (Berkeley and Los Angeles: The University of California Press, 1964), pp. 326–47. Reprinted by permission of the publisher.

that usually obtained from official and private memoranda, must also encompass public opinion and the changing moods of national psychology. The achievement of Bradford Perkins's work is that it satisfies the demands posed by his premises.

In broad perspective, he sees the three decades from 1795 to 1823 as the age of "America's search for true independence and recognition as a sovereign power, with the political, economic, and psychological implications that accompany independence and sovereignty." An effective rapprochement *was achieved during the first period, from 1795 to 1805, the product mainly of the Federalists' "realistic decision to make haste slowly," whereby they gained certain concessions from England and withstood the maritime excesses of France. The second period, 1805–1812, saw "the nearly ruinous Republican assertion of unattainable rights" and the outbreak of war in 1812. The last period, 1812–1823, saw the war itself, and then a movement toward a more secure peace, independence, and sovereignty. By 1823, says Perkins, America "had carved out a position dialectically combining the realism of the Federalists with Republican aspirations. This clearly appears in the dialogue preceding the promulgation of the Monroe Doctrine, when the administration decided to proclaim American isolation from Europe and at the same time to act independently of Great Britain in facing the challenge to Latin America."*

The selection reprinted below is the final chapter of Castlereagh and Adams. *Perkins presents a careful and absorbing account of each of the major actors in the drama that concluded with the declaration of the Monroe Doctrine: George Canning, the successor to Viscount Castlereagh as British Foreign Secretary; his cousin Stratford Canning, British minister to the United States; Richard Rush, America's ambassador to the United Kingdom; John Quincy Adams, the American Secretary of State; and, of course, President James Monroe himself. Perkins also sets right some of the errors that mar the usual account of how the basic tenets of the Monroe Doctrine were formulated. He reminds us anew, moreover, oriented as we are to the sense that the Monroe Doctrine was a categorical and permanent statement of principles, of how equivocal and tentative were the acts of the men whose interrelated moves led to its pronouncement.*

Finally, he sees the Monroe Doctrine as an outgrowth of America's quest, begun in 1776, for independence and sovereignty. Perkins demonstrates convincingly that Castlereagh's role was of the greatest moment in making the quest successful, for it was he who reversed earlier British policy and accepted both the fact of American independence and the efficacy of America's claim to being treated on the basis of parity. Canning's achievement was that he continued Castlereagh's policies, disconnecting the conduct of British affairs from that of the Continental powers, and pursuing a diplomacy of moderation and entente with America. It was on this basis, indeed, that Canning offered an alliance to the United States, when it seemed likely that France and her conservative allies would cross the Atlantic to put down the rebellion of the Spanish colonies in the New World. For Perkins, then, the significance of the Monroe Doctrine was this: ". . . the Americans, educated by the two foreign secretaries [Castlereagh and Canning] to act as equals, turned down a British offer of cooperation because they did not wish to play the role of a satellite. They struck out on their own. Monroe's message of December 2, 1823, completed the work of the Declaration of Independence."

Rush reported his exchanges with Canning in two sets of dispatches. The first, describing their correspondence but not the discouraging interviews following the Foreign Secretary's return to London, reached Washington on October 9, 1823, the very day Polignac approved in principle the memorandum Canning thrust upon him. Adams was still rattling across Pennsylvania on his return from Massachusetts, where he had visited his lonely father, a widower since 1818. President Monroe, who only awaited Adams' return before taking a short vacation of his own, interrupted preparations to scan the dispatches.

James Monroe and those he consulted agreed that Canning's offer posed "the most momentous [question] which has ever been offered . . . since that of Independence." In the early years of the republic European powers usually called the tune. The War of 1812 showed America's impatience with passive defense, while the Treaty of Ghent and Castlereagh's postwar policy revealed a growing, somewhat grudging British recognition of her power. Now Canning offered a limited alliance, an understanding nominally between equals, really an entente on British principles. Should the United States accept? The isolationist spirit, the almost universal conviction that America and Europe occupied distinct spheres, urged refusal. Yet during the Revolution, the undeclared war with France, and the Louisiana crisis, the Americans sought foreign assistance. Had Castlereagh's policy unintentionally taught them to value their own worth? Had they now the confidence to strike out on their own?

The President first turned to his old mentors, Jefferson and Madison. Forwarding the correspondence to them, Monroe stated his opinion that Britain at last found herself forced to choose between autocracy and constitutionalism, that if the Europeans succeeded in Latin America they would attack the United States, and that "we had better meet the proposition fully, & decisively," thus encouraging her to serve "in a cause which tho' important to her, as to balance of power, commerce &c, is vital to us, as to government." The President did not explicitly recommend acceptance of Canning's five points.

Thomas Jefferson and James Madison advised Monroe to accept Canning's offer even though it meant, as Jefferson pointed out, postponing Cuban ambitions. "Great Britain is the nation which can do us the most harm of any one, or all on earth," Jefferson wrote; "and with her on our side we need not fear the whole world." The separation of Europe and America would be assured. More specifically the two Virginians, ignoring gaps in Canning's proposal, expected current threats to collapse in the face of Anglo-American union. "Whilst it must ensure success, in the event of an appeal to force," Madison predicted, "it doubles the chance of success without that appeal." For the moment Monroe kept this advice secret, even from Adams.

The President, who returned to Washington on November 4, convened his cabinet on the afternoon of the seventh. Five men— Monroe, Adams, Secretary of War Calhoun, Secretary of the Navy Southard, and Attorney General Wirt—settled the reply to Britain, an important declaration to Russia, and Monroe's message at the opening of Congress on December 2. William Wirt and Samuel Southard, old friends of the President's, contributed little to the first meeting or the half dozen that followed. On Latin America, the most debated question, Calhoun spoke the language of caution and his elder, Adams, the language of bold independence. The President heard all views, at times inclined toward Calhoun's, and ultimately backed Adams'.

Until November 21, when Monroe read a preliminary version of his message, none of the secretaries expected the President to make a general declaration of principles in his message to Congress. As was then customary, each secretary prepared a few paragraphs on his department for the President's guidance. Adams' suggestions, submitted on November 13, ignored the Latin-American question, the Secretary expecting to handle this in diplomatic correspondence. His draft concentrated on the Pacific Coast. The ukase, Adams observed, had led to discussions in which the American government asserted that "the American Continents by the free and independent condition which they have assumed and maintain, are henceforth not to be considered as subjects for future Colonization by any European Power." The President accepted this passage almost verbatim.

As a maxim the noncolonization doctrine, a less acid expression of the views Adams inflicted on Stratford Canning in their worst quarrel, challenged England more than any other power. Yet although the Secretary sometimes considered it applicable to British claims in the Oregon country, the doctrine never played a major part in that dispute, nor did it have relevance to current British ambitions. Noncolonization was laid down at this time solely because of the Russian ukase.

When Monroe read his draft Adams, happy to hear the paragraph on colonization, took exception to another presidential passage. The Chief Executive cast a benevolent eye upon the Greeks, then struggling to cast off their Turkish yoke, and spoke "in terms of the most pointed reprobation of the late invasion of Spain by France, and of the principles upon which it was undertaken by the open avowal of the King of France." Like many Republicans at the opening of the French Revolution and many contemporaries as well, the President allowed enthusiasm for self-government and dislike of tyranny to undermine his devotion to isolation. A strong antimonarchist, an even stronger isolationist, Adams protested that Monroe's proposed statement, by breaking down the idea of two spheres, weakened the noncolonization doctrine and objections to European projects in the Western Hemisphere. The statement might even involve the country in serious controversy over non-American issues.

The President apparently felt the force of Adams' arguments. Despite Calhoun's contrary opinions he altered his plans. After expressing sympathy for Spain the message delivered to Congress added, "In the wars of the European powers, in matters relating to themselves, we have never taken any part, nor does it comport with our policy, so to do." Monroe thus made explicit the traditional isolationism of his people, a feeling as old as and more realistic than their prorepublicanism. This became the second tenet of the doctrine bearing his name. The third required much more discussion.

When the President returned to Washington Adams showed him a note delivered on October 16 by Baron Tuyll, the Russian minister. Tuyll announced and justified Russia's adamant refusal to recognize the rebellious colonies. He also praised the American decision to remain neutral even after recognition. This warning against American aid to Latin America, if indeed it was a warning, was temperate enough to permit Adams to reply, for the President, with a mild defense of recognition and a hope that Russia too would remain neutral. Otherwise the United States might reconsider its own neutrality.

Tuyll returned to the charge. On the afternoon of the seventeenth, after Adams had already spent a long day drafting instructions to Rush, discussing them with Monroe, and interviewing the British chargé, the Russian appeared in his office. Tuyll presented extracts from circular instructions recently received. These reviewed in "a tone of passionate exultation," Adams observed, French success in Spain, put Russia on record as opposing revolution in principle, and announced the Czar's intention to act as world policeman. Did the imperial constable, Adams asked, still consider Latin America to be Spanish property? Yes, Tuyll replied. This declaration, Adams said a few days later, was "bearding us to our faces upon the monarchical principles of the Holy Alliance." In his view and that of his colleagues, "It was time to tender them an issue."

Because Europe had no real plans the administration often dealt in rumor, and in the autumn of 1823 Tuyll and Canning tempted

Monroe and his lieutenants to forget contrary, consoling information. Months earlier Rush had reported that, although Canning's letter to Stuart did not quite say so, Great Britain would prevent French counter-revolutionary efforts in Latin America. On the heels of this wise conjecture Adams received from Gallatin, just returned from Paris, a soothing report of his last conversation with Foreign Minister Chateaubriand. Pressed by Gallatin to disavow ambitions "either to take possession of some of her [Spain's] colonies, or to assist her in reducing them under their former yoke," Chateaubriand gave categorical assurances that France had no such plans and would in no way interfere in American questions. Of course Chateaubriand and Villèle, his chief, notoriously worked at cross-purposes. Still this was as explicit an assurance as one could ask.

Adams thought Canning feigned alarm to draw the Americans to his own position. He concealed this suspicion from the British chargé, of course, but he did tell Henry Addington he considered the danger negligible. Talking of the South Americans, he told Addington "nothing could [be] more absurd than the notion that they could ever be again brought to submit to the Spanish yoke." Moreover Adams felt sure that British and American disapproval, already clear to Europe, would suffice to prevent intervention. "Any mere declaration on the part of the European Sovereigns he considered as a dead letter, and as for active and substantial interposition the bare idea was too absurd to be entertained for a moment."

Monroe and Calhoun considered the danger genuine, and so apparently did Wirt and Southard. Less than a week after receiving Rush's first reports the President asked Gallatin to return to Paris, urging the need of an experienced hand in a period of crisis. Adams tried to argue Monroe and Calhoun out of their alarm. "Calhoun," he complained, "is perfectly moon-struck by the surrender of Cadiz, and says the Holy Alliance . . . will restore all Mexico and all South America to the Spanish dominion." The Secretary of State maintained that allied forces could make no more than a temporary impression in Latin America. Did he doubt the rebels' ability to fend off attack, he said, he would advise against "embarking our lives and fortunes in a ship which . . . the very rats have abandoned." Monroe and Calhoun, who wanted to support Latin America, had no answer to this argument.

On November 16, the day after Adams found Calhoun "moon-struck," further dispatches arrived from Rush. Describing the conversations following Canning's return to London, they showed that the Foreign Secretary had markedly cooled. Monroe interpreted this to mean that Canning had somehow discovered that the danger to Latin America had become less immediate. He took comfort in this guess. During the second fortnight of November, when he framed his message and whipped it into shape, Monroe seemed less fearful than before. He never entirely abandoned his old concern, and certainly Calhoun did not, but the President's hopes rose. At least he did not fear that French troops at Cadiz would immediately board ship for South America.

This declining sense of urgency did not destroy the appeal of Canning's proposal. For some days the cabinet, aware of the cost, wrestled over the attractive, unprecedented invitation to join the club of major powers. Perhaps unnecessary at the moment, a joint declaration would certainly discourage future European plans, and all the cabinet preferred an investment of words to a later investment of force. Even more important, in the view of Monroe and his advisers, union with Britain would cement her break with the Continent.

The idea, fatuous after Verona and the Stuart letter, that Britain teetered near the brink of an understanding with the allies troubled Monroe, Wirt, Calhoun, and Jefferson. Their concern showed the depth of their distrust of England as well as a simplistic republican inability to distinguish among types of monarchy. Even the more sophisticated Adams, denying the need to bind England, merely maintained that her past actions committed her against the allies, not that her system was different.

Distrust cut both ways, arguing also against a connection with Albion. At the height of the cabinet discussions a letter from George W. Erving, a former diplomat traveling privately in Europe, came into Monroe's hands. An alliance with England horrified Erving, who was "perfectly persuaded . . . that in such alliance either her system or ours would suffer, & equally persuaded that it would not be hers." Better abandon Latin America, counseled Erving, than join England "at the imminent risk of exposing our health by the poisonous contact." Adams, who did not respect Erving, nevertheless shared his feelings, as to a lesser degree did the President. Castlereagh's years of endeavor, strikingly successful on the diplomatic level, barely touched the visceral Anglophobia of the American people.

Adams, the cabinet member most hostile to understanding with England, attached as much importance to recognition as did Rush. At an early interview with Addington, Adams permitted the chargé to hope for some way to bypass the issue. As time passed he tightened his position. English recognition of at least one of the new states, he told Addington after receiving Rush's report of the deadlock with Canning, was indispensable so that "whatever events may happen, the concord in the views and measures of the Governments may be preserved unbroken, and that confusion avoided, which a discrepancy of principle might engender." The United States denied the right of any power including Spain to challenge states already living in freedom. If a twist of events led Britain to support reconstruction of the empire, albeit on a less rigid basis, a real crisis might develop. To eliminate this possibility Monroe and Adams, like Rush, required England to take a public stand by the act of recognition.

Pointing to the statement, proposed by Canning, that neither Britain nor America had territorial ambitions, Adams argued that the Englishman sought a pledge only "ostensibly against the forcible interference of the Holy Alliance between Spain and South America; but really or especially against the acquisition to the United States themselves of any part of the Spanish-American possessions." He was not willing, although Calhoun was, to foreclose the possibility of admitting Cuba or even Texas into the union at the request of local inhabitants, and he was willing to give up the advantage of a self-denying British pledge to preserve his own country's freedom of action.

The Americans saw serious risk in acting at England's call. "Had we mov'd first in London," Monroe later observed, "we might have appeared . . . a secondary party, whereby G.B. would have had the principal credit with our neighbors" in Latin America. Adams was equally reluctant to allow her the lead. "As the independence of the South Americans would then be only protected by the guarantee of Great Britain," he said, "it would throw them completely into her arms." He urged independent action partly to strengthen political and commercial ties with the new states.

In more general form the discussion reached the heart of America's position as an independent power. At the first cabinet meeting after Monroe's return, Adams pointed out that Tuyll's *démarche* provided an opportunity "to take our stand against the Holy Alliance, and at the same time to decline the overture of Great Britain. It would be more candid, as well as more dignified, to avow our principles explicitly to Russia and France, than to come in as a cock-boat in the wake of a British man-of-war." The cabinet agreed. The day after Tuyll's second note Adams told Addington, who visited him to discuss Latin America, that "Foreign Powers . . . should not be left in ignorance of the views and opinions of the United States. . . . These views would be openly and distinctly declared to them." National self-respect urged such a course rather than action as England's junior partner.

Proceeding along these lines the President prepared a long, heated passage for his address to Congress. His diatribe against antirepublican endeavors everywhere—in Greece, in Spain, in Italy, in Latin America—upset Adams, who successfully urged the President to tone down denunciations of purely European activities, to promise to abstain from European politics, and to concentrate his fire against outside intervention in the New World. Speaking past Congress to the allies James Monroe wrote:

> We owe it . . . to candor, and to the amicable relations existing between
> the United States and those powers, to declare that we should consider any
> attempt on their part to extend their system to any portion of this hemi-
> sphere as dangerous to our peace and security. . . . With the Governments
> who have declared their independence and maintained it, . . . we could not
> view any interposition . . . by any European power, in any other light than
> as the manifestation of an unfriendly disposition toward the United
> States. . . .
> It is impossible that the allied powers should extend their political system
> to any portion of either continent without endangering our peace and
> happiness; nor can anyone believe that our southern brethren, if left to
> themselves, would adopt it of their own accord. It is equally impossible,
> therefore, that we should behold such interposition, in any form, with
> indifference.

Thus was phrased the third tenet of Monroe's famous message, the
nonintervention doctrine.

Secretary Adams, who approved the final version of Monroe's message, altered his draft reply to Tuyll to correspond with it and considered the result a "firm, spirited, and yet conciliatory answer to all
the communications lately received from the Russian Government, and
at the same time an unequivocal answer to the proposals made by Mr.
Canning to Mr. Rush." Calhoun considered the note far from conciliatory and wanted to eliminate it altogether, merely sending the
presidential message to Tuyll. Monroe found Adams' draft not a little
strong, but after the Secretary pled his case in a private interview
Monroe allowed Adams to proceed much as he had planned. The
Secretary of State read his note to Tuyll on November 27 and promised
soon to send a written copy.

Statements to the world through Tuyll and Congress made it plain
that the American government intended to act as an independent power
rather than as a British satellite. They did not make a reply to Canning
less necessary. Unwillingness to act as "a cock-boat in the wake of a
British man-of-war," in other words, made it certain Canning's plan
would not gain unconditional, immediate approval, but did not disbar
negotiations on the basis of that plan.

Adams' diary pictures the President as uncertain of the proper reply
to England, not as inclined to accept Canning's offer. Even Calhoun, the
most alarmed member of the inner circle, proposed to give Rush only
discretionary authority to accept the offer in an emergency. All apparently agreed to seek modifications if time permitted, particularly to
request or require British recognition of Latin states. At one point the
President endorsed Calhoun's suggestion. Adams rather easily talked

him out of this idea, and in the end the President adopted Adams' sterner position.

Instructions to Rush, revised several times as the President edged toward decision, bore date of November 29, a few days after Monroe had completed his forthcoming address. At Monroe's direction Adams struck out an explicit statement that until Britain granted recognition "we can see no foundation upon which the concurrent action of the two Governments can be harmonized." The instructions made the point in more diplomatic language. Only if Britain extended recognition was Rush authorized to move "in concert" with her. This last clause, whatever courses it approved, clearly did not mean joint action along the lines Canning originally proposed, even should the Foreign Secretary bring his colleagues around to recognition. Monroe and Adams promised to consider joint as opposed to parallel action only if, a new emergency arising, Rush referred home further proposals.

Adams, who never claimed credit for rejecting the British offer (he took pride chiefly in the noncolonization doctrine), stood nearer his colleagues than is often said. No one desired unconditional approval. In his first comments on Canning's offer the President merely said that his inclination was to "meet" it, not that he favored the joint manifesto Canning urged. Obviously the President wished to widen the breach between Britain and the allies and to protect Latin America. He believed the reply to Tuyll and the message to Congress did so. "We certainly meet, in full extent, the proposition of Mʳ. Canning," he wrote Jefferson. "With G. Britain, we have, it is presumed, acted fairly & fully to all her objects, & have a right to expect, a corresponding conduct on her part," he wrote his immediate predecessor. Forwarding the President's message to Rush, Adams observed, "The concurrence of these sentiments with those of the British Government as exhibited in the proposals of Mr. Canning, will be obvious to you. It will now remain for Great Britain to make hers equally public. The moral effect upon the councils of the Allies, to deter them from any interposition of force between Spain and America, will be complete." The form might differ from Canning's scheme. The effect did not, President and Secretary both believed.

On December 2, 1823, instructions having gone to Rush and a reply to Tuyll, Congress heard the President's message. Three of fifty-one paragraphs dealt with foreign affairs, an early one stating the noncolonization doctrine and two later ones mingling isolationist sentiments and warnings against intervention by Europe.

Not for thirty years did Americans name these three paragraphs the Monroe Doctrine. From the beginning, however, they valued the principles laid down by the last of the Virginia dynasty. Within a week Adams noted that the nation universally approved the message. The

British chargé agreed. "The explicit and manly tone," he informed Canning a month later, "has evidently found in every bosom a chord which vibrates in strict unison with the sentiments so conveyed. They have been echoed from one end of the union to the other." Monroe's decision to ignore the advice of his two neighbors and predecessors, to strike out boldly and independently with a declaration of principle despite possible risks, drew support throughout the nation.

Just after the message Washington received a rumor, in fact unfounded, that 12,000 French troops were about to sail for South America. This alarmed editors Niles and Gales as well as the President, who talked briefly of the need to "unite with the British Govt, in measures, to prevent the interference of the allied powers." Monroe soon cooled, perhaps under Adams' influence. New instructions to Rush, carried by a secret agent sent to Europe to ferret out allied plans, spoke only of a "concert of operations" and studiously avoided any mention of joint action.

In a few days a dispatch arrived from Daniel Sheldon, the chargé at Paris. Sheldon reported that, neither the Bourbon monarchy scheme nor any other having come to a focus, the United States need not fear an immediate descent on Latin America. A second dispatch two weeks later repeated this prediction. The scare passed. In the spring Henry Clay withdrew a resolution endorsing the nonintervention doctrine, saying, "Events and circumstances, subsequent to the communication of the Message, evinced, that if such a purpose were ever seriously entertained, it had been relinquished."

Monroe's message, aimed partly at Latin America, had no clear effect there. The leader of the fight for liberty, Simón Bolívar, completely ignored it in his correspondence. Most South American leaders continued to regard England as their chief defense against European intervention.

Europeans, who also felt that the message scarcely altered the practical situation, nevertheless reacted strongly to the President's sentiments. Liberals contrasted Monroe's enlightened views with those of their own governments. The dominant groups denounced his presumption. The noncolonization doctrine challenged international law; the warning against intervention denied legitimist ambitions; the prorepublican theme threatened traditional European doctrines. The United States, Prince Metternich complained, "have suddenly left a sphere too narrow for their ambition, and have astonished Europe by a new act of revolt, more unprovoked, fully as audacious, and no less dangerous than the former. . . . If this flood of evil doctrines . . . should extend over the whole of America, what would become of . . . that conservative system which has saved Europe from complete dissolution?"

In Britain praise outweighed criticism. The message reached Falmouth by government packet on December 24 and passed to all the kingdom. The *Caledonian Mercury,* usually friendly to the United States, scoffed at Monroe's "obscure innuendos." Other papers gave the message the attention it deserved, the *Chronicle* pronouncing it "worthy of the occasion and of the people, who seem destined to occupy so large a space in the future history of the world." No editor denounced the republican cast which so upset Metternich. All withheld comment on the isolationist passages, apparently considering them mere truisms. The papers concentrated upon the noncolonization and nonintervention doctrines.

Several editors objected to the former, a "startling general principle," a "curious idea," a "grave and somewhat novel doctrine." The *Star,* most critical of the entire message, declared: "The plain *Yankee* of the matter is, that the United States wish to monopolize to themselves the privilege of colonising . . . every . . . part of the American Continent." In the Oregon country and elsewhere Britain must not accept this proposition. Not one British voice defended Monroe, but many papers passed over noncolonization in silence.

Britons regarded the nonintervention doctrine as the heart of the message, and on the whole they liked it. Even the *Star,* which considered Monroe hypocritical "to place on the basis of a bounden duty, what is, in plain truth, a matter of the sheerest self-interest," welcomed his reinforcement of British efforts. "The President has made just such a declaration . . . as it is to the interest of this country that he should have made," opined the *Herald.* "This is plain speaking, and it is just speaking," pontificated the *Times.* Both the *Times* and the *Chronicle* contrasted America's boldness with the British government's alleged lack of courage. The latter paper even maintained that an English declaration as forthright as Monroe's would have prevented the French invasion of Spain which began the whole crisis.

The *Courier,* once bitterly anti-Yankee and long a mouthpiece of British conservatism, capped British comment. "The question of the Independence and recognition of the South American States, may now be considered as at rest," the paper declared. Europe would no longer dare to plan action against the former Spanish colonies. "Protected by the two nations that possess the institutions, and speak the language of freedom—by Great Britain on one side, and by the United States on the other, their independence is placed beyond the reach of danger." On the great issue of the day England and the United States stood together as allies for freedom.

Canning reacted less favorably to the message and the decision, unknown to the public but to him painful, to refuse the offer of joint action. Six months earlier his cousin's overoptimistic reports led to dreams of a virtual alliance, an agreement far transcending a joint statement on Latin America. In October, after discussing general negotiations with Rush and Stratford Canning, he turned to his cousin, who remained in the office, and said "he should be inclined to take this opportunity to make a clearance of all American questions." The collapse of hopes for an entente on Latin America destroyed Canning's interest in other negotiations. Rush's conversations with Stratford Canning and Huskisson dwindled slowly into nothing during the first half of 1824. Canning made little effort to stir the negotiations into life.

Nor did the Foreign Secretary show interest when Rush read Adams' instructions of November 29, laying down terms on which cooperation might develop. With the Latin-American problem anesthetized by the Polignac memorandum, Canning saw no need for a joint statement, particularly one quite different from his original proposal, and felt free to take up new questions posed by Monroe's message.

Canning particularly objected to the noncolonization doctrine. He complained so strongly that Rush quickly dropped the matter. Canning drew up but wisely did not deliver an argumentative note in which he compared Alexander's ukase with "the new doctrine of the President," concluding that "we cannot yield obedience to either." Later, in instructions to Stratford Canning and Huskisson, he declared the British government "prepared to reject [Monroe's principle] in the most unequivocal manner, maintaining that whatever right of colonizing the unappropriated parts of America had been hitherto enjoyed . . . may still be exercised in perfect freedom, and without affording the slightest cause of umbrage to the United States."

Although Canning saw advantages in acting hand in hand with the United States he shrank from appearing at St. Petersburg with a power avowing principles so different. He also did not like or even profess to understand the American proposal to limit permanent British settlements to the area between 51° and 55°, and when the American minister presented this plan Canning replied, "Heyday! What is here? Do I read Mr Rush's meaning aright?" Consequently he ordered his ambassador in Russia to negotiate separately. No harm resulted. Russia abandoned her claim to broad maritime jurisdiction and, by separate agreements with her two adversaries, abandoned the Oregon country.

George Canning considered the nonintervention doctrine in some ways useful to England. He even professed unconcern at the refusal to act jointly. After Polignac he did not fear an allied descent upon South America. He counted on Monroe's message to give pause to planners of a European congress on Latin-American affairs. "The Congress was broken in all its limits before, but the President's speech gives it the *coup de grace*," he felt, overoptimistically as events proved. "The effect of the ultra-Liberalism of our Yankee cooperators, on the ultra-despotism of our Aix la Chapelle allies, gives me just the balance that I wanted," he informed his friend Bagot.

In more important ways the presidential announcement unsettled Canning. A proud and practical politician, he disliked having Monroe steal a march on him. "Are you not," Lord Grey asked Holland, "delighted with the American speech? What a contrast to the conduct . . . of our Government. . . . Canning will have the glory of following in the wake of the President of the United States." Canning did not like to have his enemies free to speak this way, particularly since he believed, and said Rush agreed, that "his Gov^t. would *not* have spoken out, but for what passed between us." Canning felt Monroe had tricked and defeated him.

More than mere pique upset the Foreign Secretary. Canning did not want close economic and political ties between the United States and South America, partly because these might lead to discrimination against English commerce and partly because Britain, already at odds with Europe, would find herself isolated. The Foreign Secretary still hoped for negotiations between Spain and the Latin Americans, a course Monroe clearly disapproved. Because Canning, in the words of an admiring biographer, considered "constitutional monarchy . . . the true *via media* between democracy and despotism," he hoped to keep monarchist ideas alive in South America. Monroe's message was a paean on popular government. Canning felt he must regain the lead from one who blew "a blast on the republican trumpet, while sheltered behind the shield of England."

The Polignac memorandum, circulated to European diplomats shortly after its signature and sent by Canning to Rush a few weeks later, remained secret from the public until 1824. At the opening of Parliament in February, Canning, assailed for following a less decisive tack than Monroe, defended ministers with a paraphrase. On March 4 he presented the memorandum, still with deletions, to the House of Commons, and government spokesmen exploited it. Lord Liverpool asked if such a *démarche*, which the French had been forced to accept, was not "worth a thousand official declarations." The government also revealed its refusal to attend a congress on Latin America, a proposal reluctantly made by Ferdinand. These actions showed Europe and Latin America, neither of whom needed much convincing, that Britain still posed the most effective barrier to outside interference in the imperial war.

Fostering monarchical principles in Latin America proved more difficult, even impossible. After the downfall of Iturbide in Mexico they virtually disappeared. Moreover King Ferdinand, obdurate as ever, refused to countenance negotiations with his erstwhile subjects, and the continued presence of French troops in Spain angered Canning. Supported by Liverpool he decided to challenge the cabinet majority. In August, 1824, Canning forced agreement to recognize Buenos Aires, although George IV objected that "the whole proceedings . . . are premature"—at a time when, except in Peru, Spain had no armies on the mainland. On the last day of the year, after a lengthy battle during which Canning threatened to resign, the Foreign Secretary won cabinet approval of a note to Spain announcing England's intention to recognize Buenos Aires, Mexico, and Colombia. The King again objected to his ministers' precipitancy—"I have already expressed my wishes . . . & wishes when coming from the King are always to be considered & understood as Commands"—but recognition proceeded as Canning and Liverpool planned. A year and a half after Canning first approached Rush the British and American governments were aligned. They were also rivals for Latin-American favor and commerce.

Canning's efforts to counteract the nonintervention doctrine, usually carried out with a tact belying his reputation, failed to pull the wool over Richard Rush's hypercritical eyes. Late in 1824 he wrote: "It would be an entire mistake to suppose, that because of the partial and guarded approach to us by Britain last year, on the south American question, she feels any increase of good will towards us."

Most Americans disagreed, and in 1824 and 1825 Anglo-American friendship reached unprecedented levels. Early in 1824 an alliance on Latin-American questions gained wide support although, as Addington reported, it could be "attributed as much to the hope of acquiring additional security to their own institutions as from any inherent affection for Great Britain, or disinterested ardour in the cause of transatlantic Liberty." Alliance talk died with the collapse of threats to Latin America; friendship did not. The tariff debate of 1824 totally lacked the anti-British emphasis of that of 1816. At a White House reception the President, speaking in a tone to be overheard, praised British policy and welcomed the growth of Anglo-American concord.

In the spring of 1825, learning of Charles Vaughan's appointment as minister to the United States, Addington requested a leave to escape the oppressive Washington heat. He looked back upon his tenure with satisfaction. "It is scarcely possible that a man should arrive under better auspices than Vaughan," he reported, "for 2/3^{ds} of the Americans are just now well-disposed towards us, and Clay [the former war hawk now secretary of state] says that he is quite in love with Mr Canning." An honest man well aware that outstanding issues or new ones could spoil the scene, Addington added: "How long this may last I do not pretend to conjecture."

Addington's ease paid tribute to George Canning and perhaps even more to Lord Castlereagh, for Canning reaped where Castlereagh had sown. From the spring of 1814 onward, at first slowly and almost inadvertently, British policy moved toward conciliation. The Rush-Bagot agreement and the convention of 1818 were positive sides of this policy. Probably more important, Castlereagh and then Canning sought to stifle controversy before it became serious or, better, to avoid it altogether. "Let us hasten settlement, if we can; but let us postpone the day of difference, if it must come; which however I trust it need not," Canning wrote. This policy had the disadvantage of leaving issues like Oregon and West Indian trade for future dispute. In the immediate sense it paid impressive dividends.

Even Rush, hostile and suspicious, admitted, "Mine have been plain-sailing times," and in general the American political world praised England for muffling winds of controversy. An observant British traveler, no mere panegyrist of the United States, wrote in 1823 that "there are few, whose good opinion is worth having, who do not unite in good will towards the people of my native country." This much had the climate changed since 1812.

In the Liverpool speech which charmed Christopher Hughes, George Canning "express[ed] the gratification which he felt, in common with the great mass of the intelligent and liberal men of both countries, to see the animosities necessarily attendant on a state of hostility so rapidly wearing away." He welcomed the growth of friendship between "two nations united by a common language, a common spirit of commercial enterprise, and a common regard for well-regulated liberty." Appropriately, Canning did not mention contrary factors—the continuing British air of superiority, American touchiness and ambition, commercial rivalry, England's distrust of republicanism, and America's of monarchy. Still he fairly described a process taking place on both sides of the Atlantic.

Basically the new relationship reflected the growth of American power and stability and of Britain's sometimes half-reluctant recognition of this growth. America has "already taken her rank among the first powers of Christendom," the *Annual Register* observed in the volume for 1824. Few Englishmen yet placed the United States on a par with their own country. They did see that the American form of government "has survived the tender period of infancy, and outlived the prophecies of its downfall. . . . It has been found serviceable both in peace and war, and may well claim from the nation it has saved . . . the votive benediction of 'Esto perpetua.'" Perpetual or not—Calhoun and Jefferson Davis would speak to that—the union had gained a position beyond foreign challenge. Capable and bold diplomacy followed a dangerous and ill-fought war. The new American generation vindicated the aspirations of their fathers in 1776.

Jackson's Fight with the "Money Power"

BRAY HAMMOND

What was the nature of Jacksonian democracy? The question is under perennial discussion, and new answers are being constantly proposed; indeed, Lee Benson of the University of Pennsylvania, carefully analyzing voting behavior in New York state during the 1830's and 1840's, has recently argued that the whole concept of Jacksonian democracy is a specious one and ought to be discarded. In his pamphlet, Jacksonian Democracy *(1958), Professor Charles Grier Sellers, Jr., of the University of California, found that, depending on their own interests and frames of reference, historians formulated three essentially different views. A "patrician" school, drawn from Eastern middle- or upper-middle-class interests and writing largely during the latter half of the nineteenth century, saw in Jacksonian democracy the origins of a deplorable vulgarity and corruption in American public life. After 1900, an "agrarian democratic" school, with Western and Southern middle-class backgrounds and guided by the hypotheses of Frederick Jackson Turner, rehabilitated Jacksonian democracy as an egalitarian movement of the common man. "In more recent years," said Professor Sellers, "a school of 'urban' historians emerged which, from the vantage of the New Deal and American industrial progress and problems, saw Jacksonian democracy as a contest for power either between capitalists and noncapitalists or between old capitalists and new ones."*

It is this last view which is presented in the following essay by the late Bray Hammond. A former assistant secretary of the Federal Reserve Board, Mr. Hammond was the author of Banks and Politics in America *(1957), a fresh and imposing study of the political impact of business enterprise during the period from the Revolution to the Civil War, and for which he received the Pulitzer prize in history. Because of its importance for his theme, the dramatic struggle between Andrew Jackson and the Second Bank of the United States drew the close attention of Mr. Hammond. In con-*

SOURCE: *American Heritage, The Magazine of History,* VII (June, 1956), 9–11, 100–103. Reprinted by permission of the American Heritage Publishing Co., Inc.

sidering the nature and importance of the struggle, he arrived at an arresting and perspicacious analysis of what Jacksonian democracy was all about.

He explains how Jackson himself was far from being a Jacksonian democrat. He explains how the advent of the Industrial Revolution created opportunities and problems which necessarily involved banks and politics. He explains how the attack on the Bank, generally regarded as a clear expression of Jacksonian democracy, in fact expressed the principles neither of Jackson nor of democracy.

Mr. Hammond's misgivings about the role of the Jacksonians in American economic development suggest questions about the roles of other men in other times. It is a moot problem whether the economic values and policies which governed the building of American life are those which indeed should have governed. Touching as it does upon American life in our own age, the problem is no less moot today.

"Relief, sir!" interrupted the President. "Come not to me, sir! Go to the monster. It is folly, sir, to talk to Andrew Jackson. The government will not bow to the monster. . . . Andrew Jackson yet lives to put his foot upon the head of the monster and crush him to the dust."

The monster, "a hydra of corruption," was known also as the Second Bank of the United States, chartered by Congress in 1816 as depository of the federal government, which was its principal stockholder and customer. The words were reported by a committee which called on President Jackson in the spring of 1834 to complain because he and Secretary of the Treasury Roger Taney had removed the federal deposits from the federal depository into what the Jacksonians called "selected banks" and others called "pet banks." The President was disgusted with the committee.

"Andrew Jackson," he exclaimed in the third person as before, "would never recharter that monster of corruption. Sooner than live in a country where such a power prevailed, he would seek an asylum in the wilds of Arabia."

In effect, he had already put his foot on the monster and crushed him in the dust. He had done so by vetoing a new charter for the Bank and removing the federal accounts from its books. So long as the federal Bank had the federal accounts, it had been regulator of the currency and of credit in general. Its power to regulate had derived from the fact that the federal Treasury was the largest single transactor in the economy and the largest bank depositor. Receiving the checks and notes of local banks deposited with it by government collectors of revenue, it had had constantly to come back on the local banks for settlements of the amounts which the checks and notes called for. It had had to do so because it made those amounts immediately available to the Treasury, wherever desired. Since settlement by the local banks was in specie, i.e., silver and gold coin, the pressure for settlement automatically regulated local bank lending; for the more the local banks lent, the larger the amount of their notes and checks in use and the larger the sums they had to settle in specie. This loss of specie reduced their power to lend.

All this had made the federal Bank the regulator not alone of the currency but of bank lending in general, the restraint it had exerted being fully as effective as that of the twelve Federal Reserve Banks at present, though by a different process. With its life now limited to two more years and the government accounts removed from its books, it was already crushed but still writhing.

The Jacksonian attack on the Bank is an affair respecting which posterity seems to have come to an opinion that is half hero worship and half discernment. In the words of Professor William G. Sumner, the affair was a struggle "between the democracy and the money power." Viewed in that light, Jackson's victory was a grand thing. But Sumner also observed—this was three-quarters of a century ago— that since Jackson's victory the currency, which previously had owned no superior in the world, had never again been so good. More recently Professor Lester V. Chandler, granting the Bank's imperfections, has said that its abolition without replacement by something to take over its functions was a "major blunder" which "ushered in a generation of banking anarchy and monetary disorder." So the affair stands, a triumph and a blunder.

During Andrew Jackson's lifetime three things had begun to alter prodigiously the economic life of Americans. These were steam, credit, and natural resources.

Steam had been lifting the lids of pots for thousands of years, and for a century or so it had been lifting water from coal mines. But only in recent years had it been turning spindles, propelling ships, drawing trains of cars, and multiplying incredibly the productive powers of man. For thousands of years money had been lent, but in most people's minds debt had signified distress—as it still did in Andrew Jackson's. Only now was its productive power, long known to merchants as a means of making one sum of money do the work of several, becoming popularly recognized by enterprising men for projects which required larger sums than could be assembled in coin. For three centuries or more America's resources had been crudely surmised, but only now were their variety, abundance, and accessibility becoming practical realities. And it was the union of these three, steam, credit, and natural resources, that was now turning Anglo-Saxon America from the modest agrarian interests that had preoccupied her for two centuries of European settlement to the dazzling possibilities of industrial exploitation.

In the presence of these possibilities, the democracy was becoming transformed from one that was Jeffersonian and agrarian to one that was financial and industrial. But it was still a democracy: its recruits were still men born and reared on farms, its vocabulary was still Jeffersonian, and its basic conceptions changed insensibly from the libertarianism of agrarians to that of *laissez faire*. When Andrew Jackson became President in 1829, boys born in log cabins were already becoming businessmen but with no notion of surrendering as bankers and manufacturers the freedom they might have enjoyed as farmers.

There followed a century of exploitation from which America emerged with the most wealthy and powerful economy there is, with her people the best fed, the best housed, the best clothed, and the best equipped on earth. But the loss and waste have long been apparent. The battle was only for the strong, and millions who lived in the midst of wealth never got to touch it. The age of the Robber Barons was scarcely a golden age. It was scarcely what Thomas Jefferson desired.

It could scarcely have been what Andrew Jackson desired either, for his ideals were more or less Jeffersonian by common inheritance, and the abuse of credit was one of the things he abominated. Yet no man ever did more to encourage the abuse of credit than he. For the one agency able to exert some restraint on credit was the federal Bank. In destroying it, he let speculation loose. Though a hard-money devotee who hated banks and wanted no money but coin, he fostered the formation of swarms of banks and endowed the country with a filthy and depreciated paper currency which he believed to be unsound and unconstitutional and from which the Civil War delivered it in the Administration of Abraham Lincoln thirty years later.

This, of course, was not Andrew Jackson's fault, unless one believes he would have done what he did had his advisers been different. Though a resolute and decisive person, he also relied on his friends. He had his official cabinet, largely selected for political expediency, and he had his "kitchen cabinet" for informal counsel. Of those advisers most influential with him, all but two were either businessmen or closely associated with the business world. The two exceptions were Major William B. Lewis, a planter and neighbor from Tennessee who came to live with him in the White House; and James K. Polk, also of Tennessee, later President of the United States. These two, with Jackson himself, constituted the agrarian element in the Jacksonian Administration. Several of the others, however, were agrarian in the sense that they had started as poor farm boys.

Martin Van Buren, probably the ablest of Jackson's political associates, was a lawyer whose investments had made him rich. Amos Kendall, the ablest in a business and administrative sense, later made the telegraph one of the greatest of American business enterprises and himself a man of wealth. He provided the Jacksonians with their watchword, "The world is governed too much." He said "our countrymen are beginning to demand" that the government be content with "protecting their persons and property, leaving them to direct their labor and capital as they please, within the moral law: getting rich or remaining poor as may result from their own management or fortune." Kendall's views may be sound, but they are not what one expects to hear from the democracy when struggling with the money power.

Roger Taney, later Chief Justice, never got rich, but he liked banks and was a modest investor in bank stock. "There is perhaps no business," he said as Jackson's secretary of the treasury, "which yields a profit so certain and liberal as the business of banking and exchange; and it is proper that it should be open as far as practicable to the most free competition and its advantages shared by all classes of society." His own bank in Baltimore was one of the first of the pets in which he deposited government money.

David Henshaw, Jacksonian boss of Massachusetts, was a banker and industrialist whose advice in practical matters had direct influence in Washington. Henshaw projected a Jacksonian bank to take the place of the existing institution but to be bigger. (A similar project was got up by friends of Van Buren in New York and one of the two was mentioned favorably by Jackson in his veto message as a possible alternative to the existing United States Bank.) Samuel Ingham, Jackson's first secretary of the treasury, was a paper manufacturer in Pennsylvania and later a banker in New Jersey. Churchill C. Cambreleng, congressional leader of the attack on the Bank, was a New York businessman and former agent of John Jacob Astor. These are not all of the Jacksonians who were intent on the federal Bank's destruction, but they are typical.

There was a very cogent reason why these businessmen and their class generally wanted to kill the Bank of the United States. It interfered with easy money; it kept the state banks from lending as freely as they might otherwise and businessmen from borrowing.

New York, for example, was now the financial and commercial center of the country and its largest city, which Philadelphia formerly had been. The customs duties collected at its wharves and paid by its businessmen were far the largest of any American port, and customs duties were then the principal source of federal income. These duties were paid by New York businessmen with checks on New York banks. These checks were deposited by the federal collectors in the New York office of the Bank of the United States, whose headquarters were in Philadelphia and a majority of whose directors were Philadelphia businessmen. This, Amos Kendall observed, was a "wrong done to New York in depriving her of her natural advantages."

It was not merely a matter of prestige. As already noted, the United States Bank, receiving the checks of the New York businessmen, made the funds at once available to the secretary of the treasury. The Bank had therefore to call on the New York banks for the funds the checks represented. This meant that the New York banks, in order to pay the federal Bank, had to draw down their reserves; which meant that they had less money to lend; which meant that the New York businessmen could not borrow as freely and cheaply as they might otherwise. All this because their money had gone to Philadelphia.

Actually the situation was not so bad as my simplified account makes it appear. For one thing, the goods imported at New York were sold elsewhere in the country, and more money came to New York in payment for them than went out of the city in duties paid the government. But I have described it in the bald, one-sided terms that appealed to the local politicians and to the businessmen prone to grumbling because money was not so easy as they would like. There was truth in what they said, but it amounted to less than they made out.

New York's grievance was special because her customs receipts were so large and went to a vanquished rival. Otherwise the federal Bank's pressure on the local banks—all of which were state banks—was felt in some degree through the country at large. Wherever money was paid to a federal agency—for postage, for fines, for lands, for excise, for import duties—money was drawn from the local banks into the federal Bank. The flow of funds did not drain the local banks empty and leave them nothing to do, though they and the states' rights politicians talked as if that were the case. The federal Bank was simply their principal single creditor.

And though private business brought more money to New York and other commercial centers than it took away, the federal government took more away than it brought. For its largest payments were made elsewhere—to naval stations, army posts, Indian agents, owners of the public debt, largely foreign, and civilians in the government service throughout the country. In the normal flow of money payments from hand to hand in the economy, those to the federal government and consequently to the federal Bank were so large and conspicuous that the state banks involved in making them were disagreeably conscious of their size and frequency.

These banks, of course, were mostly eastern and urban rather than western and rural, because it was in eastern cities that the federal government received most of its income. Accordingly, it was in the eastern business centers, Boston, New York, Baltimore, and Charleston, that resentment against Philadelphia and the federal Bank was strongest. This resentment was intensified by the fact that the federal Bank's branch offices were also competitors for private business in these and other cities, which the present Federal Reserve Banks, very wisely, are not.

General Jackson's accession to the presidency afforded an opportunity to put an end to the federal Bank. Its charter would expire in seven years. The question of renewal was to be settled in that interval. Jackson was popular and politically powerful. His background and principles were agrarian. An attack on the Bank by him would be an attack "by the democracy on the money power." It would have, therefore, every political advantage.

The realities behind these words, however, were not what the words implied. The democracy till very recently had been agrarian because most of the population was agricultural. But the promoters of the assault on the Bank were neither agrarian in their current interests nor representative of what democracy implied.

In the western and rural regions, which were the most democratic in a traditional sense, dislike of the federal Bank persisted, though by 1829 it had less to feed on than formerly. Years before, under incompetent managers, the Bank had lent unwisely in the West, had been forced to harsh measures of self-preservation, and had made itself hated, with the help, as usual, of the state banks and states' rights politicians. But the West needed money, and though the Bank never provided enough it did provide some, and in the absence of new offenses disfavor had palpably subsided by the time Jackson became President.

There were also, in the same regions, vestiges or more of the traditional agrarian conviction that all banks were evil. This principle was still staunchly held by Andrew Jackson. He hated all banks, did so through a long life, and said so time after time. He thought they all violated the Constitution. But he was led by the men around him to focus his aversion on the federal Bank, which being the biggest must be the worst and whose regulatory pressure on the state banks must obviously be the oppression to be expected from a great, soulless corporation.

However, not all agrarian leaders went along with him. For many years the more intelligent had discriminated in favor of the federal Bank, recognizing that its operations reduced the tendency to inflation which, as a hard-money party, the agrarians deplored. Altogether, it was no longer to be expected that the agrarian democracy would initiate a vigorous attack on the federal Bank, though it was certainly to be expected that such an attack would receive very general agrarian support.

It was in the cities and within the business world that both the attack on the Bank and its defense would be principally conducted. For there the Bank had its strongest enemies and its strongest friends. Its friends were the more conservative houses that had dominated the old business world but had only a minor part in the new. It was a distinguished part, however, and influential. This influence, which arose from prestige and substantial wealth, combined with the strength which the federal Bank derived from the federal accounts to constitute what may tritely be called a "money power." But it was a disciplined, conservative money power and just what the economy needed.

But it was no longer *the* money power. It was rivaled, as Philadelphia was by New York, by the newer, more vigorous, more aggressive, and more democratic part of the business world.

The businessmen comprising the latter were a quite different lot from the old. The Industrial Revolution required more men to finance, to man, and to manage its railways, factories, and other enterprises than the old business world, comprising a few rich merchants, could possibly provide. The Industrial Revolution was set to absorb the greater part of the population.

Yet when the new recruits, who yesterday were mechanics and farmers, offered themselves not only as laborers but as managers, owners, and entrepreneurs requiring capital, they met a response that was not always respectful. There was still the smell of the barnyard on their boots, and their hands were better adapted to hammer and nails than to quills and ink. The aristocrats were amused. They were also chary of lending to such borrowers; whereupon farmers' and mechanics' banks began to be set up. These banks found themselves hindered by the older banks and by the federal Bank. They and their borrowers were furious. They resisted the federal Bank in suits, encouraged by sympathetic states' rights politicians, and found themselves blocked by the federal courts.

Nor were their grievances merely material. They disliked being snubbed. Even when they became wealthy themselves, they still railed at "the capitalists" and "the aristocrats," as David Henshaw of Massachusetts did, meaning the old families, the Appletons and Lawrences whom he named, the business counterparts of the political figures that the Jacksonian revolution had replaced. Henshaw and his fellow Jacksonian leaders were full of virtue, rancor, and democracy. Their struggle was not merely to make money but to demonstrate what they already asserted, that they were as good as anyone, or more so. In their denunciation of the federal Bank, one finds them calling it again and again "an aristocracy" and its proprietors, other than the federal government, "aristocrats."

The Jacksonians, as distinct from Jackson himself, wanted a world where *laissez faire* prevailed; where, as Amos Kendall said, everyone would be free to get rich; where, as Roger Taney said, the benefits of banks would be open to all classes; where, as the enterprising exploiters of the land unanimously demanded, credit would be easy. To be sure, relatively few would be rich, and a good many already settling into an urban industrial class were beginning to realize it. But that consideration did not count with the Jacksonian leaders. They wanted a new order. But what they achieved was the age of the Robber Barons.

The attack on the old order took the form of an attack on the federal Bank for a number of reasons which may be summed up in political expediency. A factor in the success of the attack was that the president of the Bank, Nicholas Biddle, was the pampered scion of capitalists and aristocrats. He was born to wealth and prominence. He was elegant, literary, intellectual, witty, and conscious of his own merits. When at the age of 37 he became head of the largest moneyed corporation in the world he was wholly without practical experience. In his new duties he had to rely on brains, self-confidence, and hard work.

With these he did extraordinarily well. He had a remarkable grasp of productive and financial interrelations in the economy. The policies he formulated were sound. His management of the Bank, despite his inexperience, was efficient. His great weakness was naïveté, born of his ignorance of strife.

This characterization, I know, is quite contrary to the conventional one, which makes Biddle out a master of intrigue and craft such as only the purity of Andrew Jackson could overcome. But the evidence of his being a Machiavelli is wholly the assertion of his opponents, whose victory over him was enhanced by a magnification of his prowess. One of these, however, the suave Martin Van Buren, who knew him well and was a judge of such matters, ascribed no such qualities to him but instead spoke of the frankness and openness of his nature; it was in Daniel Webster that Van Buren saw wiliness.

Nicholas Biddle's response to the Jacksonian attack was inept. He was slow in recognizing that an attack was being made and ignored the warnings of his more astute friends. He expected the public to be moved by careful and learned explanations of what the Bank did. He broadcast copies of Jackson's veto message, one of the most popular and effective documents in American political history, with the expectation that people in general would agree with him that it was a piece of hollow demagogy. He entered a match for which he had no aptitude, impelled by a quixotic sense of duty and an inability to let his work be derogated. He engaged in a knock-down-drag-out fight with a group of experts as relentless as any American politics has ever known. The picture he presents is that of Little Lord Fauntleroy, lace on his shirt and good in his heart, running into those rough boys down the alley.

In his proper technical responsibilities Nicholas Biddle was a competent central banker performing a highly useful and beneficial task. It is a pity he had to be interrupted, both for him and for the economy. For him it meant demoralization. He lost track of what was going on in the Bank, he made blundering mistakes, he talked big. These things his opponents used tellingly against him. He turned from able direction of the central banking process to the hazardous business of making money, of which he knew nothing and for which his only knack lay in an enthusiastic appraisal of America's great economic future. In the end his Bank of the United States broke, he lost his fortune, he was tried on criminal charges (but released on a technicality), and he died a broken man.

This was personal misfortune, undeserved and severe. The more important victim was the American people. For with destruction of the United States Bank there was removed from an overexcitable economy the influence most effective in moderating its booms and depressions.

Andrew Jackson had vetoed recharter in 1832 and transferred the federal accounts to the pet banks in 1833 and 1834. The Bank's federal charter expired in 1836, though Nicholas Biddle obtained a charter from Pennsylvania and continued the organization as a state bank. The period was one of boom. Then in 1837 there was panic, all the banks in the country suspended, prices fell, and business collapsed. It was all Andrew Jackson's fault, his opponents declared, for killing the federal Bank. This was too generous. Jackson was not to blame for everything. The crisis was world-wide and induced by many forces. It would have happened anyway. Yet certainly Jackson's destruction of the Bank did not help. Instead it worsened the collapse. Had the Bank been allowed to continue the salutary performance of the years immediately preceding the attack upon it, and had it been supported rather than undermined by the Administration, the wild inflation which culminated in the collapse would have been curbed and the disaster diminished. Such a course would have been consistent with Jackson's convictions and professions. Instead he smote the Bank fatally at the moment of its best performance and in the course of trends against which it was needed most. Thereby he gave unhindered play to the speculation and inflation that he was always denouncing.

To a susceptible people the prospect was intoxicating. A continent abounding in varied resources and favorable to the maintenance of an immense population in the utmost comfort spread before the gaze of an energetic, ambitious, and clever race of men, who to exploit its wealth had two new instruments of miraculous potency: steam and credit. They rushed forward into the bright prospect, trampling, suffering, succeeding, failing. There was nothing to restrain them. For about a century the big rush lasted. Now it is over. And in a more critical mood we note that a number of things are missing or have gone wrong. To be sure, we are on top of the world still, but it is not very good bookkeeping to omit one's losses and count only one's gains.

That critical mood was known to others than Jackson. Emerson, Hawthorne, and Thoreau felt it. So did an older and more experienced contemporary of theirs, Albert Gallatin, friend and aide in the past to Thomas Jefferson, and now president of a New York bank but loyal to Jeffersonian ideals.

"The energy of this nation," he wrote to an old friend toward the end of Andrew Jackson's Administration, "is not to be controlled; it is at present exclusively applied to the acquisition of wealth and to improvements of stupendous magnitude. Whatever has that tendency, and of course an immoderate expansion of credit, receives favor. The apparent prosperity and the progress of cultivation, population, commerce, and improvement are beyond expectation. But it seems to me as if general demoralization was the consequence; I doubt whether general happiness is increased; and I would have preferred a gradual, slower, and more secure progress. I am, however, an old man, and the young generation has a right to govern itself. . . ."

In these last words, Mr. Gallatin was echoing the remark of Thomas Jefferson that "the world belongs to the living." Neither Gallatin nor Jefferson, however, thought it should be stripped by the living. Yet nothing but the inadequacy of their powers seems to have kept those nineteenth-century generations from stripping it. And perhaps nothing else could.

But to the extent that credit multiplies man's economic powers, curbs upon credit extension are a means of conservation, and an important means. The Bank of the United States was such a means. Its career was short and it had imperfections. Nevertheless it worked. The evidence is in the protest of the bankers and entrepreneurs, the lenders and the borrowers, against its restraints. Their outcry against the oppressor was heard, and Andrew Jackson hurried to their rescue. Had he not, some other way of stopping its conservative and steadying influence could doubtless have been found. The appetite for credit is avid, as Andrew Jackson knew in his day and might have foretold for ours. But because he never meant to serve it, the credit for what happened goes rather to the clever advisers who led the old hero to the monster's lair and dutifully held his hat while he stamped on its head and crushed it in the dust.

Meanwhile, the new money power had curled up securely in Wall Street, where it has been at home ever since.

Calhoun: An Interpretation
CHARLES M. WILTSE

What was the age of Jackson all about? Historians today are far from agreed on its essential importance. Bray Hammond, as we have noted, finds it in the attempt to liberate business, to make available to the many the entrepreneurial opportunities that were being confined to the few. Professor Arthur M. Schlesinger, Jr., finds it in the attempt on the part of the other sections of society, including the laboring classes begotten by the new industrialism, to restrain the power of the business community. Professor Marvin Meyers finds it in the attempt to restore the virtues of an earlier republican society.

John C. Calhoun's biographer Charles M. Wiltse finds in the age of Jackson something else again. In addition to his outstanding three-volume life of the great Southern leader (which appeared 1944–51), Professor Wiltse has written The Jeffersonian Tradition in American Democracy *(1935),* The New Nation, 1800–1845 *(1961), and* The Medical Department: Medical Service in the Mediterranean and Minor Theaters *(1965), one of the multi-volume* United States Army in World War II *series. He is currently editing the Daniel Webster papers at Dartmouth College. In the following essay, Wiltse concludes that Jacksonian politics were the politics of despotism and that Jackson himself was the despot. Events before the administration of Jackson had made Calhoun apprehensive for the liberty of minority interests and had led him to formulate a doctrine of nullification. But events during that administration confirmed his worst fears and persuaded him of the dire need for sustaining his doctrine.*

Professor Wiltse pursues his argument by addressing himself to the component questions which his appraisal of Calhoun undertakes to answer. What were the larger historical conditions which formed the matrix of Calhoun's thought? What were the tenets of his political philosophy in general, and of his theory of the concurrent majority in particular? How did the activities of Jackson and his cohorts confirm Calhoun's fears for liberty and for the rights of minorities?

SOURCE: *Proceedings of the South Carolina Historical Association*, 1948, pp. 26–38. Reprinted by permission of the author.

It is fair enough to say that Wiltse's analysis of Calhoun answers many significant questions but raises many others. To what extent, for example, was Calhoun's political philosophy a rationalization both of Southern economic interests and of his own personal ambitions? How can one otherwise explain his conversion from ardent nationalism to ardent sectionalism? To what extent does the theory of the concurrent majority, in seeking to preclude the tyranny of the majority, lead inevitably to the tyranny of the minority? How fair is Wiltse's assessment of Jackson, which, regarding him from the premise of Calhoun's point of view, magnifies that which seems to be high-handed and peremptory and blurs that which may have been sincerely and effectively liberal?

Calhoun's ideas represent a significant point in the route from 1787, when the Constitution was drawn up, to 1861, when the Civil War began. Social change had made infeasible the balance of jurisdiction between the central and state governments which the Founding Fathers had devised. The Southern problem was a real one. The South was fast becoming the prisoner of a system which it had helped create and to which for many decades it had held the key. Yet it is important to remember, as Professor Charles Sellers will remind us in a subsequent essay, that during this period not every Southern state was South Carolina and not every Southerner was John C. Calhoun. He was for the Southern problem a Jeremiah and a Cassandra. Many Southern leaders held substantially different convictions. The Civil War came only when Southern leadership arrived, as it did in 1860, at the viewpoint which Calhoun had assumed in 1830.

I

When the bitterly contested subtreasury bill was before the Senate early in 1838, Clay took occasion to upbraid Calhoun for his apostasy. Calhoun replied in kind, and Philip Hone, popular Whig merchant and former Mayor of New York, watching the scene from a seat on the Senate floor, noted a greater "degree of acrimony and ill-nature" than the occasion warranted. Hone was ready to excuse the South Carolina Senator, however, on the ground that he was unusually sensitive, "like all men whose position is doubtful in their own minds."

Hone was a shrewd observer and a good judge of human nature, but he was utterly wrong about Calhoun. Whatever his faults, however great his errors, Calhoun's position was never doubtful in his own mind. He sometimes arrived at his conclusions with baffling rapidity, but the most careful and mature reflection never shook his faith in his own logic. Throughout a lifetime of controversy, as he once confessed with masterly understatement to a friend, he remained "a good deal attached" to his own opinions, and "not so much disposed, perhaps, to take advice" as he ought to be. His insufferable cocksureness made enemies of men who should have been his friends, but it was also the measure of his leadership, for in times of stress and turmoil, men who doubt themselves tend to fall in behind those who have no doubts.

The quality of his intellect led Calhoun almost inevitably to generalize from his experience, and to set up his generalizations in the form of universal laws. His unshakable self-confidence, his unquestioning certainty that he was right, led him to evaluate the actions of others and in large measure to determine his own on the basis of these general principles. His own political philosophy, in short, was a framework upon which he hung his reading of history and in terms of which he interpreted the economic and political forces of his time. By the same token it is also a pattern which gives consistency and direction to a career that appeared to his enemies and often to his friends to be erratic and without principle. His course was not determined by simple reactions to people and events, but was rather derived from a system of philosophy into which people and events had first been neatly fitted and arranged. Calhoun's career will become more meaningful if we examine the major tenets of this system, and apply them as he did to the world in which he lived.

Calhoun belonged to an age of revolution, of intellectual ferment, of political and economic experimentation. He was born before the close of the American struggle for independence. When he was a precocious lad of six his father opposed ratification of the new Constitution of the United States, because it gave too much power to a central government. The French Revolution was the overshadowing fact of his youth. He was nearing maturity when Virginia rebelled against the autocracy of the Alien and Sedition Acts, and he had already entered preparatory school when the explosive force of that rebellion carried Thomas Jefferson to the presidency. He was in college when Bonaparte completed the transition from successful military commander to First Consul to Emperor, and we know from his letters that the young Carolinian watched the process and its aftermath with interest and concern.

Equally suggestive of conflict and upheaval is Calhoun's early political career. He entered public life at a time when his country was being forced to choose sides in a world-wide struggle for power. He sat in a war Congress and grappled there with the problems of foreign invasion and internal revolt. He saw, and encouraged, the rise of industry in the northern and middle states, but in the process he had ample opportunity to observe the interaction of economic forces and political events. From the vantage point of a Cabinet seat he witnessed the first sectional rift in the smooth surface of the Union, and he recognized the Missouri Compromise for what it was: an internal balance of power. It was an age of wonderful technological advances, which seemed to go hand in hand with crumbling social institutions; an age when active minds went back to fundamentals, and thinking men sought new interpretations of the world order.

Calhoun's own search for first principles undoubtedly began at an early stage of his career, but it was the fall of 1828 before he reduced his findings to orderly and systematic form in the *South Carolina Exposition.* Thenceforth he weighed every public measure in the same scale. He added illustrations from current politics or from history as he went along, but he found nothing to justify any basic modification in the general thesis. When his theory appeared in definitive form in the post-humous *Disquisition on Government* it was still essentially the same as it had been in its initial version, save for a greater completeness in its presentation. Like the authors of the *Federalist,* Calhoun drew freely from Hobbes and Harrington and Locke, but the significance of the doctrine thus derived lay not in its seventeenth century skeleton but in its contemporary dress, and in the use to which it was put.

II

Government, for Calhoun, was inseparable from human nature, and with respect to neither was he troubled by any Utopian illusions. His major premise, derived from what he called "universal experience," was that man cannot exist without some kind of government. The law of self-preservation requires that we pursue our own interests more assiduously than we pursue the welfare of others. The natural consequence is a tendency to conflict among individuals which would destroy society and make life impossible were it not controlled. The controlling force, whatever form it takes, is government. The powers of government, however, must be exercised by men, and they are therefore liable to abuse because of the same tendency in human nature that makes government necessary. Unless safeguarded in some fashion, the power given to the rulers to prevent injustice and oppression will be used by them to oppress the ruled.

This tendency to abuse of the powers of government could be successfully resisted, in Calhoun's view, only by the internal structure of the government itself. Governments so constructed that the ruled might resist the abuses of the rulers he called limited or constitutional governments. All others were absolute. In neither category did it make any difference whether the ruler was a single individual, an oligarchy, or a majority.

A constitutional government, as Calhoun visualized it, must be based on suffrage; but the right of suffrage alone is not enough to prevent absolutism. By means of popular elections the actual seat of power may be shifted from the rulers to the body of the community, but the abuse of power will not thereby be prevented unless the individual interests of the whole citizen body are the same. Where interests are many and varied, the right of suffrage merely intensifies the tendency to conflict, for each interest strives to gain control of the powers of government as a means of protecting itself. This leads to combinations and arrangements, until the whole community is divided into two hostile parties.

Indeed, the community would be so divided, even if interests were otherwise the same, by the action of the government alone. To fulfill its purpose government must be strong. It must, therefore, employ officers, collect taxes, and spend money in numerous ways. It is difficult if not impossible to collect taxes equally from the whole community, and they are never spent in equal proportions. The community will thus be divided into opposing interests by the fiscal action of the government alone. The majority, moved by the same self-interest as the individuals who compose it, will inevitably seek to aggrandize itself at the expense of the minority. The fact that, by means of the ballot, the two may change places only intensifies the tendency to conflict and disorder.

Suffrage, then, is not enough to prevent the abuse of power. There must be some other provision which will prevent any single interest or combination of interests from gaining exclusive control of the machinery of government. Calhoun's solution of the problem was the theory of the concurrent majority. Where the action of the government might affect the various portions of the community unequally, he would give to each portion, through its own majority, either a concurrent voice in the making of the laws, or a veto on their execution. To act at all the government would thus require the consent of the various interest groups of which it was composed. Its guiding principle would therefore be compromise, whereas the only principle underlying absolute governments is force.

Such, in broad outline, is Calhoun's system of political philosophy. The dogma of state sovereignty, with its correlatives of nullification and secession, was but an application of this more general doctrine, restated in terms of familiar American institutions. He found a classical basis for his theory in the separate representation of patricians and plebeians in ancient Rome, under a system that gave to each a veto on the acts of government, and a more recent illustration in the balance of classes in British parliamentary practice. In his own country he found that the basic distinction between interests, though still along economic lines, followed an essentially geographical pattern. They were not stratified as classes or estates, but were localized as sections or regions in terms of the prevalent source of livelihood, this in turn being based on climate and natural resources. The States were most nearly representative of this division, so it was to the States, in their character as members of a confederacy, that Calhoun accorded a concurrent veto power.

The controversies of the preceding three decades pointed the way so clearly to this particular application that it would have been the part of political wisdom to use it even if logic had directed otherwise. Ever since the Alien and Sedition Acts, and the countering resolutions from the legislatures of Kentucky and Virginia, a debate as to the true construction of the Constitution had been in progress. The Virginia school, for which both Jefferson and Madison had argued, held the instrument to be in fact a compact among independent sovereignties. From this it followed, under accepted principles of international law, that each party to the compact had a right to judge of its own powers, and to interpose to arrest a patent violation of the agreement. Calhoun's own intensive study during the summer and early fall of 1828 when he was preparing to write the *Exposition* convinced him of the validity of the compact theory, and served as his point of departure in his subsequent writings and speeches on the question. The Roman Tribunate had been established by agreement between warring factions. First the temporal lords and then the commons derived their equal power in Britain from contracts, signed and witnessed in due form. The concurrent veto—the great conservative principle of a society—did not just happen, but came into existence to protect each of the parties to a compact from violation by the others.

Having fitted the Constitution of the United States into its proper niche in his political philosophy, it was no difficult matter for Calhoun to reason that the House of Representatives was the organ of the numerical majority, but that the Senate, with its representation by States, was intended to give a concurrent voice to the various interests that made up the body politic. His own function in the Senate was thus to maintain the interests, economic and political, of South Carolina, and by extension the interests of the whole region of which the State was a part. He could change sides on major issues, he could change party allegiance, he could pursue a seemingly erratic course on any phase of public policy, and still be entirely consistent with his own political philosophy. He represented a minority interest, threatened with extinction by the action of a government in control of a numerical majority. Nor was it alone for South Carolina's benefit that he asserted her sovereignty against the weight of numbers. It was also for the good of the whole; for in that way alone, so he believed, could the Union endure.

III

The major tenets of this theory of the state—that governments tend to become absolute, that rulers tend to abuse their powers, that the honors and emoluments of government are in themselves enough to fix party lines and precipitate a struggle for power—all of these propositions were deductions from the nature of man. But they were far more than that. They were also obvious facts that anyone could see for himself in the day-to-day operations of the government of the United States. So clear were they to Calhoun that they gave validity to a theory otherwise abstract, and justified extremes that a man of less positive convictions might have hesitated to invoke.

History may be interpreted in many ways, according to the preconceptions of the historian, the material he elects to accept, and the sources he chooses to ignore. The age of Jackson may, indeed, have been the forerunner of later social movements in which the welfare of the common man was pitted against intrenched privilege and greed. Certainly Amos Kendall and Francis Blair, among the ablest if not the most truthful journalists of the century, strove mightily to provide the contemporary voter (and incidentally, posterity) with just such a picture. But to Calhoun, and unquestionably to a majority of the middle class of his day, Jackson's career was one unbroken march toward despotism. It proved every point in Calhoun's political theory, offered new and pertinent illustrations of the nature of the governmental process, and justified the most vigorous forms of opposition. Let us strip the Jackson era of its supporting propaganda, forget the idealism of the glosses that have been written on it, and look at it as nearly as we may with Calhoun's eyes.

The tools of power were ready to Jackson's hand when that extraordinary man took office, and his political lieutenants were thoroughly skilled in their use. The tools had been thoughtfully provided by unwitting rivals going back for nearly a decade. The four-year tenure law of 1820, conceived by the political genius William H. Crawford, was a potent engine for securing partisans. Under this innocent-looking statute district attorneys, officers of the customs service, registers of the land offices, naval agents, and a few less numerous officials were made removable at the will of the President. Their terms of office, moreover, were specifically limited to four years, so that as each presidential election rolled around, virtually the entire civilian personnel of the Federal Government would have to seek reappointment. The more numerous group of postal employees already served for limited periods, defined by the contracts under which the mails were carried.

The four-year law was in fact one element in a closely knit political machine that Crawford had built up on the foundations of the old Jefferson-Burr alliance, and which was expected to make him President in 1824. When ill-health thwarted Crawford's hopes, Martin Van Buren succeeded to control of the machine, which he deftly turned to the service of Andrew Jackson. John Quincy Adams, meanwhile, though he had less than a third of the popular vote, had been elected President early in 1825 by a House of Representatives in which tariff sentiment predominated. Immediately thereafter the leading exponent of the protective policy received the first place in the Cabinet, and the President propounded a legislative program whose maximum benefits would accrue to those states to which he owed his election. He did his best to divert former Crawford partisans to his own cause by judicious reappointments under the four-year law; and in the skillful hands of Secretary of State Henry Clay, the printing and other public contracts were given out with a view to Adams' re-election.

It was not the officeholders, however, but the beneficiaries of the tariff who made up the core of Adams' strength, and shortly before the election of 1828 he prepared to insure their loyalty with still higher duties. Calhoun was already in opposition, since his state and section were the primary victims of the administration policy. He had allied himself perforce with the Jacksonians, even though it brought him into the same camp as the bulk of the Crawford Radicals, his bitter foes of a few years earlier. Calhoun and other Southern followers of Jackson tried to block this new attempt to increase the tariff by introducing provisions deliberately obnoxious to Adams' New England supporters; but when the critical moment arrived Van Buren, Eaton, Benton, and others among the Jackson inner circle voted to pass the measure they had pledged themselves to defeat. The strength of the tariff interest had not been lost upon the Democratic managers, and with the election approaching in the fall, they made their own peace with the manufacturers. They courted both sides and won.

It was at this point that Calhoun wrote the *South Carolina Exposition*. To him, the relation between the dominant economic interest and the partisan majority was clear. In subtle, indirect, but entirely legal ways, the latter had been bought by the former. The government was already in the exclusive control of the stronger interest, and the destruction of the weaker, which was also his own, must inevitably follow, unless Jackson chose to cast the influence of his vast personal popularity into the opposite scale.

Jackson, surrounded as he was by some of the ablest party strategists ever produced in this or any other country, preferred to consolidate his power. His methods were simple, direct, and effective. He began by reappointing to office only known and proven partisans, and by removing those who were not whole-hearted in his cause in favor of men whose personal loyalty was undeviating. When the process of patronage distribution was well advanced, in December 1829, a New York paper devoted to Van Buren's interests announced its support of Jackson for a second term, and of Van Buren for the succession. From the beginning of his campaign, Jackson had been committed to a single term, but before another year was out his candidacy for re-election was acknowledged and a new "official" newspaper had been established in the capital to advance it. The Washington *Globe,* edited publicly by Blair and behind the scenes by Kendall, became thereafter an almost irresistible vehicle for party propaganda. Its financial support came from office-holders, who were required to subscribe for it—and pay in advance—or resign their places to men who would.

Another important milestone on Jackson's march to autarchy was the Maysville Road veto in 1830. The action was received with initial approbation in the South because it appeared to put an end to federal spending for public works. It could therefore be used as an argument for reducing the revenue, which meant the tariff. But it presently appeared, as other internal improvement bills received the President's approbation, that the question was still open. The only real change was that the use of public funds for improvement purposes was made subject in each case to the personal judgment of the executive. The Maysville Road was in Kentucky, whose legislature had sent Henry Clay to the Senate. Highways and canals in more compliant states might perhaps prove to be for national purposes.

Year after year McDuffie introduced into the House bills for tariff reduction in accordance with what he and Calhoun believed to be Jackson's pre-election pledge to South Carolina; and year after year they came to nothing. The vote was manipulated by the same economic interest that had elected Adams and now supported Jackson. The cost of manufactured products rose, the price of cotton fell, and Southern leaders, particularly the younger group in South Carolina, threatened revolt. So in July 1831 Calhoun restated his theory, with embellishments looking to positive action. He pointed out that although a substantial minority believed the tariff to be unconstitutional, the majority continued to pursue that policy to the economic ruin of the cotton states. So he claimed for the interest he represented a concurrent veto, but at the same time expressed his great preference for an adjustment of the point at issue by Congress.

Again the national legislature refused to make concessions, and in that refusal gave further evidence of the validity of Calhoun's premises. For there was actually strong sentiment in many parts of the country for tariff reduction, but to yield to it would have been to concede a political triumph to Calhoun. This neither Jackson nor Clay would do; so at the risk of civil war the Jacksonians and the National Republicans voted together to maintain a prohibitive scale of duties, lest the pretensions of a rival be advanced. Throughout the whole controversy the actions, motives, and purposes of Calhoun and his followers were deliberately misrepresented and distorted by Blair and his satellite editors to arouse public indignation against South Carolina and her leaders.

The issue was joined in the fall of 1832. Calhoun stated the case for state action to arrest the tariff in a letter to Governor Hamilton late in

August. It was timed immediately to precede state elections whose outcome would determine whether South Carolina would interpose her sovereignty to restrain the protective system. Calhoun showed how the majority always has an interest in enlarging the powers of government, and how human nature itself would impel the rulers to oppress the ruled, unless they were in some manner prevented from so doing. Majority rule was in fact only rule by the stronger interest, whose cupidity and ambition would inevitably hasten the government along the road to absolutism. The only barrier lay in the original sovereignty of the states.

To those who lost money by the protective policy the argument was convincing. The Nullifiers won their two-thirds majority. The convention was duly called, and the tariffs of 1828 and 1832 were declared null and void within the limits of South Carolina.

Jackson's answer to nullification was a proclamation explicitly claiming for the Federal Government—which is to say, for the majority—precisely the powers that George III had claimed over the colonies in 1776: the power to judge of its own limits, to pass laws within those limits, and to compel obedience to those laws. The partisan majority then ratified these claims by voting to the President full control over army, navy, militia, and for all practical purpose public treasury, any or all of which might be used to assist in the collection of import duties in the rebellious state. An act, Calhoun called it, to "enforce robbery by murder." He did not doubt that Jackson, like Macbeth, saw in his dreams the vision of a crown.

The compromise of 1833 put an end for the time being to the controversy between South Carolina and the general government, but it impeded not at all Jackson's progress toward undisputed power. In the summer of 1832 the President had vetoed a bill renewing the charter of the Bank of the United States. The Bank threw its influence to Clay in the fall election, and for this political opposition, Jackson undertook to destroy the "monster of corruption" without waiting for its charter to expire. In the fall of 1833, with no economic justification and the flimsiest of legal pretexts, the public funds were removed from the custody of the Bank and placed with various State institutions where they were directly under executive control. Two Secretaries of the Treasury were dismissed before one who would sign the necessary order was found, and the action was deliberately timed to precede the meeting of Congress, so that it could not be blocked.

In the Senate, where Calhoun and Clay had temporarily joined forces against the administration, the removal of the deposits was denounced as the ultimate act of tyranny. Clay read from Plutarch the description of Caesar entering the Roman Treasury sword in hand. Calhoun showed that whatever the motive, the result in this case was the same. For the

Roman had seized the public treasure to buy partisans with which to consolidate his power; and the public funds in the pet banks were being recklessly loaned out to speculators who were thereby converted into partisans. The Senate voted a resolution censuring the President. Jackson replied with a sharp protest, which the Senate refused to receive.

As of the spring of 1834 the record, in the eyes of Calhoun and those who thought with him, was something like this: First the patronage had been perverted, by instituting the general practice of removal from office without cause—the principle of the Albany Regency that "to the victors belong the spoils." The total number of employees and pensioners of the Federal Government had doubled since 1825, and expenses exclusive of payments on the public debt had likewise doubled, although the population increase was no more than 25 percent. The revenue had been enormously increased in the same interval, largely through a form of taxation which fell unequally on the different sections of the country, and the President had been given by a subservient Congress the power to perpetuate this inequality by military force. A large and unscrupulous press had been suborned to do the bidding of the party leaders. The public money had been removed without adequate reason or even plausible excuse from the depository established and safe-guarded by law, and had been placed in a group of favored banks where it was under the exclusive control of the executive. This money was being used by the banks that held it, not as a deposit but as capital, and the amount of it was loaned out three and four times over, the profits going to the pet banks and the loans going to partisans, present or prospective. Yet when the Senate condemned the final act of power, though it had sanctioned everything that went before, the President, in language skillfully chosen to inflame popular prejudices, accused the Senate of violating his rights. In the Cherokee case two years earlier Jackson had ignored a decision of the Supreme Court. Who but the most blinded partisan could fail to see in this challenge to the Senate the first step toward subverting the legislative arm as well?

All this would have been more than enough to convince men less predisposed in that direction than Calhoun that the Constitution was in fact a dead letter and Andrew Jackson a dictator of unrestrained power. But there was more to come. Jackson decreed that Martin Van Buren should be his successor, and a party convention made up of officeholders and pensioners unanimously ratified the choice. There was no subtlety about it. The President was openly and shamelessly designating his successor, and would use all the vast patronage at his command to insure the election of his favorite. To Calhoun it was as "open and palpable usurpation of the supreme executive power" as though it had been brought about by military force. Force had in fact been threatened for the collection of a relatively trifling debt from France, and that matter still hung fire early in 1836 when Van Buren's cause looked none too bright. So Jackson indulged once more in vigorous saber-rattling, until Calhoun thought him bent upon war to justify himself in accepting a third term. Napoleon was not the first who had risen to imperial estate through successful foreign war, nor was he likely to be the last.

Jackson also decreed that the resolution of censure should be expunged from the Senate Journal, and the faithful Benton, himself designated for the presidential succession at one remove, undertook the task. He was not "single-handed and alone" for long. The party machinery, reaching down to the smallest hamlet and out to the remotest reaches of a far-flung domain, was set in motion. Senators who had voted to condemn the President were marked for the slaughter, and those members of their State Legislatures who had supported them were the preliminary victims. Against each of these local representatives a campaign was waged on his home ground, with all the persuasions that a powerful and wealthy central government could command. In half a dozen states the political complexion of the legislature was changed, and Senators were "instructed" to expunge the hated judgment. Some obeyed, others resigned; but the result was the same. In less than three years the Senate majority was reversed, and Jackson was vindicated in January 1837. Not without reason Calhoun called it "the melancholy evidence of a broken spirit, ready to bow at the feet of power."

IV

To a generation accustomed to a liberal evaluation of the Jackson era, this picture will seem exaggerated and overdrawn. It was nevertheless the picture that a substantial and talented portion of King Andrew's subjects saw. Calhoun's writings and speeches only add more detail to the skeleton presented here. Substantially the same view will be found in the columns of Duff Green's *United States Telegraph*, of Richard Craillé's Richmond *Jefferson and Virginia Times*, and in many other anti-Jackson papers. It was ably and clearly expressed by many prominent actors on the scene, like John Tyler of Virginia, George Poindexter of Mississippi, Willie P. Mangum of North Carolina, even by Clay and Webster themselves. In literary form Judge Beverley Tucker's novel, *The Partisan Leader*, first published by Duff Green in 1836, traces the same forces through three hypothetical Van Buren administrations, and might have come even closer to prophecy than it did had not the panic of 1837 put an abrupt end, for the time being, to the hand-picked Jackson dynasty.

Calhoun's analysis of the political process was complete long before he gave his own support to Van Buren's program in the special session of 1837. The administration, through the normal reaction of the average man to economic catastrophe, had been thrown into the minority, and Calhoun knew that the interests of South Carolina were no safer in the hands of the Clay-Webster combination than they had been under Jackson or Adams. As the advocate of a special interest it was clearly his duty to go with whichever party was most likely to advance his cause.

The theory, to repeat, was fully matured before Jackson left office, every tenet of it having been in one way or another confirmed by the career of the Hero. It was thereafter a glass through which Calhoun observed the passing scene. The logcabin-and-hard-cider campaign of 1840 merely showed once more how partisans were lost when the well of patronage ran dry, and were won by promises, however specious. He had reasoned from the start that the struggle for place would tend to become more violent until control changed hands at every election, to be retained at last by force. He saw the partisan majority change with each election from Van Buren's day until his own death in 1850. Believing as he did that the need for new sources of political reward would force the partisan majority to seek new forms of power, he could hardly have been surprised at Polk's venture into aggressive war.

Had Calhoun been less sure of himself, less ready to pursue his own reasoning to the ultimate end, and less ingenious in fitting the facts as he saw them into the pattern as he himself had laid it down, he might perhaps have reached a different explanation of his times, and followed in consequence a different course. Being the type of man he was, and in the environment that was his, like Luther at the Diet of Worms, he could do no other. To him and to a majority of his generation liberty was the most precious possession of mankind. It was for liberty that a revolution had been fought and a new nation established—not to substitute after half a century the absolutism of a successful general for that of a demented British king. History, philosophy, and his own experience taught him that the natural tendency of government was to whittle away the sphere of liberty, and that this tendency could be resisted only by power. Calhoun was simply realist enough to know that the greatest power in any state, next to military might, is the organized power of its economic interests.

24

Who Were the Southern Whigs?
CHARLES GRIER SELLERS, JR.

In our study of history we tend to use convenient schemes. The past is wrapped up in a tidy package. It becomes considerably more teachable if also considerably less true. One can better understand results that are known to follow if one has causes that clearly explain them. Nothing would more baffle the student or distress his mentor than to have an imperfect matching of causes and results.

A notable case in point is the analysis we give, in our courses and in our textbooks, of the coming of the Civil War. To account for a conflict so dire, so bloody, and so regrettable, we have settled upon causes that could lead into it clearly, cosmically, understandably, inevitably. The North and South must have been, for several decades, moving farther and farther apart into sharply defined attitudes of increasing mutual hostility. It would untidy our package and confuse our scheme to consider that the process had not been one of decades, that hostility was not ever-increasing, and that, indeed, the attitudes were far from being clearly defined or clearly sectional.

That, however, is the lesson we can learn from the following essay by Charles Grier Sellers, Jr., of the University of California. Professor Sellers is one of the scholars who are doing so much to restudy the complex pattern of politics during the decades after the War of 1812. He has contributed considerably to an understanding of those decades through his perceptive articles as well as through his award-winning biography of James K. Polk, the first two volumes of which have thus far appeared.

In the essay below, Professor Sellers asks us to reconsider Southern politics in the 1830's and 1840's. We may give up several of our stereotypes, he submits, if we look again and more closely at the program and activities of the Southern Whigs. We may find that we have erroneously projected the Solid South of the decades after the Civil War to those before it. We may find too that we may have to replace our clear and certain explanation of why the war came with one that is appreciably more complex and certainly less convenient.

SOURCE: *The American Historical Review*, LIX (January, 1954), 335–346. Reprinted by permission of the author.

Students of the Old South have spent much of their time in recent years dispelling myths about that fabled land of moonlight and magnolias. Our understanding of the social, intellectual, and economic life of the ante-bellum South has been considerably revised and immeasurably widened by the work of a large number of able scholars.

Political history, however, has been unfashionable, and one of the results has been the survival of a series of myths about the political life of the South in the 1830's and 1840's. The key myth may be called the myth of a monolithic South: a section unified as early as the 1820's in its devotion to state rights doctrines and its hostility to the national-istic, antislavery, capitalistic North. The result of approaching ante-bellum history by way of Fort Sumter and Appomattox, this point of view found its classic statements in the apologias of Jefferson Davis and Alexander H. Stephens, but it was made respectable in the first genera-tion of professional scholarship by such historians as Herman Von Holst and John W. Burgess. It colored such early monographs as U. B. Phillips' "Georgia and State Rights" and H. M. Wagstaff's *States Rights and Political Parties in North Carolina, 1776–1861,* and is to be seen in most of the more recent works on the pre-Civil War South. It has also given rise to the corollary myths that Calhoun was the representative spokesman and political leader of the South after about 1830, and that the Whig party in the South mainly reflected the state rights proclivities of the great planters.

These myths have been strengthened by Frederick Jackson Turner's sectional analysis of our early national history. Turner's approach has been extremely fruitful, but its sweeping application has tended to exaggerate differing sectional tendencies into absolute sectional differences. The application of geographic sectionalism to individual states, moreover, has fostered the further myth that political strife within the Old South was confined largely to struggles over intrastate sectional issues between up-country and low country, hill country and "black belt."

All of these myths have some basis in fact. They are, however, the product of a misplaced emphasis which has permeated nearly all the studies of pre-Civil War southern politics. Sectionalism and state rights have been made the central themes of southern political history for almost the entire ante-bellum period. Southern opposition to nation-alistic legislation by Congress has been overemphasized. And the social, economic, and ideological lines of political cleavage within the slave states have been obscured. The early history of the Whig party below Mason and Dixon's line shows the character of these distortions.

It is too often forgotten that in the ante-bellum period the South had a vigorous two-party system, an asset it has never since enjoyed. Until at least the later 1840's, the voting southerner was much more interested in the success of his own party and its policies than in banding together with southerners of the opposite party to defend the Constitution and southern rights against invasion by the North. The parties were evenly matched and elections were bitterly contested. It was rare for any southern state to be regarded as absolutely safe for either party. Of the 425,629 votes cast in the slave states at the election of 1836, the Whigs had a majority of only 243 popular votes. In this and the three succeeding presidential elections, a total of 2,745,171 votes were cast, but the over-all margin, again in favor of the Whigs, was only 66,295, or 2.4 per cent of the total votes. In these four elections the Whigs carried a total of twenty-seven southern states and the Democrats twenty-six.

An equally close rivalry is evident in congressional representation. In the five congressional elections between 1832 and 1842, southern Democrats won an aggregate total of 234 seats, while their opponents captured 263. Whigs predominated among southern representatives in three of these five Congresses, and Democrats in two. In three of them the margin between the southern wings of the parties was five or less. We have then a picture of keen political competition, with a vigorous Whig party maintaining a slight ascendancy.

What did this Whig party stand for? The pioneer account of the southern Whigs was the essay by U. B. Phillips which, significantly, appeared in the *Festschrift* to Frederick Jackson Turner [New York, 1910]. This study shows Phillips' characteristic tendency to generalize about the entire South on the basis of conditions in his native Georgia. "The great central body of southern Whigs," he declares, "were the cotton producers, who were first state-rights men pure and simple and joined the Whigs from a sense of outrage at Jackson's threat of coercing South Carolina."

Two years after Phillips' essay appeared, Arthur C. Cole published his exhaustive monograph on *The Whig Party in the South*. Less than a third of the Cole volume is concerned with the period before 1844, when Whiggery was of greatest importance in the South, and he generally follows the Phillips interpretation of its origins. His account of the birth of the party devotes three pages to early National Republicanism in the South, twenty to the anti-Jackson sentiment aroused during the nullification crisis, and only four and a half to the fight over the national bank and financial policy. "Various interests," he says, "linked in political alliance with the few southerners whose interests and inclinations led to the support of latitudinarian principles, a still larger faction made up of those who supported constitutional doctrines on the opposite extreme and whose logical interests seemed to point against such an affiliation."

An analysis, however, of the record of the Twenty-second Congress (1831–1833) leads to somewhat different conclusions. It was this

Congress which dealt with the tariff, nullification, and national bank questions, and it was during this Congress that the groundwork for the Whig party was laid. Of the ninety southerners in the House of Representatives, sixty-nine had been elected as supporters of Andrew Jackson, while twenty-one, nearly a fourth, were National Republicans. Of the sixty-nine Democrats, twenty-five were subsequently active in the Whig party. Eighteen of the latter were state rights Whigs, while seven were not identified with the state rights wing of the opposition. These twenty-five men then, together with the twenty-one National Republicans, may be regarded as representative of the groups which formed the Whig party in the South.

These incipient Whigs voted twenty-four to twenty-one in favor of the tariff of 1832, a measure denounced by state rights men and nullified by South Carolina. They also voted twenty-four to nineteen for the Force Bill, which was designed to throttle the nullifiers. This backing of administration measures was hardly a portent of an opposition state rights party. The real harbinger of Whiggery was the vote on the national bank bill, which this group supported twenty-seven to seventeen.

The Whig party actually took shape during the Twenty-third Congress (1833–1835), in which it gained the allegiance of fifty-two of the ninety-nine southern members of the House. They voted twenty-nine to sixteen in favor of rechartering the national bank and unanimously in favor of restoring the government deposits to Biddle's institution. By a closer vote of twenty-two to twenty they supported repairing and extending the Cumberland Road. In the Twenty-fourth Congress (1835–1837) the forty-eight Whig Representatives from the South divided thirty-eight to three in favor of Clay's bill to distribute the proceeds from sales of public lands to the states. Other votes showing similar tendencies might be cited, but enough has been said to suggest that, even in the beginning, a majority of southern anti-Jackson men were far from being state rights doctrinaires.

In the light of this record it is not so surprising that only a handful of southern Whigs followed Calhoun when he marched his supporters back into the Democratic household during Van Buren's administration. The record also prepares one for the increasing manifestations of nationalism among southern Whigs which Phillips and Cole found so difficult to explain. The southern wing of the party backed Clay almost unanimously for the Presidential nomination in 1840. Tyler's nomination for Vice President was more a sop to the disappointed Clay men, of whom Tyler was one, than a concession to the state rights proclivities of southern Whiggery, the reason usually given for his choice.

The nature of southern Whiggery had its real test when Tyler challenged Clay for leadership of the party. Of the fifty-five southern Whigs in the lower house of the Twenty-seventh Congress (1841–1843), only three stuck by the Virginia President and his state rights principles, whereas Mangum of North Carolina presided over the caucus which read Tyler out of the party, and southern Whig editors joined in castigating him unmercifully. Southern Whigs supported Clay's legislative program—repeal of the Subtreasury, a national bank, distribution, and tariff—by large majorities. Even the Georgians, Berrien, Toombs, and Stephens, defended the protective features of the tariff of 1842.

Having said so much to the point that the Whig party in the South did not begin as and did not become a state rights party, it is necessary to add that neither was it consciously nationalistic. State rights versus nationalism simply was not the main issue in southern politics in this period. It is readily apparent from the newspapers and correspondence of the time that, except for Calhoun and his single-minded little band, politicians in the South were fighting over the same questions that were agitating the North—mainly questions of banking and financial policy.

It is hard to exaggerate the importance of the banking question. State and federal governments, by their policy in this sphere, could cause inflation or deflation, make capital easy or difficult to obtain, and facilitate or hinder the marketing of staple crops and commercial activity generally. And by chartering or refusing to charter banks, they could afford or deny to the capitalists of the day the most profitable field of activity the economy offered.

The banking issue is the key to an understanding of southern as well as northern Whiggery. Merchants and bankers were most directly concerned in financial policy, but their community of interest generally included the other business and professional men of the towns, especially the lawyers, who got most of their fees from merchants, and the newspaper editors, who were dependent on the merchants for advertising revenues. The crucial point for southern politics, however, is that the large staple producers were also closely identified economically with the urban commercial groups. These were the principal elements which went into the Whig party.

The Whigs generally defended the national bank until its doom was sealed, then advocated a liberal chartering of commercial banks by the states, and finally, after the Panic of 1837, demanded a new national bank. The Democrats fought Biddle's institution and either favored state-operated banks to provide small loans for farmers, as distinguished from commercial banks, or tried to regulate banking strictly or abolish it altogether.

Much of the misunderstanding about the Whig party in the South may be traced to the technique of plotting election returns on maps. Such maps tell us much, but they may also mislead. They show, for example, that the "black belts" of the lower South were the great centers of Whig strength. This has led scholars to reason: (1) that the Whig party was a planters' party *par excellence*, (2) that planters were necessarily rigid state rights men, and (3) that the Whig party was, therefore, a state rights party. *Q. E. D.!*

What the maps do not illustrate, however, is the dynamics of the political situation—the elements of leadership, impetus, financing, and propaganda, which are the real sinews of a political organization. In the case of the Whig party, these elements were furnished mainly by the commercial groups of the cities and towns, with their allied lawyers and editors. Lawyers were the practicing politicians for both parties, but the greater incidence of lawyers among the Whigs is an indication of the commercial affiliations of the party. Seventy-four per cent of the southern Whigs who sat in Congress from 1833 to 1843 are identified as practicing attorneys, as compared with fifty-five per cent of the Democrats. In the lower house of the Tennessee legislature of 1839, farmers predominated, but a fourth of the Whigs were lawyers, as compared with only a tenth of the Democratic membership.

The size and importance of the urban middle class in the Old South has yet to be fully appreciated. As early as 1831, Nashville, for example, contained twenty-two wholesale houses and seventy-seven retail stores, not to mention numerous other businesses, such as the sixty taverns and tippling houses. Even the little county seat town of Gallatin, Tennessee, boasted in 1840 ten mercantile firms, a grocer, a merchant tailor, three hotels, five lawyers, five doctors, a paper and grist mill, and eighteen artisans' establishments of one kind or another.

Businessmen dominated the towns socially, economically, and politically, and the towns dominated the countryside. This was particularly true of the "black belts" of the lower South, since the great cotton capitalists of this region were especially dependent on commercial and credit facilities for financing and carrying on their extensive planting operations. In recognition of the urban influence on politics, congressional districts were commonly known by the names of the principal towns in each—as, for example, the Huntsville, Florence, Tuscaloosa, Montgomery, and Mobile districts in Alabama.

Other evidence points in the same direction. A large majority of the stockholders in Virginia banks in 1837 lived in the areas of heaviest Whig voting. The principal commercial towns of the state—Richmond, Petersburg, and Norfolk—gave unbroken Whig majorities throughout the period 1834–1840. In North Carolina twenty of the twenty-one directors of the two principal banks in 1840 were Whigs. The first

Whig governor of North Carolina was a railroad president; the second was a lawyer, cotton manufacturer, and railroad president; and the third was one of the wealthiest lawyers in the state.

Similar party leadership obtained elsewhere. In Virginia, younger men of the type of John Minor Botts of Richmond and Alexander H. H. Stuart of Staunton actually directed the party of which Tyler and Tazewell were nominal leaders. Senators George A. Waggaman and Judah P. Benjamin were typical of the New Orleans lawyers who guided Louisiana Whiggery. Poindexter and Prentiss in Mississippi were intimately associated both personally and financially with the bankers and businessmen of Natchez. The Tennessee Whigs were led by John Bell, Nashville lawyer and iron manufacturer, who had married into the state's leading mercantile and banking house; Ephraim H. Foster, bank director and Nashville's most prominent commercial lawyer; and Hugh Lawson White, Knoxville lawyer, judge, and bank president.

This commercial bias of the Whig party did much to pave the way for the industrial development of the South after the Civil War. It was no accident that former Whigs provided a large part of the leadership for the business-minded Conservative-Democratic parties which "redeemed" the South from Republican rule and then proceeded to make the conquered section over in the image of the victorious North, often in the interest of northern capital.

Commercial considerations and the banking question did not, of course, determine political alignments in the Old South by themselves. Pro-tariff sentiment made for Whiggery among the sugar planters of Louisiana, the hemp growers of Kentucky, and the salt and iron manufacturers of western Virginia and Maryland. The more liberal policy of the Whigs toward internal improvements by both the state and federal governments won them support in landlocked interior sections and along the routes of projected transportation projects. And the fact that the Democrats generally championed a broadened suffrage, apportionment of congressional and legislative seats on the basis of white population, and other measures for extending political democracy, inclined propertied and conservative men to rally to the Whig party as a bulwark against mobocracy.

These factors, however, merely reinforced the commercial nature of southern Whiggery. The business orientation of the Whigs and the relative unimportance of their state rights wing become quite apparent if the party is described as it actually developed in the various states, rather than on the basis of general assumptions about southern politics.

A state by state analysis would indicate that, in the four border slave states and Louisiana, Whiggery was simply National Republicanism continued under a new name. The National Republicans were also strong in Virginia, but here they were joined in opposition to the

Democrats by a body of state rights men alienated from Jackson by his attitude toward nullification. The National Republican and commercial wing of the party, however, was the dominant one, especially after the business-minded Conservative Democrats joined the Whigs on the Subtreasury question. In North Carolina and Tennessee, the Whig party was formed by the secession of pro-Bank men from the Democratic party, aided in Tennessee by the local popularity of Hugh Lawson White as a Presidential candidate in 1835–1836.

The state rights element was more conspicuous in the four remaining states of the lower South. But it was by no means the majority wing of the Whig party in all of them. Both Alabama and Mississippi had an original nucleus of pro-Clay, anti-Jackson men, and in both states the nullification episode caused a substantial defection from the Jackson ranks. In Mississippi, however, a greater defection followed the removal of government deposits from the national bank. The state rights men were clearly a minority of the opposition party, which elected an outspoken foe of nullification to the governorship in 1835 and sent the ardent Clay partisan, Seargent S. Prentiss, to Congress two years later.

The state rights defection seems to have been more important in Alabama, where it was led by the able Dixon H. Lewis. The Lewis faction, however, maintained only a tenuous connection with the regular Whigs, and in 1837 Lewis and his supporters followed Calhoun back into the Democratic party. The significant fact is that in neither Alabama nor Mississippi were the Whigs greatly weakened by the departure of Calhoun's admirers.

Only in South Carolina and Georgia did avowed state rights men make up the bulk of the anti-Jackson party. When the real nature of the new party alignments became apparent, the politicians of Calhoun's state gave proof of their sincerity (and of the Presidential aspirations of their chief) by moving back to the Democratic ranks at the first decent opportunity.

The principal Whig leader in Georgia was John M. Berrien, a Savannah lawyer and attorney for the United States Bank who had been forced out of Jackson's cabinet by the Peggy Eaton affair. At the time of the election of 1832, Jackson's Indian policy was so popular in Georgia that Berrien did not dare oppose the President openly. Instead, he went about stirring up anti-tariff and state rights sentiment, while secretly trying to prevent anti-Bank resolutions by the legislature. Immediately after Jackson's re-election, however, Berrien and his allies managed to reorganize the old Troup political faction as an openly anti-Jackson state rights party. In view of Berrien's pro-Bank attitude and his subsequent staunch support of Clay's policies, it seems probable that he was merely capitalizing on state rights sentiment to defeat Democratic measures which he opposed on other grounds. At any rate, the Georgia Whigs were soon arrayed against the Jackson financial program, and they held their lines nearly intact in the face of the desertion of state rights Whigs to the Democrats on the Subtreasury issue. By 1840 Berrien had brought his Georgia followers into close harmony with the national party.

This summary sketch of southern Whiggery raises, of course, more questions than it could possibly answer definitively. It has attempted to suggest, however, that preoccupation with the origins and development of southern sectionalism has led to distortions of southern political history in the 1830's and 1840's. Specifically, it is suggested:

That only John C. Calhoun and a small group of allied southern leaders regarded state rights as the most important issue in politics in this period.

That the southern people divided politically in these years over much the same questions as northern voters, particularly questions of banking and financial policy.

That the Whig party in the South was built around a nucleus of National Republicans and state rights men, but received its greatest accession of strength from business-minded Democrats who deserted Jackson on the Bank issue.

That the Whig party in the South was controlled by urban commercial and banking interests, supported by a majority of the planters, who were economically dependent on banking and commercial facilities. And finally,

That this alliance of the propertied, far from being inherently particularistic, rapidly shook off its state rights adherents and by 1841 was almost solidly in support of the nationalistic policies of Henry Clay.

There is a great need for intensive restudy of southern politics in the 1830's and 1840's, and particularly for critical correlation of local and national developments. The story as it comes from the contemporary sources is full of the resounding clash of solid interests and opposing ideologies, hardly having "the hollow sound of a stage duel with tin swords" which one historian seems to detect. And recent events should make the student wary of state rights banners, especially when raised by conservative men against national administrations not conspicuously devoted to the interests of the propertied.

Maritime Factors in the Oregon Compromise
NORMAN A. GRAEBNER

A decade in history is seldom as integrated as mere chronology would seem to suggest or as the convenience of having the past neatly divided would seem to require. The 1840's, however, have about them a distinct unity. Clearly, this was the decade of expansion. The United States achieved virtually all of the borders that we have since then come to accept as its natural fulfillment. The Webster-Ashburton Treaty of 1842 defined the Maine boundary, Texas entered the Union in 1845, the Oregon Treaty of 1846 extended the northern boundary of the United States along the 49th parallel to the Pacific, and the war with Mexico added the great Southwest to the national domain.

Attention has naturally centered on the headlong thrust to the Pacific. Why did it occur at this time? Among the many factors responsible, which was the most important? What in particular decided the way in which the United States acquired its Pacific empire?

A noteworthy answer to these questions has been made by Professor Norman A. Graebner of the University of Virginia, who has established himself as an authority on the middle period of American history as well as on American foreign policy. His writings on the latter subject include The New Isolationism *(1956) and* Cold War Diplomacy *(1962). In his* Empire on the Pacific: A Study in American Continental Expansion *(1955), Professor Graebner suggests that, in explaining that expansion, too much has been made of the role of American settlers in the Far West, of the spirit of manifest destiny, and of the consequences of the Mexican War. The movement to the Pacific was precise, calculated, and limited in its goals. Above all, it sought specific outlets on the Coast, in the hope that they would become foci for a great Far Western trade. The accession of land was entirely incidental to the accession of ocean ports. "Any interpretation of westward*

SOURCE: *Pacific Historical Review*, XX (November, 1951), 331–345. Reprinted by permission of the author and publisher.

expansion beyond Texas," submits Professor Graebner, "is meaningless unless defined in terms of commerce and harbors."

He interprets the Oregon compromise, which pushed the American frontier to the Pacific Ocean, in precisely such terms in the following essay. Professor Graebner makes some very interesting points. He shows how widespread was the sentiment for compromise, how it focused on three specific harbors on the Pacific coast, how the relative strength of the particular program of compromise meant also the relative weakness of the general spirit of manifest destiny, and how the remarkable thing about the Oregon treaty was not so much why the Americans accepted the compromise as why the British did.

Professor Graebner's essay suggests many questions. How much did American expansion to the West proceed under the banner of national ideals, how much under the auspices of particular interests and private gain? Is it correct to set up a contrariety, as Professor Graebner's thesis does, between the manifest destiny of the United States and its pursuit of commerce, or has our destiny always been to be a nation of shopkeepers and tradesmen?

What did our Pacific advance signify diplomatically? Did it not mean that the Americas were recognized as the domain of the United States and that therefore the independence guaranteed the Latin American republics by the Monroe Doctrine was itself dependent on the territorial and commercial ambitions of the colossus of the North? What were the consequences for our foreign relations of having become a Pacific power?

What was the impact of the great territorial advance of the 1840's upon our domestic affairs? What significance did it have for the nation's commerce and transportation? What did the opening up of a new empire of land mean for American values? To what extent, moreover, did it begin the course toward civil war? The milestones of that course—the Wilmot Proviso, the Compromise of 1850 and its failure, "bleeding Kansas," and the breakdown of intersectional politics in 1860—are arrayed in a close and inevitable sequence which seems to have begun when the United States unfurled its flag on the Pacific.

Of those factors in American expansionism which sought solution in the Oregon negotiations of 1846, none appeared of greater concern to the people of the United States than the disposition of Asiatic trade. Historians have detected a persistent commercial motivation in this nation's expansion to the Pacific. Foster Rhea Dulles, for example, developed the theme that Oregon and California were not ends in themselves, but rather a "point of departure" for an Asiatic commercial empire. Richard Van Alstyne held that American expansion can be only partly explained in terms of a continental domain. Frederick Jackson Turner also took the broader view of American acquisitions on the Pacific Ocean, the mastery of which, he said, "was to determine the future relations of Asiatic and European civilization."

Mercantile interests in the Pacific, however, explain more than one powerful motive in American expansionism. Maritime calculations augmented the strong inclination of American commercial interests to seek a peaceful solution of the Oregon controversy and actually defeated the movement for 54° 40' quite as effectively as the threat of war with Great Britain or Mexico. This ardent quest for ports on the Pacific, moreover, fused Oregon and California into one irreducible issue in the minds of the commercial enthusiasts and thereby played an intensely persuasive role in the eventual delineation of this nation's western boundaries.

When the 29th Congress met in December, 1845, there was still little indication that within six months the settlement of the disturbing Oregon question would be assured. Enthusiasm for the whole of Oregon, engendered by the President's message, rapidly translated United States claims to the Far Northwest into what Albert K. Weinberg has termed a "defiant anti-legalism." It no longer mattered that the American title to territory north of the Columbia was far from conclusive, and above the 49th parallel practically nonexistent. It had become, wrote John L. O'Sullivan of the New York *Morning News,* "our manifest destiny to occupy and to possess the whole of the Continent which Providence has given us. . . ." To 54° 40' proponents that seemed to settle the issue.

It quickly becomes evident from a study of the great debate that this expanding outlook was doomed from the beginning by the patent interests of American commercialism. Too many Congressional eyes were narrowly trained on ports to permit the triumph of agrarian nationalism. For almost a half century the trading empire of Boston and New York had given to Oregon's waterways a peculiar significance in America's future economic growth. Countless early spokesmen for Oregon from John Jacob Astor to Hall J. Kelley had viewed the region primarily as an American window on the Pacific. A decade of attention to trappers, missionaries, and pioneers, furthermore, had not obscured to Congressmen the strategic importance of Oregon to the trade of Asia. Samuel Gordon of New York phrased for the House in January, 1846, his district's cogent evaluation of Oregon: "It is the key to the Pacific. It will command the trade of the isles of the Pacific, of the East, and of China." Similarly Washington Hunt, also of New York, stated this repetitious theme: "Its possession will ultimately secure to us an ascendency in the trade of the Pacific, thereby making 'the uttermost parts of the earth' tributary to our enterprise, and pouring into our lap 'the wealth of Ormus and of Ind.'"

Salt spray had also conditioned New England's outlook toward Oregon. Even before the introduction in January, 1846, of the resolution to terminate the convention of 1827, Robert Winthrop of Massachusetts had defined clearly the objectives of commercial America. "We need ports on the Pacific," he shouted. "As to land, we have millions of acres of better land still unoccupied on this side of the mountains."

During the preceding year William Sturgis, the noted Boston merchant and pioneer in the Northwest fur trade, had popularized such particularistic notions in the Bay State. In his famous lecture to the citizens of Boston in January, 1845, Sturgis admitted that the Willamette Valley was both attractive and productive, but he added that he had never seen or heard of any Oregon lands which were superior to millions of uncultivated acres east of the Rockies. His three decades of intense commercial activity in the Pacific had channeled his attention to ports and not to land. Sturgis indicated, moreover, which ports in Oregon the United States would require to assure fully her future position in oriental trade. The Columbia, he warned, was always dangerous for large ships and almost inaccessible for a considerable portion of each year. Instead, this nation's maritime greatness in the Pacific would derive from the possession of the Straits of San Juan de Fuca and its numerous branches which were "easy of access, safe, and navigable at all seasons and in any weather."

Writings of such leading authorities on Oregon as Robert Greenhow, Thomas J. Farnham, and Charles Wilkes merely affirmed Sturgis' conclusions. They likewise had convinced the representatives of commerce that the Columbia, although traditionally associated with the Northwest trade, was of questionable value as an ocean port. Their writings had made axiomatic the dangers of the sand bar between Cape Disappointment and Point Adams. "Mere description," wrote Wilkes, "can give little idea of the terrors of the bar of the Columbia: all who have seen it have spoken of the wildness of the scene, and the incessant roar of the waters, representing it as one of the most fearful sights that can possibly meet the eye of the sailor."

In sharp contrast was their description of the Fuca Straits and the sea arms to the east of them. "No part of the world," wrote Farnham, "affords finer inland sounds or a greater number of harbours than can be found here. . . ." Wilkes' description was equally glowing: "Nothing can exceed the beauty of these waters, and their safety: not a shoal exists within the straits of Juan de Fuca, Admiralty Inlet, Puget Sound, or Hood's Canal, that can in any way interrupt their navigation by a seventy-four gun ship. I venture nothing in saying, there is no country in the world that possesses waters equal to these." Herein lay the primary objectives in Oregon of the commercial Northeast.

Agrarian spokesmen of the Middle West also debated the Oregon question in maritime terms, for Oregon held a special commercial significance for their constituents. The Straits of Fuca, saw these ardent expansionists, were the future link between the Mississippi Valley, with its surplus of grain, and the teeming millions of the Orient who in exchange could enrich the great valley with cargoes of tea, porcelain, silks and satins, velvets, sugar, and spices. Through possession of the Straits, moreover, the United States would challenge the commercial supremacy of England in the Pacific. Andrew Kennedy of Indiana sought to erase all doubts as to the tangible value of Oregon to the Middle West:

> It is the inch of ground upon which we can place a fulcrum, giving us the lever by which to overturn the world of British commerce. It will give us a cluster of manufacturing and commercial states on the Pacific corresponding with our New England States upon the Atlantic. Then the inhabitants of the great Mississippi Valley, who have in their possession the garden of the world and the granary of the universe, will stretch out one hand to the East Indies through the Pacific chain, the other to Europe through the Atlantic channel, grasping the trade of the civilized earth, as we now hold in possession the means of subsistence of the whole human family.

What alarmed these nationalists, however, was the fact that the constant reiteration of the commercial value of Oregon bespoke compromise at the 49th parallel, for that boundary would give the United States access to the Straits. Representatives of commerce who wished to settle the issue and secure permanent title to the magnificent inlet pointed out that the United States could acquire all the excellent harbors in Oregon and still proffer an olive branch to England. Sturgis, for example, had argued effectively that a settlement at 49°, with the granting of Vancouver Island to Great Britain, would secure the maritime objectives of the United States and still not deny to England the navigation of the Fuca Straits, a right which she would not relinquish. On the other hand, Wilkes had described the Pacific coast north of the 49th parallel as being devoid of good harbors or any extensive commercial inducements. His writings simply substantiated the particularistic view that everything of value in Oregon lay to the south of that line. Bradford Wood of New York assured Congress that it "knew nothing of the country north of that parallel. All that had been said of its value and beauty were mere draughts on the imagination."

Uncompromising Democrats were driven by the logic of the commercial argument to assume the task not only of proving the value of Oregon north of 49°, but actually of doing so in realistic commercial terms. The acquisition of the Straits alone, they sought to illustrate, hardly touched the commercial possibilities of the Northwest coast. They reminded Congress that a compromise would lose the islands of Vancouver and Washington with their sturdy forests for American shipbuilding, their excellent harbors, their unparalleled fisheries, and their commanding position on the sea lanes. With such a settlement would go also other valuable islands and the bays and harbors which indented the coast. They demanded to know why the United States would voluntarily grant such enormous commercial advantages to Great Britain. John McClernand of Illinois impressed upon the commercial spokesmen of the House the fatal error of compromise when he declared:

> Commercially, indeed, by such a concession, we voluntarily decapitate ourselves upon the Pacific seaboard; we lose that portion of Oregon which bears the same relation to the Pacific, in furnishing a commercial marine upon that ocean, which New England now bears upon the Atlantic. . . . The American or British marine, which will whiten the Pacific, and carry direct trade to Asia, Polynesia, and South to the Atlantic capes, will be built, owned, and navigated by a similar people, who shall dwell north of the 49th parallel. This must naturally come to pass, because the harbors, bays, timber, and material, to give existence to a marine, exist there in combination; and there, too, are fisheries which nurse seamen.

Similarly warned Edward Hannegan, the Indiana Senator: "Let England possess Nootka Sound, the finest harbor in the world, commanding as it does the Straits of Fuca, and consequently the access to Puget's Sound, and she has all of Oregon worth possessing in a commercial and maritime point of view." He turned his abuse on men dominated by narrow commercialism. "It is the opinion of six-sevenths of the American people," he shouted, "that Oregon is ours—perhaps I should rather say five-sevenths, for I must leave out of the estimate the commercial and stockjobbing population of our great cities along the seaboard, a great portion of whom are English subjects, residing among us for the purpose of traffic. . . ."

Because of the "Bargain of 1844" and the necessity of agrarian unity in achieving the whole of Oregon, Hannegan would not write off the South or its Democratic leadership so easily. He castigated that region for losing interest in free territory after it had acquired Texas. There is more evidence, however, that southern low tariff advocates, such as John C. Calhoun, wanted to compromise the Oregon issue not only to avoid war with England, but also to facilitate the repeal of the British Corn Laws and the passage of a lower tariff in the United States. The Charleston *Mercury* gave evidence of this southern preference for free trade to the acquisition of the whole of Oregon when it declared that southern statesmen would not maintain a clear and unquestioned title to 54° 40' at the price of two million bales of cotton per annum.

Actually the South, like the Northeast, revealed its inclination to compromise in commercial terms. No American publication called the attention of its readers to the importance of Asiatic commerce in more ebullient terms than did *DeBow's Commercial Review* of New Orleans. Declared its editor in January, 1846:

> The commerce of the East Indies has for ages been a glittering object in the eyes of trading nations. They have sought it, and grown up to power and influence under its support. What, for instance, were the Italian republics, until the bounteous products of the East were thrown into their lap; and where were Venice and Genoa and Pisa, when the Portuguese, by a shorter passage to the Indies, had cut off these rich resources? Britain, too, what has been her advance since she has enjoyed an almost monopoly of this invaluable trade? If possessions on the Pacific Ocean will facilitate such a commerce—if they be necessary to its existence—then, surely, we will not be neglectful of these possessions.

Even those who believed that the trade of Oregon would accrue to the benefit of other sections insisted on the preservation of the Straits. But they would court no conflict by demanding more than 49°. To Jefferson Davis this guaranteed American interests in Oregon: "Possessed, as by this line we should be, of the agricultural portion of the country, of the Straits of Fuca, and Admiralty Inlet, to American enterprise and American institutions we can, without a fear, intrust the future."

Widening emphasis on the Fuca Straits developed public opinion for compromise in 1845 and 1846. Perhaps more significant was the role of Pacific commerce in diverting attention from Oregon to the harbors of California. Whereas the excellence of the Straits as an ocean port was widely recognized, their northern position blinded many to their potential value. All agreed that harbors were of real consequence in the development of commerce in the Pacific, but the known quality of San Francisco and San Diego harbors to the south convinced many travelers, politicians, and members of the press that the commercial growth of the United States in the Pacific was contingent upon the acquisition of the California ports. When by 1845 this ardent quest for ports encompassed the question of both Oregon and California, it increasingly motivated compromise at 49° and actually determined the fate of the Pacific coast from Lower California to Alaska.

Numerous travelers had pictured the harbor of San Francisco as the veritable answer to America's commercial dreams. Wilkes, who had also sailed the Straits of Fuca, believed that California could boast "one of the finest, if not the very best harbor in the world." It was so extensive, he added, that the "combined fleets of all the naval powers of Europe might moor in it." Farnham called it "the largest and best harbor of the earth" and "the glory of the Western world." New England's remarkable hide trade with California publicized the value not only of San Francisco but also of San Diego. Its bay, small and land-locked, free of surf, and sufficiently deep that vessels could lie within a cable's length of the smooth beach, was "tailor-made" for drying, curing, and loading hides. These facts were well known to commercial America.

Several noted writers and travelers, when they ignored the Straits of Fuca and recounted in detail the inadequacies of the Columbia, stimulated the intensive desire of Americans to acquire ports in California. Albert Gilliam warned that Oregon was so devoid of harbors that if the United States did not secure ports in California it would ultimately lack sea room. Similarly, Waddy Thompson, seeing no hope for commercial greatness in Oregon's waterways, praised San Francisco Bay in words reminiscent of Farnham and Wilkes.

It is not strange that many Americans were willing to trade off varying portions of Oregon for an opportunity to acquire California. That Daniel Webster had little interest in land empires but enormous enthusiasm for spacious ports for his Yankee constituents is well known. In 1843 he attempted to cede all of Oregon north of the Columbia in exchange for the acquisition of San Francisco from Mexico through British intercession. By 1845 the tremendous burst of enthusiasm for California which followed the passage of the Texas resolution had convinced many commercial expansionists that America's real interests lay to the south of Oregon. In March, Webster revealed his true interests in the American West: "You know my opinion to have been, and it now is, that the port of San Francisco would be twenty times as valuable to us as all Texas." In July, Thomas O. Larkin of Monterey in a letter to the New York *Journal of Commerce* found the solution of the Oregon question in the expanding commercial interest in California. He wrote: "If the Oregon dispute continues, let England take eight degrees north of the Columbia, and purchase eight degrees south of forty-two from Mexico, and exchange." The *Journal* concurred in the view that California was this nation's real objective and therefore the United States could well settle at the Columbia and still retain ten degrees of coast. John Tyler never lost the vision of Webster's tripartite proposal. He wrote to his son in December, 1845, regarding the Oregon question: "I never dreamed of conceding the country, unless for the greater equivalent of California, which I fancied Great Britain might be able to obtain for us through her influence in Mexico. . . ."

Other California enthusiasts desired to compromise the Oregon controversy but were far more sanguine in their objectives. Increasingly the American dream of empire on the Pacific included the ports of both Oregon and California. Writing to President James K. Polk in July, 1845, Charles Fletcher, the Pennsylvania railroad booster, pictured an American union expanding from the Atlantic to the Pacific and from the 30th to the 49th degree of north latitude. The St. Louis *Missourian* demanded both the Straits of Fuca and San Francisco harbor to fulfill the maritime destiny of the United States. Quite typically William Field, a Texan, advised the President to accept the parallel of 49° and then purchase California for as much as fifty million if necessary. He wrote: "I will only remark that if you can settle the Oregon difficulty without war and obtain California of Mexico, to the Gulf of California and the river Gila for a boundary, you will have achieved enough to enroll your name *highest* among those of the benefactors of the American people." By 1846 this unitary view of the Pacific coast had penetrated the halls of Congress where Meredith P. Gentry of Tennessee observed: "Oregon up to the 49th parallel of latitude, and the province of Upper California, when it can be fairly acquired, is the utmost limit to which this nation ought to go in the acquisition of territory."

Even the British press saw the impact of American interest in California on the Oregon question. Before the news of the Mexican War had reached Europe, the London *Times* insisted that "if any incident should lead to the declaration of war against Mexico, the seizure of Port St. Francis and of Upper California, would be considered all over the Union as a sufficient pretext for adjourning the discussion of the Oregon Convention."

It was more than the desire for San Francisco Bay that caused the California issue to prompt compromise on Oregon. The pervading fear that England was negotiating for California had not only designated that province as an immediate objective of Manifest Destiny in 1845, but also it now convinced certain American observers that the United States might well compromise on Oregon to diminish British pressure in California. In urging Americans to settle the Oregon question the Richmond *Enquirer* warned: "It is clearly England which retreats. But it is too much to retreat at the same time in Oregon and California. The English annals present no example of such prudence." In one terse observation the New York *Herald* summed up the entire issue: "We must surrender a slice of Oregon, if we would secure a slice of California."

By early 1846 the metropolitan expansionist press was fostering compromise vigorously. Because of its addiction to California, the New York *Journal of Commerce* succumbed early to the desire for compromise at 49°. By January, 1846, both the New York *Herald* and the New York *Sun* had joined the trend, as had also the Washington *Union* and the St. Louis and New Orleans press. The leading compromise editors stressed the maritime significance of the Pacific coast, denounced members of Congress who still favored the whole of Oregon even at the cost of war, and minimized the worth of Oregon's soil, especially as compared to that of California. The *North American Review*, quite characteristically, after citing Wilkes, Farnham, and Greenhow to prove that Oregon was an "arid and rugged waste," inhabited only by hunters and Indians, concluded in January that "it is hardly too much to say that what Siberia is to Russia, Oregon is to the United States."

Even after the outbreak of the Mexican War, expansionist editors continued uninterrupted in their commercial outlook toward the Pacific. To them the settlement with England had been made particularly acceptable by the anticipation of adding certain Mexican ports to the American union. As war broke out in May, 1846, the New York *Herald* urged the United States to seize San Francisco so that men would forget the whole of Oregon. One California correspondent predicted the result of the speedy occupation of the Pacific ports by the American naval commander: "We shall have then a country, bounded at the North latitude by 49 degrees, to the Pacific—and the South on the same ocean by 32 degrees—and the western and eastern boundaries, being what Nature intended them, the Pacific, with China in the outline, and the Atlantic with Europe in the background." Such prospects pleased the editor of the New York *Herald.* He noted that the proposed boundaries gave the United States 1,300 miles of coast on the Pacific, several magnificent harbors, and "squared off our South-Western possessions." One writer for the New York *Journal of Commerce* in December, 1846, rejoiced that with the acquisition of New Mexico and California the territory of the United States would "spread out in one broad square belt from one ocean to the other, giving us nearly as much coast on the Pacific as we possess on the Atlantic." Obviously the imaginary line of 42° meant little to the American commercial expansionists of a century ago.

American historians have analyzed thoroughly the factors which compelled Great Britain to settle the Oregon question in 1846. In fact, in British rather than American policy is to be found the key to the several well-known interpretations of the Oregon compromise. England had long since quit her claim to the regions south of the Columbia, while the United States had traditionally offered to yield all territory north of 49°. As late as July, 1845, Polk had offered to treat on that line. Viewed from diplomatic history, therefore, a compromise at 49° was a British surrender. Melvin Jacobs has stated clearly this widely accepted assumption:

> Taking into consideration the indefiniteness and weakness of claims to new territory on the basis of discovery and exploration, in contrast to occupation and settlement, instead of raising the question as to the reasons why America did not secure the whole of Oregon to fifty-four degrees and forty minutes, it appears to be more appropriate to raise the question as to why England lost the territory between the Columbia River and the forty-ninth parallel after she had both occupied and, apparently, possessed it.

Despite the many domestic pressures that drove Britain toward compromise, the British willingness to accept the 49th parallel, just as the American, was largely motivated by maritime considerations.

Two important streams of British trade met in Oregon waters, the commerce with the Orient and the northwest fur trade of the Hudson's Bay Company. To British officials and traders the Columbia River, therefore, presented a watercourse of peculiar significance, furnishing an ocean port as well as an access to the interior fur-bearing regions. For this reason the British during the early Oregon negotiations held to the Columbia boundary. George Canning, the British minister, giving evidence of his own commercial motivation during the 1826 negotiations, wrote that he would not care to have his "name affixed to an instrument by which England would have foregone the advantage of our immense direct intercourse between China and what may be, if we resolve not to yield them up, her boundless establishments on the N.W. Coast of America." Canning attempted unsuccessfully to quiet the early American demand for 49° by offering a frontage of isolated territory on the Straits. For the next two decades Britain continued to hold to the Columbia line. In 1846, however, only a British surrender of territory made possible a peaceful settlement.

Several American students of the Oregon question have attributed British conciliation to the pressure of American pioneers. It is unquestionably true that the British viewed their growing numbers south of the Columbia with dismay, for they endangered the peace and disrupted the fur trade. When in 1845 the Hudson's Bay Company moved its main depot to Vancouver Island because of the decline of the fur traffic and American immigrant pressure, it admitted that its perennial *sine qua non* in any treaty, the Columbia, was no longer its vital trade route. This surrender of the Columbia, says Frederick Merk, was the key to the Oregon settlement.

Lord Aberdeen, who as Foreign Secretary led the British government toward compromise, analyzed cogently his inclination to retreat in terms of Pacific ports. He wrote to Sir Robert Peel in September, 1844:

> I believe that if the line of the 49th degree were extended only to the waters edge, and should leave us possession of all of Vancouver's Island, with the northern side of the entrance to Puget's Sound; and if all the harbors within the Sound, and to the Columbia, inclusive, were made free to both countries; and further; if the river Columbia from the point at which it became navigable to its mouth, were also made free to both, this would be in reality a most advantageous settlement.

A year later Aberdeen admitted that England could obtain everything worth contending for in Vancouver Island, the navigation of the Columbia, and free access to all ports between the Columbia and 49 degrees.

Aberdeen's purpose in 1845 and 1846 was to propagandize the British people into an acceptance of his view. His specific task was to convince them that British claims to Oregon were imperfect, that

Oregon was not worth a dispute with the United States, that the British fur trade was dying, that the Columbia offered little security for heavy commerce, and that the United States had reasonable claims to good harbors on the Pacific. Several major British journals, especially the *Edinburgh Review*, the *Illustrated London News*, the *Quarterly Review*, and the London *Times*, spread these doctrines for him. Thus the British willingness to compromise in 1846 was in a sense a triumph for Aberdeen's maritime views.

Historians have attributed the British inclination to settle at 49° to two other factors. First, such students of the question as Thomas P. Martin and St. George Sioussat have concluded that the harvest shortage of 1845 and the corresponding need of American grain contributed to British pacificism. Merk, however, has challenged this interpretation by citing evidence that the scarcity of food in the British Isles was not sufficient to alter prices or trade considerably. A second popular interpretation, the free trade analysis, rests primarily on a variety of British statements such as one of Lord Peel: "The admission of Maize will I believe go far to promote the settlement of Oregon." Apparently certain British spokesmen believed that the opening of the British grain market would provide a market for the surplus wheat of the Old Northwest and reduce the persistent Anglophobia of the region in direct proportion. Perhaps more agrarian tempers were aggravated than soothed by this British action, however, for it removed the advantage of easy entry into the British empire trade through Canada.

The real significance of the famous British Corn Law crisis in motivating compromise rested in its creation of a realignment of British parties that brought into power in England a coalition that was willing to settle the Oregon issue for an equitable distribution of ports. The essential fact is that by May, 1846, Aberdeen, upon the passage of the resolution by the United States Congress to terminate the joint convention of 1827, was permitted by both the British government and British public opinion to proffer to the United States an acceptable treaty.

That James K. Polk without hesitation presented the British proposal to the Senate indicates that he had moved far from his December position. Historical analyses of this policy shift fall basically into two categories. Julius Pratt has developed the thesis that Polk was convinced by Minister Louis McLane early in 1846 that the British would fight and that thereafter the President was less inclined to look John Bull in the eye. Other historians such as Albert Weinberg attribute Polk's desire to compromise to the growing threat of war with Mexico.

Although it is true that there was tremendous pressure placed upon the President to avoid war with England, it must be remembered that long before Polk forced the Oregon issue upon Congress and the British ministry in his message of December, 1845, his vision of America's future position in the West had been fashioned by the Pacific. It was largely his interest in ports that turned his attention to California in 1845. He admitted to Senator Thomas Hart Benton in October that in his desire to limit British encroachment in North America he had California and the bay of San Francisco as much in mind as Oregon. He demonstrated this interest when he attempted to purchase that port from Mexico in the Slidell mission of November, 1845. Yet at no time did the President lose sight of the Straits of Fuca. In his first message to Congress he declared that the United States could never accept a settlement in Oregon that "would leave on the British side two-thirds of the whole Oregon territory, including the free navigation of the Columbia and all valuable harbors on the Pacific." Finally, in late December, 1845, Polk noted in his diary that he would submit to the Senate for its previous advice any British offer that would grant to the United States the Straits of Fuca and some free ports to the north.

This brief analysis of the maritime objectives of the national leaders would indicate that the Oregon settlement was no compromise at all, for Polk and Aberdeen were essentially in agreement over an equitable distribution of Oregon waterways even before the great debate of 1846. For large portions of both the British and American people, however, the final settlement was viewed as a sacrifice. The task of leadership in the crisis consisted of bringing public opinion in both nations to an acceptance of the 49th parallel. Since the unequivocal language of Polk's message tied his hands, the movement for compromise in the United States had to come from Congress and the metropolitan press. For Aberdeen the task of securing support was more difficult, since Britain, unlike the United States, was forced to retreat from its traditional offer.

Both nations as a whole were content with the distribution of land and ports. During the closing argument on the Oregon treaty Benton passed final judgment on the 49th parallel: "With that boundary comes all that we want in that quarter, namely, all the waters of Puget's Sound, and the fertile Olympian district which borders upon them." The Oregon treaty brought to the business community on both sides of the Atlantic relief from the evils of suspense and uncertainty. A brief poem of America's leading expansionist press, the New York *Herald*, summed up well the attitude of the English-speaking world:

> Old Buck and Pack
> Are coming back
> And will soon together dine.
> And drink a toast
> Upon their roast
> To number forty-nine.

SOCIETY IN FERMENT

26

The Frontier in Illinois History

RAY A. BILLINGTON

Westward expansion has been a central feature of American history. During the early decades of the nineteenth century this expansion reached a new peak. Impelled by many factors, principally the quest for land, men pushed the lines of settlement across the Alleghenies and along the Gulf of Mexico into the Northwest Territory and into a new South. In less than a decade, six new Western states were admitted to the Union: Louisiana (1812), Indiana (1816), Mississippi (1817), Illinois (1818), Alabama (1819), and Missouri (1821). Within each of these states a larger historical process was in motion, involving an interplay between the institutions which the new settlers brought and the frontier conditions to which they brought them.

What were the basic features of this process? Answering this question has been the object of much of the writing of Ray A. Billington, who pursued a long career in teaching at Clark, Smith, and Northwestern before becoming Senior Research Associate at the Huntington Library in 1963. Professor Billington is clearly the principal disciple of Frederick Jackson Turner, the founder and most famous teacher of American frontier history. His mentor's premises, which he has in some respects modified, have served Professor Billington as points of departure for many of his writings, including West-ward Expansion *(1949) and* The Far Western Frontier, 1830–1860 *(1956), a volume in the* New American Nation *series.*

In the essay which follows Professor Billington shows the frontier process in operation in Illinois at the time of its settlement. Here he finds an

SOURCE: *The Journal of the Illinois State Historical Society,* XLIII (Spring, 1950), 28–45. Reprinted by permission of the author and publisher.

exemplary instance of the balance between the forces of men's traditions and those of wilderness life. In defining the balance, he poses and answers some very basic questions. How much were the inherited institutions of the pioneers altered by natural conditions? Where did the society of settlers come from and what new amalgam did they form? How did man's struggle with nature affect his mechanical ingenuity? What impact did frontier living have upon the growth of democratic theory and practice in Illinois? How did the frontier people's faith in progress evidence itself? Finally, in what respects was the Illinois pioneer more an opportunist than a rationalist, more the man of practical reality than of consistent theory?

The significance of Illinois for Professor Billington therefore is that it reveals the forces at play in westward expansion and settlement. It is a commentary on the dynamic push which in the early decades of the nineteenth century thrust across the Mississippi. It adumbrates the effervescent spirit of manifest destiny which led to the farthest reaches of the continent and to the Mexican War. In Illinois might be heard too the early rumblings of the conflict which was to burst out as civil war. Certainly, as Professor Billington aptly puts it, in the Illinois frontiersman of this period one could find a perfect answer to Crèvecoeur's question: "What then is the American, this new man?" It would be well for the student to remember that the frontier moved and changed and ultimately passed away. In the process there emerged a striking succession of new Americans and new men.

The historian who attempts to isolate the unique characteristics of the people of any American region must search for clues in both their imported traits and the environmental influences operating upon them. Of the latter, none has been more influential than the impact of the frontier; in the continuous rebirth of civilization that occurred during the settlement process both men and institutions were "Americanized" as inherited practices or traits were cast aside. This mutation followed no set pattern, for in no two regions of the West were the ingredients of the new society—man and nature—blended in identical proportions. At times man was so influenced by tradition that he refused to bow completely to the forest environment; thus the Massachusetts Bay Puritans were too united by religious ties to respond to the centrifugal forces of wilderness life. At other times the environment was sufficiently overwhelming to create utterly distinct behavior patterns; the Mormons who settled the deserts of Utah exhibited few of the traits usually found on the frontier. In relatively few areas were the two ingredients sufficiently balanced to create a completely typical result. One favored spot where this occurred was Illinois.

This can best be realized by restating several general propositions concerning the frontier process, then applying them to the early history of the state.

First, the frontier was an area where man's inherited institutions were significantly altered by natural conditions. Illinois offers a unique example of this transformation, for within its borders are two differing soil areas, each of which influenced not only the settlement process but subsequent economic developments. These resulted from two of the glaciers that ground their way southward during the Pleistocene Age. One, the Illinoian Drift, covered the state as far south as the Ohio River, leaving behind as it receded a rugged hill country littered with glacial debris, and a compact clay soil marked by the absence of such essential elements as sulphur, potassium, carbon, and nitrogen. At a later day in geological history a second ice sheet pushed slowly down from the north—the Wisconsin Drift. Grinding down hills into smooth prairies, this glacier left behind a level countryside and a light loam soil rich in both the humus and chemicals needed for fertility. The Wisconsin Drift, however, did not benefit all parts of the state equally. The extreme southern limit of its advance was marked by the clearly defined Shelbyville Moraine, the most important natural boundary in all Illinois. Pioneers were quick to notice the difference between lands lying north and south of this dividing line. Above the moraine the countryside was level, the soil deep, and the swamps numerous— swamps that could readily be drained to form humus-rich fields of immense productivity. Below, the rugged hills and glacier-strewn waste discouraged frontiersmen.

For a century both land prices and agricultural yields confirmed the judgment of the first settlers. In 1904, for example, lands just north of the moraine sold for from $75 to $125 an acre; those to the south for $30 an acre. In the same year fields in Coles County, lying in the glaciated area, yielded thirty-six bushels of oats or forty of corn to the acre; in Cumberland County, just to the southward, only twenty-eight bushels of oats or thirty of corn were produced. Higher yields, in turn, allowed a greater degree of population concentration; a typical county north of the moraine contained 42 per cent more people than another to the south. This reflected a more advanced stage of urbanization, on which depended cultural progress. The counties north of the Shelbyville Moraine, with more taxable wealth, could support better schools, colleges, libraries, and similar intellectual agencies. Although twentieth-century industrialization has lessened the effect of this natural boundary, Illinois' early history provides an outstanding example of that impact of nature on man, which typified the Americanization process.

Secondly, the frontier was an area where men of all sections and all nations met to form a new society, enriched by borrowings from many lands. In few other areas of the West did the accident of migration result in such a thorough blending of many racial strains as in Illinois. From the Southeast, from the Middle States, from New England, from older states of the Northwest, and from Europe came the state's pioneers, each contributing new flavor and new strength to the social order that evolved.

The first settlers were from the South. Some came from the seaboard regions, but more left homes in the uplands of the Carolinas, Virginia, Tennessee, or Kentucky, where a mingling process had already produced a mixed population from Scotch-Irish, German, and English strains. Skilled in the techniques of conquering the wilderness, these sturdy woodsmen were crowded from their old homes by the advance of the plantation frontier during the first quarter of the nineteenth century. Moving northward over Kentucky's Wilderness Road, or drifting down the Ohio River on flatboats, they reached such embarkation points as Shawneetown by the thousands, then fanned out over the trails that led to the interior: some along the Great Western Road through Kaskaskia and Cahokia to St. Louis, others along the Goshen Road toward Alton, still others northward through Carmi to Albion after that town was founded in 1818. Filling in the rich bottom lands of the Ohio and Mississippi first, they soon spread over the forested portions of southern Illinois, seeking always the dense timber that testified to good soil. There they girdled the trees, planted their corn, raised their log cabins, split rails for their worm fences, shook through regular attacks of malaria, and steadily extended their civilization over a widening area.

The predominantly southern character of Illinois' early migration cannot be overemphasized. In 1818, when the first rough survey was taken, 38 per cent of the settlers were from the South-Atlantic Seaboard, almost 37 per cent from Kentucky and Tennessee, 13 per cent from the Middle States, 3 per cent from New England, and 9 per cent from abroad. Thus 75 per cent of the people were from the South, as opposed to 25 per cent from all the rest of the United States and Europe. Nor did this ratio change during the next decade; as late as 1830 observers believed that Illinois was on its way to becoming a transplanted southern commonwealth, with all the institutions—including slavery— of its sister states south of Mason and Dixon's Line.

Then the tide turned. The Erie Canal was responsible. The opening in 1825 of that all-water route between the Hudson River and Lake Erie shifted the center of migration northward as New Englanders and men from the Middle Atlantic States found the gateway to the West open before them. Now the Great Lakes, not the Ohio River, formed the pathway toward the setting sun. From Buffalo, New York, steamboats carried pioneers to new towns that sprang up as embarkation points: Cleveland, Toledo, Detroit, and Chicago. In 1834 80,000 people followed this route westward; eleven years later the number reached 98,000.

Michigan and Ohio attracted some, but Illinois, which was scarcely settled north of Alton, was the mecca of more. As they landed on the Chicago wharfs, that frontier hamlet blossomed overnight into a booming city. Such was the demand for buildings to house the newcomers that lots which sold in the spring of 1835 for $9,000 fetched $25,000 four months later. Most stayed in the cramped city only long enough to lay in supplies for the overland trip to the farm at the end of their rainbow. As they flooded over the countryside the statistics of the government land offices told a dramatic story: a quarter of a million acres were sold in 1834, two million in 1835, almost four million in 1836.

The newcomers were as predominantly northern as the earlier immigrants were southern; fully 75 per cent were from north of the Mason and Dixon Line. Some came in groups from their native New England, fully equipped with pastor, schoolmaster, and eastern ways of life. Rockwell, Tremont, and Lyons were planted in this way between 1833 and 1836; a year later Wethersfield was laid out by Yankees whose childhood had been spent in the shaded streets of that old Connecticut village. More came as individuals or in families, bringing with them the habits of their native New England and an insatiable thirst for land that did not, as one advertiser put it, stand on edge. As they came they transformed northern Illinois into a replica of the Northeast, just as southern Illinois was a duplicate of the Southeast. "Each of these two fountains of our civilization," wrote the editor of the *Democratic Monthly Magazine* in 1844, "is pouring forth its columns of immigrants to the Great Valley, forming there a new and third type that will reform and remold the American civilization."

Yet no frontier state could be typically American without the invigorating impact of European migration. Illinois benefited from the transfusion of this fresh blood during the 1840's. First to come were Irish peasants who drifted westward as laborers on canals and railroads; many eventually settled along the path of the Illinois and Michigan Canal. They were soon joined by German pioneers who had been driven from their homes by a devastating potato famine. Taking advantage of the cheap transportation offered by returning cotton ships, they reached New Orleans, then traveled up the river to the cheap lands of Missouri, Illinois, and Wisconsin. With them came a sprinkling of intellectuals fleeing the political tempests of 1848. Few in numbers but large in influence, these leaders injected German customs and thought into the Illinois social order to a degree rarely equalled in other states.

If an Illinoisan had paused to take stock of his state at the close of the settlement period he would have been proud of what he saw. In few commonwealths was acculturation so complete. Here in 1850 lived 334,000 native sons, 138,000 born in the South, 112,000 from the Middle Atlantic States, 37,000 from New England, 110,000 from the other states of the Old Northwest, and 110,000 foreign-born. Each group contributed something to the composite whole; each made Illinois more completely American. "The society thus newly organized and constituted," wrote a Westerner, "is more liberal, enlarged, unprejudiced, and, of course, more affectionate and pleasant, than a society of people of *unique* birth and character, who bring all their early prejudices, as a common stock, to be transmitted as an inheritance in perpetuity."

Illinois' good fortune was in marked contrast to the fate of its neighbor, Indiana. When the settlement of the two territories began, they seemed destined to follow a parallel course. To Indiana, as to Illinois, came the southern migratory stream, to fill the southern third of the state in the first quarter of the nineteenth century. If the frontier process had operated normally, New Englanders, men from the Middle Atlantic States, and Europeans would have moved into its northern portions. That they failed to do so was due to two unhappy circumstances.

One was the state's bad reputation. Travelers who entered Indiana from the northeast were forced to cross the elongated morass along the Maumee River known as the Black Swamp, then thread their way across the swampy tablelands of the upper Wabash where drainage was so poor that water frequently covered the trails even in periods of normal rainfall. They never forgot this first impression. In books, in newspaper articles, and in conversations they always referred to "the swamps and bogs of Indiana"—a phrase soon indelibly associated with the name of the state. In vain did Hoosiers protest that the prairies of Illinois were no drier; for decades northern pioneers passed over poorly advertised Indiana.

An even more effective deterrent to settlement was the activity of land speculators, of whom a Hartford businessman, Henry L. Ellsworth, was most prominent. Impressed with the beauty and richness of Indiana's prairies while on a western trip in the 1830's, Ellsworth moved to Lafayette in 1835 and promptly began amassing land until his holdings totaled 18,000 acres. He farmed them so profitably, even after the Panic of 1837, that other Easterners made similar investments. Ellsworth encouraged this; in his little book, *The Valley of the Upper Wabash* (1838), he promised to farm prairie land for any investor, paying the owner 8 or 10 per cent, and taking his own profit from half the remaining surplus. Numerous Easterners entered into such contracts with Ellsworth; others were persuaded to buy Indiana lands by his advertising. Within a few years their holdings blanketed the central and northern portions of the state, effectively discouraging settlement by the five-dollar-an-acre price demanded for resale. Not until the 1850's did mounting taxes force the speculators to unload; then purchasers were principally younger sons from southern Indiana who moved northward in search of land. Ellsworth's propaganda and poor advertising, by closing the gates to pioneers from the Northeast and Europe, deprived Indiana of that population blending that so benefited Illinois.

Thirdly, the frontier was a region where mechanical ingenuity was highly developed in the never-ending battle between man and nature. In Illinois settlers were forced to display a higher degree of adaptability than on most frontiers, for they faced a natural barrier that would have proved insurmountable to men of lesser stature: the vast central grassland. This was a forbidding obstacle to pioneers trained by two centuries of experience in the technique of clearing wooded areas. They had learned to judge the fertility of land by the density of its forests, to build their homes and fences from the plentiful wood supply, to secure their fuel from the wilderness, to obtain water from springs or streams, and to depend for shelter on the bands of timber left standing when fields were cleared. The habits of woodland pioneering were so deeply engrained in the average pioneer that any deviation was difficult if not impossible.

Yet that adjustment had to be made before Illinois could be settled. In the northern portions of the state vast fields blanketed by six-feet-tall grass were interlaced with forest lots or crisscrossed by the bands of timber that followed every stream, but in central Illinois the prairies stretched away to the horizon on every side. Every instinct told the pioneer to avoid these grasslands. How could soil that would not support trees grow crops? Where could he get wood for his cabin, his fences, and his fuel? How could he obtain drinking water in a region where sluggish streams were thick with silt? How could he farm fields that were turned into swamps by every rainfall? And, most important of all, how could he bring the prairies under cultivation when tough sod shattered the fragile cast-iron plows which had proved adequate in timbered areas? Those were the problems that had to be solved before central and northern Illinois could be settled.

Little wonder, in view of these obstacles, that the shift from forest to prairie was made slowly. Farmers in the wooded areas along the Fox and Rock rivers first began pasturing their cattle on near-by grasslands, then experimentally turned under some of the sod. When the land proved productive, others imitated their example, until a ring of farms surrounded the open grassland. Each year the cultivated fields were expanded until eventually they met. By 1850 all the grasslands of Illinois were under the plow save the central portions of the Grand Prairie. Not until the Illinois Central Railroad penetrated that region five years later was the last unsettled area occupied.

No simple account of the settlement of the state reveals the inventiveness, ingenuity, and boldness displayed by the Illinois pioneers.

They overcame one of their most deep-seated prejudices when they learned that a soil's richness could not be determined by the density of its timber. They discovered that "stone coal" could be brought in more easily than wood for heating. They learned how to sink wells, and developed both well-drilling machinery and windmills to ease the back-breaking task of providing water. They discovered that cooperative efforts were necessary for drainage. And they invented special plows, pulled by from four to six oxen, to break the tough sod. The expense involved in the use of these cumbersome contraptions, which could be hired from a local operator at a rate of from two to five dollars an acre, created a demand for more efficient equipment which sent inventors to their drafting boards; one landmark was passed in 1837 when John Deere gave the world the steel plow. They learned to plant a "sod crop" by cutting upturned furrows at intervals with an ax, then dropping in a few kernels of corn. Although these fields could not be cultivated, the good Illinois soil produced yields up to fifty bushels to the acre, while the roots helped break up the rotting sod.

Learning new techniques and inventing new implements, the Illinois farmer not only solved one of the most troublesome problems faced in the conquest of the continent but by his very ingenuity stamped himself as a typical product of the American frontier.

Fourthly, the West was a region where democratic theory was enshrined and democratic practices perpetuated. Living in a land where all men were reduced to equality by the greater force of nature, conscious of the economic opportunity that promised to make the poor rich, and impatient of restraints from uninformed Easterners who knew nothing of western problems, the frontiersman insisted that each man's right to rule himself was as fundamental as his right to good land. The Westerner made few contributions to the mechanics of democracy, for in the realm of theory he was imitative rather than inventive, but he did show a marked tendency to adopt the most liberal practices of the East he had left behind. Illinois, as a typical frontier state, exhibited this tendency admirably.

Its people's democratic faith was first reflected in the Constitution of 1818. At this time Southerners predominated; in the constitutional convention twenty-one were from the South, two had been born in Illinois of southern parents, five came from the Middle Atlantic States, and only one from New England. Despite this influence toward conservatism, despite even the perpetuation of slavery—in the form of indentured servitude—the Illinois constitution was a model of democratic practice. Based on the frames of government already adopted in Ohio, Tennessee, and Kentucky, but going beyond them in the direction of popular rule, it vested virtually sovereign power in the legislature, while reducing the governor to a mere figurehead. True, the chief executive, together with the justices of the State Supreme Court, constituted a council of revision empowered to veto acts of the assembly, but as laws could be passed over the veto by a mere majority vote, this meant nothing. Property qualifications for voting and office holding were swept away, and all adult males who had lived in the state for six months were allowed to vote. Mounting western nationalism was reflected in a provision that the governor must have been a citizen of the United States for at least thirty years.

The Constitution of 1818, democratic as it was, only paved the way for still more liberal changes during the next years; eventually even the state judges were popularly elected. Illinois, a frontier state, believed, even before Lincoln's classic statement, in rule of the people, by the people, and for the people.

Fifthly, the frontier was a region of optimism, of boundless belief in the future. The Illinois frontiersman shared with his fellow Westerners an exuberant faith in progress; like them, too, he had a rambunctious confidence in his ability to make his dreams come true. One manifestation of this spirit was his willingness to support colleges. Although primary education was not fully established until the passage of the school law of 1855, institutions of higher learning began to multiply a quarter-century earlier, many of them church-supported schools dedicated to the task of producing intelligent congregations and learned ministers. By 1840 the thinly settled, poverty-ridden Prairie State boasted no less than twelve colleges. Pioneers unable to read and write were anxious to contribute time and money to assure their children a better opportunity, their community a richer culture. In few other states were frontiersmen willing to invest so heavily in the future.

On a less elevated plane, frontier optimism in Illinois found expression in speculative land buying. In no other wilderness commonwealth were so many acres engrossed by jobbers, so many "paper towns" laid out, so much absentee capital invested, in the years before 1850.

They were legion, the starry-eyed speculators who gobbled up the forests and prairies of the state. Many were farmers who bought more land than they could use, hoping to sell off the remainder to later comers; in 1850 seven million acres of Illinois land that had been sold but not improved was largely held by such purchasers. Others were local businessmen or politicians who accumulated strategically located lands against the price rise they believed inevitable. Still others were wealthy Easterners or Southerners whose careers were devoted to speculation. Men of this ilk engrossed 6,000,000 acres in Illinois between 1847 and 1855 by buying up soldiers' warrants at from fifty cents to a dollar an acre; others of the same fraternity bought 7,000,000 acres of rich countryside near Springfield between 1833 and 1837. A favorite occupation of all these speculators was the accumulation of prospective town sites.   Scarcely a bend or fork of a stream deep enough to wade in, scarcely a bay on Lake Michigan that would shelter a rowboat, scarcely a spot on any imagined canal or railroad that might conceivably be built in the future, that was not grabbed up by some land jobber.   Most of these never got beyond the "paper" stage —where maps were drawn to induce gullible Easterners to buy town lots—yet in one northern Illinois "town" that had only one house, lots sold for $2,500 each, while a Chicago observer, witnessing the mad scramble for town sites, seriously proposed reserving one or two sections in each township for farming!

Finally, the frontier was an era where opportunism, rather than an enduring belief in any one theory or system, shaped the character of economic life and thought.   Students of the westward movement, failing to recognize this, have frequently insisted that the West was a region of economic radicalism, of *laissez faire,* of rugged individualism. True, the frontiersman was an economic radical on occasion, but he was just as likely to be found among extreme conservatives; he was an individualist if such a course seemed feasible, but he did not hesitate to embrace the cause of collectivism if that path promised greater profits. He did believe in *laissez faire*—some of the time—but he was ready to demand national or state aid, and even governmental ownership of essential services, if such a course seemed wiser. The frontiersman, in other words, was a practical realist who believed in following the path that promised greatest immediate returns, regardless of past precedents. An opportunist rather than a theorist, he showed no embarrassment when forced to shift his thought with the changing times. The Illinois pioneer reflected this point of view. His vacillating opinion on the question of state-operated transportation facilities and on matters of finance illustrated how well he fitted into the frontier mold.

He first became aware of the transportation problem in the 1820's and 1830's when accumulating agricultural surpluses in interior Illinois brought home the need for highways to the main trade arteries of the West: the Mississippi River system and the Great Lakes. Statisticians were everywhere present to demonstrate the profits that would go to the pioneer if these could be built. A bushel of corn, they pointed out, sold in the interior for from twelve to twenty cents; at Chicago or on the Ohio River that same bushel fetched fifty cents. As the average farmer produced sixty bushels to the acre, lead-pencil engineers needed only enough ciphering paper to prove the stratospheric profits that would be the farmer's with better outlets. For every hundred-acre farm the increased return would be $1,800 a year; for the ten million acres soon to be in production the saving would be $180,000,000! Roads and canals would transmute Illinois' poverty into luxurious affluence. So all agreed, and they were equally sure that these outlets could only be built by the state government, which alone boasted resources and credit adequate for the giant task. By the beginning of the 1830's all Illinois was advocating an important experiment in state socialism.

Thus was the stage set for the fabulous internal improvement program launched during the next decade. An approving populace watched delightedly as the legislature authorized construction of the Illinois and Michigan Canal, secured a land grant from Congress, and placed the credit of the state behind the canal bonds that were marketed in the East and England to finance the project. This simply whetted the popular appetite for more. The canal benefited only one corner of Illinois; why should the rest be neglected when state-constructed railroads and canals would not only pay for themselves and enrich shippers but assure such profits that taxes could be abolished? Swept along on this wave of enthusiasm, Illinois adopted its famous Internal Improvements Act of 1837. This fantastic measure pledged the 400,000 poverty-ridden inhabitants of the frontier state to spend more than $10,000,000 on a network of railroads and canals which would crisscross in every direction. If the program had been less grandiose, and the times more auspicious, Illinois' dreams of a state-operated transportation system might have been realized. Instead the mere magnitude of the plan, the lack of managerial skill among those entrusted with its administration, and the Panic of 1837, brought a speedy end to the whole project. By 1841 work was at a standstill.

The effect of this debacle on public opinion was great. As Illinois farmers viewed the visible remains of their wrecked hopes—half-completed road beds, untidy slashes that marked the beginning of canals, a $15,000,000 state debt, a 50 per cent increase in land taxes, debt repudiation—a feeling of revulsion against state ownership swept across the state. During the next few years the one completed railroad, the Northern Cross, which had cost $250,000, was sold for $21,000 without a voice being raised in protest. The people wanted no more public control; private enterprise could run the risks in the future. For the next generation the citizens of Illinois advocated *laissez faire* as strenuously as they had governmental ownership a few years before.

Their frontier-like tendency toward opportunism was even better illustrated when two panics during the pioneer period brought them face to face with an age-old question: what banking and currency system would assure security and prosperity for their state? Twice they tried to solve the problem, and each time their answers differed.

The issue first arose in the era of hard times following the Panic of 1819. What was needed to stem the downward trend, all agreed, was more money. This could best be provided by local banks, backed by the faith and credit of the state, which could issue paper currency. On the crest of this pro-bank sentiment, the legislature in 1821 chartered the Bank of Illinois, capitalized at $300,000 to be subscribed by the state, and authorized to issue bank notes in small denominations to the full extent of its capitalization. The notes were made legal tender for all public and private debts; any creditor who refused to accept them was prohibited from seizing property pledged as security for at least three years. This, in other words, was an inflationary measure, designed principally to increase the amount of circulating currency. Popular meetings in Illinois and elsewhere went even farther along the path toward inflation by demanding a complete paper currency bearing no relationship to specie.

The inflationary trend was accentuated during the prosperous 1830's when money was in great demand for land speculation, business expansion, and the internal improvement program. By this time the State Bank of Illinois, with headquarters at Springfield, had joined the Bank of Illinois in catering to the state's financial needs. Both of these institutions were called upon to aid the public works program that was launched in 1837. This was done by increasing their capitalization, turning over to them state bonds in return for shares of bank stock, and then borrowing back the bank notes issued on the basis of the state's own securities. Officials honestly believed that this flimsy process would not only supply money for internal improvements but eventually pay for all construction, as the bank stock was expected to pay annual dividends of from 8 to 10 per cent. These returns, plus tolls from canals and railroads, would soon retire the entire investment and provide so much income that taxes could be abolished! This was the talk, not of wild dreamers, but of sober businessmen and state leaders.

Illinois learned its lesson when the Panic of 1837 tumbled down its speculative house of cards. With hard times antibank feeling swept across the state. Farmers who owed money to the banks grumbled that they could not continue their payments. Others who were paid for their produce in the depreciated notes of the two institutions complained that they were being swindled. Still others lost heavily when the banks finally collapsed. More were convinced that there was a direct connection between the banks and the panic. The depression, they told themselves, was a product of the wild currency fluctuations that followed the overissue of state bank notes. These might benefit eastern capitalists, but every fluctuation drove the poor man, who could never understand such financial mysteries, deeper into debt. His only protection was to abolish banks and paper money, returning to the security of a solid gold and silver currency. "A bank of earth is the best bank," wrote one, "and a plow share the best share," while another declared: "Banks to help the farmer appear to me like feudal lords to defend the people." The Illinois farmer of the post-panic era was the most conservative of all Americans on financial questions.

The reaction of the state's pioneers to the panics of 1819 and 1837 demonstrated the opportunistic nature of frontier economic thought. In one case they moved leftward along the road to inflation; in the other they swung so far to the economic right that the nation's business leaders and bankers seemed financial radicals by comparison.

Reactions such as these stamped the Illinois frontiersman as typically American. He was typical, too, in his optimism, his democracy, his ingenuity, and his faith in progress. Molded by the frontier environment and strengthened by contacts with fellow pioneers from all the western world, he served as a perfect answer to Hector St. John de Crèvecoeur's famous query: "What then is the American, this new man?"

27

American Development Policy: The Case of Internal Improvements
CARTER GOODRICH

Our view of the American past includes many myths, and one of the most prominent is that our great economic development was the product of a policy of laissez faire. Purportedly, there was an idyllic period of the "good old days" when government abstained from participation in economic affairs. The truth, however, as such scholars as Oscar Handlin, Louis Hartz, and Milton S. Heath have shown in recent years, is that on both the local and national levels governmental action was more than merely accepted, it was requested. By means of its fiscal policies, its tariff regulations, its financing of roads, canals, and railroads, government played a central role in the great age of business expansion between 1815 and 1860, an expansion which George Rogers Taylor has so aptly called "the transportation revolution."

SOURCE: *The Journal of Economic History*, XVI (December, 1956), 449–460. Reprinted by permission of the author and publisher.

Using the development of internal improvements as a case in point, Professor Carter Goodrich, who has taught at Columbia University and at the University of Pittsburgh, explores in the following essay the question of how and why government activity contributed to American economic growth. Having served for some three decades in various capacities with the League of Nations, the United Nations, and in administration agencies of the United States government, Professor Goodrich is eminently qualified to answer this question. His essay was originally delivered as the presidential address before the Economic History Association in 1956 and is a distillation of studies in this area over many years.

As Professor Goodrich points out, the problem of governmental participation in national economic development carries particular interest for such an age as our own, when the new and revolutionary nations of both hemispheres have thrown their energies into the cause of economic advance. What lesson can they learn from American development policy? What was the nature of that policy? How much did it change as development proceeded and why? In what respects was this policy similar to that of the other major industrial powers of the nineteenth century—Great Britain and Germany? In what respects was it different? What were the shortcomings of the policy we pursued? What were its unique features? From the perspective of our own experience, Professor Goodrich arrives at conclusions that are highly relevant to today's world of nascent and striving nationalities.

The root problem confronting them now, as it confronted us more than a century ago, is how to amass sufficient capital to erect a modern structure of industry and commerce. Inevitably the way they proceed is in large measure governed by the traditions of their polity and by the ratio of the advance they want to make to that which they have already made. When Americans accepted the government aid in pursuing their economic growth, the circumstances of their acceptance were the substantial capital they had amassed on their own, the individuality of their enterprise, and the control they ultimately held over their government.

The subject I should like to discuss grows directly out of the theme of the meetings as a whole.[1] They have been concerned with the Ameri-

---

[1] The author's study has been carried on under the auspices of the Council for Research in the Social Sciences of Columbia University. The paper draws on the materials of articles previously published: in JOURNAL OF ECONOMIC HISTORY, "The Revulsion Against Internal Improvements," X (November, 1950), 145–169; (with Harvey H. Segal) "Baltimore's Aid to Railroads: A Study in the Municipal Planning of Internal Improvements," XII (Winter, 1953), 2–35; in the *Political Science Quarterly,* "National Planning of Internal Improvements," XLIII (March, 1948), 15–44; "The Virginia System of Mixed Enterprise: A Study of State Planning of Internal Improvements," XLIV (September, 1949), 355–387; "Local Government Planning of Internal Improvements," XLVI

can West as an Underdeveloped Region, and the title was intended to suggest the analogy between the United States of an earlier period and the so-called underdeveloped nations of the present day. To many it would suggest a contrast in policy. These other nations are now in many cases striving to achieve economic development by national planning and deliberate measures of governmental policy. On the other hand the United States achieved its massive economic development without over-all economic planning, without five-year plans or explicit national targets of input and output, and—it is sometimes believed—without the adoption of policies deliberately intended to promote development.

Yet the contrast is not as complete as this statement would suggest. It is not quite true that the United States just "growed" like Topsy or that the American empire of the West was settled and developed in a fit of absence of mind. Throughout our history statesmen have been concerned with devising measures to promote economic growth, and individuals and corporations have often come to governmental agencies with demands for encouragement and assistance. Many of the great debates on political issues have turned on what would today be described as development policy. Hamilton's *Report on Manufactures* is an obvious case in point. Its well-remembered argument for protection and its almost-forgotten plea for encouraging the importation of technical improvements from abroad are both commonly duplicated in the underdeveloped nations of today. Hamilton's plea for the Funding System, that it would in effect provide a favorable climate for foreign investment, reminds us of what is so commonly urged on capital-hungry nations today. It is perhaps more difficult to disentangle explicit developmental considerations in the bitter nineteenth-century debates over monetary and banking issues. In national policy there was nothing to suggest comparison with the Development Banks, *Corporaciones de Fomento,* and National Investment Funds that play so large a role in the current plans of the less developed countries, though on the state level Milton Heath's reappraisal of the Central Bank of Georgia and Carter Golembe's study of early Middle-Western banking may suggest that we have underestimated the influence of conscious development policy.[2] With respect to land, the great decisions down

---

(September, 1951), 411–445; "Public Aid to Railroads in the Reconstruction South," LI (September, 1956), 407–442; in the *Proceedings of the American Philosophical Society,* XCII (October 25, 1948), 305–309.

[2] Milton S. Heath, *Constructive Liberalism: The Role of the State in Economic Development in Georgia to 1860* (Cambridge: Harvard University Press, 1954), ch. 9. Carter H. Golembe, "State Banks and the Economic Development of the West, 1830–1844," unpublished dissertation, Columbia University, 1952.

through the nineteenth century were concerned with the conditions under which the national domain was to be turned over to individuals and corporations. This was the main issue of land policy, not land use, not conservation, not "land reform" in the explosive twentieth-century sense—unless you choose to regard the emancipation of the slaves as the most completely unplanned land reform in history! Yet the public domain was itself so magnificent that the manner of its disposition could not fail to be a major factor in influencing development, and explicit considerations of the rapidity and the desirable type of settlement dominated the debates from the Ordinance of 1787 to the Homestead Act, including expressions of deliberate preference for a particular type of social structure, that represented by the independent small farmer.

In an examination of American development policy, I believe that particular interest attaches to the case of internal improvements. Here the aim was directly and unmistakably developmental and the amount and variety of governmental activity quite extraordinary. Recent studies have increased our knowledge of the number of cases, and they have shown that the volume of government investment was greater than had been believed, both in absolute figures and in relation to total canal and railroad investment, to total national investment, and to the total budgets of governmental authorities.[3] Yet, half a century ago, the first modern student of the subject, Guy Stevens Callender, was able to point out that our supposedly individualistic America had had in the early and middle nineteenth century a certain world prominence as an example of the extension of the activity of the state into industry. He asked what conditions had given "rise to this remarkable movement towards State enterprise here in America where of all

---

[3] Professor Lively is right in pointing out that too little has been done with the comparison with private investment. Robert A. Lively, "The American System: A Review Article," *Business History Review*, XXIX (March 1955), 81–96. He cites Heath's figures on the ante-bellum South as a notable exception. See Milton S. Heath, "Public Railroad Construction and the Development of Private Enterprise in the South before 1861." JOURNAL OF ECONOMIC HISTORY, X (Supplement, 1950), 40–53.

An approach to the comparison with total national investment has been made in Harvey H. Segal, "Canal Cycles, 1834–1861: Public Construction Experience in New York, Pennsylvania and Ohio" (unpublished dissertation, Columbia University, 1956), which relates the canal expenditures to several estimates of capital formation and construction.

Heath, *Constructive Liberalism*, ch. 15, relates improvement expenditures to the state budget of Georgia; and Goodrich and Segal, "Baltimore's Aid to Railroads," relate them to the city budget.

places in the world"—he said—"we should least expect to find it."[4]

This movement, however, appears less paradoxical if it is examined in the light of the economics of development. The conspicuous contrast was with England. English canals and railways were built entirely by private enterprise. American canals and railways were for the most part products of governmental or mixed enterprise or the recipients of government aid. But consider the difference in economic circumstance. A railway between London and Liverpool ran through settled country and connected established centers of trade. It could expect substantial traffic as soon as completed. On the other hand, a route across the Appalachians to the largely unsettled West or a railroad running from Chicago west across almost empty plains could hardly be profitable until settlement took place along its route and at its terminus. Jerome Cranmer uses the words "exploitative" and "developmental" for these two types of enterprise.[5] Exploitative canals or railroads were built to take advantage of an existing opportunity. With them early returns could be expected and private enterprise could operate without subsidy. On the other hand the developmental undertaking depended for most of its traffic on the settlement that its own construction was to bring about. But such development could not in the nature of the case be immediate, and substantial early returns on the investment were hardly possible. The ultimate benefits might be very large but they were certain to be deferred and likely to be widely diffused. Such undertakings, therefore, could hardly be carried to success by unaided private means. They required either government enterprise, subsidy to private enterprise, or else extraordinary illusions on the part of the original investors.[6]

A survey of the history of railroad building around the world illustrates this distinction and tends to confirm these observations. Few countries copied the British example. Certainly it was seldom followed where the problem was one of opening up unsettled areas or of achieving economic development in a preindustrial region. The railroads of

---

[4] Guy Stevens Callender, "The Early Transportation and Banking Enterprises of the States in Relation to the Growth of Corporations," *Quarterly Journal of Economics*, XVII (November, 1902), 111–162. Reprinted in Joseph T. Lambie and Richard V. Clemence (eds.), *Economic Change in America* (Harrisburg: The Stackpole Co., 1954), pp. 552–559. The quotation is from p. 554.

[5] Jerome Cranmer, "The New Jersey Canals: A Study of the Role of Government in Economic Development," unpublished dissertation, Columbia University, 1955.

[6] This last alternative is noted in Frank W. Fetter, "History of Public Debt in Latin America," *American Economic Review*, XXXVII (May, 1947), 147–148.

Australia and New Zealand are state enterprises. Throughout most of the rest of the world the greater part of the railroad network has been built either on government account or with different forms of government aid or subsidy. One variant of the latter, government guarantee of return on the private investment, which Daniel Thorner has described as "Private Enterprise at Public Risk," was employed in India and Brazil as well as in France.[7] The purely private enterprises have been typically those that exploited obvious economic opportunities—to carry the produce of the pampas to Buenos Aires, or sugar from Cuban fields to the ports, or coffee to Santos. In Bolivia, for example, the pattern is precisely illustrated. The two railroads that take the tin from the great mines to the coast were built and are still owned and operated by private British interests, while the others are entirely governmental.

Nineteenth-century America displayed a similar pattern. There were certain railroad companies, particularly on the Atlantic seaboard, exploiting the opportunities of trade between established centers, which were profitable from the beginning and neither asked nor needed government aid. For New England, Kirkland described these as "dowager railroads" and cited the Boston and Lowell as one of the examples.[8] The Camden and Amboy was a similar case, and its partner the Delaware and Hudson might be described as a dowager canal—both exploiting the trade between New York and Philadelphia. But these were exceptions. Most of the canals and early railroads depended for their traffic on the growth of the areas into which they were extended. They were developmental in character and, like developmental undertakings almost everywhere, they were in considerable part built with government funds and credit.

The same distinction supplies one important clue to the understanding of the complex and apparently irregular timing of internal improvements activity. In this there were, to be sure, many crosscurrents. Reversals of state policy sometimes resulted, though less often than is sometimes believed, when power shifted from Whigs to Democrats, or vice versa, or when "Redemption" ended Reconstruction regimes in the South. More often improvements policy varied with the phase of the business cycle. Ambitious programs were abandoned in depression years, and failures were followed by "revulsion" and constitutional prohibitions. The collapse of the Illinois railroad program gave a lesson

---

[7] Daniel Thorner, *Investment in Empire: British Railway and Steam Shipping Enterprise in India, 1825–1940* (Philadelphia: University of Pennsylvania Press, 1950), ch. 7. Julian Smith Duncan, *Public and Private Operation of Railways in Brazil* (New York: Columbia University Press, 1932).

[8] Edward C. Kirkland, *Men, Cities and Transportation: A Study in New England History, 1820–1900* (Cambridge: Harvard University Press, 1948).

of caution to neighboring Iowa. On the other hand, New York's success with the Erie Canal had earlier inspired imitation up and down the entire Atlantic seaboard. Aid was given by local authorities, in varying amounts, in every state that formed part of the Union before 1890;[9] and in some fourteen states it continued to be given after the abandonment of state programs.[10] It may be said that governmental participation at one level or another persisted in most sections of the country as long as "developmental" conditions continued to exist, and perhaps in some cases beyond that point.

In general the relationship between developmental conditions and the various waves of government activity can be readily traced. For the Federal Government the building of the National Road and the formulation of the comprehensive internal improvement plans of Gallatin and Calhoun took place when the geographical obstacle to development was the Appalachian Mountains; and the major extension of actual aid to the transcontinental railroads took place when the obstacle was that of the Rocky Mountains and the Great Plains. Government activity in internal improvements was in large measure a frontier phenomenon, a great instance of frontier collectivism. In any given area it tended to diminish and die out as settlement and traffic became more dense and also as the business corporations themselves grew in strength and in the ability to raise large sums of money and commit them for long periods. As early as the 1850's, the *American Railroad Journal* was emphasizing this distinction. "In the infancy of our railroads," it said, "it was frequently necessary for the community to aid them in its collective capacity." Such a need continued in the South and in the West, declared the *Journal*, but in the North and East there was "abundant capital . . . for all legitimate enterprise," and public aid was no longer required.[11] To this doctrine it was not a real exception that Maine should vie with Oregon in furnishing some of the very latest cases of local government aid, since eastern Maine remained no less of a frontier than the Far West. Somewhat more surprising were the large amounts of money that Massachusetts poured out after the Civil War for the construction of the Hoosac Tunnel route and the extraordinary outpouring of municipal bonds for the building of the New York Midland. Yet in each case this represented an improvement for

---

[9] In Colorado only during the territorial period.

[10] States of which this was substantially true include Georgia, Illinois, Indiana, Maryland, Michigan, Minnesota, Mississippi, Missouri, Nebraska, New York, North Carolina, South Carolina, Tennessee, and Virginia. Local aid was also given in states that had not had state programs. On the other hand, Alabama, Arkansas, Colorado, Ohio, and Pennsylvania adopted constitutional prohibitions against local aid at the same time as against state aid.

[11] *American Railroad Journal*, XXVII (1854), 449; XXVIII (1855), 281.

the less developed part of a highly developed state; and it may be added that in the case of the latter a new bankruptcy and the failure of plans for reorganization, occurring since the publication of Harry Pierce's book, tend to confirm his account of the selection of the route![12]

If, then, we think of nineteenth-century America as a country in process of development, the experience of other countries in a similar situation suggests that extensive government investment in the means of transportation was not paradoxical but something entirely to be expected. What would really have been surprising would have been the spectacle of communities eager for rapid development but waiting patiently for their canals and railroads until the way was clear for prudent private investment to go forward without assistance. Yet neither an analysis of the economics of development nor analogy from foreign experience would account for all the peculiar forms and shapes taken by the American movement for internal improvements. Among its characteristics were three general shortcomings that would at once be obvious to anyone attempting to advise the underdeveloped countries of today on the organization of their programs of public improvement.

The first of these deficiencies was the failure to develop a workable economic criterion for the selection of projects for government support. Perhaps the sheer abundance of developmental opportunities made the question seem less crucial than it is for countries with more limited resources. There was, to be sure, no lack of statements of the reasons why short-run return on the investment itself was not a sufficient test. In addition to arguments based on the political advantages of closer connection between sections, which would strike a familiar note in many underdeveloped countries, expenditure on developmental transportation was defended on economic grounds. These statements called attention, often in thoroughly sophisticated terms, to its various benefits, not all of which could be appropriated by the collection of tolls or fares and freight charges. These included gains to the government itself in the enlargement of its tax base and the enhanced value of its lands, the diffused gains to the population at large in opportunities for income and employment, and in general the external economies provided to business as a whole by the provision of adequate transportation. But how should these broader and vaguer benefits be balanced against the expected costs? How were expenditures on unnecessary projects to be prevented? If prospective profit was not to be the conclusive test, how much immediate loss—and under what conditions—should the public authorities be prepared to

---

[12] Harry H. Pierce, *Railroads of New York: A Study of Government Aid, 1826–1875* (Cambridge: Harvard University Press, 1953).

incur in order to obtain these general advantages? On these questions I have so far found no serious contemporary statement.

A second shortcoming was the failure to develop and apply criteria for the assignment of projects to the different levels of government authority—federal, state, and local. Gallatin's admirable attempt to define a national project had little or no practical effect, and his program of federal action foundered largely on unresolved conflicts of state and regional interests. Within the several states, the problem of competing local interests was hardly less acute. Virginia attempted to operate on the theory of state support on equal terms to all local projects meeting certain specified conditions. In Pennsylvania and elsewhere there were bitter conflicts between proponents of a main or trunk line development and the advocates of aid to miscellaneous minor projects. Ante-bellum Georgia offered the unique example of confining its contribution almost entirely to a single strategically located state railroad, leaving connecting lines to local aid and private enterprise.[13] The extensive resort to the agencies of local government, the several thousand cases of railroad subscriptions and subsidies on the part of cities, counties, towns, and villages, can hardly be explained as the result of the application of any reasoned criteria as to which authorities were best fitted to make the necessary decisions. Aside from the early projects of the ambitious eastern seaports, each eager to carve out its part of the western empire, the recourse to local aid was in most cases a final expedient adopted after state aid had been prohibited, but when public demand for improvements, skillfully abetted by the companies themselves, still remained irrepressible. The extreme example of this type of causation is that of the citizenry of Cincinnati who, discovering that prohibition against *aiding* a railroad did not prevent them from *building* one, proceeded to construct the Cincinnati Southern as a successful municipal enterprise.

The third shortcoming lay in the nature of the government agencies themselves. They were sometimes subject to corruption, the danger of which increased as the railroad corporations graduated from the stage of infant enterprises. Moreover, they were in most cases poorly equipped to discharge the responsibilities of planning programs of internal improvement and of operating the undertakings effectively or of protecting the public interest in those that received public support. There were, to be sure, a considerable number of notable exceptions. The Gallatin Plan, prepared by the Secretary of the Treasury and a few clerks, would stand comparison with any twentieth-century plan for the development of a nation's communications. The present location of the trunk line railroads is eloquent testimony to its geographic fore-

---

[13] Heath, *Constructive Liberalism*, ch. 11.

sight. New York's state enterprise, the Erie Canal, was both a financial and a technological success. The engineers who learned the job on the Erie carried their technique to other undertakings. The United States Army Engineers gave technical assistance to a large number of railroads;[14] and, in its early days, the Virginia Board of Public Works furnished engineering services to local enterprises. Georgia's state railroad, the Western and Atlantic, not only earned a good return on its investment but also provided for the other railroads of the state their indispensable connection with the West. Baltimore's City Council made serious and persistent efforts to guard its railroad investments. Cincinnati's success has already been cited. Other examples could of course be named. Yet it can hardly be denied that in general the governments of the time, with small budgets and small staffs, with little expert personnel and without civil service traditions, lacked what would now be regarded as the essential means for the effective supervision of improvement programs. The deficiency became more glaring as public aid came more and more to rest on the decisions of local authorities. Little planning could be expected of village or township boards deciding whether to recommend "whacking up" the contribution demanded by the railroad agent, or to risk letting the road go through the neighboring crossroads instead. Their chance to protect the public interest consisted mainly in making sure that the company really ran cars through their village in exchange for the contribution.

To contemporaries the lightness or feebleness of the supervisory hand of government did not always appear a disadvantage. Shortly after the Federal Government had begun the practice of making land grants to railroads, a British official, reporting enthusiastically to the Privy Council's Committee for Trade and Foreign Plantations, suggested its adoption in the British colonies precisely on the ground that it gave needed assistance without imposing the penalty of interference with management. The *American Railroad Journal* often advocated public aid but consistently argued that governments should not take a direct part in improvement enterprises. As president of the Baltimore and Ohio Railroad, John W. Garrett protested indignantly against what he regarded as interference by the public directors at a time when a substantial majority of the company's stock belonged to the State of Maryland and the City of Baltimore. If these attitudes are to be discounted as *ex parte,* there is evidence that legislators often shared these views and argued for them on grounds of public interest.

Virginia's system of mixed enterprise was explicitly based on the principle that the purpose of the state subscription was to draw out

---

[14] Forest G. Hill, "Government Engineering Aid to Railroads before the Civil War," JOURNAL OF ECONOMIC HISTORY, XI (Summer, 1951), 235–246.

individual wealth for purposes of public improvement, and that the Commonwealth's control over the enterprises should extend no further than the correction of obvious abuses. With this in view, the state's participation in stock and voting rights was first limited to two fifths of the whole. When it appeared necessary to raise the state contribution to three fifths, the voting power of the state proxy in the stockholders' meeting was deliberately limited to two fifths, in accordance with the philosophy of the original law. A similar attitude was illustrated in the local aid statutes of a number of states that provided that the shares of stock subscribed to by the local governments should be distributed pro rata to the individual taxpayers. It was believed inexpedient to leave the administration of this stock in the hands of the local authorities, and that its distribution to private individuals would stimulate them to a vigilant supervision of the conduct of the work.[15]

As long as the common purpose was that of getting the much-desired improvement made, those who took part in the movement were not very much concerned if in many cases the method employed came close to being public enterprise under private management. To the Missourians on whom James N. Primm reports, as to many other Americans of the period, "The details of ownership and control were secondary . . . to the principal objective, the establishment of a comprehensive system of public improvement in the interests of the general welfare."[16]

Popular interest in this objective was very widely diffused. This was conspicuous in the support given to the many state programs and perhaps even more clearly in the willingness of the citizens to vote to assume local taxes in so many local elections. In these campaigns the appeals were typically couched in terms of public spirit and local patriotism. "Call meetings," urged a Mississippi paper. "Vote county, city, corporation and individual aid in bonds, money and land." A newspaper from a neighboring state added its plea: "Let the Mississippians come up strong to the work" on election day.[17] Projects were planned and campaigns organized in state or regional railroad conventions and in innumerable local railroad meetings. Boards of trade and chambers of commerce took leading parts in the movement. In a number of cases, after local government aid had been made illegal,

---

[15] An alternative explanation, that of evading a constitutional prohibition against government stock ownership, has been suggested for the Iowa statute. See Earl S. Beard, "Local Aid to Railroads in Iowa," *Iowa Journal of History,* L (1952), 1–34.

[16] James Neal Primm, *Economic Policy in the Development of a Western State: Missouri, 1820–1860* (Cambridge: Harvard University Press, 1954), p. 113.

[17] Jackson *Mississippi Daily Pilot,* May 15, 1871. Mobile *Register,* October 24, 1871.

unofficial bodies like these raised subscriptions in the same spirit and by appeal to the same arguments. It was they who took over the function of negotiating with the railroads over the location of their lines, shops, or roundhouses.

Throughout the developmental period individual citizens donated land for railroad rights of way, permitted the use of stone and timber from their lands, and supplied the labor of their slaves or their teams—occasionally even their own labor—to what was considered the common cause. Often, though not always, these services were paid for in shares of the stock of the enterprise. Appeals for cash subscriptions to canal or railroad stock were frequently based on grounds of civic duty as well as on prospects of financial return. Citizens were urged to bear an honorable part in what was often described as a great state or national work. In 1857 the president of a North Carolina railroad reproved his private stockholders for clamoring for dividends as if they had invested as capitalists rather than as citizens eager to promote the development of their state. As late as 1870, the editor of a Nashville paper declared that "no individual in this country outside of the Lunatic Asylum ever subscribed to the capital stock of a railroad expecting to receive a profit on the investment in the way of dividends." This is of course not to be taken as literal truth. By the time the editor wrote, many investors had received good returns on railroad stock, and no doubt others were bitterly disappointed that they had not done so. But it remains true that for many private subscribers, as well as for those who urged government action, "the object," as he said, or at least one great object, "was to develop the country, enhance the value of their lands, and create cheap transportation of their produce."[18]

I am sure that no one would urge the underdeveloped countries of today to pattern their programs of transportation development upon the very disorderly history of American action in the field. One may hope that they will succeed in avoiding the three shortcomings I have noted, though they will not find it easy to do so. Most students believe that they will need to use the powers and the borrowing power of government even more than in the American case. But they would be fortunate indeed if they found their citizens as ready to support the undertakings with their own savings and the forced savings of taxation, and if they could enlist as widespread an interest and participation in transportation development as was taken by the people of the United States. In this the local governments, for all their mistakes and inadequacies, and also the voluntary associations, played a considerable part. The building of the American network of transportation gained support

---

[18] Nashville *Union and American,* February 11, 1870.

from the local patriotism and the booster spirit of the city, town, and small community. It may be pointed out that the Communist practice of carrying regimentation and the party apparatus down into the smallest units, and the very different methods of "community development" of India and other countries, represent deliberate efforts to obtain popular participation at the local level in the processses of economic development. In the United States, vigorous local participation took instead the spontaneous forms that have been described.

On this occasion it is customary to consider The Tasks of Economic History. May I suggest that one such task is the examination of the economic effects of this American "boosterism," of this local civic pride, and to ask how much of its rather noisy activity canceled out in cross-purposes and duplication of effort,[19] and to what extent its energy made a positive contribution to economic development. Since a large part of this activity has been carried on by voluntary and unofficial organizations, the subject has rather fallen between the stools of the historians of politics and the historians of business. The records of these bodies are less accessible than those of governments, and their accomplishments are less measurable than those of business firms. Yet exploration of the subject, whatever the difficulties, seems to me essential for the understanding of a unique characteristic of American life.

My discussion of internal improvements began by citing the comment that the amount of government activity and expenditure in this field appeared astonishing in so individualistic a country. It ends on a quite different note, by suggesting that the nature and manner of this extensive government activity have been in close conformity with certain special characteristics of American development. Our record demonstrates a preference, though by no means universal or doctrinaire, for government partnership or subsidy rather than for purely public enterprise, and for leaving management largely in the hands of individuals and corporations. In this American experience differs from that of many foreign countries but not of all. Our record also shows that a large amount of this government action was taken by local governments, often of small communities. In this American experience is unique. In our case, moreover, governmental effort has been accompanied and abetted by the voluntary activity of a host of unoffi-

---

[19] The effect of local rivalries in impeding the formation of a fully connected national railroad system, by perpetuating differences in gauge and delaying physical connections between lines, is discussed in George Rogers Taylor and Irene D. Neu, *The American Railway Network, 1861–1890* (Cambridge: Harvard University Press, 1956). The text refers to the "long continued parochialism of the cities" (p. 51) and quotes a comment on "village peevishness" (p. 53).

cial civic organizations, for which I am sure no parallel can be found in the history of other developing countries. Our policy with respect to internal improvements has thus been profoundly affected—for better or worse—by the traditional American characteristics of individualism, of localism, and of the habit of voluntary association.

28

Patent-Office Models of the Good Society: Some Relationships Between Social Reform and Westward Expansion

ARTHUR BESTOR

America during the ante-bellum decades was in a ferment of reform. Education, from the elementary level to the college, was caught up in the zeal for change. The temperance movements, through meetings, tracts, songs, and hundreds of societies, argued the sinfulness of drinking and the need for moral restraint. Abolitionists by the thousands, radical and moderate, clamored for the end of slavery. Reformers pleaded for the rights of women, for a more humane treatment of the insane, for the improvement of prison conditions, for the permanent termination of war. In this active and multifarious world of reform belonged the communitarians, secular and religious, the Shakers, the Rappites, the Owenites, the Fourierists, and others, with their small-scale experiments in model communities and their many plans for the good society.

But just how did they belong? Were they Utopians? What was their place in early nineteenth-century social thought? What in particular was their relevance to the westward movement, considering that so many of them took root in the area of the Middle West? These are questions which Professor Arthur Bestor of the University of Washington answers in the following

SOURCE: *The American Historical Review*, LVIII (April, 1953), 505–526. Reprinted by permission of the author. All but two of the footnotes that originally appeared with the article have been omitted.

essay. Professor Bestor has long studied the communitarian movements and is the author of Backwoods Utopias *(1950), which is concerned in the main with the ideas of Robert Owen and the attempt to realize them in America. In two other volumes,* Educational Wastelands *(1953) and* The Restoration of Learning *(1955), Professor Bestor has also distinguished himself as a critic of certain tendencies in modern American education and as the proponent of a broad program of educational reform.*

Professor Bestor's essay makes the important point of placing communitarian thought in the context of the expanding society of the early nineteenth century. His comments will inevitably evoke questions that will demand the attention of the student, though it is beyond the scope of his essay to answer them. What was the substance of the plans to establish the good society? In what way was the good society good? How did communitarian thought relate to other reform movements of the period? In what way did it share with them qualities that were pragmatic, individualistic, sectarian, and moral? How did these various movements spring from a society undergoing a major redefinition of social and economic values and institutions? How do the reform movements of the ante-bellum decades fit into the larger pattern of American reform?

Of course it is a matter of interest to us to know our place in that pattern and to understand in what respects our own age has been one of reform. Certainly the slogans of our recent Presidents—Kennedy's "New Frontier" and Johnson's "Great Society"—indicate an ideal of reform. But how far has the ideal been realized? Were not Kennedy's frontiers left largely unexplored, because of congressional opposition as well as recurrent crises in our foreign relations, and was not Johnson's great society essentially unattained, because of our deep involvement in Vietnam? If reform is inherent in the American political ethos, may it not be because we compensate by professions and advertisements for what we know to be the inadequacies and inequities in American life? Has the nature of American reform changed? Did the ante-bellum generation strive to perfect man's condition, and do we now hope merely to ameliorate it? In a basic way, American history is a narrative of American reform, and it is therefore important for us to understand the substance and meaning of the programs by which we have perennially sought to make American life better.

In the mechanical realm, nineteenth-century American inventiveness left as its most characteristic record not a written description or a drawing but a working model, such as the Patent Office then required. In somewhat similar fashion, the societal inventiveness of the first half of the nineteenth century embodied itself in a hundred or so cooperative colonies, where various types of improved social machinery were hopefully demonstrated. Patent-office models of the good society we may call them.

To build a working model is not the same thing as to draw a picture. Hence it is necessary, at the outset, to distinguish between communitarianism, or the impulse which constructed these hundred model communities, and utopianism, or the impulse to picture in literary form the characteristics of an ideal but imaginary society. The distinction is more than verbal. A piece of utopian writing pictures a social order superior to the present, and it does so, of course, in the hope of inspiring men to alter their institutions accordingly. But a utopian work (unless it happens also to be a communitarian one) does *not* suggest that the proper way of going about such a reform is to construct a small-scale model of the desired society. Edward Bellamy's *Looking Backward,* for example, was a utopian novel, but definitely *not* a piece of communitarian propaganda, because the social transformation that Bellamy was talking about could not possibly be inaugurated by a small-scale experiment; it could come about only through a great collective effort by all the citizens of the state.

The communitarian, on the other hand, was by definition the apostle of small-scale social experiment. He believed that the indispensable first step in reform was the construction of what the twentieth century would call a pilot plant. The communitarian was not necessarily a utopian; few of the religious communities, for example, attempted to visualize an ideal future society this side of heaven. When the communitarian did indulge in utopian visions, the characteristic fact about them was that they always pictured the future as something to be realized through a small-scale experiment indefinitely reduplicated. The communitarian conceived of his experimental community not as a mere blueprint of the future but as an actual, complete, functioning unit of the new social order. As the American communitarian Albert Brisbane wrote:

> The whole question of effecting a Social Reform may be reduced to the establishment of one Association, which will serve as a model for, and induce the rapid establishment of others. . . . Now if we can, with a knowledge of true architectural principles, build one house rightly, conveniently and elegantly, we can, by taking it for a model and building others like it, make a perfect and beautiful city: in the same manner, if we can, with a knowledge of true social principles, organize one township rightly, we can, by organizing others like it, and by spreading and rendering them universal, establish a true Social and Political Order.

This is a fair summary of the communitarian program.

Historically speaking, the idea of undertaking social reform in this particular way—by constructing a patent-office model or a pilot plant—is not a common idea but a distinctly uncommon one. No other period comes close to matching the record of the first half of the nineteenth century, which saw a hundred communitarian experiments attempted in the United States alone. The vogue of communitarianism can be delimited even more sharply than this. During a period of precisely fifty years, beginning in 1805, when the first communitarian colony was planted in the Old Northwest, at least ninety-nine different experiments were actually commenced in the United States. Nearly half of these—forty-five to be exact—were located in the Old Northwest, strictly defined.[1] Another twenty-eight were in areas which belonged to the same general cultural region—that is, western New York, the parts of the Ohio River valley outside the Old Northwest, and certain adjoining areas on the other side of the upper Mississippi.[2] A total of seventy-three communities—roughly three quarters of the total—thus belonged to what can be described, without undue geographical laxness, as the Middle West.

Such a clear-cut localization of communitarian ideas in time and place can hardly be fortuitous. It is the kind of fact that cries aloud for explanation in terms of historical relationships. What, then, were the unique elements in the historical situation of the Old Northwest that help to explain why communitarianism should have reached its peak there during the first half of the nineteenth century?

Twenty years ago an answer would have been forthcoming at once, and would probably have gone unchallenged: *the frontier.* If, however, the frontier is given anything like a satisfactorily limited definition— if, in other words, the term is taken to signify primarily that "outer margin of the 'settled area'" which figured in Frederick Jackson Turner's original essay—then a close relationship between the frontier and communitarianism is hard to find.

In the first place, communitarian ideas cannot be said to have arisen spontaneously among any groups living in actual frontier zones. The leading communitarian philosophies, in point of fact, were elaborated in Europe—not only those of Robert Owen, Charles Fourier, and Etienne Cabet but also those of most of the religious sects. The Moravians in the eighteenth century found their "general economy" well adapted to new settlements, but its principles were ones the sect had worked out and partially practiced before they came to America. The Shakers faced frontier conditions when they first arrived in America, but they worked out their communistic polity later. It was, in fact, their way of settling down after the frontier stage had passed. The non-

---

[1] That is, twenty-one in Ohio, eleven in Indiana, eight in Wisconsin, four in Illinois, and one in Michigan.

[2] That is, eleven in western New York, seven in western Pennsylvania, one in what is now West Virginia, two in Kentucky, two in Missouri, and five in Iowa.

religious communitarianism of the nineteenth century drew its ideas from sources even more obviously unconnected with the frontier. Robert Owen's plan was a response to conditions which the factory system had created in Britain, and it made no significant impression in America until Owen himself brought it to this country. Americans did take the initiative in importing certain communitarian theories, but here again frontier motivation was absent. Albert Brisbane, though the son of a pioneer settler of western New York, became aware of social problems gradually, first in New York City, then in the ancient but impoverished realms of eastern Europe. He finally brought back from the Continent the most sophisticated social theory of the period, Fourierism, and made it the leading American communitarian system of the 1840's, by dint of propaganda directed largely from New York and Boston.

If the ideas of the communitarians did not arise on the frontier, neither did the impulse to put them in practice. The handful of communities that were actually located in or near true frontier zones were all planted there by groups from farther east or from Europe. They were not established there with the hope or expectation of gaining recruits from among the frontiersmen; on the contrary, communitarian leaders were often warned against accepting local settlers. Finally, communitarians were misled if they expected greater toleration of their social nonconformity in the West than in the East. The mobs who attacked the Shakers in Ohio, at any rate, were indistinguishable from those who attacked them in Massachusetts.

Nothing created by the frontier contributed positively to the growth of communitarianism. Only as a passive force—as an area of relatively cheap land or relatively few restrictions—could the frontier be said to have had anything to do with the communitarian movement. These passive advantages of the frontier were, as a matter of fact, almost wholly delusive. The Shakers afforded an excellent test case, for their villages were to be found in regions of various types. The most successful were in long-settled areas, reasonably close to cities. The one Shaker settlement on the actual frontier—at Busro on the Wabash River above Vincennes—had a dismal history of discontent, hostility, and failure, from the time of its founding in 1810, through its evacuation at the time of the War of 1812, until its abandonment in 1827. The withdrawal of the Rappites from their westernmost outpost—in the very same region and at the very same time—may be taken as evidence that they too felt the frontier to be basically unfavorable to communitarianism. Thomas Hunt, a British Owenite who led a colony to Wisconsin in the 1840's, had to admit that whatever physical advantages the frontier might offer could "be secured, not only by bodies of men, but by private individuals." This fact was quickly discovered by members of co-operative communities which moved to the frontier. "On their arrival here," Hunt observed, "they . . . find many opportunities of employing their labour *out of the society they are connected with.*" Though Hunt saw advantages for communitarianism in the cheaper lands of the frontier, he saw none in the state of mind which the frontier engendered. Among the factors prejudicial to success, he listed, with emphasizing italics, "the *influence which the circumstances of this country may exert over their minds, in drawing them again into the vortex of competition.*"

Hunt was probably wrong in regarding even the cheap lands of the frontier as a real economic boon to communitarianism. They proved to be the exact opposite, according to the shrewdest of all the nineteenth-century historians of the movement. This was John Humphrey Noyes, himself founder of the successful Oneida Community (located, incidentally, far from the frontier), who reached the following conclusions after carefully analyzing the history—particularly the record of land-holdings—of communitarian ventures contemporaneous with his own:

> Judging by our own experience we incline to think that this fondness for land, which has been the habit of Socialists, had much to do with their failures. Farming is . . . the kind of labor in which there is . . . the largest chance for disputes and discords in such complex bodies as Associations. Moreover the lust for land leads off into the wilderness, "out west," or into by-places, far away from railroads and markets; whereas Socialism, if it is really ahead of civilization, ought to keep near the centers of business, and at the front of the general march of improvement. . . . Almost any kind of a factory would be better than a farm for a Community nursery. . . . Considering how much they must have run in debt for land, and how little profit they got from it, we may say of them almost literally, that they were "wrecked by running aground."

The frontier, then, did not generate communitarianism. It did not inspire its inhabitants to join communitarian ventures. It did not show itself particularly hospitable to communitarian ideas. It did not even offer conditions that could contribute substantially to communitarian success. Communitarianism, in other words, cannot be explained as an outgrowth of the conditions of frontier life.

In point of fact, communitarianism developed in a fairly normal environment of settled agricultural and commercial life. The foreign-language sectarian communities, it is true, were not indigenous to the localities in which they were established. The Rappites, for example, were conducted as a body from Germany to Harmonie, Pennsylvania, then to Harmonie, Indiana, and finally back to Economy, Pennsylvania. None of the original members had any previous connection with these places, and the number of members recruited in the neighborhood was negligible. The same could be said of communities like Zoar, Ebenezer, and Amana. In the history of the communitarian movement as a whole, however, this pattern was the exception rather than the rule. The Shakers illustrated a more typical development. Each village of theirs was "gathered" (the phrase was a favorite one with them) from among the converts in a given locality, and was established upon a farm owned by one of the group or purchased with their combined resources. When communitarianism assumed a secular character, beginning in the 1820's, this local pattern became even more characteristic of the movement.

Of the thirty-six Owenite and Fourierist communities established in the United States during the half century under consideration, only one —Hunt's colony in Wisconsin—represented an immigrant group comparable to the Rappites or Zoarites. Only ten others involved any substantial migration of members, and in many of these the recruits from the immediate vicinity clearly outnumbered those drawn from a distance. At least two thirds of the Owenite and Fourierist communities were experiments indigenous to the neighborhood in which they were located. Sometimes groups in a small village or on adjoining farms threw their lands together or traded them for a larger tract nearby. Sometimes groups in a larger town moved to a domain which they acquired a few miles out in the country. It is difficult to distinguish between the two processes, and unnecessary. In neither case did the moving about of men and women constitute anything like a true migration to a new environment. Clearly enough, communitarianism as a secular doctrine of social reform made its impact in already settled areas and it inspired its adherents to act in their own neighborhoods far more frequently than it led them to seek the frontier.

Yet the fact remains that the great outburst of communitarian activity occurred during the period when the frontier of agricultural settlement was pushing ahead most rapidly, and it tended to concentrate in the area lying in the wake of that forward thrust. Some connection obviously existed between the idea and the situation. The true nature of that relationship must be explored.

In his original statement of the so-called frontier thesis, Frederick Jackson Turner enumerated certain ideas and habits of mind that he deemed characteristically American. "These," he exclaimed, "are traits of the frontier, or traits called out elsewhere because of the existence of the frontier." The latter half of the sentence has a rather off-hand air about it, suggesting that Turner did not fully recognize how radically different were the two types of causation he was bracketing together. Indeed, if the implications of the second part of the statement had been followed out fully and carefully by Turner and his disciples, the frontier thesis itself might have been saved from much of the one-sidedness that present-day critics discover in it. Be that as it may, the second part of the quoted sentence does describe the kind of relationship that existed between westward expansion and the vogue of such an idea as communitarianism. The latter was one of the "traits called out elsewhere because of the existence of the frontier."

This paper purposes to explore the process through which communitarianism—and, by extension, a variety of other social ideas— were "called out" by the mere existence of the frontier. The statement we are using is, in part, a figurative one. For the sake of precision it ought to be restated at the outset in completely literal terms. Three points require brief preliminary discussion. In the first place, ideas are not produced by the mere existence of something. They result from reflection upon that something, reflection induced either by direct observation or by knowledge derived at second hand. We are, by definition, interested in the reflections of men and women who did not participate in, and did not directly observe, the frontier process. In the second place, ideas rarely, if ever, spring into existence fresh and new. Reflection upon a new occurrence does not produce a set of new ideas. It exercises a selective influence upon old ones. It represses some of these. It encourages others. It promotes new combinations. And it may infuse the whole with deeper emotional feeling. The resulting complex of ideas and attitudes may be new, but the newness lies in the pattern, not in the separate elements. Finally, though we have adopted Turner's phrase, and with it his use of the word "frontier," we will find that it was really the westward movement as a whole, and not the events at its frontier fringe, that the men and women "elsewhere" were meditating upon.

With these three considerations in mind, we are ready to restate the subject of our inquiry in distinct, if prosaic, terms. The rephrasing will be clearer if cast in the form of a series of questions, although these will not have to be taken up in order or answered separately in the discussion that follows. How, then, did the expansion of population into unsettled areas, and the planting of civilized institutions there, strike the imaginations of those who took no direct part in the process? What ideas of theirs about the nature of social institutions were confirmed and amplified by their reflections upon this continuing event? Which of their hopes were encouraged, which desires rendered more certain of fulfillment, by what they conceived to be taking place? And how did this new pattern of ideas and aspirations correspond to the pattern embodied in a doctrine of social reform like communitarianism?

Now, communitarianism involved, as we have seen, certain very definite convictions about the way social institutions are actually created. It assumed the possibility of shaping the whole society of the future by deliberately laying the appropriate foundations in the present.

And it called upon men to take advantage of this possibility by starting at once to construct the first units of a new and better world.

In this set of beliefs can we not immediately detect certain of the ideas that took shape in the minds of men as they contemplated—from near or far—the upbuilding of a new society in the American West?

First among these ideas, certainly, was the sense of rapid growth and vast potentiality.   No theme was so trite in American oratory and American writing; quotations of a general sort are not needed to prove the point.   But one particular aspect of this belief in the future greatness of the United States requires special notice.   The point in question was enshrined in a couplet which was composed in New England in 1791 and which quickly became one of the most hackneyed in the whole of American verse:

> Large streams from little fountains flow;
> Tall oaks from little acorns grow.

American civilization, to spell out the interpretation which hearers instinctively gave to these lines, was destined for greatness, but this greatness was growing, and would grow, out of beginnings that were small indeed.

The converse of this idea formed a second important element in the reflections which the westward movement induced.   The habit of tracing greatness back to its tiny source led easily to the conception that every beginning, however casual and small, held within it the germ of something vastly greater.   In a stable society, small happenings might have no consequences.   But to men who pondered the expansion going on in the West, there came a sense that no event was so insignificant that it might not affect the future character of an entire region—perhaps for evil (if men lacked vigilance), but more probably for good.

A third idea, closely linked to these others, provided the most distinctive element in the entire pattern.   Human choice could play its part in determining the character of the small beginnings from which great institutions would in future infallibly grow.   But—and this is the uniquely important point—an organized effort to shape them would be effective only during the limited period of time that institutions remained in embryo.   This concept is not, of course, the obvious and quite unremarkable idea that what one does today will affect what happens tomorrow.   On the contrary, it assumed that there was something extraordinary about the moment then present, that the opportunity of influencing the future which it proffered was a unique opportunity, never to be repeated so fully again.

The corollary to all this—the fourth element in the complex of ideas —was a moral imperative.   Men and women were duty-bound to seize, while it still existed, the chance of building their highest ideals into the very structure of the future world.   When men spoke of "the mission of America," it was this particular idea, more than any other, that imparted to their words a sense of urgency. This moral imperative applied to the transplanting of old institutions as well as the establishment of new. The link between reformer and conservative was their common belief that institutions required positively to be planted in the new areas. Naturally the *best* institutions were the ones that should be so planted. For most men and women this meant the most familiar institutions, or at least the most respected among the familiar ones. Consequently the greater part of the effort which this concept inspired went into reproducing old institutions in the new West. A few men and women, however, always sought these best institutions not among those that already existed but among those that might exist. Hence the concept gave scope for reform as well as conservation.

Even when it assumed a reformist character, however, this concept must not be equated with reform in general. That is to say, it was not identical with the sense of duty that urges men to remedy social injustices and to remake faulty institutions wherever they find them. The present concept was much narrower. Without necessarily overlooking abuses hoary with age, those who thought in this particular way concentrated their attention upon institutions at the rudimentary stage, believing that the proper shaping of these offered the greatest promise of ultimate social reformation.

The group of four concepts we have been considering formed an altruistic counterpart to the idea of the West as a land of opportunity for the individual. The dreams of wealth, of higher social station, and of greater freedom were doubtless the most influential ideas which the West generated in the minds of those who reflected upon its growth. The action which such dreams inspired was participation in the westward movement. But all men who thought about the West did not move to it. There were also dreams which men who remained in the East might share, and there were actions appropriate to such dreams. Throughout the world, as men reflected upon the westward movement, they grew more confident that success would crown every well-intended effort to create a freer and better society for themselves and their fellows. And many of them felt that the proper way to create it was to copy the process of expansion itself, by planting the tiny seeds of new institutions in the wilderness.

What men thought about the West might or might not conform to reality. But in the fourfold concept we have analyzed, there was much that did correspond with developments actually taking place in America. At the beginning of the nineteenth century the vast area beyond the Appalachians was in process of active settlement, yet its future social pattern was still far from irrevocably determined. Different ways of living existed within its borders: aboriginal, French, English, Spanish, Southern, Yankee, the ways of the fur trader and the ways of the settled farmer. The pressures from outside that were reinforcing one or another of these patterns of life were vastly unequal in strength, and this fact portended ultimate victory to some tendencies and defeat to others. But the victory of no one of the contending social systems had yet been decisively won. And the modifications which any system would inevitably undergo as it spread across the region and encountered new conditions were beyond anyone's predicting. Half a century later this indeterminateness was no longer characteristic of the West. Many of the fundamental features of its society had been determined with such definiteness as to diminish drastically the range of future possibilities. Just as the surveyors had already laid down the township section lines which fixed certain patterns irrevocably upon the land, so the men and women of the region, in subtler but no less certain fashion, had by the middle of the nineteenth century traced and fixed for the future many of the principal lines in the fundamental groundplan of their emergent society.

The consciousness that they were doing this was stronger in the minds of Americans during the first fifty years of the nineteenth century than ever before or since. The idea had found expression earlier, of course, but never had it been validated by so vast a process of institutional construction as was taking place in the Mississippi Valley. The idea might linger on after the middle of the nineteenth century, but every year it corresponded less with the realities of the American scene, where social institutions were being elaborated or painfully reconstructed rather than created fresh and new. The first half of the nineteenth century was the period when it was most natural for Americans to assert and to act upon the belief that the new society of the West could and should be shaped in embryo by the deliberate, self-conscious efforts of individuals and groups.

This conviction received clearest expression in the pulpit and in the publications devoted to missions. An eastern clergyman, addressing the American Home Missionary Society in 1829, called upon the imagination of his hearers, asking that they place themselves "on the top of the Allegheny, survey the immense valley beyond it, and consider that the character of its eighty or one hundred million inhabitants, a century hence, will depend on the direction and impulse given it now, in its forming state." "The ruler of this country," he warned, "is growing up in the great valley: leave him without the gospel, and he will be a ruffian giant, who will regard neither the decencies of civilization, nor the charities of religion."

The tone of urgency increased rather than diminished as the great valley filled up and men sensed the approaching end of the time during which its institutions might be expected to remain pliant. "The next census," wrote the editor of *The Home Missionary* in 1843, "may show, that the majority of votes in our national legislature will belong to the West." The myriads there, in other words, "are soon to give laws to us all." The conclusion was obvious: *"Now is the time when the West can be saved; soon it will be too late!"*

> Friends of our Country—followers of the Saviour—[the editor continued] . . . surely the TIME HAS COME . . . when the evangelical churches must occupy the West, or the enemy will. . . . The way is open—society in the West is in a plastic state, worldly enterprise is held in check, the people are ready to receive the Gospel. . . .
>
> When the present generation of American Christians have it in their power, instrumentally, to determine not only their own destiny and that of their children, but also to direct the future course of their country's history, and her influence on all mankind, they *must* not be—we hope they *will not be*—false to their trust!

If one is tempted to regard this as the attitude only of easterners seeking to influence western society from outside, listen for a moment to a sermon preached before the legislature of Wisconsin Territory in 1843:

> It will not answer for you to fold your hands in indolence and say "Let the East take care of the West. . . ." The West must take care of itself—the West *must* and *will* form its own character—it must and will originate or perpetuate its own institutions, whatever be their nature. . . . Much as our brethren in the East have done, or can do for us, the principal part of the task of enlightening and evangelizing this land is *ours;* if good institutions and virtuous principles prevail, it must be mainly through our own instrumentality. . . . In the Providence of God, you have been sent to spy out and to take possession of this goodly land. To *you* God has committed the solemn responsibility of impressing upon it your own image: the likeness of your own moral character—a likeness which . . . it will, in all probability, bear through all succeeding time. Am I not right then in saying that you . . . occupy a position, both in time and place, of an exceedingly important nature?

The same evangelical fervor began to infuse the writings of educational reformers in the second quarter of the nineteenth century, and the same arguments appeared. When Horace Mann bade his "official Farewell" to the school system of Massachusetts, he too spoke in terms of "a futurity rapidly hastening upon us." For the moment this was "a futurity, now fluid,—ready, as clay in the hands of the potter, to be moulded into every form of beauty and excellence." But, he reminded his fellow citizens, "so soon as it receives the impress of our plastic touch, whether this touch be for good or for evil, it is to be struck into . . . adamant." "Into whose form and likeness," he asked, "shall we fashion this flowing futurity?" The West was explicitly in his mind.

In settlements already planted, the lack of educational provision posed problems of peculiar exigency, for "a different mental and moral culture must come speedily, or it will come too late." Nor was this all.

> Beyond our western frontier [he continued], another and a wider realm spreads out, as yet unorganized into governments, and uninhabited by civilized man. . . . Yet soon will every rood of its surface be explored. . . . Shall this new empire . . . be reclaimed to humanity, to a Christian life, and a Christian history; or shall it be a receptacle where the avarice . . . of a corrupt civilization shall . . . breed its monsters? If it is ever to be saved from such a perdition, the Mother States of this Union,—those States where the institutions of learning and religion are now honored and cherished, must send out their hallowing influences to redeem it. And if . . . the tree of Paradise is ever to be planted and to flourish in this new realm; . . . will not the heart of every true son of Massachusetts palpitate with desire . . . that her name may be engraved upon its youthful trunk, there to deepen and expand with its immortal growth?

Religious and educational ideals were not the only ones which Americans cherished and whose future they were unwilling to leave to chance. In establishing their political institutions, they were weighed down with thoughts of posterity, and of a posterity that would occupy lands as yet almost unexplored. At the Constitutional Convention James Wilson of Pennsylvania spoke to the following effect: "When he considered the amazing extent of country—the immense population which is to fill it, the influence which the Govt. we are to form will have, not only on the present generation of our people & their multiplied posterity, but on the whole Globe, he was lost in the magnitude of the object."

Such ideas as these found embodiment in the great series of documents which provided for the extension of government into the American West. Usually the purpose was so self-evident as to require no explicit statement. The Northwest Ordinance of 1787, for example, was without a preamble. It proceeded directly to the task of providing frames of government for the Northwest Territory, through all the stages up to statehood, and it concluded by setting forth certain "articles of compact" which were to "forever remain unalterable" and whose manifest purpose was to determine irrevocably for the future certain institutional patterns of the region. The framers of this and similar constitutional documents were proclaiming, by actions rather than words, their adherence to the set of beliefs under discussion here, namely, that the shape of western society was being determined in their own day, and that they possessed both the opportunity and the responsibility of helping to direct the process. "I am truly Sensible of the Importance of the Trust," said General Arthur St. Clair in 1788 when he accepted the first governorship of the Northwest Territory. He was aware, he continued, of "how much depends upon the due Execution of it—to you Gentlemen, over whom it is to be immediately exercised—to your Posterity! perhaps to the whole Community of America!"

Economic and social patterns, Americans believed, could also be determined for all future time during a few crucial years at the outset. Nothing was of greater concern to most inhabitants of the United States than the pattern of landownership which was likely to arise as a consequence of the disposal of the public domain. In this as in other matters, the present interests of the persons involved were naturally more compelling than the prospective interests of unborn generations. Nevertheless, concern for the latter was never pushed very far into the background. "Vote yourself a farm" was doubtless the most influential slogan of the land reformers. But not far behind in persuasiveness were arguments that dwelt upon the kind of future society which a particular present policy would inevitably produce. The argument was often put in negative form; propagandists warned of the evils that would inescapably follow from a wrong choice made during the crucial formative period.

> The evil of permitting speculators to monopolize the public lands [said a report of the land reformers in 1844], is already severely felt in the new states. . . . But what is this evil compared with the distress and misery that is in store for our children should we permit the evil of land monopoly to take firm root in this Republic? . . .
>
> Time rolls on—and in the lapse of a few ages all those boundless fields which now invite us to their bosom, become the settled property of individuals. Our descendants wish to raise themselves from the condition of hirelings, but they wish it in vain . . . and each succeeding age their condition becomes more and more hopeless. They read the history of their country; they learn that there was a time when their fathers could have preserved those domains, and transmitted them, free and unincumbered, to their children.

If once lost, the opportunity could never be regained. But if seized upon "by one bold step," the report continued, "our descendants will be in possession of an independence that cannot fail so long as God hangs his bow in the clouds."

Certain aspects even of the slavery controversy grow clearer when examined in the light of this characteristic American belief. One central paradox, at least, becomes much more understandable. "The whole controversy over the Territories," so a contemporary put it, "related to an imaginary negro in an impossible place." This was in large measure true. Even the admission of new slave states or of new free ones—and such admissions were occurring regularly—aroused no such controversy as raged about the exclusion of slavery from, or its extension to, unsettled areas where no one could predict the possible economic utility of the institution or its ability to survive. The violence of this controversy becomes explicable only if one grasps how important in the climate of opinion of the day was the belief that the society of the future was being uniquely determined by the small-scale institutional beginnings of the present.

From the Missouri crisis of 1819–21 onwards, practically every major battle in the long-continued contest was fought over the question of whether slavery should go into, or be excluded from, territories whose social institutions had not yet crystallized. So long as both sides could rest assured that the existence or nonexistence of slavery was settled for every inch of territory in the United States, then the slavery controversy in politics merely smoldered. Such a salutary situation resulted from the Missouri Compromise, which drew a geographical dividing line across the territories. But when the Mexican War opened the prospect of new territorial acquisitions, the controversy burst into flame again with the Wilmot Proviso, which aimed to nip in the bud the possibility that slavery might ever become an institution in the new areas. The Compromise of 1850 composed the dispute with less definitiveness than had been achieved thirty years before, for the question of slavery in New Mexico and Utah was left open until those territories should be ripe for statehood. Though the Compromise was, for this reason, intrinsically less stable than the earlier one, the uncertainties that it left were in areas which settlement was hardly likely to reach in the near future. Comparative calm thus ensued until the Kansas-Nebraska Act of 1854. By opening to slavery the territories north of the old Missouri Compromise line, this measure threw back into uncertainty the character of the future social order of an area now on the verge of rapid settlement. Bleeding Kansas resulted from the effort to settle by force what could no longer be settled by law, namely, the kind of social institutions that should be allowed to take root in the new territory and thus determine its future for untold ages to come.

Abraham Lincoln in his speech at Peoria on October 16, 1854, made perfectly clear his reasons for opposing the doctrine of popular sovereignty embodied in the new act:

> Another important objection to this application of the right of self-government, is that it enables the first FEW, to deprive the succeeding MANY, of a free exercise of the right of self-government. The first few may get slavery IN, and the subsequent many cannot easily get it OUT. How common is the remark now in the slave States—"If we were only clear of our slaves, how much better it would be for us." They are actually deprived of the privilege of governing themselves as they would, by the action of a very few, in the beginning.

Four years later Lincoln restated the argument in a letter to an old-time Whig associate in Illinois. His point of departure was a statement of Henry Clay's. "If a state of nature existed, and we were about to lay the foundations of society, no man would be more strongly opposed than I should to incorporate the institution of slavery among its elements," Clay was quoted as saying. "Exactly so," was Lincoln's comment.

> In our new free ter[r]itories, a state of nature *does* exist. In them Congress lays the foundations of society; and, in laying those foundations, I say, with Mr. Clay, it is desireable that the declaration of the equality of all men shall be kept in view, as a great fundamental principle; and that Congress, which lays the foundations of society, should, like Mr. Clay, be strongly opposed to the incorporation of slavery among it's [*sic*] elements.

These statements come as close as any to explaining the true nature of the issue which neither side was willing to compromise in 1860–61. In the midst of the crisis, it will be remembered, Congress passed and transmitted to the states for ratification a proposed constitutional amendment forever prohibiting any alteration of the Constitution that would permit Congress to interfere with slavery in the states. This provision was acceptable to Lincoln and the Republicans even though they were refusing to concede a single inch to slavery in the territories. On the other hand, the complete guarantee of slavery where it actually existed was insufficient to satisfy the southern leaders, so long as permission to extend slavery into new areas was withheld. For both sides the issue was drawn over potentialities. But this does not mean that it involved unrealities. In the mid-nineteenth-century climate of opinion, potentialities were among the most real of all things. The issue of slavery in the territories was an emotionally potent one because it involved a postulate concerning the creation and development of social institutions, and a corresponding ethical imperative, both of which were woven into the very texture of American thought.

How communitarianism fitted into this tradition should now be clear. The communitarian point of view, in simplest terms, was the idea of commencing a wholesale social reorganization by first establishing and demonstrating its principles completely on a small scale in an experimental community. Such an approach to social reform could command widespread support only if it seemed natural and plausible. And it was plausible only if one made certain definite assumptions about the nature of society and of social change. These assumptions turn out to be precisely the ones whose pervasive influence on American thought this paper has been examining.

A belief in the plasticity of social institutions was prerequisite, for communitarians never thought in terms of a revolutionary assault upon a stiffly defended established order. To men and women elsewhere, the West seemed living proof that institutions were indeed flexible. If they failed to find them so at home, their hopes turned westward. As Fourierism declined in the later 1840's, its leaders talked more and more of a "model phalanx" in the West. George Ripley, founder of Brook Farm in Massachusetts, defended this shift, though it belied his earlier hopes for success in the East:

> There is so much more pliability of habits and customs in a new country, than in one long settled, that an impression could far more easily be produced and a new direction far more easily given in the one than in the other. An Association which would create but little sensation in the East, might produce an immense effect in the West.

But it was more than pliancy which communitarians had to believe in. Their doctrine assumed that institutions of world-wide scope might grow from tiny seeds deliberately planted. Such an assumption would be hard to make in most periods of history. The great organism of society must usually be taken for granted—a growth of untold centuries, from origins wrapped in obscurity. Rarely does experience suggest that the little projects of the present day are likely to develop into the controlling institutions of the morrow. Rarely has society been so open and free as to make plausible a belief that new institutions might be planted, might mature, and might reproduce themselves without being cramped and strangled by old ones. In America in the early nineteenth century, however, men and women believed that they could observe new institutions in the making, and they were confident that these would develop without check and almost without limit. Large numbers of Americans could be attracted to communitarianism because so many of its postulates were things they already believed.

Large numbers of Americans *were* attracted to communitarianism. If the experimental communities of the Middle West had been exclusively colonies of immigrants, attracted to vacant lands, then communitarianism would have had little significance for American intellectual history. But for the most part, as we have seen, communitarian colonies were made up of residents of the region. Though such experiments did not arise spontaneously on the frontier itself, they did arise with great frequency and spontaneity in the settled areas behind it. There men possessed a powerful sense of the plasticity of American institutions but were at the same time in contact with the social ideas circulating throughout the North Atlantic world. One strain of thought fertilized the other. In a typical communitarian experiment of the Middle West, men might pay lip service to Owen or Fourier, but their central idea was the conviction that a better society could grow out of the patent-office model they were intent on building.

On the whole, the fact that communitarianism stood in such a well-defined relationship to a central concept in American thought is perhaps the most important thing which the intellectual historian can seize upon in attempting to assess the significance of the communitarian movement. This movement has been looked at from many different points of view: as part of the history of socialism or communism, as a phase of religious history, as one manifestation of a somewhat vaguely defined "ferment" of democratic ideas. Communitarianism was relevant to these different categories, of course, but its true nature is hardly made clear by considering it within the limits of any one of these classifications. The only context broad enough to reveal the true significance of the communitarian point of view was the context provided by the early nineteenth-century American way of thinking about social change.

This way of thinking was summed up and applied in the manifesto with which Victor Considerant launched his ambitious but ill-fated colony of French Fourierites in Texas in 1854:

> If the nucleus of the new society be implanted upon these soils, to-day a wilderness, and which to-morrow will be flooded with population, thousands of analogous organizations will rapidly arise without obstacle and as if by enchantment around the first specimens. . . .
>
> It is not the desertion of society that is proposed to you, but the solution of the great social problem on which depends the actual salvation of the world.

The last sentence stated an essential part of the true communitarian faith. A remaking of society, not an escape from its problems, was the aim of communitarian social reform during the period when it exerted a real influence upon American social thought. The dwindling of the ideal into mere escapism was the surest symptom of its decline. Such decline was unmistakable in the latter half of the nineteenth century. By 1875 a genuinely sympathetic observer could sum up in the following modest terms the role which he believed communitarian colonies might usefully play in American life;

> That communistic societies will rapidly increase in this or any other country, I do not believe. . . . But that men and women can, if they *will*, live pleasantly and prosperously in a communal society is, I think, proved beyond a doubt; and thus we have a right to count this another way by which the dissatisfied laborer may, if he chooses, better his condition.

In the late nineteenth century, it is true, numerous communitarian experiments were talked about and even commenced, and their prospectuses echoed the brave old words about planting seeds of a future universal social order. But such promises had ceased to be credible to any large number of Americans. Industrialism had passed beyond the stage at which a community of twenty-five hundred persons could maintain, as Owen believed they could, a full-scale manufacturing establishment at current levels of technological complexity and efficiency. Before the end of the nineteenth century, even communitarian sects like the Rappites and Shakers were in visible decline. The impulse to reform had not grown less, but it had found what it believed were more promising methods of achieving its ends. Men and women who were seriously interested in reform now thought in terms of legislation, or collective bargaining, or organized effort for particular goals, or even revolutionary seizure of power. Rarely did they consider, as so many in the first half of the century instinctively did, the scheme of embodying their complete ideal in a small-scale experimental model. When they did so, it was almost always a temporary move, a way of carrying on in the face of some setback, or a way of organizing forces for a future effort of a quite different sort. Such revivals of the communitarian program were apt to be sternly denounced as escapism by the majority of up-to-date socialists. In America, as in the world at large, communitarianism had become a minor eddy in the stream of socialism, whose main channel had once been defined by the communitarian writings of Robert Owen, William Thompson, Charles Fourier, Albert Brisbane, Victor Considerant, and Etienne Cabet.

The decline of communitarian confidence and influence paralleled the decline of the cluster of beliefs or postulates which this paper has been exploring. These intellectual assumptions faded out, not because the so-called free land was exhausted nor because the frontier line had disappeared from maps of population density, but simply because social patterns had become so well defined over the whole area of the United States that the possibility no longer existed of affecting the character of the social order merely by planting the seeds of new institutions in the wilderness.

How quickly and completely the old set of beliefs vanished from the American mind was revealed by certain observations of James Bryce in 1888. In a speech to a western legislature Bryce reminded his hearers of "the fact that they were the founders of new commonwealths, and responsible to posterity for the foundations they laid." To his immense surprise, he discovered that this point of view—"trite and obvious to a European visitor," so he believed—had not entered the minds of these American legislators. In this instance it was not Bryce but his hearers who showed the greater perception. The idea he expressed had once been held with tenacity. In the end, however, it had grown not trite but anachronistic. No longer did it state a profound reality, as it might have done half a century before. By the 1880's there was no point in talking about laying the foundations of new commonwealths within the United States. The reforms in American life which Bryce thought necessary were not to be achieved that way. Serious social reformers in the later nineteenth century were faced with the task of altering institutions already firmly established. Henry George and Edward Bellamy recognized this in their writings; Grangers and trade unionists in their organizations; opponents of monopoly in the legislative approach they adopted. For most American reformers in an industrialized age, communitarianism was a tool that had lost its edge, probably forever.

29

The Emergence of Immediatism in British and American Antislavery Thought
DAVID BRION DAVIS

No one will gainsay the importance of the antislavery movement of the ante-bellum period. Its participants espoused it as a moral crusade. It brought the temper of politics to an angry boil. It led the nation into a bitter civil war. And its repercussions are being felt even today. Yet in the usual text-book account, abolitionism does not make its appearance until 1831, when William Lloyd Garrison sounded his famous words in the first issue of the Liberator. The movement's context is left obscure and amorphous. Indeed, little more than a few details about the whole institution of American slavery are offered the student to fill out the story of its development during the two centuries before Garrison's passionate appeal. It generally suffices to say that the first Negroes—twenty in number—were brought to the English mainland colonies in 1619 by a Dutch man-of-war, that slavery seemed to be, on its way to extinction during the eighteenth century, and that it was revived and expanded by Whitney's invention of the cotton gin and the tremendous expansion of cotton production which the invention made possible.

But what explains the great prominence which the antislavery movement gained in the 1830's, and why in particular was it immediatist in its call

SOURCE: *The Mississippi Valley Historical Review,* XLIX (September, 1962), 209–230. Reprinted by permission of the publisher.

for abolition? Indeed, just what did "immediatism" mean? How did it differ from the gradualist approach to abolitionism? In what ways did gradualism coincide with the premises of eighteenth-century thought, both in America and Europe? How far, and for what reasons, did the appearance of American immediatism parallel a similar movement in Great Britain? In what ways did this appearance reflect, in both countries, a new perspective on human history, nature, and progress?

These are the questions to which David Brion Davis of Cornell University addresses himself in the following essay. The subject of immediatism is part of a larger comparative study of the British and American antislavery movements in which Professor Davis is presently engaged. In pursuing his study, he found that abolitionism could be seen in proper perspective only by understanding that slavery had been, since its introduction and institutionalization in the New World, a source of social and psychological tension in Western thought. The nature of this tension has been very carefully explored by Professor Davis in a major monograph, The Problem of Slavery in Western Culture *(1966), for which he won a Pulitzer prize, and which is the first of a projected multi-volume series on the larger theme he is studying.*

The book is rich in insights about American and European attitudes in the seventeenth and eighteenth centuries toward Negro bondage. Particularly rewarding is the first chapter, "Slavery and the Meaning of America," in which Professor Davis notes the profound moral contradiction that contemporaries found between the practice of slavery and the mission of America as a harbinger of liberty and democracy. This contradiction characterized American thought from the colonial period up to the Civil War. Indeed, its latter-day expression troubles us even today, involving as it does a condition of general equality and well-being for white Americans and a denial of both to the slaves' descendants.

In the history of reform few slogans have brought forth such confusion and controversy as "immediate emancipation." To the general public in the 1830's the phrase meant simply the abolition of Negro slavery without delay or preparation. But the word "immediate" may denote something other than a closeness in time; to many abolitionists it signified a rejection of intermediate agencies or conditions, a directness or forthrightness in action or decision. In this sense immediatism suggested a repudiation of the various media, such as colonization or apprenticeship, that had been advocated as remedies for the evils of slavery. To some reformers the phrase seemed mainly to imply a direct, intuitive consciousness of the sinfulness of slavery, and a sincere personal commitment to work for its abolition. In this subjective sense the word "immediate" was charged with religious overtones and referred more to the moral disposition of the reformer than to a particular plan for emancipation. Thus some reformers confused immediate abolition with an immediate personal decision to abstain from consuming slave-grown produce; and a man might be considered an immediatist if he were genuinely convinced that slavery should be abolished absolutely and without compromise, though not necessarily without honest preparation. Such a range of meanings led unavoidably to misunderstanding, and the antislavery cause may have suffered from so ambiguous a slogan. The ambiguity, however, was something more than semantic confusion or the unfortunate result of a misleading watchword. The doctrine of immediacy, in the form it took in the 1830's, was at once a logical culmination of the antislavery movement and a token of a major shift in intellectual history.

A belief in the slave's right to immediate freedom was at least implicit in much of the antislavery writing of the eighteenth century. If Negro slavery were unjust, unnatural, illegal, corrupting, and detrimental to the national interest, as innumerable eighteenth-century writers claimed, there could be no excuse for its perpetuation. Several of the *philosophes* held that since masters relied on physical force to impose their illegal demands, slave revolts would be just; Louis de Jaucourt went so far as to argue that slaves, never having lost their inherent liberty, should be immediately declared free. Anthony Benezet advanced a similar argument, asking what course a man should follow if he discovered that an inherited estate was really the property of another: "Would you not give it up immediately to the lawful owner? The voice of all mankind would mark him for a villain, who would refuse to comply with this demand of justice. And is not keeping a slave after you are convinced of the unlawfulness of it—a crime of the same nature?"

In England, Granville Sharp denounced slavery as a flagrant violation of the common law, the law of reason, and the law of God. After exhorting Lord North to do something about the plight of the slaves, he warned: "I say immediate redress, because, *to be in power*, and to neglect . . . even a day in endeavoring to put a stop to such monstrous injustice and abandoned wickedness, must necessarily endanger a man's *eternal* welfare, be he ever so great in *temporal* dignity or office." Sharp, who argued that "No Legislature on Earth . . . can alter the Nature of Things, or make that to be lawful, which is contrary to the Law of God," secured a judicial decision outlawing slavery in England. Americans like James Otis, Nathaniel Appleton, and Isaac Skillman took a similarly uncompromising stand before the Revolution; by the 1780's the doctrine of natural rights had made the illegality of slavery an established fact in Vermont and Massachusetts.

But the natural rights philosophy was not the only source of immediatism. Officially, the Society of Friends showed extreme caution in encouraging emancipation, but from the time of George Keith a latent impulse of moral perfectionism rose to the surface in the radical testimony of individual Quakers, who judged slavery in the uncompromising light of the Golden Rule. For such reformers, slavery was not a social or economic institution, but rather an embodiment of worldly sin that corrupted the souls of both master and slave; emancipation was not an objective matter of social or political expediency, but a subjective act of purification and a casting off of sin.

Immediatism, in the sense of an immediate consciousness of the guilt of slaveholding and an ardent desire to escape moral contamination, is similarly evident in the writings of men who differed widely in their views of religion and political economy. John Wesley's combined attack on the opposite poles of Calvinism and natural religion could also be directed against slavery, which some defended by arguments similar to those that justified seeming injustice or worldly evils as part of God's master plan or nature's economy. In 1784 Wesley's antislavery beliefs were developed into a kind of immediatism in the rules of American Methodists: "We . . . think it our most bounden duty to take immediately some effectual method to extirpate this abomination from among us." A related source of immediatism can be traced in the development of the romantic sensibility and the cult of the "man of feeling," which merged with Rousseau and the French Enlightenment in the writings of such men as Thomas Day and William Fox.

In the light of this evidence we may well ask why immediatism appeared so new and dangerously radical in the 1830's. The later abolitionists charged that slavery was a sin against God and a crime against nature; they demanded an immediate beginning of direct action that would eventuate in general emancipation. Yet all of this had been said at least a half-century before, and we might conclude that immediatism was merely a recurring element in antislavery history.

But if immediatism was at least latent in early antislavery thought, the dominant frame of mind of the eighteenth century was overwhelmingly disposed to gradualism. Gradualism, in the sense of a reliance on indirect and slow-working means to achieve a desired social objective, was the logical consequence of fundamental attitudes toward progress, natural law, property, and individual rights.

We cannot understand the force of gradualism in antislavery thought unless we abandon the conventional distinction between Enlightenment liberalism and evangelical reaction. It is significant that British opponents of abolition made little use of religion, appealing instead to the need for calm rationality and an expedient regard for the national interest. Quoting Hume, Lord Kames, and even Montesquieu to support their moral relativism, they showed that principles of the Enlightenment could be easily turned to the defense of slavery. A belief in progress and natural rights might lead, of course, to antislavery convictions; but if history seemed to be on the side of liberty, slavery had attained a certain prescriptive sanction as a nearly universal expression of human nature. Men who had acquired an increasing respect for property and for the intricate workings of natural and social laws could not view as an unmitigated evil an institution that had developed through the centuries.

Though evangelicals attacked natural religion and an acceptance of the world as a divinely contrived mechanism in which evils like slavery served a legitimate function, they nevertheless absorbed many of the assumptions of conservative rationalists and tended to express a middle-class fear of sudden social change. Despite the sharp differences between evangelicals and rationalists, they shared confidence, for the most part, in the slow unfolding of a divine or natural plan of historical progress. The mild and almost imperceptible diffusion of reason, benevolence, or Christianity had made slavery—a vestige of barbarism—anachronistic. But while eighteenth-century abolitionists might delight in furthering God's or nature's plan for earthly salvation, they tended to assume a detached, contemplative view of history, and showed considerable fear of sudden changes or precipitous action that might break the delicate balance of natural and historical forces.

There was therefore a wide gap between the abstract proposition that slavery was wrong, or even criminal, and the cautious formulation of antislavery policy. It was an uncomfortable fact that slavery and the slave trade were tied closely to the rights of private property, the political freedom of colonies and states, and the economic rewards of international competition. Yet from the 1790's to the 1820's British and American reformers were confident that they understood the basic principles of society and could thus work toward the desired goal indirectly and without infringing on legitimate rights or interests. Frequently they seemed to think of slavery as a kind of unfortunate weed or fungus that had spread through the Lord's garden in a moment of divine inattention. As expert horticulturalists they imagined they could gradually kill the blight without injuring the plants. The British reformers focused their attention on the slave trade, assuming that if the supply of African Negroes were shut off planters would be forced to take better care of their existing slaves and would ultimately discover that free labor was more profitable. In America, reform energies were increasingly directed toward removing the free Negroes, who were thought to be the principal barrier to voluntary manumission. Both schemes were attempts at rather complex social engineering, and in both instances the desired reform was to come from the slaveowners themselves. Antislavery theorists assumed that they could predict the cumulative effects and consequences of their limited programs, and since they never doubted the goodness or effectiveness of natural laws, they sought only to set in motion a chain of forces that would lead irresistibly to freedom.

This gradualist mentality dominated antislavery thought from the late eighteenth century to the 1820's. Though French thinkers had been among the first to denounce slavery as a crime, the emancipation scheme which they pioneered was one of slow transformation of the slave into a free laborer. Even the *Amis des Noirs* feared immediate emancipation; and the French decree abolishing slavery in 1794, which was the result of political and military crisis in the West Indies, seemed to verify the ominous warnings of gradualists in all countries. The years of bloodshed and anarchy in Haiti became an international symbol for the dangers of reckless and unplanned emancipation.

British abolitionists were particularly cautious in defining their objectives and moving indirectly, one step at a time. When outlawing the slave trade did not have the desired effect on colonial slavery, they then sought to bring the institution within the regulatory powers of the central government by limiting the extension of slavery in newly acquired islands and by using the crown colonies as models for gradual melioration; and when these efforts failed they urged a general registration of slaves, which would not only interpose imperial authority in the colonies but provide a mechanism for protecting the Negroes' rights. By 1822 these methods had proved inadequate and the British reformers began agitating for direct parliamentary intervention. Even then, however, and for the following eight years, British antislavery leaders limited their aims to melioration and emancipation by slow degrees.

Between British and American antislavery men there was a bond of understanding and a common interest in suppressing the international slave trade and finding a home in Haiti or western Africa for free Negroes. But in America the antislavery movement was given a distinctive color by the discouraging obstacles that stood in the way of even gradual emancipation. While states like New York and Pennsylvania provided tangible examples of gradual manumission, they also showed the harsh and ugly consequences of racial prejudice. Americans, far more than the British, were concerned with the problem of the emancipated slave. Even some of the most radical and outspoken abolitionists were convinced that colonization was the inescapable prerequisite to reform. Others stressed the importance of education and moral training as the first steps toward eventual freedom.

In America the gradualist frame of mind was also related to the weakness and limitations of political institutions. British abolitionists could work to enlist the unlimited power of a central Parliament against colonies that were suffering acute economic decline. But slavery in

America was not only expanding but was protected by a sectional balance of power embodied in nearly every national institution. A brooding fear of disunion and anarchy damped down the aspirations of most American abolitionists and turned energies to such local questions as the education and legal protection of individual Negroes. Antislavery societies might call for the government to outlaw slavery in the District of Columbia or even to abolish the interstate slave trade, but in the end they had to rely on public opinion and individual conscience in the slave states. While British abolitionists moved with the circumspection of conservative pragmatists, their American counterparts acted with the caution of men surrounded by high explosives. For many, the only prudent solution was to remove the explosives to a distant country.

But if British and American abolitionists were gradualist in their policies and expectations, they did not necessarily regard slavery as simply one of many social evils that should be mitigated and eventually destroyed. The policy of gradualism was related to certain eighteenth-century assumptions about historical progress, the nature of man, and the principles of social change; but we have also noted a subjective, moral aspect to antislavery thought that was often revealed as an immediate consciousness of guilt and a fear of divine punishment. During the British slave trade controversy of the 1790's the entire system of slavery and slave trade became identified with sin, and reform with true virtue. Though antislavery leaders adopted the gradualist policy of choosing the slave trade as their primary target, they bitterly fought every attempt to meliorate or gradually destroy the African trade. It was the determined opponents of the slave trade who first gave popular currency to the slogan, "immediate abolition," which became in the early 1790's a badge of moral sincerity. When uncompromising hostility to the slave trade became a sign of personal virtue and practical Christianity, the rhetoric of statesmen acquired the strident, indignant tone that we associate with later American abolitionists. Charles James Fox made scathing attacks on those who pled for moderation; he even said that if the plantations could not be cultivated without being supplied with African slaves, it would be far better for England to rid herself of the islands. "How shall we hope," asked William Pitt, "to obtain, if it is possible, forgiveness from Heaven for those enormous evils we have committed, if we refuse to make use of those means which the mercy of Providence hath still reserved to us for wiping away the guilt and shame with which we are now covered?"

This sense of moral urgency and fear of divine retribution persisted in British antislavery thought and was held in check only by a faith in the certain and predictable consequences of indirect action. Whenever the faith was shaken by unforeseen obstacles or a sense of crisis, there were voices that condemned gradualism as a compromise with sin. Granville Sharp, who interpreted hurricanes in the West Indies as supernatural agencies "to blast the *enemies* of *law* and *righteousness*," called in 1806 for direct emancipation by act of Parliament, and warned that continued toleration of slavery in the colonies "must finally draw down the Divine vengeance upon our state and nation!" When William Allen, Zachary Macaulay, and James Cropper became disillusioned over the failure to secure an effective registration scheme and international suppression of the slave trade, they pressed for direct though gradual emancipation by the British government. The British Anti-Slavery Society remained officially gradualist until 1831, but individual abolitionists, particularly in the provinces, became increasingly impatient over the diffidence of the government and the intransigence of colonial legislatures. From 1823 to 1832 the British Caribbean planters violently attacked the government's efforts to meliorate slavery. They not only devised schemes to nullify effective reform but threatened to secede from the empire and seek protection from the United States. Though the evils of West Indian slavery were probably mitigated in the 1820's, the planters' resistance convinced many abolitionists that gradual improvement was impossible.

The most eloquent early plea for immediate emancipation was made in 1824 by a Quaker named Elizabeth Heyrick, who looked to the women of Great Britain as a source of invincible moral power, and who preached a massive consumers' crusade against West Indian produce. The central theme in Mrs. Heyrick's pamphlet, *Immediate, Not Gradual Abolition,* was the supremacy of individual conscience over social and political institutions. Since antislavery was a *"holy war"* against "the very powers of darkness," there was no ground for compromise or for a polite consideration of slaveholders. Like the later American immediatists, she excoriated gradualism as a satanic plot to induce gradual indifference. It was a delusion to think that slavery could be gradually improved, for "as well might you say to a poor wretch, gasping and languishing in a pest house, 'here will I keep you, till I have given you a capacity for the enjoyment of pure air.'" For Mrs. Heyrick the issue was simple and clearcut: sin and vice should be immediately exterminated by individual action in accordance with conscience and the will of God.

In 1824 such views were too strong for British antislavery leaders, who still looked to direct government action modeled on the precedent of the Canning Resolutions, which had proposed measures for ameliorating the condition of West Indian slaves as a step toward ultimate emancipation. Abolitionists in Parliament continued to shape their strategy in the light of political realities, but by 1830 several prominent reformers had adopted the uncompromising stand of Elizabeth Heyrick. The shift from gradualism to immediatism is most dramatically seen in James Stephen, who possessed a mind of great clarity and precision and who, having practiced law in the West Indies, had acquired direct experience with slavery as an institution. For a time Stephen adhered to the principle of gradualism, transferring his hopes from the slave registration scheme to a "digested plan" of abolition by stages, beginning with domestic servants. By 1830, however, he was convinced that debate over alternative plans merely inhibited action and obscured what was essentially a question of principle and simple moral duty. It would be a tragic mistake, he felt, for the abolitionists to propose any measure short of "a general, entire, immediate restitution of the freedom wrongfully withheld." Lashing out at the moral lethargy of the government, he denounced the principle of compensation to slave-owners and rejected all specific gradualist measures such as the liberation of Negro women or the emancipation of infants born after a certain date. Stephen's immediatism was based ultimately on a fear of divine vengeance and an overwhelming sense of national guilt. "We sin remorselessly," he said, "because our fathers sinned, and because multitudes of our own generation sin, in the same way without [public] discredit."

On October 19, 1830, the Reverend Andrew Thomson, of St. George's Church in Edinburgh, delivered a fire-and-brimstone speech that provided an ideology for George Thompson and the later Agency Committee. Beginning with the premise that slavery is a crime and sin, Thomson dismissed all consideration of economic and political questions. When the issue was reduced to what individual men should do as mortal and accountable beings, there was no possibility of compromise or even controversy. The British public should "compel" Parliament to order total and immediate emancipation. With Calvinistic intensity he exhorted the public to cut down and burn the "pestiferous tree," root and branch: "You must annihilate it,—annihilate it now,— and annihilate it forever." Since Thomson considered every hour that men were kept in bondage a repetition of the original sin of man-stealing, he did not shrink from violence: "If there must be violence, . . . let it come and rage its little hour, since it is to be succeeded by lasting freedom, and prosperity, and happiness."

Taking its cue from men like Stephen, Thomson, and Joseph Sturge, the Anti-Slavery Society reorganized itself for more effective action and focused its energies on raising petitions and arousing public feeling against slavery. While Thomas Fowell Buxton sought to make the fullest use of public opinion to support his campaign in Parliament, he found himself under mounting pressure from abolitionists who refused to defer to his judgment. People's principles, he told his daughter, were the greatest nuisance in life. When the government finally revealed its plan for gradual and compensated emancipation, the Anti-Slavery Society committed itself to vigorous and aggressive opposition. But once the law had been passed, the antislavery leaders concluded that they had done as well as possible and that their defeat had actually been a spectacular victory. They had achieved their primary object, which was to induce the people to support a tangible act that could be interpreted as purging the nation of collective guilt and proving the moral power of individual conscience.

In America the developing pattern was somewhat similar. Despite the conservatism of most antislavery societies, a number of radical abolitionists branded slaveholding as a heinous sin, which, if not immediately abandoned, would bring down the wrath of the Lord. A few early reformers like Theodore Dwight, David Rice, Charles Osborn, and John Rankin, were well in advance of British antislavery writers in their sense of moral urgency and their mistrust of gradualist programs. As early as 1808, David Barrow, although he denied favoring immediate abolition, anticipated the later doctrine of the American Anti-Slavery Society by refusing to recognize the lawfulness of slavery or the justice of compensation. Holding that slavery was the crying sin of America, he urged a prompt beginning of manumission in order to avert the retribution of God. Three years earlier Thomas Branagan, who opposed "instantaneous emancipation" if the freed Negroes were to remain within the United States, contended that his plan for colonization in the West would bring a speedy end to slavery and avert the divine judgment of an apocalyptic racial war. In 1817 John Kenrick showed that colonization could be combined with a kind of immediatism, for though he proposed settlement of free Negroes in the West, he went so far as to suggest that the powers of the central government should be enlarged, if necessary, in order to abolish slavery. "If slavery is 'a violation of the divine laws,'" Kenrick asked, "is it not absurd to talk about a gradual emancipation? We might as well talk of gradually leaving off piracy—murder—adultery, or drunkenness."

The religious character of this radical abolitionism can best be seen in the writings of George Bourne, an English immigrant who was to have a deep influence on William Lloyd Garrison. In 1815 Bourne condemned professed Christians who upheld the crime of slavery. "The system is so entirely corrupt," he wrote, "that it admits of no cure, but by a total and immediate, abolition. For a gradual emancipation is a virtual recognition of the right, and establishes the rectitude of the practice." But while Bourne associated slavery with the very essence of human sin, his main concern was not the plight of Negroes but the corruption of the Christian church:

> Had this compound of all corruption no connection with the church of Christ; however deleterious are the effects of it in political society, however

necessary is its immediate and total abolition, and however pregnant with danger to the *Union*, is the prolongation of the system; to Legislators and Civilians, the redress of the evil would have been committed. But *Slavery* is the *golden Calf*, which has been elevated among the Tribes, and before it, the Priests and the Elders and the *nominal* sons of Israel, *eat, drink, rise up to play, worship and sacrifice.*

Thus for Bourne "immediatism" meant an immediate recognition of the sin of slavery and an immediate decision on the part of Christians to purge their churches of all contamination. He was far more interested in the purification of religion than in slavery as an institution.

In 1825 the Boston *Recorder and Telegraph* published a long correspondence that further clarifies the origins of immediatism. After arguing that slavery was unlawful and suggesting that slaves might have a right to revolt, "Vigornius" [Samuel M. Worcester] asserted that *"the slave-holding system must be abolished;* and in order to the accomplishment of this end, immediate, determined measures must be adopted for the ultimate emancipation of every slave within our territories." This was the position of the later Kentucky and New York abolitionists, but Vigornius combined it with strong faith in the American Colonization Society. He was bitterly attacked by "A Carolinian," who accused him of believing in "an entire and immediate abolition of slavery." "Philo," the next contributor, said he opposed immediate emancipation on grounds of expediency, but recognized the right of slaves to immediate freedom; he advocated, therefore, "immediate and powerful remedies," since "We are convinced, and if our Southern brethren are not convinced, we wish to convince them, and think with a little discussion we could convince them, that to postpone these prospective measures a day, is a great crime . . . and moreover, we wish to state directly, that this postponement is that, in which we consider the guilt of slavery, so far as the present proprietors are concerned, to consist."

A Southerner, who called himself "Hieronymus," defended Vigornius and tried to avoid the ambiguities that were later to cloud discussions of immediate abolition. Vigornius, he wrote,

> pleads, it is true, for *speedy* emancipation, and immediate preparatory steps. But immediate and speedy are not synonimous [*sic*] expressions. One is an absolute, the other a relative or comparative term. An event may in one view of it be regarded as very speedy, which in another might be pronounced very gradual. If slavery should be entirely abolished from the United States in 30, 40, or even 50 years, many . . . will readily admit, that it would be a speedy abolition; while every one must perceive, that it would be far, very far, from an immediate abolition. In a certain sense abolition may be immediate; in another, speedy; and in both, practicable and safe. There are not a few blacks now at the South, qualified for immediate emancipation, if Legislatures would permit, and owners would confer it.

Hieronymus, who had read and been impressed by Elizabeth Heyrick's pamphlet, agreed with Vigornius that colonization was the only practicable solution to the nation's most critical problem.

These ardent colonizationists believed that slavery was a sin that would increase in magnitude and danger unless effective measures were adopted without delay. Yet by 1821 Benjamin Lundy and other abolitionists had come to the opinion that the American Colonization Society was founded on racial prejudice and offered no real promise of undermining slavery. Lundy thought that slavery could not be eradicated until his fellow Americans in both North and South were willing to accept the free Negro as an equal citizen. But in the meantime the institution was expanding into the Southwest and even threatening to spread to such states as Illinois. In the face of such an imposing problem, Lundy called for the swift and decisive use of political power by a convention of representatives from the various states, who might devise and implement a comprehensive plan for emancipation.

The American antislavery organization absorbed some of this sense of urgency and mistrust of palliatives. The Pennsylvania Society for the Abolition of Slavery was cautious in its approach to the national problem, but in 1819 it approved a declaration that "the practice of holding and selling human beings as property . . . ought to be *immediately* abandoned." In 1825 the Acting Committee of the American Convention for Promoting the Abolition of Slavery advocated the "speedy and entire" emancipation of slaves, a phrase later used by the British Society. The Convention showed little confidence in any of the specific proposals for gradual abolition but at the same time rejected direct emancipation by act of Congress as an impossibility. Alert always to the need for conciliating the South and remaining within the prescribed bounds of the Constitution, the Convention considered every conceivable plan in a rationalistic and eclectic spirit. In the South, however, there was an increasing tendency to see the most conservative antislavery proposals as immediatism in disguise. By 1829 the gradualist approach of the American Convention had reached a dead end.

It is a striking coincidence that both the British and American antislavery movements had come to a crucial turning point by 1830. In both countries the decline of faith in gradualism had been marked in the mid-1820's by enthusiasm for a boycott of slave produce, a movement which promised to give a cutting edge to the moral testimony of individuals. In both countries the truculence and stubborn opposition of slaveholders to even gradualist reforms brought a sense of despair and indignation to the antislavery public. To some degree immediatism was the creation of the British and American slaveholders themselves. By accusing the most moderate critics of radical designs and by blocking the path to many attempted reforms they helped to discredit the gradualist mentality that had balanced and compromised a subjective conviction that slavery was sin. The sense of crisis between 1829 and 1831 was also accentuated by an increasing militancy of Negroes, both slave and free. In 1829 David Walker hinted ominously of slave revenge; groups of free Negroes openly repudiated the colonization movement; and in 1831 bloody revolts erupted in Virginia and Jamaica. In that year a new generation of American reformers adopted the principle of immediatism, which had recently acquired the sanction of eminent British philanthropists. But while American abolitionists modeled their new societies and techniques on British examples, the principle of immediatism had had a long and parallel development in both countries.

In one sense immediatism was simply a shift in strategy brought on by the failure of less direct plans for abolition. Earlier plans and programs had evoked little popular excitement compared with parliamentary reform or Catholic emancipation in England, or with tariff or land policies in the United States. As a simple, emotional slogan, immediate abolition would at least arouse interest and perhaps appeal to the moral sense of the public. As a device for propaganda it had the virtue of avoiding economic and social complexities and focusing attention on a clear issue of right and wrong. If the public could once be brought to the conviction that slavery was wrong and that something must be done about it at once, then governments would be forced to take care of the details.

But immediatism was something more than a shift in strategy. It represented a shift in total outlook from a detached, rationalistic perspective on human history and progress to a personal commitment to make no compromise with sin. It marked a liberation for the reformer from the ideology of gradualism, from a toleration of evil within the social order, and from a deference to institutions that blocked the way to personal salvation. Acceptance of immediatism was the sign of an immediate transformation within the reformer himself; as such, it was seen as an expression of inner freedom, of moral sincerity and earnestness, and of victory over selfish and calculating expediency. If slaveholders received the doctrine with contempt and scathing abuse, the abolitionist was at least assured of his own freedom from guilt. He saw the emergence of immediatism as an upswelling of personal moral force which, with the aid of God, would triumph over all that was mean and selfish and worldly.

There are obvious links between immediate emancipation and a religious sense of immediate justification and presence of the divine spirit that can be traced throught the early spiritual religions to the Quakers, Methodists, and evangelical revivals. The new abolitionism contained a similar pattern of intense personal anxiety, rapturous freedom, eagerness for sacrifice, and mistrust of legalism, institutions, and slow-working agencies for salvation. It was no accident that from the late seventeenth century the boldest assertions of antislavery sentiment had been made by men who were dissatisfied with the materialism and sluggish formality of institutionalized religion, and who searched for a fresh and assuring meaning of Christian doctrine in a changing world. To the extent that slavery became a concrete symbol of sin, and support of the antislavery cause a sign of Christian virtue, participation in the reform became a supplement or even alternative to traditional religion. As a kind of surrogate religion, antislavery had long shown tendencies that were pietistic, millennial, and anti-institutional. By the 1830's it had clearly marked affinities with the increasingly popular doctrines of free grace, immediate conversion, and personal holiness. According to Amos A. Phelps, for example, immediatism was synonymous with immediate repentance: "All that follows is the carrying out of the new principle of action, and is to emancipation just what sanctification is to conversion."

Immediate emancipation was also related to a changing view of history and human nature. Whereas the gradualist saw man as at least partially conditioned by historical and social forces, the immediatist saw him as essentially indeterminate and unconditioned. The gradualist, having faith in the certainty of economic and social laws, and fearing the dangers of a sudden collapse of social controls, was content to wait until a legal and rational system of external discipline replaced the arbitrary power of the slaveowner. The immediatist, on the other hand, put his faith in the innate moral capacities of the individual. He felt that unless stifling and coercive influences were swept away, there could be no development of the inner controls of conscience, emulation, and self-respect, on which a free and Christian society depended. His outlook was essentially romantic, for instead of cautiously manipulating the external forces of nature, he sought to create a new epoch of history by liberating the inner moral forces of human nature.

It falls beyond the scope of the present essay to show how immediatism itself became institutionalized as a rigid test of faith, and how it served as a medium for attacking all rival institutions that limited individual freedom or defined standards of thought and conduct. It is enough to suggest that immediatism, while latent in early antislavery thought, was part of a larger reaction against a type of mind that tended to think of history in terms of linear time and logical categories, and that emphasized the importance of self-interest, expediency, moderation, and planning in accordance with economic and social laws. Immediatism shared with the romantic frame of mind a hostility to all dualisms of thought and feeling, an allegiance to both emotional sympathy and abstract principle, an assumption that mind can rise above self-interest, and a belief that ideas, when held with sufficient intensity, can be transformed into irresistible moral action. If immediate emancipation brought misunderstanding and violent hostility in regions that were charged with racial prejudice and fear of sectional conflict, it was nevertheless an appropriate doctrine for a romantic and evangelical age.

30

The Antislavery Myth

C. VANN WOODWARD

So much of our history is written under the auspices of the American myth that the condition itself testifies both to an unawareness of the sponsorship and an ignorance of the myth. Here then are initial questions for the student of the American past: What are the components of the American myth? What needs in American society does the myth serve? What have been the myths of other nations and societies? How far do different national myths share ideas, personages, and values? What have been the divergences between social myth and social reality? How far may it be said that the viability of a society is directly proportional to the difference between its myths and its realities?

To a nation of conscience such as ours, founded as a Zion in the wilderness and a city upon a hill, understanding the function of the national myth is important. A myth does not merely project reality; it compensates for it. It reduces our view of experience (the way we distill reality) and of the future (the way we anticipate it) to a moral code. Thus a social myth speaks social conscience and atones for social guilt. Its real importance is that it expiates past sins and makes possible—by atoning regularly and in advance for them —present and future ones. A social myth is thus the way a society accommodates fact to fancy, what is to what should be, the evil that men do in fact to the good they would like to do.

SOURCE: *The American Scholar*, XXXI (Spring, 1962), 312–328. Copyright © 1962 by the United Chapters of Phi Beta Kappa. Reprinted by permission of the publisher.

In this light, history-writing is the staged re-enactment of the national story before the tribunal of the national values. Far from being the past wie es eigentlich gewesen, such history is the past wie es eigentlich hätte sein sollen. In writing history, we pass reality through the filter of conscience, judging the way life did go against how it should have gone. We become then not merely judges after the fact, but actors in it.

Here then is the importance of the following essay on the antislavery myth by C. Vann Woodward of Yale University. A specialist in the history of the American South, on which he has written many books, Woodward is one of our outstanding historians and a consummate essayist. To his writing he consistently brings a broad-ranging knowledge, a catholic temperament, a discriminating judgment, and a sense of the irony of human history. In the review essay that appears below, Woodward shows how writing about ante-bellum slavery has proceeded from two opposing sets of myths about its justifiability. He shows too how both sets—the proslavery myth of the South and the antislavery myth of the North—are coming under the closer scrutiny of our historians.

Woodward hopes that the historian will be less a protractor of myths and more their challenger, less their instrument and more their analyst. He finds cause for reassurance in the works of Larry Gara and Leon Litwack, which reveal the glaring discrepancies between the antislavery myth and the actual facts. He is less happy about the work of Dwight L. Dumond, which, far from subjecting the myth to critical analysis, embraces and glorifies it. Woodward would wonder too about recent books on the movement against slavery; the most important of these, surely, is a volume of essays by younger historians, **The Antislavery Vanguard** (edited by Martin L. Duberman, 1965), which tends to see yesterday's abolitionists in the light of today's civil rights leaders. Woodward's point is that a program of conscience is not in and of itself a valid basis for historical inquiry and that, if the historian ought hardly to be insensitive to moral questions, history cannot become merely a tale told by moralists.

It is not too difficult to understand why the antislavery myth has persisted so long, indeed why it is currently being revitalized. It has long suited the American temper, and admirably expresses the temper of our times. The antislavery myth coincides with our national conscience. It realizes our ideal of equality. It articulates our hope for freedom. It expresses our rejection of the Old World, with its earlier societies of castes and distinctions and its trafficking in human bondage. It sums up our sense of history as the continuous improvement of the human condition. It validates our belief that American experience has followed a course of moral good. It redeems us from our sense of sin against the Negro, and redefines our worst war as a war of faith and justification. Woodward's plea for an honest understanding of our past is essentially that of Socrates. Self-knowledge begins where mythology leaves off. This is no less true for a nation than for an individual.

Slavery and the Civil War were prolific breeders of myth, and their fertility would seem to wax rather than wane with the passage of time. Neither the proslavery myths of the South nor the antislavery myths of the North ceased to grow after the abolition of the Peculiar Institution. In fact they took on new life, struck new roots and flourished more luxuriantly than ever. Both myths continually found new sources of nourishment in the changing psychological needs and regional policies of North and South. The South used the proslavery myth to salve its wounds, lighten its burden of guilt and, most of all, to rationalize and defend the system of caste and segregation that was developed in place of the old order. The North, as we shall see, had deeply felt needs of its own to be served by an antislavery myth, needs that were sufficient at all times to keep the legend vital and growing to meet altered demands.

In late years the proslavery myth and the plantation legend have been subjected to heavy critical erosion from historians, sociologists and psychologists. So damaging has this attack been that little more is heard of the famous school for civilizing savages, peopled with happy slaves and benevolent masters. Shreds and pieces of the myth are still invoked as props to the crumbling defenses of segregation, but conviction has drained out of it, and it has been all but relegated to the limbo of dead or obsolescent myths.

Nothing like this can be said of the antislavery myth. Its potency is attested by a steady flow of historical works by journalists and reputable scholars. It is obvious that the myth can still dim the eye and quicken the pulse as well as warp the critical judgment. Apart from the fact that it is a creation of the victor rather than the vanquished, there are other reasons for the undiminished vitality of the antislavery myth. One is that it has not been subjected to as much critical study as has the proslavery myth.

Before turning to certain recent evidence of the exuberant vitality of the antislavery myth, however, it is interesting to note two penetrating critical studies of some of its components. Larry Gara, in *The Liberty Line: The Legend of the Underground Railroad,* addresses himself to a limited but substantial element of the myth. No aspect of the myth has so deeply engaged the American imagination and entrenched itself in the national heritage as the underground railroad, and no aspect so well reflects what we fondly believe to be the more generous impulses of national character. It is a relief to report that Mr. Gara is a temperate scholar and has avoided handling his subject with unnecessary rudeness. By the time he finishes patiently peeling away the layers of fantasy and romance, however, the factual substance is painfully reduced and the legend is revealed as melodrama. Following the assumptions that the better critics of the proslavery legend make about the slave, he assumes that "abolitionists, after all, were human," and that the "actual men and women of the abolition movement, like the slaves themselves, are far too complex to fit into a melodrama."

One very human thing the authors of the melodrama did was to seize the spotlight. They elected themselves the heroes. It was not that the abolitionists attempted to stage *Othello* without the princely Moor, but they did relegate the Moor to a subordinate role. The role assigned him was largely passive—that of the trembling, helpless fugitive completely dependent on his noble benefactors. The abolitionist was clearly the hero, and as Gerrit Smith, one of them, put it, the thing was brought off by the "Abolitionists and the Abolitionists only." As Mr. Gara points out, however, it took a brave, resourceful and rebellious slave to make good an escape, not one temperamentally adapted to subordinate roles—no Uncle Tom, as abolitionists often discovered. Moreover, by the time he reached the helping hands of the underground railroad conductors—if he ever did in fact—he had already completed the most perilous part of his journey, the southern part.

Another important actor in the drama of rescue who was crowded offstage by the abolitionists was the free Negro. According to the antislavery leader James G. Birney, the assistance of the fugitives was "almost uniformly managed by the colored people. I know nothing of them generally till they are past." The fugitive slaves had good reason to mistrust any white man, and in the opinion of Mr. Gara the majority of those who completed their flight to freedom did so without a ride on the legendary U.G.R.R.

Still another human failing of the legendmakers was exaggeration, and in this the abolitionists were ably assisted by their adversaries, the slaveholders, who no more understated their pecuniary losses than the abolitionists underestimated their heroic exploits. Under analysis the "flood" of fugitives diminishes to a trickle. As few as were the manumissions, they were double the number of fugitives in 1860 according to the author, and by far the greater number of fugitives never got out of the slave states. Another and even more fascinating distortion is the legend of conspiracy and secrecy associated with the U.G.R.R. The obvious fact was that the rescue of fugitive slaves was the best possible propaganda for the antislavery cause. We are mildly admonished that the U.G.R.R. was "not the well-organized and mysterious institution of the legend." "Far from being secret," we are told, "it was copiously and persistently publicized, and there is little valid evidence for the existence of a widespread underground conspiracy."

But there remains the haunting appeal and enchantment of the secret stations, the disguised "conductors," and the whole "underground" and conspiratorial aspect of the legend that is so hard to give up. "Stories are still repeated," patiently explains Mr. Gara, "about underground tunnels, mysterious signal lights in colored windows, peculiarly placed rows of colored bricks in houses or chimneys to identify the station, and secret rooms for hiding fugitives." These stories he finds to be without basis in fact. While we must continue to bear with our Midwestern friends and their family traditions, we are advised that, "Hearsay, rumor, and persistent stories handed down orally from generation to generation are not proof of anything."

The most valuable contribution this study makes is the revelation of how the legend grew. It was largely a postwar creation, and it sprang from a laudable impulse to be identified with noble deeds. Family pride, local pride and regional pride were fed by abolitionist reminiscences and floods of memoirs and stories. "Every barn that ever housed a fugitive, and some that hadn't," remarks Mr. Gara, "were listed as underground railroad depots." There were thousands of contributors to the legend, but the greatest was Professor Wilbur H. Siebert, whose first book, *The Underground Railroad from Slavery to Freedom,* appeared in 1898. In the nineties he painstakingly questioned hundreds of surviving antislavery workers, whose letters and responses to questionnaires Mr. Gara has reexamined. Mr. Siebert accepted their statements at face value "on the ground that the memories of the aged were more accurate than those of young people." The picture that emerged in his big book was that of "a vast network of secret routes," connecting hundreds of underground stations, operated by 3,200 "conductors"— the very minimum figure, he insisted. This work fathered many subsequent ones, which borrowed generously from it. There has been no lag in legend-building since. "The greater the distance," observes Mr. Gara, "the more enchantment seems to adhere to all aspects of the underground railroad, the legend that grew up around it, and its role in America's heritage."

A second and more elaborate aspect of the antislavery myth is the legend that the Mason and Dixon Line not only divided slavery from freedom in antebellum America, but that it also set apart racial inhumanity in the South from benevolence, liberality and tolerance in the North. Like the Underground Railroad Legend, the North Star Legend (for lack of another name) was a postwar creation. Looking back through a haze of passing years that obscured historical realities, the myth-makers credited the North with the realization in its own society of all the war aims for which it fought (or eventually proclaimed): not only Union and Freedom, but Equality as well. True, the North did not win the third war aim (or if it did, quickly forfeited it), but it nevertheless practiced what it preached, even if it failed to get the South to practice it, and had been practicing it in exemplary fashion for some time.

For a searching examination of the North Star Legend we are indebted to Leon F. Litwack, *North of Slavery: The Negro in the Free*

States, 1790–1860. He starts with the assumption that, "The inherent cruelty and violence of southern slavery requires no further demonstration, but this does not prove northern humanity." On racial attitudes of the two regions he quotes with approval the observation of Tocqueville in 1831: "The prejudice of race appears to be stronger in the states that have abolished slavery than in those where it still exists." White supremacy was a national, not a regional credo, and politicians of the Democratic, the Whig and the Republican parties openly and repeatedly expressed their allegiance to the doctrine. To do otherwise was to risk political suicide. "We, the Republican party, are the white man's party," declared Senator Lyman Trumbull of Illinois. And, as Mr. Litwack observes, "Abraham Lincoln, in his vigorous support of both white supremacy and denial of equal rights for Negroes, simply gave expression to almost universal American convictions." These convictions were to be found among Free Soil adherents and were not unknown among antislavery and abolitionist people themselves.

One reason for the unrestrained expression of racial prejudice from politicians was that the Negro was almost entirely disfranchised in the North and was therefore politically helpless. Far from sharing the expansion of political democracy, the Negro often suffered disfranchisement as a consequence of white manhood suffrage. By 1840 about 93 per cent of the free Negroes in the North were living in states that excluded them from the polls. By 1860 only 6 per cent of the Northern Negro population lived in the five states that provided legally for their suffrage. In only three states were they allowed complete parity with whites in voting. Even in those New England states doubts lingered concerning the practical exercise of equal political rights. As late as 1869, the year before the ratification of the 15th Amendment, New York State voted against equal suffrage rights for Negroes. Four Western states legally excluded free Negroes from entry.

In Northern courtrooms as at Northern polls racial discrimination prevailed. Five states prohibited Negro testimony when a white man was a party to a case, and Oregon prohibited Negroes from holding real estate, making contracts or maintaining lawsuits. Only in Massachusetts were Negroes admitted as jurors, and that not until the eve of the Civil War. The absence of Negro judges, jurors, witnesses and lawyers helps to explain the heavily disproportionate number of Negroes in Northern prisons.

Custom, extralegal codes and sometimes mob law served to relegate the Negro to a position of social inferiority and impose a harsh rule of segregation in Northern states. According to Mr. Litwack:

> In virtually every phase of existence, Negroes found themselves systematically separated from whites. They were either excluded from railway

cars, omnibuses, stagecoaches, and steamboats or assigned to special "Jim Crow" sections; they sat, when permitted, in secluded and remote corners of theaters and lecture halls; they could not enter most hotels, restaurants, and resorts, except as servants; they prayed in "Negro pews" in white churches, and if partaking of the sacrament of the Lord's Supper, they waited until the whites had been served the bread and wine. Moreover, they were often educated in segregated schools, punished in segregated prisons, nursed in segregated hospitals, and buried in segregated cemeteries.

Housing and job opportunities were severely limited. A Boston Negro wrote in 1860 that "it is five times as hard to get a house in a good location in Boston as it is in Philadelphia; and it is ten times as difficult for a colored mechanic to get work here as it is in Charleston." The earlier verdict of Tocqueville continued to ring true. "Thus the Negro is free," he wrote, "but he can share neither the rights, nor the pleasures, nor the labor, nor the afflictions, nor the tomb of him whose equal he has been declared to be; and he cannot meet him upon fair terms in life or in death."

In Northern cities with large Negro populations, violent mob action occurred with appalling frequency. Between 1832 and 1849 mobs touched off five major anti-Negro riots in Philadelphia. Mobs destroyed homes, churches and meeting halls, and forced hundreds to flee the city. An English Quaker visiting Philadelphia in 1849 remarked that there was probably no city "where dislike, amounting to hatred of the coloured population, prevails more than in the city of brotherly love!"

The Southern historian will be struck with the remarkable degree to which the South recapitulated a generation later the tragic history of race relations in the North. Once slavery was destroyed as a means of social control and subordination of the Negro, and Reconstruction was overthrown, the South resorted to many of the devices originally developed in the North to keep the Negro in his "place." There was more delay in the resort to segregation than generally supposed, but once it came toward the end of the century it was harsh and thorough. One important difference was that in the antebellum North the Negro was sometimes free to organize, protest and join white sympathizers to advance his cause and improve his position. His success in these efforts was unimpressive, however, for by 1860, as Mr. Litwack says, "despite some notable advances, the Northern Negro remained largely disfranchised, segregated, and economically oppressed." The haven to which the North Star of the legend guided the fugitive from slavery was a Jim Crow haven.

While these two studies of the antislavery myth are valuable and significant, they are slight in scope and modest in aim when compared with the far more ambitious—and traditional—book of Dwight Lowell

Dumond, *Antislavery: The Crusade for Freedom in America*. Elaborately documented, profusely illustrated and ornately bound, this massive volume is easily twice the bulk of an average-sized book. It covers the entire scope of the organized antislavery movement in this country, as well as preorganizational beginnings, and is the most extensive work on the subject in print. Represented as the result of "more than thirty years" of research by the Michigan historian, it is the outcome of a lifetime absorption in antislavery literature. It is doubtful that any other scholar has lavished such devoted study upon this vast corpus of writings.

The author's total absorption with his source materials is, indeed, the key to the theory of historiography upon which this remarkable work would appear to be based. That theory is that the purest history is to be derived from strict and undivided attention to source materials —in this case chiefly the writings, tracts and propaganda, running to millions upon millions of words, of the antislavery people themselves. If the author is aware of any of the scholarly studies of slavery and antislavery that have appeared in the last generation or more, he does not betray awareness by reference to the questions they have raised, by use of methods they have developed, or by incorporation of findings they have published. Neither the problems of slavery and antislavery that have been pressed upon the historian by new learning in psychology, anthropology, sociology and economics, nor the questions that have been raised by fresh encounters with Africa and Afro-Americans and by new experience with reformers and revolutionists and their motivation, receive any attention from the author. It is difficult to comment intelligently upon a work that so persistently and successfully avoids engagement with the contemporary mind, its assumptions, its preoccupations, its urgent questions, its whole frame of reference.

Mr. Dumond's treatment of slavery and the abolitionists admits of no complexities or ambiguities beyond the fixed categories of right and wrong. All of his abolitionists are engaged in a single-minded crusade wholly motivated by a humanitarian impulse to destroy an evil institution and succor its victims. They are moral giants among the pygmies who cross their will or fail to share their views. The single exception is William Lloyd Garrison, for whom he shares the strong distaste of his onetime collaborator Gilbert H. Barnes, the Midwestern historian. "In fact," writes Dumond (the italics are his), *"he was a man of distinctly narrow limitations among the giants of the antislavery movement."* Why Garrison falls so far short of the stature of the giants is not quite clear, but we are assured that he was "insufferably arrogant," given to "cheap cynicism" and withal "a timid soul except when safely behind the editorial desk."

Apart from Garrison, the antislavery leaders command Mr. Dumond's unqualified admiration, and his praise of them is unbounded. "What a combination of intellect, courage, and Christian faith!" he exclaims in describing the founders of the American Anti-slavery Society. The abolitionists are indeed due a redress of grievances at the hands of the historians, for they have had something less than justice from the craft. They are remembered more as pictured by carica-tures such as Henry James drew in *The Bostonians* than for their good works and genuine merits. The wild eccentricities, the fierce come-outerism, the doctrinaire extravagancies and the armchair bloodlusts of some of the abolitionists have been stressed and repeated to the neglect of the dedicated and fearless work they did in the face of ridicule, mob violence and all the pressures that wealth and established order can bring to bear upon dissenters. Their cause was just, and among their numbers were men and women of courage, intelligence and moral force. They deserve their due and need a sympathetic defender.

The trouble with Mr. Dumond as historian of the antislavery move-ment is his total involvement. This involvement extends beyond hatred of slavery and approval of abolition. It commits him as well to the style and tone and temper, the immediacy of indignation, the very idiom and rhetoric of a movement of thought that took its shape from intellectual influences and social conditions existing nearly a century and a half ago. The effect is startling. The rhythm and color of his prose is in perfect keeping with the style and tone of the scores of lithographs and prints from old abolitionist tracts that serve appro-priately to illustrate the book. The author paints just what he sees, but he sees everything through the eyes of the 1830's. The result is more than an anachronism. It gives the effect of a modern primitive, a Henri Rousseau of historiography.

Any treatment of the antislavery movement necessarily involves some treatment of the institution it opposed. Mr. Dumond's conception of slavery would seem to have taken shape in considerable degree from the antislavery literature he has so thoroughly mastered. At any rate, he quotes liberally from this literature in characterizing slavery. Among other things, he quotes a poem by Timothy Dwight, published in 1794, the year before he became president of Yale. The last stanza of it reads as follows:

> Why shrinks yon slave, with horror, from his meat? / Heavens! 'tis his flesh, the wretch is whipped to eat. / Why streams the life-blood from that female's throat? / She sprinkled gravy on a guest's new coat!

"Poetic license?" asks the historian. "Exaggeration? Fantasy? *Only half the truth, if a thousand witnesses are to be believed.*" And they, he assures us, are to be believed.

Mr. Dumond selects Theodore Dwight Weld's *American Slavery As It Is*, published in 1839, as "the greatest of the antislavery pamphlets," and still the best historical authority on slavery. "It is an encyclopedia of knowledge. It is a book of horrors," he writes. Weld himself correctly described it as "a work of incalculable value" to the abolitionist cause. "Facts and testimonies are troops, weapons and victory, all in one," he wrote. The principles governing its composition are suggested by a letter to Weld from two editorial advisors, Sereno and Mary Streeter: "Under the head of personal cruelty [you] will be obliged to reject much testimony; and this is not because the facts are not well authenticated but because those which are merely *horrid* must give place to those which are absolutely diabolical." Absolutely diabolical or not, in the opinion of Professor Dumond, "It is as close as history can come to the facts." According to his theory of historical evidence, "Diaries and plantation records are largely worthless because slaveholders never kept a record of their own evil ways."

The strong sexual theme that pervades antislavery literature often took a prurient turn, but in Mr. Dumond's hands the pruriency is transmuted by bold treatment. The presence of miscegenation is attested by the Census of 1860 and the proportion of the colored population of the South that was of mixed blood. But to Mr. Dumond, sexual exploitation becomes very nearly the basis of the institution of slavery. "Its prevalence leads to the inescapable conclusion," he writes, "that it was the 'basis—unspoken to be sure—of much of the defense of the institution." Ulrich B. Phillips, the Southern historian of slavery, doubtless betrayed a certain blindness when he reported that in all the records he studied he could find only one instance of deliberate "breeding" of slaves, and that an unsuccessful one in colonial Massachusetts. To Mr. Dumond, however, it is plain as day that the "breeding" was practiced by *all* slaveholders: "That is exactly what slave owners did with the slaves, and there were no exceptions." To the Georgia historian there were no instances, to the Michigan historian no exceptions! What is one to tell the children?

Mr. Dumond's main subject, of course, is not slavery but antislavery. In his treatment of this great theme the myth is slightly muted, but it nevertheless pulses powerfully through the whole narrative. The Underground Railroad is described as "a highly romantic enterprise" that became "well organized." In these pages it operates with all the enchanting conspiracy and secrecy of the legend, with fugitive slaves "secreted in livery stables, in attics, in storerooms, under featherbeds, in secret passages, in all sorts of out of the way places." There was one hayloft in Detroit that "was always full of Negroes."

In Professor Dumond's history the North Star Legend is given very nearly full credence. In striking contrast with the account rendered in detail by Mr. Litwack, we are informed that Negroes "continued to vote without interruption in New Hampshire, Vermont, Rhode Island, and in the two slave states of New York and New Jersey," and that there were never "any distinctions whatever in criminal law, judicial procedure, and punishments" in any New England states. "Negroes were citizens in all of these [free?] states," he writes (leaving it unclear how many). "They were citizens by enjoyment of full political equality, by lack of any statements to the contrary in any constitution or law, by complete absence of legal distinctions based on color, and by specific legal and constitutional declaration, and any statements to the contrary by courts, federal or state, were contrary to historical fact and are worthless as historical evidence." There is no hint of the thoroughgoing system of Northern segregation described by Mr. Litwack. It is admitted that one might "find a less liberal attitude toward free Negroes" in the Midwestern states, but that is easily accounted for: "There was a preponderance of Southern immigrants in the populations." In spite of this, we learn that in Jackson's time, "the Northern people, freeing themselves of the last vestiges of slavery, moved forward in a vast liberal reform movement."

The theory Mr. Dumond applies to the antislavery movement colors and coerces his reading of the whole of American history from the Revolution through the Civil War. This reading amounts to a revival of the long discredited theory of the Slave Power Conspiracy, a dominant hypothesis two or three generations ago. Slavery, we are told, "gave clay feet to Patrick Henry . . . and I suspect to Washington and Jefferson as well." Of the Revolutionary leaders he writes: "Those men were perfectly willing to spread carnage over the face of the earth to establish their own claim to freedom, but lacked the courage to live by their assertion of the natural rights of men." Of the Presidential contest of 1800 we are told: "This election enabled Jefferson to lay solidly the foundations of the party of agrarianism, slavery, and decentralization." Any mention of Jefferson is accompanied by a reminder that he owned slaves. The achievement of a group is discredited with the phrase, "slaveholders all." The Virginia Dynasty, its heirs and successors of the next three decades, and most of their acts and works including the Constitution, fare pretty harshly under this restricted historical criterion.

The whole sectional conflict that eventually erupted in the Civil War is construed, of course, in terms of right versus wrong, North against South. Civil War historians will be interested to learn that "there was complete co-ordination by the Congress, the President, and the field commanders of the Army" in their mutual determination to abolish slavery at the earliest possible moment. This revelation will require a good deal of revision in accepted views, which take into account a great lack of coordination among those distracted branches of the wartime government.

It is possible that Professor Dumond's interpretations of American history might be traced directly to an unfortunate theory of historical method. Neither this nor the extended criticism of his work already undertaken would be worth the effort, however, were it not for what the book reveals about the present vitality and amazing persistence of the antislavery myth. His book is the latest and fullest embodiment of the myth. Yet it comes with endorsements of unqualified praise from leading authorities in the field. The wide flaps of the dust jacket bear such recommendations from the three foremost present-day historians of the American Civil War, followed by the equally enthusiastic praise of prominent historians from four of our most respected universities. These are not men who share Mr. Dumond's restrictive concepts of historiography, nor are they given to bestowing praise lightly. They undoubtedly mean what they say. What two of them say is that this book is "definitive," and all agree that from their point of view it is wholly satisfying.

One would like to know more about their reasoning. Several of them refer directly or obliquely to present-day social problems that are a heritage of slavery, meaning segregation and the movement for Negro rights. But surely one can establish his position upon such clear-cut contemporary moral problems as these without compromising the standards of historical criticism. And by this time, one hopes, it is possible to register a stand on the slavery issue without feigning the apocalyptic rages of a John Brown. No, these are not adequate or convincing explanations, at least for the reactions of these particular historians.

In all probability the real reason why this ponderous, fierce and humorless book is handled with such piety and solemnity is the very fact that it does embody one of the great American myths. We have never faced up to the relationship between myth and history. Without tackling the semantic difficulties involved, we know that *myth* has more than pejorative usages and that it can be used to denote more than what one deems false about the other man's beliefs. In the non-pejorative sense myths are images, or collections of them, charged with values, aspirations, ideals and meanings. In the words of Mark Schorer, they are "the instruments by which we continually struggle to make our experience intelligible to ourselves." Myths *can* be, in short, "a good thing." No man in his right mind, and surely not a responsible historian, will knowingly and wantonly destroy a precious thing. And no doubt some would hesitate to lay hands on a book that, improperly though it may be, got itself identified as a repository of cherished values.

Serious history is the critique of myths, however, not the embodiment of them. Neither is it the destruction of myths. One of the great national myths is the equality of man, embodied in the Declaration of Independence. Tocqueville's study of equality in America is a valid critique of the myth, with neither the intention nor the effect of de-

stroying it or doing it injury. Henry Nash Smith's *Virgin Land* provides
a valid critique of the West's Myth of the Garden and symbols of the
frontier without succumbing to impulses of iconoclasm. There is no
comparable critique of the more elaborate myth—one might say mythology—of the South. What has been done in this respect has been
mainly the work of imaginative writers rather than historians of the
South.   Historians have made a beginning, however, and a recent
contribution by William R. Taylor, *Cavalier and Yankee,* which illumi-
nates the legend of aristocratic grandeur, is an excellent illustration
of what is needed.

As a result of such studies, intelligent, contemporary Americans
can speak of the myth of equality without self-consciousness or cynicism, and embrace it without striking the pose of a defiant Jacksonian
of the 1830's. Contemporary westerners are able to cherish and preserve
frontier values without assuming the role of a Davy Crockett. And
southerners can even salvage some of the aristocratic heritage without
wallowing in the Plantation Legend.

As yet, however, the Yankee remains to be fully emancipated from
his own legends of emancipation. Confront him with a given set of
symbols and he will set his sense of humor aside, snap to attention and
come to a full salute. In the ensuing rigidities of that situation, conversation tends to lag. The pertinent interjections by Mr. Gara on the
U.G.R.R. and by Mr. Litwack on the North Star Legend, already noticed,
may help to break the ice, but the thawing will probably be slow. The
provocative suggestions of Stanley M. Elkins, in *Slavery: A Problem in
American Institutional and Intellectual Life,* have been gravely rebuked
for impropriety, if not impiety. The orthodox text is obviously still
the gospel according to Mr. Dumond.

The big assignment on the Antislavery Myth still awaits a taker.
The eventual taker, like any historian who would make myth the proper
subject of his study, should be involved without running the risks
of total involvement. It would help a great deal if he could contrive
to bring detachment as well as sympathy to his task. It is also to be
hoped that he might make legitimate use of irony as well as compas-
sion. And, finally, no aspirant with inappropriate regional identifi-
cations need apply.

The Search for the Individual: 1750–1850
RUSSEL B. NYE

America is the covenanted community. It is a society of purposes that have
been consciously articulated and agreed upon. The slogans that sum up
these purposes are statements of promise. Lacking reference to the past,
they are written against the future, offering the covenanters new freedoms,
new deals, new frontiers. Written for a people of plenty, they project a
vision of increasing plenitude, of full dinner pails, and of great societies.
The recurrence of the word "deal" in so many of the slogans discloses that
the business of the American covenant is business.

In pursuing the work of the covenant, we have regularly understood two
premises: that the community was an enterprise for realizing its aims, for
achievement, for improving its condition, in effect, for "progress"; and that
the fulfillment of the aspirations of the community was the fulfillment of
those of the individual, and vice versa. But if the premises have been constant, the particulars with which they have dealt have not. If the perennial
goal has been progress, just what has constituted progress—what society
has considered to be its aims within a specific historical context—has undergone variation from one age to the next. And if the individual has always
been central to the covenant, just who and what he is—his nature, his
potentiality, his relation to God, truth, and the goals of the community—has
also been subject to redefinition by each succeeding generation. Indeed, it
is these changing views of the American's nature and of his community's
aims that make up the history of American thought.

That these views went through a basic reformation during the century
from 1750 to 1850 is the theme of the following essay by Russel B. Nye.
Professor of English at Michigan State University, Nye is the author of
many books on American history that are mainly concerned with reformers
and progressives and the evolution of American social thought. He won a
Pulitzer prize for his biography of the famous nineteenth-century historian

SOURCE: The Centennial Review, V (Winter, 1961), 1–20. Reprinted by permission of the author and the publisher.

and politician, George Bancroft. His most recent volume, This Almost Chosen People *(1966), traces the development of several of America's principal ideas—nationalism, progress, free enterprise, individualism, mission, equality—"to show how they have given an ideological backbone to American thought and activity. . . ."*

In The Cultural Life of the New Nation, 1776–1830 *(1960), Professor Nye sought to answer the same questions that he considers in the essay reprinted below: What were the respective ideas, concerning the individual, of the revolutionary age and of the age of Jackson? What were their respective ideas concerning progress? Why did these ideas change from one age to the next? How in effect do we diagram and explain the great transition from the American Enlightenment to American Romanticism and Transcendentalism? How much did this transition owe to the growth of an independent, increasingly democratic American society?*

One has but to peruse our journals of opinion and the books that command our attention these days to know that we very much remain a covenanted community, a polity self-consciously dedicated to certain goals and preoccupied with our national purpose. But if we are to a great extent engaged in discussions of our goals and purpose, we are to no lesser extent confused about what they should be. What has become of the covenant? What are our purposes today, and how different are they from what they were in Emerson's day? What is the American's present concept of truth and progress? How far has his Romantic view of truth—in the sense of transcendental, universal, divine, intuitive—been replaced by one that regards truth as finite, particular, relative, existential? How much has the liberal idea—that what is good for the individual is also good for the community—survived? Has the hope that the idea of progress as it was once expressed been robbed of relevance and meaning by American experience since 1850?

What is the significance for the premises upon which the covenant so long rested—individualism and progress—of some of the salient developments of our times: the extending forms and values of mass society and their fettering of the individual; the revolution of the Negro against the inequities of American life and the irrelevance, to him, of the conditions of the covenant; the increasing addiction to drugs of American youth, and the pursuit of happiness in hedonistic rather than moral terms; the growing sense that the slogans of the community's leaders have not been realized, that the summons to new frontiers and a great society has been an empty ritual; the spreading view that the mission of America in Vietnam is the infliction of our idea of national purpose upon another nation with another purpose? It is a moot question for the student of American thought as to whether the ideology we fashioned out of our premises is at all consonant with today's realities, and whether it has not in fact been an ever-increasing burden that is making it more and and more difficult for us to run the course of relations with the other polities of the late twentieth-century world.

This essay is concerned with an exploration of certain aspects of American intellectual life during the period 1750 to 1850. Its thesis is not complicated. Stated simply, it is that because of certain major changes in what men believed about human nature and truth, there were corresponding changes, between 1750 and 1850 in the United States, in American concepts of individualism and progress—and that the social, political, religious, and cultural thought of this period reflects these changes. To phrase it differently, life in the United States from the middle of the 18th century to the Civil War can be most clearly read in terms of a pervasive popular faith in the individual's adequacy to fulfill all his aims and functions. The framework of American thought in the United States during these years was constructed about this principle.

This belief in individualism and progress, one must hasten to point out, is congruent with the American acceptance of the Romantic movement. But it must be noted first that the United States emphasized certain aspects of Romanticism in a manner, and to a degree, not true of contemporary England or Europe. And second, by reason of its historical and intellectual environment, American thought in the decades after 1750 would naturally have centered about these twin principles of individualism and progress, even had no Romantic movement existed to reinforce them.

These two related doctrines of perfectibility and progress, which provided the foundation for American thought from 1750 to 1850, were part of the great ideological legacy bequeathed to America from the 17th- and 18th-century philosophers. What the 19th century believed to be true about the nature of man, of course, was not the same as the 18th century's heritage, which, like all such legacies, underwent a sea-change. A great deal happened after 1750—in philosophy, politics, society, and in the quality of life itself after the Revolution—to make the generation of Emerson and Jackson much more assured and enthusiastic about mankind's present and future than the age of Franklin and Jonathan Edwards could afford to be. It happened in this way.

I

First, the American belief in the perfectibility of mankind rested on a powerful faith in the intrinsic goodness of human nature. Many Americans of the late 18th century—among them Paine, Barlow, Jefferson, Rush, and Franklin in his more sanguine moments—conceived their fellowmen to be perfectly capable of infinite progress and unlimited knowledge, because they believed that mankind was essentially trustworthy. Americans of their generation, in fact, tended to hold far fewer reservations about the reliability of ordinary man than did the Europeans or British. This was the result, perhaps, of a long frontier heritage, a successful revolution, and a new, incomplete, open society of opportunity. Whatever the reason, American thinkers of the later 18th century were much more confident of man's virtue and rationality than the majority of contemporary British philosophers— much closer, in their faith, to the French. What the British Romantics considered a *qualified* trust in humanity's *ultimate* goodness, the Americans (and the French *philosophes*) took as absolute conviction.

There was no reason, many Americans believed, why the heavenly city of the 18th-century philosophers could not be built by good men on this earth, on this side of the Atlantic, here and now. "No definite limits," Thomas Jefferson wrote, "can be assigned to . . . the improve-ability of the human race." Dr. Benjamin Rush, throwing caution aside, was "fully persuaded that it is possible to produce such change in the moral character of man, as shall raise him to a resemblance of angels— nay more to the likeness of God himself." When Joel Barlow asked rhetorically in *The Columbiad* (1809), "Where shall we limit the progress of human wisdom, and the force of its institutions?" he implied his own answer.

Out of this confidence in humanity, the political theorists of the new republic contrived a government built about the individual's "natural" rights, his inherent wisdom, and his ability to rule himself. There were those, of course, such as Timothy Dwight of New England, or John Adams, or Alexander Hamilton, or Fisher Ames, who did not fully share the easy confidence of the times; even the usually optimistic Franklin, now and then, had uneasy glimpses of men as "a set of Beings badly constructed." Nevertheless, there were more believers than doubters in the young United States. They agreed with Pope that the "proper study of mankind" was man, but not Pope's 18th-century man.

It was the individual, free-standing man in whom they believed, not man the pebble in Pope's social aggregate, and it was also *American* man. This confidence lent excitement to the times. Philip Freneau, the poet, writing in 1771 of *The Rising Glory of America,* impatiently awaited the day when in America

> A new Jerusalem, sent down from Heaven,
> Shall grace our happy earth,

while "the future situation of America" filled Joel Barlow's mind with "a peculiar dignity" and opened "an unlimited field of thought."

The change which took place in American thought after 1750 in the attitude toward the individual was the result, among other things, of certain new decisions reached by philosophers and theologians about the availability of truth. The 18th century was convinced that man, by exercise of his reason, could locate truth and act upon it. To that century, however, the apprehension of truth was to a great degree a social process, for social ends. As individuals seized upon fragments of truth, society put them together in coherent order to provide patterns and standards for life and belief. The early 18th century, quite certain of this, placed its reliance on Reason as the prime quality of mind by which the truth was found. Later 18th-century thinkers, though still confident of man's rationality, began to have doubts.

At the same time, the generation of Americans who were busy justifying a revolution and building a government on "self-evident" principles, found some difficulty in substantiating those so-called "self-evident truths." What the revolutionary philosophers should have been able to prove "true" by reason, they could not; how could one "prove" the right to the pursuit of happiness, when there was still some legal question about his right to liberty? Since they were forced by necessity to accept and act upon *unproveable* truths—self-evident truths —American thinkers revised their opinions of how one located truth, and the qualifications for its discovery.

This "self-evident truth" posed a bothersome problem to the thinkers of the post-Revolutionary years. If a truth were self-evident, how could it be verified? Could it be also self-originated, perhaps not a product of the reason or subject to it? It is interesting to see the Age of Reason proving the unproveable. John Harris, when he included the term "self-evident axiom" in his *Dictionary of Arts and Sciences,* defined it as "a generally-received principle or rule in any art or science." Not satisfied, he retreated a step and tried again; such an axiom could not be demonstrated "because 'tis itself much beter known than anything that can be brought to prove it." Joel Barlow, the American poet-soldier-diplomat-philosopher who had a facility for phrasing intellectual issues, wrestled with the same problem. He finally concluded that there were three kinds of truth—*rational* truth (capable of proof by logic within the mind), *scientific* (capable of empirical demonstration), and *self-evident,* which Barlow defined as those truths "as perceptible when first presented to the mind as our age or world of experience could make them."

James Wilson, the brilliant Pennsylvania jurist, grappled with the problem, too, concluding, like Barlow, that there were three kinds of verifiable truth. First, Wilson accepted those "truths given in evidence by the external senses," which provided knowledge of the physical world. Second, he said, were truths "given in evidence by our moral faculty," which supplied men with moral and ethical knowledge. And third, he recognized a puzzling kind of truth "which we are *required* and determined by the constitution of our nature and faculties to believe." But neither Barlow nor Wilson, nor others who struggled with the problem, could quite define this unproveable truth; they simply knew such truths existed, and that men somehow possessed the power to find them. So while the 18th century read Locke and dutifully tested its ideas by reason and experiment, it was also aware that there were more things than one dreamed of beyond the empirical philosophy.

By degrees, then, the "self-evident truth" turned into a kind of knowledge which no one needed to justify. The intuitive and unproveable, in the opening years of the 19th century, became as valid to the philosopher as the rational. And as American thinkers revised their ideas of what truth was and how men might find it, so they concluded that individual man himself was the *source* of truth. From where else, they asked, might "self-evident" truth come? The standards of society, the codes of tradition, the rules of universal reason, all these might serve as the bar to which ordinary logic could be brought, but to judge the validity of the self-evident truth, only a man's inner sense could suffice.

For example, James Marsh of the University of Vermont thought in 1829 that one might discover truth "by those laws of the understanding which belong in common to all men" (a good, orthodox, 18th-century dictum), but he also suggested that one must always "try the conclusions by one's own consciousness as a final test." "It is by *self-inspection*," he continued, "that we can *alone* arrive at any rational knowledge. . . ." Young Sylvester Judd, at divinity school in the twenties, believed that one could find truth only in "the impersonal, boundless, authoritative depths of his own nature." Philosopher Caleb Sprague Henry explained that "the instantaneous but real fact of spontaneous apperception of truth" took place only in "the intimacy of individual consciousness." Theodore Parker believed that truth could be perceived best in those "great primal Intuitions of Human Nature, which depend on no logical process of demonstration, but are rather facts of consciousness given by the instinctive action of human nature itself." Orestes Brownson recognized in man "the capacity of knowing truth intuitively, or of attaining to a scientific knowledge of an order of existence transcending the reach of the senses, and of which we can have no sensible experience." George Bancroft, the historian, writing in 1835, explained that each man possessed "an internal sense . . . not that faculty which deduces inferences from the experience of the senses, but that higher faculty which from the infinite treasures of its own consciousness, *originates* truth and assents to it by the force of intuitive evidence." Henry David Thoreau, of course, lived out at Walden Pond the experiment by which he tested the entire concept of self-determined values.

By the eighteen-thirties, then, the existence of self-evident truth—meaning that truth evident only to the individual self-consciousness

—was an accepted and accomplished fact in American thought. In such fashion Coleridge, Kant, Carlyle, and Cousin displaced the great Mr. Locke and the 18th-century world of Reason; in such manner the world of Jefferson, Paine, and Rush gave way to the world of Emerson. In this context George Bancroft could quite reasonably write, as he did, an essay titled "The Promise, the Necessity, and the Reality of the Progress of the Human Race," basing it on a generally-approved belief in the unlimited capacity of man to discover truth in, by, and for himself. Few of his contemporaries would have disputed him.

This change in the concept of the nature of truth, and in the individual's ability to identify it, powerfully influenced the 19th century's estimates of the theory of progress. The majority of American colonists had believed, of course, that the world improved by grace of God and Reason. To the 18th-century view, this forward movement of man and society was a slow, inevitable, divinely-ordained progression. Men could hasten it somewhat by revising their ideas and institutions, and they could retard it by their follies, but not by much. The drive for betterment, the 18th century thought, was inherent in the nature of life. The universal perfection of which the 18th century dreamed, however, was the ultimate substance of things hoped for, to be approached a step at a time as divinity willed it. The "melioration" of man's problems, to use a favorite contemporary word, *would* come. Men should do nothing to impede it, of course, but whether they would or not, progress was part of a huge cyclic change, a wave in the tide of affairs that could neither be stopped nor diverted.

After the turn of the 19th century, the American idea of progress became much more kinetic and positive. Emerson, quite typically, in his essay on *Fate,* believed that the "indwelling necessity" and "central intention" of all creation was nothing less than universal "harmony and joy." His friend, William Ellery Channing, felt that a man need only "to trust, dare and be," to have "infinite good ready for your asking." The thinkers of the thirties made the principle of progress into a rule of life; theirs was no tentative acceptance, but a fervent, clear belief.

There were a number of reasons for this. First, some of the responsibility for improving the world had shifted from God to man, who was held much more accountable than before for determining his future. Second, the *rate* of advancement in human affairs, it was assumed, could be accelerated by man's own efforts. Progress was conceived not simply to be part of a remote, ageless cycle, but something accessible, responsive to manipulation. As Albert Brisbane wrote, men could find ways of *"hastening* this progress, and of anticipating results, which if left to the gradual movement of society would require centuries to effect." Third, by using government as an instrument of change, many Americans believed that in the United States, at least, one might obtain "progress by legislation"—that is, a kind of self-willed boot-strap-lifting by statute.

In science and technology, the United States believed that they had a powerful ally for betterment, not only of material life but of the intellect and spirit as well. The progress of science, wrote the geologist James Dwight Dana, "is upward as well as onward." New machinery, Salmon P. Chase wrote in *The North American Review* in 1832, represented "an almost infinite power, brought to bear on the action of the social system . . . producing almost unmingled benefit." And, too, the 19th century discovered another effective aid to progress in the principle of *association*. Men could join in societies to multiply their strengths, to do in decades (or less) by concerted effort what God and time might take eons to accomplish. William Ellery Channing explained in *The Christian Examiner* in September, 1829:

> The union of minds and hands works wonders. Men grow efficient by concentrating their powers. . . . Nor is this all. Men not only accumulate power by union, but gain warmth, and earnestness. . . . Union not only brings to a point forces which before existed, and which were ineffectual through separation, but by the feeling and interest which it rouses, it becomes a creative principle, calls forth new forces, and gives the mind a consciousness of forces, which otherwise would have been unknown.

To summarize, it may be said that after approximately 1790, the pattern of American thought had polarized about certain ideas of human nature, and progress. Men generally believed in the goodness of human nature, in their capacity to find truth of a verifiable though intuitive kind, and in their ability to act upon it. They believed in progress, decreed by divine benevolence, which could be hastened by individual and cooperative effort, with the assistance of science and government. Since it was assumed that all men, not merely a few or those of a certain class, profited from this upward trend, the idea of progress was thus integrated into American democratic idealism, built into its social and intellectual framework. The consideration of almost every issue of general interest to the early 19th century was formulated and influenced in some way by these twin assumptions of individualism and progress. The acceptance of these principles thrust new responsibilities on the American individual, casting him in a new role as shaper and director of his future.

II

In the remainder of this essay, it is my intention to trace the effects of this cluster of beliefs in three important areas of 19th-century American thought—politics, religion, and social reform. To represent the prevailing concepts of individuality and progress as they appeared in ideas and events, I shall use Andrew Jackson, Ralph Waldo Emerson, and William Lloyd Garrison. Each, in his way, represents one side of an equilateral triangle—Jackson the political leader, Emerson the ethical philosopher, Garrison the activist crusader for reform. All three centered their lives about these contemporary convictions about human nature and progress.

What the history books label "Jacksonian democracy," historians generally agree, was much more than Andrew Jackson's creation. Whether Old Hickory led a procession of common men to political triumph, or whether he stepped in at the head of a parade already marching, need not concern us here. However, it is important to understand that Jacksonian democracy was the *political* manifestation of the current belief that individual man was his own master, and that *American* man, certainly, was able to control and to improve his government almost without limitation.

There were non-ideological factors involved in the rise of Jacksonism, indeed—the westward shift of population, the beginnings of western sectionalism, the rise of an urban laboring class, and so on. But there also was current in Jacksonian politics an acute awareness, never before so precisely defined in American political thinking, of the supreme consequence of the individual in government. Jefferson's trust in man, properly qualified and controlled, was well known. The Age of Jackson deified the individual—or very nearly so—and made of individual man an oracle never intended by even the most optimistic of the 18th-century philosophers. Evidence of this lies not so much in the practical politics of his time, but rather in what the American public used Jackson to symbolize and his movement to represent.

To the American public, Andrew Jackson became Individual Man incarnate.[1] His admirers claimed that he embodied personally all the virtues of *natural* American man, invigorated with "natural genius," free of artificiality and European taint, liberated from false tradition. Jackson was a man of *intuitive* wisdom, his biographers said; study of his life revealed how an individual could find truth out of his own mind and experience. *The Illinois Gazette* in 1824 thought Jackson "gifted with genius—with those great powers of mind that can generalize with as much ease as a common intellect can go through detail." He possessed, according to another of his eulogists, "instinctive superiority, self-reliance, and impulsive energy." He was, said another, "a master spirit . . . the architect of his own fortunes" who from an orphaned, poverty-stricken boyhood rose to eminence by relying on himself, "by

---

[1] See John W. Ward, *Andrew Jackson: Symbol for An Age* (New York: Oxford University Press, 1955) for a more thorough treatment of this idea.

standing and acting alone."[2]   In 1834, *The New York Times*, almost exactly paraphrasing Bancroft's essay on popular intuitive truth, found in Old Hickory

> . . . a mysterious light which directs his intellect, which baffles all speculation upon philosophy of mind. . . . He arrives at conclusions with a rapidity which proves that his process is not through the tardy avenues of syllogism. . . . His mind seems clogged by no forms, but goes with lightning's flash and illuminates its own pathway.

Certainly not until the later essays of Emerson, Channing, Parker, and the transcendentalists was there such lucid exposition of the superiority of Reason (in the Kantian sense) over Understanding.

The Jacksonians were politicians, not philosophers, of course, but as surely and as clearly as Emerson, they placed at the base of their political creed the same pervasive faith in the individual—as symbolized by Jackson—and in his intuitive perception of self-evident truth. John O'Sullivan, the Jacksonian editor, attempted to define this faith in an article he wrote for *The United States Magazine and Democratic Review* in September, 1839:

> (Democracy) recognizes the distinct existence of man in himself as an independent end, not barely as a means to be merged in a mass, and controlled as a thing by public caprice or policy. His instinctive convictions, his irrepressible desires, his boundless capacity for improvement, conspire with all the indications of Providence, with all the teachings of history, and all the designs of his internal condition and adjustments, to make the doctrine of individual rights the greatest of political truths. . . .

If each man were given full freedom to take care of himself, the Jacksonians seemed to say, then God and Nature would take care of the rest. If the individual were granted his liberty, a kind of fundamental order would spontaneously arise, as O'Sullivan wrote, for there are "natural laws which will establish themselves and find their own level" if men are free.

George Bancroft, who like Barlow had a knack for expressing the popular mind, was a better writer than O'Sullivan and expressed this belief in a better metaphor. As each person contained within him the ability to improve himself, he explained, so the sum of individual advancements combined for total human progress, much as particles of water merged to make a wave. Bancroft was convinced that the study of history, especially American history, proved that mankind moved steadily upward. What check-point, he asked, what standard might

---

[2] Any of these admiring descriptive phrases, it is worth noting, could easily have been quoted from Emerson's *Self-Reliance*, which did not appear until 1841.

the historian use to measure that progress and its rate? He chose the status of the *individual,* his rights, dignity, and happiness; by this standard one might judge man's progress at any selected point in history. The movement of humanity could always be measured, he believed, by the *individual's* advance. For as he wrote in his essay *The Office of the People in Art, Government, and Religion* (1835), it is certain that "The irresistible tendency of the human race is therefore to advancement. . . . The movement of the species is upward, irresistibly upward." Judged by this standard, Jacksonian America, as Bancroft observed it, represented the highest point yet reached in the species' upward march. (It is not surprising that some critics accused his *History of the United States from The Discovery of the Continent. . . . ,* the first volume of which appeared in 1834, of "voting for Jackson.")

Jacksonian democracy's exalted estimate of Individual Political Man, and its confident convictions of progress, found its religious analogy in the unitarian-transcendentalist movement which culminated with Emerson's ringing celebration of self-reliance in theology and ethics. Beneath the doctrinal complexities of the controversy among Calvinists, Unitarians, and transcendentalists which occupied much of the first four decades of the 19th century, there ran a single line of argument—what is the nature of man, and how may he perceive God's truth? There were a number of issues on which religious opinion was divided after 1790, but this was the most critical, since it involved agreement on the source of true revelation.

The various disputants were willing to concede that the Bible was *one* source of general religious truth, but few could arrive at agreement about the degree and manner of its reliability. If the Bible contained truth, it must stand the test of reason; it must agree with the "facts of inward consciousness" of which Bancroft spoke and with those "self-evident" truths which entranced and puzzled the 18th century. But what if it did not? What if the Bible and the individual reason did not "speak with the same voice"? The time came when a choice had to be made between the Scriptures and the intuitions of the individual's own mind. William Ellery Channing, before Emerson the leader of the theological liberals, chose to trust the individual. "I am surer of my rational nature from God," he wrote, "than that any book is."

Channing's was a decisive step. It was not far from his position to Emerson's, which placed complete reliance on the individual in ethical and theological decisions—as the Jacksonians in the political sphere placed their confidence in the common man. And this step, too, forced a closer inspection of the nature and attributes of this self-reliant individual; the result led the New Englanders directly to that unique mixture of theology, philosophy, moralism, and sermonizing loosely called transcendentalism.

From the mid-18th century to the mid-19th in American thought, therefore, the accepted version of the individual's power to grasp and interpret God's truth underwent a complete change—from Calvin's dependence on the Bible and emphasis on the sovereignty of God, to deism's grant to man of equal sovereignty in a universe of reason, to Channing's transfer of sovereignty from Bible and church to man, and finally to the *self*-reliance of Emerson, Parker, and Thoreau. The line of thought moved from Mather's distrust of man, to Jefferson's qualified confidence in him, to Emerson's and Jackson's deep and abiding faith in his capacity to find and act upon divine truth. It was a long journey from John Cotton's struggle with man's inward dark angel, to Edwards' reluctant submission to God's rule, to Emerson's proud, confident "Know thyself! Every heart vibrates to that iron string!" The 19th century's deification of human nature reached its climax in the essays of the Sage of Concord. *The American Scholar* deified the Individual in art and intellect; *The Divinity School Address* exalted the Individual in religion; *Self-Reliance* granted each man the right and duty to find his own moral and ethical guides.

Confidence in man (and men) runs like a bright thread through the pattern of American thought in the first half of the 19th century. The Enlightenment sought the measure of things outside man; Jefferson, who yielded to none in his respect for his fellowman, thought of him in terms of his relationships to the whole. The Age of Reason, to phrase it differently, with all its esteem for men, found them most comprehensible in group terms, most explicable in the aggregate. But Jacksonians and transcendentalists found the measure of things *within* the individual. What the Age of Reason hoped to establish as truth by empiricism and experiment, the Age of Emerson and Jackson located inside human nature, in the personal, intuitional act of cognition. Bronson Alcott explained succinctly, "It is the still, small voice of the private soul that is authentic . . . the single man's oracle." What Emerson defined as the absolute, basic fact of truth, "the coincidence of an object with a subject," was something to be privately perceived—or as he explained it in another way, one "solved the metaphor of Nature alone." What a man must do to find the truth, he wrote in *The American Scholar*, was "to learn to detect and watch that gleam of light which flashes across his mind from within." Out of secluded, intimate moments of perception, he believed, came that sudden conviction of enlightenment which men knew was true.

Because they believed in this concept of human nature, the Age of Emerson and Jackson believed it understood the world, and could control it. Viewed in these terms, the old problems of state, society, church, ethics, art, and morality seemed simplified and soluble. All human problems, in fact, according to Theodore Parker, really could be reduced to one problem, which was simply "no less than this, to reverse the experience of mankind and try its teachings by the *nature* of man." It was perhaps the last time in history that a generation could look about, understand its universe so clearly, and embrace it with such supreme assurance.

In effect, the Jacksonians and the Emersonians gave man domain over what the 17th and 18th centuries assumed to be God's. Calvinism and deism set their Gods beyond the individual's reach—as Parker said, in realms where he "could not meet God face to face." The 19th century made deity immanent in man and deified human nature. "The idea of God," William Ellery Channing wrote, ". . . is the idea of our own spiritual nature, purified and enlarged to infinity." God became individual man infinitely projected; conversely, the individual became God. American theology and philosophy, so to speak, turned Pope's phrase into a palindrome, wherein the proper study of mankind was God, and of God, mankind.

Emersonian-transcendental thought therefore provided a philosophy, once-removed, for Jacksonism. It was unfortunate that Emerson and his followers could not accept Jackson himself as the embodiment of Transcendental Man in Politics (though logically they should have) for Jacksonism, give or take a few unphilosophical rudenesses, provided an outlet and expression for the spirit of self-reliance in a way that the Concord philosophers could not. Theodore Parker recognized this when he said that "All American history is an attempt to prove by experience the transcendental proposition of man, to organize the transcendental idea of politics." But transcendentalism was not for the Jacksonian masses, nor could Jackson's men probably have grasped the sophisticated message of *Self-Reliance* or *Politics* had they read it. The message belonged to the times, nevertheless, and what Emerson said to intellectuals, others said to the crowds.

Within the context of the early 19th century's attitudes toward the individual, his nature, and his progress, the relationships among Jacksonism, perfectionism, and transcendentalism (as well as among other lesser movements of the time) thus become visible and understandable. Spiritualism, millenialism, New Thought, Andrew Jackson Davis, the Fox Sisters, Abner Kneeland, and Phineas Quimby, among others, reflect the current faith in man's ability to find truth directly, by his own act. All of them drew strength from the same principles. Even phrenology, pseudo-science though it may have been, found a place within the pattern. For phrenology insisted that each person was unique, and that each individual, by determination and self-training, could weaken his evil propensities and strengthen his good ones. The design of thought in the early 19th century is really, then, of one piece. William Miller's pathetic band, waiting on a New York hilltop for the coming of judgment, were poor relations of Emerson's Concordians, Finney's Perfectionists, Jackson's army of "common men," Quimby's New Thinkers, and Spurzheim's skull-scientists. Their concepts of man, progress, and truth they held in common—loosely, but in common.

A third strand in this pattern of 19th-century American thought was social reform. The preceding century, despite its Enlightenment, displayed a surprisingly callous indifference toward pain, poverty, and injustice. The 19th century saw things quite differently. Its philosophers recognized much more clearly the reality of human rights and human duties, and most important of all, they generally believed that something could be done to make society better. Institutions, like men, were vastly improveable. European observers such as Harriet Martineau rarely failed to remark on the Americans' confidence in their power to remake men and society quickly—so different, she wrote, from the "paralyzing hopelessness" of European reformers who struggled against apathy and traditionalism.

To the American reformer, the *individual* counted for everything, whether he be poor, oppressed, maladjusted, unfortunate, helpless, or even sinful. The great wave of American reform that swept through the first half of the 19th century derived from a single great purpose—to establish individual integrity and maintain individual worth. The dozens of widely disparate reform movements in the country from 1800 to 1850 held this motive in common, from the mildest of food faddists to the most relentless of abolitionists. As the editors of *The Dial* summarized the reforming spirit of the times, "The final cause of human society is the unfolding of *individual man*, into every form of perfection, without let or hindrance, according to the inward nature of each."

This emphasis on the individual as the focus of reform, however, posed a problem to some of the reformers. Reform was best accomplished through societies, by the joint efforts of individuals working together in common cause. The principle of "association," many believed, was the greatest reform weapon of all; the age simply proliferated associations. But how did one avoid losing the individual identity in collective action? Might not the group swallow the person? William Ellery Channing, who praised "association" one moment, also warned against it at the next. "The truth is," wrote Channing,

> that our connexion with society, as it is our greatest aid, so it is our greatest peril. We are in constant danger of being spoiled of our moral judgment, and of our power over ourselves. . . . We insist on these remarks, because not a few Associations seem to us to be exceedingly exceptionable on account of their tendency to fetter men, to repress energy, to injure the free action of individuals.

For this reason, Emerson avoided societies, including those of which he approved; as Thoreau once remarked, "God does not approve of popular movements." For this reason, too, William Lloyd Garrison, who founded the first influential abolitionist society, found it very hard to cooperate even with his own friends and followers.

William Lloyd Garrison, possibly the most famous of all American reformers, provides the third symbol for the 19th century's concepts of individualism and progress as they appeared in social reform. He disliked societies, distrusted institutions, and felt trapped by organizations. His fierce personal individualism confused the crusade against slavery for more than a decade and eventually split it. Though Garrison centered his life on the task of liberating the slave, his struggle was to free *individuals*, not a race or a people. Slavery violated many natural and divine laws, but most of all, in Garrison's book, it violated the sanctity of the individual. As he said more than once, he "wanted freedom for persons, not a class." Garrison was once asked, "Why do you work so hard for the black man when white men too are enslaved in other ways?" His reply is revealing. "I do not fight for colored men, but for *man*, whatever his complexion," he said. "So long as *one* man, black or white, remains in fetters anywhere, I fight for *him*." He saw the evils of slavery in individual terms.

This intense individualism was always part of Garrison's reforming outlook. He believed deeply in progress, as his age did, and lacking Emerson's philosophical mind or Jackson's political skill, he strove in his own angry, almost arrogant way to force it on his own society by making the individual conscience the battleground for reform. "Individual effort," he once wrote, "is the true foundation of society," a principle with which he never compromised. He was a "no government" man who once disclaimed "allegiance to any government, refused to recognize state or national boundaries, and rejected all distinctions of class, sex, or race made by society." Garrison went far beyond Thoreau in repudiating "every legislature and judicial body, all human politics, worldly honors, and stations of authority," a position which made Thoreau's mild misdemeanors seem conservative. Garrison, after all, once burned a copy of the United States Constitution in public on Independence Day and ground the ashes under his heel.

Garrison was not a man of ideas (Emerson said Garrison "neighed like a horse" whenever he tried to discuss abstract principles), but he personified better than others in the reform movement the doctrine of self-reliant individualism as it appeared in 19th-century reform. "What is a man born for, but to be a Reformer, a Remaker of what man has made?" asked Emerson, in what was almost a definition of Garrison's life. Jackson served his age as an emblem of the power of the individual in re-shaping his state. Garrison personified the power of

the individual to re-form his society. Philosophically, Emerson justified them both.

III

This, then, is the stream of ideas which lies beneath the surface of
events in the Age of Jackson, Emerson, and Garrison. Faith in the merit
of individual human nature, faith in the inevitability of human progress
—these beliefs provided, during this interval, spirit, character, and
distinctive temper for American thought. There was nothing else like
it in American life, before or after. "Every spirit builds its own house,"
wrote Emerson, speaking to the men of his era, "and beyond its house
a world, and beyond its world a heaven. Know then that the world
exists for you."

Yet there were those who saw neither life nor man with the un-
clouded vision of an Emerson or the confidence of a Jackson. Even
some of the faithful, now and then, expressed doubts about what
Emily Dickinson aptly called "freckled human nature." Alcott argued
for years with Emerson and Channing over what he called their
"excessive individuality." Orestes Brownson, rebel though he was,
decided that the individual must be subject to some sort of authority,
joined the Catholic church, and concluded that individual freedom was
to be obtained only within the realm of the imaginative.

The early 19th century had its Nay-sayers, men who saw shadows in
the universe, and knew the power of blackness. The Yea-sayers lacked
a sense of the past. Emerson did not need it; the Jacksonians rejected
it; Garrison and the reformers hoped to escape it by remaking the
future. But where Emerson could say that "God himself culminates in
the present moment" and concern himself solely with his intuitive
instant, Hawthorne instead spoke of "that visionary and impalpable
now, which if you look at it closely, is nothing." Melville's Pierre followed Longfellow's confident advice to "Act, act in the living present!"
and found only sheer disaster. In the same way, as Thoreau found
certainty and sufficiency in the Individual Self, so Melville's theme is
the insufficiency and alienation of Self. Neither Hawthorne nor Melville could accept the Emersonian dictum, "Know thyself," for what
they found, when they searched within, was the desperate self-destruc-
tion of Ahab and Ethan Brand. *Pierre, Moby Dick, Young Goodman
Brown,* and *The Marble Faun* were dark books that did not belong with
the optimism and hopefulness of *The American Scholar* or *Self-Reliance*,
and it is equally true that behind the drums and tramplings of the
Jacksonian torchlight parades there was always the cold, hard realism
of John C. Calhoun, or the shadow of secession and war. These things
were the underside of the intellectual pattern of the age.

Yet the dominant design of American thought in the Age of Emerson, Jackson, and Garrison was one of hope and faith. These men symbolized it. Somewhat later, at midcentury, the design was rudely shattered and the dream suddenly died. Emerson, when he read Darwin's *Origin of Species,* wrote angrily in his journal, "I refuse to be caught in the trap of biological science." But he was caught, and so was his era. At almost the same time, John Brown attacked Harper's Ferry. The Golden Age was over.

32

An Excess of Democracy: The American Civil War and the Social Process

DAVID DONALD

33

The Needless Conflict

ALLAN NEVINS

In the history of the national state there is often a turning point, a point of crisis at which two ideas come into conflict. Although the conflict is resolved in a superficial way, it passes, on a deeper level and in subsequent redefinitions, into the current politics of the state. In France, the turning point came with the Revolution of 1789; in England, with the Puritan Revolution of the 1640's; in the United States, with the Civil War. In each instance, the issue to be decided was the relevance of the polity to the people. In each instance, the source of sovereignty, and therefore the very nature of the state, was being redefined. In this sense, every great revolution has been a civil war and every civil war a great revolution. Crises of such profundity become part of the mythology of the state. They are mirrors in which the changing face of the real present is variously seen, by different groups, in different ages, and for different purposes.

This is why historians have failed to come to any agreement on a very basic question about the American Civil War—what caused it? From the time of the war until the present day, opinions on this question have differed widely, and often indeed have clashed harshly. These differences of opinion have been surveyed in two very useful studies: Howard K. Beale's essay, "What Historians Have Said About the Causes of the Civil

War," in the Social Science Research Council's Bulletin 54, Theory and Practice in Historical Study (1946) and Thomas J. Pressly's Americans Interpret Their Civil War (1954). The war has been attributed to a conflict between a ruthless "Slave Power" in control of the South and an aggressive Northern group of "Black Republicans," intent on inflicting their views upon the South. It has been attributed to antagonistic economies and class struggles, to irreconcilable theories concerning the nature of the Union and the rights of the states, and to the whipping up of sectional passions by irresponsible and selfish leaders.

While a final analysis of what caused the Civil War is therefore beyond the hope of historical scholarship, for the present certainly, some very excellent suggestions have been made. Two of these are offered in the following essays by Professors David Donald of the Johns Hopkins University and Allan Nevins of the Huntington Library, whom we have had occasion to read before (pp. 3–13). A student and onetime assistant of the late James G. Randall, who was the principal Lincoln scholar of his day, Professor Donald is himself an outstanding figure in the field of Civil War scholarship. He has taught at Columbia and Princeton, and was Harmsworth Professor of American History at Oxford. Each of his works has been a signal contribution to the study of its subject. He won a Pulitzer prize for his Charles Sumner and the Coming of the Civil War (1960), the first of a two-volume biography. His other works include a biography of Lincoln's law partner (Lincoln's Herndon, 1948), a book of wide-ranging, stimulating essays on the Middle Period (Lincoln Reconsidered, 1956), a superb revision of Randall's authoritative text (The Civil War and Reconstruction, 1961), and a fresh, suggestive view of Congress and the re-admission of the South (The Politics of Reconstruction, 1863–1867, 1965).

The following essay of David Donald's affords us an insight into the origins of the Civil War that is most rewarding. Noting that earlier historians have not explained the outbreak of the war so much as they have helped us to understand why war could break out, Donald takes his vantage ground outside the frame of American life, hoping thereby to gain the broader view of how our society functioned that some of our perspicacious foreign observers had. His analysis of the social process in ante-bellum America significantly enhances our understanding of the crisis that the American polity had to face. And yet, his analysis, while answering many basic questions, would seem to raise others in turn. Is it not fair to say that Donald's thesis about why the war came stresses fundamental factors, and is thus a kind of explanation that, in his introductory statement of the problem, he considers to be not "intellectually satisfying?" And does his thesis really fulfill his initial hope for discovering why hostilities actually broke out? Does the thesis, in fact, do more than what other theses have done: explain why war could have come, not why it actually did? To put the *question another way: To what extent does Professor Donald leave us still having to call on the explanations that he tends to dismiss in the introductory section of his article? Moreover, if much is to be gained from consulting foreign views in order to understand the operations of American society, is there not also something that may be lost? Few foreign commentators have had the temperament of a Tocqueville, who brought balance to his assessment of our institutions, though he did not necessarily approve them; more tended to the temperament of a Mrs. Trollope, who made a commerce of disapproval, and possibly of imbalance. Is it not a fact that Europeans, on the whole, found America no more to their sense of what order and stability should be than Americans found Europe?*

Professor Nevins's portrait of the nation in the years before and during the Civil War (six volumes have thus far appeared) is probably, in the field of American history, the outstanding work of our times. It is history in the grand manner, on a theme of epic dimensions. Professor Nevins's conclusions on the causes of the war are certainly noteworthy.

"The war, when it came, was not primarily a conflict over State Rights, although that issue had become involved in it. It was not primarily a war born of economic grievances, although many Southerners had been led to think that they were suffering, or would soon suffer, economic wrongs. It was not a war created by politicians and publicists who fomented hysteric excitement; for while hysteria was important, we have always to ask what basic reasons made possible the propaganda which aroused it. It was not primarily a war about slavery alone, although that institution seemed to many the grand cause. It was a war over slavery **and** *the future position of the Negro race in North America. Was the Negro to be allowed, as a result of the shift of power signalized by Lincoln's election, to take the first step toward an ultimate position of general economic, political, and social equality with the white man? Or was he to be held immobile in a degraded, servile position, unchanging for the next hundred years as it had remained essentially unchanged for the hundred years past? These questions were implicit in Lincoln's demand that slavery be placed in a position where the public could rest assured of its ultimate extinction."* (The Emergence of Lincoln, *New York: Charles Scribner's Sons, II, 470-71.)*

The issue which lay at the bottom of the war cannot, to the mind of Professor Nevins, be separated from the men who were called upon to make important decisions about that issue. Weak Presidents were leading the nation when it most needed men of strength. Lacking in statesmanship, unimaginative, irresolute, Fillmore, Pierce, and Buchanan were incapable of facing up to the great demands of the presidency; and of the three, Buchanan was the weakest. At a time of great trial, submits Professor Nevins in the essay below, when the struggle in Kansas over slavery dramatized the national problem, Buchanan failed dismally. If leadership had been in the hands of men of conviction and strength, the war might have been averted. In this sense, Professor Nevins feels, it was a needless conflict. His analysis of the coming of the Civil War differs from David Donald's in at least three ways. Donald, it will be seen, does not regard the question of the evitability or inevitability of the war as one that the historian can sensibly entertain or successfully answer. In explaining why the war started, moreover, Donald is reluctant to attribute central importance to the role and activities of individuals. Thirdly, he sees the conflict as arising from the very nature and operation of a whole society, while Nevins traces it to a particular institution and a particular problem.

However the question of what caused the war may ultimately be resolved, there can be little doubt that the whole subject of the war is the most commanding point of interest in our history for both the professional historian and the general public. The centenary celebrations which we witnessed a few years ago were merely quickenings of a concern that has always been there. The issues which dominated the war continue, in newer forms, to have vitality; the myth we have made of the war is very much alive. For one thing, the Old South, despite its defeat, continues to have meaning for us: in that efficient remembrance of things past by which we remember what we will and how we will, we have reformed the Old South from a transient and divided society into one that is resolved and permanent; we have restyled it in feudal garb and invested it with what we consider to be the romance and simplicity of a pre-industrial age; we are caught in the paradox of applauding the triumph of the Northern ideal while regretting the defeat of the Southern one, which in the national myth represents aristocracy, order, chivalry, and the uncomplicated love of mannered men for beautiful women. Moreover, if the North won the war, the South, in a distinct way, won the peace; and the Civil War sustained itself long after Appomattox because the Northern ideal would have to triumph again. Another reason for interest is that the real civil war is being fought today, not so much in a clash of arms or legal decisions as in the impact of deeper economic and social forces upon the mind of the South; it is being fought internally, in individual and group consciences, in a scene of rapidly changing institutions and values. Finally, the Civil War has its own meaning for an age of international struggle between two systems and two worlds. It signifies two ideas in conflict, and the shorthand of the phrases "free world" and "unfree world" may aptly summarize both the American conflict of the 1860's and the world conflict of a century later.

DAVID DONALD

About few subjects do historians become so excited as about the causes of wars. War is by its nature such a monstrous evil that rational man seeks desperately to "explain" it. Most Western historians, mild men with humane intentions, can but instinctively regard war as a hideous aberration, a foul blot in the human copybook.

American historians have been especially concerned with this problem. Nearly all nurtured in a comfortable belief in progress, they have found it necessary to face the fact that the United States has not always marched onward and upward but has repeatedly backslid into the abyss of savagery. For most American wars, our historians have a comforting explanation: they were caused by somebody else. It was the British, we say, who provoked the American Revolution and the War of 1812; it was the Mexicans who incited the War of 1846; it was Spanish barbarities in Cuba which produced the War of 1898; it was German submarine atrocities which caused American entrance into World War I; it was the Japanese attack at Pearl Harbor which brought us into World War II; it was Communist aggression in Korea which sent American soldiers to fight in that God-forsaken land.

But the most sanguinary of American conflicts does not lend itself to such an explanation. The American Civil War of 1861-1865 can be blamed upon nobody but the American participants themselves. It is partly for this reason that the causes of our Civil War have had an irresistible fascination for Americans. Virtually every imaginative writer of any importance in the United States since the 1860's has felt obliged to deal with this brothers' war and the subsequent reconciliation. Novelists as diverse as Mark Twain and Henry James, Stephen Crane and Thomas Nelson Page, Margaret Mitchell and William Faulkner have exhibited a recurring, almost obsessive interest in this wholly American war. Almost every major historian of the United States has also been concerned with the problem; one thinks, for example, of Henry Adams, Edward Channing, James Ford Rhodes, John Bach McMaster, James Schouler, Hermann E. von Holst, Albert J. Beveridge, James G. Randall and Allan Nevins.

Though united in concern to explain the appalling catastrophe that befell America in the 1860's, historians of the United States have agreed upon very little else about that conflict. Many have continued to support James Ford Rhodes's flat contention that the American Civil War had "a single cause, slavery"; others have accepted Allan Nevins's modification that the cause was not Negro slavery alone but the concomitant problem of race adjustment. Disciples of Frederick Jackson Turner have found the cause of the Civil War in the growth of sectionalism, especially in the competition between sections for the newly

SOURCE: *The Centennial Review,* V (Winter 1961), 21–39. Reprinted by permission of the author. This article was originally published by the Oxford University Press, 1960, and was delivered by Professor Donald as his inaugural lecture as Harmsworth Professor of American History at the University of Oxford.

opened West. Followers of Charles A. Beard, on the other hand, have traced the essential origin of the war to the clash of economic classes, chiefly to the inevitable conflict between Northern capitalism and Southern agrarianism. The "Revisionists" of the 1930's and 1940's, headed by Avery O. Craven and James G. Randall, argued that the Civil War had no basic causes; that it was a "repressible conflict," a "needless war," precipitated through want of wisdom in the "blundering generation" of the 1850's. More recently, critics, who styled themselves "New Nationalists," have replied sharply that the Revisionists were blind to the enormous evil of slavery and sought "in optimistic sentimentalism an escape from the severe demands of moral decision."

Acrimoniously American historians have argued over the degree to which individual politicians and statesmen were responsible for the Civil War. Presidents Franklin Pierce, James Buchanan, and Abraham Lincoln have all been accused of bringing on the war, but all three have had vigorous defenders. George Fort Milton and other scholars rehabilitated the reputation of Stephen A. Douglas as the statesman of sectional conciliation, but Allan Nevins has continued to brand the Illinois "Little Giant" as a morally obtuse and disastrously shortsighted politician. Frank L. Owsley, a Southern-born historian, squarely blamed Northern abolitionists; "neither Dr. Goebbels nor Virginia Gayda nor Stalin's propaganda agents," he wrote in 1941, "were able to plumb the depths of vulgarity and obscenity reached and maintained by . . . Wendell Phillips, Charles Sumner, and other abolitionists of note." Historians of Northern origin retorted angrily that the blame should more properly fall upon Southern "fire-eaters," who precipitated secession. Craven and Randall attacked with equal vigor the "extremists" and "agitators" of all sections, the disciples of John C. Calhoun along with the followers of William Lloyd Garrison.

It is sometimes mistakenly maintained that the basic issue over which these historians have so confusingly argued is that of the inevitability of the Civil War. Such a view is an oversimplification, for, as the Dutch historian Pieter Geyl sensibly remarks, "The question of evitability or inevitability is one on which the historian can never form any but an ambivalent opinion." So much depends upon speculations which historians are properly reluctant to make. If Jefferson Davis's government had refused to fight for independence, there could, of course, have been no war. Similarly, if Lincoln's administration had acquiesced in the peaceful secession of the South, there would have been no conflict. The question of inevitability is also partly a matter of timing. Virtually no one would argue that a Civil War was inescapable as early as 1820 or 1830; hardly anyone would suggest that it was avoidable after the first gun was fired on Fort Sumter.

The real cleavage in American historical thought is, instead, between those who see the Civil War as the result of the operation of grand elemental forces and those who attribute it to the working of accidental or random factors. The former discuss the war as the result of deep national urges, basic social or economic cleavages, and fundamental nationalistic drives; the latter argue that these alleged fundamental "causes" have no demonstrated connection with the course of events in the 1850's and stress the importance of accident, of personality, and of propaganda in shaping history.

Neither of these rival interpretations is entirely satisfactory. The "Fundamentalists" (if we may so call them) have failed to prove that their underlying "causes" produced the actual outbreak of hostilities. They talk impressively about Southern economic grievances—but never demonstrate that such issues as the tariff or international improvements played any significant part in bringing on the actual secession crisis. The rise of Southern nationalism is another of these general explanations that sound impressive—until one realizes, after making a study of the Confederacy, that Southern nationalism during the Civil War was anything but a strong unifying force. It is plausible to stress slavery as the cause of the Civil War, but, as Revisionists have repeatedly pointed out, no responsible political body in the North in 1860 proposed to do anything at all about slavery where it actually existed and no numerous group of Southerners thought their peculiar institution could be extended into the free states. As for Allan Nevins's emphasis upon the problems of race adjustment, one must note that virtually nobody, North or South, was concerned with such matters in the 1850's.

The problem with all these Fundamentalist explanations is that they rely upon stereotypes which have little relation to the complex social reality of the United States in the 1850's. Writers speak of the Southern interest in slavery, even when they perfectly well know that in the "plantation" South only one-fourth of the white families owned slaves at all. They talk of "industrial" New England, though over half of the population of that region still lived on farms. They write of the small farmers of the "frontier" West, even though that section had a remarkable urban development and even though it was partly settled by men like Michael Sullivant, "the world's largest farmer," who owned 80,000 acres of rich Illinois soil, employed between 100 and 200 laborers, and had 5,000 head of cattle grazing in his own pastures.

On the other hand, it is equally difficult to accept the Revisionist argument that happenstance developments—such as the introduction of the Kansas-Nebraska Bill in 1854 or John Brown's raid—produced the war, if only because one dislikes to give up the old maxim that great events have great causes. If it is true that the hottest issue of the

1850's was not race adjustment or the future of slavery itself but the spread of slavery into the few remaining territories of the United States, do we not have to inquire why public opinion, North and South, grew so sensitive over what appears to be an abstract and unimportant point? If we must admit that propagandists and agitators, abolitionists and fire-eaters, whipped up sentiment in both sections, are we not required to ask further why that public opinion could be thus roiled, and why on these specific issues? And if we are bound to agree that the 1850's saw a failure of American statesmanship, do we not have to seek why this disaster afflicted the United States at this particular time and in this peculiar manner?

I

Since neither Revisionism nor Fundamentalism offers an intellectually satisfying explanation for the coming of the Civil War, perhaps the problem should be approached afresh. The Civil War, I believe, can best be understood neither as the result of accident nor as the product of conflicting sectional interests, but as the outgrowth of social processes which affected the entire United States during the first half of the 19th century.

It is remarkable how few historians have attempted to deal with American society as a whole during this critical period. Accustomed to looking upon it as a pre-war era, we have stressed divisive elements and factors of sectional conflict. Contemporary European observers, on the whole, had a better perspective. Some of these foreign travelers looked upon the American experiment with loathing; others longed for its success; but nearly all stressed the basic unity of American culture, minimizing the ten percent of ideas and traits which were distinctive to the individual sections and stressing the ninety percent of attitudes and institutions which all Americans shared.

It is time for us to emulate the best of these European observers and to draw a broad picture of the common American values in the early 19th century. Any such analysis would have to start with the newness of American life. Novelty was the keynote not merely for the recently settled regions of the West but for all of American society. Though states like Virginia and Massachusetts had two hundred years of history behind them, they, too, were affected by social changes so rapid as to require each generation to start anew. In the Northeast, the rise of the city shockingly disrupted the normal course of societal evolution. Boston, for example, grew from a tidy, inbred city of 40,000 in 1830 to a sprawling, unmanageable metropolis of 178,000 by 1860; New York leaped from 515,000 to 805,000 in the single decade of the 1850's. This kind of urban life was as genuinely a frontier experience as settling on the Great Plains; to hundreds of thousands of

European-born immigrants and American farm boys and girls, moving to the big city was an enormously exhilarating and unsettling form of pioneering. In the Old South, the long-settled states of the Eastern coast were undergoing a parallel evolution, for the opening of rich alluvial lands along the Gulf Coast offered bonanzas as surely as did the gold mines of California. In the early 19th century all sections of the United States were being transformed with such rapidity that stability and security were everywhere vanishing values; nowhere could a father safely predict what kind of world his son would grow up in.

Plenty was another characteristic of this new American society. From the richness of the country's basic resources, Americans, as David M. Potter has observed, ought to be called "The People of Plenty." The land begged to be developed. Immigrants from less privileged lands found it almost impossible to credit the abundance which everywhere surrounded them. As settlers in the Wabash Valley sang:

> Way down upon the Wabash
> Such lands were never known.
> If Adam had passed over it,
> This soil he'd surely own.
> He'd think it was the Garden
> He played in when a boy,
> And straight he'd call it Eden
> In the State of Illinois.

Mineral wealth surpassed men's dreams. And there was nothing to divert Americans from the exploitation of their resources. As Tocqueville pointed out, the absence of strong neighbors to the north and the south gave the United States a peculiar position among the 19th-century powers; she alone could devote her entire energies to the creation of wealth, instead of wasting them upon arms and warlike preparations. Some Americans made their fortunes in manufacturing; others in cotton and rice plantations; still others in the mines and lands of the West. Not everybody got rich, of course, but everybody aspired to do so. Both the successful and those less fortunate were equally ruthless in exploiting the country's natural resources, whether of water power, of fertile fields, of mineral wealth, or simply of human labor.

Rapid social mobility was another dominant American trait. Though some recent sociological studies have correctly warned us that the Horatio Alger stories represent a myth rather than a reality of American society and that, even in the early 19th century education, family standing and inherited wealth were valuable assets, we must not forget that there was nevertheless an extraordinary opportunity in the United

States for poor boys to make good. Surely in no other Western society of the period could a self-taught merchant's apprentice have founded the manufacturing dynasty of the Massachusetts Lawrences; or a semi-literate ferry-boatman named Vanderbilt have gained control of New York City's transportation system; or the son of a London dried-fish shopkeeper named Benjamin have become Senator from Louisiana; or a self-taught prairie lawyer have been elected President of the nation.

Such vertical mobility was not confined to any class or section in the United States. Though most of us are willing to accept the rags-to-riches version of frontier society, we often fail to realize that every-where in America the early 19th century was the day of the self-made man. The Boston Brahmins, as Cleveland Amory has wittily pointed out, were essentially *nouveaux riches;* the Proper Bostonians' handsome houses on Beacon Hill, their affectations of social superiority, their illusions of hearing ancestral voices concealed the fact that most of them derived from quite humble origins, and within the last genera-tion or two. In the South there were, of course, a few fine old families—but not nearly so many as the F.F.V.'s fondly fancied—but these were not the leaders of Southern society. The typical figure of the antebellum South is not Robert E. Lee but tight-fisted Thomas Sutpen, William Faulkner's fictional character, whose unscrupulous rise from hard-scrabble beginnings to the planter class is traced in *Absalom, Absalom.*

II

A new society of plenty, with abundant opportunities for self-advance-ment, was bound to leave its hallmark upon its citizens, whether they lived in North, South, or West. The connection between character and culture is still an essentially unexplored one, but it is surely no accident that certain widely shared characteristics appeared among Americans in every rank of life. In such a society, richly endowed with every natural resource, protected against serious foreign wars, and structured so as to encourage men to rise, it was inevitable that a faith in progress should be generally shared. The idea of progress is not, of course, an American invention, and no claim is even suggested here that 19th-century Americans were unique. Indeed, the American experience is merely a special case of the sweeping social transforma-tion which was more slowly changing Europe as well. But American circumstances did make for a particularly verdant belief that better-ment, whether economic, social, or moral, was just around the corner. Surely Mark Twain's Colonel Beriah Sellers is, if not a unique American type, the representative American citizen of his age.

Confidence in the future encouraged Americans in their tendency to speculate. A man of even very modest means might anticipate making his fortune, not through exertions of his own but through the waves of prosperity which seemed constantly to float American values higher and higher. A small initial capital could make a man another John Jacob Astor. "I have now a young man in my mind," wrote C. C. Andrews from Minnesota in 1856, "who came to a town ten miles this side of St. Paul, six months ago, with $400. He commenced trading, and has already, by good investments and the profits of his business, doubled his money." It was no wonder that Americans rejected the safe investment, the "sure thing," to try a flier into the unknown. In some cases, the American speculative mania was pathological. A writer in November, 1849, described the frenzied state of mind of Californians:

> The people of San Francisco are mad, stark mad. . . . A dozen times or more, during the last few weeks, I have been taken by the arm by some of the *millionaires*—so they call themselves, I call them madmen—of San Francisco, looking wondrously dirty and out at elbows for men of such magnificent pretensions. They have dragged me about, through the mud and filth almost up to my middle, from one pine box to another, called mansion, hotel, bank, or store, as it may please the imagination, and have told me, with a sincerity that would have done credit to the Bedlamite, that these splendid . . . structures were theirs, and they, the fortunate proprietors, were worth from two to three hundred thousand dollars a year each.

But one does not have to turn to the gold rush of California to learn what abundance can do to social values. A sympathetic contemporary Southerner, Joseph G. Baldwin, described "The Flush Times in Mississippi and Alabama," when the virgin lands in that region were first opened to settlement.

> . . . the new era had set in—the era of the second great experiment of independence: the experiment, namely, of credit without capital, and enterprise without honesty. . . . Every crossroad and every avocation presented an opening,—through which a fortune was seen by the adventurer in near perspective. Credit was a thing of course. To refuse it—if the thing was ever done—were an insult for which a bowie-knife were not a too summary or exemplary means of redress . . . prices rose like smoke. Lots in obscure villages were held at city prices; lands, bought at the minimum cost of government, were sold at from thirty to forty dollars an acre. . . . Society was wholly unorganized: there was no restraining public opinion: the law was well-nigh powerless—and religion scarcely was heard of except as furnishing the oaths and *technics* of profanity. . . . Money, got without work, . . . turned the heads of its possessors, and they spent it with a recklessness like that with which they gained it. The pursuits of industry neglected, riot and coarse debauchery filled up the vacant hours. . . . The . . . doggeries . . . were in full blast in those days, no village having less than a half-dozen all busy all the time: gaming and horse-racing were polite and well patronized amusements. . . . Occasionally the scene was diversi-

fied by a murder or two, which though perpetrated from behind a corner, or behind the back of the deceased, whenever the accused *chose* to stand his trial, was always found to have been committed in self-defence. . . . The old rules of business and the calculations of prudence were alike disregarded, and profligacy, in all the departments . . . , held riotous carnival. Larceny grew not only respectable, but genteel, and ruffled it in all the pomp of purple and fine linen. Swindling was raised to the dignity of the fine arts. Felony came forth from its covert, put on more seemly habiliments, and took its seat with unabashed front in the upper places of the synagogue. . . .

"Commerce was king"—and Rag, Tag and Bobtail his cabinet council. . . . The condition of society may be imagined: — vulgarity — ignorance — fussy and arrogant pretention—unmitigated rowdyism—bullying insolence. . . .

Allowance must, of course, be made for a writer of imaginative fiction, but there is a basic truth in Baldwin's observations. In 19th-century America all the recognized values of orderly civilization were being eroded. Social atomization affected every segment of American society. All too accurately Tocqueville portrayed the character of the new generation of Southerners: "The citizen of the Southern states becomes a sort of domestic dictator from infancy; the first notion he acquires in life is that he was born to command, and the first habit he contracts is that of ruling without resistance. His education tends, then, to give him the character of a haughty and hasty man—irascible, violent, ardent in his desires, impatient of obstacles." William H. Herndon, Lincoln's law partner, graphically depicted the even cruder settlers in the West:

These men could shave a horse's main [sic] and tail, paint, disfigure and offer him for sale to the owner in the very act of inquiring for his own horse. . . . They could hoop up in a hogshead a drunken man, they being themselves drunk, put in and nail down the head, and roll the man down New Salem hill a hundred feet or more. They could run down a lean, hungry wild pig, catch it, heat a ten-plate stove furnace hot, and putting in the pig, could cook it, they dancing the while a merry jig.

Even the most intimate domestic relations were drastically altered in 19th-century America. For centuries the Western tradition had been one in which females were subordinate to males, and in which the wife found her full being only in her husband. But in the pre-Civil War United States such a social order was no longer possible. In Massachusetts, for example, which in 1850 had 17,480 more females than males, many women could no longer look to their normal fulfillment in marriage and a family; if they were from the lower classes they must labor to support themselves, and if they were from the upper classes they must find satisfaction in charitable deeds and humanitarian enterprises. It is not altogether surprising that so many reform movements had their roots in New England. In the West, on the other hand, women were at a great premium; however old or ugly, they found themselves marriageable. One reads, for example, of a company of forty-one women who traveled from the East to frontier Iowa. Before their steamship could reach the wharf, the shore was crowded with men using megaphones to make proposals of marriage; "Miss with the blue ribbon in your bonnet, will you take me?" "Hallo thar, gal, with a cinnamon shawl; if agreeable we will jine." It was, consequently, extremely difficult to persuade these ladies that, after marriage, they had no legal existence except as chattels of their husbands. Not surprisingly, woman's suffrage, as a practical movement, flourished in the West.

Children in such a society of abundance were an economic asset. A standard toast to wedding couples was: "Health to the groom, and here's to the bride, thumping luck, and big children." Partly because they were so valuable, children were well cared for and given great freedom. Virtually every European traveler in the 19th century remarked the uncurbed egotism of the American child: "Boys assume the full air of full grown coxcombs." "Parents have no command over their children." "The children's faces were dirty, their hair uncombed, their disposition evidently untaught, and all the members of the family, from the boy of six years of age up to the owner (I was going to say master) of the house, appeared independent of each other." "The lad of fourteen . . . struts and swaggers and smokes his cigar and drinks rum; treads on the toes of his grandfather, swears at his mother and sister, and vows that he will run away . . . the children govern the parents."

This child was father of the American man. It is no wonder that Tocqueville, attempting to characterize 19th-century American society, was obliged to invent a new word, "individualism." This is not to argue that there were in pre-Civil War America no men of orderly, prudent, and conservative habits; it is to suggest that rarely in human history has a people as a whole felt itself so completely unfettered by precedent. In a nation so new that, as President James K. Polk observed, its history was in the future, in a land of such abundance, men felt under no obligation to respect the lessons of the past. Even in the field of artistic and literary endeavor acceptance of classical forms or acquiescence in the dictates of criticism was regarded as evidence of inferiority. Ralph Waldo Emerson set the theme for 19th-century Americans: "Let me admonish you, first of all, to go alone; to refuse the good models, even those which are sacred in the imagination of men. . . . Imitation cannot go above its model. The imitator dooms himself to hopeless mediocrity. . . . Yourself a newborn bard of the Holy Ghost, cast behind you all conformity. . . ."

Every aspect of American life witnessed this desire to throw off precedent and to rebel from authority. Every institution which laid claim to prescriptive right was challenged and overthrown. The church, that potent instrument of social cohesion in the colonial period, was first disestablished, and then strange new sects, such as the Shakers, Mormons, and Campbellites, appeared to fragment the Christian community. The squirearchy, once a powerful conservative influence in the Middle States and the South, was undermined by the abolition of primogeniture and entails and then was directly defied in the Anti-Rent Wars of New York. All centralizing economic institutions came under attack. The Second Bank of the United States, which exercised a healthy restraint upon financial chaos, was destroyed during the Jackson period, and at the same time the Supreme Court moved to strike down vested monopoly rights.

Nowhere was the American rejection of authority more complete than in the political sphere. The decline in the powers of the federal government from the constructive centralism of George Washington's administration to the feeble vacillation of James Buchanan's is so familiar as to require no repetition here. With declining powers there went also declining respect. Leonard D. White's scholarly works on American administrative history accurately trace the descending status and the decreasing skill of the federal government employees. The national government, moreover, was not being weakened in order to bolster the state governments, for they, too, were decreasing in power. The learned historians of Massachusetts during these years, Oscar and Mary Handlin, find the theme of their story in the abandonment of the idea of "Commonwealth," in the gradual forgetting of the ideal of the purposeful state which had once concerted the interests of all its subordinate groups. By the 1850's, the authority of all government in America was at a low point; government to the American was, at most, merely an institution with a negative role, a guardian of fair play.

Declining power of government was paralleled by increased popular participation in it. The extension of the suffrage in America has rarely been the result of a concerted reform drive, such as culminated in England in 1832 and in 1867; rather it has been part of the gradual erosion of all authority, of the feeling that restraints and differentials are necessarily antidemocratic, and of the practical fact that such restrictions are difficult to enforce. By the mid-19th century in most American states white manhood suffrage was virtually universal.

All too rarely have historians given sufficient attention to the consequences of the extension of the franchise in America, an extension which was only one aspect of the general democratic rejection of authority. Different appeals must necessarily be made to a broad electorate than to an elite group. Since the rival parties must both woo the mass of voters, both tended to play down issues and to stand on broad equivocal platforms which evaded all subjects of controversy. Candidates were selected not because of their demonstrated statesmanship but because of their high public visibility. The rash of military men who ran for President in the 1840's and 1850's was no accident. If it is a bit too harsh to say that extension of the suffrage inevitably produced leaders without policies and parties without principles, it can be safely maintained that universal democracy made it difficult to deal with issues requiring subtle understanding and delicate handling. Walter Bagehot, that shrewd English observer, was one of the few commentators who accurately appreciated the changes that universal suffrage brought to American life. Writing in October, 1861, he declared: "The steadily augmenting power of the lower orders in America has naturally augmented the dangers of the Federal Union. . . . a dead level of universal suffrage runs, more or less, over the whole length of the United States. . . . it places the entire control over the political action of the whole State in the hands of common labourers, who are of all classes the least instructed—of all the most aggressive— of all the most likely to be influenced by local animosity—of all the most likely to exaggerate every momentary sentiment — of all the least likely to be capable of a considerable toleration for the constant oppositions of opinion, the not infrequent differences of interest, and the occasional unreasonableness of other States. . . . The unpleasantness of mob government has never before been exemplified so conspicuously, for it never before has worked upon so large a scene."

One does not, of course, have to accept the Tory accent to recognize the validity of Bagehot's analysis. Simply because Americans by the middle of the 19th century suffered from an excess of liberty, they were increasingly unable to arrive at reasoned, independent judgments upon the problems which faced their society. The permanent revolution that was America had freed its citizens from the bonds of prescription and custom but had left them leaderless. Inevitably, the reverse side of the coin of individualism is labeled conformity. Huddling together in their loneliness, they sought only to escape their freedom. Fads, fashions, and crazes swept the country. Religious revivalism reached a new peak in the 1850's. Hysterical fears and paranoid suspicions marked this shift of Americans to "other-directedness." Never was there a field so fertile before the propagandist, the agitator, the extremist.

III

These dangerously divisive tendencies in American society did not, of course, go unnoticed. Tocqueville and other European observers were aware of the perils of social atomization and predicted that, under shock, the union might be divided. Nor were all Americans indifferent to the drift of events. Repeatedly in the Middle Period conservative statesmen tried to check the widespread social disorganization. Henry Clay, for example, attempted to revive the idea of the national interest, superior to local and individual interests, by binding together the sections in his American System: the West should produce the nation's food; the South its staples; and the East its manufactures. The chief purpose of Daniel Webster's great patriotic orations was to stimulate a national feeling based on shared traditions, values, and beliefs. Taking as his twin maxims, "The best authority for the support of a particular provision in government is experience . . . ," and "Because a thing has been wrongly done, it does not therefore follow that it can now be undone . . . ," Webster tried to preserve the Union from shocks and rapid change. John C. Calhoun, too, argued for uniting "the most opposite and conflicting interests . . . into one common attachment to the country" through protecting the rights of minorities. With suitable guarantees to vested sectional interests (notably to slavery), Calhoun predicted that "the community would become a unity, by becoming a common centre of attachment of all its parts. And hence, instead of faction, strife, and struggle for party ascendency, there would be patriotism, nationality, harmony, and a struggle only for supremacy in promoting the common good of the whole."

Nor did conservative statesmanship die with the generation of Webster, Clay, and Calhoun. Down to the very outbreak of the Civil War old Whigs like John Jordan Crittenden, John Bell, and Edward Everett argued for adjustment of sectional claims to the national interest. Abraham Lincoln, another former Whig, tried to check the majoritarianism of his fellow-countrymen by harking back to the Declaration of Independence, which he termed the "sheet anchor of our principles." In the doctrine that all men are created equal, Lincoln found justification for his belief that there were some rights upon which no majority, however large or however democratic, might infringe. Majority rule, he maintained, could no more justify the extension of slavery to the territories than majority rule could disenfranchise the Irish, or the Catholics, or the laboring men of America. Soberly he warned that in a country like America, where there was no prescriptive right, the future of democratic government depended upon the willingness of its citizens to admit moral limits to their political powers.

None of these attempts to curb the tyranny of the majority was successful; all went too strongly against the democratic current of the age. American society was changing so rapidly that there was no true conservative group or interest to which a statesman could safely appeal. Webster, it is clear, would have preferred to find his following among yeoman farmers, holding approximately equal wealth; instead he was obliged to rely upon the banking, manufacturing, and speculative interest of the Northeast, the hard, grasping, arriviste element of society, a group which had itself risen through the democratic process. These special interests used Webster to secure tariffs, banking acts, and internal improvement legislation favorable to themselves, but they selfishly dropped him when he talked of subordinating their local particularism to the broad national interest.

Similarly, Calhoun sought a conservative backing in the plantation aristocracy, the same aristocracy which in a previous generation had produced George Washington, James Madison, and John Marshall. But while Calhoun prated of a Greek democracy, in which all white men, freed by Negro slavery of the burdens of menial labor, could deliberate upon statesmanlike solutions to the nation's problems, the conservative aristocracy upon which his theories depended was vanishing. Political and economic leadership moved from Virginia first to South Carolina, then to Mississippi. The educated, cosmopolitan plantation owners of the 1780's disappeared; in their place emerged the provincial Southron, whose sentiments were precisely expressed by an up-country South Carolinian: "I'll give you my notion of things; I go first for Greenville, then for Greenville District, then for the up-country, then for South Carolina, then for the South, then for the United States; and after that I don't go for anything. I've no use for Englishmen, Turks and Chinese." These slavemasters of the new cotton kingdom endorsed Calhoun and his doctrines so long as their own vested interests were being protected; after that, they ignored his conservative philosophy.

Possibly in time this disorganized society might have evolved a genuinely conservative solution for its problems, but time ran against it. At a stage when the United States was least capable of enduring shock, the nation was obliged to undergo a series of crises, largely triggered by the physical expansion of the country. The annexation of Texas, the war with Mexico, and the settlement of California and Oregon posed inescapable problems of organizing and governing this new empire. Something had to be done, yet any action was bound to arouse local, sectional hostilities. Similarly, in 1854 it was necessary to organize the Great Plains territory, but, as Stephen A. Douglas painfully learned, organizing it without slavery alienated the South, organizing it with slavery offended the North, and organizing it under popular sovereignty outraged both sections.

As if these existential necessities did not impose enough strains upon a disorganized society, well intentioned individuals insisted upon adding others. The quite unnecessary shock administered by the Dred Scott decision in 1857 is a case in point; justices from the antislavery North and the proslavery South, determined to settle the slavery issue, once and for all, produced opinions which in fact settled nothing but only led to further alienation and embitterment. Equally unnecessary, of course, was the far ruder shock which crazy John Brown and his little band administered two years later when they decided to solve the nation's problems by taking the law into their own hands at Harpers Ferry.

These crises which afflicted the United States in the 1850's were not in themselves calamitous experiences. Revisionist historians have correctly pointed out how little was actually at stake: slavery did not go into New Mexico or Arizona; Kansas, after having been opened to the peculiar institution for six years, had only two Negro slaves; the Dred Scott decision declared an already repealed law unconstitutional; John Brown's raid had no significant support in the North and certainly roused no visible enthusiasm among Southern Negroes. When compared to crises which other nations have resolved without great discomfort, the true proportions of these exaggerated disturbances appear.

But American society in the 1850's was singularly ill equipped to meet any shocks, however weak. It was a society so new and so disorganized that its nerves were rawly exposed. It was, as Henry James noted, a land which had "No sovereign, no court, no personal loyalty, no aristocracy, no church, no clergy, no army, no diplomatic service, no country gentlemen, no palaces, no castles, nor manors, nor old country houses, nor parsonages, nor thatched cottages, nor ivied ruins; no cathedrals, nor abbeys, nor little Norman churches; no great universities nor public schools . . . ; no literature, no novels, no museums, no pictures, no political society"—in short, which had no resistance to strain. The very similarity of the social processes which affected all sections of the country—the expansion of the frontier, the rise of the city, the exploitation of great natural wealth—produced not cohesion but individualism. The structure of the American political system impeded the appearance of conservative statesmanship, and the rapidity of the crises in the 1850's prevented conservatism from crystallizing. The crises themselves were not world-shaking, nor did they inevitably produce war. They were, however, the chisel strokes which revealed the fundamental flaws in the block of marble, flaws which stemmed from an excess of democracy.

ALLAN NEVINS

When James Buchanan, standing in a homespun suit before cheering crowds, took the oath of office on March 4, 1857, he seemed confident

SOURCE: *American Heritage, The Magazine of History,* VII (August, 1956), 5–9, 88–90. Reprinted by permission of the American Heritage Publishing Co., Inc.

that the issues before the nation could be readily settled. He spoke about an army road to California, use of the Treasury surplus to pay all the national debt, and proper guardianship of the public lands. In Kansas, he declared, the path ahead was clear. The simple logical rule that the will of the people should determine the institutions of a territory had brought in sight a happy settlement. The inhabitants would declare for or against slavery as they pleased. Opinions differed as to the proper time for making such a decision; but Buchanan thought that "the appropriate period will be when the number of actual residents in the Territory shall justify the formation of a constitution with a view to its admission as a State." He trusted that the long strife between North and South was nearing its end, and that the sectional party which had almost elected Frémont would die a natural death.

Two days after the inaugural Buchanan took deep satisfaction in a decision by the Supreme Court of which he had improper foreknowledge: the Dred Scott decision handed down by Chief Justice Taney. Its vital element, so far as the nation's destiny was concerned, was the ruling that the Missouri Compromise restriction, by which slavery had been excluded north of the 36°30' line, was void; that on the contrary, every territory was open to slavery. Not merely was Congress without power to legislate *against* slavery, but by implication it should act to protect it. Much of the northern press denounced the decision fervently. But the country was prosperous; it was clear that time and political action might change the Supreme Court, bringing a new decision; and the explosion of wrath proved brief.

Buchanan had seen his view sustained; slavery might freely enter any territory, the inhabitants of which could not decide whether to keep it or drop it until they wrote their first constitution. In theory, the highway to national peace was as traversible as the Lancaster turnpike. To be sure, Kansas was rent between two bitter parties, proslavery and antislavery; from the moment Stephen A. Douglas' Kansas-Nebraska Act had thrown open the West to popular sovereignty three years earlier, it had been a theater of unrelenting conflict. Popular sovereignty had simply failed to work. In the spring of 1855 about five thousand invading Missourians, swamping the polls, had given Kansas a fanatically proslavery legislature which the free-soil settlers flatly refused to recognize. That fall a free-soil convention in Topeka had adopted a constitution which the slavery men in turn flatly rejected. Some bloody fighting had ensued. But could not all this be thrust into the past?

In theory, the President might now send out an impartial new governor; and if the people wanted statehood, an election might be held for a new constitutional convention. Then the voters could give the nation its sixteenth slave state or its seventeenth free state—

everybody behaving quietly and reasonably. Serenity would prevail. Actually, the idea that the people of Kansas, so violently aroused, would show quiet reason, was about as tenable as the idea that Europeans would begin settling boundary quarrels by a quiet game of chess. Behind the two Kansas parties were grim southerners and determined northerners. "Slavery will now yield a greater profit in Kansas," trumpeted a southern propagandist in *De Bow's Review*, "either to hire out or cultivate the soil, than any other place." He wanted proslavery squatters. Meanwhile, Yankees were subsidizing their own settlers. "I know people," said Emerson in a speech, "who are making haste to reduce their expenses and pay their debts . . . to save and earn for the benefit of Kansas emigrants."

Nor was reason in Kansas the only need. Impartiality in Congress, courage in the presidential chair, were also required. The stage was dressed for a brief, fateful melodrama, which more than anything else was to fix the position of James Buchanan and Stephen A. Douglas in history, was to shape the circumstances under which Lincoln made his first national reputation, and was to have more potency than any other single event in deciding whether North and South should remain brothers or fly at each other's throats. That melodrama was entitled "Lecompton." Douglas was to go to his grave believing that, had Buchanan played an honest, resolute part in it, rebellion would have been killed in its incipiency. The role that Buchanan did play may be counted one of the signal failures of American statesmanship.

To hold that the Civil War could not have been averted by wise, firm, and timely action is to concede too much to determinism in history. Winston Churchill said that the Second World War should be called "The Unnecessary War"; the same term might as justly be applied to our Civil War. Passionate unreason among large sections of the population was one ingredient in the broth of conflict. Accident, fortuity, fate, or sheer bad luck (these terms are interchangeable) was another; John Brown's raid, so malign in its effects on opinion, North and South, might justly be termed an accident. Nothing in the logic of forces or events required so crazy an act. But beyond these ingredients lies the further element of wretched leadership. Had the United States possessed three farseeing, imaginative, and resolute Presidents instead of Fillmore, Pierce, and Buchanan, the war might have been postponed until time and economic forces killed its roots. Buchanan was the weakest of the three, and the Lecompton affair lights up his incompetence like a play of lightning across a nocturnal storm front.

The melodrama had two stages, one in faraway, thinly settled Kansas, burning hot in summer, bitter cold in winter, and, though reputedly rich, really so poor that settlers were soon on the brink of starvation. Here the most curious fact was the disparity between the mean actors and the great results they effected. A handful of ignorant, reckless, semi-drunken settlers on the southern side, led by a few desperadoes of politics—the delegates of the Lecompton Constitutional Convention—actually had the power to make or mar the nation. The other stage was Washington. The participants here, representing great interests and ideas, had at least a dignity worthy of the scene and the consequences of their action. James Buchanan faced three main groups holding three divergent views of the sectional problem.

The proslavery group (that is, Robert Toombs, Alexander H. Stephens, Jefferson Davis, John Slidell, David Atchison, and many more) demanded that slavery be allowed to expand freely within the territories; soon they were asking also that such expansion be given federal protection against any hostile local action. This stand involved the principle that slavery was morally right, and socially and economically a positive good. Reverdy Johnson of Maryland, in the Dred Scott case, had vehemently argued the beneficence of slavery.

The popular sovereignty group, led by Douglas and particularly strong among northwestern Democrats, maintained that in any territory the issue of slavery or free soil should be determined *at all times* by the settlers therein. Douglas modified the Dred Scott doctrine: local police legislation and action, he said, could exclude slavery even before state-making took place. He sternly rejected the demand for federal protection against such action. His popular sovereignty view implied indifference to or rejection of any moral test of slavery. Whether the institution was socially and economically good or bad depended mainly on climate and soil, and moral ideas were irrelevant. He did not care whether slavery was voted up or voted down; the right to a fair vote was the all-important matter.

The free-soil group, led by Seward and Chase, but soon to find its best voice in Lincoln, held that slavery should be excluded from all territories present or future. They insisted that slavery was morally wrong, had been condemned as such by the Fathers, and was increasingly outlawed by the march of world civilization. It might be argued that the free-soil contention was superfluous, in that climate and aridity forbade a further extension of slavery anyhow. But in Lincoln's eyes this did not touch the heart of the matter. It might or might not be expansible. (Already it existed in Delaware and Missouri, and Cuba and Mexico might be conquered for it.) What was important was for America to accept the fact that, being morally wrong and socially an anachronism, it *ought* not to expand; it *ought* to be put in the way of ultimate eradication. Lincoln was a planner. Once the country accepted nonexpansion, it would thereby accept the idea of ultimate extinction. This crisis met and passed, it could sit down and decide when and how, in God's good time and with suitable compensation to slaveholders, it might be ended.

The Buchanan who faced these three warring groups was victim of the mistaken belief among American politicians (like Pierce, Benjamin Harrison, and Warren G. Harding, for example) that it is better to be a poor President than to stick to honorable but lesser posts. He would have made a respectable diplomat or decent Cabinet officer under a really strong President. Sixty-six in 1857, the obese bachelor felt all his years. He had wound his devious way up through a succession of offices without once showing a flash of inspiration or an ounce of grim courage. James K. Polk had accurately characterized him as an old woman—"It is one of his weaknesses that he takes on and magnifies small matters into great and undeserved importance." His principal characteristic was irresolution. "Even among close friends," remarked a southern senator, "he very rarely expressed his opinions at all upon disputed questions, except in language especially marked with a cautious circumspection almost amounting to timidity."

He was industrious, capable, and tactful, a well-read Christian gentleman; he had acquired from forty years of public life a rich fund of experience. But he was pedestrian, humorless, calculating, and pliable. He never made a witty remark, never wrote a memorable sentence, and never showed a touch of distinction. Above all (and this was the source of his irresolution) he had no strong convictions. Associating all his life with southern leaders in Washington, this Pennsylvanian leaned toward their views, but he never disclosed a deep adherence to any principle. Like other weak men, he could be stubborn; still oftener, he could show a petulant irascibility when events pushed him into a corner. And like other timid men, he would sometimes flare out in a sudden burst of anger, directed not against enemies who could hurt him but against friends or neutrals who would not. As the sectional crisis deepened, it became his dominant hope to stumble through it, somehow, and anyhow, so as to leave office with the Union yet intact. His successor could bear the storm.

This was the President who had to deal, in Kansas and Washington, with men of fierce conviction, stern courage and, all too often, ruthless methods.

In Kansas the proslavery leaders were determined to strike boldly and unscrupulously for a slave state. They maintained close communications with such southern chieftains in Washington as Senator Slidell, Speaker James L. Orr, and Howell Cobb and Jacob Thompson, Buchanan's secretaries of the Treasury and the Interior. Having gained control of the territorial legislature, they meant to keep and use this mastery. Just before Buchanan became President they passed a bill for a constitutional convention—and a more unfair measure was never put on paper. Nearly all county officers, selected not by popular vote but by the dishonestly chosen legislature, were proslavery men. The bill provided that the sheriffs and their deputies should in March, 1857, register the white residents; that the probate judges should then take from the sheriffs complete lists of qualified voters; and that the county commissioners should finally choose election judges.

Everyone knew that a heavy majority of the Kansas settlers were anti-slavery. Many, even of the southerners, who had migrated thither opposed the "peculiar institution" as retrogressive and crippling in character. Everybody also knew that Kansas, with hardly thirty thousand people, burdened with debts, and unsupplied with fit roads, schools, or court-houses, was not yet ready for statehood; it still needed the federal government's care. Most Kansans refused to recognize the "bogus" legislature. Yet this legislature was forcing a premature convention, and taking steps to see that the election of delegates was controlled by sheriffs, judges, and county commissioners who were mainly proslavery Democrats. Governor John W. Geary, himself a Democrat appointed by Pierce, indignantly vetoed the bill. But the legislature immediately repassed it over Geary's veto; and when threats against his life increased until citizens laid bets that he would be assassinated within forty days, he resigned in alarm and posted east to apprise the country of imminent perils.

Along the way to Washington, Geary paused to warn the press that a packed convention was about to drag fettered Kansas before Congress with a slavery constitution. This convention would have a free hand, for the bill just passed made no provision for a popular vote on the instrument. Indeed, one legislator admitted that the plan was to avoid popular submission, for he proposed inserting a clause to guard against the possibility that Congress might return the constitution for a referendum. Thus, commented the *Missouri Democrat,* "the felon legislature has provided as effectually for getting the desired result as Louis Napoleon did for getting himself elected Emperor." All this was an ironic commentary on Douglas' maxim: "Let the voice of the people rule."

And Douglas, watching the reckless course of the Kansas legislators with alarm, saw that his principles and his political future were at stake. When his Kansas-Nebraska Act was passed, he had given the North his solemn promise that a free, full, and fair election would decide the future of the two territories. No fraud, no sharp practice, no browbeating would be sanctioned; every male white citizen should have use of the ballot box. He had notified the South that Kansas was almost certain to be free soil. Now he professed confidence that

President Buchanan would never permit a breach of fair procedure. He joined Buchanan in persuading one of the nation's ablest men, former Secretary of the Treasury Robert J. Walker, to go out to Kansas in Geary's place as governor. Douglas knew that if he consented to a betrayal of popular sovereignty he would be ruined forever politically in his own state of Illinois.

For a brief space in the spring of 1857 Buchanan seemed to stand firm. In his instructions to Governor Walker he engaged that the new constitution would be laid before the people; and "they must be protected in the exercise of their right of voting for or against that instrument, and the fair expression of the popular will must not be interrupted by fraud or violence."

It is not strange that the rash proslavery gamesters in Kansas prosecuted their designs despite all Buchanan's fair words and Walker's desperate efforts to stay them. They knew that with four fifths of the people already against them, and the odds growing greater every year, only brazen trickery could effect their end. They were aware that the South, which believed that a fair division would give Kansas to slavery and Nebraska to freedom, expected them to stand firm. They were egged on by the two reckless southern Cabinet members, Howell Cobb and Thompson, who sent an agent, H. L. Martin of Mississippi, out to the Kansas convention. This gathering in Lecompton, with 48 of the 60 members hailing from slave states, was the shabbiest conclave of its kind ever held on American soil. One of Buchanan's Kansas correspondents wrote that he had not supposed such a wild set could be found. The *Kansas News* termed them a body of "broken-down political hacks, demagogues, fire-eaters, perjurers, ruffians, ballot-box stuffers, and loafers." But before it broke up with the shout, "Now, boys, let's come and take a drink!" it had written a constitution.

This constitution, the work of a totally unrepresentative body, was a devious repudiation of all the principles Buchanan and Douglas had laid down. Although it contained numerous controversial provisions, such as limitation of banking to one institution and a bar against free Negroes, the main document was not to be submitted to general vote at all. A nominal reference of the great cardinal question was indeed provided. Voters might cast their ballots for the "constitution with slavery" or the "constitution without slavery." But when closely examined this was seen to be actually a piece of chicanery. Whichever form was adopted, the 200 slaves in Kansas would remain, with a constitutional guarantee against interference. Whenever the proslavery party in Kansas could get control of the legislature, they might open the door wide for more slaves. The rigged convention had put its handiwork before the people with a rigged choice: "Heads I win, tails you lose."

Would Buchanan lay this impudent contrivance before Congress, and ask it to vote the admission of Kansas as a state? Or would he contemptuously spurn it? An intrepid man would not have hesitated an instant to take the honest course; he would not have needed the indignant outcry of the northern press, the outraged roar of Douglas, to inspirit him. But Buchanan quailed before the storm of passion into which proslavery extremists had worked themselves.

The hot blood of the South was now up. That section, grossly misinformed upon events in Kansas, believed that *it* was being cheated. The northern freesoilers had vowed that no new slave state (save by a partition of Texas) should ever be admitted. Southerners thought that in pursuance of this resolve, the Yankees had made unscrupulous use of their wealth and numbers to lay hands on Kansas. Did the North think itself entitled to every piece on the board—to take Kansas as well as California, Minnesota, Iowa, Nebraska, Oregon—to give southerners nothing? The Lecompton delegates, from this point of view, were dauntless champions of a wronged section. What if they did use sharp tactics? That was but a necessary response to northern arrogance. Jefferson Davis declared that his section trembled under a sense of insecurity. "You have made it a political war. We are on the defensive. How far are you to push us?" Sharp threats of secession and battle mingled with the southern denunciations. "Sir," Senator Alfred Iverson of Georgia was soon to assert, "I believe that the time will come when the slave States will be compelled, in vindication of their rights, interests, and honor, to separate from the free States, and erect an independent confederacy; and I am not sure, sir, that the time is not at hand."

Three southern members of the Cabinet, Cobb, Thompson, and John B. Floyd, had taken the measure of Buchanan's pusillanimity. They, with one northern sympathizer, Jeremiah Black, and several White House habitués like John Slidell of Louisiana, constituted a virtual Directory exercising control over the tremulous President. They played on Buchanan's fierce partisan hatred of Republicans, and his jealous dislike of Douglas. They played also on his legalistic cast of mind; after all, the Lecompton constitution was a legal instrument by a legal convention—outwardly. Above all, they played on his fears, his morbid sensitiveness, and his responsiveness to immediate pressures. They could do this the more easily because the threats of disruption and violence were real. Henry S. Foote, a former senator from Mississippi and an enemy of Jefferson Davis, who saw Lecompton in its true light and hurried to Washington to advise the President, writes:

> It was unfortunately of no avail that these efforts to reassure Mr. Buchanan were at that time essayed by myself and others; he had already

become thoroughly *panic-stricken;* the howlings of the bulldog of secession had fairly frightened him out of his wits, and he ingloriously resolved to yield without further resistance to the decrial and vilification to which he had been so acrimoniously subjected.

And the well-informed Washington correspondent of the New Orleans *Picayune* a little later told just how aggressively the Chief Executive was bludgeoned into submission:

> The President was informed in November, 1857, that the States of Alabama, Mississippi, and South Carolina, and perhaps others, would hold conventions and secede from the Union if the Lecompton Constitution, which established slavery, should not be accepted by Congress. The reason was that these States, supposing that the South had been cheated out of Kansas, were, whether right or wrong, determined to revolt. The President believed this. Senator Hunter, of Virginia, to my knowledge, believed it. Many other eminent men did, and perhaps not without reason.

Buchanan, without imagination as without nerve, began to yield to this southern storm in midsummer, and by November, 1857, he was surrendering completely. When Congress met in December his message upheld the Lecompton Constitution with a tissue of false and evasive statements. Seldom in American history has a chief magistrate made a greater error, or missed a larger opportunity. The astute secretary of his predecessor, Franklin Pierce, wrote: "I had considerable hopes of Mr. Buchanan—I really thought he was a statesman—but I have now come to the settled conclusion that he is just the damndest old fool that has ever occupied the presidential chair. He has deliberately walked overboard with his eyes open—let him drown, for he must."

As Buchanan shrank from the lists, Douglas entered them with that *gaudium certaminis* which was one of his greatest qualities. The finest chapters of his life, his last great contests for the Union, were opening. Obviously he would have had to act under political necessity even if deaf to principle, for had he let popular sovereignty be torn to pieces, Illinois would not have sent him back to the Senate the following year; but he was not the man to turn his back on principle. His struggle against Lecompton was an exhibition of iron determination. The drama of that battle has given it an almost unique place in the record of our party controversies.

"By God, sir!" he exclaimed, "I made James Buchanan, and by God, sir, I will unmake him!" Friends told him that the southern Democrats meant to ruin him. "I have taken a through ticket," rejoined Douglas, "and checked my baggage." He lost no time in facing Buchanan in the White House and denouncing the Lecompton policy. When the President reminded him how Jackson had crushed two party rebels, he was ready with a stinging retort. Douglas was not to be overawed by a man he despised as a weakling. "Mr. President," he snorted, "I wish you to remember that General Jackson is dead."

As for the southern leaders, Douglas' scorn for the extremists who had coerced Buchanan was unbounded. He told the Washington correspondent of the Chicago *Journal* that he had begun his fight as a contest against a single bad measure. But his blow at Lecompton was a blow against slavery extension, and he at once had the whole "slave power" down on him like a pack of wolves. He added: "In making the fight against this power, I was enabled to stand off and view the men with whom I had been acting; I was ashamed I had ever been caught in such company; they are a set of unprincipled demagogues, bent upon perpetuating slavery, and by the exercise of that unequal and unfair power, to control the government or break up the Union; and I intend to prevent their doing either."

After a long, close, and acrid contest, on April 1, 1858, Lecompton was defeated. A coalition of Republicans, Douglasite Democrats, and Know-Nothings struck down the fraudulent constitution in the House, 120 to 112. When the vote was announced, a wild cheer rolled through the galleries. Old Francis P. Blair, Jackson's friend, carried the news to the dying Thomas Hart Benton, who had been intensely aroused by the crisis. Benton could barely speak, but his exultation was unbounded. "In energetic whispers," records Blair, "he told his visitor that the same men who had sought to destroy the republic in 1850 were at the bottom of this accursed Lecompton business. Among the greatest of his consolations in dying was the consciousness that the House of Representatives had baffled these treasonable schemes and put the heels of the people on the neck of the traitors."

The Adminstration covered its retreat by a hastily concocted measure, the English Bill, under which Kansas was kept waiting on the doorstep—sure in the end to enter a free state. The Kansas plotters, the Cobb-Thompson-Floyd clique in the Cabinet, and Buchanan had all been worsted. But the damage had been done. Southern secessionists had gained fresh strength and greater boldness from their success in coercing the Administration.

The Lecompton struggle left a varied and interesting set of aftereffects. It lifted Stephen A. Douglas to a new plane; he had been a fighting Democratic strategist, but now he became a true national leader, thinking far less of party and more of country. It sharpened the issues which that summer and fall were to form the staple of the memorable Lincoln-Douglas debates in Illinois. At the same time, it deepened the schism which had been growing for some years between southern Democrats and northwestern Democrats, and helped pave the way to that disruption of the party which preceded and facilitated the disruption of the nation. It planted new seeds of dissension in Kansas—seeds which resulted in fresh conflicts between Kansas free-soilers or jayhawkers on one side and Missouri invaders or border ruffians on the other, and in a spirit of border lawlessness which was to give the Civil War some of its darkest pages. The Lecompton battle discredited Buchanan in the eyes of most decent northerners, strengthened southern conviction of his weakness, and left the Administration materially and morally weaker in dealing with the problems of the next two and a half critical years.

For the full measure of Buchanan's failure, however, we must go deeper. Had he shown the courage that to an Adams, a Jackson, a Polk, or a Cleveland would have been second nature, the courage that springs from a deep integrity, he might have done the republic an immeasurable service by grappling with disunion when it was yet weak and unprepared. Ex-Senator Foote wrote later that he knew well that a scheme for destroying the Union "had long been on foot in the South." He knew that its leaders "were only waiting for the enfeebling of the Democratic Party in the North, and the general triumph of Free-soilism as a consequence thereof, to alarm the whole South into acquiescence in their policy." Buchanan's support of the unwise and corrupt Lecompton constitution thus played into the plotters' hands.

The same view was taken yet more emphatically by Douglas. He had inside information in 1857, he later told the Senate, that four states were threatening Buchanan with secession. Had that threat been met in the right Jacksonian spirit, had the bluff been called—for the four states were unprepared for secession and war—the leaders of the movement would have been utterly discredited. Their conspiracy would have collapsed, and they would have been so routed and humiliated in 1857 that the Democratic party schism in 1860 might never have taken place, and if it had, secession in 1861 would have been impossible.

The roots of the Civil War of course go deep; they go back beyond Douglas' impetuous Kansas-Nebraska Bill, back beyond the Mexican War, back beyond the Missouri Compromise. But the last good chance of averting secession and civil strife was perhaps lost in 1857. Even Zachary Taylor in 1850 had made it plain before his sudden death that he would use force, if necessary, to crush the secessionist tendencies which that year became so dangerous. A similar display of principle and resolution seven years later might well have left the disunionist chieftains of the Deep South so weakened in prestige that Yancey and his fellow plotters would have been helpless. The lessons of this failure in statesmanship, so plain to Douglas, ought not to be forgotten. The greatest mistake a nation can make is to put at its helm a man so pliable and unprincipled that he will palter with a clean-cut and momentous issue.

Abolitionists and the Freedman:
An Essay Review
DAVID BRION DAVIS

"*The book is dedicated to all those who are working to achieve the aboli-*
tionist goal of equal rights for all men." With this inscription, James M.
McPherson opens his recent study of the abolitionists' attempt to achieve
equality for the Negro after *the Civil War had begun. The words signify*
several things. They relate the past to the present, indicating how the
present uses the past, and how, in the differing perspective of its own values,
today's America differently perceives the America of yesterday. They
show that American history, as we read and write it, is a tale of moral
struggle, and that our most trying war was a struggle over the moral
issue of equality. They link the civil rights movement of the 1960's to the
abolitionist movement for Negro equality in the 1860's. They reflect a new
view of the abolitionists, one that regards them as redeemers of American
ideals rather than as disturbers of American consensus. In connection with
the subject of Professor McPherson's book, the words indicate that the
abolitionist crusade for Negro equality became most meaningful once the
Civil War had begun: that is, once the actual clash of arms made it possible
for its participants to realize palpably what had hitherto been a crusade of
hopes.

The 1860's are in fact coming under a new view, as the following review
essay of David Brion Davis's illustrates. About Professor Davis's long-
standing interest in abolitionism and his own contribution to the study
of slavery, we have already spoken (pp. 431–32). His review essay per-
ceptively analyzes two important studies that deal with attempts during the
1860's and 1870's to give the Negro freedom and equality: McPherson's
The Struggle for Equality: Abolitionists and the Negro in the Civil
War and Reconstruction *(1964) and Willie Lee Rose's* Rehearsal for
Reconstruction: The Port Royal Experiment *(1964). Both books show how*
the men of that generation confronted the nagging questions posed by

SOURCE: *The Journal of Southern History,* XXXVI (May, 1965), 164–70. Copyright © 1965 by the Southern Historical Association. Reprinted by permission
of the Managing Editor.

the Negro problem: Should the North's war with the South become a war of slave emancipation? In those Southern areas which had fallen into Northern hands while the war was being waged, how should the hitherto enslaved Negroes be treated? How should the captured areas be controlled? What, in fact, should be the guidelines for reconstructing the South? Could liberty and civil rights be granted the Negro? Was he innately inferior, or was he in fact the white man's equal? How far would it be necessary to educate the freed Negro to prepare him for citizenship? How should those who were committed to achieving Negro equality act with respect to the ascendant Republican Party, many of whose members did not share their commitment?

Viewing the way men addressed themselves to the issue of Negro freedom and equality a century ago, both books are fraught with significance for us. They offer us the assurance that men of vision have anticipated us and made our task easier by taking their own first steps toward solving the kinds of problems we are facing today. To the degree that we are a nation born of conscience and a desire to set right social conduct that we feel to be wrong, we may surely agree with C. Vann Woodward that we are at last, in acts designed to give the Negro the full measure of his rights, coming to fulfill America's commitment to equality.

But there is an improbability about construing recent developments this way. For one thing, the construction is itself part of a theory of progress, and there is something specious not only about seeing the American past as one of progress but also about expecting that the future is a reliable and infinite treasury against which we can mortgage our perhaps innocent beliefs. More significantly, the sense that we are at least fulfilling our commitment to equality ignores the respects in which, despite our pronouncements, ours is a society of great inequalities. The bases of these inequalities are many: wealth, education, occupation, ethnic identity, religious affiliation, genealogy, to name some of the more obvious ones. A particularly significant basis of inequality is one which is particularly visible: color. It is not fortuitous in our society of proclaimed equality that those who are black are, for the majority, also those who are poor.

If ideological commitment is part of the American story, so too is the dichotomy between what we have preached and what we have practiced. How far does what we preach compensate for what we do not practice? To pose the question from another angle: How far does the tendency to discriminate inhere in human nature, and how successfully can a democracy, despite its ideology, successfully legislate or guarantee equality? To answer this question in the negative is not to condone America's present wavering on its commitment to equality. It is merely to help identify and explain it.

According to our conventional periodization, the antislavery crusade comes to an abrupt end in 1861; the drama of Reconstruction begins in the summer of 1865. In viewing the intervening four years we have quite naturally been distracted by the smoke of battle, the glint of bayonets against the dogwood blossoms, and the debatable effects of war on Northern industry. The Civil War has long been a kind of special preserve for military and economic historians. The time has come, however, when more connecting roads must be built through even the most hallowed sanctuary of our past. For as James M. McPherson and Willie Lee Rose brilliantly demonstrate in recent books,* we shall never understand our greatest failure, or what their common teacher, C. Vann Woodward, has called our "deferred commitment to equality," unless we recognize the 1860's as our truly crucial decade. It is Mr. McPherson's thesis that abolitionism retained its moral vigor during the decade-long "struggle for equality." Mrs. Rose pushes Reconstruction back to the beginning of the war, when the curtain opened on an all-important "dress rehearsal" in the Sea Islands of South Carolina.

Contrary to the usual picture of abolitionists whose thinking stops with a negative and abstract ideal of freedom, the reformers in Mr. McPherson's book emerge as genuine revolutionaries, intent on realizing the goals of racial equality and social justice. Far from being naïve fanatics, they were aware of the depth of Northern racial prejudice and of the compromising character of politics, and were accordingly prepared to adjust their tactics to changing circumstances. In the beginning of the war, for example, many prominent abolitionists remained in the background, letting less controversial figures publicize the ideas of emancipation and enlistment of colored troops as military necessities. As the war became critical and public opinion grew more favorable to radical measures, they took to the lecture stand, secured a voice in leading newspapers, and were courted by political factions on both state and national levels. They were ready to support Lincoln and even Johnson so long as there was hope of counteracting the glacial forces of prejudice and caution. But abolitionists had reason to fear that Lincoln, who comes off rather badly in both books, would never consent to emancipation so long as there was hope of winning back the South. In the spring of 1862 fugitive slaves were still being caught in Washington. As late as the following December, the President was proposing a constitutional amendment that would give compensation to any state agreeing to abolish slavery by 1900. Never-

---

* *The Struggle for Equality: Abolitionists and the Negro in the Civil War and Reconstruction.* By James M. McPherson. (Princeton: Princeton University Press, 1964. Pp. ix, 474. Bibliographical essay, index.)

Rehearsal for Reconstruction: The Port Royal Experiment. By Willie Lee Rose. (Indianapolis: Bobbs-Merrill Company, 1964. Pp. xviii, 442. Map, illustrations, notes on sources, appendix, index.)

theless, abolitionists were shrewd enough to use Lincoln as a symbol of the Great Emancipator, and hence contributed to his undeserved reputation for moral leadership.

Mr. McPherson shows that some abolitionists were surprisingly realistic in their expectations regarding the Negro. Confident that American culture would be enriched by the Negroes' passion for music and social spontaneity, they also knew, as Wendell Phillips said, that the effects of slavery would last for one or even two more generations: "It [slavery] were a very slight evil if they could be done away sooner." For this reason abolitionists took a leading role in the wartime education of human "contrabands." And while this work was largely carried on by private societies, the reformers realized that a problem of such magnitude demanded a uniform and co-ordinated governmental program. Yet abolitionists had a legitimate mistrust of any halfway stations between slavery and freedom. They knew of the failure of apprenticeship in the British West Indies; their desire to prove the natural equality of Negroes made them suspicious of paternalism in any guise. Mr. McPherson brings out these points, but he appears to mute the poignant conflict in values which the abolitionists faced. They might agitate for a Freedmen's Bureau and a national program of aid and rehabilitation; but they could not at the same time admit the disturbing truth which alone could justify such a program, and give immediate proof to their countrymen that Negroes were the equals of whites.

But Mr. McPherson argues persuasively that abolitionists were more farsighted than has been generally supposed. They knew that without political and economic power the Negro could never be truly free. They perceived the dangerous loopholes in the Fourteenth Amendment and grasped the essential fact that racial discrimination could not be tolerated in the North if Southern freedmen were to secure their rights. Ultimately they came to see that mere laws were not sufficient. Only military occupation could ensure the social and economic revolution necessary to prevent the freedmen from falling back into a hopeless state of bondage.

The chief merit of Mr. McPherson's book does not lie in bold generalization or in the application of new techniques, but rather in a highly readable narration of fresh and important material. His cast of abolitionists includes both the more radical reformers like Phillips and Parker Pillsbury and men of more moderate views like James Miller McKim and Edmund Quincy. He has digested a prodigious quantity of manuscript sources—his bibliography is the most thorough guide to abolitionist manuscripts yet to appear. He writes in a crisp, economical style, and has a remarkable eye for the telling quotation.

Unfortunately, he seldom probes into the motives and interpersonal influences which constitute the dynamics of organized reform. Occasionally, indeed, he lapses into a moralistic tone that detracts from the force of his argument. A more serious flaw can be found in his attempts to relate abolitionism with changing public opinion. One is never quite sure when the times are "ripe" or "unripe" for reform. On page 82, for example, we are told that by December 1861 "the powerful idea of universal freedom was taking deep root in America. As lifelong champions of this idea, abolitionists began to reap the benefits of its growing popularity." Yet nine pages and one month later we are startled to find that a new "emancipation journal," *Continental Monthly,* believes that " 'This is not now a question of the right to hold slaves, or the wrong of so doing. . . . All of that old abolition jargon went out and died with the present aspect of the war. So far as nine-tenths of the North ever cared, or do now care, slaves might have hoed away down in Dixie' forever, if their masters had not rebelled and sought to destroy the Union." Much of Mr. McPherson's later evidence would seem to support that view. And this makes one dubious about the supposedly great shifts in public opinion for which the abolitionists are given credit.

But the important thing is that Mr. McPherson has demolished the stereotyped view of the abolitionist who is content to abandon the Negro with the outbreak of war. He properly stresses the revolutionary implications of mass emancipation, the enrollment of freedmen in the Union army, and the reformers' ideal of full social equality. It is clear, however, that Lincoln's administration and much of the Northern public had no such aims in view. The revolution, after all, misfired. By showing that many abolitionists were working for the same goals as the present proponents of civil rights, Mr. McPherson has made it all the more imperative for us to know what went wrong.

The Struggle for Equality gives a brief description of the early experiment in reconstruction at Port Royal, and both Mr. McPherson and Mrs. Rose have obviously profited from the other's researches. It would be a mistake, however, to suppose that Mr. McPherson's summary can be a substitute for reading Mrs. Rose's book. *Rehearsal for Reconstruction,* which won the Allan Nevins History Prize, is at once a work of art and a triumph of historical analysis. Far narrower in scope than Mr. McPherson's book, it furnishes a detailed re-creation of some of the Civil War's noblest hopes and greatest tragedies. Mrs. Rose has gone through a mass of manuscript sources with a fine sensitivity to the subtleties of character and the nuances of personal relationships. Even more impressive is her ability to see the role of individuals in larger situations—to relate the small canvas of Port

Royal to the panorama of slavery, war, and Reconstruction. And though well aware of the grim seriousness of her subject, she has a quiet sense of humor. She is, in short, more relaxed than Mr. McPherson.

In November 1861, Union forces captured and occupied a cluster of sea islands between Charleston and Savannah. The abandoned property, including rich cotton plantations and some 10,000 slaves, fell under the jurisdiction of the Treasury Department. Despite the coolness of Lincoln and the rest of the cabinet, Secretary Salmon P. Chase looked upon the Port Royal area as the stage for the first experiment in reconstruction. With incredible speed a kind of Peace Corps was recruited in the North. Mainly from New England and New York, the original fifty-three missionaries included twelve women and an impressive number of young graduates from Harvard, Yale, and the divinity schools. If the "Gideonites," as they were called, were of mixed backgrounds and lacking in practical experience, they were dedicated to the great task of proving that Negro slaves could be converted into responsible citizens. In Mrs. Rose's words, "On these islands, within gunshot and shouting distance of the Confederate pickets, American antislavery men and women had met the American slave on his home ground and were asking him to work out his own salvation by working cotton—voluntarily."

Cotton was the problem. As might be expected, the government was more interested in contraband cotton than in contraband slaves. From the beginning the experiment presupposed that slaves could be educated and uplifted while the government appropriated the Southern system of one-crop agriculture. Not only would Negroes continue to toil in the cotton fields as before, and ultimately be judged by the success or failure of a precarious economic system, but the government's fiscal policies clashed with the efforts of reformers at every point. Treasury agents confiscated furniture and buildings at the very moment when Gideonites were trying to settle on the islands. And just as the reformers were beginning to prove that Negroes could support themselves by growing provisions, tax commissioners arrived with the intent of selling land under the confiscatory tax law of June 1862.

The conflict between reform and revenue is only a part of Mrs. Rose's picture. Armies of occupation are always a demoralizing influence, and the Union army was hardly an exception. In the eyes of tough soldiers the Gideonite's idealism was a preposterous joke. Supplementing the common prejudice which most Americans held against Negroes, the troops harbored "an ill-defined notion that the Negro was somehow, at bottom, the cause of the war." With this insight Mrs. Rose helps to explain the outrageous treatment of Negroes at the hands of Union soldiers. The problem worsened considerably with the arrival of thousands of starving refugees, who hit the islands in wave after wave both in advance and in the wake of Sherman's army. And if Sherman's combat troops were hardened to the sight of dying Negro children, they were shocked to the quick by the glimpse of a Northern white woman riding in a wagon with a colored man. In the deep-rooted prejudice of Sherman's soldiers one sees how much education was yet to be accomplished in the North and West, and how far abolitionist reformers had moved beyond the mass of their countrymen.

The Gideonites knew that, like the Puritans of Massachusetts Bay, they were engaged in a great errand into the wilderness, and were building the city on a hill. If they could prove that even the most oppressed slaves could be educated and could work as free laborers, the foundations for a successful reconstruction would be secure. But while divided by personal animosities, denominational conflict, and a puritanical "mutual watchfulness," their greatest problem arose from the very logic of their situation. As abolitionists they were prepared to accept the fact that slavery degraded the human soul; but as reformers and uplifters, they could not help but minimize the deep scars of bondage. They were alert to the dangers of paternalism, but found themselves replacing Southern masters in positions of authority over dependent Negroes. As they fell into the mold of a governing class, they could not accept the full implications of freedom. Harriet Ware, for example, said she was glad to see Negroes losing some of their old servility, but was distressed to find that they were no longer so obedient!

The insight and objectivity with which Mrs. Rose handles the reformers are nowhere more evident than in her treatment of Edward Philbrick, a young Boston abolitionist who also had a hardheaded interest in cotton manufacturing. Philbrick wanted to *do* something "in this great work which is going on," but his moral earnestness was tempered by a conviction that the Negro's interest could best be served by a concrete demonstration that free labor could compete in the open market. Buying large tracts of confiscated land for a New England syndicate, Philbrick proposed to show that Negroes could voluntarily grow cotton in sufficient quantities to attract Northern capital. Because he made substantial profits for himself and tried to keep wages as low as possible, he is an easy target for the cynical historian. Mrs. Rose shows, however, that he was sincere in his laissez faire convictions, and that he devoted large sums to Negro education. Philbrick's failure arose not from his lack of good will or self-sacrifice, but from his blindness to the inadequacies of ante bellum agriculture. He helped to build the framework for tragedy by identifying the cause of the Negro with an economic system that was artificially sustained by war and that was bound to collapse when world competition reduced the price of cotton.

Perhaps Mrs. Rose's richest contribution to our understanding of the first phase of Reconstruction lies in her portrayal of the Negro himself. At times gently questioning Stanley Elkins' recent theories, she provides a subtle analysis of the diverse effects of slavery on the Negro's personality, and of the difficulties he faced in adjusting to the uncertain policies of his new masters. One ex-slave remembered that when he was a boy on the Sea Islands and heard the roar of the first Union guns, his mother assured him "dat ain't no t'under, dat Yankee come to gib you Freedom." Yet the Yankee intended no such thing, and after the capture of the islands the contrabands' status was anything but clear. Unable even to promise future freedom, the Gideonites were faced by the problem of an edgy and suspicious population that was no longer subject to the disciplinary controls of slavery. Despite the prevalence of apathy and ignorance, the Negroes were highly sensitive to breakthroughs in opportunity and to the changing attitudes and policies of Northerners. Many were eager for education, and some were well informed and partly literate. When General Rufus Saxton began to implement a plan for pre-emption of land, many Negroes became successful independent farmers. Some bought plantations and town houses in Beaufort. One group pooled their resources to purchase a plantation which they ran collectively without white direction. After the war certain Southern planters found themselves borrowing funds from their former slaves.

Yet the story of Port Royal is a story of inflated hopes and broken promises. The Sea Island Negroes were among the small minority of slaves actually freed by the Emancipation Proclamation. They were among the first to be enrolled in the Union army. But though they served with honor, Negro soldiers were paid at a rate far below that of white soldiers, when they were paid at all. Lincoln, one may note, defended this discriminatory policy. Even worse was the forcible impressment of colored troops, who were brutally seized and often shot without provocation. And the betrayal of promises that accompanied emancipation and military service hardly matched President Johnson's reversal of the land policy embodied in Sherman's Special Field Order Number 15; after Johnson's action, Negroes were evicted from their farms unless they agreed to sign labor contracts with the prewar owners.

For all the bungling, shortsightedness, and cross-purposes of the Port Royal experiment, Mrs. Rose points out that the missionaries did prove their case. They showed that the most degraded slaves could support themselves on the land, fight against their former masters, and make heartening progress in education. If the lives of the Gideonites had been full of illusion, frustration, and disappointment, they had prepared the way for a reconstruction program that recognized a national responsibility for the freedmen. But in the last analysis, Mrs. Rose maintains, such gains had been possible only because of the exigencies of war. The nation was ready to use the Negro in any way that seemed likely to bring the war to an end; aside from this, it was not prepared to follow the path of the small band of Gideonites toward slow and painful progress. As Mr. McPherson concludes, the failure was ultimately one of the American people. Mrs. Rose leaves one with a sad appreciation of the magnitude and contingencies of that failure.

35

Did the Civil War Retard Industrialization?
THOMAS C. COCHRAN

The war of ideas between the "free" world and the "communist" world has centered on the growth and productivity of their respective economic systems. Which system provides more goods and services for its nation's citizens? Which affords a nation greater potential for defending itself and making war? Which can best serve as a model certain to be emulated by the many new nations of the world? The ideological conflict over economies, particularly the disputation between the United States and the Soviet Union, has been lively and basic because it is also one over national power and the course of international politics.

Here is why so much discussion has been proceeding in recent years about the rate of a country's economic growth and the factors that could help to increase it. Here is also why so much interest attaches to the development of the American economy—which has clearly produced more in goods and services than that of other nations—and to the particular conditions which have encouraged it. To consider a very basic question: What accounts for our industrial revolution? Or, to phrase this somewhat differently, in the words recently popularized by Walt W. Rostow: What

SOURCE: *The Mississippi Valley Historical Review,* LVIII (September, 1961), 197–210. Reprinted by permission of the publisher.

circumstances were responsible for the "take-off" of our economy into industrialism? In the traditional view, the role of the Civil War was basic. The war, it was said, was a dividing line between an era of small beginnings and limited growth, and one of rapid expansion and massive industrial formations. The war brought about highly favorable government policies toward business, extensive orders for equipping the Union armies, and a prosperity that gave northern business the incentive to expand production.

This view was recently challenged by Thomas C. Cochran, of the University of Pennsylvania, in a talk which he delivered before the Mississippi Valley Historical Association and which is reprinted below. One of our principal writers on American economic history, Professor Cochran is the author of several important studies, including Railroad Leaders, 1845 to 1890: The Business Mind in Action *(1953),* The American Business System: A Historical Perspective, 1900-1955 *(1957), and* The Inner Revolution: Essays on the Social Sciences in History *(1964). When the U. S. Bureau of the Census and the National Bureau of Economic Research made available statistics on long-run industrial trends during the nineteenth century, Professor Cochran found adequate reason for disputing the usual thesis concerning the Civil War's impact on American economic development. Indeed, on the basis of the newly available data, he concluded that the war had retarded our industrial growth. In the final section of his essay, moreover, he offers several provocative "obiter dicta" (as he calls them) about the nature and extent of American economic advances during the antebellum decades.*

Since the appearance of Cochran's seminal essay, historians have been reconsidering both the larger question he raised about the Civil War's economic effects and the answer he came up with. Several of the more important by-products of this reconsideration can be found in two recent collections: Ralph Andreano, ed., The Economic Impact of the American Civil War *(1962), and David T. Gilchrist and W. David Lewis, eds.,* Economic Change in the Civil War Era *(1965). The discussion of the question by his fellow historians indicates that the greater number of them tend to agree with Professor Cochran's conclusion. It indicates something more. The increasing concern with economic growth—with progress and retardation, with rates of increase in gross national product, with "take-off" periods, and with the many factors that contribute to the one or the other— is part of a greater concern with our nation's role as the exemplar of a "free" economy. In a world of increasingly controlled or planned economies, this is no small concern.*

In most textbooks and interpretative histories of the United States the Civil War has been assigned a major role in bringing about the American Industrial Revolution. Colorful business developments in the North—adoption of new machines, the quick spread of war contracting, the boost given to profits by inflation, and the creation of a group of war millionaires—make the war years seem not only a period of rapid economic change but also one that created important forces for future growth. The superficial qualitative evidence is so persuasive that apparently few writers have examined the available long-run statistical series before adding their endorsement to the conventional interpretation. The following quotations taken from the books of two generations of leading scholars illustrate the popular view.

"The so-called Civil War," wrote Charles A. and Mary R. Beard in 1927, " . . . was a social war . . . making *vast changes* in the arrangement of classes, in the accumulation and distribution of wealth, *in the course of industrial development.*" Midway between 1927 and the present, Arthur M. Schlesinger, Sr., wrote: "On these tender industrial growths the Civil War *had the effect of a hothouse.* For reasons already clear . . . nearly every branch of industry grew lustily." Harold U. Faulkner, whose textbook sales have ranked near or at the top, said in 1954: "In the economic history of the United States the Civil War was extremely important. . . . In the North *it speeded the Industrial Revolution* and the development of capitalism by the prosperity which it brought to industry." The leading new text of 1957, by Richard Hofstadter, William Miller, and Daniel Aaron, showed no weakening of this interpretation: "The growing demand for farm machinery as well as for the 'sinews of war' led to American industrial expansion. . . . Of necessity, *iron, coal, and copper* production boomed during the war years." A sophisticated but still essentially misleading view is presented by Gilbert C. Fite and Jim E. Reese in a text of 1959: "The Civil War proved to be a boon to Northern economic development. . . . Industry, for example, was not created by the war, but wartime demands *greatly stimulated and encouraged industrial development* which already had a good start." In a reappraisal of the Civil War, in *Harper's Magazine* for April, 1960, Denis W. Brogan, a specialist in American institutions, wrote: "It may have been only a catalyst but the War *precipitated the entry* of the United States *into the modern industrial world,* made 'the take-off' (to use Professor W. W. Rostow's brilliant metaphor) come sooner."

In all of these reiterations of the effect of the Civil War on industrialism, statistical series seem to have been largely neglected. None of the authors cited reinforce their interpretations by setting the war period in the context of important long-run indexes of industrial growth. Since 1949, series for the period 1840 to 1890 that would cast doubt on the conventional generalizations have been available in *Historical Statistics of the United States, 1789-1945.* In 1960 a new edition of *Historical Statistics* and the report of the Conference on Research in Income and Wealth on *Trends in the American Economy in the Nine-*

teenth Century have provided additional material to support the argument that the Civil War retarded American industrial development. These volumes give data for many growth curves for the two decades before and after the war decade — in other words, the long-run trends before and after the event in question. The pattern of these trends is a mixed one which shows no uniform type of change during the Civil War decade, but on balance for the more important series the trend is toward retardation in *rates* of growth rather than toward acceleration. This fact is evident in many series which economists would regard as basic to economic growth, but in order to keep the discussion within reasonable limits only a few can be considered here.

Robert E. Gallman has compiled new and more accurate series for both "total commodity output," including agriculture, and "value added by manufacture," the two most general measures of economic growth available for this period. He writes: "Between 1839 and 1899 total commodity output increased elevenfold, or at an average decade rate of slightly less than 50 per cent. . . . Actual rates varied fairly widely, high rates appearing during the decades ending with 1854 and 1884, and a very low rate during the decade ending with 1869." From the over-all standpoint this statement indicates the immediately retarding effect of the Civil War on American economic growth, but since most of the misleading statements are made in regard to industrial growth, or particular elements in industrial growth, it is necessary to look in more detail at "value added by manufacture" and some special series. Gallman's series for value added in constant dollars of the purchasing power of 1879 shows a rise of 157 per cent from 1839 to 1849; 76 per cent from 1849 to 1859; and only 25 per cent from 1859 to 1869. By the 1870's the more favorable prewar rates were resumed, with an increase of 82 per cent for 1869-1879, and 112 per cent for 1879-1889. Thus two decades of very rapid advance, the 1840's and the 1880's, are separated by thirty years of slower growth which falls to the lowest level in the decade that embraces the Civil War.

Pig-iron production in tons, perhaps the most significant commodity index of nineteenth-century American industrial growth, is available year-by-year from 1854 on.   Taking total production for five-year periods, output increased 9 per cent between the block of years from 1856 to 1860 and the block from 1861 to 1865.   That even this slight increase might not have been registered except for the fact that 1857 to 1860 were years of intermittent depression is indicated by an 81 per cent increase over the war years in the block of years from 1866 to 1870. If annual production is taken at five-year intervals, starting in 1850, the increase is 24 per cent from 1850 to 1855; 17 per cent from 1855 to 1860; 1 per cent from 1860 to 1865; and 100 per cent from 1865 to 1870. While there is no figure available for 1845, the period from 1840 to 1850 shows 97 per cent increase in shipments, while for the period 1870 to 1880 the increase was 130 per cent. To sum up, depression and war appear to have retarded a curve of production that was tending to rise at a high rate.

Bituminous coal production may be regarded as the next most essential commodity series. After a gain of 199 per cent from 1840 to 1850 this series shows a rather steady pattern of increase at rates varying from 119 to 148 per cent each decade from 1850 to 1890. The war does not appear to have markedly affected the rate of growth.

In the mid-nineteenth century copper production was not a basic series for recording American growth, but since three distinguished authors have singled it out as one of the indexes of the effect of the war on industry it is best to cite the statistics. Before 1845 production of domestic copper was negligible. By 1850 the "annual recoverable content" of copper from United States mines was 728 tons, by 1860 it was 8,064 tons, by 1865 it was 9,520 tons, and by 1870 it was 14,112 tons. In this series of very small quantities, therefore, the increase from 1850 to 1860 was just over 1,000 per cent, from 1860 to 1865 it was 18 per cent, and from 1865 to 1870 it was 48 per cent.

Railroad track, particularly in the United States, was an essential for industrialization. Here both the depression and the war retarded the rate of growth. From 1851 through 1855 a total of 11,627 miles of new track was laid, from 1856 through 1860, only 8,721 miles, and from 1861 through 1865, only 4,076 miles. After the war the rate of the early 1850's was resumed, with 16,174 miles constructed from 1866 through 1870. Looked at by decades, a rate of over 200 per cent increase per decade in the twenty years before the war was slowed to 70 per cent for the period from 1860 to 1870, with only a 15 per cent increase during the war years. In the next two decades the rate averaged about 75 per cent.

Next to food, cotton textiles may be taken as the most representative consumer-goods industry in the nineteenth century. Interference with the flow of southern cotton had a depressing effect. The number of bales of cotton consumed in United States manufacturing rose 143 per cent from 1840 to 1850 and 47 per cent from 1850 to 1860, but *fell* by 6 per cent from 1860 to 1870. From then on consumption increased at a little higher rate than in the 1850's.

While woolen textile production is not an important series in the over-all picture of industrial growth, it should be noted that, helped by protection and military needs, consumption of wool for manufacturing more than doubled during the war, and then *fell* somewhat from 1865 to 1870. But Arthur H. Cole, the historian of the woolen industry, characterizes the years from 1830 to 1870 as a period of growth "not so striking as in the decades before or afterwards."

Immigration to a nation essentially short of labor was unquestionably a stimulant to economic growth. Another country had paid for the immigrant's unproductive youthful years, and he came to the United States ready to contribute his labor at a low cost. The pattern of the curve for annual immigration shows the retarding effect of both depression and war. In the first five years of the 1850's an average of 349,685 immigrants a year came to the United States. From 1856 through 1860 the annual average fell to 169,958, and for the war years of 1861 to 1865 it fell further to 160,345. In the first five postwar years the average rose to 302,620, but not until the first half of the 1870's did the rate equal that of the early 1850's. Had there been a return to prosperity instead of war in 1861, it seems reasonable to suppose that several hundred thousand additional immigrants would have arrived before 1865.

In the case of farm mechanization the same type of error occurs as in the annual series on copper production. "Random" statistics such as the manufacture of 90,000 reapers in 1864 are frequently cited without putting them in the proper perspective of the total number in use and the continuing trends. Reaper and mower sales started upward in the early 1850's and were large from 1856 on, in spite of the depression. William T. Hutchinson estimates that most of the 125,000 reapers and mowers in use in 1861 had been sold during the previous five years. While the business, without regard to the accidental coming of the war, was obviously in a stage of very rapid growth, the war years presented many difficulties and may actually have retarded the rate of increase. Total sales of reapers for the period 1861-1865 are estimated at 250,000—a quite ordinary increase for a young industry —but the 90,000 figure for 1864, if it is correct, reinforces the evidence from the McCormick correspondence that this was the one particularly good year of the period. During these years William S. McCormick was often of the opinion that the "uncertainties of the times" made advisable a suspension of manufacturing until the close of the war.

For a broader view of agricultural mechanization the series "value of farm implements and machinery" has special interest. Here the census gives a picture which, if correct, is explicable only on the basis of wartime destruction. Based on constant dollars the average value of machinery per farm *fell* nearly 25 per cent in the decade of the war and showed nearly a 90 per cent gain in the 1870's. Differing from these census figures is a series prepared by Marvin W. Towne and Wayne D. Rasmussen based on the production of farm machinery. While this obviously does not take account of destruction of existing equipment or the rapid increase in the number of farms, the record of new production is hard to reconcile with the census figures. The production of implements and machinery reckoned in constant dollars is a sharply rising curve from 1850 on, with increases of 110 per cent from 1850 to 1860; 140 per cent from 1860 to 1870; and 95 per cent from 1870 to 1880. Meanwhile the number of farms increased by about one third in each of the decades of the 1850's and 1860's and by one half in the 1870's. Whatever interpretation is given to these figures, it does not appear that the war greatly increased the trend of agricultural mechanization. The series for gross farm product in constant dollars shows wide variations in increase from decade to decade, with the 1860's in the low group. The gains were 23 per cent, 1840 to 1850; 42 per cent, 1850 to 1860; 21 per cent, 1860 to 1870; 52 per cent, 1870 to 1880; and 20 per cent, 1880 to 1890.

Much American business expansion was financed by short-term bank loans continuously renewed. Thus major increases in business activity should be mirrored in increases in bank loans, both for financing short-term transactions and for additions to plant and working capital that would, in fact, be paid off gradually. If there was a really great Civil War boom in business activity it should be indicated in the series "total loans" of all banks. But it is not. In constant dollars, bank loans fell slightly between 1840 and 1850, and rose nearly 50 per cent by 1860. It should be noted that none of these three decadal years were periods of high prosperity. During the war Confederate banking statistics were not reported by the comptroller of the currency, but by 1866 there is a comparable figure for the nation as a whole, and in constant dollars it is some 35 per cent below that of 1860. Even by 1870 the constant dollar value of all loans was more than 15 per cent lower than just before the war. If instead of examining loans one looks at total assets of all banks the decline in constant dollars from 1860 to 1870 is reduced to 10 per cent, the difference arising from a larger cash position and more investment in government bonds.

Net capital formation would be a more proper index of economic growth than bank loans or assets. Unfortunately, neither the teams of the National Bureau of Economic Research nor those of the Census Bureau have been able to carry any reliable series back of 1868. From colonial times to 1960, however, the chief single form of American capital formation has undoubtedly been building construction. Farm houses, city homes, public buildings, stores, warehouses, and factories have year-by-year constituted, in monetary value, the leading type of capital growth. Gallman has drawn up series for such construction based on estimating the flow of construction materials and adding what appear to be appropriate markups. Admittedly the process is inexact, but because of the importance of construction in reflecting general trends in capital formation it is interesting to see the results. The rate of change for the ten-year period ending in 1854 is about 140 per cent; for the one ending in 1859 it is 90 per cent; for 1869 it is 40 per cent; and for 1879 it is 46 per cent. Taking a long view, from 1839 to 1859 the average decennial rate of increase was about 70 per cent, and from 1869 to 1899 it was about 40 per cent. The *rate* of advance in construction was declining and the war decade added a further dip to the decline.

Since the decline in rate is for the decade, the exact effect of the war years can only be estimated, but the logic of the situation, reinforced by the record of sharp cut-backs in railroad building, seems inescapable: the Civil War, like all modern wars, checked civilian construction. The first year of war was a period of depression and tight credit in the Middle West, which checked residential and farm construction in the area that grew most rapidly before and after the war. In both the East and the West the last two years of the war were a period of rapid inflation which was regarded by businessmen as a temporary wartime phenomenon. The logical result would be to postpone construction for long-term use until after the anticipated deflation. The decline in private railroad construction to a small fraction of the normal rate exemplifies the situation.

Lavish expenditure and speculation by a small group of war contractors and market operators gambling on the inflation seem to have created a legend of high prosperity during the war years. But the general series on fluctuations in the volume of business do not bear this out. Leonard P. Ayres's estimates of business activity place the average for 1861 through 1865 below normal, and Norman J. Silberling's business index is below its normal line for all years of the war. Silberling also has an intermediate trend line for business, which smooths out annual fluctuations. This line falls steadily from 1860 to 1869. Much of Silberling's discussion in his chapter "Business Activity, Prices, and Wars" is in answer to his question: "Why does it seem to be true that despite a temporary stimulating effect of war upon some industries, wars are generally associated with a long-term retarding of business growth . . . ?" He puts the Civil War in this general category.

Collectively these statistical estimates support a conclusion that the Civil War retarded American industrial growth. Presentation of this view has been the chief purpose of this article. To try to judge the nonmeasurable or indirect effects of the war is extremely difficult. But since further discussion of the conventional qualitative factors may help to explain the prevailing evaluation in American texts, it seems appropriate to add some conjectural *obiter dicta*.

Experience with the apparently stimulating effects of twentieth-century wars on production makes the conclusion that victorious war may retard the growth of an industrial state seem paradoxical, and no doubt accounts in part for the use of detached bits of quantitative data to emphasize the Civil War's industrial importance. The resolution of the paradox may be found in contemporary conditions in the United States and in the nature of the wartime demand. The essential wastefulness of war from the standpoint of economic growth was obscured by the accident that both of the great European wars of the twentieth century began when the United States had a high level of unemployment. The immediate effect of each, therefore, was to put men to work, to increase the national product, and to create an aura of prosperity. Presumably, the United States of the mid-nineteenth century tended to operate close enough to full employment in average years that any wasteful labor-consuming activities were a burden rather than a stimulant.

By modern standards the Civil War was still unmechanized. It was fought with rifles, bayonets, and sabers by men on foot or horseback. Artillery was more used than in previous wars, but was still a relatively minor consumer of iron and steel. The railroad was also brought into use, but the building of military lines offset only a small percentage of the over-all drop from the prewar level of civilian railroad construction. Had all of these things not been true, the Confederacy with its small industrial development could never have fought through four years of increasingly effective blockade.

In spite of the failure of direct quantitative evidence to show accelerating effects of the war on rates of economic growth, there could be long-run effects of a qualitative type that would gradually foster a more rapid rate of economic growth. The most obvious place to look for such indirect effects would be in the results of freeing the slaves. Marxists contended that elimination of slavery was a necessary precursor of the bourgeois industrialism which would lead to the socialist revolution. The creation of a free Negro labor force was, of course, of great long-run importance. In the twentieth century it has led to readjustment of Negro population between the deep South and the northern industrial areas, and to changes in the use of southern land.

But economically the effects of war and emancipation over the period 1840 to 1880 were negative. Richard A. Easterlin writes: "In every southern state, the 1880 level of per capita income originating in commodity production and distribution was below, or at best only slightly above that of 1840. . . . [This] attests strikingly to the impact of that war and the subsequent disruption on the southern economy." In general the Negroes became sharecroppers or wage laborers, often cultivating the same land and the same crops as before the war. In qualification of the argument that free Negro labor led to more rapid industrialization it should be noted that the South did not keep up with the national pace in the growth of non-agricultural wealth until after 1900.

Two indirect effects of the war aided industrial growth to degrees that cannot accurately be measured. These were, first, a more satisfactory money market, and, secondly, more security for entrepreneurial activity than in the pre-war period. The sharp wartime inflation had the usual effect of transferring income from wage, salary, and interest receivers to those making profits. This meant concentration of savings in the hands of entrepreneurs who would invest in new activities; and this no doubt helps to explain the speculative booms of the last half of the 1860's and the first two years of the 1870's which have been treated as the prosperity resulting from the war. Inflation also eased the burdens of those railroads which had excessive mortgage debts. But a great deal of new research would be needed to establish causal connections between the inflationary reallocation of wealth, 1863 to 1865, and the high rate of industrial progress in the late 1870's and the 1880's.

The National Banking Act, providing a more reliable currency for interstate operations, has been hailed as a great aid to business expansion although it would be hard to demonstrate, aside from a few weeks during panics, that plentiful but occasionally unsound currency had seriously interfered with earlier industrial growth. The existence of two and a half billion dollars in federal bonds also provided a basis for credit that was larger than before the war. This led to broader and more active security markets as well as to easier personal borrowing. But two qualifications must be kept in mind. First, local bank lending to favored borrowers had probably tended to be too liberal before the war and was now put on a somewhat firmer basis. In other words, since 1800 a multiplication of banks had made credit relatively easy to obtain in the United States, and in the North this continued to be the situation. Second, the southern banking system was largely destroyed by the war and had to be rebuilt in the subsequent decades. It should also be remembered that by 1875 some 40 per cent of the banks were outside the national banking system.

Because of a few colorful speculators like Jay Gould, Daniel Drew, and Jim Fisk, and the immortality conferred on them, initially by the literary ability of the Adams brothers, the New York stock exchange in the postwar decade appears to have mirrored a new era of predatory wealth. But one has only to study the scandals of the London and New York stock exchanges in 1854 to see that there was little growth in the sophistication or boldness of stock operators during these fifteen years. In any case, the exploits of market operators were seldom related in a positive way to economic growth. Even a record of new issues of securities, which is lacking for this period, would chiefly reflect the flow of capital into railroads, banks, and public utilities rather than into manufacturing. Very few "industrial" shares were publicly marketed before the decade of the 1880's; such enterprises grew chiefly from the reinvestment of earnings.

There was strong government encouragement to entrepreneurial activity during the Civil War, but to ascribe to it unusual importance for economic growth requires both analysis of the results and comparison with other periods. Government in the United States has almost always encouraged entrepreneurs. The federal and state administrations preceding the Civil War could certainly be regarded as friendly to business. They subsidized railroads by land grants, subscribed to corporate bond issues, and remitted taxes on new enterprise. Tariffs were low, but railroad men and many bankers were happy with the situation. Whether or not American industrialism was significantly accelerated by the high protection that commenced with the war is a question that economists will probably never settle.

The building of a subsidized transcontinental railroad, held back by sectional controversies in the 1850's, was authorized along a northern route with the help of federal loans and land grants when the southerners excluded themselves from Congress. Putting more than a hundred million dollars into this project in the latter half of the 1860's, however, may have had an adverse effect on industrial growth. In general, the far western roads were built for speculative and strategic purposes uneconomically ahead of demand. They may for a decade, or even two, have consumed more capital than their transportation services were then worth to the economy.

To sum up this part of the obiter dictum, those who write of the war creating a national market tied together by railroads underestimate both the achievements of the two decades before the war and the ongoing trends of the economy. The nation's business in 1855 was nearly as intersectional as in 1870. Regional animosities did not interfere with trade, nor did these feelings diminish after the war. By the late 1850's the United States was a rapidly maturing industrial state with its major cities connected by rail, its major industries selling in a national market, and blessed or cursed with financiers, security flotations, stock markets, and all the other appurtenances of industrial capitalism.

But when all specific factors of change attributable to the war have been deflated, there is still the possibility that northern victory had enhanced the capitalist spirit, that as a consequence the atmosphere of government in Washington among members of both parties was more friendly to industrial enterprise and to northern-based national business operations than had formerly been the rule. It can be argued that in spite of Greenbackers and discontented farmers legislation presumably favorable to industry could be more readily enacted. The Fourteenth Amendment, for example, had as a by-product greater security for interstate business against state regulation, although it was to be almost two decades before the Supreme Court would give force to this protection. By 1876, a year of deep depression, the two major parties were trying to outdo each other in promises of stimulating economic growth. This highly generalized type of argument is difficult to evaluate, but in qualification of any theory of a sharp change in attitude we should remember that industrialism was growing rapidly from general causes and that by the 1870's it was to be expected that major-party politics would be conforming to this change in American life.

Massive changes in physical environment such as those accompanying the rise of trade at the close of the Middle Ages or the gradual growth of industrialism from the seventeenth century on do not lend themselves readily to exact or brief periodization. If factory industry and mechanized transportation be taken as the chief indexes of early industrialism, its spread in the United States was continuous and rapid during the entire nineteenth century, but in general, advance was greater during periods of prosperity than in depressions. The first long period without a major depression, after railroads, canals, and steamboats had opened a national market, was from 1843 to 1857. Many economic historians interested in quantitative calculations would regard these years as marking the appearance of an integrated industrial society. Walter W. Rostow, incidentally, starts his "take-off" period in the 1840's and calls it completed by 1860. Others might prefer to avoid any narrow span of years. Few, however, would see a major stimulation to economic growth in the events of the Civil War.

Finally, one may speculate as to why this exaggerated conception of the role of the Civil War in industrialization gained so firm a place in American historiography. The idea fits, of course, into the Marxian frame of revolutionary changes, but it seems initially to have gained acceptance quite independently of Marxian influences. More concentrated study of the war years than of any other four-year span in the nineteenth century called attention to technological and business events usually overlooked. Isolated facts were seized upon without comparing them with similar data for other decades. The desire of teachers for neat periodization was probably a strong factor in quickly placing the interpretation in textbooks; thus, up to 1860 the nation was agricultural, after 1865 it was industrial. Recent study of American cultural themes suggests still another reason. From most standpoints the Civil War was a national disaster, but Americans like to see their history in terms of optimism and progress. Perhaps the war was put in a perspective suited to the culture by seeing it as good because in addition to achieving freedom for the Negro it brought about industrial progress.

Union Leadership and Discipline in the Civil War

BRUCE CATTON

If the prelude to the Civil War poses many problems for the historian, so too does the drama of the war itself. There are important questions to be asked about the resources of the combatants, their external relations, their internal policies, the lives they led behind the front, their economies, and their politics. Perhaps the most salient question is about the two great armies which grappled with each other for four long years. Who were these men? What did they think they were fighting for? How were they organized, trained, equipped? Who were their leaders? What were the larger campaign tactics of the war and how were they pursued?

Bruce Catton, centering his attention on the leadership and discipline of the Union army, offers some interesting clues to the answers insofar as the Northern armies were concerned. There is no one better qualified than Mr. Catton to do so. He established his position as our foremost writer of Civil War military history through a series of significant volumes, including the trilogy on the Army of the Potomac: Mr. Lincoln's Army *(1951),* Glory Road *(1952), and* A Stillness at Appomattox *(1953). More recently he has written the widely acclaimed three-volume* Centennial History of the Civil War: The Coming Fury *(1961),* Terrible Swift Sword *(1963), and* Never Call Retreat *(1965). He won the Pulitzer Prize in History in 1954 and is the editor of* American Heritage. *The essay which follows was delivered as a lecture before the Marine Corps Association at Quantico, Virginia.*

What Mr. Catton says is revealing and thought-provoking. One need not necessarily agree with him, however, that an army of volunteers has perforce virtues that are lacking in an army of conscripts. Does it not depend on the cause for which the army is fighting? The Union soldier,

SOURCE: *Marine Corps Gazette,* XL (January, 1956), 18–25. Reprinted by permission of the copyright holder, the Marine Corps Association, publishers of the *Marine Corps Gazette,* professional journal for Marine Officers. Copyright © 1956 by the Marine Corps Association.

*as Mr. Catton himself indicates, volunteered for reasons which by themselves hardly could have insured his victory. But the Confederate soldier, as Professor David Donald of Princeton University suggests in an interesting essay (*Journal of Southern History, *May, 1959), was himself trammeled in a cause which preached democracy but practiced aristocracy. Thus, to the degree that the outcome of the war depended on a sense of cause and the discipline it would command, it may be suggested that the North won because Johnny Reb had less of that sense and of that discipline than Billy Yank.*

What is the relevance of Mr. Catton's analysis of men at war to our own military ways and values? What is the nature of an institution that is relatively new in American history—peacetime conscription? Is our army any different for having been organized during a time of peace and for having been conscripted? How do leadership and discipline differ today from the time of the Civil War? What has been the impact on the morale of our men in Vietnam of having to fight a distant war for the nation, while the people at home were free to exploit the possibilities of peace and prosperity for themselves? The basic question, one suspects, concerns the cause for which armies are summoned and for which they would pay with their lives. Here is what needs examination when one compares the American soldier in the Armageddon of the 1860's with his counterpart in the cold and hot wars of today.

The American soldier has been much the same, probably, from the Revolutionary War down to the present day. He reflects the national character, and the national character has not changed a great deal. Weapons, tactics, strategic concepts, equipment—all of these may have changed enormously; yet the human material of which American armies are made is today very much like it was generations ago. As the battle record of many wars attests, this material has uniformly been pretty good.

Yet the ways in which this material has been used have undergone many changes. It may be instructive to note some of these changes, to see what happened in an earlier, more informal period, and to reflect on some of the lessons which can be deduced.

The Civil War was fought a century ago. At this distance it is apt to look like a romantic museum piece. It was fought by men who went into battle in close formation, with waving flags and beating drums. Generals went about on horseback in those days, they frequently rode into the middle of the fighting line, and their contacts with private soldiers tended to be direct and intimate. It is easy to think of the Civil War as a story-book affair which was not really very much like modern warfare, and in which officer and enlisted man alike somehow operated under much less pressure than is the case today.

Yet the fact remains that when the total number of casualties caused by that war are matched against the country's total population, the Civil War emerges as the costliest, deadliest war America ever fought. Five hundred thousand soldiers lost their lives, in a country whose entire population, north and south together, numbered less than 30 millions. If battle losses in the Second World War had been in proportion, we would have 2,500,000 men killed—exclusive of those wounded and missing. Some of the individual battles of the Civil War cost each army engaged more than 25 per cent of its total numbers, including the men in non-combat details. Individual tactical units met even more appalling losses. In a surprising number of cases, a regiment might lose as many as 75 or 80 per cent of the men engaged; and the fight in which such losses were incurred might last no longer than an hour or so.

All of this took place, furthermore, in the era of muzzle loaders. With rare exceptions, infantrymen used muzzle-loading muskets— usually rifled, but by no means invariably so—with which the best man could hardly get off more than 2 shots a minute. Artillery was equally primitive. Indirect fire was unheard of; the gunner had to see his target with his own eyes in order to fire at it, and shell fuses were so unreliable that it was often an even chance whether the shell he fired would burst over the enemy or over his own infantry. To all intents and purposes there were no rapid fire guns. Land mines, known then as torpedoes, were used only in a very few cases and were no more than minor nuisances.

The contrast between the primitive nature of the weapons and the deadly character of the fighting is striking. It is worth emphasizing because it proves that that far-off war was as deadly and as frightening, for the man engaged in it, as any war ever fought. And what makes the case even more astounding is the fact that the system of drill and discipline which took Civil War soldiers into action had nothing like the hard, impersonal tautness with which we are familiar today. The Civil War army tended to be loose-jointed, informal, almost slap-dash. Yet somehow it got results. Any system of discipline which would hold men together through the impact of a battle like Gettysburg or Chickamauga must have had its virtues.

So it may pay us to have a close look at the way in which the basic tactical unit of the Civil War armies, the regiment, was brought together and led.

The very way in which the ordinary Civil War regiment was organized was an obstacle to strict military discipline. While the Federal government, of course, controlled the raising of troops, and had complete supervision over them once they were mustered-in, the matter of raising and organizing the regiments was up to the state authorities.

Most regiments were recruited locally. In the ordinary course, some citizen would be commissioned by the governor to raise a regiment. He would open recruiting offices, deputize a number of men to help him, and go about looking for volunteers. If one of his helpers brought in a substantial number, that man would possibly be rewarded with a commission as lieutenant or captain; and the man in charge of the whole effort would, of course, become the colonel. In a great many cases, the individual companies would elect their own officers; very often, the colonel himself was elected by the men.

What all of this meant was that in the average regiment the officers were people whom the enlisted men had known all of their lives. The colonel or the major might, indeed, be a "leading citizen" of such stature that few of the recruits had ever been intimate with him, but the company officers had usually been on a first-name basis with their men for years. The same, of course, was true of the NCOs.

It goes without saying thus, that the private soldier was not likely to treat his officers with any undue amount of military formality. Perfectly typical is the account of a New York regiment toiling at infantry drill on a dusty field on a hot summer day. Presently one of the soldiers turned to his captain and said: "Say, Tom, let's quit this dern foolin' around and go over to the sutler's." An Illinois veteran wrote after the war: "While all of the men who enlisted pledged themselves to obey all the commands of their superior officers, and ought to have kept their word, yet it was hardly wise on the part of volunteer officers to absolutely demand attendance on such service, and later on it was abandoned." An Indiana soldier was even more explicit about it, declaring: "We had enlisted to put down the rebellion and had no patience with the red-tape tomfoolery of the regular service. Furthermore, the boys recognized no superiors, except in the line of legitimate duty. Shoulder straps waived, a private was ready at the drop of a hat to thrash his commander—a thing that occurred more than once."

It is perfectly obvious that an army organized in this way required rather special qualities of leadership from its officers. In general terms, the Civil War officer led his men, not because he wore shoulder straps, but because the men came to recognize and accept him as a qualified leader. This meant, above everything else, that in battle the officer had to be absolutely fearless. Even a major general would immediately lose control over his men if they found reason to suspect his courage. From army commander on down, he had to show physical courage rather ostentatiously. If he could not do this he could not do anything.

The officer also had to realize that he was dealing with citizen soldiers who, even after 2 years of war, would insist on remaining more citizen than soldier. They could be led anywhere, but they could hardly be driven at all. West Point training seemed to work 2 ways, in this connection. At its best, it turned out officers who knew instinctively how to induce obedience; at its worst, it produced officers who simply could not command volunteers at all.

It is interesting to look at U. S. Grant himself, when in the early summer of 1861 he became colonel of a rowdy Illinois regiment which had just run one colonel out of camp and which was doing so much drinking, fighting and chicken-stealing that it was known all around its training camp as "Governor Yates' Hellions." One of Grant's first jobs was to get his regiment over from Springfield to a point on the Mississippi River. Trains were available, but there was plenty of time and Grant decided to take his men over on foot. The march would take 4 or 5 days.

The first day's march was a shambles, with no more than half a dozen miles accomplished. That evening, Grant announced that the regiment would resume the march at 6 the next morning. Morning came, reveille was sounded—and at 6 o'clock most of the men were just starting to cook breakfast, no tents had been struck and no wagons had been loaded, and all in all it was an hour and a half longer before the march could begin.

That evening, again, Grant announced that they would march at 6 in the morning. Again, when 6 o'clock came two-thirds of the regiment was still frying bacon, tying its shoes or otherwise engaged. No matter: Grant ordered the regiment paraded and got the march started, leaving most of the men behind, frantically trying to get organized. After marching a few miles he had the men who were on the road fall out for a breather, and he extended this breather until the rest of the regiment could catch up. That evening, as before, he announced that the march would begin at 6 the next morning.

And on this morning, when 6 o'clock came, the regiment was pretty largely ready to go. It got on the road at the proper time, with only a few stragglers and the rest of the way to the Mississippi it moved on schedule. After that Grant had no trouble with it.

Now the common sense quality that enabled Grant to get this regiment in hand may seem too obvious to be worth mentioning; but not all professional soldiers had it, and those who did not failed miserably. There is something instructive about the case of Major General C. C. Gilbert, a soldier in one of the western armies who in the fall of 1862 was jumped from captain of regulars to corps commander of volunteers, and who lasted in that high position only for a few weeks.

Gilbert was one of those starchy, take-his-name-sergeant old regulars who never understood the volunteer soldier. While Buell's army was pursuing Bragg's in Kentucky, that fall, making long forced marches day after day and driving on at a man-killing pace, an Indiana regiment late one evening fell out by a dark roadside for a 5-minute rest. The men dropped in their tracks, naturally, and went sound asleep. Past this sleeping regiment, presently, came General Gilbert and his staff, clanking along on horseback; and Gilbert was incensed by the regiment's failure to stand up and salute. He grabbed the first officer he could find awake—a company commander—and demanded:

"What regiment is this?"

"12th Indiana."

"Humph. Damn pretty regiment. Why in hell don't you have your men line the road and salute when I pass by?"

"Who in hell are you?"

"Major General Gilbert, by God, sir. Give me your sword—you are under arrest."

At this point the regiment's colonel woke up and came over to take a hand in the game. Gilbert repeated his demand, and the colonel announced that his men had marched 15 hours that day and he "wasn't going to hold a dress parade at midnight for any damn fool living." Most of the regiment was awake and listening by now, and Gilbert spotted the color bearer. He reached for the flag, announcing that he was going to seize it and disgrace the regiment.

Now the color bearer told him to keep his hands off the flag or he would be killed. Someone fired a musket in the air; someone else called out "Shoot the SOB!" and a third party jabbed a bayonet into the haunch of General Gilbert's horse, which caused the beast to take off down the road at a gallop, bearing a fuming general, his staff trailing out behind him. He never did get the salute, and he lasted as a general only a few weeks after that.

It is simple enough to remark that Grant was an officer with common sense and that Gilbert was not, but the two anecdotes do tell something about the state of discipline in Civil War armies. It was a discipline which rested largely on the officer himself. It was not something he could very easily enforce; it had to come out of his own qualities of leadership. If he lacked those qualities, he had no discipline.

There were points on which the Civil War soldier simply refused to submit to restraint no matter what the source. This was especially true in respect to the matter of foraging and looting civilian property in occupied territory.

The northern soldier was pretty much unindoctrinated, when he enlisted. He usually joined up because it seemed like an adventurous, romantic thing to do, or because everybody else was doing it—or, in a great many cases, simply for fun. Mostly he liked camp life, once he got into it. A Massachusetts soldier recalling his career early in the war wrote that "Our drill consisted largely of running around the Old

Westbury town hall, yelling like devils and firing at an imaginary foe."
A Chicago boy wrote home from training camp: "It is fun to lie around,
face unwashed, hair uncombed, shirt unbuttoned and everything un-
everything-ed. It sure beats clerking." Another Illinois boy wrote
to his parents: "I don't see why people will stay at home when they can
get to soldiering. A year of it is worth getting shot for to any man."

Yet if he tended to enjoy camp life—right at first, anyway—the
northern soldier usually had no very clear notion of what he was
fighting for, except that he believed he was fighting to save the Union.
As he figured it, that meant that all southerners were trying to destroy
the Union; were, in other words, traitors, to whom the worst that could
happen was far too good. Figuring that way, he resolutely refused to
respect southern farmers' rights to their chickens, hogs, green corn,
fence rails or other property. It is interesting to note that the ravages
northern soldiers inflicted on southern territory came much more from
the impulse of the common soldier than from the orders of men like
Sherman and Sheridan.

Indeed, Sherman himself, during the first 2 years of the war, worked
himself almost to a frazzle trying to keep his men from stealing Confederate hams and burning Confederate barns. He tried all sorts of
ferocious disciplinary measures to stop it, including ordering enlisted
men tied up by the thumbs, but without the slightest success. His
men simply did not feel that there was anything wrong with what they
were doing. Furthermore, the regimental officers, as a rule, felt the
same way the enlisted men did, and flatly refused to enforce orders
against looting and foraging. It was common for a colonel, as a regiment
made camp, to address his men, pointing to some nearby farm, and
say: "Now boys, that barn is full of pigs and chickens. I don't want to
see a one of you take any of them"—upon which he would fold his
arms and resolutely look in the opposite direction. It is equally common
to read of a colonel, imposing punishment on men who had been
caught looting, saying sternly: "Boys, I want you to understand that I
am not punishing you for stealing but for getting caught at it, by God!"

The point of course is that Civil War discipline was never tight
enough to keep the men from doing something which the men themselves believed to be justified. Sherman's orders could not be enforced,
partly because the men were not disposed to obey them, and partly because the regimental officers who were primarily responsible did not try
to enforce them. In broad areas of conduct the Civil War soldier tended
to go his own way regardless of what the man at the top had to say.

As a matter of fact, it was this rowdy approach to southern property
which, as much as any other single thing, killed slavery.

The average northern soldier was not fighting to free the slaves.
He did not care about slavery one way or the other, and he had very
little fondness for the colored man as such. But he did have the feeling

that when he got down south it was up to him to put a heavy hand on the men who had rebelled against his government. He would destroy the property of such men whenever he got a chance—and the most obvious, visible, easily-removed piece of property of all was the slave. He might have very little sympathy with the Emancipation Proclamation—some of the western regiments, as a matter of fact, came very close to mutiny when the thing was read to them—but he did understand that the institution of slavery supported the Confederacy, and so he went to work to dismantle it, chattel by chattel, in precisely the same spirit that he killed pigs and burned corn-cribs. It is hardly an over-statement to suggest that if all northern armies had operated under strict discipline, so that orders against interfering with southern property had been rigidly obeyed, the institution of slavery would have had a much better chance to survive the war.

Perhaps the most surprising part about the defective discipline of the Civil War regiment is that it nevertheless sent to the front a great many fighting regiments of amazing effectiveness.

Partly this was because the men did, after all, know each other well. They had a solid feeling that they could count on one another—and, no doubt, a reluctance to show fear or hesitancy before men they had known all their lives. If a man was wounded, he knew perfectly well that even if the stretcher parties missed him some of his pals would hunt him up, if they possibly could. There was a powerful feeling of comradeship in most of these regiments, and it was a prodigious factor in battle.

In addition, many of those Civil War units built up a very high esprit de corps. The soldier identified himself first of all with his regiment, and he tended to be very proud of it. If his brigade or division had made a good name in some battle, he was equally proud of that. General Phil Kearny, the one-armed soldier who was killed in the summer of 1862, started something when he made all the men in his division wear a diamond-shaped patch of scarlet flannel on their caps. He did this simply in order that when he saw stragglers in the rear areas he could tell at once whether the men belonged to his outfit; but in no time at all the red patch became a badge of honor, Kearny's men felt they were something special because they wore it, and when a new regiment was assigned to the division the men in the other regiments refused to warm up to it until they had a chance to see it in battle—and, as one veteran put it, see "whether the regiment was worthy of belonging to the red diamond division." Six months later, Joe Hooker had similar patches made for each army corps in the Army of the Potomac, and before long the idea had spread to the western armies. Today's shoulder patches are direct descendants of those devices.

The eastern armies adopted the corps badge ahead of the westerners. In 1863, when eastern troops were sent west to bolster Grant's army in front of Chattanooga, some of the westerners in the XV Corps looked in wonder at General Slocum's XII Corp boys, whose badge was a red star. A XV Corps Irishman finally accosted one of the easterners:

"Are you all brigadier generals, with them stars?" he asked.

"That's our corps badge," explained the easterner loftily. "What's yours?"

"Badge, is it?" snorted the Irishman. He slapped his cartridge box. "Here it is, be Jazus—40 rounds!"

His corps commander heard the story and promptly adopted the device; and for the rest of the war, the XV Corps wore for its badge a replica of a cartridge box with the words "40 rounds" printed under it.

Soldiers would quickly take their tone from a commanding officer, if the officer had enough force and leadership. There was an old Regular Army man, General Charles F. Smith—tall, slim, straight as a ramrod; with long flowing white mustachios—who knew instinctively how to lead men in action. He showed up at Fort Donelson with a division of green troops who had never before been under fire, and he had to lead them up a hill, through tangled woods and underbrush, in a charge on a Confederate line of trenches. He stuck his cap on the point of his sword, got out in front of his frightened greenhorns and started off. Confederate bullets began to come through pretty thickly and Smith's men wavered. He turned about in his saddle and called out:

"Damn you, gentlemen, I see skulkers. I'll have none here. Come on, you volunteers, come on. This is your chance. You volunteered to be killed for love of your country and now you can be. You damned volunteers—I'm only a soldier and I don't want to be killed, but you came to be killed and now you can be!"

The line went on up the hill and captured its objective. One soldier wrote: "I was pretty near scared to death, but I saw the Old Man's mustache over his right shoulder and I kept on going."

Discipline or no discipline, enough men would respond to that sort of leadership to put up an excellent fight.

Old Man Smith, incidentally, was an interesting soldier. He had been Commandant of Cadets when both Grant and Sherman were in West Point, and although both of them later out-ranked him—he was a division commander under Grant at Fort Donelson—both confessed that they always felt like school boys in his presence. He seems to have led his volunteers by storming at them, so that they were scared to death of him, and by going in ahead of them when there was danger.

One very junior officer in his division told how, in that spring of 1862, his regiment was camped on a farm where a lot of mint was growing. He and another officer plucked a lot of it, got some commissary whiskey, obtained ice from the farmer's ice house, and made some excellent mint juleps. Then it occurred to them that "Old Smith" would like one, so they took one and went to his tent. The tent flaps were closed, but there was a light inside; Old Smith was propped up in his cot, reading.

One of the officers rapped on the tent pole. Out came Smith's rasping voice: Who was it, and what did he want?

These officers were so much in awe of the old soldier that they did not dare announce themselves. But the one who carried the julep finally worked up his nerve and without saying a word thrust his arm through the tent flaps, the julep glass in his fist.

Inside there was a dead silence. Then the beautiful truth dawned on the old general, and they heard him rumble: "Well, by God, this is kind!" He took the glass, they could hear him sniffing and tasting, and his voice repeated: "Kind, indeed!" Then he drained the glass at a gulp, put the empty glass in the officer's still-extended hand and relaxed. The two officers went away without having said a word, and to the end of his days Old Smith never knew where he got that drink.

From whatever source he got his battle morale, the Civil War soldier somehow learned how to handle himself under fire. Sometimes he had to learn the hard way, for he was often thrown into action almost totally untrained. Perhaps the best illustration of this comes in the terrible battle of Shiloh, where 2 completely green armies ran into each other head-on and fought for 2 days.

It is almost impossible nowadays to understand how pathetically unready for battle were the men who were pushed into the great fight at Shiloh. A Confederate brigadier general confessed afterward that until the moment the fight began he had never heard a gun fired, nor had he ever read a book or heard a lecture on tactics. There were Confederate batteries in that battle which had never fired their guns before; ammunition had been too short to allow practice firing. Many Union infantry regiments received their muskets on the way to the field, and loaded and fired them for the first time in action.

There is one revealing picture of a pea-green Ohio regiment which was in that fix, drawn up in line of battle under a heavy fire. The colonel had run for the rear at the first shock; the men were leaderless, not knowing what they were supposed to do or how they were supposed to do it, but game enough to want to stick around and find out. From somewhere there came a private soldier from another regiment. He had fought at Fort Donelson, and compared with these recruits he was a veteran. He carefully went along the firing line, showing the boys how to load these muskets and how to use them; and as he went, he kept explaining: "It's just like shooting squirrels, only these squirrels have guns—that's all."

And the regiment stayed there, unled, and fought all day long.
Civil War officers quickly learned one thing about green troops
which were shoved into battle that way. They would either run away
quickly, after the first volley — or they would not run away at all.

At Shiloh, a great many did run; after the battle was a couple of hours
old, probably a fourth of Grant's army was huddled under the shelter
of the river bank in the rear, completely leaderless and useless. But
the rest stayed and fought, and few soldiers have ever fought in a more
vicious battle. All military order and tactical formation was quickly
lost. A battle line might contain elements from half a dozen different
regiments, huddled together, somehow drawing from one another's
presence the courage to stay and fight. An advance would be a rush
forward by a mob; a retreat would be the same, with the men sticking
close to whoever seemed to show the qualities of leadership. We read
of one Indiana lad who got a flesh wound in his arm, showed it to his
colonel, and was told to drop his rifle and go to the rear. He started
off, found Rebel troops in the rear, and presently came back to his
colonel.

"Gimme another gun, Cap," he said. "This blame fight ain't got any
rear."

Some of these undisciplined private soldiers developed strong
qualities, as the war wore along. In the battle of Champion's Hill,
during the Vicksburg campaign, General John A. Logan, commanding
a Federal division, was sitting on his horse on a hill-top, watching the
fight, when a lanky enlisted man—who seems to have been prowling
around more or less on his own hook—sauntered up to him and said:

"General, I've been over on the rise yonder, and it's my idea that
if you'll put a regiment or 2 over thar, you'll get on their flank and lick
'em easy."

Logan looked where the man pointed, decided that the advice was
good, sent a couple of regiments over—and, as the man had predicted,
won his fight.

One of the most striking things about the average Civil War regiment
was the high degree of manpower wastage that afflicted it. Every
regiment contained a certain number of men who would fade back to
the rear when the fighting began. No colonel could count on all of his
men; there was a steady leakage back from the firing line, even in the
veteran regiments, from the beginning of the war to the end.

Worse yet was the toll taken by disease. Medical examinations for
recruits were very sketchy. Some regiments got in without any medical
examinations at all; and in any case, medical care was so imperfect
that there was a steady, remorseless drain on combat strength, month
after month. The Civil War regiment had a paper strength of 1,000
men; the regiment that could bring as many as 500 to the field, after 6
months in camp, was very lucky, and the average strength of a veteran

regiment would usually be between 200-300.   One veteran remarked that a third of a regiment's strength would usually be lost by desertion or straggling, and another third by sickness.   The remaining third—the men too stout to run away and too tough to get sick—had to do the fighting.   It was right there, probably, that the loose discipline and informal organization of the volunteer army proved most costly.

Yet in the long run these odd combat organizations did what they were supposed to do.   If it is possible to dredge up any number of stories revealing slipshod organization and peculiar military habits, it is also possible to show fantastic instances of solid bravery and endurance which no professional soldiers could have improved upon.

On the second day of the battle of Gettysburg, for instance, when the left end of the Union line on Cemetery Ridge had more or less dissolved, and Confederate troops were swarming up the slopes with nothing much to stop them, the 1st Minnesota came marching up from the rear to get into the fight.   General Winfield Scott Hancock, corps commander in charge of that part of the line, saw a Confederate assault wave coming, and galloped over to the Minnesota's colonel.   This colonel had been under arrest for several days; on a forced march to Gettysburg he had halted his troops, against Hancock's orders, so that they could take off their shoes and socks before fording a little stream, and Hancock had punished him for it.   The colonel was feeling rather bitter about it.

Hancock pointed toward the oncoming Confederates, whose battle flag was visible.

"Do you see those colors?" he demanded.   The colonel nodded. "Well, take them!" demanded Hancock belligerently.

The 1st Minnesota went in, head on.   It numbered only 262 men, but it swung into line and made its fight.   It stopped the Confederate charge, captured the battle flag, and an hour later it had just 47 men left—for a loss of 82 per cent, which seems to have been a record for the Union army for the entire war.   Next day, incidentally, those 47 who remained stayed in line and helped repel Pickett's charge.

Any military system which can produce combat units that will stay and fight after a loss of 82 per cent seems to me to be a pretty good system, no matter how many surface defects it may have.

And the military system that prevailed in the Civil War was, with all of its defects, a pretty good system.   The worst thing about it, probably, was that it gave the willing horse all of the load.   It never controlled the stragglers and the faint-hearts.   The good men got all the worst of it, and the gold-bricks mostly got off easy.   But a tremendous job of fighting did get done.

At the bottom, the system drew its strength from several things.

The comradeship that prevailed in the ranks was a prime element.

The men knew each other; regiments were pretty largely homogeneous; out of this they built a very high morale. Pride in the regiment, and sometimes in the brigade, division or army corps grew up naturally and became an immense stimulus to good performance. And the very looseness of army organization seems to have brought forward uncommon qualities of leadership in the officer corps. There was an enormous amount of wastage, to be sure, as the test of battle weeded out the unfit, but in the end those regiments were extremely well led.

Last of all, the human material was very, very good. By and large, I think, it was the same sort of material we have nowadays; I don't think the American people have changed a great deal. And the great lesson of the Civil War, to me, is simply this: that with volunteer American soldiers, the right leadership can do anything.

37

The Dark and Bloody Ground of Reconstruction Historiography
BERNARD A. WEISBERGER

38

The South's New Leaders
JOHN HOPE FRANKLIN

The years which followed Appomattox were no less dramatic or important than those which had preceded it. Appomattox meant an end of the trials of war and a beginning of the problems of peace. How would the victory of the North be translated into deeper economic and social terms? Would the

SOURCE: *The Journal of Southern History*, XXV (November, 1959), 427-447. Copyright © 1959 by the Southern Historical Association. Reprinted by permission of the Managing Editor.

triumph of arms also be a triumph in peace? Would the South lose the war but win the peace? What commercial and industrial policies would the new nation pursue? What would be the status of the freedman? What would the defeat of the Southern aristocracy mean for the social structure of the new America? How much had the compound of American society been altered by the chemism of war? Whatever the deeper problems resulting from the war, the most immediate one was that of Reconstruction. How were the defeated states to be governed? On what terms were they to be brought back into the Union?

Because Reconstruction dealt with problems that had been central to the war, its history has been as much a matter of controversy as the war itself. For many decades, historians tended to view Reconstruction as an age of political failure, a regrettable period in our history, in which the North inflicted a humiliating, almost barbarous rule upon the South. Seen in a bleak retrospect, the "reprehensible" deeds of the Radical Republicans in Congress and of "carpetbaggers," "scalawags," and Negroes in the Southern states appeared to be the outward and visible signs of the grace-lessness of a generation. It is true enough that this unfavorable view has, in certain respects, been increasingly modified during the past decade, but until very recently historians have resisted a comprehensive reappraisal of the age. The reason is suggested by Professor Bernard A. Weisberger, of the University of Rochester, in the first of the following essays. An excellent writer on the history of American journalism, Professor Weisberger is also a specialist in the Civil War and Reconstruction era. With regards to what he calls "the dark and bloody ground of Reconstruction historiography," he pleads for historians to come to terms with some basic problems in the American past.

To understand the age of Reconstruction, submits Professor Weisberger, we must answer questions which go to the root of all American history. What, to begin with, is our view of the Negro, his nature, his potentialities, his personality? How far, moreover, does the corruption that seems to have been so widespread during Reconstruction tend to be part of the American democratic process? In what way were post-war relations between the federal government and the states merely a step along the road of a long-term evolution? To what extent are we still interpreting Reconstruction in the light of economic and social concepts whose validity is questionable and which we no longer apply to other areas of American history? What, in general, are the deeper personal values by which we construe the American past and what, in particular, are the values of those whose interpretations have dominated Reconstruction historiography? It is the sum of Professor Weisberger's suggestion that our views on one part of American history ought to be consistent with our views on the rest of it.

The answers to Professor Weisberger's questions rest, in the main, on what historians think about such fundamental issues as the nature of the

Civil War, the justifiability of the Southern cause, and the whole issue of race relations. The new orientation that has been emerging in recent years is more positive in its assessment of the Radical Republican program and policies, and of the achievements of Reconstruction. The first major book to offer a comprehensive statement of this orientation was John Hope Frank-lin's Reconstruction: After the Civil War *(1961). Professor Franklin is one of our most distinguished scholars in the field of Southern and Negro history, and the author of several notable volumes, including* From Slavery to Freedom *(third edition, 1967),* The Militant South *(1956), and* The Emancipation Proclamation *(1963). His* Reconstruction, *as Daniel J. Boorstin has noted, sees the era in broad perspective, as a phase in national development, rather than "as a chapter in regional history—or, we might even say, in regional punishment or crucifixion. . . ."; it gives an account in refreshing detail of the forward steps taken, in the South, in important areas of social and economic life during the late 1860's and early 1870's. In the chapter reprinted below, Professor Franklin undertakes to correct the errors of fact and understanding that have for a long time affected our view of the South's new leaders after the Civil War: the Negroes, the "carpetbaggers," and the "scalawags."*

The South has been in a state of radical transition in recent years; it is being made over by powerful internal forces and by the impact on American policy of the opinion of a largely non-white world. Industrialization and desegregation are two significant aspects of the restyling of Southern life. In this sense we are witnessing a second and more profound Reconstruction. It is imperative for an honest consideration of what is occurring today that we review the first Reconstruction and that we understand what its men, its problems, and its achievements really were.

BERNARD A. WEISBERGER

Twenty years ago, as the exciting thirties drew to a close, the dry bones began to stir in that notable valley of historical skeletons, the Reconstruction period. In February 1939, the *Journal of Southern History* carried an article by Francis B. Simkins describing a number of "New Viewpoints of Southern Reconstruction."[1] Frankly facing the fact that "the main issue of the Reconstruction period, the great American race question," like Banquo's ghost, would not down, Simkins asked for a fairer analysis of Reconstruction's achievements and failures and an end to the notion that encouraging the Negro in voting and officehold-ing was somehow a crime of crimes. By adopting a more "critical, creative and tolerant attitude," he said, historians of the South could better discharge their "great civic obligation."

---

[1] *Journal of Southern History*, V (February 1939), 49–61.

In the following year, Howard K. Beale took up this theme with a brisk, provocative essay, "On Rewriting Reconstruction History," in the *American Historical Review*.[2] Forthrightly, Beale asked if it were "not time that we studied the history of Reconstruction without first assuming, at least subconsciously, that carpetbaggers and Southern white Republicans were wicked, that Negroes were illiterate incompetents, and that the whole white South owes a debt of gratitude to the restorers of 'white supremacy'?" He then posted a list of questions previously ignored except in scattered numbers of the *Journal of Negro History* and in W. E. B. Du Bois' 1935 volume, *Black Reconstruction*. What was the *whole* story of popular government in the South from 1865 to 1900? What were the economic connections of the so-called Redeemers? How much of the famed Reconstruction debt went for gilt spittoons and legislative boodle, and how much for social, educational, and industrial rebuilding? Where did the poor white fit into the picture? What lessons could be learned by considering Reconstruction anew, this time as a short-lived revolution which placed power in inexperienced hands.

These questions struck to the heart of the prejudiced version of Reconstruction laid down around the turn of the century by Rhodes, Burgess, and Dunning, developed by Fleming and some of the individual state historians of the period, and widely popularized, in 1929, by Claude Bowers' zestful work of imagination, *The Tragic Era*.[3] That story is familiar. It told of how "Vindictives" and "Radicals" in Congress shouldered aside Johnson and the Supreme Court and imposed "Carpetbag" and "Scalawag" and "Negro" governments on the South by the bayonet. These new governments debauched and plundered a proud but helpless people until finally, desperately harried whites responded with their own campaigns of violence and persuasion. These respectable folk at last took advantage of mounting Northern disgust with "carpetbag crimes" to restore "home rule" unopposed.

The Beale and Simkins articles seemed to indicate that professional historians were ready to overhaul this operatic version of events—perhaps to use the perspective gained at the end of one decade of swift

---

[2] *American Historical Review*, XLV (July 1940), 807-27.

[3] Claude G. Bowers, *The Tragic Era; the Revolution after Lincoln* (Boston, 1929). To particularize individual monographs on Southern Reconstruction here would involve the compilation of a virtually complete critical bibliography of works on the subject up to 1939, whereas this article aims at a detailed examination only of studies appearing since that date. Accordingly, the reader's familiarity with the earlier works is assumed. They are conveniently listed in a number of places, notably in James G. Randall, *The Civil War and Reconstruction* (Boston, 1953), 881-935.

social change in the careful examination of an earlier period of up-heaval. Yet now, twenty years after these premonitory signs, the indicated tide of revision has not fully set in. Certainly the work still needs to be done. The New Deal, the Second World War, and the Cold War have all set in motion what some have called a "New Reconstruction" of the South—with fresh patterns in industry, urban life, population movement, agrarian practice, social and political leadership, and capitalization forming almost faster than the census takers can reveal them. The school desegregation crisis has, since 1954, moved the race question into disturbing but unescapable prominence. It is more important than ever that progress be made towards understanding the issues raised in the "old" Reconstruction of 1865 to 1877. Yet something seems to have blunted the purpose of the historical guild, and the discovery of what this something is deserves professional attention.

Certainly it is no lack of revisionary work on the monographic level. There is plenty of that, some of it brilliant. One is almost tempted to cite the leading journals *passim* for fear of overlooking meritorious pieces, but short of that, one may point to at least half a dozen books and twice that many articles of genuine significance. There are, for one thing, three path-breaking books by C. Vann Woodward dealing with economic leadership, political organization, and racial adjustment in the post-Appomattox South.[4] Among articles on more specialized topics, there is, to begin with, an outstanding survey of the attitudes dominating the historical approach to Reconstruction by T. Harry Williams, fit to stand in the good company of the Beale and Simkins articles.[5] David Donald gave impetus to a study of Southern Republicans, in 1944, with a piece on Mississippi "scalawags," and he has since given fresh scrutiny to the relationships between the Radicals, Lincoln, and Johnson.[6] Thomas B. Alexander surveyed the role of the Whigs in Tennessee Reconstruction and found a more complex story than had hitherto been suggested.[7] The oft-maligned agents of the Freedmen's Bureau have been made the subjects of a judicious plea in defense by

[4] *Reunion and Reaction; the Compromise of 1877 and the End of Reconstruction* (Boston, 1951); *Origins of the New South, 1877–1913* (Baton Rouge, 1951); *The Strange Career of Jim Crow* (New York, 1955).

[5] An Analysis of Some Reconstruction Attitudes," *Journal of Southern History*, XII (November 1946), 469–86.

[6] "The Scalawag in Mississippi Reconstruction," *Journal of Southern History*, X (November 1944), 447–60; "Why They Impeached Andrew Johnson," *American Heritage*, VIII (December 1956), 20–25; "The Radicals and Lincoln" in *Lincoln Reconsidered* (New York, 1956), 103–27.

[7] "Whiggery and Reconstruction in Tennessee," *Journal of Southern History*, XVI (August 1950), 291–305.

John and LaWanda Cox.[8]   Northern philanthropists and educators, alternately hailed as agents of progress and damned as Yankee marplots, have also undergone dispassionate examination by such scholars as Henry L. Swint and Ralph Morrow.[9] Both Swint and Morrow have published full-dress books on the subjects of their articles, and, indeed, monographs continue almost regularly to break up the fallow ground.[10] George R. Bentley has brought up to date Paul Pierce's half-century-old work on the Freedmen's Bureau.[11] Otis Singletary has submitted the fullest report so far on Negro militiamen in the occuped states of the South.[12] Vernon Wharton has, it may be hoped, provided a pilot project for the studies of the Negro as voter and officeholder in his book on Negroes in Mississippi during and after the Radical heyday.[13] Fresh biographies, both of major and minor actors, have also appeared. Robert Durden has revealed the paradox of a Negro-hating Radical in his life of James S. Pike, and Jonathan Daniels has contributed a portrait of a "carpetbagger," Milton S. Littlefield, the delicious wickedness of which should not obscure its real importance.[14] At least two writers

---

[8] "General O. O. Howard and the 'Misrepresented Bureau,'" *ibid.,* XIX (November 1953), 427–56.   The Coxes believe that "even the most friendly studies of the Bureau have exaggerated its weaknesses and minimized its strength." LaWanda Cox has also contributed fresh material on the motivation of postwar reformers in "The Promise of Land for the Freedman," *Mississippi Valley Historical Review,* XLV (December 1958), 413–40.

[9] Henry L. Swint, "Northern Interest in the Shoeless Southerner," *Journal of Southern History,* XVI (November 1950), 457–71; Ralph Morrow, "Northern Methodism in the South during Reconstruction," *Mississippi Valley Historical Review,* XLI (September 1954), 197–218.

[10] Henry L. Swint, *The Northern Teacher in the South, 1862-1870* (Nashville, 1941); Ralph Morrow, *Northern Methodism and Reconstruction* (East Lansing, 1956).   Before leaving the subject of periodical articles, it is well to note that this sampling takes no note of articles in the journals of various state historical societies or of professional associations for the study of economics, sociology, and political science.   Nor is any attempt made here to list new works of which the author is aware on subjects related to Reconstruction indirectly—studies of pardon, amnesty, and loyalty oaths after the war, of railroad financing in the Southern states, or of aspects of the national battles over land, currency, and tariff reforms.   Such a listing would unduly prolong this article, but would also add support to one of its contentions, that abundant material for a fresh synthesis of the period is available.

[11] George R. Bentley, *A History of the Freedmen's Bureau* (Philadelphia, 1955).

[12] *Negro Militia and Reconstruction* (Austin, 1957).

[13] *The Negro in Mississippi, 1865-1890* (Chapel Hill, 1947).

[14] Robert F. Durden, *James Shepherd Pike: Republicanism and the American Negro, 1850-1882* (Durham, 1957), a significant part of which appeared as "The Prostrate State Revisited: James S. Pike and South Carolina Reconstruction," *Journal of Negro History,* XXXIX (April 1954), 87–110; Jonathan Daniels, *Prince of Carpetbaggers* (Philadelphia, 1958).

have grappled, since 1940, with the contradictions of Thaddeus Stevens: Richard Current in a sharply critical book, and Ralph Korngold in a rather saccharine tribute.[15] Two recent biographies of Benjamin F. Butler also bear witness to the dangers of attempting to "typecast" an important Radical.[16] Still more light on Reconstruction may be expected when David Donald's forthcoming life of Sumner appears.

Varied as are all these works in quality, aim, and scope, their total impact clears the air. They show, first of all, that the so-called "scalawags" were not all the ragged underlings of Southern society, but included—at least early in the period—many erstwhile Southern Whigs, high in status and thoroughly baptized in the church of the Lost Cause. The nucleus of a Southern Republican party, they were displaced by extremist pressure from overardent Radicals, both Negro and white, on the one hand, and die-hard "white line" supporters on the other. Often, however, the issues on which they were challenged had as much to do with patronage and with profit as with race.[17] Secondly, the Republican state governments chosen under the operation of the Reconstruction Acts of 1867 were not composed exclusively of corruptionists, white or Negro, and achieved a number of praiseworthy social and educational reforms.[18] Thirdly, such corruption as did

---

[15] Richard N. Current, *Old Thad Stevens; A Story of Ambition* (Madison, 1942); Ralph Korngold, *Thaddeus Stevens; A Being Darkly Wise and Rudely Great* (New York, 1955).

[16] Robert Holzman, *Stormy Ben Butler* (New York, 1954); Hans L. Trefousse, *Ben Butler, the South Called Him Beast!* (New York, 1957).

[17] Evidence for this statement is scattered widely through the works already referred to. Donald, "Scalawag in Mississippi Reconstruction," 60, declares that in that state, "the importance of the former Whigs has generally been neglected." Alexander, in "Whiggery and Reconstruction in Tennessee," 305, suggests "the possible value of reviewing Reconstruction in all southern states to appraise the role of persistent Whiggery." Insofar as the business community of the South was identified with the Whigs, this view finds support in T. Harry Williams' study, "The Louisiana Reunification Movement of 1873," *Journal of Southern History*, XI (August 1945), 349–69, wherein he finds in Reconstruction "still another group whose importance has not been recognized—the business men, not closely affiliated with politics, who saw the strife of parties and races destroying the stability they desired. . . ." (369). Woodward, in *Reunion and Reaction*, significantly entitles one chapter "The Rejuvenation of Whiggery," and begins his *Origins of the New South* with a quotation from a contemporary Southern source concerning a marriage whose "high contracting parties were Whiggism and Democracy," and whose presumable offspring was Conservatism.

[18] This point was so widely conceded as early as 1939 as to require little documentation here. It is cogently stated in Simkins, "New Viewpoints of Southern Reconstruction," Beale, "On Rewriting Reconstruction History," and Williams, "An Analysis of Some Reconstruction Attitudes," already cited. Vernon Wharton, after a close study of one "reconstructed" state, reaches a

exist was shared in by many white and respectable Southerners, later to become "Bourbons," who did not scruple to profit by the lavish gifts of the sinful "carpetbag" governments to Southern development companies. Moreover, when restored to control, these "Conservatives" continued to keep the doors of the state treasuries hospitably open to businessmen who had formerly supported the Radicals.[19] Fourthly, the restored "Conservatives" were willing to live with Negro suffrage, provided they could control its outcome. The "sin" of enfranchising the illiterate freedman was apparently washed whiter than snow, once he switched to the Democratic ticket.[20] Fifthly, life somehow went on under "bayonet rule." Crops, capital, and order *were* restored, after all, and there were cakes and ale as well as heartbreak and ugliness. Violence there was; but the legend of Negro militiamen's "atrocities," perpetuated in Thomas Dixon's *The Klansman,* is as baseless as the implication in Albion Tourgée's *A Fool's Errand* that every square Southern mile contained a secretly buried victim of the Klan.[21] Lastly, neither in Congress nor in the South were the Radicals the purposeful and unified group of conspirators that they have been made out to

---

conclusion probably applicable to most of the former Confederate commonwealths: "Altogether, as governments go, that supplied by the Negro and white Republicans·in Mississippi between 1870 and 1876 was not a bad government." *The Negro in Mississippi,* 179.

[19] This point forms almost the entire thesis of Woodward's *Reunion and Reaction,* and is explored in depth in *Origins of the New South,* 1–74, as well as in the opening chapters of the same author's *Tom Watson, Agrarian Rebel* (New York, 1938). Daniels' *Prince of Carpetbaggers* is an excellent detailed account of the financial relationships between white Democrats and "carpetbaggers" in North Carolina and Florida.

[20] Negroes "continued to vote in large numbers in most parts of the South for more than two decades after Reconstruction." Woodward, *Strange Career of Jim Crow,* 35.

[21] E. Merton Coulter, who most certainly believes Reconstruction to have been a severe time of trial for the South, nevertheless thoroughly documents the return to normal life in *The South during Reconstruction, 1865-1877* (Baton Rouge, 1947). He declares (ix): "There were . . . with all the political and constitutional abnormalities of the times, the ordinary activities of the people, as they sowed and reaped, went to church, visited their neighbors, sang their songs, and sought in a thousand ways to amuse themselves." As for the question of placing the role of the Negro militia in its true proportions, Singletary observes that the Radical governors rarely used the troops available to them under state law, and notes that the real affront, for white Southerners, was the simple presence of Negroes in uniform. "For even had the militia refrained from committing a single act antagonistic to the whites, in all probability they would still have been destroyed." *Negro Militia and Reconstruction,* 152. The use of Federal troops is a matter deserving greater study, and as for riots and incidents not involving the use of uniformed soldiery, the responsibility is not easily pinned on one side or the other.

be by friendly biographers of Andrew Johnson.[22] Johnson himself, pilloried though he was by his enemies, added to his own woes by personal hardheadedness, political stumbling, and a blind belief that the incantation of constitutional formulas could change the brute facts of power distribution.[23]

This is a good record of piecemeal accomplishment. Yet in two significant areas, the professional record remains poor. For one thing, there has been no synthesis of this material in a good general history of Reconstruction. The one full-scale treatment by an academic historian since 1940 is E. Merton Coulter's *The South during Reconstruction, 1865-1877*. Regrettably, Professor Coulter chose to begin with a veteran's indignant rejection of the entire notion of revision. There could be, he said, "no sensible departure from the well-known facts of the Reconstruction program as it was applied to the South. No amount of revision can explain away the grievous mistakes made in this abnormal period of American history."[24] This attitude seems ex-

---

[22] David Donald notes, in *Lincoln Reconsidered*, 103–27, that the concept of the "malevolent Radical" comes in part from the need to find new antagonists, in every generation, for the noble figure of Lincoln in the Lincoln-myth. Certainly close study of the lives of eminent Radicals reveals plenty of dissension among them; as for the Southern Radicals in the statehouses, their factional feuds in every state suggest, in the words of a recent article, "a much more complex social, economic and political evolution than is found in partisan accounts." Jack B. Scroggs, "Southern Reconstruction: A Radical View," *Journal of Southern History*, XXIV (November 1958), 428. Both Williams and Donald warn against facile generalization. "Southerners differed among themselves on the issues of Reconstruction in about the same degree as did groups in the North," says Williams in "An Analysis of Some Reconstruction Attitudes," 486, while Donald reports that the "difficulties of making an adequate study of a Reconstruction election in the South have seldom been realized." "The Scalawag in Mississippi Reconstruction," 458. James M. Dabbs, a temperate Southerner of today, also underscores the complexity of the story in *The Southern Heritage* (New York, 1958), 105.

[23] The most intelligent critical discussion of Johnson to appear recently is David Donald's "Why They Impeached Andrew Johnson," *American Heritage*. A good, new biography of the impeached President is needed. The two most frequently cited nowadays suffer from the vigor of their efforts to defend him unreservedly. They are, George F. Milton, *The Age of Hate; Andrew Johnson and the Radicals* (New York, 1930) and Lloyd P. Stryker, *Andrew Johnson; A Study in Courage* (New York, 1929). An interesting minor revision of the Johnson story has lately been contributed by Ralph J. Roske, "The Seven Martyrs?" *American Historical Review*, LXIV (January 1959), 323–30, who challenges the view that the seven Republicans who voted for his acquittal were "relentlessly persecuted . . . until they were forced altogether from the American political scene" (323). He denies that their later careers were marked by "unrelieved martyrdom."

[24] Coulter, *South during Reconstruction*, xi.

cessively conservative.   If modern historical scholarship teaches anything, it teaches that "well-established" facts are constantly changed
in implication as new facts are unearthed, and that there are several
sensible departures from any set of facts, depending upon whose
definition of "sensible" is employed.[25]   Rich though it may be in
material, *The South during Reconstruction* is no contribution to understanding.   In point of fact it is something of a setback.   Appearing as
it does in the *History of the South* series published by the Louisiana
State University Press—a set of works which must long remain the
standard repository of Southern history—it would have been more
enduring had it maintained a more judicious attitude. Since 1947 the
only other general book on Reconstruction is Hodding Carter's *The
Angry Scar; the Story of Reconstruction*.[26]   Carter, a literate and "moderate" Mississippi editor, provides a book which is a distinct improvement in fairness on the earlier "nonprofessional" study of Bowers.
Yet it is still marked by a defensive spirit, and more to the point,
its incorporation of fresh research is at best uneven.

The other failure of historians to deal adequately with Reconstruction is evident in textbooks, many of which play old tunes on worn
keys. This is especially lamentable since the text is so often the college
graduate's only exposure to the literature of history.   Some volumes
designed for classroom use attempt balanced discussions—notably
(though not exclusively) the works of Freidel, Current, and Williams,
of Hofstadter, Aaron, and Miller, of Billington, Loewenberg, and Brockunier, and of Leland D. Baldwin.[27]   Others lean heavily on stereotyped

---

[25] A searching critique both of Coulter's "facts" and his deductions there-
from is John Hope Franklin's "Whither Reconstruction Historiography,"
Journal of Negro Education, XVII (February 1948), 446–61. For a briefer statement
of Coulter's conventional view of Reconstruction, see A. B. Moore, "One Hundred Years of Reconstruction of the South," *Journal of Southern History,* IX (May
1943), 153–80.

[26] New York, 1959.

[27] Frank Freidel, Richard N. Current, and T. Harry Williams, *A History of the
United States* (2 vols., New York, 1959), II, 23–27; Richard Hofstadter, Daniel
Aaron, and William Miller, *The United States: The History of a Republic* (Engle-
wood Cliffs, N.J., 1957), 404–405; Ray A. Billington, Bert J. Loewenberg, and
Samuel Brockunier, *The United States; American Democracy in World Perspective* (New York, 1947), 261–85; Leland D. Baldwin, *The Stream of American
History* (2 vols., New York, 1953), I, 911–15. The first two of these books stress
economic turmoil as the basis for a good deal of political misbehavior usually
imputed to "carpetbag" villainy or Negro ignorance.   Baldwin declares that
one "can find what he seeks when he examines the role of the Negroes in the
reconstruction period. . . . If it was Negro votes that made some astonishing
steals possible, it should be remembered that it was white men who got the
bulk of the swag." Billington, Loewenberg and Brockunier point out that the
"reconstruction record, written under the tutelage of scholars of Bourbon

reactions. For one thing, the terms "Carpetbagger" and "Scalawag" are sometimes used as if they were genuine proper nouns and not cartoonists' labels. It is true that they are now so familiar as perhaps not to need quotation marks, and yet by the same token we should expect to find Jacobin, Doughface, and Gold Bug in current and unqualified usage to describe certain groups in our history. Negro suffrage is generally deplored and credited only to opportunistic, if not openly base, motives. Thus, John D. Hicks traces "an infinite amount of abuse" to "premature" voting by the freedmen, while Morison and Commager explain that it was instituted by the Radicals "to secure the colored vote at the earliest opportunity," which is partly true but does not explain why the Fourteenth Amendment offered the South the opportunity to reject Negro enfranchisement if Southerners were willing to pay the price of reduced representation in Congress.[28] Riegel and Long deplore the handiwork of the "'ill-trained Negro freedman, intoxicated by his first breaths of liberty," while Carman and Syrett, generally fair, nevertheless ring the changes on the gross extravagance of the "black and tan" legislatures.[29] Thomas A. Bailey's *The American Pageant,* a highly popular one-volume text, belongs to the Burgess era. "The Radicals," it declares, "would 'Republicanize' the South by making the freedman an unwitting tool of their own schemes, and ride into power on his lash-scarred back." The "gun-supported reconstruction of the South, begun so brutally in 1867 . . . under the stern eye of bayonet-bearing Union soldiers," resulted in Southern legislatures which sometimes "resembled the comic opera."[30] No doubt this is as stirring, for students, as a showing of *The Birth of a Nation,* but it is not much more accurate.

In sum, although the foregoing survey does not pretend to cover the textbook situation completely, teachers of American history have not taken into account the newest modifications of the "Carpetbag—bayonet rule—Negro domination" legend either in general works for

---

lineage seeking a gentlemanly road to reunion, has long demanded reappraisal." Another sympathetic and careful presentation of the Reconstruction period is to be found in Carl N. Degler, *Out of Our Past* (New York, 1959).

[28] John D. Hicks, *The American Nation; a History of the United States from 1865 to the Present* (Cambridge, 1955), 30; Samuel E. Morison and Henry S. Commager, *The Growth of the American Republic* (2 vols., New York, 1950), II, 38–43.

[29] Robert E. Riegel and David F. Long, *The American Story: Volume One: Youth* (New York, 1955); Harry J. Carman and Harold Syrett, *A History of the American People* (2 vols., New York, 1952), II, 20–31.

[30] Thomas A. Bailey, *The American Pageant: A History of the Republic* (Boston, 1956), 467–74.

the broad public or in texts designed for college students. The question of "why" is a challenging one. Part of the answer appears to lie in a professional conservatism which we historians of America too often permit to close our minds to new approaches in the entire range of our work. "He that is unjust in the least," Scripture says, "is unjust also in much." If we have been unjust to some actors in the Reconstruction story, it is because we have not come to terms with some larger problems of United States history.

In the first place, white historians have shied away from grasping the nettle of race conflict, mainly because of the difficulty of recognizing their own emotional involvement in the problem. Yet this unwillingness to dwell on the almost universal nineteenth-century conviction of the Negro's innate inferiority often leads to a slipshod evaluation of materials. It is proper to take account of the frankly political motives of many Radical defenders of the Negro voter. It is equally proper to bear in mind the frankly racial motives of some of the Radicals' opponents. A glance at source materials of the sixties, for example, shows that many so-called conservatives opposed the Radical program for the South not because they were devoted to states' rights, or agrarianism, or the Constitution, or the Democratic party alone, but plainly and simply because they thought it was sinful to give so-called Africans the right to share in governments framed by a clearly superior Anglo-Saxon race. In combing the Civil War files of such northern Democratic papers as the New York *World,* Chicago *Times,* and Cincinnati *Enquirer,* one finds diatribes against "niggers" and the "Republican niggerocracy" quite as fulsome as anything ever concocted by today's racists.[31] Instincts of decency as much as anything else prompt the suppression of such material, but silence on the subject covers up some of the ignobler motives of men who are now and then lauded as brave opponents of "Radical tyranny." It is hardly correct to judge "Radicals" by their worst motives and "Redeemers" only by their best.

Negro historians, from the venerable days of George Williams to the modern times of John Hope Franklin, Rayford W. Logan, and others, have had, perforce, to recognize a conflict between the status conservatism of a dominant white race and the aspirations of the Negro people. Reviewers sometimes tend to patronize their works as restricted by adherence to a minority point of view. But white historians, naturally enough, write from a majority point of view which is sometimes confused with objectivity—and which leads even the fairest

---

[31] Abundant documentation of this statement is available in the newspapers mentioned. For a brief sample drawn from the news columns only, see Bernard A. Weisberger, *Reporters for the Union* (Boston, 1953), 265–70.

of them on occasion into unrecognized value judgments. Take, for example, the simple matter of suffrage. Many textbooks deprecate the enfranchisement of freedmen almost immediately after emancipation. While by no means "naturally" inferior, they argue, the victims of slavery were as yet too ignorant and irresponsible to be trusted with political power. The statement is true in part, but the historian who demands intelligence and responsibility as prerequisites for the ballot is, wittingly or not, making the Federalist and Whig case against universal suffrage. Unique as was the experience in slavery, it would be difficult to prove that the freedman was inherently less ready to vote than the illiterate backwoodsman or the freshly-arrived immigrant. Yet the same historian who has doubts about the freedman as voter often votes in earlier chapters *for* the Jacksonians and *against* the Know-Nothings. It would be a good thing, in fact, if more historians examined critically the libertarian and equalitarian assumptions, both romantic and rationalistic, which have governed our experiment in democracy, but the examination ought to extend to all groups, localities, and periods, and not merely to Reconstruction Negroes. The members of the James Ford Rhodes school of historians were more consistent in this regard. Often they *did* distrust the immigrant as a voter, and if they supported universal suffrage, it sometimes seemed to be on the ground that illiterate Anglo-Saxons were by nature better citizens than men of lesser breeds without a "genius for self-government." Their views should not be perpetuated nowadays by mixing them with the base alloy of hypocrisy. It would be better to discuss the Negro vote in terms of public resistance to it and of what parties gained by it—in terms of motive and expediency—rather than by Olympian judgments on how "good" a voter the Negro made. Evaluations of the political records of entire groups of citizens are at best difficult, and at worst dangerous.

Historians are not obliged, of course, to support the Negro's case unreservedly wherever it appears. They ought, nonetheless, to walk humbly when talking of the American Negro as slave, freedman, voter, or worker. He is known to us almost exclusively through the writings of white men, who, whether well-intentioned or not, were interested parties to a conflict.[32] Conflicts may be solved peaceably,

---

[32] One basic historiographical problem, in fact, revolves around the question of whether "the Negro" revealed by the documents is the true image of himself or the man whom whites want him to be. One may hope that not all Negroes feel like the grandfather in Ralph Ellison's *Invisible Man* (New York, 1952), whose dying words were: "Son . . . I never told you, but our life is a war and I have been a traitor all my born days, a spy in the enemy's country ever since I gave up my gun back in the Reconstruction" (13–14). But considering the Negro's position in American society, one may also wonder if there

but not wished away. The conflict between white Southerners' determination to be the architects of their own society and black Southerners' desire for a place of dignity in that society did not disappear in 1877. It was "solved" by Northern acquiescence in the subordination of the Southern Negro. Paul Buck's well-known "road to reunion" was paved with the broken ambitions of the freedmen.[33] If Reconstruction is to be correctly branded as a failure, it is just to point out that its aftermath also represented a great failure of democracy. But American historians do not, to judge by their works, like the word "failure" any better than the word "conflict." Neither fits the textbook myths of underlying unity, of unceasing progress, of all problems ultimately coming out right, somehow, in the pendulum swings of time. In the case of the knotty race problem, however, only a hardheaded approach to distasteful truths will yield real understanding.

Secondly, it is time for a fresh look at the "abnormal corruption" of Reconstruction, which has long colored the period's image. True, it is now often palliated by comparison with the general fraudulence of the Grant era—the grafting of a Tweed, the gaudy robberies of the Erie gang, the copious cheats practiced by the appointees and favorites of the Hero of Appomattox. Yet this does not get at the *basic* historical question. Where does "corruption" begin and "lawful business" end in our society, which has encouraged unlimited gainfulness and freedom from restraint as legitimate goals, and insisted meanwhile that these characteristics can readily be combined with public virtue and civic responsibility. Tocqueville, acute as usual, saw the catch. "When the taste for physical gratifications" among a democratic people outgrew their wisdom and experience, he prophesied in warning of dangers to democratic states, some men would "lose all self-restraint. . . . In their intense and exclusive anxiety to make a fortune they [would] lose sight of the close connection that exists between the private fortune of each . . . and the prosperity of all."[34] From the beginning, the United States has liberally rewarded enterprise and industry

---

is not a certain applicability to him in words used by a president of the Southern Historical Association to describe white ex-Confederates in Reconstruction: "Southerners were being forced, like the peoples in any conquered and occupied country, to resort to deception, violence, and intrigue. Double standards and non-moral attitudes were inevitable results." Avery Craven, "The Price of Union," *Journal of Southern History*, XVIII (February 1952), II.

[33] This fact is underscored by contrasting the optimistic and conciliatory statements reported in *Road to Reunion* (Boston, 1937) with the unpleasant facts noted in Rayford W. Logan, *The Negro in American Life and Thought: The Nadir, 1877–1901* (New York, 1954).

[34] Alexis de Tocqueville, *Democracy in America*, tr. by Henry Reeve, revised by Francis Bowen, ed., by Phillips Bradley (2 vols., New York, 1945), II, 140–41.

—one form of the pursuit of private fortune—and assumed that the public prosperity would flourish in consequence. But with unerring periodicity some businessmen have run so far and so fast in their quest that they have found even our few legal safeguards of the public weal in their way. Then they have tried to evade, hurdle, or destroy them, producing, in consequence, what is called "fraud."

Let the judicious historian of Reconstruction consider the widespread land frauds involved in the sale of portions of the public domain in the old Northwest. Let him recall the fragrant Yazoo scandals, and reflect on Joseph G. Baldwin's description of the Southwest of Jackson's day:—"What country could boast more largely of its crimes? What more splendid role of felonies! . . . What more magnificent operations in the land-offices! . . . And in INDIAN affairs!—the very mention is suggestive of the poetry of theft—the romance of a wild and weird larceny!"[35] Let those who read Reconstruction history recall the banking swindles and internal improvement bubbles and repudiations of the period just before 1837, and then, skipping ahead five or six decades, dwell on the state house gangs and municipal rings with whom the Progressives did battle. Let all American scholars contemplate the Harding regime, and then ponder soberly our own society, with its expense-account millionaires, its depletion allowances, its licensing scandals, its much-advertised union corruption, its much *less* well-advertised business corruption and tax evasion, its paid "amateur" university athletes, its call girls hired to "entertain" key "accounts," and its numerous other evidences of the conflicts that can arise between "good business" and "good morals." In the face of all this, can the Reconstruction legislatures which showered the resources of their states on promoters and developers be properly called "abnormal"? What manner of historical "abnormality" is it which recurs every twenty years or so, if not oftener?

This is not to suggest that students of the national past should now turn to the writing of a running record entitled *Main Currents in American Larceny*. The matter is not that simple. Yet it has been made so; our use of the word "corruption" in connection with Reconstruction and other periods supports the faith that our institutions are fundamentally whole and sweet, and that only when "dishonest men" get control of them are the times out of joint. We could do with a rereading of Lincoln Steffens. And we could do more good by asking ourselves questions than by condemning rascals. Is this cycle of so-called "corruption" and "purification" inherent in our marriage, during the last century, of the acquisitive mentality and the liberal

---

[35] Joseph G. Baldwin, *The Flush Times of Alabama and Mississippi* (New York, 1853), 238.

state? Did we thus, to borrow from Shaw's definition of marriage, combine "the maximum of temptation with the maximum of opportunity?"

Certainly the "carpetbaggers," for example, deserve a fresh look. Remarkably few of them are well-known to history. Mostly they were young men winging into undeveloped territory in search of profitable opportunities, with a light load of moral as well as of personal baggage. Such enterprise was praised when it carried "civilization" into the West, where only aborigines were dispossessed of their birthright. It was condemned in the South when it resulted in the impoverishment of disfranchised whites. Yet was not the "carpetbagger" as much a product of nineteenth-century America's values of "get" and "build" and "hustle" as was, say, the frontiersman? Or the industrial tycoon? Or the "Bourbon" who took over where the "carpetbagger" left off— without bothering to plow back some of the loot into vote-getting social services as the "carpetbagger" had done? There is no need to rehabilitate the "carpetbagger"—although it may be unjust to leave him in outer darkness when some historians are telling us once more that his counterparts in Northern business circles were creative capitalists. But chroniclers of America will do American democracy better service if they examine it with true impartiality and do not dismiss its contradictions as merely accidental, or as the work of powers of darkness.

A third error in compiling the Reconstruction record has been its treatment as an almost isolated episode in federal-state relations. The national fetish of Constitution-worship is partly to blame here. "Constitutional history" is not valid as a study of inviolable principles, but rather as an examination of how men adapt their principles to the actual shifts of power within a political system. Thus, to talk of Reconstruction's "constitutionality" is not very useful except as theoretical exercise. The real question is one of just how the Constitution itself was reconstructed. Historians ought to beware of the snare which entangled Andrew Johnson. Some of his supporters have praised his "realism" in contrast to the alleged Radical bemusement with the "abstraction" of Negro equality. Yet it was Johnson and some other "conservatives" who believed that the victors, after the bloodiest civil war of modern history, would restore the defeated enemy to a share in national power immediately—and out of respect for a compact whose interpretation had been one of the very causes of the war. This is a high order of abstraction! Yet it was fundamentally American. Even the Radicals showed a surprising concern for the maintenance of the forms of the federal system, whatever the realities, and for the appearances of constitutionalism. Otherwise why did this "united" and "vindictive" group not choose to protect "its" national program by simply occupying and running the South as conquered territory for a dozen years, as some suggested?[36] Why, otherwise, were they so ready to undertake the bothersome (and ultimately unworkable) business of building Republican machines in the defeated states and then readmitting them?

The perspective of the present day should give us, as historians, a clearer view. We can see that throughout the modern world a massive centralization of power and a corresponding decline in localism and provincialism were in process. We need to spend less time in praising the Jeffersonian dream and more in analyzing the forces that eroded it. In 1787 the state governments were the nurseries of national statesmen. Today they are often enough, in Harry Ashmore's phrase, "the happy hunting grounds of the interests," and a state legislator is frequently "a small-town lawyer who makes no secret of the fact that he has accepted a part-time job that pays little . . . in order to run errands for his clients."[37] We need to know the extent to which this transition has taken place and how it came about. Yet there are few state studies that analyze problems and forces as probingly as those of Shugg on Louisiana, Hartz on Pennsylvania, or the Handlins on Massachusetts, to name three outstanding examples.[38] There are many "narrative" state histories—many of them monuments to local patriotism—designed to serve the needs of required courses in state history at public universities, courses too often thrust upon the most defenseless member of the department. This creates a fundamental weakness, for good history of the United States must rest on sound historical knowledge of each of them. A sound beginning would be the study of Reconstruction as an episode in the decline and fall of the states, and not as a conspiracy to overthrow a wise and good constitutional arrangement.

A fourth barrier to the writing of a sound, modern history of Reconstruction lies in the fact that historians as a group are too often bounded,

---

[36] Such a policy would have appeared logical to twentieth-century nationalism. Even John W. Burgess, no friend to the racial policies of Radicalism, defended the Wade-Davis bill, considered the idea of restoring the South to territorial status to be "sound political science," and considered the theory of Congressional (as opposed to Presidential) reconstruction "in the right, logically, morally, and legally." John W. Burgess, *Reconstruction and the Constitution, 1866-1876* (New York, 1902), 17–18, 60, 111.

[37] Harry Ashmore, *An Epitaph for Dixie* (New York, 1958), 111.

[38] Roger Shugg, *Origins of Class Struggle in Louisiana; a Social History of White Farmers and Laborers During Slavery and After, 1840-1875* (Baton Rouge, 1939); Louis Hartz, *Economic Policy and Democratic Thought: Pennsylvania, 1776–1860* (Cambridge, 1948); Oscar and Mary F. Handlin, *Commonwealth; a Study of the Role of Government in the American Economy: Massachusetts, 1774-1861* (New York, 1947). The selection of these three works is not meant to imply that they are our only valuable state histories, but to illustrate the type of analysis too rarely undertaken.

when dealing with economic and social matters, by obsolete, unsophisticated, and intellectually isolated viewpoints.   A few examples will readily illustrate this point.   Reconstruction is still frequently taught as the story of how "the North" attempted to remold "the South."   But the sectional approach so well employed by historians of a past generation has exhausted most of its utility.   Beyond a certain point, the theory of sectionalism fails to explain similarities of pattern clearly visible in "North," "South," and "West," and what is more, it stumbles over the widespread cultural and economic differences among regions *within* each section.   Nowadays, the use of a purely sectional analysis is a triumph of mere habit over critical thought.

Also noticeable is a lack of refinement in economic as well as geographical thought.   Textbooks cling yet to the well-known view— once a "radical revision" in itself—that the Civil War and Reconstruction sealed the triumph of "industry" over "agriculture," the process christened by Charles A. Beard as the "second American revolution."[39] Yet this conflict cannot be neatly packaged.   Richard Hofstadter reminds readers in an article lately published that Americans in sentimental championship of the yeoman as the staunch foe of Mammon, only pay tribute to "the fancied innocence of their origins," and Henry Nash Smith has dealt elaborately with a national image of the farming West which he calls "the myth of the garden."[40]   The facts are less picturesque.   The American farmer, perennially in search of a cash crop, had never, in Parrington's words, "been a land-loving peasant, rooted to the soil and thriving only in daily contact with familiar acres.   He had long been half middle-class, accounting unearned increment the most profitable crop, and buying and selling land as if it were calico."[41]

---

[39] Charles A. and Mary Beard, *The Rise of American Civilization* (2 vols. in one, New York, 1930), II, 52–121.   It is interesting to note how "revisionists" are themselves revised.   Both Beard and Howard K. Beale (in *The Critical Year; a Study of Andrew Johnson and Reconstruction*, New York, 1930) assumed the triumph of "business" to be evident in the Radical plan of Reconstruction.   Yet this view is undergoing new scrutiny.   In a recent article on the money question, Irwin Unger shows an abundance of evidence to support his contention that it is "clearly not valid to speak of a single business attitude toward the money question after the Civil War."   "Business Men and Specie Resumption," *Political Science Quarterly*, LXXIV (March 1959), 46–70.   Stanley Coben, in "Northeastern Business and Radical Reconstruction: A Re-examination," *Mississippi Valley Historical Review*, XLVI (June 1959), 67–90, concludes from an examination of tariff and currency debates that "factors other than the economic interests of the Northeast must be used to explain the motivation and aims of Radical Reconstruction."

[40] Richard Hofstadter, "The Myth of the Happy Yeoman," *American Heritage*, VII (April 1956), 43; Henry Nash Smith, *Virgin Land: The American West as Symbol and Myth* (Cambridge, 1950), 123–260, but especially 123–33.

[41] Vernon L. Parrington, *Main Currents in American Thought* (3 vols., New York, 1930), III, 26.

In him we can see already outlines of today's businessman-farmer, private plane, automatic feeder, and all. As for the agrarian South in 1860, it was neither the "feudal" empire of Marxist historians (who have been as obtuse as anyone about Reconstruction), nor yet the physiocratic paradise envisioned by Jefferson, Nathaniel Macon, or John Taylor. Its prosperous planters with their wide holdings and great labor gangs were farmer-capitalists, curiously modern in some ways as they were archaic in others. Reconstruction's real economic story is in the emergence of a new *kind* of agrarian-industrial capitalism in the South, and the need of history is for studies of how this came about, to what end, and to whose advantage—not for lamentations on the disappearance of a fancied Arcadian way of life.

A last example of overly restricted outlooks among historians is in the charge that Reconstruction made the South a victim of colonialism.[42] This is a valuable insight, but its value is diminished sharply by the failure to take cognizance of comparable world developments. "Colonialism" is a complex term, describing a relationship which brings about vast changes in class structure, local leadership, resource exploitation, social mobility, and even religious belief in both colony and mother country. Few writers who employ "colonialism" as a key to Reconstruction show much familiarity with the best comparative studies of the subject by European historians, or by economists, sociologists, and geographers. Rather, they applaud or, more often, condemn on the basis of emotional reactions aroused by the word itself.

Finally, the historical profession is not likely to revise its notions concerning Reconstruction or any other phase of the American experience unless it subjects itself to the same discriminating analysis which it applies to the documents of history. Historians themselves work from implicit assumptions, measurable in the light of sociology and psychology, and it is a legitimate duty of scholars to examine those assumptions. It is surely no disparagement to the historians of the generation of Rhodes, Burgess, Dunning, and Fleming to point out that their background predisposed them towards a dim view of so-called "Black Reconstruction." The success of Rhodes in the coal business is well known. Dunning was the son of a New Jersey manufacturer. Burgess was trained to be a lawyer and studied abroad, an option not open to the lesser classes of mankind in the years just after the Civil War. Fleming's father had been a "well-to-do farmer" in Alabama before the war ruined him. It might be noted, too, that

---

[42] Thus Coulter declares that Reconstruction "riveted tighter upon the South a colonial status under which it had long suffered," *South during Reconstruction*, I, while Walter P. Webb made this complaint the basis of an entire book, *Divided We Stand; the Crisis of a Frontierless Democracy* (New York, 1937).

the authors of at least six of the "standard" monographs on Reconstruction in individual states—Garner, Hamilton, Lonn, Patton, Ramsdell, and Staples—had reached the age of twenty-one by 1901.[43] These are in no sense submitted as hostile suggestions. These men and women were fair-minded and thorough. We who write history today will do well to be as scrupulous within our own limitations. What is more, these students of sixty years ago unearthed materials which must form the basis of any future judgments on Reconstruction. Yet they *did* come from an "old-stock" background; they *were* the children of small property-owners and professional men, and in entering academic life they were themselves joining a genteel profession; they *were* taught, in the formative years of adolescence, to believe that Civil Service, a low public debt, stout constitutions, and Anglo-Saxon leadership were the pillars of a great and enduring republic which was naturally perfect, though it might sometimes be tainted by the work of wicked plutocrats or ignorant foreign voters.[44] We need not wonder that these men and their students identified themselves with the displaced and respectable leaders of the "white South," and not with the adventurers, social climbers, and black and white laborers who wielded power for what must have seemed, retrospectively, a brief and unpleasant hour. But we ought to recognize that the Reconstruction story which they left arose in part out of identification with a supposed natural aristocracy of ownership and talent.

These observations are only the framework of an answer to the question of why Reconstruction represents a challenge not met by academic historians. Underlying the problem is the fact that Reconstruction confronts American writers of history with things which they prefer, like other Americans, to ignore—brute power and its manipulation, class conflict, race antagonism. Yet these things make it an essentially modern period. Reconstruction cannot be properly "gotten at" by the well-worn roads of agrarianism, sectionalism, or constitutional analysis. It cannot be approached without perhaps requiring of American historians that they yield up some of their marvelous ability to read unity, progress, and patriotism into every page of the American record—that they face problems which all their piety and

[43] Biographical data and dates of birth are from the *Dictionary of American Biography* and its two supplements and from the 1942 and 1951 editions of the *Directory of American Scholars*. Information on Thompson, Fertig, Ficklen, and Eckenrode, not available at the time of this writing, might increase the list of writers on Reconstruction in individual states who were born before 1880.

[44] Hofstadter has sharply etched a similar group mentality in his analysis of the Progressives in *The Age of Reform; from Bryan to F. D. R.* (New York, 1955).

wit cannot dismiss or solve with credit to all. Yet those who teach and write the American story cannot be a mere priesthood of patriotism, unless they wish to invite the dominion of the second-rate. If they do not confront tragedies, paradoxes, tidal forces in the culture—if they do not show the forces eroding the compromises of the post-Civil War period and illustrate the frustrating complexity of the problems now awakened again—then Reconstruction will have added the historical guild to the list of its "victims."

JOHN HOPE FRANKLIN

The Act of March 2, 1867, was specific about the qualifications of those who were to have a voice in the new program of reconstruction. Constitutions were to be written by delegates "to be elected by the male citizens of the state, twenty-one years old and upward, of whatever race, color, or previous condition, who have been resident in said state for one year . . . except such as may be disfranchised for participation in the rebellion or for felony at common law." It was no easy task to administer satisfactorily these provisions of the Act. The commanding generals in the Southern military districts were hard pressed to find competent and qualified registrars to enroll the electorate. They used Union army officers and Freedmen's Bureau agents; and a few of them used some Negroes. Travel into remote areas was difficult, and in some instances weeks elapsed before registrations were received, compiled, and made ready for elections.

Some of the commanding generals felt a deep responsibility to provide a little political education for those voters who had never had the experience or the opportunity to participate in politics. Several of them gave explicit instructions to registration officials to provide the freedmen with adequate information regarding their political rights. Freedmen's Bureau officers and agents engaged by the generals to work in the registration program helped the new voters understand their rights and duties. When Bureau officials had no political literature of their own to distribute, they disseminated materials prepared by the Union League, which was, as we shall see, easily the most active organization in the political education of the Negro.

When the criteria for becoming electors were applied to the people of the South, three groups qualified. One group was the vast majority of Negroes whose loyalty to the Union was unquestioned and who

---

SOURCE: John Hope Franklin, *Reconstruction: After The Civil War* (Chicago: The University of Chicago Press, 1961), pp. 85–103. Reprinted by permission of the University of Chicago Press. Copyright © 1961 by the University of Chicago.

merely had to prove that they were not felons and had lived in the state one year. Another was the Northerners who had taken up residence in the South. If they met the residence requirements, they were enrolled. Finally, there were the native Southerners who qualified to take the "ironclad oath," and who were scrutinized with the greatest care. The rank and file among these groups was to be the center of the controversy that raged over the ensuing decade. Out of these groups were to come the leaders who bore the majority responsibility for both the good and the evils flowing from the difficult task of rebuilding the South.

The entrance of Negroes into the political arena was the most revolutionary aspect of the reconstruction program. Out of a population of approximately four million, some 700,000 qualified as voters, but the most of them were without the qualifications to participate effectively in a democracy. In this they were not unlike the large number of Americans who were enfranchised during the age of Jackson or the large number of immigrants who were being voted in herds by political bosses in New York, Boston, and other American cities at this time. They were the first to admit their deficiencies. Beverly Nash, an unlettered former slave sitting in the South Carolina convention, expressed the views of many when he said: "I believe, my friends and fellow-citizens, we are not prepared for this suffrage. But we can learn. Give a man tools and let him commence to use them, and in time he will learn a trade. So it is with voting. We may not understand it at the start, but in time we shall learn to do our duty."

Like Nash most of the Negroes were illiterate. A slave existence could hardly be expected to prepare one for the responsibilities of citizenship, especially when there were laws, as there were in all slave states, banning the teaching of slaves. Even if Negroes were free, as were more than 200,000 in the slave states before the war, laws forbade their being taught to read and write. Indeed, when they came out of slavery many Negroes did not know their own names; many did not even have family names. It goes without saying that a considerable number had not the vaguest notion of what registering and voting meant.

None of this is surprising. It had been only two years since emancipation from a system that for more than two centuries had denied slaves most rights as human beings. And it must be remembered that in these two years the former Confederates, in power all over the South, did nothing to promote the social and political education of the former slaves. What is surprising is that there were some—and no paltry number—who in 1867 were able to assume the responsibilities of citizens and leaders.

Among South Carolina's Negro leaders was state treasurer Francis
L. Cardozo, educated at Glasgow and London, who had been a minister
in New Haven and, after the war, was principal of a Negro school in
Charleston. Robert B. Elliott, born in Massachusetts, trained at Eton
College in England, and elected to Congress in 1870, was urbane and
articulate. J. J. Wright, a state supreme court justice, had studied at
the University of Pennsylvania and had been a respected member of
the Pennsylvania bar before moving to South Carolina after the war.
Congressman James Rapier's white father sent him to school in Canada, and when he returned to his native Alabama after the war he had
not only an ample formal education but a world of experience gained
from travel and work in the North. Florida's secretary of state, Jonathan
C. Gibbs, graduated from Dartmouth College and had been a Presbyterian minister for several years when reconstruction began. Among
the Negro leaders of North Carolina James W. Hood, assistant superintendent of public instruction, and James H. Harris, an important figure
in the 1868 constitutional convention, were educated, respectively,
in Pennsylvania and Ohio. Many others, among them Henry M.
Turner of the Georgia legislature, Hiram Revels, United States senator
from Mississippi, and Richard H. Gleaves, member of Congress from
South Carolina, had much more than the rudiments of a formal education when they entered upon their official duties.

Significant among Negro leaders were those who were almost
wholly self-educated. Robert Smalls of South Carolina pursued his
studies diligently until he had mastered the rudiments. Later he went
to the United States House of Representatives. In Mississippi, John
Roy Lynch regularly took time off from his duties in a photographer's
studio to gaze across the alley into a white schoolroom, where he kept
up with the class until he had mastered the courses taught there.
When he became speaker of the Mississippi house and later a member
of Congress, he relied on this earlier training. Before Jefferson Long
went into Congress from Georgia, he had educated himself and had
become a merchant tailor in Macon. There were numerous other self-
educated Negro leaders, including John Carraway and Peyton Finley
of Alabama, James O'Hara and A. H. Galloway of North Carolina,
and James W. Bland and Lewis Lindsay of Virginia. From this educated
element came the articulate, responsible Negroes who contributed
substantially to the writing of the new constitutions and the establishment of the new governments in the former slave states.

Most of the Negro leaders were ministers. A fair number taught
school. Some were employees of the Freedmen's Bureau or another
federal agency. Here and there one found a Negro who had been
trained in the law. There were, of course, farmers; and there were

some artisans engaged in a variety of occupations. The economic
interests and aspirations of the Negro leaders varied widely. It would
be wrong to assume that they had no economic interests or that they
had no views regarding the economic future of the South.

On of the really remarkable features of the Negro leadership was the
small amount of vindictiveness in their words and their actions. There
was no bully, no swagger, as they took their places in the state and
federal governments traditionally occupied by the white planters of
the South. The spirit of conciliation pervaded most of the public
utterances the Negroes made. In his first speech in the South Carolina
convention Beverly Nash asserted that the Southern white man was
the "true friend of the black man." Pointing to the banner containing
the words "United we stand, divided we fall," Nash said, "If you could
see the scroll of the society that banner represents, you would see the
white man and the black man standing with their arms locked together,
as the type of friendship and union which we desire."

Negroes generally wished to see political disabilities removed
from the whites. In South Carolina several Negroes presented a
resolution asking Congress to remove all such disabilities, and it was
passed. In Louisiana the Negroes requested that former Confederates
be permitted to vote but, for the time being, not to hold office. In
Alabama James T. Rapier, a Negro delegate to the constitutional
convention, successfully sponsored a resolution asking Congress to
remove the political disabilities of those who might aid in reconstruction. In Mississippi a Democratic paper, the Jackson *Clarion,* admitted
that in their general conduct Negroes "have shown consideration for
the feelings of the whites. . . . In other words, the colored people had
manifested no disposition to rule or dominate the whites, and the only
Color Line which had existed, grew out of the unwise policy which
had previously been pursued by the Democratic Party in its efforts
to prevent the enjoyment by the newly-emancipated race of the rights
and privileges to which they were entitled, under the Constitution
and laws of the country." In South Carolina Beverly Nash declared
that in public affairs "we must unite with our white fellow-citizens.
They tell us that they have been disfranchised, yet we tell the North
that we shall never let the halls of Congress be silent until we remove
that disability."

Negroes attempted no revolution in the social relations of the races
in the South. Francis B. Simkins in his "New Viewpoints of Southern
Reconstruction" has accurately observed that "the defiance of the traditional caste division occasionally expressed in an official reception
or in an act of the legislature was not reflected generally in common
social relations." Negroes, as a rule, conceded to the insistence of
whites that they were a race apart; and they made little or no attempt

to invade social privacies. They did not even attempt to destroy white supremacy except where such supremacy rejected Negroes altogether as human beings, and there was almost nowhere any serious consideration given to providing legal approbation of interracial marriages. While Negroes sought equality as human beings, they manifested no desire to involve themselves in the purely social relations of whites as individuals or as groups. "It is false, it is a wholesale falsehood to say that we wish to force ourselves upon white people," declared the near-white P. B. S. Pinchback of Louisiana.

Nor did any considerable number of Negroes seek to effect an economic revolution in the South. Henry McNeal Turner, the fearless Negro leader who was almost universally disliked by white Georgians, did what he could to assist the whites in recovering their economic strength. In the Georgia convention he secured the passage of two resolutions that indicated a remarkable willingness to stabilize the economic life of the white community. One sought to prevent the sale of property whose owners were unable to pay their taxes; the other provided for the relief of banks. In South Carolina Negro leaders such as Robert DeLarge and Francis Cardozo supported relief measures with the full knowledge that whites would benefit as much as Negroes.

The movement of Northerners into the South after the Civil War is a part of the exciting drama of the migrations that had seen the continent populated from ocean to ocean and had taken Americans, new and old, wherever opportunity beckoned. The movement into the South was greatly stimulated by the favorable observations of scores of thousands of Union soldiers who had seen action on Southern battlefields. Some were mustered out of the army while still in the South and, despite some Southern feelings of hostility against them, decided to adopt the South as their home. Others, back in their Northern homes, waited only for the first opportunity to return to the South. By the fall of 1866, for example, more than five thousand Union soldiers had settled in Louisiana alone. The movement was also stimulated by the large number of industrialists and investors who saw in the underdeveloped South an important new economic frontier. Those committed to the view that the South's recovery from the war would be accompanied by an era of unparalleled expansion began to move into the region, bringing with them their own resources, and often the resources of others, with which to build railroads and factories and to purchase farm land and other properties.

Many federal agents—some from the Department of the Treasury, others from the Freedmen's Bureau—settled in the South and called it home. Northern teachers, men and women, braved numerous indignities at the hands of hostile whites in order to teach Negroes, and they cast their lot with the South. There were those from the

North, moreover, who saw new political opportunities in the South. They hoped to use the newly enfranchised element and the problems arising out of reconstruction to achieve political power and economic gain. For them the South was a "happy hunting ground" that they could not resist. As to any frontier, there went to the South the adventurers, those who wanted to "get rich quick," and ne'er-do-wells who were fully prepared to embrace *any* cause, including Radical Reconstruction, that would benefit them.

These were the people who have been called "carpetbaggers" for the last ninety years. This opprobrious term, used as early as 1846 to describe any suspicious stranger, was applied indiscriminately to all Northerners in the South during reconstruction. It has generally implied that as a group they had nothing in the way of worldly possessions and were thoroughly unprincipled in their determination to fleece and exploit the South until their carpetbags fairly bulged with the possessions of Southerners and they were forced to acquire new coffers in which to place their ill-gotten gains. They have been described as a group at work on a grand master plan to Africanize the country. One historian described them as "gangs of itinerant adventurers, vagrant interlopers" who were "too depraved, dissolute, dishonest and degraded to get the lowest places in the states they had just left." These descriptions fall far short of the mark. They impugn the integrity and good intentions of thousands whose motives were otherwise. Even more important, perhaps, is the fact that such descriptions show no understanding of the variety and complexity of the motives underlying the migrations and no appreciation for the economics and political relationships that grew out of such motives.

There is no evidence that even the considerable number of Negro migrants from the North were interested in "Africanizing" the country. Indeed the term was an extravagance, a flourish—like "Negro rule"—used to express disgust. The other common descriptions are equally inaccurate. As Thomas Conway pointed out a few months after the war, many Northerners, including the teacher, preacher, merchant, husbandman, mechanic, laborer, and discharged Union soldier, were ready to move South. He had persuaded Northern men to take $3,000,000 into the South to purchase land, make loans, and advances on crops. Their only fears were whether there was sufficient law and order to maintain security for their investments. But they went South, and they continued to go all during the reconstruction period. In November, 1865, Sidney Andrews observed that already several Massachusetts men were in business in Charleston; and he estimated that at least half the stores on the principal streets of the city were run by Northern men.

The careers of Captain H. S. Chamberlain and General John T. Wilder, both of Ohio, illustrate the kind of activities in which numerous so-called carpetbaggers were engaged. When Chamberlain was mustered out of the Union army in Knoxville, Tennessee, in 1865, he at once entered the iron and coal business in Knoxville and is regarded by some as the real founder of the modern iron industry south of the Ohio. In 1867 Chamberlain joined with General Wilder, late of Wilder's Lightning Brigade of Ohio, to organize the Roane Iron Company, which bought large tracts of coal and iron land and engaged extensively in the operation of coke works, iron mines, and furnaces. Together they became involved in many industrial and financial ventures, including the Dixie Portland Cement Company, the Brookside Cotton Mills of Knoxville, and the First National Bank of Chattanooga.

That all so-called carpetbaggers were not simply Radicals with no consideration for the welfare and development of the South can be seen also in the life of Willard Warner, planter, politician, and iron manufacturer. Born in Granville, Ohio, and educated at Marietta College, Warner served in the Union army and went to the Ohio senate in 1865. Two years later he moved to Alabama, and with his ample resources engaged in cotton planting for several years. He became active in Republican politics and served in the United States Senate from 1868 to 1871. Then he organized the Tecumseh Iron Company and served as president and manager until 1873. For this venture more than $100,000 was supplied by his Northern associates. Later he moved to Tennessee, where he had extensive investments and blast furnaces. The overthrow of reconstruction seems not to have affected this "carpetbagger," for as late as 1900 the Conservatives (the Democrats) in his adopted state elected him to the Tennessee legislature.

If recent historians have reviled Northerners who settled in the South after the Civil War, their Southern contemporaries were inclined to be grateful to them for their contributions to Southern development. Clinton A. Cilley, born in New Hampshire and a Harvard graduate, settled in North Carolina in 1866. After a career in the law, including several years as a judge of the Lenoir Superior Court, he was called in 1900 "one of North Carolina's ablest lawyers and finest citizens." General Wilder, the iron manufacturer, was very popular among Southerners, including former Confederates. During the Spanish-American War the governor of Tennessee named the training camp near Knoxville "Camp Wilder," in honor of the carpetbagger from Ohio. Lieutenant B. H. True of the 136th New York Volunteers, who settled in Georgia in 1865, was consistently popular with his new neighbors; they not only supported his newspaper, the *Appeal and Advertiser*, but elected him, as the "celebrated farmer from Morgan County," to the State Agricultural Society.

The interest of such men and groups of men in the political future of the South was real. With so much at stake in the way of investments and with full appreciation of the economic potential of the South they could not be indifferent to the uncertain political winds that were blowing across their adopted home. Their interest transformed itself into a strong desire to attain certain specific political goals for the South. One was the achievement and maintenance of law and order. They had seen enough hostility and lawlessness in many Southern communities to cause considerable uneasiness about the safety of their investments. They wanted governments that would insure this safety; and if they could facilitate the establishment of such governments, they would certainly do so. Another was the maintenance of a close alliance between government and the business community. They had seen the importance of such an alliance in numerous developments in Washington during the war and in the effective service that several state governments in the North had rendered the business community. Favorable banking and insurance laws, tax exemptions or rebates, land grants and other assistance to railroads were among the favors the government could and would, under certain desirable circumstances, grant to business and industry. If at all possible, Northerners would see that this was done in the South.

Finally, most Northerners in the South were convinced that their goals could best be attained through a vigorous, well-organized Republican party throughout the South. This was, after all, the party responsible for the intimate relationship between government and business on the national level and in several Northern state governments. They knew that there was little chance of luring the former Confederates into the Republican party and that the Democratic party would oppose at every turn whatever Republicans attempted to do. Southern Democrats tended to equate Republicans with abolitionists and thus to regard them as the destroyers of the South's cherished economic and social system. Northern Republicans had to look to others in the South for political support.

A Republican in the South did not have to belong to the Thaddeus Stevens–Charles Sumner wing of the party to reach the conclusion that Negro suffrage was not only desirable but imperative. For the conclusion was inescapable that the party's strength would come from Negroes and from whatever support they could secure from loyal native Southerners. They did all they could to promote the enfranchisement of the Negro and draw him into the Republican party. This did not mean, however, that the so-called carpetbaggers were interested in "Africanizing" the South. Even when they undertook to "Northernize" the South, there was no revolution in the general social relations between Negroes and whites. B. H. True, a New Yorker living in Georgia, said that he was as friendly toward the Negro as anyone, "but there is an antagonism which we all have against the race; that I cannot get rid of; I do not believe any man can." Had these Radicals been radical on social questions, they would have opposed the laws against intermarriage that were enacted during the Radical regime. They would also have stood for one system of public schools open to all races, but their infrequent expressions in favor of such a system were feeble indeed. These matters—unlike Negro suffrage—were not among their primary interests, and they gave them scant attention.

It was only natural that Northerners in the South could wield political influence and exercise power far out of proportion to their numbers. They were the best prepared to step into the vacuum created by the disfranchisement of the former Confederates. They had training and experience in political and economic matters that neither Negroes nor loyal native Southerners had. They clearly knew what their interests were and how best they could be secured. Finally they had the support of the powerful, victorious party that was in control of affairs in Washington. While their influence in the South was not always decisive or even critical, it was invariably a factor in the determination of affairs, present and future, in the Southern states.

No group of postwar Southern leaders has been reviled or castigated —or misunderstood—more than loyal native Southerners, commonly known as "scalawags." The term came in all likelihood from Scalloway, a district in the Shetland Islands where small, runty cattle and horses were bred. It was used in western New York before the Civil War in referring to a "mean fellow, a scape grace." In the South the term was used by the opponents of reconstruction to describe those they regarded as the lowest, meanest element in society. These were the Southerners who could swear that they had never voluntarily given aid, countenance, counsel, or encouragement to persons in rebellion and had exercised or attempted to exercise the functions of no office under the Confederacy. They were largely men who had opposed secession. The votes against secession in some state legislatures, together with the known sentiment against such drastic action, indicates that a considerable number of Southerners dragged their feet or refused to have any part in the Confederate cause. Many had for years smarted under a system that gave every advantage to the planter class, to which very few of them belonged. They bitterly resented the course of action, pursued by the planter class, which had led to a war that, from their point of view, became more and more a "poor man's fight."

It is impossible to determine how many so-called scalawags were qualified to participate in reconstruction under the terms of the several acts of Congress. Likewise it is impossible to determine the extent to which those who took the "ironclad oath" were eligible to do so. After June, 1867, those who took the oath were, as President Johnson had indicated to the commanding generals, judges of their own honesty. Since the machinery as well as the personnel of registration was of questionable efficiency, it is entirely possible that many who were clearly not eligible registered anyway. There were some eligibles who refused to register, and many who were not eligible advised the loyal Southerners to have no part in the Radical regime. Others advised the eligibles to register and then defeat the Radical effort by voting against it. "If we are to wear manacles," said Governor Perry of South Carolina, "let them be put on by our tyrants, not ourselves."

But there were those in the South who counseled loyal Southerners to participate in the new reconstruction program and then to restrain any excessive or revolutionary tendencies that might militate against the best interests of the South. The fact that Negroes were to participate did not degrade white Southerners or diminish their influence unless they purposely abandoned the field to Negroes. The New Orleans *Picayune* told its readers that promptness in registering and voting would convince the North "that we mean to take care of our own affairs." The Savannah *News* gave similar advice when it declared that Georgia expected every man to do his duty and register without delay to show his reverence for his "noble commonwealth." The Charleston *Daily Courier* echoed the same view: "That you should register is an imperative duty which each man owes to himself, to his community and to his state."

A curious assortment of native Southerners thus became eligible to participate in Radical Reconstruction. And the number increased as the President granted individual pardons or issued new proclamations of amnesty. It became increasingly difficult to make a distinction between the views of the loyal Southerners and the views of those whose citizenship was being restored. On political and social questions they ranged from the radicalism of James W. Hunnicut of Virginia, who stood for the full legal and social equality of Negroes and whites, to the conservatism of Milton Candler, a Georgia senator who claimed that Negroes were not citizens and therefore were not eligible to hold office. Certainly the majority of these loyal Southerners could not be described as Radicals in the sense of embracing the policies and programs for Negroes set forth by the Radicals in Congress. Often they advocated segregation of Negroes and whites in educational and other institutions. Often they spoke as vigorously for the right of the South as did any former Confederate. Their primary interest was in supporting a party that would build the South on a broader base than the plantation aristocracy of ante-bellum days. They found it expedient to do business with Negroes and so-called carpetbaggers; but often they returned to the Democratic party as it gained sufficient strength to be a factor in Southern politics.

These were the people who were called scalawags by their adversaries. They hardly deserved the name, nor did they deserve the numerous other opprobrious labels pinned on them by hostile critics. Wade Hampton called them "the mean, lousy and filthy kind that are not fit for butchers or dogs." Another called them "scaly, scabby runts in a herd of cattle." Even the historians have joined in the verbal assault on these loyal native Southerners. One describes scalawags as "vile, blatant, vindictive, unprincipled." Perhaps during the period of their ascendancy the scalawags committed many offenses against the social order; for the graft and corruption they must take at least a part of the blame. But their most serious offense was to have been loyal to the Union during the Civil War or to have declared that they had been loyal and thereby to have enjoyed full citizenship during the period of Radical Reconstruction.

It is extremely difficult to determine the strength of the three groups that dominated the South during Radical Reconstruction. There was constant fluctuation in the show of strength, particularly among the native Southerners and the Northerners living in the South. And there was constant defection, with Negroes dropping out of the picture under Ku Klux Klan or other pressures, with Northerners leaving or going over to the Conservatives, as the opponents of Radical Reconstruction were called, and with "loyal" Southerners deviating from or deserting the Radical cause altogether. The best that one can do is look at the comparative numerical strength of the three groups and draw some inferences from the observation. A likely time for such a comparison is 1867-68, when the several state conventions wrote the new constitutions required by the Reconstruction Acts (see table).

The figures in the table illustrate several significant points. In the first place, except for South Carolina, Negros enjoyed no numerical domination in the conventions. The only other state in which they were nearly a majority was Louisiana, where by agreement they were to constitute 50 per cent of the delegates. Thus "Negro rule," as reconstruction has been erroneously described, had an inauspicious beginning and, indeed, was never to materialize. Second, the so-called carpetbaggers were in the minority in every state except Mississippi. Many were so preoccupied with personal undertakings, or with setting up schools and churches, that they had no time for public service. Their position, however, was adequately represented by those new settlers who did find time to serve. Finally, the native whites had a larger numerical representation in the conventions than is usually recognized. Dominating several conventions, such as those in Alabama, Georgia, and North Carolina, and having substantial numbers in others, they were prepared to play a significant part in the deliberations and in the administration of affairs in their states.

Although leadership in the South came from these three groups, at least in the early days of congressional reconstruction, it does not follow that the leaders invariably worked together in promoting a

MEMBERSHIP OF STATE CONVENTIONS, 1867–68

STATE	NEGRO	WHITE			TOTAL	PERCENTAGE		
						Negro	White	
		Native	North-ern	Total			Native	North-ern
Alabama	18	59	31	90	108	17	55	28
Arkansas	8	35	23	58	66	13	52	35
Florida	18	12	15	27	45	40	27	33
Georgia	33	128	9	137	170	19	74	7
Louisiana	49	*	*	49	98	50	*	*
Mississippi	17	29	54	83	100	17	29	54
North Carolina	15	100	18	118	133	11	75	14
South Carolina	76	27	21	48	124	61	22	17
Virginia	25	33	47	80	105	24	31	45
Texas	9	*	*	81	90	10	*	*

* Further breakdown unavailable.

Radical program. Their motives, values, and goals were not the same and their effort to work together was often strained because of these differences. Far from entering into any conspiracy to degrade and destroy the Southern way of life, they frequently worked at cross purposes. At times the position of the Negro leaders approached that of the crusading abolitionists. Meanwhile, the so-called carpetbaggers frequently preoccupied themselves with building up the alliance between the business community and the Republican-controlled state government. All too often, moreover, the loyal Southerners talked and acted like the conservative former Confederates whom they presumably opposed. Cooperation was at best loose and irregular, forced at times only by the threat of their common destruction. It was under these circumstances that the three groups of leaders forged a program for the reconstruction of the Southern states. How such a program actually emerged is one of the fascinating chapters in American history.

Correlation of American History: Recent
Interpretations, Book I,
with American History Texts

	John M. Blum et al., THE NATIONAL EXPERIENCE, 2nd ed.	Carman, Syrett, and Wishy, A HISTORY OF THE AMERICAN PEOPLE, 3rd ed., Vol. I	John A. Garraty, THE AMERICAN NATION
Text Chapters	Related selections in *American History: Recent Interpretations*		
Preface	1	1	1
1	2, 4, 5	2	2
2	3, 6	4	3–6, 8–11
3	7, 8, 9, 10, 11	3, 6, 8	7, 12, 13
4	12, 13	5, 9, 10	14
5	14, 15, 16	7	15, 16, 17, 18
6	17, 18, 19	11, 12, 13	19
7	20	14	20, 21
8	21, 26	15, 16	26
9	22, 23, 24	17, 18, 19	
10	28, 29, 30, 31		22, 23
11	25	20	24, 25
12	27	26	27
13	32, 33	21	29, 30, 31
14	34, 35, 36	22, 23	32, 33
15	37, 38	27	34, 35, 36
16		28, 29, 30, 31	37, 38
17		25	
18		24	
19		32, 33	
20		34, 35, 36	
21		37, 38	

Text Chapters	Oscar Handlin, AMERICA: A HISTORY	Hicks, Mowry, and Burke, A HISTORY OF AMERICAN DEMOCRACY, 3rd ed.	Hofstadter, Miller, and Aaron, THE UNITED STATES, 2nd ed.
	Related selections in *American History: Recent Interpretations*		
Preface	1	1	1
1	2	2, 3	2
2	4	4, 5, 6, 8, 9	3, 4, 5, 6
3	3	8, 10, 11	7, 9, 12
4	9	7, 12	8, 10, 11
5	5, 6, 8	11, 12, 13, 14	11, 12, 13, 14
6	6	15, 16	13, 15, 16
7	7	15, 16, 17, 18	17, 18, 19
8	10, 11	17, 19	20, 21
9	12	20	26, 27
10	13	21, 26	22, 23, 24
11	13	31	28, 29, 30, 31, 32
12	14	22, 23, 27	25
13		22, 24	30
14	15, 16	28, 31	26, 27
15	15, 16	29, 30	32, 33
16	17, 18	25	34, 35, 36
17	19		35, 36, 37
18	19	32, 33	
19	20	34, 35, 36	
20		37, 38	
21	21		
22	22		
23	26		
24	27		
25			
26	22, 23		
27	31		
28	28, 29, 30		
29			
30	25		
31	32, 33		
32	34, 35, 36		
33	37, 38		

	Morison, Commager, and Leuchtenburg, THE GROWTH OF THE AMERICAN REPUBLIC, 6th ed., Vol. I	Williams, Current, and Freidel, A HISTORY OF THE UNITED STATES, 2nd ed., Vol. I	Williams, Current, and Freidel, AMERICAN HISTORY: A SURVEY, 2nd ed.
Text Chapters	Related selections in *American History: Recent Interpretations*		
Preface	1	1	1
1	2	2	2, 3
2		3, 4	4–6, 8–10
3	3, 4, 5	6, 9	7, 12
4	5, 6, 7	5, 8, 10	11, 13
5	8, 9, 10, 12	7, 12	14
6	11, 12, 13	11, 13	15, 16
7	11, 13	14	17, 18, 19
8	11, 13	15, 16	
9	11, 13	17, 18	
10	11, 13	19	20
11	14		21
12	11, 13		22, 23
13	13, 15	20	24
14	13, 15, 16	26	26, 27
15	15, 17	21	28, 29, 30, 31
16	17, 18	27	
17	17		25
18	19	23	33
19		22	32
20	20	28, 29, 30, 31	34, 35, 36
21		27	37, 38
22	21		
23	22, 23	24	
24	27	25	
25			
26	28, 29, 30, 31	32, 33	
27	24	33	
28	25		
29			
30		36	
31	32	37, 38	
32	32, 33		
33	32, 33		
34	36		
35			
36	34, 35		
37			
38	34, 35		
39	37, 38		
40	37, 38		
41			

	L. B. Wright *et al.*, THE DEMOCRATIC EXPERIENCE, revised
Text Chapters	Related selections in *American History: Recent Interpretations*
Preface	1
1	2, 3, 7, 9
2	11–14
3	4, 5, 6, 8, 10, 11
4	15–19
5	20, 21
6	11, 31
7	22, 23, 24, 25
8	26, 27, 28
9	28, 29, 30, 31
10	32, 33
11	34–38

Index